DOWN
AND DIRTY
PICTURES

**Miramax, Sundance and the Rise of
Independent Film**

PETER BISKIND

BLOOMSBURY

First published in Great Britain in 2004

This paperback edition published 2005

Copyright © 2004 by Peter Biskind

The moral right of the author has been asserted

Bloomsbury Publishing, Plc, 38 Soho Square, London W1D 3HB

A CIP catalogue record for this book is available from the British Library

ISBN 0 7475 6571 6

10 9 8 7 6 5 4 3 2 1

nted in Great Britain by Clays Ltd, St Ives plc

bury Publishing are natural, recyclable products made from wood
aged forests. The manufacturing processes conform to the
vironmental regulations of the country of origin.

www.bloomsbury.com/peterbiskind

For Betsy and Kate as always

Contents

DOWN
AND DIRTY
PICTURES

Preface

This book is a sequel, of sorts, to *Easy Riders, Raging Bulls,* my history of that exuberant, fecund decade, the 1970s, that gave us the so-called New Hollywood—a wave of mostly film school–educated kids who, under the influence of drugs, European cinema, and the anti-war movement, exploited a nearly bankrupt studio system to produce the best American films of the second half of the century. The New Hollywood lasted a scant ten years or less, but it left a rich legacy, not the least of which is a loose collection of spiritual and aesthetic heirs, collectively known as the "independents."

"Independent film" brings to mind noble concepts like "integrity," "vision," "self-expression," and "sacrifice." It evokes the image of struggling young filmmakers maxing out their credit cards to pay their actors and crews, who work long hours for little or no compensation because they believe in what they're doing. As Quentin Tarantino puts it, "Independent filmmakers don't make money. They'll spend all the money they have to make the movie. Money they don't have. Their parents' money. Steal money, go into debt for the rest of their lives. The movie can be as good as it's gonna be, or as bad as it's gonna be, but it's theirs."

Although there is more than a little truth to this conventional notion, it's important to remember that it's not the whole truth. Life in the indie world can be nasty, brutish, and short. It was once said, if Hollywood is like the Mafia, indies are like the Russian mob. In both cases, the bad guys will cap the good guys, but in Hollywood they do it with a certain degree of finesse—they send a basket of fruit over for your assistant afterward—while the indies just whack you—and your wife and kids for good measure. In the studio world, you're imprisoned in a gilded cage. In the indie world, you're in the hole, which is darker, dirtier, and a lot smaller. With less at stake, fewer spoils, little food and water, the fighting is all the more ferocious, and when times are tough, the rats (let's be nice—the mice) feed on one another. And because there's no place to run, there's neither respite nor recourse. People get away with even worse behavior than they do in Hollywood.

In *Easy Riders, Raging Bulls,* the challenge was to hack a path through the thicket of embroidered memory, recollections encrusted by legend, tall tales that had been told so often they enjoyed the ring of truth. Here, in res-urrecting the 1990s, the enemy is hydra-headed: lies, fear, and lack of his-torical perspective. The disconnection between appearance, as it is presented in the media, and the reality of what actually occurs behind the scenes is as great in Hollywood as it is in Washington, if not greater, be-cause the high glamour of the movie industry—even the lowly indies—lies on entertainment reporting like a blanket, smothering whatever errant in-clinations to poke about may emerge now and then, while at the same time, the issues at stake lack the gravitas that ignites, at least occasionally, the ambitions of political journalists. Moreover, Hollywood stories have an internal life cycle that conspires against disclosure. They begin in conflict, and if a journalist is lucky enough to catch an angry player in the heat of battle, the truth may out. But no matter what atrocities have occurred on the set or in the editing room, by the time the release date rolls around, the concerned parties have been convinced that public airing of dirty laundry helps no one and achieves nothing, least of all for the picture, protection of which is front and center. The principals, who may have been ripping out one another's aortas just weeks before, appear on televsion, smiling and ti-died up, fielding softball questions lobbed by Allison Anchor, sounding like those robotic sports figures who mumble, modestly, "I'm just taking it one game at a time," or, "My opponent, he's a real competitor." If the picture bombs, nobody cares how much blood was spilled making it; if it does well, success—Oscar nominations, big grosses—makes lovebirds of them all. In both cases, the truth becomes a casualty of the calendar, old news, swept aside by the next big release.

Miramax, and to a lesser extent Sundance, dominate this story, as they do the indie world. Many filmmakers (in mid-career) and staffers inter-viewed for this book were reluctant to speak the truth about either. The Sundance Film Festival in January is the most important event on the indie calendar. Filmmakers arrange their shooting schedules so that their films will be out of the lab in time to be seen by festival director Geoff Gilmore the preceding fall. There are other festivals—Telluride, Toronto et al.—but Sundance is far and away the foremost showcase for indie films, the best place to see and be seen, to rub shoulders with Hollywood honchos and network with peers. Again, Tarantino, speaking about submitting *Reservoir Dogs*: "I've never had anything in my life like that, the fever of, Are we gonna get in, are we gonna get in, are we gonna get in, like every American independent filmmaker, sweating and growing bald, thinking about it." If you're turned down, it's back to the convenience store or social work school. Moreover, if you cross Sundance, you won't be able to take advantage of the labs or the tender loving care it offers. Even though Robert Redford's record as the jefe of the institute has been checkered at best, he has rarely known bad press, especially after he was first able to wrap himself in the Sundance banner. Except once, in 1991, when yours truly wrote a critical article that was published in *Premiere* magazine. Even though I was able to interview him at that time, Redford, who has a long memory and seems to hold on to grudges like a drowning man, refused to cooperate with this book, and more or less restricted my access to at least one key person who works for him.

Then there's Miramax, run by the Weinstein brothers, Harvey and Bob. They have a reputation for brilliance, but also for malice and brutality. Even though, properly speaking, Miramax is not an indie, it was at one time, and until very recently bestrode that world like the proverbial colossus. Questions about Harvey Weinstein tend to elicit stock responses, like, "He's passionate about movies," or, "He may be difficult, but he's all about the work," accompanied by rolling of the eyeballs. So while there are many, many attributed quotes in this book, there are unattributed ones as well. Weinstein likes to go on in the press about the unattributed quote, implying that it is the last refuge of the scoundrel, a dagger wielded under cover of night. And it's true that in a perfect world, sources would freely speak out—without fear of retribution. But unfortunately, we don't live in a perfect world.

Each year Miramax releases as many films as a couple of studios combined. By virtue of the volume of its output, it is by far the largest employer of above-the-line talent and below-the-line crew in New York City, and it has a significant presence in Los Angeles as well. Staffers are afraid that if they talk they will lose their jobs and find themselves blackballed from future employment. Directors fear that if they put themselves on the Weinsteins' bad side, they won't be handed that next hot Nicole Kidman film, or any film at all. Writers wonder if they'll be able to sell their latest script, actors worry that they won't be hired for the coveted role in the upcoming Lasse Hallström picture. As director James Ivory puts it, "A lot of people are afraid to speak out. Directors, actors and actresses, and other people who eventually might end up in his hands again, might want to make another movie with him even though they've had a bad experience; they're not going to talk." The Coen brothers, perhaps the quintessential indie team working today, recently produced a picture called *Bad Santa* set up at Bob Weinstein's Miramax division, Dimension, starring Billy Bob Thornton and directed by Terry Zwigoff (*Crumb, Ghost World*). After some ugly disputes, Bob took the film away from Zwigoff and had a different director reshoot the ending. (Zwigoff subsequently returned to the picture.) The Coens, one or both, reportedly remarked, dourly, "We've spent our whole careers avoiding Miramax, and this is the reason." The brothers generally approach the press like a patient under a dentist's drill, but they have been unusually closemouthed, even for them. Would he care to confirm the remark? "No comment," says Ethan Coen. Would he care to comment on *Bad Santa*? "No." Would he care to comment after the picture is out? "No." Would it make sense to talk to Joel? "No." While many badmouth the Weinsteins in private, it's the rare filmmaker who will say, like Spike Lee, "I'll speak my mind. I'm not scared a' that fat fuck, he can't whiteball me out of the industry."

The Weinsteins have been quick to sue or threaten to sue people who cross them. When a key staffer leaves the company, or when the brothers settle a lawsuit, the severance or settlement terms, like those that Sundance imposes, often contain gag clauses, prohibiting people from speaking out. And when the Weinsteins get wind of a critical article in the offing, or hear that someone has broken the code of omertà, Miramax publicists rise from their desks like a swarm of locusts, and have been known to employ intimidation before the fact and/or spin control after. They are particularly skilled in turning bad news into good. *Talk* magazine failed? Lost the company $27 million? It allowed Harvey to "return to [his] roots." *Gangs of New York* hemorrhaged money? Miramax can't lose; its exposure is limited to $15 million. MGM, partnered with Miramax on *Cold Mountain*, suddenly pulls out because it fears the budget is heading north, leaving the already hard-pressed mini-major with a $90 million hot potato? No problem. As sole owner, Miramax will make more money. The Lizzie Grubman of the movie business, Harvey is like a drunk driver who jumps the curb, maims a few pedestrians, swerves crazily back into traffic, and screeches to a halt inches from a stroller, whereupon he leaps out, grabs the baby and holds it up for everyone to see as he takes credit for saving its life.

But the Weinsteins are too smart to rely solely on the stick. They dangle the carrot as well, occasionally flying favored editors about in the Miramax jet, winning hearts and minds with elaborate parties, flattering journalists with early screenings and courting their opinions. Over the last decade, the brothers have become adept at having their way with the press. In 1991, when I was working at *Premiere* magazine, I was asked to write an investigative piece about the brothers, who even then were notorious for their outré behavior. Before I had made a single phone call, Miramax had agitated the publisher by threatening to withdraw its advertising from the magazine, and the next thing I knew, Harvey was writing columns for *Premiere* and I was his editor. The hard-hitting exposé? Forgotten.

When I was in the middle of this book—happily laboring away, I thought, under the radar—I received a call summoning me to the third floor of 375 Greenwich—the Miramax office—for a meeting with the brothers. Harvey was unhappy. I had told him that I wasn't going to pry into his private life—the 1990s were not, after all, the 1970s; drugs, sex, and rock 'n' roll were not creative stimulants or career busters as they were then—but he had received word from his network of informants who curry favor with him by picking up the phone and conveying what they've heard, that I was nosing about.

The Miramax offices are a disconcerting place. There are plenty of smart, good-hearted people there, like Matthew Hiltzik, VP of corporate publicity, and some of them have been associated with Miramax for years, like marketing maven Arthur Manson, a distinguished-looking man with a mane of white hair who is beloved in the industry, or Irwin Reiter, a CPA and fifteen-year veteran of the company, whose shy smile and open face make him instantly likable. I found myself thinking, If these guys work here, it can't be as bad as legend has it. But then there are the others, the ones with heads bowed over their desks who look up long enough to shoot furtive glances full of mute appeal like messages stuffed in bottles thrown into the sea. The place reminded me of those old movies, like *The Desperate Hours*, where a psycho holds a family hostage, and when the cops finally show up at the door and ask the quaking mother, "Everything okay, ma'am?" she plasters a smile on her face and hisses through clenched teeth, "Everything's fine, officer," while her eyes scream otherwise.

Harvey was seated behind a vast desk made out of some kind of polished wood with a high red gloss. Although it has taken a long time, he has finally found his look: a black golf shirt open at the neck—revealing the tracheotomy scar from his Christmas 1999 illness—and dark pants held up by wide suspenders. I couldn't help noticing the baseball bat in the corner, leaning against the wall. Reading my mind, he quickly moved to disarm with the self-deprecating humor that's become his trademark, shouting, "Matthew, get in here! It's time for your flogging!" Bob, dark and brooding, sat slumped in a chair to the left in front of the desk, playing Caliban to Harvey's Prospero, while I sank into a bottomless black leather couch so low it had me staring up at him, all too aware of the mini-Mussolini-ness of it all. The odor of menace hung in the air like the smell of burning tires. I felt like the guy from one of those bomb-in-the-building pictures, Bruce Willis in *Die Hard*, perhaps, careful not to cut the wrong wire, the red one instead of the yellow, for fear of setting them off.

To spend even a little time with Harvey is to become acquainted with a preternaturally charming man who is nevertheless a roiling cauldron of insecurities, in which self-love and self-hatred contend like two demons, equal in strength, canniness, and resolve. To listen to him for any length of time is to be continuously entertained, but battered as well by relentless waves of hubris, and drowned by apologia, false humility, and self-pity, reminiscent of Richard Nixon.

Harvey, donning his publisher hat—he also runs Miramax Books—

began by deprecating my project, explaining, as if for my own good, that books like this one don't make any money. It was fine if I was satisfied with a pat on the back at cocktail parties, but essentially it was a loser and so was I. By way of contrast, he mentioned several Miramax books, then on the *New York Times* best-seller list, and asked, "What do you really want to write?" As he guessed—he's eerily skilled at finding the right buttons and pushing them—I did have a project that I was secretly nursing, and I told him what it was, all the while feeling like a schmuck for letting him play me. What I said seemed to excite him. His face lit up, and he bellowed, "That's a terrific idea, that could make millions. We'll do it, won't we, Bob? Why don't you just give up the book you're writing now and do this one." I declined, and he seemed genuinely sorry for me as I confirmed for him that I was indeed a loser.

Sundance and Miramax are by no means anomalous. Everyone in the movie business tries desperately to get his or her way, in this case to control their press. But at least in part because of his publishing holdings—at that time, *Talk* magazine was still limping along, and he has an interest in *Gotham* magazine and *Los Angeles Confidential* as well—Harvey's carrot patch is large. In the end Harvey, smarter than Redford, and a believer in Don Corleone's dictum—"Hold your friends close and your enemies closer"—decided to sit for a series of interviews, for which I am grateful. Ditto the small army of former staffers who have passed through the Miramax doors. Since I was not in a position to promise them haven in the Witness Protection Program, some people I approached were too fearful to talk, but many more agreed, either on the record or off, or both, and I thank them as well.

I owe a special debt of gratitude to Lynda Obst, one of the sharpest participant-observers of the Hollywood scene I know, and a gifted writer, who urged me to embark on this book, and when I was on the edge, unsure if I could get the story, shoved me over. I would also like to thank friends and colleagues to whom I turned for help, the old *Premiere* gang, now scattered to the four winds, Susan Lyne, Rachel Abramowitz, Corie Brown, John Clark, Nancy Griffin, Holly Millea, Howard Karren, Kim Masters, Christine Spines, and Mark Malkin, as well as Carl Bromley, James Greenberg, Michael Cieply, Charles Lyons, Dana Harris, David Carr, and researcher Stephen Hyde. Many players on the indie scene, who fled from these acknowledgments, as if they were on fire, went out of their way to connect me with their contacts, but it must be stressed that the opinions expressed here are my own, not theirs.

Sara Bershtel and Lisa Chase read the manuscript and gave me the benefit of their editorial advice, as did my editor at *Vanity Fair*, Bruce Handy.

As they have done in the past, Bob Bender, my editor at Simon & Schuster, and my agent, Kris Dahl at ICM, both helped enormously. And I must thank my wife, Elizabeth Hess, and my daughter, Kate, for leaving cookies and milk in front of my office door.

Introduction:
The Story Till Now

"In the late '60s and early '70s, the studios didn't know how to market films for the youth culture, and they turned to new young filmmakers to figure it out for them. The exact same thing happened across the '90s, and when this generation came of age, it put out very original, distinctive, mature work. They revitalized American films after a decade of it being pretty fuckin' flat. It was the first real American New Wave since the late '60s."

—EDWARD NORTON

On a crisp November morning in 1979, Robert Redford, one of the 1970s' brightest stars, inaugurated a three-day conference of filmmakers and arts professionals at his home, a big-beamed ski lodge high up on the slopes of Mount Timpanogos, in the North Fork of Provo Canyon, Utah. It was only a decade since *Easy Rider* had exploded across the screens of America and kicked off the new Hollywood revolution of the 1970s, changing everything forever—or so it seemed. As that extraordinary era was drawing to a close, *Kramer vs. Kramer* became the number one grosser of the year, breaking $100 million; Bob Fosse's *All That Jazz* was a hit, and so was Francis Coppola's *Apocalypse Now*. One of that generation's greatest pictures was still in the pipeline, Martin Scorsese's *Raging Bull*, but so was Michael Cimino's *Heaven's Gate*, which is to say, the palace of wisdom to which that decade's road of excess had led would soon come crashing down. In a preview of things to come, the kids who went to the movies that year also lined up to see the first *Star Trek*, and the second *Rocky*, *The Amityville Horror*, *10*, *Buck Rogers in the 25th Century*, *Hurricane*, and *Meteor*.

The new Hollywood had ended, more or less, by 1975, when Ho Chi Minh's armies marched into Saigon, Mike Ovitz—to go from the sublime to the ridiculous—founded CAA, Robert Evans vacated the executive suite at Paramount, and Universal released Steven Spielberg's *Jaws*, the first mega-blockbuster. By the second half of the decade, the rising tide of the civil rights and anti-war movements that had floated the films of the new Hollywood had receded, exposing a muddy expanse of shallows littered with studio junk. When the Ronald Reagan tsunami swept everything before it, the market replaced Mao, the *Wall Street Journal* trumped *The Little Red Book*, and supply-side economics supplanted the power of the people. The boomers who fought the war against the war were staring at the face of middle age, getting ready to move aside for the next demographic wave, the grasping, me-generationists of the 1980s to be followed by the "Gen-Xers" or "Slackers" of the early 1990s, who couldn't be bothered with either the Yippies of the 1960s or the yuppies of the 1980s.

In Hollywood, the new television regime at Paramount reclaimed the asylum from the movie brat inmates who, like Jack Nicholson's Randle McMurphy in *Cuckoo's Nest*, had disappeared with the medication cart. Studio heads, sitting happily astride bags of cash labeled *Saturday Night Fever* and *Superman*, had raised the drawbridge, stranding marginally commercial directors like Peter Bogdanovich, Bob Rafelson, Billy Friedkin, Hal Ashby, and even, eventually, Scorsese and Coppola, on the far side of the moat. When *E.T.* burned through the summer of 1982, finishing what *Star Wars* started, the studios went off on a trip of their own, fueled by cash, not drugs.

In the perennial tug-of-war between art and commerce that is Hollywood, muscular producers were dragging skinny, coked-out directors through the wreckage of the 1970s onto their own turf, which is to say, commerce had won. In the coming decade, Hollywood would fly first class on the Simpson/Bruckheimer Gulfstream. Genres that used to be studio staples—like the family film—migrated to TV, pushing the majors in the direction of "event" pictures in an attempt to cash in.

Roger Corman, who produced B movies in the 1960s and early 1970s, used to complain that he'd had a hard time in the 1980s because the B movies had become A movies, with bigger budgets and real stars. Hollywood abandoned the experimentation of the previous decade, losing interest in how-we-live-now small films about real people—*The Last Picture Show, Carnal Knowledge, Five Easy Pieces*—in favor of megabuck fantasies. Everything that had been turned upside down in the 1970s was set right side up again. Cops regained their glow, even if they were black and therefore fish out of water like Eddie Murphy in the *Beverly Hills Cop* cycle. G.I.s were top guns again, and comic strip characters like Rambo, pumped up like balloons in the Macy's Thanksgiving Day Parade, got a shot at winning the Vietnam War, while Superman and Batman refought battles that Dirty Harry and Paul Kersey (*Death Wish*) had won a decade earlier—sans capes. With the bland leading the bland, Spielberg's suburban fantasies replaced Scorsese's mean streets. The utopian attempts to defy the system launched by the most visionary of the New Hollywood directors—Coppola and George Lucas—had either failed, in Coppola's case, or succeeded all too well, like Lucas's Skywalker empire. You couldn't really blame people like Redford for just turning their backs on the whole sorry mess.

Redford was not your garden-variety celebrity. Even though he was virtually synonymous with Hollywood glamour, he saw himself as an outsider. Too straight and conservative in his personal habits, and too much the prisoner of the star vehicles crafted by George Roy Hill and Sydney Pollack, Redford was not about to volunteer for the next Dennis Hopper flick, which is to say, he was not going to hop aboard the New Hollywood's sex, drugs, and rock 'n' roll express. He remained married to the same woman, Lola Van Wagenen, for many years and was a stranger to the gossip columns. On the other hand, he was too liberal to embrace the old Hollywood establishment, and throughout his career, he devoted himself to deploying the power that celebrity confers to effect progressive social change, showing a particular affinity for environmentalism and Native American rights.

Still, despite his contempt for Hollywood and disregard for the trappings of celebrity, and despite the noises he made about being a regular Joe, he remained very much the star. Although soft-spoken and courteous, he was notorious for keeping people waiting, breaking appointments, and failing to follow through on commitments. In Hollywood, it was widely known that to make a deal with Redford was to fall into development hell—script notes, rewrites, and more rewrites—often going nowhere. Used to being flattered, deferred to, and yessed, he mistrusted the people around him. He valued loyalty, and gave it back—sometimes. He refused to delegate power to others but was indecisive and slow to act himself. Cautious by nature and almost paralyzed by perfectionism, he continually second-guessed the people around him. He could be charming and entertaining but, as one former employee put it, "He's not a people person."

Although Redford had been one of Hollywood's leading box-office earners for a decade, when he looked around him at the end of the 1970s, he didn't like what he saw. A decade earlier, the studios had been so desperate that directors like Scorsese and Robert Altman, who would have been—and virtually were—indies in the 1980s, could work inside the system, so that an institution such as Redford contemplated would have been superfluous. But the landscape had changed so dramatically since then that now it was a necessity. Redford understood that the most creative filmmakers were being increasingly shut out of the system. He also recognized that if a would-be filmmaker were brown, black, red, or female—forget it; his or her chances of getting a project produced were virtually nil. He knew that indie filmmaking was generally a trust-fund enterprise, because outside of a few federal grants and cash from the proverbial family friends, orthodontists, eye doctors, and so on, there was precious little money available to produce them. Raising money, not to mention writing, casting, shooting, and editing, was brutal, teeth-grinding work that could take years, and if by some miracle it all somehow came together, directors often found, *pace* the thimbleful of tiny, struggling distributors, that they had to release their films themselves, leaving them broke, exhausted, and disillusioned. In short, indies needed help.

Redford believed that American film culture could contribute more than stale sequels and retreads, that historically, before the renewed hegemony of the studios, film had been a medium for genuine artists and could be again if only they could be sheltered from the marketplace long enough to nurture their skills and find their voices. Oddly enough, he had or thought he had some firsthand experience with the problems they encountered. As he has said repeatedly, "I knew what it was like to distribute a film that you produced. In 1969, I carried *Downhill Racer* under my arm, fighting the battles that most people face." He came to understand, as he puts it, the dilemma of the "filmmaker who spends two years making his film, and then another two years distributing it, only to find out he can't make any money on it, and four years of his life are gone. I thought, *that's* who needs help."

In the mid-1960s, Redford had bought some land, semiwilderness nestled in a deep gorge some 6000 feet up in the Wasatch Mountains of Utah. Then he bought the lot next door, and the lot next door, and after he made some money on his big hit, *Butch Cassidy and the Sundance Kid,* on August 1, 1968, he and his partners bought the Timp Haven ski and recreation area. He must have thought, Build a ski resort and they will come. What he didn't know was that because of its comparatively low elevation, his resort got less snow and therefore enjoyed a shorter ski season than its competitors. Despite the money he poured into it, nobody, or almost nobody came. In fact, the no-snow zone he had purchased would become a running joke. But the hemorrhage of red ink wasn't funny.

Redford knew that Aspen, Colorado, had become the seat of the Aspen Institute, transforming the sleepy town into a Mecca for coneheads with a taste for skiing and a winter getaway de rigueur for Hollywood stars and investment bankers. By building an Aspen-like infrastructure on his land, he hoped to turn a white elephant into an arts colony that at best might enhance the value of the for-profit ski resort and at worst could do a whole lot of good. It was a brilliant stroke, allowing Redford to kill a multiplicity of birds with one not-for-profit stone.

The purpose of Redford's conference was to lay the groundwork for a novel organization that would nurture indie filmmakers. It would be called the Sundance Institute, after the bank robber Redford had played in *Butch Cassidy and the Sundance Kid*. The whiff of outlawry that came with the name flattered his sense of himself as a Hollywood maverick. Or better, the new enterprise suggested a movie like *The Magnificent Seven,* with Redford like Steve McQueen, the golden-haired Hollywood star with his band of outlaws protecting the powerless farmers (read, indies) against the depredations of vandals and looters (read, the studios), so they could raise their crops (read, films) in peace.

The Redford name attracted an impressive array of brain power, but this convocation of like-minded souls was all very informal. The participants—many bearded, sporting the down jackets, plaid wool shirts, Levi's, and shit-kicker boots that later would become de rigueur at Sundance— stayed at the nearby resort. It was an idyllic spot. Rough-hewn cabins played peekaboo among the spiky stands of mountain pine and aspen that covered the slopes, while a bubbling brook meandered downhill, paused for a moment to form Bob's Pond, and continued on its way. On a clear day, the air was so crystalline it felt like you could raise your hand and touch the heavens.

Self-effacing as always, Redford, surrounded by his collection of Kachina dolls, diffidently served beer to his guests from behind the bar. His modest posture—"I'm here to listen and learn"—along with his Oscar- winning turn as director of *Ordinary People* a year later, would earn him the fond sobriquet, "Ordinary Bob," but in fact, it was all a bit much, teetering on the edge of kitsch, an Eddie Bauer theme park, Bobworld. (Later, the gift shop at his resort would be stocked with "Sundance" coolers.) Still, Redford had charisma and passion to spare, and they created a powerful gravitational field.

Explaining the lure of Redford's dream, Liz Manne, who would work for him many years later at the Sundance Channel, speaks for many when she says, "It was a combination of politics and aesthetics. He would talk a lot about the independent vision, and diversity, and the importance of unique voices. You wanted to believe in the shining city over the horizon. There aren't many opportunities in this world to do good work that you really be- lieve in. So to be able to work for a guy who stands for what he stands for, who puts his money where his mouth is, and uses his power and his celebrity in a way that is not ignorant, but very informed, that's fuckin' great. At the beginning, I just felt honored to be a part of the mission. I was one of the true believers, I was a moonie."

At the end of the three days the participants, framed by the snow- capped peaks rising picturesquely behind them, posed for pictures in front of a split-rail fence below his home. When the photo op was over, Redford extended his arm to receive a golden eagle that had been nursed back to health after an injury. He removed its hood and thrust it into the air. As the great bird spread its mighty wings and took flight, catching the updraft and soaring high above them, none of the conferees could have been oblivious to the symbolism—Redford wasn't a movie star-cum-director for nothing—and even the most cynical among them could hardly help blinking back a tear. They were present at the creation. Like the eagle, Sundance was going to fly.

THAT SAME YEAR, across the country in Buffalo, two frizzy-haired, unprepossessing brothers from Queens named Weinstein, more at home with pigeons than with eagles, were preparing to move their tiny film company, Miramax, named after their parents, Miriam and Max, down to New York City where the action was. The brothers were anomalies in the world of indie distribution. In contrast to many of their peers, the distributors who began their careers running college film societies in the 1970s, the Weinsteins had come up through the rough-and-tumble world of rock and roll promotion. Says Tom Bernard, co-president of Sony Classics, "We all reflect where we came from. The rock promotion business is cutthroat. You're fighting for your territory and using intimidating tactics."

In the late 1970s, Harvey Weinstein had acquired the Century Theater in downtown Buffalo, and to keep the seats warm when it was not being used for concerts, he and Bobby, as his brother was then known, began showing movies. When they moved their act to New York City, Bobby became president. But despite his lofty title, he was still Harvey's kid brother. Harvey always stuck up for him, saying things like, "You might not think Bobby's valuable to this company, but he is. And if you don't believe it, you can get the hell out. Don't fuck with my brother." But Bobby wanted to be his own man. One day he announced, "My name is Bob. Call me Bob." The two small-time music promoters set up an office in a cramped, two-bedroom apartment at 211 West 56th St., on the corner of Broadway. It was not a distinguished address. There was a madam working out of the building.

Harvey Weinstein, born in 1952, was a paler, doughier version of Bob, who was two years younger. He looked like what he was, the first pancake off the griddle, before it's quite hot enough. At six feet, 300 pounds and counting, he was larger in every respect than Bob, with eyes like olive pits staring out of a round, pasty face, neck like a fireplug, and hands as big as lamb chops. Someone, in other words, it might be prudent to cross the street to avoid. With his collar open, shirttails out, and dark crescents of sweat under his armpits, he looked like Broderick Crawford in *All the King's Men*.

Harvey could always be found with a Diet Coke in one hand and a True Blue in the other, chain-smoking, not so much inhaling as vacuuming up the entire cigarette, smoke, paper, tobacco, and all, one after another, pack after pack. The assistants learned to buy Coke by the case, cigarettes by the carton, candy bars by the gross, or at least it seemed that way, as if Harvey were a founding member of Sam's Club. He was a man of large appetites. Watching him feed was an experience not easily forgotten. It brought to mind the great scenes of movie gluttony—anything from *La Grande Bouffe* or the spectacular sequence in Monty Python's *The Meaning of Life* where a ravenous diner explodes like an overblown balloon. Always working on his weight, Harvey in the early days ate lunches that consisted of a tunafish salad sandwich on rye, toasted, a slice of American cheese, and the inevitable Diet Coke. But then he would chase it with a side or two of french fries as if to reward himself for his restraint. As Bingham Ray, a founding partner of October Films and now head of United Artists, once put it, bending over to mime a close look at an imaginary chest, " 'So Harvey, what did you have for lunch today? Let's see, pea soup, pizza, salad, custard.' That's why Harvey has started wearing black shirts."

Rather than trying to smooth the rough edges, Harvey flaunted them, tried to turn them into pluses. Even though he was known as someone whose word at times meant nothing, he fashioned a reputation for truth telling. He knew that the sweat, the food stains, the slovenly dress, the inner demons writ large on his battered face could be made to send a message, one that went, to quote Popeye, "I yam what I yam." And in the world of appearances—of Armani suits and 500SLs—in which he operated, as often as not, it worked. People admired his fidelity to his nature and often forgave him his sins. As Matt Damon puts it, "It's the old tale of the scorpion and the frog. The scorpion's sitting on the bank of a river, and a frog walks by, and the scorpion says, 'Take me to the other side.' The frog replies, 'No, because when we get to the other side, you're gonna sting me, you're gonna kill me.' The scorpion says, 'I would never do that, please, I'm asking you for a favor, I can't swim, I need your help to get me to the other side of the river.' The frog finally agrees, takes him across on his back, and just as they get to the other side, the scorpion stings the frog. As the frog is dying, he says, 'Why did you do that?' The scorpion just looks down at him and says, 'Because I'm a scorpion, it's my nature.' It's the same with Harvey. It's his nature."

Harvey loved the limelight and could make himself extremely appealing. He liked, in fact, to be liked. He was funny, wielding a wicked, slashing wit that he could use on himself when he wanted to or just as easily turn against others, reducing grown men to tears. When he was on a roll, no one was funnier. Speaking of somebody or other, he once said, "He's the kinda guy, you gotta hold his hand when you're chopping off his head!"

And dwelling somewhere within Harvey's breast was the heart of—if not a poet, at least a cinéaste. He genuinely loved movies, A movies, B movies, horror, sci-fi, comedy, musicals, kung-fu, all kinds of movies, but particularly he adored foreign films, art films, "specialty" films. He loved to tell the story about going to see *The 400 Blows* when he was fourteen, which he believed, for reasons best known to himself, to be a sex film, but during the course of the hour and a half he spent in the theater, he was transported by the magic of François Truffaut. Says Mark Lipsky, Miramax head of distribution in the late 1980s, "I've heard that story—'I saw *400 Blows*, it changed my life'—a zillion times. It's significant that Harvey tells that story, not Bob."

Bob, dressed in black, always seemed a little off, uncomfortable in his own skin, as if he were not in the right place, but in some world of his own. If Harvey was bigger than life, Bob was smaller, more intense, a reduction, *l'essence d'Herve*. If Harvey was the outside guy, Bob was the inside guy. He was quieter, preferred to stay in the shadows. It didn't matter to Bob if he were liked or not.

Despite what Bob told the press—"We're artists. We're not interested in money"—he didn't much care about Truffaut. As former Miramax executive Patrick McDarrah succinctly put it, "This business is about ego and greed. Harvey is ego, Bob is greed." Bob liked exploitation flicks, commercial product that could go direct to video. He was focused on the bottom line. Whatever the movie, he always wanted to know, "Are we gonna make money on it, Harve?"

If Harvey wore his heart on his sleeve, Bob was opaque, subject to extreme mood swings. "You can't really tell what's going on in Bob's mind," says Mark Tusk, who would become one of the most effective of the acquisitions shock troops in the mid-1990s. "He will turn on a dime."

SUNDANCE AND MIRAMAX, the twin towers of the indie world, will cast long shadows across this tale. But in 1979, they were no more than dreams. Around the same time that Redford's eagle had taken wing and the Weinsteins had come to ground in New York, three modest indie features opened quietly to respectful reviews and decent business. None had the seismic impact of Dennis Hopper and Peter Fonda's not-just-a-biker-movie, and all wore their earnestness conspicuously on their sleeves, but for those who hungered for an alternative to the slick, overproduced, and empty studio fare, they were cause for rejoicing. One was called *Alam-*

brista! (1978), directed by Robert M. Young, and produced by Michael Hausman; the second was *Northern Lights* (1978), written and directed by Rob Nilsson and John Hanson; and the third was *Heartland* (1979), directed by Richard Pearce and produced by Annick Smith. *Alambrista!* told the story of the struggles of a Mexican illegal to find work in the United States. *Northern Lights* paid tribute to the hardscrabble radicalism of the immigrant farmers who settled North Dakota and formed the Non-Partisan League to protect themselves against the big banks, granaries, and railroads. *Heartland* focused on the trials and tribulations of a stouthearted widow who braves the harshness of the turn-of-the-century West to homestead on her own. Whereas the twitchy, paranoid *Easy Rider* regarded the vast expanse of country between the two coasts as a redneck free-fire zone, Nilsson and Hanson, Pearce and Smith, celebrated it as, precisely, the heartland. All three films were made by Vietnam generation filmmakers, and all were marbled by a residue of its politics. Later, in the 1980s, the kind of salt-of-the-earth regionalism these films celebrated would degenerate into mindless boosterism for barnyards and square dancing, Garrison Keillor-style, but in the beginning they stood out like lonely sentries against the Hollywood hordes.

In 1978, Sandra Schulberg, the associate producer of *Northern Lights*, helped found the Independent Feature Project, the first institutional brick in the indie infrastructure. IFP conducted a series of seminars about working outside the system—how to raise money, how to produce, how to distribute yourself—it was like inventing the wheel. The goal was simple—to plug American indies into the distribution system already in place for foreign films—but the execution was anything but. Still, in 1980, the indies' *Easy Rider* finally appeared in the modest guise of John Sayles's *The Return of the Secaucus 7*, which, championed by the *New York Times*'s Vincent Canby, played to surprisingly strong box office—an extraordinary $2-million gross. Despite their obvious differences, the two films were strikingly similar, with the autumnal *Secaucus 7* mourning a revolution that failed, a gloss on Fonda's famous line, "We blew it." Unlike *Rocky, Superman,* and *Porky's* et al., Sayles's film dealt with a serious subject—the post-war exhaustion of the peace movement—that affected and might conceivably interest real people. "Financing really didn't exist when we started," says Sayles. "It was hard to get an independent script to an actor, and you didn't bother going to a studio unless your script was commercial. And even then if you weren't connected through an agent, they wouldn't read it. Independent films were truly on the outside." *The Secaucus 7* cost a mere $60,000 out of pocket, was entirely financed by Sayles himself, and could never have been made at a studio—although, in a preview of things to come, it was appropriated by Columbia and morphed into *The Big Chill*.

The Secaucus 7 was followed by films like Louis Malle's *My Dinner with André* (1981) that grossed $1.9 million; Wayne Wang's *Chan Is Missing* (1982) that did $1 million; Paul Bartel's *Eating Raoul* (1982) that did $4.7 million; Greg Nava's *El Norte* (1984) that took in $2.2 million; and a string of John Waters pictures featuring Divine, Mink Stole, and the rest of his patented menagerie of weirdos. In 1984, Jim Jarmusch made *Stranger Than Paradise*, which cost almost nothing and grossed $2.5 million. The same year, the Coen brothers, Joel, who had gone to NYU film school, and Ethan, who did not, made a wonderfully nasty film noir called *Blood Simple* for next to nothing that grossed $2.1 million. And another NYU graduate, Spike Lee, broke through with *She's Gotta Have It* in 1986 that grossed a phenomenal $7.1 million. David Lynch made his mark with *Eraserhead* (1977), and then *Blue Velvet* in 1986. It soon became clear that where before there had been a trickle of poorly funded documentaries, supplemented by the occasional underfinanced grainy feature, there was now a comparative flood of slick, reasonably well-produced theatrical pictures, some of which benefited from the unprecedented level of public support by the National Endowments during the Jimmy Carter years. Suddenly, there seemed to be an indie *movement* that had people who care about film practically dancing in the streets. For the organizers of Sundance, the hope was that these home-grown filmmakers would generate the energy, excitement, and box office that Ingmar Bergman, the Italians, and the French New Wave had enjoyed in the 1960s.

But the few distributors with enough clout to command decent screens, like UA Classics, where Ira Deutchman, Tom Bernard, and Michael Barker cut their teeth, still primarily dealt in foreign films, which were successful enough that by the early 1980s, almost every studio had its own classics division. For the most part, American indies were still a curiosity, without a demonstrable audience. In 1982, Deutchman left UA Classics to team up with Amir Malin and John Ives to form a new company called Cinecom. "The studios were bidding up the price on the name-brand foreign films, the Truffauts, Fellinis, Bergmans, way out of proportion to what they could earn," he recalls. "As a startup, we said, 'We can't compete with what all these other people are doing. What can we do that's different?' We started tapping into what was just beginning to be called American independent films. It wasn't, 'This is the next big thing,' it was really just running away from what we knew we couldn't afford." As former Miramax distribution VP Eamonn Bowles puts it, "Specialized film was a rarefied little field. If a film did a couple of million dollars, 'Wow, that was great!' You could manage your assets, make sure you didn't get hurt, and eke out a modest profit."

But indie films had one advantage that would turn out to be decisive.

Cinecom had the good fortune to open its doors right at the beginning of the video boom. "Many of these startup video companies were so hungry for product to put on their shelves that anything with sprocket holes was worth a certain amount of money to them," explains Deutchman. "Those folks had no interest whatsoever in foreign language films because people didn't want to read subtitles. These American films, despite the fact that they didn't reach a large audience theatrically, were worth something on video."

Video wiped out the foreign film market overnight and, along with cable and European public television, fueled the explosion of American indies with a gusher of money. Companies like Vestron, RCA/Columbia Home Video, and Live Entertainment began funneling cash directly into the production pipeline. Meanwhile, with Deutchman in charge of acquisitions, Cinecom released a string of hits, including Jonathan Demme's Talking Heads documentary *Stop Making Sense*, which took in $5.5 million; Spalding Gray's monologue film, *Swimming to Cambodia*, which did $1 million; and Sayles's third film, *Brother from Another Planet* (1986), which only cost Cinecom $400,000 and grossed $3.7 million.

Older distributors, like New Yorker Films, New Line, and the Samuel Goldwyn Company, also fattened themselves at the video trough, while litters of newbies scampered between their legs. UA Classics had been started by Arthur Krim's United Artists, a company known for its good taste and talent-friendly attitude. When Krim walked out to start Orion Pictures in 1978, UA Classics's Barker and Bernard went with him to form Orion Classics. Says Bernard, "We followed the same theory that Krim did when we had our first job at UA. Once the script and the director were set and it was clear the movie could be made for the budget they wanted, then we stepped aside and let the artists do their work. We didn't interfere in the creative process, like, 'We're going to fix it for you, recut it for you.' The last thing we wanted to do is influence the director's vision." The other indie distributors shared the same attitude. Unlike the studios where, before and after the 1970s, fiddling with films was de rigueur, these companies served the directors.

By the mid-1980s, indie films were starting to build an identity and an audience. Grosses spiraled upward. In 1985, *Kiss of the Spider Woman* racked up a very sweet $17 million for Island, and *The Trip to Bountiful* grossed $7.5 million. The following year Ismail Merchant and James Ivory's *A Room with a View* broke out and grossed $23 million for Cinecom, while a trio of British films—*Sid and Nancy*, *My Beautiful Laundrette*, and *Mona Lisa*— also enjoyed strong box office. The field was getting so crowded that there was bound to be a correction, and it happend in October 1987, when the stock market crashed. That, combined with the overexpansion of the most successful distributors, led to a shakeout. At the end of the decade, the heavens parted to let loose a black rain of dying companies, including some, like Cinecom and Vestron, that had seemed most healthy but had made the mistake of turning away from acquisitions to make their own films.

GENUINE CHILDREN of the New Hollywood, the indies absorbed, at least in the beginning, their anti-Hollywood aesthetic. What defines an indie film has been argued ad nauseam, but in those days, despite quibbles about this or that film, there existed something of a consensus. The purists reigned. As director/producer Sydney Pollack puts it, "Independent usually meant anything that was an alternative to recipe films or mainstream films made by studios." They were anything Hollywood was not. If Hollywood made "movies," indies made "films." If Hollywood sold fantasy and escapism, indies thrived on realism and engagement. If Hollywood avoided controversial subjects, indies embraced them. If Hollywood movies were expensive, indie films were cheap. If Hollywood used stars, indies preferred unknowns, even nonactors. If Hollywood retained final cut, indies demanded it for themselves. If Hollywood strip-mined genres and dropped movies out of cookie cutters, indie films expressed personal visions and were therefore unique and sequel-proof. If Hollywood made movies by committee, indies were made by individual sensibilities who wrote as well as directed, and sometimes shot and edited as well. While Hollywood employed directors, hired to do a job, indies were filmmakers who worshipped at the altar of art. While directors accumulated BMWs and homes in Malibu, filmmakers made unimaginable sacrifices and lived in New York, preferably on the Lower East Side. They scammed and hustled, lied and cheated, even sold drugs or their own blood, to finance their films.

Hollywood favored spectacle, action, and special effects, while indies worked on a more intimate scale, privileging script and emphasizing character and mise-en-scène. Allison Anders (*Gas Food Lodging*) put it nicely when she described her own aesthetic: The story, she said, is like "a clothesline. I'm interested in what's on the clothesline, not the clothesline itself. For the most part, Hollywood is all about the clothesline." If Hollywood both reflected and pandered to popular taste, indies worked without an audience in mind, and if they found one, it was serendipitous and likely to be a niche, not a mass audience. Likewise, if Hollywood movies were embedded in an economic system that cushioned risk with ancillary markets,* indies marched ahead—often foolishly—without a thought to distribution. They worked without a net.

---

* "Ancillary markets": video, DVD, television, cable, etc.

Indie films existed in the space between the shots of Hollywood movies, which is to say, they concerned themselves with what Hollywood left out. The converse was true as well: they left out what Hollywood included, not only because they weren't interested, but because they couldn't afford it. Poverty inspired its own aesthetic. Hollywood reproduced conventional wisdom and mainstream ideology, whereas indies challeged both—sometimes. Like Young, Pearce, Sayles, and Lee, the first group of indie filmmakers which came up in the 1980s was forged in the crucible of the civil rights and anti-war movements, which had enough staying power to survive into the 1970s, and animate its values. Sayles in particular had absorbed the politics of the 1960s, while Lee's work is influenced by the Black Power movement. Both filmmakers carried political chips on their shoulders, and others breached sexual taboos, like Gus Van Sant in *Mala Nocha*, or explored unconventional aesthetic territory like Jarmusch, or just displayed an ironic, smart-ass sensibility, like the Coen brothers. Indie films were never programatically left wing, or even "political" except in the most attenuated fashion, but many were infused with an Us/Them attitude toward the studios and other American institutions similar to that held by the movie brats of the 1970s. The preoccupations of the 1960s and 1970s—class, work, race, American imperialism, and gender—were eventually, with a few exceptions, more or less forgotten, but by virtue of the democratizing thrust of the movement, as a succession of disenfranchised groups—gays, women, people of color—gained some access to the camera, in addition to the circumstances of their production (passing the hat), they were almost by definition outsider films, and therefore—however tenuously—oppositional in nature.

Many of the successful indie films of the 1980s told the story of literal outsiders, the halt and the lame (*The Waterdance*), angry blacks (*Do the Right Thing*), undocumented workers (*El Norte*), AIDS-infected gays (*Parting Glances*), pushers and petty hoods (*Drugstore Cowboy*), and even the obese (*Heavy*). On a sexual or gender level, a good number of them were mildly kinky—transgressive, to use a buzzword—giving viewers a glimpse of subject matter rarely treated in mainstream movies, say, Lynch's *Blue Velvet*, or Lizzie Borden's *Working Girls* versus Disney's *Pretty Woman*. Since the pioneers held mainstream films in contempt, the worst sin was to "sell out." Jarmusch always worked outside the system, while Sayles, Lee, and the Coens made forays into the studios, most of which ended badly. The studios, prosperous once again, were not about to bend over a second time for maverick filmmakers with their own ideas about how things should be done.

This having been said, with certain exceptions, like Jarmusch's work, these films were untouched by the kind of aesthetic antics that informed the anti-narrative underground directors of the 1950s and 1960s, like Stan Brakhage, Michael Snow, Andy Warhol, and even the New Hollywood. "The original sin of the American independent cinema, when it shifted away from the avant-garde, was the introduction of narrative," says writer/producer James Schamus, now co-president of Focus Features. "Once you do that, you're inserting yourself into a commodity system. At that point, whether or not you have seized the means of production, à la Karl Marx, doesn't matter, because what you haven't done is seize the means of exhibition, marketing, and distribution, and so you end up having to play by the rules of the big boys."

Looking backward, it's obvious that the 1980s was the great primordial swamp out of which the indies crawled, flopped onto land, and slithered off into the jungle. As Sayles puts it, "It's like looking at a fossil record of all these animals that once existed." The Darwinian drama of unbridled eat-or-be-eaten corporate competition that destroyed promising companies like Cinecom and Vestron as soon as they got into production, made breathing room for vigorous, younger outfits that were just emerging, which in turn allowed the next wave of indies to rise up on their two hind legs and splash mud in the faces of the studio dinosaurs.

By the 1990s, Hollywood had become even more focused on comic book, event pictures than it had been in the previous decade, creating a space, not to say an entire continent, for filmmakers who wanted to tell stories with a human scale. Although it might be argued that the 1990s—a decade in which indies reached a détente with their historical enemy, Hollywood—marked the end of the movement, this is too harsh. For our purposes it was a time when the seeds planted in the previous decade grew and blossomed. The pioneers—Sayles, Lee, Lynch, Demme, Van Sant, Wang, Waters, and the Coen brothers—continued to evolve, but within a few short years they were joined by a veritable swarm of films and filmmakers, including Anders with *Gas Food Lodging*; Steven Soderbergh with *sex, lies, and videotape*; Hal Hartley with *The Unbelievable Truth*; Rick Linklater with *Slacker*; Todd Haynes with *Poison*; Gregg Araki with *The Living End*; Quentin Tarantino with *Reservoir Dogs*; David O. Russell with *Spanking the Monkey*; Ang Lee with *Eat Drink Man Woman*; Kevin Smith with *Clerks*; Neil LaBute with *In the Company of Men*; Robert Rodriguez with *El Mariachi*; James Gray with *Little Odessa*; James Mangold with *Cop Land*; Tom DiCillo with *Living in Oblivion*; Carl Franklin with *One False Move*; Nick Gomez with *Laws of Gravity*; Todd Solondz with *Welcome to the Dollhouse*; Larry Clark with *Kids*; Nicole Holofcener with *Walking and Talking*; Alexander Payne with *Citizen Ruth*; the Andersons, Wes and P. T. with *Bottle Rocket* and *Boogie Nights*; Lisa Cholodenko with *High Art*; Kim Peirce with *Boys Don't Cry*; and

Darren Aronofsky with *Pi*. Not to mention the British, Irish, and Australian filmmakers who enjoyed wide U.S. distribution, like Michael Caton-Jones with *Scandal*; Jim Sheridan with *My Left Foot*; Jane Campion with *The Piano*; Neil Jordan with *The Crying Game*; and later Danny Boyle with *Trainspotting*.

Like the New Hollywood, with its Jack Nicholsons, Robert De Niros, Harvey Keitels, Al Pacinos, and Dustin Hoffmans, the indies introduced a whole new generation of character actors like Steve Buscemi, John Turturro, Tim Roth, Joaquin Phoenix, Tim Blake Nelson, Billy Bob Thornton, James Spader, and John C. Reilly, as well as actresses like Lili Taylor, Parker Posey, Catherine Keener, Janeane Garofalo, Gwyneth Paltrow, Annabella Sciorra, and Uma Thurman. It's a testimony to the differences between the two decades that for the most part, unlike their predecessors, these actors—particularly the ethnic ones—were unable to cross over and become stars. In fact, the movement was in the other direction, with Hollywood stars stooping to conquer by playing character roles in indie films.

Like the 1970s, the 1990s was pregnant with change. "I remember the New York Film Festival where *Blood Simple* and *Stranger Than Paradise* premiered," said producer Ted Hope. "All of a sudden the Coen brothers get up on stage, and I recognized them from my local supermarket. . . . I was like, 'Oh my God, it's those stoners from the neighborhood!' And like two days later, after seeing *Stranger Than Paradise*, there was Jim Jarmusch on the subway. Somehow it just felt really possible." "I was just getting out of college in 1991," recalls Edward Norton. "I was twenty-two. There was a sense that anything was possible. I was kicking around New York, doing theater, and I had this friend, Connie Britton, who lived across the street from me. I ran into her, asked, 'What are you up to?'

" 'I'm supposed to be going to this audition for some little independent this kid is making. It's out in Brooklyn, and I really don't want to go.'

" 'Read the script?'

" 'Yeah.'

" 'Like it?'

" 'Yeah, I did, actually.'

" 'What the hell are you moaning about? You gotta hunk out to those kinda things.' Later, she told me, 'This guy wants me to do it, it's nine or ten weekends, at his parents' house, he's got $25,000.'

" 'Connie, you've never been in a movie. Just do it for the experience.' She did it, and five months later she told me, 'I saw this movie I did, it's pretty good, and we just heard that it got into the Sundance Film Festival.' It was *The Brothers McMullen!* That's the way it felt, that there was this new vortex that you could head toward that had nothing to do with Hollywood, the sense that, holy shit, some kid with $25,000 from his parents could end up at Sundance Film Festival, and then the doors opened to that new spring."

The indies of the 1990s were a diverse lot, ranging from Haynes, with his astringent exercises in theoretically inflected gay cinema on the one hand to Smith, with his twenty-something gross-out comedies on the other, and with every conceivable variety of film in between. They lacked the cohesiveness of the movie brat generation of the 1970s, and a lot of the latter-day indies missed the feeling of community they imagined the movie brats shared, the sense that they were destiny's children. Says Anders, "It's so exciting when you're starting to make films and you first learn about Scorsese and his peers, when they all started making films together, the stories about Brian De Palma coming in and cutting one of his scenes for *Mean Streets*, it's like, those guys were all part of a historical moment." In fact, the New Hollywood inhabits the indies of the 1980s and 1990s like a haunting. "I've been pretending that we're in the late '60s and early '70s for my whole career, actually," said Soderbergh. "I've tried to adopt the idea of infusing American material with a European film aesthetic. I mean, that was their great contribution." In the 1980s, there still existed a network of revival houses that gave the larval indies access to New Hollywood movies, as well as foreign classics and the greats of the Hollywood past. "I remember seeing *Taxi Driver* at one of those Landmark theaters," recalls Linklater, who grew up in Texas. "It was right after the assassination attempt on Reagan. I walked out of the theater, and I was in a daze for the next two days. I'll never forget those years. I was just in love with cinema, and there was something every night—*Badlands*, *Days of Heaven*, revivals like *Ambersons*, *Grand Illusion*, *Los Olvidados*. There was really something magical about sitting in a theater and watching these beautiful 35mm prints. That's all gone now."

With the benefit of hindsight, it's clear that the generation of the 1990s was a movement, however ill-defined and unlike the New Hollywood. But their films, with the exception of Quentin Tarantino's, aren't so flamboyant as those of their predecessors; they don't have "Look at me" written all over them, and some of the most prominent filmmakers have even rejected the auteur label. "I certainly didn't feel like I was going to grow up to be Steven Spielberg, but nor did I think I was going to grow up to become Martin Scorsese," says Soderbergh. "I'm not one of those visionary types. I'm sort of in the middle. I want John Huston's career. I want to work for a long time and make all kinds of films." Consequently, their achievement is deceptively understated. Again Schamus: "Most of the filmmakers are aesthetically audacious, but austere and rigorous at the same time. They get up in the morning, and they go to work. They have unique voices, but

they're not necessarily staking their claim to their potential greatness on them. The aesthetic work is focused, targeted, and modest."

WHILE THE INDIE ROCKET lifted a whole new generation of gifted film-makers into orbit, it never would have gotten off the launching pad were it not for the scrappy, talented entrepreneurs who took chances on pictures that no one thought would sell. As Project Green Light has taught us, when budgets are low and shooting schedules short, the drama behind the camera is as compelling as the drama in front of the camera. That drama is often about deals, getting the picture financed before it is shot and into the theaters afterward. As veteran distributor Ray Price puts it, "A good deal is smarter than a good film. You can have the world's best film, and no-body cares. But a good deal never betrays you." "To make a film, all you need is a girl and a gun," Jean-Luc Godard once famously said. He might have added, "If you want someone to see it, you need a distributor." Says Kevin Smith, "Independent films punched through based on the sales-manship of the distributors that were repping them and the personalities of the people who made the films, and not even so much the personalities as their backstory. Robert Rodriguez is a fantastic example of that. *El Mari-achi.* So is Billy Bob Thornton. The '90s seemed to be all about the back-story."

The people who gave us that backstory were the distributors, the mar-keters, and if the 1970s was a directors' decade, the 1990s was their decade. Historically, marketing has always been at the heart of the indie business. If "specialized product," wasn't going to make money, it wasn't going to exist, and most of the distribution companies were run by marketing people, like Deutchman at Cinecom and later Fine Line; Barker and Bernard at UA, Orion, and finally Sony Classics; and Bingham Ray and Jeff Lipsky at Oc-tober. Of course, starting as early as the late 1970s, when marketers mus-cled production at the studios, gaining the last word over what could or could not be green-lit, it was cause for the wringing of hands and the gnash-ing of teeth. The bean counters took charge, snuffing the flames of origi-nality that still flickered among the proponents of the easily digested, "high concept" pictures that were being packaged with recognizable faces for pre-existing audiences and tested to death in previews administered by the increasingly influential National Research Group.

But indie marketing was as distinct from studio marketing as indie films were from studio movies. Where studios spent freely on advertising, indies relied on publicity, which was free. Whereas studios practiced saturation booking and launched expensive campaigns that included massive TV buys, newspaper ads, radio, billboards, and so on, aimed at attracting as many people to as many theaters as possible in the shortest amount of time—usually the first weekend—indie distributors did the opposite. Instead of taking the money and running, they understood that the first week was going to be weakest, so they depended on good reviews and word of mouth gradually to build an audience for films booked into lengthy engagements at few theaters. (At its maximum exposure, A *Room with a View* went out on no more than 150 screens, while Cinecom cautiously marked the one-year anniversary of its run at the Paris theater in New York by taking out its first full-page ad in *The New York Times*.) Whereas the studios adhered to the law of large numbers, releasing a lengthy slate of pictures each year, gambling that a handful would break out while dumping the rest, indie distributors released few pictures, could ill-afford even a single flop, much less two or three, and consequently lavished tender loving care on each one.

But by the end of the 1980s, distributors had hit a wall. None of the indie hits had been able to crack the $25 million ceiling. They had reached, apparently, the limit of their audience. Enter Harvey and Bob Weinstein, who transformed the indie landscape. As Harvey himself—never one to hide his light under a bushel—put it, "If I didn't exist, they'd have to invent me—I'm the only interesting thing around." Perhaps. Had the Weinsteins never existed, others might have been invented to fill their shoes, but on the other hand, perhaps not, and the 1990s might have been more like the 1980s, with art films still prisoners of the art houses.

Jarmusch's *Stranger Than Paradise* is a logical place to begin a book like this because, shot in basic black and white with barely a nod toward a plot, it looked deceptively easy to make, almost a home movie—just get hold of a camera and shoot your friends. Like John Cassavetes's *Shadows* in 1959, it was one of those "I can do that" films that inspired a decade of filmmakers, convincing them that they, too, could make movies. But under the pressure of the frantic quest for the Next Big Thing, the American film scene changes so quickly that to the second wave of indies, the 1980s already seemed like ancient history; it might as well have been the silent era, with Jarmusch its D. W. Griffith, so irrelevant had it become. In the go-go climate of the 1990s, the refusal of many of that generation's filmmakers to accept the rules of the game as laid down not only by the studios, but seemingly by audiences as well, made them look like fools and losers. Of course, endorsing this view is bad history and does the pioneers an enormous injustice, but it is true that the indie explosion of the 1990s was so dramatic and so distinctive that it deserves a book of its own. And if this story is as much about the indie business as it is about films and filmmakers, it makes sense to start a few years later, and take 1989—the *sex, lies, and videotape* year at the Sundance Film Festival—as the big bang of the modern indie film movement. *Sex, lies* not only marked the arrival of Soderbergh, one of the brightest stars in this new galaxy of filmmakers, but it also signaled the emergence of the Sundance Film Festival (then officially still the U.S. Film Festival), which showcased the film, and Miramax, which distributed it. On the face of it, Redford and the Weinsteins would seem to be poles apart— class versus trash, to put it crudely, with Sundance the finishing school that teaches young filmmakers how to dress for success, and Miramax the reform school where they are cuffed and cudgeled into shape. Sundance and Miramax are the yin and yang of the indie universe, the high road and the low, the sun and the moon, Luke Skywalker and Darth Vader. But the two had more in common than appeared at first blush. Sundance never would be able to shed its baleful twin, and eventually it would go over to the dark side. That may or may not have been a good thing, but either way, it is the story of this decade.

One
Made in USA
1989

• **How Robert Redford hatched his institute but drove his chicks crazy, until *sex, lies, and videotape* saved the festival he never wanted and launched Miramax on the road to world conquest.**

"In the '80s, the studios could predict what worked and what didn't. And that's what the '80s were—one movie you'd already seen after another. Suddenly, that's not working anymore. . . . When the audience is fed up with the standard stuff and crying out for something different is when exciting things happen in Hollywood."

—QUENTIN TARANTINO

When Steven Soderbergh stepped off the plane at the Salt Lake City International Airport headed for the U.S. Film Festival, thirty miles to the northeast in Park City, it was January 21, 1989, a Saturday afternoon, and he was just seven days past his twenty-sixth birthday. He was hand-carrying the print of his film *sex, lies, and videotape*, which he had just picked up from the lab in Hollywood that morning. The weather was cloudy, with occasional snow flurries, and the thin mountain air cut like a blade, but he was feeling good. The sutures in his gums had finally healed after painful surgery to correct his exaggerated overbite, the Soderbergh family curse. And having grown up in the oppressive heat and dampness of Baton Rouge, Louisiana, he liked cold weather. He was looking forward to screening his film for the first time in front of real people.

In those days Park City was a struggling, sub-Aspen ski resort, a huddle of drab buildings ringed by a dark necklace of high-priced condos splayed across the snow-covered hills around it. A mining town in the previous century, it was well on its way to becoming a theme park, with faux Wild West wooden facades jammed together like teeth up and down both sides of Main Street. The restaurants bore names like the Grubstake, the Eating Establishment, and so on, spelled out in Gold Rush signage that featured the faces of scowling men in bowler hats and stringy handlebar mustaches staring down from wooden shingles hanging out front. It looked like the set of *McCabe & Mrs. Miller*, directed by Walt Disney instead of Robert Altman. The town's tarnished crown jewel was the Egyptian Theater, located at the top of Main Street and the festival's screening venue of choice, built in 1926 apparently as a replica of the old Warner's Egyptian in Pasadena. Everywhere the young director turned were puffy, down-clad filmmakers looking like so many Pillsbury Doughboys flogging their films.

Sundance had taken over the ailing U.S. Film Festival in 1985, despite Redford's publicly stated objection to festivals. They involved too much hype, they were too competitive, and so on. But he was finally persuaded by the logic of the argument: so far, the institute had only addressed the development part of the filmmaking equation. By ignoring marketing, distribution, and exhibition, it was virtually relegating itself to irrelevance. "There was a real fear that Sundance would be perceived as this utopian thing in the mountains, without making any impact on independent filmmaking in the United States," explains former Sundance executive director Sterling Van Wagenen. And, wonders director Sydney Pollack, "If a tree falls in the forest, and nobody hears it, does it make a noise? There is no noise with a movie unless somebody watches it."

Wearing several layers of sweaters, jeans, scuffed leather boots, and a threadbare black cotton duster so long the hem flirted with his ankles, Soderbergh made his way carefully down the icy streets banked with mounds of filthy snow. His hair was long, his prominent ears nestled in the nimbus of auburn ringlets that surrounded his face like an aureole of cotton candy. Soderbergh wore glasses with thick lenses that sat like a saddle on an aquiline nose cantilevered over a thin mouth. He was tall, about six feet, and skinny, with long graceless limbs. He looked, as one journalist unflatteringly described him, like a "stork with red hair." He always thought he was unattractive. Once, watching a scene from his own picture, he ran his fingers over his face, plucking at his cheeks. "Look at Jimmy [Spader] and Andie [MacDowell]," he exclaimed. "I mean, they have cheekbones. You could plane doors with my face." Still, despite a certain lack of harmony among the parts, the overall effect was not displeasing. His eyes radiated intelligence. He had a quick, disarming smile, and a dark, self-deprecating sense of humor.

The festival was one of the few devoted exclusively to American indies, which in those days existed well beneath the radar of all but a small band of dedicated enthusiasts. It was a sleepy gathering, not yet the make-or-break event for filmmakers that it would soon become. Few of the films that played the festival got distributed; even fewer scripts that went through the labs got produced, and when by some fluke one did, it was hardly likely to set the world on fire. No agents showed up, few publicists, and fewer press. There was no reason to; the films, with a few exceptions, were eminently forgettable. Even the critics, who dutifully approached each festival like an obligatory visit to a sick friend, were running out of patience. John Powers, writing in *Film Comment*, had dismissed the 1987 festival as more interesting for "the skiing and the parties" than the movies, and charged that independent film had "settled into a complacent mediocrity whose axiom is 'Play it safe.' "

Soderbergh's film, which had cost $1.2 million, a hefty budget for an indie feature in those days, had been a tough sell to the festival. Outside of the fact that it had been shot in Baton Rouge, and might therefore qualify as regional, it didn't fit the profile. By design as well as default, Sundance had become wedded to the kind of watered-down populism that was still hanging around from the 1960s, the kind that animated, if that's the right word, *Northern Lights* and *Heartland.* The politically correct, regional Americana ran thinly through the veins of the "granola" films, Sundance warhorses like *Gal Young 'Un, El Norte,* and *The Ballad of Gregorio Cortez,* what Lory Smith, one of the programmers, admiringly described as "feel-good, socially responsible" pictures. They were content-driven, not director-driven, often about less-than-pressing social issues. They were like *Anne of Green Gables* for adults, often featuring Colleen Dewhurst, Richard Farnsworth, Wilford Brimley, or equivalents. Occasionally, if a filmmaker got lucky, he might land a weathered Sam Shepard squinting into the sun while spitting tabakky through his crooked teeth and kicking cow patties at the lens with his boot.

The Grand Jury Prize rarely went to the best film, but rather to the most worthy film, and was therefore regarded as the kiss of death. In 1987, the dramatic award went to Jill Godmilow's paralytic *Waiting for the Moon,* and the following year to Rob Nilsson's *Heat and Sunlight.* That same year, the festival had reached a nadir of mediocrity unprecedented even in its history of mediocrity, featuring films where you needed a magnifying glass to find the plot, like *Rachel River,* or *The Silence at Bethany,* set among Mennonites, which concerned itself with a crisis set off by milk delivery on Sunday. The festival was regarded by many distributors as toxic. If Cinecom, say, or the Samuel Goldwyn Company had a film it thought might cross over, they would withhold it from Sundance lest it be stigmatized as an "art" film. (It was a sign of things to come that, even by 1989, to be known as an "art" film was to have been kissed by death. Soderbergh had been admonished to refer to *sex, lies* as a "specialty" film.)

But nobody in *sex, lies* wore bib overalls. Rather, the film was set among urban yuppies in Baton Rouge. The picture had been pushed by Marjorie Skouras, director of acquisitions for Skouras Pictures, whose breakthrough release had been Lasse Hallström's *My Life as a Dog* in 1985, a film that grossed a very healthy $9.1 million. In the 1980s, the few indie distributors who sank money into production, like Cinecom, went bankrupt; the rest bought the rights to finished films financed by others that they discovered at festivals. Acquisitions was a relaxed, gentleman's business, and veterans look back on that era fondly. Skouras loved her job. She recalls, "People were passionate for the right reasons. It was about the art and the filmmakers and the excitement of reaching a community. We acquired interesting films at a very low cost. The business wasn't driven by the big money."

Skouras was a member of the festival selection committee. Nancy Tenenbaum, a friend and one of *sex, lies*'s producers, asked her to take a look. The film was still in rough shape and boasted of no actors of any renown. Not expecting much, Skouras popped the tape into her VCR at 11:30 one night before she went to sleep, and she wasn't disappointed. There was not much in the way of plot or action, and no sex to speak of, despite the provocative title—just people sitting around talking about sex. She went, Huh?

Tenenbaum understood. She too had passed when she first scanned the script. "It read like a first draft," she says, "long speeches, tons of monologues." But then Soderbergh called her, convinced her to meet him. She remembers him as an Elvis Costello look-alike, wearing shirts buttoned all the way up to the Adam's apple, geeky or maybe retro if you were inclined to be generous. His mouth was sewn up, courtesy of the dental surgeon, and he talked through clenched teeth. He lived like the single guy he was, ate out of cans, Dinty Moore, franks and beans. But Tenenbaum liked him. He told her exactly what he thought, and he was very serious about making movies, a diamond in the rough. "He doesn't hedge his words, is extremely rational," she says. "Doesn't gush sentimentality. Doesn't like to dumb things down or explain them ad nauseam." She agreed to help him. But Tenenbaum had a lot of trouble raising money for a movie about an impotent guy who videotapes women talking about their sexual experiences and then gets off watching the tapes. "*Sex, lies* was passed on by just about everyone out there," she recalls. "A lot of people thought it was perverted. One friend of mine who isn't prudish found it vile. She said to me, 'It's pretty disgusting, Nancy, what are you doing getting involved in a movie like that?' I felt self-conscious, thinking, Maybe I'm doing something wrong."

In any event, a few days later, Skouras had lunch with Larry Estes, the senior vice president for feature film acquisitions at RCA/Columbia Home

Video, which had put up the biggest chunk of cash for *sex, lies,* and hence numbered, along with Bobby Newmyer and Nick Wechsler, as another of the five producers the picture had accumulated—like the sticky trail left by a snail—in the course of its slow and tortuous journey to the screen. Although Soderbergh's backers were politely encouraging, nobody had said, "I think you've made a great film." It was more like, "Well, it's okay," or, "You haven't embarrassed yourself—and it's still too long." None of them thought his film had much commercial potential. Estes, who retained what he assumed was the film's most valuable asset—the video rights—was just looking to break even, especially since he felt Soderbergh had welched on his promise to include some skin. Months before, when Estes looked at Laura San Giacomo's audition tape, he had asked Soderbergh, "Is she going to have a problem with the nudity?" Without hesitation, Soderbergh assured him that she wouldn't, saying, "No. She's in this play called *Beirut* where she is naked on the stage most of the time." But Estes was watching the dailies, and hadn't seen what he was looking for. He called Soderbergh, asked him, "Are you sure I've gotten all the footage? Because I'm not seeing any flesh. Why is that?"

"Because there isn't any."

"Why not?"

"Because I decided it wasn't necessary. It will be more erotic if it's not so explicit."

"You have a commitment to shoot what's written in the script. We may have a problem." Soderbergh was annoyed that Estes wasn't congratulating him on his great-looking footage instead of saying, "What happened to the tits?"

Estes asked Skouras to distribute it, even offered her a service deal.* Says Jeff Lipsky, who was head of distribution at Skouras Pictures, "That's how confident RCA/Columbia was that this film was a bomb." Margie was dubious, but she discovered that the more she thought about Soderbergh's film, the more she liked it. Lipsky, who was given to powerful enthusiasms, also saw a tape and was wild about it, thought, This is *the* best American indie film ever made. I'm completely blown away. He went to Tom Skouras, and said: "I would bet the company on this film." But his boss wouldn't give him the green light to buy it. Tom, Margie's step-father, was the nephew of the legendary Spyros Skouras, who made his fortune in exhibition and controlled Twentieth Century Fox well into the 1960s. Some thought Tom was more passionate about restoring classic racing cars than distributing pictures. Says Lipsky, "He was so risk-averse that Margie knew

---

* Service deals are a form of vanity distribution, in which the producers not only get no advance, they pay the costs of prints and advertising.

it was a Sisyphean task to persuade him to buy a film where the home video
rights weren't even available, when it was like pulling hair out of her head
to get him to put up a whopping $45,000 advance three years earlier for *My
Life as a Dog*."

Margie thought the film was good enough to go into the festival, told
Tony Safford, the festival director, "You should really see it, something
new." Safford, who was smart, confident in his taste, and just short of arrogant, agreed to look at it. Although he hated the regional films that Sundance loved, and boasted of an eclectic, quirky taste, *sex, lies* left him cold.
Still, Margie pressed him, said, "As a favor to me, take this film, I really feel
that strongly about it." Safford gave in, and *sex, lies, and videotape* became
the last entry accepted into the sixteen-film competition of the 1989 U.S.
Film Festival.

This would prove to be a banner year in the short, lusterless history of
the festival. Among the other films in competition were Nancy Savoca's
True Love, with Annabella Sciorra; Martin Donovan's *Apartment Zero*,
with Colin Firth and Hart Bochner; Jonathan Wacks's *Powwow Highway*,
executive-produced by George Harrison; Jeffrey Noyes Scher's *Prisoners of
Inertia*, with Amanda Plummer; and Michael Lehmann's *Heathers*, with
Winona Ryder, Shannen Doherty, and Christian Slater, a truly questionable choice, given its Hollywood pedigree. Even in that relatively innocent,
pre-cell-phone era, most of the films featured entry-level Hollywood stars
or star-wannabes. The budgets ranged from $15,000 for Rick Schmidt's
Morgan's Cake to $3 million for *Heathers*. Safford honored John Cas-
savetes—regarded by many as the godfather of the American indie film—
with a retrospective.

Sex, lies premiered on Sunday night, January 22, at ten o'clock at
Prospector Square, a small, cramped theater a couple of miles out of town.
Before the lights went down, Soderbergh stood up, cleared his throat, and
made the usual disclaimers: the film was still long, he was using a temp mix,
and the titles were Xeroxed. Personal encounters always made him nervous and uncomfortable, but public occasions like this one didn't seem to
faze him. He was fatalistic. The picture was what it was. As the opening
scenes unreeled, with Andie MacDowell's character Ann talking to her
shrink (Ron Vawter), at least one person in the audience thought, Oh, no,
another droning indie film, and promptly dozed off. But after the first
twenty minutes, the pace picked up, and by the end, the audience seemed
to be with it. Soderbergh made his way to the front of the theater and answered questions. He was still uncertain about the title, a matter of contention between him and RCA/Columbia Home Video, which worried
that it was too generic, and reeked of straight-to-video. He recalled, "It got
to the point where they were saying, 'You know, we can keep the first two

words, sex, lies—that's fine. But the third word—maybe we could change the third word.' And I'm like, 'What—sex, lies, and magnetic oxide?' " Soderbergh had fooled around with other titles, facetiously coming up with *Hair and Plants* (the actors all had great hair and continually exchanged plants as gifts), but nothing seemed right. About half the audience voted to change it. It was too early in the festival to have much basis for comparison, but Soderbergh was relieved. At least he hadn't been hooted off the stage. In fact, two young producers, Ron Yerxa and Albert Berger, impressed with his film, took him to lunch two days later and asked him if there was anything he wanted to do. Soderbergh gave them a novel, *King of the Hill*, a coming-of-age story set in depression-era St. Louis, by A. E. Hotchner.

SEX, LIES came along at a particularly propitious moment for the U.S. Film Festival and its not-for-profit parent, the Sundance Institute. Only two years away from its tenth birthday, it was fighting for its life after nearly a decade of false starts, wrong turns, and dead ends. The institute was in the midst of a longterm and seemingly endless crisis of leadership. Redford, a control freak, was not in a position to run the institute himself, but neither, it seemed, was he able to let anyone else run it. The first executive director was his wife's cousin, Sterling Van Wagenen. Van Wagenen was a charming, boyish-looking man with tousled blond hair and more passion than experience. He was the former head of the U.S. Film Festival, but better, he was family, which reassured the suspicious star. "Bob's very paranoid, and doesn't trust anyone who does not do the 'Yes Bob' shuffle," says Maria Schaeffer, who would be general manager of the institute for four years before she was fired, leaving her bitter and disillusioned. "Sterling was a real charming, trainwreck kind of person—he could give good Sundance."

At the outset, Van Wagenen was little more than an administrator, deferential to the board—a mix of indie filmmakers, Hollywood figures, and foundation executives. But he was a quick study. According to one source, "Sterling was a very ambitious guy who understood from the beginning that the original board members, all of whom had considerably more experience in film than he did, were potential problems for him in terms of pulling together his power base."

The board's terms were renewable, but some were more renewable than others, and within a very few years, certain terms—those of the indies— didn't get renewed at all. Several of the original board members felt betrayed. One of those original board members, Annick Smith was part of the Sundance "family." Her film *Heartland* was a model for the kinds of films

Sundance hoped to develop and possibly produce. She attended every lab in the early years, either with a project or as a resource person. "Sundance started out as one thing and changed into something else," she said in 1990. "It became more Hollywood. I haven't been back there since. I haven't been asked." Adds another board member, "They eliminated the people who created the institute, that gave blood and sweat, and had a real stake in it, the people who had the vision and the passion. A lot of us put in a tremendous amount of time, and what we got out of it was a silver-plated ashtray."

Moreover, for some of the board, Redford's "Ordinary Bob" routine was wearing thin. Says one who worked closely with the star, "He wants to be seen as part of a group, but he's also the king. There are lots of subtle ways he'll let you know that: the way he walks out on the middle of your presentation, the way he writes a note while somebody else is speaking, the way he doesn't say anything for half an hour, then talks for forty-five minutes, and then leaves, as if that's the last word. Bob used to say, 'This is not Robert Redford's Sundance, this is all of you.' We appreciated the intention of the remark, but we all knew it was bullshit."

Despite his detractors, Van Wagenen was a decent man and a key player in those early years. But it wasn't too long before he began to get restless. In the beginning, he had been content to do Redford's bidding, and he had done it well. But if Redford believed Van Wagenen had no ambitions of his own, he was mistaken. The two men nearly came to blows over a script called *The Giant Joshua*, which surfaced at the very first lab in 1981. The filmmakers' labs, held once a year in June, were the heart of Sundance. The assumption governing the lab process was that indies have something to say but lack the skills to say it, and that Hollywood has nothing to say, but says it with great skill. The lab was a place where the twain met. Indies would come with promising scripts that they would proceed to rewrite, direct, tape, and edit with the help of topflight Hollywood talent, known as "resource people." Sundance was a fresh air camp for Hollywood's deserving poor. Seven or so scripts were chosen for the 1981 trial run. At the beginning, there was a distinctly "We've got the barn, let's put on a play" air to the labs. Every day was an adventure in improvisation as a ski resort was transformed into a jerrybuilt backlot. The ski-rental shed was used as a screening room. "We'd convert the restaurant into a place to stage scenes during the daytime," Redford remembered fondly in 1990. "At night, we'd put the furniture back. We'd move the fire engine out of the firehouse and use the building as a soundstage. It was really rough."

The Giant Joshua was written by John and Denise Earle. It was based on a sprawling three-generational account of a pioneer Mormon family, written by Maureen Whipple in the 1940s, that the Earles had optioned. According to Denise, one week after the lab was over, they got a call from a Redford representative who wanted to buy their script. She recalls, Redford "was irritated when we bought the option. His attitude was, 'The script is worthless; let us take it off your hands.' We were supposed to be happy that he was interested and walk away. It made us feel small." Then, still according to Denise, along came Van Wagenen offering more money to buy the very same script to produce himself, with some sort of financial participation for both of them. The Earles made a deal. In 1984, John Earle died of a heart attack, and everything was put on hold. In October of that same year, Van Wagenen took a leave of absence to produce *The Trip to Bountiful*, written by institute darling Horton Foote and directed by Peter Masterson. With Van Wagenen gone, there was no one but Redford to pick up the slack. But "Redford was not there when you needed him," says Safford. "It's not just that he's unavailable, but getting to him is a complicated game of cat and mouse, approach avoidance." In January 1985, the star decamped for Africa to make *Out of Africa*. As one former board member puts it, Sundance "had become a ship without a rudder."

Trip to Bountiful was a success (it won an Oscar for Geraldine Page) and Van Wagenen returned to Sundance in 1986. Redford, who had not been pleased to see him go, did not seem pleased to see him return. Emboldened by *Bountiful*'s success, Van Wagenen moved ahead on *Giant Joshua*. "This project was like Merlin—it was like a sorcerer's tool—and what it did to people was sort of amazing," Redford recalls. "Sterling asked me if I would do the film. I said 'Yes.' He said, 'Can I work on the production?' And I said, 'Yes.' After he got the rights, Sterling developed his own ambitions. The next thing I know, it jumped from him wanting to develop it for me while I was busy on other projects, to him producing it with me directing it, to him directing it. I was suddenly out of it and being asked to have my company make it. Basically, that's leveraging off of me. So we had a disagreement about it."

Redford's backing had enabled Van Wagenen to put the financing together with Carolco, which was eager to shed the image of being the house that *Rambo* built, in the spring of 1987. Van Wagenen had selected Vanessa Redgrave for the female lead. "It was a perfect set of circumstances, if Bob would have supported me as a director," Van Wagenen complains. "We got right to the edge—ten days before the start of preproduction. Then Bob pulled the plug." According to Michael Hausman, who was set to produce, "Redford said to Carolco, 'I don't think it can be made.' He didn't think we had enough money, which was ridiculous. He created [so many] obstacles that the money fell out." Says Earle, "Redford never wanted Sterling to go out on his own. He wanted him to be his gofer." Van Wagenen stayed on as a board member until 1988. Ironically, looking backward at what he helped wrought, his position has changed. "Maybe because so many of us came of age in the '60s, we envisioned an open infrastructure that had the rigorous participation of independent filmmakers where there would be debate," he says. "I remember those early meetings with Victor Nuñez, Moctezuma Esparza, Larry Littlebird, and Annick Smith, who had very strong opinions about where Sundance should go. Those people got weeded out. My last Sundance board meeting was held in a conference room at CAA Beverly Hills. Joe Roth was sitting on one side of me and Mike Ovitz on the other, and I looked around, and there were no independent filmmakers in the room at all." With Van Wagenen preoccupied by producing, and his relationship with Redford virtually ended—today, Redford does not take his phone calls—the institute suffered. Says former board member Howard Klein of the Rockefeller Foundation, "In 1984, '85, and '86, no one was in charge."

In 1985, Redford hired Gary Beer, a former Washington lobbyist to solve the management muddle. Beer was a pudgy, unremarkable looking man who wore oversize aviator glasses and his dun-colored hair fashionably long and disordered, a lock falling casually over his forehead. He came from a different world, and struck some people like a breath of fresh air. Says Suzanne Weil, who was executive director of Sundance from 1989 to 1990, "He was funnier and hipper than most of the people on the staff."

Beer became executive vice president, and it wasn't long before the contradiction between the realities of the day-to-day grind of running an underfinanced nonprofit and the Hollywood glitter of the fund-raising side, which required hobnobbing with celebrities, became more acute. According to several sources Beer, who was making about $100,000 a year, displayed the wasteful habits of a studio executive. Maria Schaeffer, whom Beer hired, says, "The reason Gary Beer lives is to tell people he works for Bob Redford. He was willing to do whatever he thought Bob wanted. It was, 'Yes Bob, yes Bob.' " Many blamed Redford for Beer. "Bob had blinders on about Gary," says a source. Beer was like "the hunchback who manipulates the handsome prince."

Beer, who is now CEO of Smithsonian Business Ventures, emphatically denies any improprieties. The institute "is not like one of these organizations where 90 percent of the budget goes to overhead. It's way under the national average of 15 or 17 percent." There was nothing illegal about anything Beer did, and Johann Jacobs, a former Sundance financial officer, argues that the problem was not so much Beer as that "it was never clear where the difference lay between the institute, the resort, and the Sundance Group [a for-profit entity set up to develop commercial business opportunities for Redford]. It was hard to say, 'Yes, this is right, or no, this isn't right.' "

Indeed, the expenses may have been justified and the accounting procedures accurate, but correctly or incorrectly, there was a general perception of waste, and it was a huge morale factor. A chasm opened up between Sundance's high-flying executives, who breathed the rarefied air of wealth and celebrity, and its young, poorly paid, idealistic staff, which felt underappreciated. "I worked there for a year and one half before Bob spoke my name," says Schaeffer. The people who actually did the work running the programs struggled to make ends meet. Adds Cathy Schulman, who worked as a programmer at the festival in the early 1990s, "There was a lot of resentment, because you had people on the corporate side living this glitzy life, while at the festival and the lab the penny-pinching was really extraordinary. No expense accounts. You couldn't take a filmmaker to lunch. We were always flying on the worst planes at the worst times with the most connections." Schulman even had to share a hotel room with a male colleague. "That was weird, a man and a woman, even though he was gay. He'd say, 'Just pretend I'm another girl.' If his boyfriend came to stay with him, it was the two of them and me!"

Originally, the idea was that the resort, a Redford-owned for-profit business, would support the institute. But the resort had never been a big money maker, and so it turned out that the institute was the resort's single biggest customer, spending a little less than half of its annual lab budget for rental of cottages and food services. "We could have gotten comparable services [from outside vendors] for less, but we weren't allowed to because we had to help finance the resort," says Schaeffer. Thus, the original model was turned on its head: a nonprofit institution helped support an unprofitable business.

Redford was acutely aware of the discontent. "It drove me crazy," he says. "The whole point was to have an egalitarian tone. I don't take kindly to fat-cat behavior. I'd caution Gary about it." Still, the animus toward Beer may have been misplaced. As one former Sundance executive puts it, "To make Gary, or anybody else, the lightning rod for conflict within the organization is a bit of a shell game. Bob is unbelievably talented at deflecting blame, because at the end of the day, he is the man behind the curtain. All roads lead to Bob."

In 1988, Redford appointed Tom Wilhite, who had been vice president of production at Disney, executive director, and Beer was "Sundanced" over to the Sundance Group. Wilhite did not bother to cultivate much of a relationship with Redford, never sought his permission to blow his nose like his predecessors, and before long the two men butted heads. Oddly enough, the tipping point that sent Wilhite into outer darkness may well have been the highly successful series of "Great Movie Music" events which took place from March of 1988 through 1989 and were organized by Wilhite and composer David Newman. By all accounts, what should have been a fund-raising watershed at New York's Lincoln Center turned into a traumatic and contentious fiasco. A gaggle of celebrities was on hand at the glittering occasion, and top Hollywood composers like Maurice Jarre, Marvin Hamlisch, and Henry Mancini donated their services.

But Redford was unhappy. According to one staffer, "Redford thought it was too Hollywood." He reportedly had a hissy fit because he didn't want to wear a tuxedo and was angered by the involvement of Charlton Heston, the National Rifle Association standard bearer, although staffers say he was informed on numerous occasions in advance of the event and never objected. In any case, he refused to come out of the green room at Lincoln Center to greet donors. The star explained, "I said, 'Don't put me in the center of this evening.' And I suddenly found myself smack in the center of it. I resented it." Van Wagenen, who probably knew Redford better than most, explains his behavior this way. "Bob does have a fundamental sense of integrity. His instinct said, Something needs to be done by somebody with visibility and power in the industry to support the independents. But he is not naturally a public person, and when he's put in positions where he has to function publicly, he can get irritable, and sometimes that turns into anger."

Redford was such a magnet for money that from the start, the institute was dependent on him to raise it. But he found it humiliating to hold out the tin cup. Once, in the early 1980s, he visited Marvin Davis, who then owned Fox, to hit him up for a gift. Davis was watching football on TV and seemed more interested in the game than in Redford. "He said. 'Hey, look, I'm going to give you the money, because you cared enough to come see me,' " recalls Redford. "Then he said, 'There's a few ladies out in the pool. Why don't you go jump in?' What's really bad is I did. But in those days we needed all the help we could get."

Although the concert was a huge success, raising $600,000, Redford tried to cancel a similar event in Los Angeles (he relented only after the Hollywood Bowl, which had already sold tickets, threatened him with a law-suit), and did succeed in cancelling the Chicago concert which featured the Chicago Symphony. Proud of their work, staffers regarded this as a "slap in the face," says former accountant Gary Burr. Adds Mary Cranney, associate director of development, Redford's attitude was often perceived this way: "It was like Bob was saying, 'This is my dream, but don't bother me—I want you to fund it.' "

"Redford doesn't fire people, he just stops talking to them," says Safford. He stopped talking to Wilhite. When his head rolled, Sundance staffers were irate, but not surprised. Sundance was again without a director. As 1988 drew to a close, a gloomy Redford addressed the staff in the *Sundancer*, the institute's newsletter. "Sundance," he wrote, "is a place with no luck, where the birds refuse to nest, where there is no local support beyond lip service, where water dries up, snow avoids us like the plague, and unpaid bills pile up like soot on a city fire escape. But by God I love it, and I love you, and that's all that counts. Merry Christmas."

EVEN THOUGH he had spent a couple of years knocking out scripts in Los Angeles, doing what he could do to keep change in his pocket and move his career to the next square, Soderbergh didn't know a soul in Park City. He was broke, having gone through the $35,000-odd he got to write, shoot, and edit *sex, lies*. He couldn't even afford to rent a car and was forced to use the shuttle bus or walk. He had nothing to do but wait for the next screening, on Wednesday, when he expected to be joined by a handful of friends, along with two cast members, Peter Gallagher and Laura San Giacomo. Much to his surprise, the tickets were gone a half hour before showtime, and the lobby was packed with excited moviegoers. This was also the first screening to be attended by distributors, which wasn't saying much, because in those days, few bothered to take the long flight to Salt Lake City. Among the ones who showed up were Michael Barker and Tom Bernard, who were running Orion Classics. The two men alarmed Soderbergh by walking out after twenty minutes. He thought, Oh well, I guess we're going straight to video.

Sitting on the floor in the back of the theater was Ira Deutchman, a short, slight, good-natured young man with an open face who appeared altogether too young to have been one of the troika that had founded Cinecom. Just a few weeks earlier, in mid-December, Deutchman had been ignominiously forced out, and now he was at Sundance on his own dime trying to regain his footing. Coming in from the airport, he had asked the driver, "So what have you heard about that's really good?" Without missing a beat, the young man replied, "There was a movie that screened last night that has everybody buzzing, called *sex, lies and videotape*." Deutchman made a beeline for the next screening. He noticed Newmyer, one of the producers, standing in the back of the theater. Deutchman knew that neither he nor video companies like RCA/Columbia that had gotten into production had any experience marketing movies. He saw a niche: he would help them find a distributor, then consult on the marketing. With that in mind, he went up to Newmyer and offered to work on *sex, lies*. Newmyer replied, "Great idea, really interesting."

Soderbergh was a glass-half-empty kind of guy, and he discounted the favorable response as one from a "festival" audience, that is, one predisposed to be generous. He was worried that the good word of mouth his film was generating would backfire, raise the expectations of the audience so high that future viewers would inevitably be disappointed. But he could not have been insensible of the fact that strangers began to accost him on the street. One man asked, "Can my girlfriend kiss your feet?"

A week after Soderbergh arrived, *sex, lies* was finally screened at the Egyptian. The tickets were scalped, a first for the festival. The crush was so bad that Soderbergh felt like he'd been "flypapered." He recalls, "It was the first time I really felt a concentrated kind of energy coming at me. I had to fight my way out. At one point, some woman handed me a business card saying, if I need a place to stay in L.A. I could stay with her. My agent, Pat Dollard, was standing right next to me. We exchanged a look as if to say, This is very, very weird."

The appeal of *sex, lies* was so palpable, it was like a contagion. With the benefit of hindsight, it is not hard to understand. It was the paradigmatic indie film. Soderbergh not only directed it, he wrote the script as well, rendering him a genuine "filmmaker." Moreover, the story was personal, based on aspects of his own life to which he darkly alluded. In 1987, at the age of twenty-four, he had an epiphany. He recalled, "I was involved in a relationship with a woman in which I was deceptive and mentally manipulative. I got involved with a number of other women simultaneously—I was just fucking up. Looking back on what happened, I was very intent on getting acceptance and approval from whatever woman I happened to pick out, and then as soon as I got it, I wasn't interested anymore. . . . There was one point at which I was in a bar, and within a radius of about two feet there were three different women I was sleeping with. Another six months of this behavior—this went on for the better part of a year—and I would have been, bare minimum, alcoholic and, going on from there, mentally screwed up. . . . I just became somebody that, if I knew them, I would hate. Then one day it hit me that there was no bottom. It would just keep going until I drank myself into a grave or someone shot me." He tried therapy, but it didn't take. Had he been able, he would, he said, have joined a twelve-step program for recovering liars.

Coming at the end of the 1980s, *sex, lies* was the first Gen-X picture, taking shots at the predatory, suspender-wearing, Reagan-era yuppie (played with just the right degree of preening entitlement by Gallagher), in favor of Spader's version of Soderbergh, a recovering liar who is withholding and impotent, to boot, yet soft and sensitive, a feminized man racked by the kind of guilt that was obviously a stranger to the freewheeling Oliver Norths of the decade about to be past. A premature slacker, aimless, and lacking money, career, or ambition, Spader's character, Graham, can fit the entirety of his worldly possessions into the trunk of his car. Still, in Soderbergh's hands, his preoccupation with moral issues ennobles him, particularly in contrast to the venality of Gallagher's Me Generation avatar.

Despite its diagrammatic, audience-flattering Manichaeism (the good slacker versus the bad yuppie, complemented by good and bad sisters, played by MacDowell and San Giacomo), *sex, lies* hit a nerve. To Edward Norton, it was his generation's *The Graduate*. Recalling the film's impact, he says, "There's a zeitgeist, there's a generational energy being expressed in that movie. Spader has a hesitancy, a reluctance to engage, a shell-shockedness in the face of the collective cynicism of our parents about how messed up things were, that many of us connected with. It's about a guy who's just closed down from what he's expected to engage in, a guy who just wants to keep things simple. I'll always remember this line, 'I just want one key.' People just plugged right into that sentiment."

If *sex, lies* was not a great film, it was a very good one. Characteristically, Soderbergh himself, always his own harshest critic, couldn't or wouldn't do it justice: "When I look at it now, it looks like something made by someone who wants to think he's deep but really isn't. To me the fact that it got the response it did was only indicative of the fact that there was so little else for people to latch onto out there."

The festival was winding down, but still there were no offers. "It was different then," the filmmaker continues. "There wasn't that sense, on the part of the studios, like, If I don't close this today, it's gonna be gone. The sensation was more, We'll see what happens after the festival."

As award night approached, the buzz was that *sex, lies* was going to win the Grand Jury Prize in the dramatic competition. Fearing the worst, as usual, Soderbergh didn't want to hear about it, and this time he was right. The prize went to *True Love*, Nancy Savoca's inspired homage to romance in the Bronx. Then Paul Mazursky, the master of ceremonies, dramatically announced, "I've seen it and I loved it: *sex, lies, and videotape!*" Soderbergh's film won the Audience Prize. The director, his face flushed and his ears bright red, stumbled up to the podium and muttered a few words, thanked Marjorie Skouras, and went out to celebrate. The next day he caught the flight back to L.A.

To Soderbergh, the ten days in Sundance seemed like a dream. He was still broke, and he was still in dental hell. When he was growing up, his parents had never bothered to take him to the dentist. "I got a toothache when I was nine and went to the dentist essentially for the first time," he recalls. "The guy just went, 'Oh my God!' During the period of *sex, lies*, the orthodontist said, 'Your jaw's out of alignment.' They took tissue out of the roof of my mouth and grafted it along the portions of my gum line that needed shoring up. It was a disaster, a four-year process. I had to have braces for a year."

Then a friend thrust into his hands five copies of the *Variety* review of *sex, lies*, written by Todd McCarthy, a rave. His agent got a call from Pollack. He had read the review and wanted to see the picture. Right on the heels of that call, Soderbergh heard from Barbara Maltby, a producer with a deal at Wildwood, Redford's production company. Yerxa and Berger had alerted her to *sex, lies* and passed along *King of the Hill*. She told him that Redford wanted to be in business with him.

Don Simpson and Jerry Bruckheimer's office phoned. For someone like Soderbergh, the uber-producers represented everything that was toxic about the business, and he didn't even bother returning their calls. "They're slime, just barely passing for humans," he told *Rolling Stone*'s Terri Minsky some months later. But he didn't actually know Simpson and Bruckheimer, and subsequently had to issue an embarrassing apology.

Dollard, who took five hundred calls concerning Soderbergh in the course of a month, had to work into the small hours of the morning to find time for his other clients. "It's like being the manager of the Doors in 1967," he said at the time. Dollard raised Soderbergh's asking fee from $35,000 to $250,000 to write, $100,000 for a rewrite, and $500,000 to direct.

Soderbergh knew he had to take advantage of the heat around him before he was hit with a blast of arctic air, which he expected momentarily. On March 8, he met with Pollack. He was excited, thought, Wow, Sydney Pollack! Soderbergh suggested a book called *The Last Ship*, set among a handful of survivors of World War III, a sort of *On the Beach* on the water. Then he got a call from Mark Johnson who ran Baltimore Pictures, director Barry Levinson's company. Soderbergh told him he was interested in Lem Dobbs's *Kafka* script. *Kafka* had been circulating for years and enjoyed a considerable underground cachet, but no one would touch it because it had "uncommercial" written all over it. Meanwhile, Pollack had pitched *The Last Ship* to Casey Silver at Universal, who went for it in the third week of April. Soderbergh was suddenly juggling three projects. His brilliant career was getting complicated.

Meanwhile, the indie distributors were not idle. The sky over Larry Estes's RCA/Columbia office in a spanking new building at the corner of Olive and Riverside in Burbank was dark with buyers circling overhead. The parlous finances of some of these companies just made them more eager; they grasped at *sex, lies* like a lifeline. Moreover, with their film almost incandescent with heat, Estes and Newmyer were in the enviable position of being able to pick and choose. The two producers, seated in the RCA/Columbia conference room with its imposing stone-topped table, slotted in every buyer in town and watched them perform their dog-and-pony shows at one-hour intervals. Barker and Bernard from Orion Classics, Janet Grillo from New Line, Lipsky from Skouras. Bingham Ray made an impassioned pitch for Alive Films: "We're not as well-heeled as some of these other companies, but we're hungrier, because it's me, and I'm really, really hungry," he pleaded. "This film, I'm drooling. I would chop my left arm to do it. I'll make the best possible offer, but . . . ah . . . ah . . . I don't have any money to offer you! Thank you very much." Of course he didn't get it.

New Line offered a couple of hundred thousand dollars but was deterred by the absence of video rights and regarded Savoca's *True Love* as a better bet. Goldwyn, too, was breathing heavily. Like Tom Skouras, Sam Goldwyn was a scion of Hollywood royalty. He had a reputation for looking over his shoulder at the studios, worrying about their opinion, staying in the good graces of the Lew Wasserman crowd. Goldwyn was a gentleman—genteel, magnanimous, and gracious. His company had a policy against giving advances without video rights. But there was one small, struggling company that contacted Estes and Newmyer that was not genteel, magnanimous, or gracious. It was called Miramax.

IN THE BEGINNING, back in 1979, the Weinsteins were bottom-feeders, trolling for movies—anything on celluloid—that no one else would touch. Like many in the film business, they have soft-core skeletons rattling around their closet, movies with titles like *I'm Not Feeling Myself Tonight* and *A Thousand and One Arabian Nights*. They understood that sex sells. If *The 400 Blows* changed Harvey's life, as he claims, for Bob it was *I Am Curious Yellow*, rated X for full frontal nudity. The brothers noticed, as Bob wrote in *Vanity Fair*, "a packed audience of 'art-lovers' who never would have set foot in a movie with subtitles but for the fact that there was a little something extra added," namely, sex. They took films, often British, X-rated, and priced so that they could afford them, altered them to make them more palatable to the U.S. audiences, then sold them to hungry home-video distributors and to the burgeoning cable networks like Showtime or Cinemax. When Harvey stumbled on *Goodbye, Emmanuelle*, the third of the endless (and profitable) series of soft-core movies starring Sylvia Krystel, he must have grinned broadly and helped himself to another tuna on rye.

The brothers drifted into distribution with a couple of concert films, including one that featured Genesis, and another Paul McCartney. On his way back from Cannes in June 1981, Harvey stopped off in London and acquired *The Secret Policeman's Ball (SPB)*, the film version of a benefit concert for Amnesty International that featured comic turns by members

of Britain's two biggest comedy groups, Beyond the Fringe and the Pythons, who were hot off *The Life of Brian* (1979), along with music by Pete
Townshend, among others. The folks at Amnesty, which was nearly bankrupt, knew precious little about the movie business, did not have high
expectations for the film, and did not expect an advance—a situation
ready-made for the Weinsteins. They exploited it to the hilt.

The picture's producer, Martin N. Lewis, a flamboyant, speed-rapping
Brit and would-be stand-up comic, met Harvey at a hotel in Mayfair. Even
though he hadn't seen the picture, Harvey was wildly enthusiastic, gushed,
in a raspy, Queens-inflected growl that rarely escaped the register of a tuba,
"This is fantastic, we can really promote this, we're gonna play this big, we
did this for Paul McCartney!!!" Lewis was nonplussed but grateful that
someone was showing interest in his baby, and after listening to Harvey
spritz for thirty seconds, surprise turned to love, and he exclaimed, "OK,
you gotta deal." Years later, he recalls, "It was an impulsive gesture. There
was something about the energy of the guy. I was not unaware that there
were bullshit merchants in the world, but I felt he was a bullshit merchant
who was gonna deliver."

Lewis, however, made one mistake. He happened to mention to Harvey
that he was working on a sequel. Harvey exclaimed, "Great, fantastic!" and
then every week the call would come: "How's the sequel going?"

"Well, we're gonna do it—"

"When, when are you gonna do it?"

"In September. We may give you the sequel, but let's see how you do
with this one."

"Martin, we need to make a few edits."

"You need to edit?"

"Well, some of this stuff is not gonna play well with an American audience. You gotta trust me on this. We're gonna have to cut it back." Lewis
demurred. After all, this was original Python material, never before seen.
But Harvey cut and cut, and cut some more. Before long, a movie that had
been about 110 minutes long was reduced almost by half, to about 65 minutes. Still, Lewis didn't understand why Harvey was so anxious to get hold
of the sequel. When it was finally ready, it contained more Python material,
much more music—Sting, Eric Clapton, Jeff Beck, Phil Collins—and it
was made by a real director, Julien Temple, for about $120,000. It was
called *The Secret Policeman's Other Ball (SPOB)*. By this time Harvey was
calling Lewis several times a day. Solicitously, he asked, "How's everything
doing, how's the new show coming? Are the rights available?" Lewis's first
obligation was to Amnesty, and he had a duty to get the best deal that he
could. He was confident *The SPB* would be a smash hit and was hoping to
sell the sequel to an American major for a huge advance. So he always

made the same reply: "Let's see how you do with *The Secret Policeman's Ball*."

Lewis brought *SPOB* to Los Angeles's film festival, Filmex, in March of 1982, hoping to find a buyer. Instead, he ran into Harvey, who again began the drumbeat: "We gotta get *The Secret Policeman's Other Ball*, we gotta have it, you gotta give it to us." Worn down, Lewis agreed. Still in denial, Lewis asked, "It's a double bill, isn't that what you're thinking about?" Harvey replied, "No, no, no, that would be three hours, people aren't going to spend three hours watching two movies, you've got to boil it down to one film. You can make a lot more money if you can make one movie that plays like gangbusters." That was his favorite phrase in those days, "plays like gangbusters." After six weeks in the editing room, they succeeded in reducing two movies to one, 240 minutes to about 100 minutes. They called the combined version *The Secret Policeman's Other Ball* and hoped it would play like gangbusters.

Harvey had sold Lewis on the basis of his experience with rock 'n' roll concert films, McCartney and Genesis, but Lewis started looking at the marketing campaigns they'd done. He thought, Jesus, what the hell is this? *Spaced Out? Goodbye, Emmanuelle?* What have I got myself into here? "I discovered that they knew nothing about movie distribution," he says. "They had the passion, but there was a lot of bluster there. I looked at the mocked-up ads, and I was appalled. They were terrible, tasteless. One of them involved quotes from various film critics on a roll of toilet paper." Lewis told the brothers, "Your campaign is shit, if you don't mind me saying so."

"Look, I may be fat, but I'm not stupid. You know better, do you?"

"Yeah, I think I do." Lewis was aware that Jerry Falwell had recently campaigned against the Pythons' *Life of Brian* when it was released in 1979. In an effort to create some controversy of his own by tweaking the Moral Majority, he designed a TV spot around Python Graham Chapman, dressed conservatively in a three-piece suit, seated at a desk with an American flag directly behind him. Chapman says something like, "My fellow Americans, I'm from the Oral Majority. I want to protest strongly against this disgusting new motion picture, *The Secret Policeman's Other Ball*. It is without doubt the most lewd, lascivious, tasteless movie since *The Sound of Music*. This movie must be banned before it turns us all into a nation of perverts!" At which point he stands up, revealing a pink tutu and black fishnet stockings. Lewis presented his idea to the brothers, saying, "Let's get the movie banned." He recalls, "There was this blank look on Bob and Harvey's faces. They didn't understand publicity. They didn't know about stories, angles, hypes, stunts. To them, publicity was just film reviews. Advertising, buying space. They were concert promoters."

But the Weinsteins gave Lewis the green light. At most, he hoped to get lucky with a few column items. He didn't bank on Donald Wildmon's Coalition for Better Television, which at the time was on a rampage against the networks. The skittish NBC affiliate in New York turned down the ad, citing a 1941 joint resolution of Congress banning the use of the American flag in advertisements. Lewis promptly called *Saturday Night Live,* which, though a bit long in the tooth, was still flush with the success of its early years, and asked them to run the spot. They did, on Weekend Update. Recalls Lewis, "We had a huge story! Bob's and Harvey's eyes popped out on stalks. 'Aha, aha, aha!' They got it, they understood what publicity was: 'Martin, we were going to spend $5,000 on a local TV spot, this is running nationally, this is worth $100,000.' " Suddenly, Lewis, whom the Weinsteins hadn't entirely trusted, could do no wrong. "Harvey called me the third brother," he continues. "It was like the fifth Beatle. There's been a million since, but I was the first."

The SPOB premiered in New York on May 21, 1982. According to an ad the brothers later ran in *The Hollywood Reporter,* the film grossed $6 million. Amnesty apparently saw very little of that money. Says Lewis, "We didn't make much money on the theatrical, is my memory. Did Amnesty get every single penny they probably should have had? I don't know. There was a fair amount that came off in expenses, and they probably were high, but we [at Amnesty] didn't know how to gauge them. Do I think Harvey and Bob baldfaced stole $4 million from a human rights organization, that they ripped off Amnesty International? No, I do not. What they'd said to us was that the theatrical was going to generate more publicity and heat for the home video and TV. Was Amnesty unhappy? Our expectations on this were minimal, zero. Amnesty was thrilled beyond words."

Thinking he was being smart, Lewis had held on to the TV and video rights, imagining he could sell them for more money after the film opened. Harvey wanted them desperately, and he wouldn't give up. He was like a hair in the back of your throat that swallowing won't get rid of. He bellowed, "You're going to sell me the rights—"

"I'm not going to sell you the rights. I want to wait till the movie opens."

"But they belong to me . . ."

"That wasn't the deal we did."

"We've put so much effort into this, we've been a team." Continues Lewis, "He browbeat me and guilt-tripped me. At the end of it I was completely drenched with sweat. I thought, That was like the most intense sex I've ever had in my life. It felt horrible and pleasurable at the same time. My girlfriend will kill me." By the time Lewis got off the phone, he had agreed to sell Harvey the TV and video rights.

Harvey and Bob squeezed blood out of every frame of film, shuffling and reshuffling *The Secret Policeman/Other Ball* deck, recycling and resectioning the material like the Plains Indians of grade-school fame who were commended for making use of every part of the buffalo, the flesh for food, the skin for clothing, the hooves for whatever. In 1983, the Weinsteins apparently acquired theatrical rights to *Monty Python and the Holy Grail,* which was then eight or nine years old, put it on a double bill with *SPOB,* which had already been out for a year, distributed buttons that read, "Get Pythonized," and made even more money. Feeding the hungry video maw, they took the outtakes from the two *Secret Policeman* pictures and edited them into a 90-minute straight-to-video film called *The Secret Policeman's Private Parts* that they sold to Media Home Entertainment. Harvey and Bob even resliced *The Secret Policeman* pie into two best-of films (comedy and music), *The Secret Policeman's Private Party* and *The Secret Policeman's Rock Concert* and sold them to a company in Japan.

Unlike most distributors who started like the Weinsteins, picking over the refuse discarded by their betters, Harvey aspired to intellectual and aesthetic respectability, and when in Cannes he stumbled across *Eréndira* (1983), a Brazilian film directed by Ruy Guerra based on a Gabriel García Márquez short story, he snapped it up. Explains Robert Newman, now an agent at ICM, but then a kid fresh out of NYU film school gofering for Miramax at $3.50 an hour, "While they were still trying to acquire a film, they would already have sold the home video rights to somebody, and they would already be preselling it to the movie theaters. It was very much buying the cow with her own milk." *Eréndira* featured the legendary Greek actress Irene Papas and an unknown but sexy newcomer named Cláudia Ohana. Newman asked, skeptically, "How do you sell it?"

"Easy!" Harvey responded. "You got a Nobel prize winner and you got sex. You work both ends."

Harvey knew that García Márquez, an outspoken left-wing critic of the United States, had been denied an entry visa by the American government, and he used it to his advantage, creating a stink about the fact that the State Department wouldn't let the Nobel prize winner visit the U.S. for the premiere of his own film. Says Newman, the idea was to "get the message out without necessarily having to write checks." Playing the Papas card, he managed to get *Eréndira* into the New York Film Festival, at the same time that he slipped Ohana into *Playboy.* Says veteran indie publicist Reid Rosefelt, whom Harvey hired to work on the film, Miramax "retouched Ohana's chest to give her cleavage! I thought, This is different. They just had an unabashed willingness to sell that I had not seen within the specialty markets."

Eréndira became a modest hit. But more important, with the mix of sex, controversy, and prestige that accompanied the Márquez imprimatur, it became a model for the kinds of films Miramax wanted to distribute and the kinds of marketing campaigns they would use to launch them.

From the beginning, it was clear that the Weinsteins would not be satisfied with merely distributing other people's movies. These two cinemabesotted young men, like many who labored in the vineyards of indie distribution, were frustrated filmmakers. Bob, who fancied himself a screenwriter, wrote a baseball script called *Grand Slam*, with Harvey's help, that went nowhere. In 1980, the brothers made a knockoff of John Carpenter's *Halloween* series starring Jamie Lee Curtis, a slasher movie called *The Burning*, which features a summer camp caretaker slicing and dicing horny teens with pruning shears. Harvey produced, and Bob took co-writing credit.

In the late '70s, Harvey had bought a getaway cottage up at Crystal Beach, in Canada, just north of Buffalo, and it was there that the brothers started writing the script for the film they hoped would launch their filmmaking careers. The film was part John Hughes movie, part musical. As the story evolved—teenagers inherit a dilapidated, white elephant of a house in a small town and turn it into a rock and roll hotel—it became more autobiographical, loosely based on the Weinsteins' days and nights at the Century Theater in Buffalo. The boys' friends considered *Playing for Keeps* a kind of Freudian Rosetta Stone for parsing the puzzle of the brothers' perplexing emotional development.

Neither of them had ever directed, so they shot a twenty-minute promo reel, which they took to Cannes in an effort to raise money. Recalls Harvey's childhood friend Alan Brewer, who supervised the picture's music and was supposed to get a producer credit, "People said that they were crazy for trying to do this with the limited experience they had, yet that just motivated them, especially Harvey. 'You think I'm crazy? Just watch me!' " Harvey pitched the film on the basis of the soundtrack album, which he promised would be packed with the superstar acts they had promoted in Buffalo. It didn't matter if the movie itself bombed, he argued; the soundtrack would be solid gold, not to mention the music video spinoffs. A London-based company called J&M Films bought his pitch and agreed to finance the movie to the tune of about $4 million.

Built into the structure of most productions is a system of checks and balances—the director against the producer, the star against either or both, and the studio against all of them. But whether from megalomania, paranoia, or some other, more exotic "ia" disorder, the brothers, in their infinite wisdom, decided to do it all, direct and produce. And to make matters worse, much worse, each would do both, co-produce and co-direct.

The film, called *Playing for Keeps*, was shot on a farm in Bethany, Pennsylvania, near Wilkes-Barre. The Weinsteins had had the entire script story-boarded in L.A., so in theory it should have been an easy shoot; all they had to do was connect the dots. In practice, it was anything but. Recalls Jeff Silver, who is now a partner at Outlaw Productions, and was then hired by the production manager to *be* the production manager, "I've always called *Playing for Keeps* the Noah's Ark of films because there was two of everything."

Needless to say, the two-headed beast ate through the budget double time. The financial problems were severe and started early, even before the beginning of principal photography. Silver remembers, "When I was brought in, two weeks before the shooting started, it was, Help, we're sinking here, and I was supposed to find out who and where the problem was. I went through each department asking, 'Why are you so far over budget here?' They'd say, 'We get one decision from Bob, one decision from Harvey.' Harvey and Bob mostly disagreed with each other, except where it came to hammering the production team on costs, and there they were in perfect harmony. They did a lot of yelling and screaming about the costs, but they would be the biggest instigators of cost increases owing to their inability to decide anything. My report was, 'It's the boys, it's the brothers that are mucking everything up here.' I was brought in as a detective, but I found out that the culprit was the client."

The cameras rolled in mid-September 1984. Co-directors are as rare as two-headed mules, and *Playing for Keeps* was Exhibit A in why that is so. Whenever it came time to make a decision, it was, Should we shoot this way? Should we shoot that way? "They would have behind-the-monitor arguments incessantly, to the point where we'd all be standing around kind of wondering if we were supposed to be doing something, because the arguments would go on for fifteen and twenty minutes," Silver recalls. "On the set, that's an eternity." When they couldn't agree, which was most of the time, they shot it both ways, thinking they'd resolve it in the editing room.

The promo reel to one side, the Weinsteins had virtually no track record with actors, sensitive souls who require a lot of tender loving care, particularly these actors, who were young, inexperienced—and cheap. (Mary Ward played the "love interest," and Marisa Tomei in her second movie, was also featured.) They don't respond particularly well to bullying and belittling, the only directing skills in the Weinsteins' arsenal. Recalls a source who was often on the set, "It was, Okay, Bob's been sitting at the video monitor for two hours, relaxing, getting energized, then he's gonna come kick your ass. Now Harvey's gonna go and relax, and then he's gonna come kick your ass. It was like tag-team directing. One day, they made Mary Ward burst into tears, cry hysterically. They were both ganging up on her, yelling. It was, Now, I'm not only being yelled at by one director, I'm being yelled at by two."

Adds Silver, "It wasn't limited to Mary Ward. I saw tears in the editing room, I saw tears in the art department. Those guys were tyrannical and emotionally manipulative. They would yell at you for something that they told you yesterday, and the next day tell you that's not what they said at all. Something was great one minute and horrible the next. I'm professionally accustomed to cutting directors a whole lot of slack in the temper department. People undergo personality changes in the midst of productions. It's a war-like mentality. The first half a dozen times, I figured, I get it guys, you're just in over your heads and having a bad time, that's okay, we're here to help. But this went beyond that. These were desperately angry men. There was no way to get through to them. When they started turning on you and acting like you're there to harm them, that's where you throw up your hands and go, 'OK, maybe I can't help.' They made all of our lives miserable." In the end, Silver just gave up. "My job description was, 'Get this sucker under control.' Nobody could do that."

And because the Weinsteins were producing as well as directing, there was no one to say "No." Recalls Brewer, who was also onboard as a producer, "It was hard for them to listen to anyone saying, 'But if you do that, it's gonna cost you. We don't have it in the budget.' They'd say, 'I don't care, take it from somewhere else!' But eventually there was no place to take it from." Silver continues, "No one knew what the budget was. In truth, there was no budget. It was a real mess." Even today, it is impossible to determine what the film ultimately cost. Adds Silver, "I would not be surprised if it was twice the $4 million budget going in. It ran over weeks, and millions."

Alarmed, Film Finances, the completion bond company, sent David Korda, the son of Zoltan Korda, who directed the 1939 version of *The Four Feathers*, and was a member of the famous British film family, to the set. J&M, meanwhile, sent former United Artists executive Chris Mankiewicz to lie down on the tracks in front of the runaway train. Like Korda, Mankiewicz was a scion of cinema royalty. His father was Joe Mankiewicz, who directed classics like *All About Eve*, and his uncle was Herman J., who wrote *Citizen Kane*. "It was amateur night in Dixieville," Mankiewicz recalls. "Neither Harvey, the Otto Preminger of the two, the ranter and the screamer, nor Bob, the gnome-like brother, who was very stubborn, very tough-minded, had any idea how to direct a movie, and they couldn't admit that. These louts, these crude barbarians from Buffalo showed not the slightest aptitude for filmmaking. They didn't know what they wanted to do or how to do it. I remember a glacial pace of production and massive indecision. This was a film of a very dubious screenplay. Extremely dreadful, unfunny comedy business. The Weinsteins directing that Frank Capra kind of comedy—no. I thought of them as charlatans. I couldn't believe anybody would have given these people money to do it. They were very brutal customers in those days. Harvey would hiss at me every time I got into his eyesight. Hell hath no fury like a Weinstein scorned. He was ferocious. He was like Mike Tyson was when he first came up, when he would rush out at the opening bell, and everybody would hold their breath thinking that he would just crush his opponent. I'd never met somebody with that kind of animal intensity."

Nor did Harvey impress Mankiewicz as being particularly interested in film. "There was nothing about film history or films that I felt he had any respect for," he continues. "Imagine having a Korda and a Mankiewicz around, and never asking, 'Gee, tell me something about your dad or your uncle.' I don't think he had any idea who David Korda's family was or my family or cared. I've grown up knowing a lot of great screenwriters. There's a sense of the poet or a storyteller about them, an artistic sensibility. [With Harvey] you never felt that there was an artistic muse involved. Whether he was going to be making films, or donuts, or machine gun parts, it was a product, and there was just a sense of ferocious ambition. He was a guy who wanted to have a career or make a lot of money."

The production dragged on and on, days, weeks past the scheduled stop date, until Film Finances pulled the plug on November 10, 1984, after forty-eight days. According to Martin Lewis, the brothers knew the picture wasn't much good: "They were trying to make it better. Their way to make it better was soundtrack. They called in every favor in Christendom—and Jew-dom. They went to Townshend. Peter Townshend! And they got a song from him. "Life to Life." Simon Le Bon from Duran Duran. They got a song from Phil Collins, an outtake from one of his albums, but not a bad song. Still the boys still weren't satisfied with that. They wanted to get the older crowd, so they got Peter Frampton. They wanted to get the African-American crowd, so they went to Sister Sledge. They covered every fucking demographic known to mankind. Bob and Harvey didn't have pictures of these guys having sex with animals; they were given the songs because of the relentless charm, pressure, cajoling, 'Please give us a break, we've done a movie, we need your help.' Their drive was far in excess of their creativity as directors, but you couldn't help admiring it. They would not take no for an answer. They were like the Terminator. They just wouldn't stop."

Harvey had left Robert Newman and his Buffalo-era pal Jim Doyle to mind the store in New York. But without the brothers' full attention, the business was suffering, especially with editing dragging on for another year or so, and with *Playing for Keeps* sucking the air—not to mention the cash—out of the room. Says Brewer, "*Playing for Keeps* definitely weakened the finances of Miramax, and put it in a very tenuous position. The atmosphere was tense and scary." Adds Lewis, choosing his words carefully, "Their passion to make *Playing for Keeps* succeed was out of proportion to the quality of the movie, more intense than their friendship with me. I felt not burned, but singed. When you're giving a party, and you've invited everybody, you've done all the preparation, at a certain point you've got to sit back and say, 'That's it. It's gonna be what it is.' They weren't like that. They could not stop. If it had succeeded, it would have been a big coup for them. They were chasing that success."

Universal, which had picked up the film in the waning days of the Frank Price regime, probably for its soundtrack, unceremoniously dumped it. Says Tom Pollock, who succeeded Price, "What was done to it is what Harvey has done to so many other movies since." Lewis continues, "Really dumb people would have said, This is a great movie, Universal screwed us, we'll make another movie. Here comes *Playing for Keeps 2*. Instead, they said, 'We're not Steven Spielberg, we have to find a niche for ourselves.' Their skills were that they understood movies, and they had a passion for them, they could market them. And they went that route."

Harvey and Bob turned back to Miramax, but it was not the same Miramax. *Playing for Keeps* had taken its toll. As Ed Glass, who cut trailers for the Weinsteins, puts it, "That movie was like World War II. It just went on and on and on and on. They shot it, they edited, they went out and shot new scenes, they re-edited. There was lots of yelling and screaming. [The brothers] were fighting with each other. It destroyed everybody who came in contact with it." Gradually, the old gang dribbled away. Recalls Doyle, "Within days or weeks after the film was released we all left one by one. Harvey and Bob were just so angry and so disappointed about the failure of the film. They were [always] tough to work for, but during that time it was just awful." Brewer, who had known Harvey since junior high school, left. So did Lewis. Continues Doyle, "Newman also decided he didn't want any part of it anymore. He moved on. I was listening to them telling me stories—'Bob said this, Harvey did that, I can't stand it, Jimmy, I got to get out.' Now it was just me. Everyone else was bailing. So I said, 'I don't want to do this anymore.'"

The first stage of the Miramax rocket had fallen away.

After the *Playing for Keeps* debacle, the Weinsteins circled the wagons. The first order of business was to repopulate the depleted ranks of the company. The brothers were too poor or too penurious to employ people with experience; they preferred to hire young and hire cheap, took in kids off the street or just out of college. Having taken Lewis's lessons to heart, the brothers made sure they were well stocked with publicists, at least twice as many as companies of comparable size. They were the shock troops, the marines, the first to go in and ignite the word of mouth that would drive the film. Once they created the heat, money for advertising would follow, first local, and then, if the film caught on, national. As the frontline, they were under fierce pressure, and inevitably passed that pressure along. Largely female, they were known as the Furies.

The second order of business was to find a new Robert Newman to head up distribution. In the dark, at the back of Dan Talbot's Lincoln Plaza theater—the prime exhibition site for indie films in New York City—Bob approached Bingham Ray and asked him if he wanted the job. Ray turned him down, suggested Jeff Lipsky's kid brother, Mark. Mark didn't know much about Miramax, had only heard that it was run by these two crazy brothers. He recalls, "I called everybody I knew in the business to ask for advice, and there wasn't a single person I called who didn't say, 'Whatever you do, don't work for them.'" When Bob offered him the job, he took it.

It wasn't long before Lipsky discovered that Miramax was in desperate straits. He recalls, "We couldn't walk into a single screening room in New York without the money to pay for it. I was literally turned away from one: 'Come back with a check in your hand.'" Adds post-production staffer Stuart Burkin, "If you said you worked at Miramax, it closed doors. It was the last thing you would tell someone when you were trying to book a stage or trying to get an actor to dub lines: 'We need to go back and rerecord your voiceover, but we can't pay you anything.' 'Who are you again? Miramax? Oh, Harvey Weinstein owes me money!'" Moreover, the Weinsteins had no idea how to run a business. "Getting the phone answered was a nightmare," Lipsky continues. "The Weinsteins didn't let their employees do their jobs. Too many people were doing the same thing, and things had to be done over and over. If they had spent $500 on a mail-order management course, they would have doubled their income overnight." When Marty Zeidman was hired two years later to head distribution, that is, book films into theaters, his wife, who worked there briefly, discovered that there was a desk in the office stuffed with unopened envelopes containing checks. He recalls, "They sat there for months. Nobody was even going through the mail."

That same year, 1986, Miramax hired Eve Chilton, a blonde from an old WASP family with a house on the West Chop, on Martha's Vineyard. Eve was stunning, with perfect features marred only by a small, wine-colored birthmark on one side of her face. She became Harvey's new assistant, and he was instantly smitten. "It seemed like not even a day [passed] before he was all over her," Lipsky remembers. "For possibly a couple of weeks or more, there were a dozen roses on her desk when we walked into work, to the point where we had to confront him and say, 'You can't do this, it's an office, not your personal sexual playground.' In no time he took her to the Venice Film Festival or one of the European markets, and from that moment on they were inseparable. It was a bolt of lightning, very intense, very fast."

Immaculately turned out, Chilton was an anomaly in the Miramax pigsty, but people liked her, even though she was shy, quiet, and reserved, not about to let anyone in. They appreciated that she didn't take advantage of her connection to Harvey. Which is not to say they weren't cynical about the relationship. What did a woman as beautiful as Eve see in a guy like him? they wondered. They were equally fascinated that he fe.t for her. It was as if the blemish humanized her, put her within reach, gave him some kind of leverage over her. Behind their backs, of course, they referred to the couple as the Beauty and the Beast.

Alison Brantley, a southern girl well brought up in North Carolina whom Harvey had hired to head up acquisitions, believed she understood. "I thought they genuinely loved each other. When she met him, he was just struggling, a nobody, and there was something about him she liked, something about beauty within him." When you were in his presence, you understood the package, or should have. As Brantley puts it, "If you walked into his office and you didn't think he was gonna try to screw you every which way to Sunday, you were a fool. So deal with it. And that's part of the charm. That's part of what Eve liked about him."

The relationship thrived, and he promoted her, putting her in charge of the children's division. Eventually, Harvey and Eve got married at a posh club on the East Side in the 70s. They went to St. Bart's on their honeymoon.

Chilton was the first rung of the ladder that helped Harvey to climb out of the Queens shtetl where he grew up, and it seemed like some of the new hires reflected the brothers' desire to give Miramax a veneer of class. In addition to Brantley, the brothers brought on Trea Hoving, the daughter of Metropolitan Museum of Art head Tom Hoving, in acquisitions. Brantley herself came from Granada, the crème de la crème of British production companies. She recalls, "My background and theirs were so diametrically opposed that for me it was like walking into the jungle. There are lions there, and I was just what they wanted to eat. But from the moment I met Harvey, I loved him. I adored this movie Alain Corneau had made, *Indian Nocturne*. Harvey screened it, and rather than yelling at me, like, 'Whaddya crazy?' he said, 'You know, Alie, sometimes you fall in love with a movie, and that's okay. Don't be afraid to use your instincts. You're not going to be right all the time. That's why we have a group of people, that's why we talk about it.' He encouraged me. I was never afraid of telling him exactly what I thought, because I knew that's what he paid me for. No matter how much he tried to intimidate me, it didn't stop me."

Harvey and Bob went to Cannes in May of 1986. In the bar of the Petit

Carlton, Harvey struck up a conversation with a tall, disheveled Brit named Nik Powell. Powell and his partner, Steve Woolley, a clever, boyish-looking young man with fine features who wore his brown hair gathered into a ponytail, ran Palace Pictures. Palace was more Miramax than Miramax. A freewheeling, we'll-trying-anything duo, Woolley and Powell had a keen eye for films and talent, and had cherry-picked the best of films of the 1980s for British distribution, pictures as diverse as *Pixote; The Evil Dead; Diva; Blood Simple; Merry Christmas Mr. Lawrence; Stop Making Sense;* and the *Nightmare on Elm Street* series. It didn't take long for the Weinsteins to recognize in Powell, and especially Woolley, kindred spirits. Says Paul Webster, who later headed up production for Miramax and who worked for Palace in those days, "Harvey got the idea for Miramax from Palace. The relation between him and Steve was key." Woolley recalls, "I came out of the punk scene of the '70s and he came out of band promoting, and we both loved movies. A breakfast meeting turned into a whole day of just chatting. Harvey's thinking in modeling Miramax on Palace was to try to acquire movies like we did—*Paris, Texas* or *Kiss of the Spider Woman*—quality films that had a certain prestige, a certain European cachet so that they could cross over. What he learned from us was the kind of bravura showmanship, 'We really love this film, we're gonna be as passionate about this film as the filmmakers were when they made it.' I really took to Harvey, admired his spirit. We kind of formed an unwritten alliance."

If the *Playing for Keeps* fiasco had taught the Weinsteins anything, it was that they didn't have a clue about production, and Harvey was hungry to learn. When he ran into Robert Hakim in Paris, the powerful and intimidating French producer behind films like *Belle de Jour* and *Isadora,* he seized the opportunity, exclaiming, "Look, I want to make movies, can you teach me?"

"If you come to the Georges V every Wednesday, I'll give you four hours." Harvey went, sat at Hakim's knee. One day, the Frenchman told him a story about producing *Plein Soleil,* aka, *The Talented Mr. Ripley,* with Alain Delon, at the time a huge star. Delon didn't like the way things were going, and two weeks into the production he gave Hakim an ultimatum: "If things don't change around here, that's that."

"You walk off, I'm going to close the movie down."

"How can you? You've shot two weeks of footage, you'll lose millions!"

"I don't care. I'm not going to have my movie blackmailed by you." Hakim explained to Weinstein, "If you're going to be a great producer, you have to be the boss of the movie, and you have to take a threat like that and just say, 'Forget it.'" Says Harvey now, "This was one of the lessons I learned early."

The Weinsteins saw *Working Girls* at the Directors' Fortnight where

Spike Lee's *She's Gotta Have It* also made a splash. It was a down and dirty feature about the lives of hookers in New York City, an exercise in zero-budget filmmaking—$100,000 in the can—whose rawness lent it the conviction of a documentary. The director, Lizzie Borden, a small, slender woman dressed from head to toe in black, and dramatically made up with blood-red lipstick and heavy eyeshadow, was a feminist and fixture in the downtown scene, a bubbling cauldron of art, politics, and theater. In those days, before Ronald Reagan clamped down, films like *Working Girls* could get money from the federal and state arts endowments, and the $40,000 Borden collected in grants made up almost half the budget. "I would get shortends* free and developing free," she recalls. "You spent 90 percent of your time borrowing and begging."

To Borden, *Working Girls* was "not about sex, but about labor"; to the Weinsteins it was about sex, and Bob in particular was desperate to acquire it, although, as Mark Lipsky says, "He was squeamish about it. It was a lesbian movie. They are both very conservative guys. They went after these kinds of movies but cringed inside." Lipsky and the brothers met with John Pierson, whom the producers had hired to rep the film. Pierson was tall and thin. With flying hair and a prominent Adam's apple, he looked a little like Ichabod Crane. He knew the Weinsteins only slightly, but he liked them. The brothers left the meeting elated, thinking, We got the movie. Then they got a call from the producers. "We would, but we can't," they said, revealing that they had a prior commitment to Circle Releasing, which had made an offer of $100,000. But Bob would not take no for an answer. He kept calling, demanding that they meet with him again. They replied, "No, Bob, we've sold the movie, we have a deal." Bob insisted: "No, you don't understand, you gotta meet with us one more time." Says Borden, "Bob kept appearing with a suitcase full of a little bit more money every time we said no. I didn't trust them, but I liked them. I visited them in the apartment they were working out of. The thing that got me turned around was when I met Harvey's assistant Eve, who was the sweetest girl ever. The fact that this woman could be in love with that man made me think, Oh, okay." When Miramax doubled the Circle offer, putting $200,000 on the table, Borden gave in, saying, "Fuck, these guys want it more than anyone else, why not give them a shot."

Miramax, like every distributor, took its costs off the top, and was accused of "grossing up" movies, spending what would have been the filmmaker's cut on marketing to drive up grosses, thus swelling its share of the profits, while raising the profile of the company—a not uncommon practice in the industry. Directors loved the publicity and the grosses—and

* "Shortends": The unexposed film left over after a portion of a reel is shot.

only later did they recognize the ugly truth: a goose egg at the bottom of the profit statement. But the brothers did a good job with *Working Girls*. It grossed nearly $1.8 million when it was released in March 1987, very impressive considering its cost, and earned about $750,000 for the director and producers. But after going over the statements, Borden's producers demanded an audit and found charges for a ski rental during the Sundance Film Festival, and a $1,000 bill from the Mark Hopkins Hotel in San Francisco two months after the film had opened there. Miramax had to reimburse Borden. It was small change but, as Pierson wrote later, "Distribution costs on an independent film should always be *only* direct, out-of-pocket costs—the cash spent on that one, specific movie. Second, there should be real, documented, invoiced expenses." The flap did not help the Weinsteins' reputation.

There were other films on the runway waiting to take off, among them *Pelle the Conqueror*, which Harvey had acquired at Cannes the previous May. *Pelle*, directed by Bille August, was a grim and gritty, albeit ravishingly photographed film set in nineteenth-century Denmark. It told the tale of a Swedish boy's struggle to free himself from serflike servitude to a hidebound family of landowners and at the same time escape the shadow of his beloved but feckless father, beautifully acted by Max von Sydow, an Ingmar Bergman stalwart who most memorably played chess with Death in *The Seventh Seal*. Bleak and uncompromising, *Pelle* was a tough sell. Unlike *Working Girls*, there was no sex to speak of. But Harvey was determined to push the picture across the art house divide. As publicist Christina Kounelias puts it, "They were trying to unghettoize art house films, get them out of the teeny theaters at the edge of town where the beatniks live, and make them accessible to a broader, more mainstream audience."

In practice, that meant once again putting a commercial spin on the film. There's a scene where a ghostly fishing boat that has been battered by heavy seas and long given up for lost, washes up on the rocks near shore, its sails in shreds. Glass included a shot of the boat in his trailer. Zeidman recalls, "Harvey was ranting, during the trailer, 'I want a happy boat! I want a happy boat!' It was beyond me. I said to Ed, 'A happy boat?' The film was just so bleak and they were trying to find some way to make it not so dark." But somehow they managed to do it. "Their father was a diamond merchant," explains Glass. "There's millions of diamonds out there. But once he put the diamond down on the black velvet, you went, 'Wow, look at that stone!' Compared to all the commercial junk, their movies were like diamonds. They knew how to display them very well."

Zeidman, who arrived in October 1988, was one of the few new hires who actually had real experience. He had given up a big corner office at

Lorimar/Columbia and taken a cut in pay to work for Miramax. "From the very first, Harvey believed he could get Max von Sydow a nomination for an Academy Award," he remembers. "This was a very small Scandinavian film, and it was almost inconceivable. At that time, I was not a true believer. I just didn't get it."

Pelle was released December 21, 1988, but the picture stalled. Harvey used a shot of a nearly topless peasant girl (who appeared for a nanosecond in the picture) in the ads. One of Miramax's sub-distributors even tried to sell *Pelle* below the Mason-Dixon line, historically a graveyard for foreign language films. Recalls David Dinerstein, who would eventually head marketing, "We sold it as a genre film—*Pelle the Conqueror*, this action hero—and we booked it as such into some multiplexes. It was their way of getting to those places you were never able to get to in the past, maybe not in a truthful manner, but still getting the film out there. This was Harvey at his best."

When Academy nominations for 1988 were announced, von Sydow got one for Best Actor, and *Pelle* was nominated as well for Best Foreign Film—and won, giving Miramax its first Oscar. Zeidman understood he had been wrong. "It was one of the first times I realized that Harvey could make things happen that were way beyond what you would think was in the realm of possibility. In a lot of ways I believe Harvey has a certain genius." The long march had begun.

Two
The Anger Artists
1989

- **How the Weinsteins terrorized their staff but took *sex, lies* out of the art houses into the multiplexes, while the Sundance Kid nearly rode his institute into the ground and competed with Sydney Pollack for Steven Soderbergh's next film.**

"Bob and I grew up as underdogs, and if there's a theme to the movies we make, it's about the outsider who can come in and change things."

— HARVEY WEINSTEIN

When Miramax threw its hat into the *sex, lies* ring shortly after Sundance, the brothers were still searching for the breakthrough hit they needed to propel them into the front ranks of the business. In 1988, the New York office of a British bank called Midland Montague had bought, in effect, a 45 percent interest in Miramax for $3.5 million, $2.5 million of which was a direct loan to the company. On this basis, Miramax got a $10 million line of credit from Chase Bank. The company was perhaps best known for Errol Morris's groundbreaking documentary *The Thin Blue Line*, still in theaters. Randall Adams, the subject of Morris's film, a victim of Texas "justice" was in jail for a murder he very likely did not commit and had just been released, as a result, Miramax claimed, of the blizzard of press it had stirred up around the issue. *Scandal*, for which it had high hopes, was in the pipeline, slated to open later in the year, as was *My Left Foot*, directed by Jim Sheridan and starring Daniel Day-Lewis.

The Weinsteins had paid $400,000 for Errol Morris's documentary. From a marketing standpoint, the film presented some of the same problems as Miramax's other pictures, namely, to get butts in seats, the true nature of the film had to be concealed. If *The Secret Policeman's Other Ball* could not be sold as a concert film—concert films were supposed to be box office poison—*The Thin Blue Line* could not be sold as a documentary. The "D-word" had to be avoided at all costs, and it was sold as a "nonfiction feature," whatever that meant, with an emphasis on the miscarriage of justice and crusading journalism. "A documentary has a limited, narrow audience," explains publicist Christina Kounelias. "The sell was, he's a detective figuring out the clues to a mystery. 'The director detective.' "

Harvey caught Morris being interviewed on National Public Radio and hated him. He sent the director a "Dear Errol" letter, dated August 13, 1988, in which he wrote, "You were boring," and led him through a Socratic dialogue, that went in part: "Let's rehearse:

"Q: What is this movie about?

"A: It's a mystery that traces an injustice. It's scarier than *Nightmare on Elm Street*. It's a trip to the Twilight Zone . . ." Harvey continued in this vein, furnishing Morris with his lines. He concluded with, "If you continue to be boring, I will have to hire an actor in New York to pretend that he's Errol Morris."

The Thin Blue Line opened on August 26, 1988, and grossed $1.2 million, unheard of for a documentary in those days.

Meanwhile, the Weinsteins' friends across the Atlantic, Steve Woolley and Nik Powell, had come up with an ambitious slate of films in which Harvey would invest. Says Donna Gigliotti, who was then with Orion Classics and would join Miramax in 1993, "Harvey was an outsider in Hollywood, so he looked to where everybody else wasn't. It was just smart." *Scandal* was the first. It was based on a true story of "tarts, titles, and tits," as one wag put it, that rocked Britain in the 1960s and led to the resignation of Secretary of State for War John Profumo. Palace had sunk about £200,000 into the project and attached Michael Caton-Jones, a first-time director with a pay-or-play* deal. Like *Working Girls*, *Scandal*, with plenty of sex and controversy, was the perfect Miramax title, and the Weinsteins came in to the tune of $2.35 million. Joanne Whalley-Kilmer played call girl Christine Keeler, and Bridget Fonda took the role of Mandy Rice-Davies, Keeler's best friend. The film went into production in late June of 1988. Harvey, dressed in a black aertex T-shirt and black pants and carrying a plastic bag full of scripts so as not to lose a moment of work time, traveled regularly to London to keep an eye on things. The furor caused by Alan Parker's X-rated *Angel Heart* had deeply impressed the Weinsteins, and Harvey insisted that Powell and Woolley deliver *Scandal* as an X. He repeatedly muttered in Caton-Jones's ear, "Michael, you gotta get her to take her clothes off." At the same time, he was badg-

---

* "Pay or play": a director, actor, etc., is paid regardless of whether the movie is made or not.

ering Woolley: "Steve, you're making all the decisions, I'm your executive producer, I gotta do something. I wanna work on the movie." Finally, Woolley replied, "All right, you want to make decisions? Look, this weekend I'm going to take some time off, why don't you take over." Be careful what you wish for. Woolley knew that Whalley-Kilmer's skinny-dipping scene was coming up. After speaking to her husband, Val Kilmer, on the phone, the actress abruptly refused to do it, saying, "Val doesn't want me to." But Harvey, having anticipated this eventuality, had hired a body double. Whalley-Kilmer stood by while the cameras rolled. Finally, she had enough, complained, "Boy, that girl's got a big ass! I can't let her do that." She ended up doing most of the scene herself.

Scandal wrapped in late summer 1988. Post-production proceeded through the fall. Harvey demanded that the film be recut for American audiences. He explains, "I'm a kid who was born in Queens. If I could grow up the way I grew up, with a dad in the jewelry business and a mom who worked as a secretary, and I could love these movies—Truffaut, Fellini, De Broca, Visconti—why can't a guy in Kansas City love these movies? Why make it so difficult?" Harvey had never forgotten showing *And Now My Love,* a film by one of his favorite directors, Claude Lelouch, at the Century Theater in Buffalo. The long-haired crowed jeered, screaming, "Fuck this movie, fuck ... subtitles." If he was going to succeed, he had to make foreign films palatable to American audiences. Says Ed Glass, "We re-edited *Scandal.* Harvey said, 'Nobody fucking knows who Profumo is, nobody knows who Christine Keeler is, you're dealing with Americans! You've gotta tell them upfront.' Woolley and Caton-Jones thought he was insane. The auteurs felt like they were swallowing poison. They didn't want to cut a frame. But Harvey made the movie more accessible to more people."

In November 1988, Alison Brantley accompanied Harvey to London where they saw *My Left Foot,* a story about a man who overcomes cerebral palsy to become an artist. Harvey sat on one side of the aisle and Brantley on the other. When the shaking little boy writes "mother" in chalk with his foot on the floor, they both burst into tears. She says, "A lot of the movies Harvey liked had an underdog quality to them. It appealed to all the things he wanted to prove."

Harvey was desperate to acquire the film, which had been produced by Brantley's former employer, Granada. "They'd never heard of Miramax, or whatever they'd heard wasn't good," she continues. "I was the perfect front person for them, and I told Granada, 'You should really take this meeting. You may not like some things about these guys, but they're good at what they do.' " Harvey knew he had to put on a show, act like he was a powerful indie even though he wasn't. He rented a suite at the posh

Savoy and invited Steve Morrison, Granada's head of programming, to meet with him there. Morrison thought the film would sell itself because of Daniel Day-Lewis. Harvey had to demonstrate his enthusiasm for the picture while at the same time convincing Morrison that it had to be marketed hard because Day-Lewis was a romantic lead, and nobody wanted to see him folded up on himself like an accordion. Along the way, of course, he promised he would get the actor an Oscar. It was one of Harvey's patented I'm-going-to-lock-the-doors-and-keep-you-here-until-you-sign numbers. The fact that Day-Lewis played a disabled character and didn't want to have his picture taken out of character was something Harvey was going to have to deal with later. Morrison was persuaded and agreed to take $3 million for worldwide rights.

Back in New York, Harvey screened *My Left Foot* for the staff. When the lights came up, half the audience was crying and the other half was going, "Are you crazy? A drunk Irish cripple? Daniel Day-Lewis may be a love object, but he's in a wheelchair and he's all crumpled up. You think this is going to work?" Harvey did think it was going to work, at least after he had "fixed" it. Speaking of *My Left Foot,* he says, "I had tested it. The audience loved it, but they didn't understand certain things. Rather than Alan Parker's approach on *The Commitments*—I couldn't follow half that movie—I straightened out some of those rough Irish accents. What's a 'jar,' what's a this, what's a that? I went back and revoiced some of it. A 'jar' became a 'glass.' Isn't the intention to communicate? And if it is, let's find a way to do it, without compromising the integrity of the suffering. We didn't say, 'Okay, Daniel's singing and dancing Fred Astaire.' Nobody changed the ending, the pain. The essence of the movie is preserved, and it went on to play thirty-two weeks in Kansas City."

Harvey knocked on doors all over town trying to find a studio partner to share the costs. He recalls, "I said, 'I would love your help.' They said, 'You're crazy to even release this movie.' " It was impossible at that time for an indie distributor like Miramax to start a dialogue with the studios. "When you're talking to Universal or Paramount, and they were doing $40 million on a weekend, and you said, 'I just did $2 million on *Pelle the Conqueror* in fourteen, sixteen weeks,' they think you're retarded," says Jack Foley, VP of distribution in the mid-1990s, who came from MGM. "It just demonstrated the obdurate, incapacitating, heedless, ineffective thinking that goes on in the major studios. Their attitude was, 'I'm more powerful than you, my cock is bigger than yours.' " In Harvey, however, they'd met a cock they couldn't elbow off the walk. He says, "It pissed me off, and that anger fueled my belief in the film even further."

The MPAA slapped *Scandal* with an X rating in the spring of 1989, demanding a two-second excision from the orgy scene. An X rating was bad for business because most newspapers would not advertise it. Nor would video retailers like the family-fixated Blockbuster megachain stock the tapes. But the board was just playing into Harvey's hands, because by the time he caved, the fight had generated a bounty of free publicity. Since *SPOB*, Harvey's strategy was always the same: come in as an X, make as much noise as possible, and go out as an R. In this case, he substituted an outtake that showed, according to Woolley, "Christine gazing gooey-eyed at a naked black man in place of a bit of dry humping."

Neither of the Weinsteins had bothered to show up at Park City that year. Mormons? Skiing? It wasn't their scene. But after the festival, Miramax went after both *sex, lies* and *True Romance*. The brothers screened Soderbergh's film at Magno on 49th Street and Seventh Avenue, in New York. They loved it. If there was anything they could understand, it was duplicity.

In those days, Miramax was small enough to be free of the hierarchical pecking order that characterizes most companies. It was the brothers and then everybody else. Each employee, no matter what the title—vice president of this or that—was essentially an assistant and could easily find him or herself licking envelopes, answering the phone, or taking notes at a meeting. Titles were merely ego candy meant to stand in for decent salaries. By the same token, the Weinsteins threw their babies into the deep end and let them sink or swim. Lowly assistants or even interns could be invited to screenings and canvassed for their reactions to a movie the brothers were thinking of acquiring. This was flattering and fun for some but an ordeal for others, since the process often took the form of a police interrogation. You couldn't get away with yessing them, because if you just said, "Yes, Harvey, yes Bob," they thought you were stupid or not to be trusted, and in either case didn't want you around. If they suspected you were afraid to say something, they'd just push and push and push, intimidate you until you blurted it out. Then they made you feel like an idiot if you didn't agree with them. One or both would always say, "Thaat's a stupid answer. *I* can do better than that. *I* can do your job and my job." Although they prided themselves on being truth sayers, the brothers were surprisingly thin skinned. As former acquisitions executive Mark Tusk puts it, "It was easier to say, 'Yeah Harvey, that's a great idea,' than to say 'No,' so the people who worked around him ended up being yes men."

When the lights came on, Harvey said, "Whaddya think?" There was total silence. "Whaddya think?" One brave soul said, "I really liked it." Harvey bore in, "Whaddya like about it? What exactly?"

"I just liked—"

"Be specific, tell me, tell me."

"I liked the ending."

"Whaddya like about the ending? Did you like the whole ending?" And on and on. Bob in particular was hot for *sex, lies*. When it was his turn to ask, "Whaddya think?" several people chimed in with opinions about how the critics might react. Bob interrupted and said, "Don't tell me what I just saw, what'll it gross? Whaddya think of that title? Do you think we should keep it?" Somebody demurred. He exclaimed, "Whaddya crazy? That's the best title I've ever heard. That title alone will sell the movie." From a marketing point of view, just the fact that it contained the word "sex" was golden. Continues Tusk, "At that point it was pedal to the metal to get the film. Cover every angle, be as aggressive as possible."

Both Weinsteins were outstanding negotiators. They had sure instincts about what to fight for and how to get it from the other side. Harvey was especially skilled at closing, constructing circumstances favorable to himself, making sure he had all the information relative to who was making the key decisions and why, figuring out who was against him and how to neutralize them. As David Linde, who did acquisitions and international sales in the mid-1990s puts it, "People will say all kinds of shit about you in this business, so you want to be there, you want to be physically within the process. If Miramax was in a negotiation and one of the producers was in L.A., then you sent your guy to L.A., and you sat in front of them, got in their face and made sure that they were not negotiating with somebody else. You got their home phone number and you called them and called them until you got the picture. If the brothers lost a movie, then they got very pissed off and very angry, and on occasion, vituperative."

Larry Estes was impressed by Harvey. He recalls, "Everybody who called us said, 'We saw the movie, we think it's great, but we have to show it to our people.' Harvey called from New York and said, 'Can we meet tomorrow?' The next day he was in L.A." Like the other buyers, Harvey and his entourage made a pilgrimage to the RCA/Columbia conference room. He was on his best behavior, polite, dressed in a suit, although he visibly chafed at the no-smoking rule. "Harvey had three posters ready and some ads, mounted on boards, with translucent covers," Estes recalls. "He'd done the marketing work. They were charged up." Harvey told him and producer Bobby Newmyer, "I'm not going back to New York until I have this movie," and he promised to best anybody else's bid by $100,000. Says Newmyer, "At that time, they were rated fourth or fifth among distributors. We had a feeling that they were hungrier."

All the other buyers badmouthed Miramax, called Harvey and Bob every name in the book, implied that Miramax would be out of business by the end of the year. Nancy Tenenbaum remembers that Estes and

Newmyer "seemed a little nervous, based on their reputation. I brought up the idea, 'What if we had someone there who's representing us.' " She was thinking Ira Deutchman. Deutchman and Harvey were polar opposites. Deutchman was buttoned down, fiscally conservative, and principled to a fault. He wouldn't spend a dime unless he knew he could get it back. He explains, "There was paranoia about Miramax. They had a reputation for recutting and feeling like they knew best what the final form of the film should be. Filmmakers were shying away from their crassness, how they promoted films inappropriately, leading people to believe that the film was something that it wasn't. Soderbergh was particularly sensitive about that with *sex, lies*, because of the title. My job was to make sure that Harvey didn't dump the movie or, conversely, didn't go overboard."

Newmyer and his attorney, Linda Lichter, decided to call Harvey's bluff, if bluff it was, to see how badly he wanted the picture. They drew up a list of seven demands. Recalls Estes, "It was one of those dream situations, like, 'OK what do we want? We want $1 million in advance.' Harvey said, 'OK.' 'We want $1 million for P&A.'* 'OK.' 'We want you to hire Ira as the marketing consultant, and you have to pay for it.' 'OK.' We went through the whole list and eventually, when the guy keeps saying 'OK,' he's going to say, 'So we have a deal now?' So I said, 'I have to run it by the boss but—we have a deal!' "

Still, the *sex, lies* gang hemmed Miramax in with conditions. Says Tenenbaum, "Estes insisted that Miramax pay the advance upfront and put the money into an escrow account so we were assured we'd get it. We said they had to take the movie as is. There wasn't going to be any additional cutting." Miramax agreed. Estes was thrilled. "At the time $1 million just for theatrical and television on a film that you couldn't have video rights to was unheard of, plus a million dollars on top of that for P&A, basically a $2 million deal for theatrical only. None of the independent companies we talked to was aggressive enough to say, 'Tell me what you want, I want to make this deal.' Everybody else was just blah blah blah. And I really felt more comfortable with Ira being involved to tattle on them." The Weinsteins estimated that *sex, lies* would make between $5 and $10 million. Soderbergh was floored. "The whole thing made me uncomfortable," he recalls. "I thought, These guys are out of their fucking minds. People went, 'Jesus Christ! What am I missing here? What's the catch?' I guess the catch was they saw a way to do it." Says Mark Lipsky, "They probably did overpay, but they had to because nobody wanted to give them movies. In their minds, they were being extremely liberal, giving the filmmakers large advances which they were putting in their

* "P&A": Prints and advertising.

pockets, and in addition the brothers were driving the competition away. They were getting what they wanted."

The other bidders were stunned. Recalls New Line's Janet Grillo, "Hearing that Harvey was offering a million, I thought, That's ridiculous. It can't possibly be true. When we heard it was true, I was just in a state of shock, and thought, Let him be an idiot and lose his money. He's either just destroyed his company, or he knows something that we don't."

It turned out, of course, that Miramax did know something that neither New Line, nor anyone else, knew. "It was so audacious of him to do that, because it changed everything," continues Grillo. "We all knew what films were coming on the market, and we would queue up politely, take the producers' reps out to lunch, go to the screenings with everyone else, have coffee afterwards—until Harvey came along. He didn't have manners." Harvey just wasn't about to sit in the back of the classroom politely raising his hand in the air until he was called on. Adds Tony Safford, "Up until then, companies tended to sit back and wait and see what showed up on their fax machine. That kind of extremely aggressive approach to finding, getting, negotiating materials changed the business." One day, in a screening at the Toronto film festival, Margie Skouras found herself sitting on the floor because the room was packed. She recalls, "I looked around, and who's sitting next to me but Harvey. On the floor! Tom Skouras would never sit on the floor. Sam Goldwyn would never sit on the floor. They wouldn't even wait in line! That was the first time I realized that we were going to have trouble competing with Harvey and Bob."

SCANDAL OPENED on April 28, 1989. As was his custom, Dan Talbot insisted on exclusivity ("clearance") over the entire city for his Lincoln Plaza on the Upper West Side, until the picture had played for a number of weeks. But Scandal was such a draw that it enabled Marty Zeidman to break Talbot's monopoly and play three runs in Manhattan—on the Upper West Side, the East Side, and Greenwich Village, tripling the gross. "With Scandal I realized you could start playing upscale commercial movie theaters with these films," instead of just the art houses, he says. "When I first got there, the playdates for all the films they were working on [fit on] a chalk board. That's how few films they had, and they were dealing with [no more than] 10 or 15 prints of each movie, nationally. We probably got onto a few hundred screens with Scandal. That doesn't sound like a lot, compared to today, but there weren't the number of screens that there are now." As a result of Marty Zeidman's aggressiveness, Scandal grossed $8.8 million in the U.S.

With Scandal up and running, Zeidman cut a new deal that allowed him to open a Miramax office in L.A. He became the envy of everyone in the New York office. As Mark Lipsky puts it, "Nobody wanted to be in the same state, much less the same office building with Harvey and Bob. He was the first to put an entire continent between himself and them."

Miramax had pulled itself back from the brink. The 56th Street apartment was bursting at the seams, and in the late 1980s, Miramax moved to 18 E. 48th Street, between Madison and Fifth, a dank, dark, midblock building. When you exited the elevator on the sixteenth floor, the office was on the right, half a floor, but already full, even as they were still moving in, a rabbit warren of tiny spaces, with chilly fluorescent lights, drop ceilings, few windows, and walls that were so pitted and scarred it looked like they'd taken a couple of barrels of bird shot. It was only a little more roomy than the between-the-floors space occupied by John Cusack in *Being John Malkovich*. The carpet buckled in one place, tripping people up as they started down a corridor maybe 30 feet long and 12 feet wide and so choked with desks that Deutchman wondered how Harvey could thread his bulk past them to reach his office at the far end. Bob and Harvey's area was hung with production stills and posters from *The Burning* and *Playing for Keeps*. Ed Glass used to visit a dentist in the same building. "I'd go in there, and it was either my dentist or Harvey and Bob," he recalls. "I don't know which one was more painful. They were very intense. It was like getting hit by a ten-ton truck that kept going forward and backing up on top of you."

Once, the elevators broke down, and Harvey had to walk up the stairs. Says one staffer, "He was huffing and puffing so hard that we thought he was going to die then and there." Harvey's type A personality, lack of sleep, chain-smoking, and diet from hell, along with the sheer poundage he was lugging around made him a coronary waiting to happen. Periodically, Miriam, the brothers' elfin mother, would drop by with rugulah. Says Lipsky, "Bob sniped at her. They'd keep her waiting, sometimes as much as an hour, then not show up, or if they did, they'd cut her short— 'Your time's up.' It was, 'Just give out the rugulah!' "

Miriam was so sweet, "you couldn't imagine these two guys came out of her and were raised by her," observes one former employee. The brothers' relationship with her and their father was complicated. According to childhood friend Alan Brewer, Miriam was a "demanding, aggressive, pushy Jewish mother." When they were kids, she was in the habit of making invidious comparisons between her sons and the other kids in the neighborhood along the lines of, "How come David got an A when you didn't?" or "Oh, you didn't have time to do your homework? How come Mikey had time?" Harvey used to call her "Mama Portnoy." The brothers grew up in a development called Elechester, built by the electricians' union, next door to Queens College. Brewer, who first met Harvey in 1964 in Campbell Junior High School 218, in Kew Gardens, is of the opinion that Miriam's relentless nudging was the goad that eventually flowered in Harvey's competitiveness. With some jocularity, Brewer observed, referring to DreamWorks's Best Picture Oscars in the late 1990's, "I could see her calling him up, saying, 'Those DreamWorks people, what makes them better than you? Stevie Spielberg's mother, maybe she did a better job? You coulda done it if you pushed a little harder.' It motivated him, challenged him to prove, 'I am the best, I am the king.' "

Their father, Max, was a diamond cutter who worked in Manhattan's diamond district. But to the boys' friends, Miriam appeared to be the one who wore the pants in the family; she barked out the orders, browbeat her husband. When the boys got together with Max, it was "Ach, your mother, don't worry about that." There was a certain amount of disdain for Miriam and, according to Brewer, deep down the boys regarded Max as the cool one. He admitted he had made mistakes, and used the saga of his own disappointments to motivate them. Again, according to Brewer, the lesson they learned at the paternal knee was, "Don't screw up like I did. Don't let anyone tell you you can't do it, don't let anyone get in your way, and if they do, fuck 'em"—words the boys apparently took to heart. The other lesson they took to heart was that it was them against the world.

Max served in World War II, posted in Cairo, and when the hostilities ended, he remained in the area and worked with the Zionist underground in Palestine. Growing up, Harvey tore through the novels of Leon Uris. The Holocaust wisdom stereotyped Jews as victims, filing into cattle cars with nary a murmur. This mortified him. The Jews he identified with were the ones who drove the British out of Palestine, beat back a larger army of Arabs, and founded the State of Israel. He once told the *New York Times*, "Instead of growing up to be a professor, a lawyer, or a doctor, you could grow up to be a soldier, you know, for your people. You can be tough. You can be John Wayne, too." Likewise, he admired the movie adapted from Uris's *Exodus* by blacklisted writer Dalton Trumbo. "Trumbo's great theme [was] the power of the few against the mighty," he observed. "It's a theme of my life: you can beat the mighty, you can go against the majors, and you can win." As an adult, he liked to say, "I'm not the kind of Jew who marches politely off to the gas chamber. I'm the kind of Jew who says, I'm gonna track you down and kill you, you SS fuck— and your family." Perhaps the best glosses on the Weinsteins, metaphorically speaking, are Ang Lee's *The Hulk*, and Rich Cohen's lyrical ode to New York's Jewish gangsters, *Tough Jews*. More Meyer Lanskys than

Woody Allens, had the Weinsteins been born seventy-five years earlier, they might have been found running numbers on Hester Street, bootlegging whiskey, or sitting across a card table from Louis Lepke, the head of Murder Incorporated.

The success of *Scandal* and the new digs did little to improve the brothers' dispositions. Both had volcanic tempers. They were wizards of abuse, excelling in the exotic art of public humiliation, lashing staffers in front of their peers. Says Stuart Burkin, who started in post-production in 1991, "Miramax ran on fear. They're intimidating, they shout a lot, they foam at the mouth." And Amy Hart, who worked at Miramax as a marketing coordinator for three years, "Anything anybody ever says about them being monsters is true."

Finesse was never part of Harvey's arsenal. He tore phones out of walls and hurled them. He slammed doors and overturned tables. Almost anything within reach could become a weapon—ashtrays, books, and tapes, the framed family photographs sitting on his desk that he'd heave at some hapless executive and watch as they hit the wall, exploding in a shower of glass, because the reality was, they rarely, if ever, hit their targets. It was theater—of cruelty. The joke was, get in the way, so you could settle out and be paid to leave. Recalls Hart, "I've sat outside of that conference room and seen those glass walls just shudder with his profanity." Staffers would occasionally expostulate with him, saying, "How can you treat people that way? You'll get more out of them if you treat them nicely, even if you don't like them." He'd sigh, and reply, "Yeah, I know, I know, but I can't help myself. I try, but I just have a bad temper."

If the brothers liked you, there was a familial aspect to life at Miramax. David Dinerstein lived on the Upper West Side at 101st Street and Amsterdam. There was a basketball court there, across the street from the projects. Bob was a pretty good basketball player for a short, Jewish guy, and every once in a while they'd get their car service to drive them uptown for a pickup game against the black kids from the neighborhood. Harvey preferred softball, but he wasn't the athlete Bob was; he just enjoyed his times at bat, and then replaced himself with a pinch runner. He brought the designated hitter to softball. Bob would captain one squad, and Harvey the other, and the competition between them was fierce. Bob once offered a staffer coming up to bat $100 if she made it to first base. She did, and he paid her. He once fired one of his employees for dropping the ball—the unfortunate man looked like he was going to burst into tears—and rehired him half an inning later.

Still, even for the favored few, it was no picnic. Indeed, "The culture at Miramax was very fierce," observes Mark Urman, a publicist who worked on and off with Miramax for years, and is now head of U.S. distribution at

ThinkFilm. "It was all about aggression. Nothing was ever good enough, nothing was ever enough, period." They liked Myrna Chagnard, who worked in the small L.A. office for five years. She was a hard woman with a don't-fuck-with-me attitude, but eventually she too snapped. "I was having a nervous breakdown," she recalls. "I couldn't take the stress anymore, of having Bob say, 'You're fired!' I would get my stuff and go down to my car, and then he would call me back. I started to lose weight, I was moody, depressed, it almost destroyed me. I went on workmen's comp, and stayed out for three or four months. I was a basket case." Recalls Eleanor Reznikoff, who was a publicist in the L.A. office in those days, "Working there was like having your feet held to the fire. Everyone had terrible stories, everyone was petrified of them. My first experience with Harvey was when he was flying out for a premiere. He would usually arrive the day of the screening, and he called from the plane, and said, 'When my flight lands, if I don't have twenty-five tickets in my hand, you're fired!'"

If they didn't like you, life inside the Weinstein bunker could be hell. Large and burly, Jeff Rose looked like he'd been dipped in the Weinstein gene pool, and for a while he was a favorite, another third brother, even accompanying Harvey when he visited his grandmother, who was dying. (Rose waited in the car.) "In the end, there are no third brothers," he says. One year at Cannes, in Harvey's hotel suite, Rose continues, "we were in a staff meeting at 7:00 A.M., I think Harvey was in his towel, and he said something about some deal. I disagreed, and instead of saying, 'Hey, you know what? We're gonna do it my way because I'm the boss,' he took a table, set for breakfast, and just tossed it on me." From then on, Rose could do no right. Over the course of the next six months, he got thinner, more haggard, until he apparently had some sort of nervous breakdown. Rose refuses to comment, beyond saying, "He pushed me to the edge—I definitely looked over—and I left."

Some people were just too nice to work there, and the Weinsteins tortured them. Like Harvey, Mark Silberman was a big bear of a man, but unlike Harvey, he was a gentle soul. It was St. Patrick's Day in March 1988. The 48th Street office was so close to Fifth Avenue that it sounded like the marchers were parading right through the space. Suddenly, there was a loud commotion, so loud they assumed it was drunken revelers outside in the street. Recalls Lipsky, "There was very scary yelling, somebody screaming, 'Call the police,' and several minutes after that, Mark came into my office with a look that was sort of otherworldly. I've never seen anything like it before or since." There had been an incident. Soon after, without explanation, Silberman was gone. Perhaps it's no accident that at the end of the 1990s it would be the *Scream* franchise that would drive the company, with its plot premise—victims serially picked off, one by one—an increasingly apt metaphor for life at Miramax.

Employees argued over which one was worse, Bob or Harvey. Says Paul Webster, who headed production in the mid-1990s, "Bob is the scary one, for me. Bob had a great fury inside him, a great anger." Brantley agrees. "Bob scared me much more," she says. "For the first three months I didn't even walk into his office. The air in there was so weird." Adds one person who knew them both in those days, "If you could consider Harvey as the light one, Bob was the dark one. I've never walked down death row, but that's the feeling I got around Bob. He was spooky." As Tina Brown is said to have quipped, years later, "Bob's the one who hasn't been house broken."

But some people liked Bob better. In the view of former marketing executive Eamonn Bowles, "You don't want to get Bob on a bad day. But he's more of a mensch. Bob would flip out, he'd get all pissed off, but it would be, The guy's got a reason." Adds former marketing head Dennis Rice, "When it churned up inside of Bob it was all about business. It was nothing personal. He just doesn't want to be fucked."

For others, it was Harvey who made their stomachs turn, provoked that trip to the bathroom. He let you know that when he was out of control, he might do anything. Says Brantley, when Harvey got angry, "He would kind of puff up, like the barometric pressure had changed, so you'd think he was gonna explode. Sometimes he would explode. His face got really red, and his whole expression would go to stone. It wasn't like he was gonna throw chairs, it was more you thought he was gonna go right for you, strangle you."

Bowles continues, "I'm really susceptible to people trying to flatter me, and Harvey can be the most charming person you ever met in your life. I'd spend forty-five minutes with him, and think, Wow, what a great guy, and two minutes later he'd be the most fearsome person you ever met in your life. It's scary as all hell." And Lipsky, "When Harvey [lashes out], he wants to hurt people. He has moments where he really loses it—he gets so into whatever it is, he's not thinking straight. There isn't a woman in that office that wasn't made to cry. Could be anything, even a marketing concept. Once I saw him so flummoxed and so bent out of shape about something that he was screaming at a woman, just berating her beyond belief, and calling her some man's name—he didn't even know who he was talking to. It's weird with Harvey, because he does want to be the padrone, an old Hollywood mogul. But when he turns on you, it's with venom. And it is personal."

Harvey's rages struck some Miramaxers as more calculated than spontaneous. Bowles continues, "He's obviously got a really bad temper, but I do think there are instances where there's a set up, get somebody into a room and pummel him verbally. He always tries to find out what makes people tick. What motivates them. He'll poke a bunch of different areas to see if you'll light up, and then use that." Safford, who worked for Miramax in the mid-1990s, agrees, adding, "His emotions are completely calculated. I would tell people, 'Don't be put off by his anger, because it's strategic. On the other hand, don't be fooled by his compliments, because they're equally strategic. But people were devastated by his attacks and fooled by his compliments." Is Harvey a decent guy who can't help himself? "I don't think he's a decent guy," Safford continues. "I think he's a bad guy who can't help himself."

The Weinsteins exploited their volatility, turned it into a good cop/bad cop routine that they used to keep the little people cowed and quivering. "They drove everybody crazy," says Lipsky. "Their MO from the time I've known them, was to stomp on you, then help you up, brush you off, and apologize." You could have produced a small film on the money Miramax must have spent on Harvey-didn't-mean-it flowers. As Rice puts it, "Some days Harvey would verbally abuse you, and other days he would verbally stroke you, and treat you to baubles, a bonus to make amends, and the next thing you know, he had you. For me it was the analogy of a cat with a mouse. The mouse would think it's getting away, only for the cat to put its paw on its tail and stop it." Says one source, "One of them would throw things, kick you out of the office, fire you. Then the other one will call you back, and say, 'Oh, did he do that?' as if he were trying to help you out. 'My brother didn't mean it. Come back.' There was no winning."

Some staffers thought that fighting back worked. Lipsky recalls incurring Bob's wrath over a "horrible" Australian movie called *The Quest* (1986), with Henry Thomas: "I had promised [the producers] we would buy $10,000 of TV, because it was the only way we were going to get the movie. Two days before the movie opened, Bob came into my office and said, 'Pull the TV.' It was killing him that we were gonna spend that $10,000 when he knew the movie was gonna gross less than nothing. I said, 'No. I made the commitment, and we're gonna do it.' Bob got in my face, very close, very intense, and he actually reached into a pencil cup on the desk and started pulling out pencils and breaking them. I started laughing, said, 'Bob, what are you doing, man?' He walked out of the office, never mentioned it again. And they never did the TV."

But standing your ground or returning blow for blow could often make it worse, provoking the brothers to ratchet up the rage. "There's a hesitancy to wave a red flag in front of Harvey, because he'll just go apeshit, and he'll do things irrationally to hurt you," says Safford. Adds Bowles, "If you got on an emotional level with them, you were gonna lose, you were dead. They were gonna have much more combativeness than just about anybody."

The WASPs thought the Jews had it easier. The Jews thought the brothers treated the WASPs better. Says John Schmidt, who was CFO in the early 1990s, "They were equal opportunity abusers. If they wanted to pound on someone, it didn't matter what race, creed, ethnic origin, or color they were. It was lights out!" But there is general agreement that the brothers were tougher on male employees. "I always felt sorrier for the men, because without it even having to be over an issue, with men Harvey would get like a dog, that moment right before it actually bites," recalls Brantley. "He would test them all the time. He just wanted you to know he was the big guy." To a degree, Harvey and Bob indulged employees whose expertise fell in areas they didn't know anything about. If, on the other hand, you had the misfortune to work in marketing, which Harvey considered his backyard, you were doomed to be micromanaged, second-guessed, and carpet bombed with criticism. Worse, you were spending *their* money. If you were a *male* in marketing, you were at ground zero, and you might as well pack it in. Once, angered by the poor placement of an ad in *The New York Times*, Harvey roared at Dinerstein, "I'm gonna fuckin' throw you outta that window, right now."

Still, Miramax was an exciting place to be. Says Rice, articulating a sentiment so often expressed by ex-staff that it seems like a consensus, "People hate working there, but they love what Miramax stands for, they love the magic they created in the independent film world. It's a very intoxicating feeling, and to be associated with that is addictive, so you found a way to turn a blind eye to how they did it, and to the people who became casualties along the way." Adds Foley, "They were nuclear in their energy and in their anger, even in their malevolence, but to be out there with them, that was the best."

THE MANAGEMENT CRISIS that afflicted Sundance throughout the 1980s was bad enough, but there were other problems that were even more serious. Throughout the decade, Redford had been unhappy with the quality of the projects coming into the labs. Explains Sterling Van Wagenen, "Bob was constantly critical of the selection process. He felt American films were getting worse and worse, especially in relation to what was happening in Australia and Germany." The promise of production might be first, a way of luring better projects into the labs, and second, of nudging them in a more commercial direction. But Redford feared that production would corrupt the Sundance process, turn it into a snakepit of competition and backbiting. Moreover, production is expensive. The institute would have to raise more money or involve itself in dicey alliances with the studios—or both. Van Wagenen continues, "Bob said, 'Don't get involved.' His view was that by getting entangled with the studios we would be making a pact with the devil." Eventually, Redford changed his mind. He recalls, "I'd heard filmmakers say, 'I need money.' So I thought, Maybe if we put more emphasis on the commercial aspect for awhile, give them some incentive to get their picture made, that would allow us to go in and hammer them and make it more commercial."

But, as would immediately become apparent, there was one big problem: the idealistic filmmakers themselves, for whom "commercial" was a dirty word. The Production Assistance Fund was an accident waiting to happen, and it did happen in 1984. *Desert Bloom* was a girl's coming-of-age story set in Las Vegas against a background of the A-bomb tests of the 1950s. It was one of the best films to come out of Sundance in those years, and although it slipped into oblivion after a limited release in 1986, many thought Jon Voight should have been nominated for an Oscar for his role as the abusive father. The script was written by Eugene Corr, who was set to direct, and Linda Remy, on whose life it was loosely based. At the time, she was involved with Corr.

Remy and Corr went to the June lab in 1983. "In the beginning, Sundance was wonderful," Remy recalls. "They opened doors for us. We talked to the top cinematographers, set designers, costume designers. We were the flavor of the week." Sundance helped set the project up at Tri-Star. But it didn't take long for things to get ugly. As Safford puts it, "Redford's name attached would guarantee funding, but then he would meddle from beginning to end." Continues Remy, "We could interview everyone we wanted, as long as we went with their choices. [If we didn't] they would pull back their support. Sterling said, 'Trust me.' I said, 'But you're asking us to jump off a cliff.' He said, 'But I'll be there with you.' In the end, nobody jumped off but me and Gene."

By that time, *Desert Bloom* had moved over to (Johnny) Carson Pictures, and the production degenerated into a pitched battle among Corr and Remy, on the one hand, Sundance, and Carson president Richard Fischoff on the other—over locations, casting, editing, you name it. The crowning blow came when, says Remy, "Redford took over the film from Gene and locked him out of the editing room. It was worse than a studio. I thought Sundance would protect us. I was utterly naive. Redford hated our film. He would have liked something slicker, glossier."

From the other side of the desk, Fischoff, who denies that Corr was locked out of the editing room, adds, "It might have worked if only Sundance had honored its commitment to help Gene with the production, but it didn't. Redford never came to the set and never reassured the actors, who had taken pay cuts because of him, put themselves in the hands of an inexperienced director because of him. Instead, he went to work on *Out of Africa*. We wanted to make this film for the right reasons, not because we thought we were making a killing. The moral is, in the words of Oscar Wilde, 'No good deed goes unpunished.' "

Safford says Redford tried to have *Desert Bloom* pulled from the 1986 festival after it was accepted. When Safford threatened to resign, Redford backed down, although he refused to go to the premiere.

There were other complaints as well. *Animal Behavior* was a romantic comedy directed by Jenny Bowen and produced by Kjehl Rasmussen. Rasmussen understood that it had been developed at Wildwood for Redford to star in and had gone through the lab, but Redford decided he was too old to do it. "Our investors were putting up $3.5 million in cash to finance the film," he says. "Our concern was, We love the script and we have a great cast, but we have a first time director. Redford had dinner with the investors and said, 'She's great, I love her, and I'm here, I'll be standing behind it, if you have any problems, I'll be a guiding light.' We moved forward on his representation, and then of course he went off and made *Out of Africa*. When we had problems, he was not there to help."

If production was supposed to be the carrot that would induce filmmakers to make more commercial choices, it was not working. Corr and Remy, like many other indies of their generation, had little investment in careers; fighting for their artistic vision was more important. As Van Wagenen puts it, "The problem was, we had been dealing with idealistic filmmakers who had no interest in accessing the studio system. I began to search for people who were looking to work within it."

Sundance did search for people who were looking to work inside the system, but it paid a price. "The institute has really missed the boat," concluded Safford in 1990. "The kinds of filmmakers Sundance tends to attract fall into the 'mushy middle.' Sundance hasn't censored political stuff, but it has censored stylistic stuff. The projects have all been very conservative." It was becoming increasingly impossible to ignore the fact that the stars of the indie movement who emerged in the mid-1980s— Spike Lee, John Sayles, Jim Jarmusch, Gus Van Sant, the Coen brothers, and David Lynch—had no use for Sundance and never participated in the labs. Some of those who did, skinny and pale New Yorkers plucked from their railroad flats to find themselves gulping thin mountain air and blinking in the bright Utah sun, complained they were being browbeaten into making Hollywood movies by the Oscar-winning resource people. Tom DiCillo, who had shot Jarmusch's *Stranger Than Paradise* and would go on to make his best film, the razor-sharp, wickedly on-target *Living in Oblivion* several years later, went in 1989 with the script for what would become his first feature, *Johnny Suede*. "It was helpful to take a scene, shoot it on video, work with actors and then look at it," he says. "It's something you never get a chance to do on an independent film. But it was the first time I heard, 'Plot point A does not intersect with plot point B at the right page.' I said, 'I'm sorry, what is a plot point?' Everyone was saying to me, 'This is not a screenplay.' It was insane, destructive, and negative. It was, This is how you get to Hollywood. I never had any interest in doing that. It really pissed me off."

"Independents" had once been an umbrella term for filmmakers and companies outside the studio system that made all sorts of films, from art to porn. Sundance built a firewall between art films and the rest, appropriated the term "independents" for itself, and dismissed the others as junk. But in reality, the festival was schizophrenic. Safford, bored with programming the competition, had turned it over to his protégé, Alberto Garcia, a young, former volunteer driver who wore granny glasses and his hair in a ponytail, while he devoted himself to mounting tributes to just the kind of déclassé schlockmeisters Redford didn't get and didn't much like, such as Sam Fuller. Redford's distaste for the pulpy, tabloid underbelly of mass culture was probably a function of his own insecurities. A college drop-out (he had gone to the University of Colorado on a baseball scholarship), he suffered from the intellectual anxieties of the undereducated and consequently sought the imprimatur of literary or museum culture, which is why so many of the films he directed himself (*A River Runs Through It, The Horse Whisperer,* and *The Legend of Bagger Vance*), with their lacquered veneer of exquisite pictorial beauty, are as lifeless as insects preserved in amber.

Redford's tilt toward Native American and minority projects may have won points for him with People for the American Way, but it was not in and of itself a recipe for exciting filmmaking. Given the sorry spectacle that passed for Hollywood filmmaking at that time, Redford, peering down from his aerie in the clouds, could not have been blamed entirely for turning his back on genre films of all sorts—cops and robbers, vampires and werewolves, time and space travelers, visitors from Mars in their flying saucers, G.I.s and Asian guerrillas, narcs and inner city drug traffickers, South American drug lords, gross teenagers, their acne, and their dating problems. The only trouble was, his unwritten prohibitions covered a vast territory, and when all was said and done, there wasn't a whole lot of ground left on which to plant your flag if you wanted to make indie films with the institute's help. As Michelle Satter, who was director of the feature film program, admitted at the time, "There was a mandate to work with regional, human stories, Americana, but there aren't that many really unique stories in any given category. We began to support too many mediocre projects."

SEX, LIES, AND VIDEOTAPE went to Cannes in May. Harvey had been to Cannes before, of course, but he still impressed publicist Mark Urman, whom the brothers hired to promote the company there, as a rube. Urman recalls that to save money, "They literally brought their own fax machine, plugged it into the wall, and it blew up, because they didn't realize that it was a different electric current in France." Still, he was impressed by "their innate sense, from the begining, that there was no such thing as a small film. You could make a film as big as you wanted it to be, or you could try."

Brantley was the minder Harvey had assigned to Steven Soderbergh, his skittish young director. They shared a southern background. She first met him at a dinner Miramax threw for him and the cast. She recalls, "My impression of him when I first met him was of an incredibly nice, self-deprecating person. None of this stuff was happening to him. Here he was the toast of the town, but we were being really southern and making jokes with each other, like, 'We're in Cayunnes.' He had a healthy perspective on all that stuff. His Eeyoreness kept him sane." The two of them hit it off and it seemed like they might be on the edge of a romance.

Also in competition in 1989 was Spike Lee's Do the Right Thing, a powerful exploration of race relations in an urban neighborhood on the verge of insurrection that ends with the character played by Lee himself heaving a trash can through the window of a pizza parlor owned by Sal (Danny Aiello). Do the Right Thing was originally set up at Paramount. "Paramount wanted me to change the ending," the director recalls. "They thought it was too down, not enough hope, they wanted Mookie and Sal to join hands and sing 'We Are the World' or some shit like that. We weren't doin' it." Paramount dropped the picture, and Lee took it to Universal, at that time run by Tom Pollock. Lee continues, "Tom said, 'Spike, I'm not gonna mess with your content. You got $6.5 million, you got final cut, do what you wanna do,' and he let me run with it." The result was Lee's finest picture. Soderbergh worried that Lee would dismiss sex, lies as a "white-plight" movie, but he claimed to like it. Wim Wenders, still riding the success of Wings of Desire, chaired the jury.

The awards ceremony was held on May 23, in the Palais. Harvey wouldn't let Brantley sit next to Soderbergh and relegated her to a lesser seat, farther back. Soderbergh thought *Do the Right Thing* would walk away with the top prize, the Palme d'Or. But as he and the Weinsteins strode down the aisle, they passed the *Do the Right Thing* gang and noticed that they looked glum. They had already been told that they had won nothing. Festival President Gilles Jacob advised Harvey that he was going to have a "good night." Soderbergh had already won the International Critics Prize and was expecting to win the award for new directors, the Camera d'Or. Once seated, and so nervous he was almost insensible, he heard James Spader's name announced. Spader had already left Cannes, and the young director rose to accept the acting award for him from Sally Field. Then he walked off stage where he figured he would watch the remainder of the proceedings, but he was hustled back to his seat in time to see Wenders getting ready to bestow the Palme d'Or. As he made his remarks about "a film by a young filmmaker," Soderbergh tried to connect the dots with the other entries. Suddenly, the words "*sex, lies, and videotape*" escaped Wenders's lips. More, he praised the film extravagantly, saying, "[This movie gives] us confidence in the future of cinema." Soderbergh recalled, "It's like a door opened and every sound in the world came out and I'm on my feet again, and my heartbeat is throbbing in my surely red ears. This time Jane Fonda hands me the Palme d'Or, and I stand there for a moment, waiting for the applause to stop and trying to figure out what to say and trying not to fall apart. I looked out and said 'Well, I guess it's all downhill from here.' " Later, he said it was as if a fairy had waved a wand and said, "You're John Lennon for three hours." When the ceremony was over, Soderbergh, surrounded by well-wishers and still in a daze, slowly made his way out of the Palais. He left the Palme d'Or under his seat.

Spike Lee was vocal about his disappointment. He apparently was told that Wenders had said there were no heroes in *Do the Right Thing*. He replied that he had a Louisville Slugger with Wenders's name on it, and added, referring to Spader's self-abusing character, "What's so heroic about a guy taping women?" In fact, the triumph of *sex, lies* over *Do the Right Thing* ratified the turn away from the angry, topical strain of the indie movement that had its roots in the 1960s and 1970s toward the milder aesthetic of the slacker era.

Soderbergh returned to L.A. to find that the squabbling over his next film had intensified. Redford had given Barbara Maltby the go-ahead on *King of the Hill*. He would executive produce, with Maltby, Ron Yerxa, and Albert Berger producing. But Soderbergh met with producer Mark Johnson and writer Lem Dobbs. They made a handshake deal to do *Kafka* together. Redford continued to romance the young director, inviting him to a get-to-know-you meeting. The actor was late as usual, but Soderbergh was so overcome he barely noticed. He memorialized the occasion in his journal, writing of Redford, "He's extremely smart and very candid, and I think we spent as much time talking about non-film related issues as we did about business. . . . We talked about *King of the Hill*, and he said he was very enthused about the project and I left thinking that the time had gone by very quickly." Soderbergh basked in the glow of Redford's attention. He knew nothing about the actor's checkered relationship with independents.

"Both Redford and Pollack were really competing for Steve's next movie," recalls Newmyer. Redford seemed irritated that his pal Pollack was muddying the waters. He had always said, "This is not Robert Redford's Sundance," but now he was acting as if it were, and he was merely exercising his royal prerogative. According to a source close to Redford, he said, "What the hell's going on here? Why does Sydney have a deal with Steven, and we don't? It's my festival."

But despite the fact that Soderbergh was eager to have Redford mentor him, he insisted on doing the projects in the order they were presented to him. He told Maltby that Redford would have to get in line behind Pollack and now maybe even Johnson. The Wildwood folks were flabbergasted. When the Berlin Wall came down in 1989, *The Last Ship*, a Cold War drama, came down with it; and *Kafka* moved up a slot. There was something Kafkaesque about Soderbergh fastening on this project as his next film, something self-destructive, as if he were doing penance for the undeserved success of *sex, lies*. "I was going to get my head handed to me on my second film, pretty much no matter what I did," he explained. "That's what I was prepared for. In a way, I decided I would go out in flames by making a film that really had a big red bull's-eye on its chest."

Anticipating disaster, Soderbergh courted it. Years later, Soderbergh's pal and partner George Clooney speculated that the director suffered from a fear of success.

Redford was not happy about having to wait out *Kafka*. The rumor mill was saying that Soderbergh had decided not to do *King of the Hill* after all. Every once in awhile, Maltby would put it to him, and he'd say, "Don't you trust me? I told you, it's my next picture, and it will be my next picture."

Soderbergh was looking for an actress to cast in *Kafka*. Peter Gallagher recalled that he had once appeared in a Clifford Odets play with Betsy Brantley, Alison's sister, and recommended her for the part. The role eventually went to Theresa Russell, but Soderbergh had found a new girlfriend. In a flagrant case of life copying art, he moved from Alison and took up with Betsy. She was seven years older than he, but he liked "mature" women, he said, who didn't need him to complete their lives. Betsy explained herself in the press: "He liked to bowl. So it means he had to be kind of real."

Meanwhile, the August release date of *sex, lies, and videotape* was approaching like an onrushing train, and Miramax set about preparing the marketing materials. Recalls Deutchman, "Their marketing instincts were always towards going for the jugular, which in this case meant sex, sex, sex. Steven was horrified. He felt Miramax was promising way more than the movie delivered." Adds Liz Manne, who then worked for Deutchman, "It was an exploitative Miramax thing, titillating, with the implication that the tapes were home porn tapes. It crossed the line."

The marketing meetings were tense. Soderbergh sulked, and Harvey looked like he was barely keeping himself under control. When the director stalked out of the room, steaming, Harvey threw up his hands in frustration, saying, "How are we supposed to sell this movie? This is completely unrealistic." His attitude was, It's our money, it's our film, I don't give a shit what the director thinks. These people will love us if the film does well, and if it doesn't, so what. There's always another one. But Harvey had a lot invested in *sex, lies,* more than just money, and when Soderbergh asked him if he could try his own version of the trailer, he said, "Yes." Soderbergh delivered a cut that Harvey hated, dismissed as "art house death." With Deutchman thrusting his body between the two—"I helped keep them from killing each other"—they reached a compromise: Miramax's structure with some of Soderbergh's clip selections.

Soderbergh had had it with instant fame—"Everybody wants to know me," he complained. On July 9, he dumped his Palme d'Or in the trunk of his Rambler and headed into the desert east of L.A. bound for Charlottesville, Virginia, driving at night so his car wouldn't overheat. Says Alison, "Steven's one of those people who has difficulty being happy where he's living. If he's living in L.A., he's wants to live in New York. If he's living in New York, it's, I guess I better go to L.A." His family had once lived in Charlottesville, and he had pitched a no-hitter there when he was eight years old. "He wanted to go back to where he had that moment of joy," Alison continues. "But ultimately, he can't really enjoy life." As Soderbergh has since admitted, "There's a difference between experiencing success on the scale I had it on *sex, lies,* and wanting it. I didn't expect it, and I didn't want it. When *sex, lies* happened, I martyred myself out of enjoying it. And you know, it's disingenuous and borderline offensive not to enjoy it."

Miramax premiered *sex, lies* on August 4, 1989, in what turned out to be a clever bit of counterprogramming—the summer blockbusters were winding down, and audiences who weren't brain dead by that time were hungry for something to chew on. The response was so enthusiastic that at the after party, Soderbergh felt like he was having an out-of-body experience. He confided to his diary, "I think the reason a lot of suddenly successful people get screwed up is because they think they should feel better and be happier, and when they aren't, they think there must be something wrong with themselves, so they indulge in self-destructive behavior. What has happened to me is really great, but I don't feel any happier personally than I was eighteen months ago. I think it's a bad idea to tie your self-image to your perceived success in the film business. Could make one bitter."

To break the big-city, $10 million barrier, an independent has to play the suburban multiplexes. Zeidman had blazed a path with *Scandal*, and *sex, lies* followed where *Scandal* led. "Up to that point, and even today, there are a lot of people distributing films, like the guys at Sony Classics, who think film is holy," reflects Jack Foley. "The films were cloistered in the Orson Welles in Cambridge or the Landmark Theaters or the Laemmles in L.A. You didn't put art films in certain theaters, because you bastardized them, you commercialized them. Like malls. It was a dimwitted, stupid, elitist point of view. Until Marty Zeidman said, 'Stop this preciousness and let's go. Whore of Babylon or not, this is a business. Let's make money.' Harvey molded art film into smart film. But they would have never have had the success that they did without Marty breaking the rules."

"It was like pouring water on the floor," says Zeidman. "How far will it expand? You don't know, it just kept going and going." Driven by the ambition of the Weinsteins and the media's hunger for something new and different, *sex, lies* did no more than a handful of exclusive engagements before it went wide to every major city on five hundred, six hundred screens. "It played everywhere, Corpus Christi, cities that never played specialized movies before, theaters that wouldn't have normally played a specialized movie," Zeidman continues. "But you can never [over]estimate exhibitor greed. When they saw the numbers, they jumped all over it." The expanding release pattern was accompanied with an expensive publicity blitz. Says Bingham Ray, up to that point "you'd take a four inch ad on opening day, and people would notice it. You could open a film in New York for $15,000, all in. You wouldn't think to advertise an independent or a foreign language film on TV. It was strictly in print. Or if you were really adventurous and had a little more money to spend, classical radio. With *sex, lies*, Harvey started to spend advertising dollars on TV." Larry Estes adds, "To earn $25 million—you don't do that with a million bucks. They spent over $2.5 million in P&A. They went crazy with publicity." In addition to the $24.7 million domestic gross, *sex, lies* did another $30 million worldwide.

Soderbergh was delighted with the Weinsteins. He said at the time, "I'm stunned with how deeply they were able to penetrate with the film. They're willing to go out there and pound the pavement. The amount of money they made compared to the P&A cost is amazing." The beauty of Miramax was that when everything was going right, it offered the best of both worlds, giving the films the tender loving care indie distributors excelled at and spending big money buying the TV spots. But everything didn't always go right. Harvey and Bob were like the little girl in the Mother Goose tale: when they were good they were very very good, but when they were bad they were awful.

REDFORD'S 1988 CHRISTMAS LETTER to staffers appeared to mark the nadir of the institute's fortunes, but things would get worse, and soon. Festival head Safford left what seemed like a sinking ship in 1990 and moved on to New Line; Geoff Gilmore, who arrived in April 1990, succeeded Safford but had little to do with that year's festival. Held under the cloud of the management meltdown and plunging morale, it represented a distinct falling off from the previous year. In the absence of another *sex, lies,* Sundance clung to Soderbergh himself, who headed the jury for dramatic films and was fast becoming something of a poster boy for the festival, allowing himself to be used in its promos. This festival became known as the Afro-American year for Charles Burnett's *To Sleep with Anger* and the Hudlin brothers' *House Party,* which went on to become a big hit for New Line. Other standouts included Hal Hartley's *The Unbelievable Truth,* which had been picked up by Miramax that September in Toronto, and Whit Stillman's *Metropolitan.*

Certainly, Sundance needed another *sex, lies* badly, and soon. The mediocrity of the festival seemed to confirm Redford's worst fears. As Gilmore remembers it, "There was a sense of one step forward, two steps back to the old days, where independent film was largely anonymous and marginal." Ironically, the turnaround was to come quickly, but in the dark days of 1990, no one could see around that corner, especially not Sundance, which concluded, in effect, that its mission was a failure. From the beginning, Redford had worried that indies were, well, too damn indie. Sounding like he was ready to give up, he reflected, "Maybe it's time to say, 'Are we making a mistake using the word "independent" quite so much? Should we not just say, "Film is film"?'" He had tried to use the carrot of production money to lure unruly filmmakers onto the straight and narrow of commercial production, but that failed, and he concluded that there were just not enough big fish swimming in the indie pond. Frank Daniel, who was running the labs, added his voice to the growing chorus, complaining, with a sigh, "There aren't that many independents that have talent." Thus, the institute began to favor "transitional" or "crossover" directors, which is to say, celebrities who had made their mark in areas other than filmmaking and were itching to try their hand at directing—over the "emerging" first- or second-time filmmakers who had repeatedly disappointed Redford with their clumsy efforts and disregard for his advice. Making no secret of his distaste for emerging filmmakers, Daniel continued, "The transition people are better. A guy who's spent years in theater has a better eye for a good story, a better sense of structure and character than filmmakers or screenwriters. They come with better projects." Embarrassed by its failure to produce either a succèss d'estime or a commercial hit, the institute was ready to turn its back on the indies it was created to serve.

Daniel, of course, was speaking nonsense. As director and sometime resource person Ulu Grosbard (*True Confessions*) pointed out at the time, even if it's true that your average playwright is a better writer than your average screenwriter—which is debatable—"the very thing that makes them good playwrights makes them bad screenwriters. The rules are different and the language is different." Putting his finger on one of the flaws at the heart of Sundance, he continued, "Trying to get away from commercial filmmaking, people are looking to good literature, but I'd much rather see a good pulpy genre film that's really well done than an attempt to do *War and Peace* that's flat."

Redford hired Suzanne Weil, a former PBS factotum, to succeed Tom Wilhite. In Weil, Redford presumably hoped to find a more pliable director, but once again he demonstrated his flair for hiring the wrong person. She was the opposite of Wilhite. By many accounts, she was an indifferent administrator, but she did nurture her relationship with Redford, as well as a group of "transitional" filmmakers who included such unlikely candidates as Carl Bernstein, Martha Clarke, Twyla Tharp, and Peter Weller, a.k.a. Robocop. (None of them ever did manage to make a notable film.)

Safford was a gifted programmer, but paradoxically, his most significant contribution may well have been recruiting Gilmore as his successor. Gilmore came from the Cinematèque at UCLA. With an academic background, he was not an insider. "I wasn't all that impressed with American independent cinema," he recalls, "especially the granola cinema practiced by Sundance." Gilmore couldn't have come at a worse time. The 1990 festival earned $617,000 against expenses of $546,000, for a net profit of a mere $71,000. A couple of months after he arrived, the fiscal storm broke over the institute, drenching it in red ink. The program directors were called into a meeting, told they could each keep one person, fire the rest. Staff size was abruptly cut by 50 percent, down from 35 to 12 or 13. The budget was slashed by nearly 50 percent, from about $2.7 million to approximately $1.55 million.

Later that year, Redford returned from the *Havana* production in Santo Domingo to find that the Sundance deficit had skyrocketed. "I just couldn't have it," he said, and fired Weil. Weil claimed she was unpopular because she tried to make changes. "I had a chance to mess it up," she confessed, "but I didn't have the chance to put it together again."

Once again, Sundance was adrift. Says Pollack, who was present at the creation and probably has known Redford longer than anybody, "It wasn't passive aggressive—it was more healthy than that—it was an ambivalence about wanting to dominate it himself and wanting to let go and let somebody [else] run it." As the institute's tenth anniversary approached in 1991, it was questionable whether Redford's baby would survive. Corporate sponsors were pressured to pay cash on the barrelhead lest the institute miss its payroll. The star complained, bitterly, "No matter how hard you try, somebody gets pissed off. It's time now for me to step back and see if this thing can go on its own or not. If it can't, it shouldn't." He paused. "I'd hate to think that ten years of my life have been wasted. If you say there's a leadership problem at Sundance, it's my responsibility to find someone who will run it. I haven't done it. It's as simple as that. But there's somebody who has moved into the picture right now who I think has a very good concept for raising a lot of money: Gary Beer."

Beer swept away what was left of the old guard, but the bloodletting further eroded morale. Competition programmer Alberto Garcia spoke for many when he said, "I would wish, if I'd spent years of my life with a nonprofit arts organization, to get a nice good-bye instead of a hefty boot. I find it highly ironic that the institute was created to shelter independent filmmakers from the lawyers and the money people so that they could focus strictly on the material, yet now Sundance is being run by those same people, the bean counters."

Surveying the wreckage, Redford tried to figure out how it had gone so wrong. Increasingly, he came to see himself as a drag on Sundance and Sundance as a drag on him. "A lot of people were talking about what an asset I was," he complained at the time. "I began to see it differently, that I was a distorting force, a liability. If someone says this guy is a dilettante, and he's out there in Utah trying to use this as some tax write-off, then they weren't going to be anxious to contribute. So I purposely tried to step back, because I didn't think it was healthy. Some people view that as schizophrenic leadership. That's not true. It's been conscious. I decided three years ago that I've got to go back to doing my own work. There are things I want to do and films I want to make. In the '70s, I made fourteen, fifteen films, and only four in the '80s. It was never my intention to quit my career and run Sundance."

Pace Pollack, many regard the star precisely as a passive aggressive, with a genius for snatching defeat from the jaws of victory. The final scene of *The Candidate* is vintage Redford. His character has won a grueling race for senator from California, but his last words are a querulous, "What do we do now?" as the camera holds on an empty hotel room looking for the there there. Concludes Van Wagenen, "Bob would have liked nothing better than for the institute to have worked without him. Gradually, it became clear that he was the lynchpin. He realized he would have to get involved in a central role. He got a lot more than he bargained for."

Meanwhile, Redford was impatiently waiting for Soderbergh to start work on *King of the Hill*. Soderbergh had showed up at the resort for the producers' workshop the previous August with the rest of the *sex, lies* gang. He told Estes that he was going to marry Betsy Brantley, and he did, in December 1989, before a justice of the peace in Charlottesville. The two seemed to be very much in love. A few months later, Soderbergh was shooting *Kafka* and thinking about his next film. Redford expected it to be *King of the Hill*. But Soderbergh still felt he owed Pollack a picture. While he was in post-production on *Kafka*, he was summoned by Redford to his bungalow at Universal. Redford was 45 minutes late, and since there was no one in the building, the young director sat patiently on the cement steps outside. As Soderbergh recalls the meeting, Redford said, "I understood that you might do another film before *King of the Hill*."

"Yeah, I might."

"I'm just wondering if I should carry on with this project, because I can't get a read on whether you still want to do it."

Soderbergh felt his stomach turn over. He thought, This is really strange, because they approached me, and I suggested that book. This wasn't a project they generated. It sounded to him like Redford was making a threat. "The question Redford was asking was, 'Should I do this with you or without you?' " Soderbergh replied, "No, I fully intend to do this. But these things aren't always quantifiable. All I can tell you is I absolutely intend to make this movie. I'm not bullshitting you. I'm not playing a game."

"Fine."

But Soderbergh left the meeting with an uneasy feeling, especially since Redford now owned the rights to *King of the Hill*.

HARVEY HAD PICKED UP *Cinema Paradiso* at Cannes in May of 1989.

Nobody else wanted it. Directed by Giuseppe Tornatore, it had already bombed in Italy the previous year, where it ran at a mind-numbing two-and-one-half hours plus. Most buyers were not in the habit of recutting pictures, so they just sat on their hands. Harvey was not so finicky. At the time, he maintained a primitive post-production facility that edited trailers and TV spots but also cut and revoiced. The brothers were so strapped they worked directly on the release prints, cutting and pasting, but in later days, when the company had become more prosperous, they reshot or added scenes to films that the directors who made them considered finished. The Weinsteins hired kids out of NYU film school, paid them nothing, told them Miramax was their graduate school.

Cinema Paradiso was pared down – although marketing executive Russell Schwartz claimed Tornatore cut it himself – to two hours, still long, but not interminable. Cutting pictures for length, however offensive to filmmakers, made a certain amount of sense, especially when it was done with tact, sensitivity, and in conjunction with the director. But there was more. "Harvey used to say, our job was to listen to these films, even the British ones, with an American ear," recalls Stuart Burkin. When the actors came in to dub their dialogue, "we'd ask them not to have such an overtly British accent."

Boning foreign films into easily digested fillets, safe from the kinds of cultural idiosyncrasies that might stick in the throats of American audiences made less sense; arguably, it is just those unfamiliar customs, linguistic usages, or behavioral tics that contribute to the sense of difference that makes foreign films foreign, windows onto unfamiliar worlds, and not just yet another mirror held up to ourselves. The last thing we want to do is stumble onto a McDonald's in the Forbidden City in Beijing. Harvey Keitel trying to tease words out of the mute heroine of Jane Campion's *The Piano* is, or should be, a paradigm of the relationship between American audiences and foreign films; we need to work at unlocking their secrets, and if we do, the best ones repay us with a bounty of pleasure. Besides, it is a slippery slope; the goal of big grosses all too easily tips the balance against preserving the integrity of the director's vision. Once you unzip a film, changing this and altering that, it's hard to know when to stop, and you all too easily end up at the bottom of the slope in the wreckage of those wonderful Hong Kong martial arts movies destroyed by dubbing that became Miramax staples. Harvey Weinstein insists, "We never tested the movies to change the movies." But, explains Diana Tauder, who worked at Miramax in post-production for six years, from 1993 to 1999, "Miramax did market-research screenings, and then, based on what people thought of the film, we would go back and recut it. I understood that what I was doing might not have been the most ethical thing, but it was how this movie was going to make more money. And in my opinion, most of the time, it was going to be better." By allowing audiences to play a creative role in filmmaking, however, Harvey was well down a road that led to the death of serious filmmaking—foreign films, indie films, art films, whatever—an arid desert where nothing grows save the TV networks with their lowest common denominator programming ruled by the Nielsen ratings. In short, Harvey was McMiramaxing foreign films.

Whatever the purpose, cutting for length or cutting for American eyes and ears was often a coercive procedure. As Burkin describes it, "We never put it like this, but we were saying [to the filmmaker], 'You tell us how you think you can accomplish the goals that the Weinsteins are looking for.' It went easier when they got it, because they knew that it was gonna happen anyway."

Most of the young graduates Harvey hired had been schooled to respect the auteur. Even though they believed they were helping filmmakers by improving their films, they often had little stomach for their work. "It was not fun," says Burkin. "Sometimes I thought I was cutting out the idiosyncrasies that made the film what it was just to make it move quicker. I internalized that and had a lot of stomach pain all the time." Burkin got an ulcer from the stress.

Diana Tauder felt the same way: "I just felt like it was taking someone's baby and telling the parent, I'm gonna operate on it when they think it is perfectly fine. A lot of these people were really seasoned directors. They'd obviously made a work of art. Maybe embarrassed is the right word for what I felt. At the end of my career there, I realized that it wasn't the right way for me to be creative, because I was being creative with someone else's work."

Harvey nearly got into a fistfight with Ismail Merchant, who had produced *Mr. & Mrs. Bridge* for his partner, James Ivory, to direct. The film, relatively expensive, starred Paul Newman and Joanne Woodward, and was based on two books by Evan Connell. It was produced by Cineplex Odeon. Miramax paid $4 million for it on the basis of the cast and the script, by Merchant/Ivory's regular writer, Ruth Prawer Jhabvala. "I love Ruth." Weinstein says. "She's the great talent of the trio." The filmmakers knew the brothers' reputation, but according to the contract, Ivory had final cut, so they were confident that they were protected. Harvey and Bob visited the set in Kansas City and were effusive, saying, according to Merchant and Ivory, "This is so wonderful, we're so happy to be associated with you," blah, blah. Everything remained so wonderful until Miramax saw the film, and then everything wasn't so wonderful any more.

Ivory had changed the ending, had Mrs. Bridge sitting in her car calling out, "Is anybody there?" while the snow fell silently around her. The script had ended on a more upbeat note, a flashback to their wedding. Says Merchant, "They thought it would be better that if Paul Newman comes, takes her in his arms and goes inside, with swelling music, so that the American audience feels satisfied."

Neither Cinecom, nor any of Merchant/Ivory's other distributors did test screenings, so when Miramax tested *Mr. & Mrs. Bridge*, the duo was appalled. Over the years, they had developed a high opinion of their own talents—not undeserved—and with *A Room with a View* on their résumé, they regarded themselves as well beyond the reach of preview cards and focus groups. Nevertheless, the brothers proceeded, testing *Mr. & Mrs. Bridge* at the Paris Theater, in New York. Recalls Weinstein, "It got a bad reaction, especially the ending. People gasped. Gasped!"

At a meeting with the filmmakers in the conference room at the Tribeca offices, Harvey insisted, "We have to make changes in the film." Merchant, a tough veteran of the indie wars, was disinclined to be pushed around. He told them, "The changes are not possible to do. Here you have opportunity to distribute first rate movie, and if you don't want, don't distribute." Ivory asked to see the cards from the test screening. He took one look and said, "This film's intended for sophisticated audiences. This isn't the kind of educated, upper East Side crowd you're saying it is."

"Why do you think that?" asked Harvey.

"Look at the penmanship. I can hardly read these, they've been scrawled by people who can barely write." Harvey, raised in Queens, thought, Wow, this guy is making fun of his audience. He erupted: "God, that's pretentious of you. Penmanship, goddamn it, you want fuckin' penmanship, I'll give you fuckin' penmanship." Recalled Ivory, "Harvey went mad. He started screaming, stamping around the table. I think they simply don't like to be crossed. They feel a kind of power and grandeur, sort of bullies in the schoolyard." After a flurry of "Fuck you's," Merchant leaped up from the table and said, "I'm taking film away from you. You do not deserve to distribute, Cineplex will pay you back your money." Merchant challenged Harvey and Bob to fight him outside, down on the street, and stormed out, in the process swinging his attaché case against a glass partition, which shattered noisily. He recalls, "They didn't come out, because obviously they thought that this very fiery Indian would completely—like Shiva's sword would fall on their heads, and they would have only body and head—separated."

Harvey demanded they shorten it; they refused. According to Ivory,

Miramax "withheld the last payment of the money that they'd owed to us, and of course we needed that money to pay the lab and the recording studio, and the interest on the bank loan. Even though I had final cut, he thought if he held the money back, we might cave in. We told Paul what was happening, and Paul got on the phone to Harvey and said, 'Lay off and pay 'em,' so they did." Merchant didn't talk to Harvey for ten years.

Occasionally, the filmmakers complained to the press, which made Harvey crazy, because if it got around that he reworked films willy nilly, the kinds of directors he desperately needed in his stable would steer clear. Ivory, for example, still smarting from his treatment at Harvey's hands, vented to Howard Feinstein, film editor of New York's *Village Voice*. Feinstein assigned an article on the subject. When the Miramax co-chairman got wind of it, he became apoplectic, especially since the piece was slated to appear on the eve of a benefit for the American Film Institute's National Center for Film and Video Preservation, sponsored by Miramax. According to Feinstein, Harvey called him at home on his unlisted phone number and threatened to send a film crew to his office to shoot him cutting one of his writer's pieces. Feinstein remembers, "He got pretty nasty. The way I took it at the time was as a veiled threat to me. That I could be hurt. I don't think he was stupid enough to actually say, 'I'm gonna have you killed,' but the tone was so nasty that I was quite frightened." When the article, by Elliott Stein, appeared, it cited a half dozen films that Miramax had cut, including *The Thin Blue Line, Pelle the Conqueror, Scandal,* and *The Little Thief*. Although the origins of the sobriquet are obscure, Harvey henceforth became known as "Harvey Scissorhands." Says Steve Woolley, "No one should be surprised at 'Harvey Scissorhands,' because he was always that way. Look at *The Secret Policeman's Other Ball*. He took a big knife to two films, different directors, and cut them together into one. I don't think Harvey for one minute sees it as being derogatory or negative, because he got results from doing it. 'Harvey Scissorhands' is a compliment."

Often, however, Harvey merely got the worst of both worlds: he earned the enmity of the filmmakers and reaped bad press for making cuts, but he didn't cut enough, because he either needed the directors to do publicity for their films or he wanted to work with them again, or both. Although determined, Harvey was conflicted about what he was doing. He'd worry, "Are we gonna piss 'em off? Is this stupid? Should I just let it go?" Sometimes, after a screening, he'd say, "You know what? I think I went too far. It's missing something that my brother and I loved about this movie in the first place." All in all, as Burkin puts it, "During my tenure, from 1991 to 1994, the films that did the best for us were the ones that we bought finished and never touched: *sex, lies; My Left Foot; The Crying Game.* Harvey really was a guy who loved movies, but he also loved money, and he also loved fame."

Three
Risky Business
1990–1992

• How Miramax plunged into free fall, while Todd Haynes and Christine Vachon launched the "New Queer Cinema," Quentin Tarantino unleashed his dogs on Sundance, and Bingham Ray and Jeff Lipsky gave birth to October.

"sex, lies, and videotape *was like the first time you had sex. Everybody since then has been trying to re-create that moment, but it was an aberration.*"
— TOM BERNARD, CO-PRESIDENT, SONY CLASSICS

One fine day in October 1990, Skouras Pictures' Jeff Lipsky was walking along the bank of the river Thames, when the proverbial lightbulb went off, as though in a thought balloon over the head of a character in a comic strip, which is sort of what he looked like. Bald as a cue ball—he suffers from alopecia, the Lex Luthor disease, not a hair on his body—Lipsky has an angular face and wore black-framed Mr. McGoo glasses. He was fussy and retentive, intense and intimidating. In those days he had a weakness for the color purple, sometimes wearing purple clothes exclusively, down to shoes and socks. He had purple chairs in his office when he worked at Goldwyn. But he had a reputation for being a fiery partisan of indie films, as driven as anyone at Miramax, but unlike anyone at Miramax, a passionate defender of the artistic integrity of filmmakers. The license plate on his car read, MPAA-NOT.

At that time the head of the motion picture division at Skouras, Lipsky was in London to see Mike Leigh's new film, as yet untitled. One of his triumphs at Skouras had been *High Hopes*, which he had picked up and made into a modest hit. It was the director's first feature to secure North American distribution, and Lipsky's campaign brought Leigh to the attention of U.S. critics, who applauded the film. It would not be an exaggeration to say that Lipsky was the architect of Leigh's American career, turning the underappreciated British director into a medium-sized international star. Lipsky worshipped the ground Leigh walked on and had developed a rapport with the curmudgeonly director and his producer, Simon Channing-Williams, who protected him fiercely. Leigh kept inviting Lipsky over to London to see his film. Lipsky told his boss, Tom Skouras, "We have to keep up this relationship." Skouras replied, "We'll see, we'll see." Weeks passed, and Leigh called yet again, and still Skouras dragged his feet. Lipsky thought, Well, Tom may want to sever the relationship with Mike and Simon, but I don't. He and his wife flew to London on their own dime and saw the film, which would come to be called *Life Is Sweet*. Over lunch Lipsky told the filmmakers, "This is a masterpiece—but we're not going to buy this movie." He explained the situation at Skouras. They encouraged him to start his own company, saying, "You have all this experience, you have all these connections, we'll support your acquisition of the film."

Lipsky and his wife flew back to L.A. the next morning. He walked into Skouras's office and said, impetuously, "I resign." At that point, Lipsky was a sixteen-year veteran of the business. But he knew he couldn't go it alone. Lipsky had already had several conversations with Bingham Ray, who was likewise unhappy in his current job at Avenue, about the possibility of joining forces. Recalls Ray, "We were tired of working for other people, tired of people saying, 'No, we can't buy this film,' and 'Yes we can buy this film.' I felt I was being held back. I wanted to be *the guy*." Lipsky stalked out of Skouras's office, retired to his own, and called his friend. He said, "I did it, I just resigned, I'm starting the company, I saw this great movie in England, that's our first release, are you interested?" Ray took a deep breath and said, "Yeah."

Like Lipsky, Ray, age 46, lived and breathed movies. The son of an engineer, Ray grew up in Scarsdale, a wealthy town in wealthy Westchester, just north of New York City. "I would come in from the suburbs wearing a button-down shirt to the Elgin, sit next to a guy in a raincoat," he recalls. "My father would say, 'You keep going to all these movies, you're going to turn into a bum!'" Save for a couple of fugitive WASP genes, he had the DNA of a Jewish producer. He was short, profane, and volatile. He had a famously brief attention span, made snap judgments, was proud of, and trusted, his gut. If Lipsky had a passion for purple, Ray had his own sartorial idiosyncrasies. His uniform, day in and day out, was a T-shirt, Bermuda shorts, a blazer, topsiders, and a Mets cap. He was constitutionally unable to put on a tie. "Why ties?" he wonders, rhetorically. "They're so stupid. There was this hockey coach, won Stanley Cups, who blew his nose on his tie. I was raised where you don't blow your nose on your tie. But, why not?

If you don't have a handkerchief, it's there. It's handy." Ray chain-smoked Marlboros, loved to drink, and was a real charmer, a great storyteller, expansive and flamboyant. Filmmakers loved him. He didn't have much in the way of a firewall between thought and speech, was not in the habit of biting his tongue, which flicked over friends and foes alike, sharp and tart, and often got him into trouble. Like Lipsky he was blunt and confrontational. Someone once said of Ray, "If you locked Bingham up alone in a closet, he'd pick a fight with himself."

Also like Lipsky, Ray had worked at most of the important indie companies, Island, New Yorker, Goldwyn, Alive, and Avenue. The upside of the Lipsky-Ray partnership was that neither man was in it for the money—they both carried into the 1990s the pure blue flame of passion that burned in the hearts of the young cinéastes in the 1970s and 1980s; they knew distribution and marketing inside out. The two men also shared a taste for darker, quirkier, more dangerous pictures than their competitors. Lipsky, for example, had acquired Alex Cox's grim *Sid and Nancy* for Goldwyn. "Upbeat" and "life affirming" were dirty words in their lexicon, and they were willing to take risks on movies that few believed had a prayer at the box office. As Ray explains, "I always wanted us to be able to try things that were not necessarily commercially viable. I'm not some avant-gardist, I know the difference between something that's truly experimental and something that's wholly mainstream, but I'd like to think that somewhere in the middle is a comfort zone where there's an audience. It might not be the largest, or the most lucrative, but for me the rewards there are the greatest."

The downside was that they both knew distribution and marketing inside out, that is, instead of complementing each other, their skill sets overlapped. With their hefty egos, they would be two carp in a goldfish bowl. To the outside, they appeared to be fast friends, sharing a passion for the Mets. But if their skills were identical, their personalities were not. They were an odd couple, with Ray playing Oscar to Lipsky's Felix. Lipsky was compulsive. Everything had to be in its place, just so. He got up at 5:00 A.M. and went to sleep early. Ray was just the opposite, slept late and stayed up late. Beyond that, he had spent a good chunk of his professional life in Lipsky's shadow, and as time would show, he was ready for his place in the sun.

No one was making a killing distributing indie pictures in those days, and neither Lipsky nor Ray had any money of his own. On the first of March 1991, they began working out of Lipsky's ranch-style house on Haseltine Avenue in Sherman Oaks. Every day, Ray made the long trip by car from Venice, where he lived, up the 405 to the San Fernando Valley, knocked on the door, and waited for Lipsky, who refused to give him a key, to let him in. His office was Lipsky's dining room, his desk the dining room table. When he arrived, on his chair would be the morning's "memos" "from: Jeff," "to: Bingham," re: this or that, even though the two men sat right next to each other. Ray wangled free office space from a friend at Republic Home Video but it was near the airport, that is, closer to his home, and Lipsky refused to budge. Says Ray, "Jeff is an extraordinary talent. He was involved in the distribution of dozens of successful films. That doesn't happen by accident. But he's dogmatic as the day is long. There was only one way to go about doing things, and that was Jeff's way. There was only one time, and that was Jeff's time. It had to be in Jeff's house. It was Jeff's fucking show. I was just along for the ride."

Working out of Lipsky's home was hard on both of them. One Monday, Ray arrived to find that half the furniture was gone. He exclaimed, "What the fuck happened to the furniture?" Lipsky replied, "Oh, a friend of ours moved into town. We gave him half our tables and chairs." A few days later he discovered that Lipsky's wife had walked out, taking her share of the furniture with her. Lipsky was a tightly wrapped kind of guy to begin with, and the pressure was getting to him, expressing itself in hysterical symptoms. One time, recalls Ray, "Jeff came in, he was really agitated, had his hands over his eyes, and he was yelling, 'I'm blind! I'm blind!' He was knocking into shit, and I said, 'What the fuck are you doing?' 'I can't see.' And then of course, twenty minutes later, he was fine." When Ray returned home from work that day, his wife asked, "How was your day, dear?" He replied, "Oh, Jeff went blind today!"

On another occasion, Lipsky and Ray were chatting up Bob Laemmle over lunch at a trendy Italian restaurant on Santa Monica Boulevard. Laemmle, a bear of a man whose family had owned movie theaters since the beginning of time and had also founded Universal, was a major player in indie exhibition in L.A. and hence a key to the success of their new company. Lipsky and Ray were anxious to make a good impresson, "This is who we are, our first picture is *Life Is Sweet*," and so on. But half way through the meal, Lipsky fell silent. "Jeff just stopped talking," recalls Ray. "Stared at his plate. Bob and I were looking at each other like, 'So, Jeff? You feel all right?' Nothing. He wouldn't explain his very odd behavior. Lunch wound down awkwardly. I was embarrassed." Afterward, they climbed into Lipsky's 1986 blue Thunderbird. "Jeff was driving like a bat out of hell, gripping the wheel, knuckles white. I felt like I was in *The French Connection*," Ray continues. Unable to contain himself, he finally exploded, screaming, "What the fuck is wrong with you? How do you just sit there and say nothing for almost an hour? Bob Laemmle must think we're two fucking losers, big time, you fucked everything up." Lipsky's head was getting redder and redder, a bell pepper. Squeezing out one word at a time, he said,

"Right . . . now . . . I . . . am . . . bleeding . . . to death . . . internally." Pausing for a breath, he continued, "I . . . was . . . ingesting glass . . . in that restaurant . . . that's why I wasn't . . . saying . . . anything. They put broken . . . glass in my food. And we're driving to the emergency room at Cedars Sinai." He showed Ray the "glass," which he had brought with him to give to the doctors. Ray examined it, said, "Jeff, that's not glass, that's dried pasta, the edge of the lasagna." They drove back over the hill into the Valley, and twenty-five minutes later, Lipsky was fine. "I'm going to be very kind," Ray says. "I'm going to say he is a full-blown, driven eccentric, instead of just flat-out fucking crazy."

By 1990, the ground was littered with bankrupt distribution companies that had tripped blithely down the road to production. Lipsky and Ray pitched a company that would chastely forswear making films. "We were not going to make the same mistake everybody else did, we were going to mind our knitting," explains Lipsky. "There were people at the top who for the time being had deep pockets and were doing foolhardy things like making movies, and there were the bottom-feeders who would never have the financial wherewithal to acquire any film they wanted. But the middle ground was missing, and that's the niche we intended to fill."

The two men were trying both to raise a half-million dollars for a one-off release of *Life Is Sweet*, and $7 million to capitalize their new company, which they called October, after Sergei Eisenstein's classic film of the same name, and their birthdays, both in October. In the first case, they were successful; in the second they were not. Raising money in the movie business, it sometimes seems like all roads lead to the investment house of Allen & Co., and after a good deal of to-ing and fro-ing, Lipsky and Ray indeed found themselves knocking on that door, hats in hand. "I was never an entrepreneur before this, and I didn't know Allen & Co. from shit," says Lipsky. "They read the plan, said, 'We think you're real cute and everything, but you don't have day-to-day entrepreneurial experience. Stay in touch, fellas."

The few pennies Ray and Lipsky had scraped together were gone. They were running on fumes. With thirty years of experience between them, the two men had been confident that by Cannes they'd have rounded up the cash they needed. But Cannes came and went, and they had nothing to show for their efforts. One airless, summer afternoon, in this atmosphere of gloom, the phone rang at Lipsky's home. It was Amir Malin, calling for Ray. Ray groaned inwardly. He had briefly worked at Cinecom, Deutchman and Malin's company, years ago, before leaving for Goldwyn. Malin was not his favorite person.

Indeed, Malin did not seem to be anyone's favorite person. His detractors blamed him—fairly or not—for forcing out his partners, Deutchman and John Ives, and riding a thriving company into the ground before himself being ousted by the new owner. At Cinecom, Malin was the inside man. He seemed content to stay in the shadows and proved to be something of a wizard at squeezing money out of ancillary deals. Says Sony Classics' Michael Barker, "Amir was the first guy in the independent world to see the value of television and video, how ancillaries could drive you instead of theatrical. And how libraries are the value of your company." But when someone else, namely, Deutchman, stole the spotlight, hobnobbing with filmmakers and getting the credit for the company's success, Malin seemed, although he would never admit it, jealous, hurt, and angry. He couldn't decide, in other words, if he were Bob or Harvey. He gave the impression of wanting to appear smaller than life, but inside he probably felt larger—Bob, with an inner Harvey struggling to get out.

Bart Walker, who was executive VP of Cinecom and is now an agent at ICM, explains, "I always considered Amir a good and decent person, and our business relationship has a personal quality. He is very smart, and I learned a lot from him. But a lot of our problems at the company stemmed from his inscrutability, which he cultivated. He could be an artist at making people feel uncomfortable—which is great in negotiating but a big problem in managing a small company."

Among some former colleagues, Malin had the reputation for being something less than forthright. John Shestack, who worked for Malin years later as head of production at Artisan, says, "Basically, everybody who comes in contact with the guy regrets it. The truth is just one tool in his toolbox, only to be used occasionally, when it's helpful to him. It would be little things, but over time they would aggregate. He would lie to make you feel bad. He would say, about a script, 'I read it, I'm very disappointed in it, and if you can't fix it, I'll get somebody who can,' when he hadn't read it. Then later someone else would want to buy it, and he'd say, 'No, we're keeping it.'

" 'Why are we keeping it? I thought you didn't like it.'

" 'No, I really like it, it's the one movie I really want to make.'

" 'Here's your e-mail where you said you hated it, it was really disappointing. So, which is it?' You just wouldn't get a response. He created an atmosphere of fear." Shestack referred to him as "Malach Hamavet," which means, in Hebrew, the Angel of Death.

Some filmmakers said they had trouble collecting what they believed was owed them. Cinecom's big hit was Merchant/Ivory's *A Room with a View* in 1985. The two filmmakers noticed, in Ivory's words, that "the money that we ourselves personally earned because of our percentages in the film always came from Europe and England, never from the U.S." Merchant chimes in, "When we called Cinecom's accountant, he would have all kinds of excuses, that his uncle had died, someone else was very sick in the hospital, and so on. We said, 'OK, we'll send the auditors.' " When the film broke $20 million, they say Malin sent them an expensive clock from Tiffany's. According to them, he charged it to the budget of the film, so in effect, they paid for their own gift. They also say he charged several Armani suits, claiming that they were expenses he incurred when he attended the Oscar ceremony after the film had been nominated. One time the two filmmakers, flying to L.A., ran into Malin. There's nothing like a commercial flight to make the economics of the film business crystal clear. Malin was in first class, and they were in coach. Merchant blurted out, semijoking, "I could kill you," and he says now, "It's the filmmakers' money that finances everything they do. The distributors wear Armani suits and buy huge offices on the success of a film. But the businessmen who start these companies, they have no devotion to them. It's how much money they can put in their pockets. And that's what is Amir Malin. He completely wrecked that company, which had done so well." Concludes Ivory, "We stopped making films with him."

"I don't remember sending him a Tiffany clock, I don't know anything about Armani suits, I don't charge my clothes, I don't play games with expense reports, it's totally fabricated," retorts Malin. "If there were issues with the accounting, they would have litigated it. What I do remember is that one day Ismail walked into my office with a gift for me, a beautiful framed picture of himself, me, and Denholm Elliott taken at a Sunday brunch at the Plaza Hotel, celebrating *Room with a View*'s record breaking run at the Paris Theater. I thanked him, and then a couple of days later, we got the bill, for the picture and the frame." Adds Walker, "I would never say Amir Malin bankrupted Cinecom. It was a child of his, and he was very committed to its survival. Nor do I believe Amir stabbed Deutchman in the back. From what I saw, Stephen Swid, who succeeded Amir as CEO, made that decision."

Richard Abramowitz started at Cinecom in 1983 in sales, and he left in 1992 eight and a half years later. "All those years at Cinecom, I was Amir's sole defender inside the company," he says. "We used to eat lunch together, but I gained a perspective on him as time went on. We used to refer to Amir as the poster child for anti-Semitism. This is not the guy I would want out there for—Oh yeah, that's a Jew! It was like, Do something, you're making us all look bad. He reflected most of the stereotypical characteristics that are most troubling to those of us who are sensitive to the way Jews are perceived. It always appeared that there was no such thing for Amir as a win-win negotiation. It was win-humiliate. The only way Amir considered that he'd won was if he got every fucking last nickel. People would say to me, 'He's the devil.' I would defend him, say, 'He's not the devil, you're giving him way too much credit.' The devil has a certain magnitude. You don't compare everyone to Hitler. He's not significant enough to be the devil. He's just a jerk.'"

Still, Lipsky and Ray both knew they could use a business affairs guy. Malin had convinced Cinecom's creditors that he was the best person to manage the company's only significant asset, the library. According to Ray, he told him, "I think what you guys are doing is great, I'm doing the Cinecom library, I have access to money. You guys don't do ancillary sales, that's what I do, why don't we talk about partnering." Ray was pacing and smoking, smoking and pacing, saying, "I dunno, I dunno." He couldn't even stand the sound of Malin's voice. But for Lipsky, the bad news about Malin was no more than hearsay. He and Ray were like rubberneckers standing by the side of the road gawking at a pileup of cars. They thought it couldn't happen to them. Ray said to himself, This might be a means to an end. If it gets us to the next level with Allen & Co., it might not be a bad business move. Lipsky broke the silence, said, "Let's fly to New York and see what he has to say."

MY LEFT FOOT WAS RELEASED in November 1989, *Cinema Paradiso* at the end of December in time for Academy consideration. It got killed in the *New York Times* by Vincent Canby, who compared it to a bad episode of *Growing Pains*. Nevertheless, Harvey stuck with it, and made it a hit at a time when very few if any Italian films were even being released in the United States.

When it was evident both *My Left Foot* and *Cinema Paradiso* were going to do well for Miramax, Harvey and Bob bought out the producers, making them offers they couldn't refuse. The brothers told them, We'll give you money now, maybe you're financing another picture, and who knows what you'll get later, maybe nothing, we might change our minds. It worked.

Come Oscar time, *Cinema Paradiso* even picked up a nomination for Best Foreign Film. Miramax found itself in the enviable position of receiving six additional nominations that year, five for *My Left Foot*, while Soderbergh was nominated for Best Original Screenplay.

Companies were starting to send out screener tapes to Academy members, a practice that leveled the playing field. "The tapes are what did it for *My Left Foot*," says Weinstein. "We didn't have the money to do screening after screening, busing people in, having lavish parties. That gave us parity." Harvey's campaigns were heavily dependent on personal appearances by the principals. He persuaded director Jim Sheridan and producer Noel Pearson to relocate to L.A. to work the Hollywood old-boy network, whose votes weighed so heavily in the outcome of the Academy Awards. Pearson in particular charmed them all in an incessant round of one-on-one breakfasts and lunches, topped off with small dinner parties hosted by pillars of the Hollywood Irish community like Gene Kelly and Carroll O'Connor. The dinners became items in the trades and gossip columns—Army Archerd, George Christy, and Liz Smith—which in turn generated word of mouth. He even had Day-Lewis testify in the Senate on behalf of the Disabilities Act. (His critics charged that this was a stunt to get him an Oscar but, according to Weinstein, the votes were in by that time.)

The brothers were not the first to employ these techniques. Studios had always gotten celebrities to host exclusive dinners followed by screenings of Oscar contenders at their homes in Bel Air and Brentwood, but no one had thought to do the same thing with indies and foreign films until Miramax did it—relentlessly. "In those days the studios had a lock on the Oscars, because none of the indies campaigned aggressively," Weinstein explains. "The only thing that we did to change the rules was, rather than just sitting it out and getting beat because somebody had more money, more power, more influence, we ran a guerrilla campaign." Recalls former publicist Mark Urman, "You create evening social activity where influence peddling can take place as an innocent, natural thing. More mouths to more ears." Such gatherings were particularly useful in introducing foreign actors and directors who weren't part of the community. Miramax exported the "eat, greet, and screen" practice overseas as well, to London and Rome, wherever there were pockets of Academy members.

Urman, who worked on several Miramax campaigns, continues, "They figured out that you can win an Oscar by a single vote, so they didn't consider any voting member too much trouble to seduce. They have more screenings, in more places, than anyone else. [They] set up screenings at the Motion Picture Retirement Home because Academy members live there, even if they're on life support. They find out where people holiday in the period between Christmas and New Year's, and if it's Aspen, they have screenings in Aspen. If it's in Hawaii, they have screenings in Hawaii. They actually called people at home. And now that companies aren't allowed to do that, they hire every single person who will work for them, and they do the talking for them. Many of them are part of the old Hollywood establishment who fifty-two weeks out of the year have nothing to do with a Miramax-type movie, but they know Academy members, and for the Academy season, they talk the Miramax talk, walk the Miramax walk.

"If it was important to get makeup or music score or something like that in addition to the obvious nominations—director, picture, actor, screenplay—so they could, say, claim ten nominations instead of seven, they looked at the membership roster in the applicable branch and just went into overdrive. They would sit there playing six degrees of separation—

'Who do you know who knows how to get to this person?' " Harvey worked the phones himself. Later, when Miramax was bigger and he was financing films, he might get on the line with a director or actor and say things like, "I'd love to work with you in the future. Don't you think *The Piano* is a great movie?"

But Daniel Day-Lewis was a problem. He was the son of Cecil Day-Lewis, a poet laureate of England, and he took himself very seriously indeed. On the set, he stayed in character, wouldn't eat with his hands. The Miramax co-chairman had to twist his arm to get him to do any promotion at all. Explained Weinstein, "I'm surrounded by people who never hear the truth. They are insulated beyond belief. Their asses are kissed daily. Like Daniel Day-Lewis. It's 'Yes, Mr. Lewis, No, Mr. Lewis. Your Highness. Your Lordship. Your this. Your that.' How can he judge anything? . . . I always tell him he'll end up in regional theater in Ireland with his Oscar, going, 'I was famous once . . . ' " Harvey loves to quote Day-Lewis as saying, "There's only one part of you that works—the ability to pick scripts and pick movies. Otherwise, you're a complete disaster as a person.' "

Working day to day with the Weinsteins in New York had gotten to Brantley, as it had to the others, and she had begged Harvey to let her operate out of the London office, an elegant townhouse on Redburn Street in Chelsea, between the river and Kings Road. One of her jobs was to babysit Day-Lewis, who became fond of her. His attitude was, She's the normal person in this crazy company. Harvey would never have gotten through Granada's doors had she not opened them, and he had somehow neglected to reward her with a bonus. She had never been to the Oscars and figured he owed her. After some prodding, he finally agreed to fly her to L.A. and pay for her hotel room, but he said, "Alie, I just can't get you a ticket." She replied, "Harvey, don't worry. I'll get one myself." No sooner said than Day-Lewis gave her his extra ticket. When she arrived in L.A. the day before the ceremony, she got a call from Miramax publicist Christina Kounelias, who told her, "Uh, Harvey wants to talk to you." Brantley, who had been astonished to see that the ticket was for the front row, next to Day-Lewis, couldn't help recalling that Harvey had refused to let her sit next to Soderbergh at the closing ceremony in Cannes and understood right away he wanted to sit with the nominee. She replied, "I will be damned if he's gonna get this ticket." But she had indiscreetly disclosed Harvey's intention to *My Left Foot* producer Noel Pearson, which Harvey discovered. It made him look bad, and he was furious. There was a meeting of Miramax staffers at the Beverly Hills Hotel at noon the next day. Harvey called her, bellowed, "You get yourself over here right now, down to this meeting." She thought, Oh, shit, I'm in for it. I am not walking into that meeting with this ticket in my bag. I'm going to go to my hotel and lock it up. She imagined him pawing through her purse going, "Where is that ticket?"

Twenty minutes later Brantley walked into the Miramax suite. To her chagrin she realized that everybody of any importance at the company was there. She had expected a one on one, never imagining that they would drag her in front of the whole place. She thought, He's just trying to spook me. Bob came over to her, put his arm around her, and said, "That was really dumb what you said to Noel. You must have either been stupid or disloyal. Which one was it?" She thought, This is like the Mafia. But not wanting to get herself into any more trouble, she said, in a small voice, "Oh, I guess I was really stupid." Just then, the phone rang. It was Tom Pollock, head of Universal. Harvey took the call, put on his I'm-talking-to-somebody-important voice, and after he hung up, he looked at her and said, "People at Universal would get fired for less than this." Bob put his arm around her again and walked her to the door. He was terrifying when he was being sweet. She thought, This is utterly creepy, and fully expected to hear him say, "Alie, you're finished." He didn't, but she recalls, "In my heart I knew my days were numbered. You don't stand up to Harvey." None of the people in the room said a word in her defense. "They sat there watching like in a circus," she adds. "Looking back on it, I wish I had said, 'Fuck you!' and walked out. The thing about working for them for me was, we weren't raised to be like that. We were southern." She never did give him the ticket. "I went, and I sat next to Daniel, and it was great."

Harvey may have failed to get his front row seat next to Day-Lewis at the March Academy Awards, but he found ample consolation in the outcome. Day-Lewis won Best Actor, Brenda Fricker took Best Supporting Actress, and *Cinema Paradiso* got Best Foreign Film, giving Miramax three Oscars. The awards raised the value of the films in foreign and future ancillary markets, established the brand, and lent Harvey's promises to get Oscars for his actors the ring of truth, thus helping him win acquisitions. By the time *My Left Foot* left the theaters, it had grossed $14.7 million; 1989 was indeed an annus mirabilis for Miramax. As Bob put it, "In 1989 we turned the heat up."

The Weinsteins rode *Scandal, sex, lies* and *My Left Foot,* and *Cinema Paradiso,* into 1990. *Cinema Paradiso* went wide in February. Recalls former Miramax acquistions executive Mark Tusk, "It was an experiment. Bob said, 'Why do you have to platform it like an art house movie? Why don't we do it like a genre movie? Why don't we do TV advertising, put the film on 500 screens, 700 screens, whatever.' They single-handedly pushed it onto screens that never played subtitled films."

The brothers had a genius for picking foreign films that they could cross over, that Miriam, who often accompanied them to screenings, and her friends would pay to see. As Bernardo Bertolucci, who would have occasion to waltz with Harvey a few years later, puts it, "The Italian films in particular, they are very, very sentimental. Harvey's nature is violent, and when he looks at a movie, he loves to be able to go in front of the mirror and say, 'Look, there is a tear here!' "

The Weinsteins' lineup ran from films that were unabashedly sentimental to films that were genuinely daring. The theory was, Pick up anything that provokes a reaction, positive or negative—like Peter Greenaway's *The Cook, the Thief, His Wife and Her Lover,* where half the audience walked out during the screening at the Toronto Film Festival. The important thing was that it not be boring. A violent, erotic, and blackly humorous broadside against Thatcherism run amuck, *The Cook, the Thief* was definitely not boring. Harvey wanted Greenaway to cut the film and gave him twenty-seven pages of notes to help him. Greenaway was inclined to ignore Weinstein's request, when the Miramax co-chairman called and informed him that he was so upset with Elliott Stein's article that the director needn't cut the film after all. *The Cook, the Thief* did very well, grossing $7.7 million, against the $625,000 Miramax paid for it and did a brisk business on video as well.

According to Greenaway's Dutch producer, Kees Kasander, Harvey paid the advance and some modest bonuses, but neither he nor the director ever saw a penny of the revenues. After an audit, Kasander claimed, "He owes us at least $1 million, but it would have cost more to get that money. This became a big problem for our company."

Says Harvey, The film was a "modest success, but not enough to earn overages. They were not gross participants because they had no track record. He hired a top accounting firm, but they never submitted an audit report to us. That apparently reflected that the audit did not turn up any meaningful claims. Kasander proved we owed him a million, and he voluntarily didn't take it, knowing that he was owed it? What the fuck!"

Buoyed by its success, Miramax had grown to the point where the 48th Street office resembled the subway at rush hour. In February 1990, Miramax moved down and west to Robert De Niro's hip, spanking new Tribeca Film Center on the corner of Greenwich and Franklin. Harvey's office was small. There was the obligatory TV monitor, along with stacks of video tapes, snapshots of Eve, his parents, and one of his most prized possessions, a picture of him and Bob posing with Keith Hernandez, the Mets All-Star first baseman. Weinstein's on-again, off-again dieting somehow gave him license to eat more junk food. There must have been an element of self-hatred to Harvey's eating. Every once in awhile he would drop his guard. He once complained to Steve Earnhart, who worked in post-production, "I look like a fuckin' hippopotamus, Earnhart." Still, he kept at it. If he were on his way to pick up Eve for a screening or a party, using the car service, he'd whip a tuna sandwich out of his pocket, mutter, "Eve will smell this on my breath tonight, but I don't care," gulp it down in two bites, and jam a cigarette into his mouth to mask the odor.

Undoubtedly urged on by Eve, he hired a personal trainer. At the outset, so the story goes, he told the trainer, "You better be here every day. Here's $1,000, I'm giving you in advance, don't pay any attention to what I say, make me work out." The trainer duly appeared at the apppointed hour. Harvey, on the phone, made him wait, and wait. Finally the trainer gained entry to the inner sanctum, and said, "Let's start." Harvey replied, "I don't have time now, here's a fifty, get the fuck outta my office, come back tomorrow." The trainer returned the next day, same thing. He came back day after day, week after week. Until he gave up.

The Weinsteins were tired of living on the edge, putting the entire company at risk every time they opened a movie. They knew they were in a capital-intensive business and that to succeed, they needed to have more cash at their disposal. Moreover, they were under a lot of pressure from the Chase Bank to get their act together. One route was going public, but they were leery. "We went out to one of those Allen & Co. things in Sun Valley," Harvey recalls. "You sit in a room, and there's forty guys, analysts, and they bombard you with questions. If your earnings don't move up 15 percent every year, you get lambasted. But the movie business is mercurial. What would they say if we brought in another *My Left Foot*, some weird movie. We went, Uh-uh, we're not going public. Other than my mother, going public was the one thing that terrified us."

Allen & Co. persuaded them otherwise. What with their profits from *Scandal; sex, lies; My Left Foot*; and *Cinema Paradiso*, they understood that it was now or maybe never. But the old CFO, whose job it would have been to handle the offering from the Miramax side, seemed to have disappeared. John Schmidt, the new CFO, took it over. Schmidt was an example of "hiring up." A brother of Yale president Benno Schmidt, he had sandy hair, a ready smile, and a disarming sense of humor. His father was a friend and partner of John Hay "Jock" Whitney. Schmidt arrived in the spring of 1989. Like Mark Lipsky and Marty Zeidman before him, he found the place was a mess, especially the financials. "Miramax was maybe three to six months away from chaos," he says. "The bank line had been negotiated but hadn't been closed because there was no one in place to do that or to collect our theatrical receivables or manage the company's liquidity. What's our bottom line? When do we run out of money? How much are we gonna have to borrow a year from now? They had no idea."

Still, Schmidt loved working there, at least in the beginning. "The atmosphere was electric," he recalls. "We were doing things on every front at the same time that were all new. Every day was an invention. They had an us-against-them, us-against-the-world mentality that was a lot of fun. Eventually, as we got bigger, the 'us' became more Harvey and Bob, and the 'them' became the employees."

Just a few years out of Harvard Business School, Schmidt was squeaky clean and idealistic, but he also understood that cleaning up their act was just good business, necessary to get to the next level. "I argued to Harvey and Bob that this was a point in time when our legitimacy as a growing independent company had to be based on a certain way of doing business. These were very visible films. We [had to] pay out participations and show people that if they came and worked with us, they wouldn't regret it. Because that's what getting to the next level was all about." Miramax paid out an estimated $4 million to the producers of *sex, lies,* and Harvey always boasted about it, used it as proof that indeed, Miramax did keep its word. "Usually, if they were paying out an overage, a profit to a producer, it was because there was something they wanted," Schmidt continues. Indeed, what they wanted in this case was legitimacy. He adds, "I can't say that left to their own devices they would have screwed the *sex, lies and videotape* producers out of their overages, because they had gross participation*—Harvey and Bob couldn't really fuck with that—but the discussion was all about, Look, we're making $5 or $6 million on this film, we owe this money, and these guys are going to be going around talking." (Miramax denies this.)

For a similar reason, Schmidt pushed them toward the public offering. Not only would it have allowed the Weinsteins to bring in $30, maybe $40 million in new capital and expand their debt capacity, but as a public company it would have opened them to scrutiny, thereby establishing their legitimacy in the financial community the same way that paying overages did in the film community.

At the same time, on a parallel track, Harvey and Bob were talking with studios about buying the company. If they didn't succeed in going public, they wanted a sugar daddy who could send money when they needed it. But in the midst of these maneuvers, the Miramax gusher ran dry as suddenly as it began. Three productions—*The Lemon Sisters, Strike It Rich,* and *Animal Behavior*—incautiously initiated in the wake of the company's successes, all bombed. Ironically, *Mr. & Mrs. Bridge,* released in November 1990, may have been the company's highest grossing film of that year, pulling in a very respectable $7.7 million, and Joanne Woodward was nominated for Best Actress. But as usual, this wasn't good enough. "New Line

---

* "Gross participation": a percentage of the distributor's gross.

was cleaning up with *Ninja Turtles,*" says Schmidt. "The success of New Line, always a step ahead of Miramax, killed them." *The Grifters* more or less broke even; *The Cook, the Thief* did well; Dick Pearce's *The Long Walk Home* grossed $4.8 million; Pedro Almodóvar's *Tie Me Up, Tie Me Down,* grossed $3.8 million; while a couple of critics' films—Zhang Yimou's *Ju Dou* and Michael Verhoeven's *The Nasty Girl*—made pocket money. But there was a long string of duds—something like eight straight at one particularly grim stretch, films like *The Tall Guy,* grossing $510,712; *American Dream,* grossing $269,000; and Hal Hartley's *Unbelievable Truth,* grossing $546,541. Lizzie Borden's second film, *Love Crimes,* turned into a sink hole. It was rewritten, recut, reshot, re-everything, all to no avail. Miramax entered a two-year trough which, despite the occasional hit, would lead it to the edge of the precipice.

IN THE SUNDANCE INSTITUTE'S heart of darkness, Redford sounded like he was within a hair's breadth of walking away from the project. But he stuck with it, and deserves credit for seeing it through. Says Edward Norton, "People take for granted what it takes to sustain an effort when you're finding your way. Actors get together to form theater companies all the time, and they never last, because actors by definition have to be self-involved about their own careers. They'll push the truck up the hill for a little way, but when it doesn't seem like it's gonna start, they stop. Follow through is unusual. Redford deserves a lot of credit." Ironically, it was the festival, into which Redford had to be dragged screaming and kicking, that became the tail that wagged the dog and changed the fortunes of the institute. As Sydney Pollack puts it, "It was initially almost impossible to support Sundance. The turning point came when it took over the U.S. Film Festival." Not only was it developing into a rare profit center but, in Larry Estes's words, *sex, lies* made it "the place where films came from nowhere and turned into these huge things." First under Tony Safford and then Geoff Gilmore, it proved to be an effective counterweight to the conservatism of the lab selection committee.

If 1990 was a snooze, by 1991, despite being held in the shadow of the Gulf War, the festival was starting to pick up. That year marked the tenth anniversary of the institute and was the year it officially became known as the Sundance Film Festival. Gilmore, still feeling his way, had again let Alberto Garcia program the competition, which included Richard Linklater's *Slacker,* Hal Hartley's *Trust,* John Sayles's *City of Hope,* Julie Dash's *Daughters of the Dust,* Matty Rich's *Straight Out of Brooklyn,* and Todd Haynes's *Poison,* produced by Christine Vachon. Of the sixteen films in competition, about half were released.

For *Poison*, the timing was perfect, a narrow window between the granola Sundance of the past and the cell phone Sundance to come. Shot in black and white, without stars, filled with difficult, not to say offensive content, *Poison* was a portmanteau film consisting of three stories: a parody of a '50s mad scientist B movie, a "documentary" coming-of-age tale in which a 7-year-old boy shoots his father, and a segment set in prison based on a Genet story, *Miracle of the Rose*. In Todd Haynes's words, *Poison* "contains humiliation, abuse, unabashed homoeroticism and a certain level of what I suppose you'd call masochism." It was strong stuff for the Sundance audience. People walked out in droves during a scene in which a couple of prisoners spit into the mouth of another.

The jury was leaning toward Hartley's *Trust*, but journalist Karen Durbin made a fiery appeal on behalf of *Poison*, and to everyone's surprise, it won the Grand Jury Prize. Jennie Livingston's ode to transsexuality, *Paris Is Burning*, won the documentary award, marking a sweep for a miniwave of cutting-edge gay films—instantly dubbed the "New Queer Cinema."

The New Queer Cinema was a cinema of transgression born in the flames of the AIDS epidemic. As Haynes explains it, "AIDS was a life and death issue then. A lot of gay people wanted to be accepted and treated like everybody else, but AIDS was making that impossible, so there was almost no choice but to stand up and express a more militant position. If I have any investment in being gay, it's not about just fitting in and being like everybody else, it's actually acknowledging how upsetting homosexuality is to the world, and that's why I love Genet, who articulated its criminality and rejoiced in it, rejoiced in his outsider status."

Gradually, the film culture of Sundance began to thaw. *Poison* marked a watershed for the festival. Says Gilmore, "The regional filmmaker that had been the core of what the independent world had been all of a sudden was less important. It was back to a New York/Los Angeles bias." *Poison* was worlds away from *Heartland*. The earnest, politically correct stalwarts of the 1980s, the Glen Petries, the Gregory Navas, the Annick Smiths, were swept away by a torrent of films made by a new crop of young, rowdy, nose-thumbing filmmakers. Sundance was smart enough to jump onto the train. The requirement for finished scripts was dropped, and selection committee members, some of them hoary with age, would in the future be rotated off after one year. Times were a-changin'.

Haynes and Vachon were students at Brown together in the late 1970s. The New Left may have begun to recede into the mists of time, but it had left its mark on the Brown faculty, then a hotbed of deconstructionist, Marxist-inflected film theory. Vachon was not one of those people who sat around asking, "Where is the undiscovered gay audience? Where are the films that show people like me and my friends?" And not seeing any, decide to make them themselves. For one thing, she says, "I didn't grow up gay. When I got to college it was very fashionable to be bisexual. So everybody was. It was also right before AIDS, when there was still that sense that the more 'liberated' you could be in your sexuality, the cooler and hipper you were. But I had boyfriends all through college. I even got married. To some creep! I didn't come out till well after college."

After graduating from Brown, Vachon, short and chunky, with dark hair chopped into a no-nonsense pageboy cut and a lively, determined look about her, moved back to New York, where she had grown up. At that time, the cool, downtown filmmakers like Jim Jarmusch, Amos Poe, Eric Mitchell, Beth B, Lizzie Borden, and Paul Morrissey, were orbiting the punk rockers at CBGB's on the Bowery. "I felt like it was a closed circle, and I was on the outside looking in," she continues. "I remember going to parties and just feeling, like, completely intimidated and overwhelmed by what I saw, as in, I want to be one of those people." Her older sister, Gail, was an experimental filmmaker and took her to places like the Collective for Living Cinema on White Street in Tribeca, but Vachon was bored by the films. "They were unbelievably slow and had no narrative whatsoever," she says. She was put off by her sister's friends. "They were so sanctimonious," Vachon continues. "It was either like you made these narrative-free experimental movies that were political statements by dint of their being as unentertaining as possible, or you made disgusting Hollywood movies for New Line and sold out. There was nothing in between." Indeed, she worked on a couple of low-budget New Line features like *Demon Lover* and just got condescended to for her pains. "I just wanted to learn how to do it, but those pictures were considered low class. It was like, That's fine, but if you want to make movies that matter, then you go work for free for Jim Jarmusch. I probably would have worked for him if I had the opportunity, but it was more important for me to get really good at it and be able to pay the rent."

Still, she did work on some "movies that matter," like Jill Godmilow's *Far from Poland* and Bette Gordon's *Variety*. Godmilow introduced her to Bill Sherwood, who hired her to work on *Parting Glances* in 1986. She spent two years working her way from second AD to first AD, and she constantly felt she was bucking the old-boy network. She came up at the same time as producer Ted Hope, against whom she competed for jobs. "I didn't like him," she recalls. "To me he represented a boy's club that I really wasn't into. I thought he was a thuggy fratboy. He had a certain kind of arrogance that was very exclusionary. Somebody like me was automatically labeled a bitch by them."

In the summer of 1987, Haynes, then in the MFA program at Bard College, made a film called *Superstar: The Karen Carpenter Story,* helped by a grant from the New York State Council on the Arts (NYSCA) that also provided seed money for Spike Lee's *She's Gotta Have It. Superstar* told the story of the decline and fall of pop icon Karen Carpenter as she plunged from a life of hyperreal normality to illness and death, a victim of celebrity and anorexia. The genius of the film is that Haynes used Barbie dolls to stand in for the characters and by so doing explored the mechanisms of identification and distancing. Vachon, who helped Haynes edit the sound, loved it, and critics later compared Haynes to David Lynch and John Waters for his ironic poking about among the icons of pop culture. "That movie was an epiphany for me," Vachon says. "It was like, 'Eureka!' *Superstar* works brilliantly at an intellectual level, it's provocative, it makes you think, and it's also deliciously entertaining. By the end of the movie, people are practically in tears as they watch this doll die. It kinda blows my mind every time I see it, and it summed up this feeling that you could make a movie that was as provocative as that and be entertaining too. Those were the kinds of movies I wanted to make."

Superstar made so much noise that even CAA gave the young director a call, said, "We watched that movie at lunch, we'd love to sign you up." Recalls Haynes, "But everyone got the message that I wasn't needing representation. I was writing my own material, living in New York doing that weird queer thing with that woman Christine."

Despite its Brechtian pedigree, *Superstar* was a flop downtown. Vachon remembers, "Todd was this arts/semiotics major from Brown, and he wanted Yvonne Rainer and all those people to say, 'Oh, you're a great filmmaker, that's really cool.' But they were, 'What is this shit?' When Todd tried to screen *Superstar* for the Collective for Living Cinema, they refused to show it. 'Cause it was too narrative!"

Superstar became a cult hit, and guaranteed that he'd be able to finance his next picture, *Poison.* Vachon told him she wanted to produce it. At a time when all the glory went to the auteur, and everyone was running around wanting to be a director, Vachon preferred to produce. Unlike the studio world, where the financing and distribution machinery is already in place, indies have to invent the wheel almost every time out, and producers play a much bigger role. She continues, "When the indie film movement bubbled up in New York City, there was a sense that there was business to be done, whether it was selling these movies to North American distributors like a producer's rep such as John Pierson, or shepherding them through film festivals, making deals for the director's next movie—suddenly people who had some business sense saw an opening for themselves."

James Schamus, just out of Berkeley, trying to figure out what to do with his life, sought them out. He begged them for a crumb, anything, pleading, "Please let me help, pleeease!" Wearing what would become a signature bow tie and spectacles that made him look like a benevolent Peter Lorre, he seemed a little anomalous in the rough and tumble New York film scene. But like Haynes and Vachon, he came from the hothouse world of film semiotics, spoke the language of signs and signifiers, and was a wannabe screenwriter to boot. And, says Vachon, "Screenwriting or no screenwriting, James's absolute first love was the art of the deal: how do you make one, how do you read a contract. He gets very excited at the idea of selling North American rights for a film." She brought Schamus on board as associate producer.

In December 1990, Schamus teamed up with Ted Hope to form Good Machine, which became one of three New York-based companies comprised of producers who were dedicated to director-driven films, the others being Vachon's Killer Films, with Lauren Zalaznick, and Larry Meistrich's The Shooting Gallery. When Schamus went to Sundance with *Poison*, Hope stayed home, thinking, What the fuck's Sundance, why should I go? "That's when Ang Lee walked into the office," he recalls. Lee had two grants from the Taiwanese government, and when he asked a friend, "Who can produce a film for no money?" the reply was, "You gotta meet Ted Hope." Hope told him, "You gotta meet James Schamus," and the rest is history, so to speak. Schamus and Lee went on to form a writing partnership that produced *The Wedding Banquet*, *Eat Drink Man Woman*, *The Ice Storm*, and *Crouching Tiger, Hidden Dragon*.

Poison somehow managed to get an NEA grant, along with money from the AFI and NYSCA. For the remainder of the roughly $300,000 budget, Vachon went the legendary doctor-dentist-family route.

In February, after Sundance, Haynes, Vachon, and Schamus took *Poison* to the Berlin Film Festival. It was the hip, happening film. Recalls Haynes, "Christine and I would go to festivals together, and it was all about the cult of the young, queer, groovy New York director. I was continually aware of how she wasn't included in that." To his embarrassment, Schamus, who had not actually produced the film, upstaged her. People swarmed around him, congratulating him on its success, ignoring Vachon, because she was female. North American rights went to a small company called Zeitgeist. "With great reviews, the freedom to stay in theaters, and a filmmaker who was willing to go to every city in America, you could coax it up to a million bucks," says Vachon. "Which at that time was the beacon you were striving towards as an art film. When it hit a million, we opened champagne. I got a big check for just under 200 grand, and I sent it off to the investors, and it's a good thing I did, because that's the money they invested in Todd's next film, *Safe*. Todd and I made a little bit of money, but we were so honest, and so grateful to the investors, that we hadn't built in deferments for ourselves. I still hadn't figured out how to actually make money producing."

Although Vachon says her desire to produce *Poison* "wasn't personally motivated—I never really thought about [the gay element]," it did connect with a vast gay audience. "I was savvy enough even then to be able to tell that there was a market that nobody had really tapped into yet. People who in a million years wouldn't go to see a movie that experimental, did so just because they heard there was male sex in it. Most of them came out feeling like, So I watched that whole movie for two seconds of boys fucking!"

If it was indeed Haynes's intention to offend, he succeeded. The NEA got into political trouble for giving him a grant. "Roger Ebert met Todd at the Indie Spirit Awards where *Poison* was being feted," Vachon recalls. "When Todd said, I'm Todd Haynes, Roger was, Who the hell is Todd Haynes? Todd said, I directed *Poison.* He literally snatched his hand back."

BY THE MIDDLE of the new year, Miramax was hurting. If 1990 was bad, 1991 was worse. Flush with 1989 dollars and the Chase bank line, the Weinsteins had gone on a buying spree, and they were virtually hemorrhaging releases. The highest grossing film of 1991 was Madonna's *Truth or Dare*, which did $15 million. Recalls former Miramax executive Eamonn Bowles, "Right after *Truth or Dare*, there were something like thirteen films in a row that they released, some of them wide, that were hideous failures, tank, tank, tank. You can't just suffer those kinds of losses and not be hurt."

Release after release splattered like bugs across the Miramax windshield. All in all, Miramax opened roughly forty films that year, about twice the number of a major studio. Says Schmidt, "We proceeded to try to continue to grow the company through 1990 and 1991, but it just got tougher and tougher, because the hits weren't there anymore. We were just limping along."

The Weinsteins were so desperate that they contemplated starting an exploitation division, to be called Dimension. They had watched enviously as archrival New Line cleaned up with the *Nightmare on Elm Street* series. The New Line model, with income generated by genre pictures driving the art film business, such as it was, made increasing sense to the brothers as they saw their company crumbling before their eyes. Exploitation pictures made lots of money, and because they didn't employ stars, they were cheap to make, and it wasn't necessary to give away the back end to profit participants. Ironically, the catalyst seems to have been Bob Shaye's new Fine Line division, headed by Deutchman, which they, or at least Bob, took as a direct, personal affront. Deutchman's coming out party, in effect, was the Museum of the Moving Image gala for Robert De Niro in the first week of March 1991. Deutchman spied Harvey across the ballroom, and with a smile wreathing his face, walked over and shook his hand. Harvey greeted him cordially, said, "Congratulations. It'll be fun!" Bob, standing next to him, shook his hand too, but as he did so, he hissed, "We're gonna bury you." Then, his face turning purple, he started screaming something like, "How dare you come back to the art house world! I know you started that company to get us. Not only are we gonna kill you, but we're going to go into New Line's business and kill them in their business. We're gonna do horror movies and kid movies." Bob was as good as his word, saying to Harvey, "Let's compete against those who are competing against us." (Deutchman always claimed credit for Dimension.)

In increasingly straitened circumstances, some filmmakers found it hard to collect from Miramax. Kjehl Rasmussen filed suit to collect on *Animal Behavior*, which had been released by Miramax in 1989. "It was a profitable film for Miramax, and I believe they were not properly accounting to me," he says. "It was a pretty clear cut case of they owed me money. The picture only played two weeks, and it took us three years to get our money. It wasn't a pleasant few years." According to Miramax, the film was an unmitigated disaster that did not even gross $50,000 in the U.S. Recalls Harvey, "After incurring significant legal fees, and facing the certainty of substantial additional fees if litigation continued, we thought it was best to settle, which we did. With no admission of any accounting irregularities."

Two years after *My Left Foot* had grossed $14.7 million, domestic, its producer, Noel Pearson, complained that he hadn't yet seen a cent of profit on his $2.5 million picture. "It's a bit frustrating," he said. "It's like waiting for Godot to come, and I just wish he would come a little faster." According to Weinstein, he owed Pearson nothing; if money was owed, Granada was the guilty party.

The Weinsteins sometimes bought films and then tried to better the deal. Says Mark Lipsky, "What they were then, and are today, are consummate negotiators, and even better renegotiators. They would say anything, do anything, no matter what it was or what it took, to get the deal done, and worry about it the next day. When they're in the moment, and they tell you that their life depends on acquiring your movie, they mean it. But the next minute, it never happened. And they have no conscience about it." Adds Safford, "The smarter filmmakers knew that and would insert terms into their contracts like, You must release the film theatrically in so many cities, spending so much money by such and such a date, and Harvey would happily sign it. That didn't mean he'd do it. The film would get pushed back. Or dumped. You can't believe what he says. Even he knows you can't believe what he says. What are you gonna do? Sue them? Yell and scream all you want. Take a ticket and stand in line. It's like *Citizen Kane* and Xanadu, the thrill of the hunt, of getting your hands on something, whether it's a script, a film, or a filmmaker. Once Harvey has it, he's no longer interested."

Bobby Newmyer didn't know anything about that when he sold them *The Opposite Sex*. Since 1989, Newmyer had been running Outlaw, his tiny indie production company on his share of the *sex, lies* profits, but the money was fast disappearing, and he was facing bankruptcy. *The Opposite Sex*, his second picture, was based on a screenplay he'd developed out of his own pocket, a broad romantic comedy starring Courteney Cox, Arye Gross, and Kevin Pollak. The budget was $2.5 million he'd raised in $50,000 and $100,000 chunks by begging friends and family for money. Salaries, including Newmyer's, were deferred. When the movie was done, Newmyer showed it to distributors, including Miramax. Newmyer hadn't seen much of Harvey since the *sex, lies* days, but he remembered him fondly. Harvey had done everything he said he would do and more. One summer Newmyer and his wife Debbie had run into Harvey and Eve on Martha's Vineyard. The couples had gone waterskiing together or, rather, Newmyer and Eve had gone waterskiing, while Harvey sat in the back of the boat, in shorts and an enormous Izod shirt, a tent, chain-smoking True Blues, drenched in sweat, and looking like he'd rather be anywhere but there. Newmyer was charmed. "It was totally endearing to see a guy who weighed 400 pounds sitting in that boat," he says. "That wouldn't happen with a studio head. There was something very authentic and real about him."

According to Newmyer, Harvey made a preemptive bid to take *The Opposite Sex* off the table for $5 million, an astounding price for an indie film in 1991, a million up front and four more when Newmyer turned over the elements.* Newmyer said, "Great." Elated, the producer wrote a letter to his investors, saying, "Here's a million dollars back, 40 percent of your investment. In another few months when we technically finish the picture and deliver it to Miramax, there'll be a good profit for everyone." Plus, everyone who worked on the film was going to get their deferments paid in full. He delivered the picture. "In a deal for an acquisition, the producers generally got 10 percent on signing and 90 percent on delivery," says attorney David Steinberg, who negotiated a lot of these deals for Miramax. "What they would do, often, is withhold the whole 90 percent if there was one missing thing, like a music license," harsh but a right they had under the contract. According to Linda Lichter, who was still Newmyer's attorney, "We in-

---

* "Film elements": the physical components of a movie, including picture, sound tracks, script, etc., as well as legal documents establishing the chain of ownership and various kinds of rights.

serted in the contract every form of security you could possibly have, and they still found a way around us. Outlaw had delivered all the boxes of elements, but Miramax said, 'It's not full delivery until we look through the boxes, and we don't have time to look through the boxes.' When they did go through the boxes, they said, 'You didn't get this point in this music contract.' " Adds Newmyer, "The reasons they cited became ludicrous. At one point, Harvey claimed, 'Well, there's a loose splice in Reel 8. Send someone up here to fix it. On page fifty-two of the printout of the script, there's a typo.' " Schmidt explains, "Primarily this was a cash flow management tool, a way to stretch until they could somehow find the money to pay for it."

But Newmyer got the message: To him, it was "We don't want to pay you $5 million." He talked to people who had sold films to Miramax. Everyone said, he recalls, "This is how Harvey plays it. He doesn't want to pay five, he wants to pay four. Go back and settle with him." Newmyer had "discovered" Soderbergh, had given Harvey and Bob the film—*sex, lies*—that put Miramax on the map. Another guy might have been grateful, but not Harvey. Or maybe he was, but this was business. Newmyer says he kept calling—he still wanted the film, just not for $5 million—trying to get Newmyer to agree to a lower figure. To the producer, a deal was a deal, and he refused. He went into a four-month tailspin where he never slept more than ninety minutes at a time, resumed smoking, developed a four-pack-a-day habit, and gained 30 pounds. "To every one of my thirty-two investors—my dearest friends and my family's dearest friends—I went from being the golden boy who was going to give them a tidy profit, to the moron who made this fucking deal," he remembers.

One day, Newmyer was having lunch with a friend, a prominent attorney, at the Polo Lounge of the Beverly Hills Hotel, when Harvey walked by. As Newmyer tells the story, his friend, a large man, larger than Harvey, grabbed him, and sat him down, insisted he settle. Harvey didn't want to settle, didn't even want to sit. Lighting cigarette after cigarette, he refused to look Newmyer in the eye. He finally agreed to pay $4.7 million. By this time, the producer had spent several hundreds of thousands of dollars on lawyers and a year of his life dealing with the Weinsteins. He says he agreed to givebacks not contemplated in the original understanding which allowed for Miramax to cover acquisition of music rights, etc, and still left him short.

Concludes Newmyer, "I've been in the movie business since 1982, produced fourteen, fifteen movies. I'm used to all forms of deception and manipulation, but to have someone just outright chew your face, basically say, 'I'm gonna fuck you because I can,' that was a first for me."

Harvey adamantly denies reneging on the deal and disputes Newmyer's version of events. "Newmyer signed a deal for $4.7 million, which Miramax paid. This was far in excess of the approximately $2.7 million that was represented to us as being the budget of the picture. Miramax also agreed to spend no less than $2 million in print and advertising expenditures for the U.S. theatrical release of the picture. In addition, Miramax was delivered a movie that was essentially unreleasable, and we incurred approximately $500,000 in reshoot costs. Despite our best efforts, this movie turned out to be a commercial and creative disaster. Miramax spent over $4 million, double the amount of our contractual commitment in support of the release. It grossed only $700,000 in the U.S. Miramax lost millions of dollars on this picture."

In the grip of the cash squeeze, Harvey's temper, always short, snapped like a frayed shoelace. He hired David Linde to supplement the acquisitions team of Trea Hoving and Mark Tusk. Hoving had the taste; Tusk, who was gay and hip, would go where no one else dared; and Linde's job was to do the deals. When Harvey was in a playful mood, he referred to them fondly as his "three blind mice." But he wasn't often in a playful mood. Hoving was often seen spooning Pepto-Bismol down her throat after a visit to Harvey's office.

The New York Film Festival followed right on the heels of Toronto in late September, and Harvey had executed a coup by scoring the opening night slot for Krzysztof Kieslowski's *The Double Life of Véronique*. The brothers threw a bash at the Mayflower Hotel on 62nd Street and Central Park West to celebrate. It should have been a festive occasion, but for Harvey the cheer good news brought lasted about a millisecond, and then he was back to worrying about the next catastrophe. After the screening, the Miramaxers, spruced up in formal attire, drifted in slowly, feeling good, buzzed by the champagne that flowed freely. Harvey spotted Linde, who had been riding the deal for Jocelyn Moorhouse's *Proof*, starring the young Russell Crowe. He asked, "David, you closed on *Proof?*" Suddenly the laughter died, the gaiety vanished like the sun behind a cloud. There was a collective intake of breath as staffers waited to hear Linde's response, because the deal had not been closed; the film was still in play with Linde bidding against Deutchman at Fine Line. Instantly, Harvey's Jekyll became Mr. Hyde. He pulled Linde and Tusk into the hallway, moved in a little closer on Linde, the way he always did when he wanted to use his body to intimidate. Kim Lewis was Moorhouse's agent, and Harvey barked, "Find Kim Lewis, find him now! Do you have his home number? Call him at home! Call him in L.A.! Call his office! Call!" By this time they had been joined by Linde's wife. As she watched in horror, Harvey, swollen with rage, jabbed him with his finger, while spewing a fine spray of epithets not heard since the schoolyard. Linde was shaken. (Ultimately, Miramax lost *Proof*, and even now, many years later, Linde instinctively steps backwards when he encounters Weinstein.)

With creditors nipping at their heels and the brothers' attempts to sell Miramax going nowhere, the public offering became even more important, and preparations marched ahead. There was only one problem: since Midland Montague owned a big chunk of the company, 45 percent, they too would benefit, and therefore Bob and Harvey were determined to buy them out. By that time, the streetwise bankers who engineered the deal were gone, and so was Midland Montague's New York office. The investment was being managed by a merchant banker from London named David Hutchings. Hutchings was in the classic British mold, proper and punctilious; in other words, he was a man who was completely unprepared to deal with the Weinsteins. Continues Schmidt, "They communicated with him—their largest shareholder—by saying things like, 'You will never see a cent from this company. We will take this company down before we pay any money out to you.' "

Preparing for an IPO is an arduous, time-consuming, and expensive process. The volumes of data on Miramax's finances were bound and at the couriers ready to go to the SEC to register for the offering, when Harvey and Bob stuffed themselves into a limo outside 711 Fifth Avenue, where Allen & Co. was located, on a hot August day in the aftermath of the aptly named Hurricane Bob, to make the trip downtown to their office. When they emerged twenty minutes later at the Tribeca Film Center, they blithely announced, "Look, we've changed our minds, we're not doing it." Schmidt, who had just risked his life flying down from Nantucket in perilous weather, said, "Fuck you all, I'm outta here."

The Weinstein's about-face stunned everyone. "There was a constant effort to move towards a more enlightened business environment that was ultimately unsuccessful," Schmidt explains. "To me it was a watershed decision. They decided to stay on the treadmill, chasing the next film and living off bank debt. Essentially, they said, 'We want to run the company in the same old way, our way, the way that got us here. And if it means we'll screw people, so be it." Adds one source, "They couldn't accept the idea that these British guys would make a big check off their sweat. Made 'em crazy." Schmidt continues, "Like all IPOs for small companies, theirs included an option plan for employees. So it was not just Midland Montague that got cut off at the knees, it was producers who were owed money, and the employees who worked very hard to get them to the point where their company could be a success. There could have been a way for them to take a little less into their pocket and spread it around more to the people that helped them get there. But that was never part of their thinking, because from their point of view, they were the ones who got them there. It was very sad."

Schmidt understood that the brothers were not about to let someone who was not a Weinstein dip his hand into the honey pot, and he resigned, effective March 1, 1992. He explains, "The fact that there was a good deal of abuse and pressure that went along with the job, and no equity position for the lead managers that were helping them build the company, no bonus, meant that the writing was on the wall. I left Miramax because my mother and father were not named Miriam and Max." Schmidt was sitting around, twiddling his thumbs, and wondering what to do next when he got a call from his pals at Allen & Co. They told him they were discussing a business idea with some guys they liked, who wanted to start a new company. Was he interested? A few days later, Schmidt met the two men. They hit it off, and he agreed to join October Films.

EVEN THOUGH Quentin Tarantino was still a nobody, when he arrived in Park City for the 1992 Sundance Film Festival with his new film, *Reservoir Dogs*, his reputation preceded him. He had been to the June lab the year before, and almost everyone in town had read the *Dogs* script. Allison Anders, whose second film, *Gas Food Lodging*, was in the competition, first heard his name at a pitch meeting for one of her own projects, when her partner, Kurt Voss, interrupted his spiel to digress about Tarantino for half an hour. Anders recalled, "I couldn't believe it. Goddamn it, this is *my* meeting, and I don't know who the hell they're talking about. OK, so he's a great writer, can we get back to our meeting here?"

Tarantino had never been to a film festival, had rarely been out of L.A., had never seen snow. He was walking around in a T-shirt in 20 degree weather until Live Entertainment executive Ronna Wallace bought him a parka. He was like a kid at his birthday party, not knowing what to go for first, plunge his hand into the bowls of candy, rip the wrapping off the presents, or stuff his mouth with cake. A cartoony-looking character with a high forehead and prominent jaw, he came across like Martin Scorsese in the body of Popeye. He was wired all the time, surfing an adrenaline rush, speed rapping about the gay subtext to *Top Gun*, how the contrails of the jets suggested anal entry, and he would cite chapter and verse, shots, and scraps of dialogue from any Tony Scott movie you could name, to anyone who was interested, and often to those who weren't. His bubbly enthusiasm, lack of pretension, and apparent guilelessness made him irresistible. Anders met him for the first time at Z Place, a club on Park City's Main Street, and was pleased to discover in him a warmth, a sweetness, and a generosity that she had not expected. "People would gush and make him sound so huge that I thought he was going to be ten feet tall, with a beard and all the filmmaker obnoxious ego stuff," she continues. "He came up to me and said, 'Are you Allison? My name's Quentin, and I loved your movie.' I thought, Oh my God, this is the guy."

Each year Sundance became more crowded, more frantic, more Hollywood. Suddenly, everyone had cell phones glued to their ears. During one screening, an agent was even observed calling another agent a few rows away. Ford Explorers and Jeep Cherokees full of buyers, producers, agents, and press still looking—so far in vain—for the next Soderbergh, rubbed fenders in the clogged streets of Park City and made it impossible to find— yes, parking. The 1992 lineup had been put together by Gilmore and Garcia. (Garcia, burned out and disillusioned, resigned later that year.) Sixty submissions in 1987 had become three to four hundred by 1992. Soderbergh, still the festival mascot, was once again in attendance. He told one journalist, "Obviously, I think Park City is the greatest place in the United States!"

The New Queer Cinema was still cresting, with Vachon returning for the second year in a row, this time with Tom Kalin's stylish *Swoon*, in addition to newcomers Gregg Araki, with *The Living End*, an HIV-positive lovers-on-the-run romp, and Christopher Münch with *The Hours and Times*, a fictionalized account of the relationship between John Lennon and Beatle manager Brian Epstein on vacation together in Barcelona. Says Vachon, "When you had movies in it like *The Living End*, that then got bought and had a successful commercial run, it changed people's expectations of what they could send to Sundance." Or, as Gilmore puts it, "It was becoming clear that the young nobody directors, the Gregg Arakis of the world, were really important."

Vachon, along with Haynes, Kalin, Araki, critic Ruby Rich, and others appeared on a panel devoted to the New Queer Cinema. Like *Poison*, these films were more interested in shocking straight audiences than reassuring them with the we're-just-like-you portraits of Land's End–clad gay yuppies who populated films like *Parting Glances* that just a few years earlier had seemed so daring. The new generation of gay directors was looking to Gus Van Sant's *Drugstore Cowboy* instead. *The Living End* was an exercise in agitprop that mocked the positive role models so dear to the gay activists who made such a fuss over Sharon Stone's homicidal lesbian in *Basic Instinct*, and substituted in their stead proto-criminals who fantasized about infecting then-President George Bush with their diseased blood. Recalls Vachon, "It was an insane time. Most of these people were members of some activist group or another, and both *Poison* and *Swoon* remember people in their titles who had recently died. We were all really young, and in your twenties you have a sense of righteousness. Urgency. You have to speak now, because time is running out."

Other films in competition included Alexandre Rockwell's *In the Soup*, a very low-budget, very charming tale about a filmmaker hustling money from an over-the-hill hood, winningly played by Seymour Cassel and shot in black and white, by then a rare and exotic format; and Anders's *Gas Food Lodging*. *Gas Food Lodging* was an off-kilter coming-of-age portrait of two sisters (Fairuza Balk and Ione Skye) making their way down the bumpy road of adolescence under the worried eye of their single working mother (Brooke Adams) in a trailer park in New Mexico. It sounds like a recipe for a Sundance PC pudding, but it's so richly observed, so understated, and so finely executed that it transcends its genre.

Anders was a force of nature, a tremendously appealing woman who was a single mother herself. She was born in Ashland, Kentucky, in 1955, and it hadn't been so long ago that she herself lived on welfare. Ray Price, the indie veteran whose IRS Releasing distributed the picture, says, "Everybody liked Allison. She made that film work. When she talked to women in the audience, they totally connected. Allison transcends her films. She's a morally driven person, and she makes you sit up straight, become a more moral person yourself. I loved being in the room when she was in the room. I felt better about myself." Anders was totally free from artifice and pretension. What you saw was what you got. Says Rockwell, "She's a human mood ring. She walks in the room the shade she is."

Price continues, "Critics are harder on women directors, and *Gas Food Lodging* was a little soapy for some of them, but women are more comfortable talking in the syntax of daytime TV; it's more a part of their lives. The guys have their language, and the women have theirs. I have always thought the important thing about a movie was, you know there is somebody there. You can really feel the filmmaker coming through the screen. And that was true of Allison." Anders, Rockwell, Araki, Kalin, and many of the other filmmakers in the competition that January were "emerging" directors, the very people Sundance had written off only a year before.

Miramax's Trea Hoving and Mark Tusk had been at the first screening of *Dogs* on Saturday at 10:30 P.M. at the Holiday Village Cinema and loved it. David Linde caught the second screening. "Everybody was freaked out about it," he recalls. "It was an intense movie, and in those days, that kind of intensity didn't happen in independent films." To say the least. The rumors about the *Dogs* script were correct. Tarantino, it turned out, could write like an angel. Although he was working in a different idiom, his work was reminiscent of the great Robert Towne scripts of the 1970s, providing a heady mix of B movie attitude and Nouvelle Vague cool—the apotheosis of movie geek chic.

Watching guys with guns was a guilty pleasure at Sundance and a rare one as well. Festival programmers endlessly discussed whether genre films could be art films as well. *Dogs* nicely embodied this dilemma. It was very much a genre film, and then again it wasn't. Purposely written in such a way that it could be made on the cheap, its plot is tailored to its budget. *Dogs* is a case study in the aesthetics of poverty, a heist film without a heist, just the events before and after. *Dogs* is all backstory—mostly dialogue, with few locations. The conceit is conventional, but the execution is not, nor is the time hopping, the mischievous conflation of the literary and the lurid—gangsters debating the fine points of popular culture like graduate students—electrified by the vicious kick of high-voltage violence. Tarantino's films are a walk on the wild side, and he could be depended upon to be a veritable fount of political incorrectness. The breathtaking un-PCness of his body of work, the white maleness of it all—the inventive obscenities, the rat-tat-tat of taboo words like "nigger," the butt fucking, the mainlining, the pleasure his films seem to take in casual killing, theatrically staged (for laughs, yet), their sadistic, almost baroquely creative bloodletting along with their apparent absence of redeeming social value, and the insouciantly indulgent attitude he displays toward his deadbeat characters—all combine to give them a dangerous charge. They flirted with sexism, racism, and homophobia, and as such were a slap in the face to everything Sundance stood for. Sneeringly, Tarantino once referred to white liberals as "the most sensitive human beings on the planet," and he loved nothing more than to thumb his nose at their bleeding hearts. *Dogs* was an equal opportunity offender.

It is easy in retrospect to dismiss the brouhaha *Dogs* provoked as no more than the squealing of stuck Lynne Cheneys and William Bennetts— this was 1992, after all, when George Bush père was still exploiting the euphoria of the Gulf War. Moreover, Anthony Hopkins had sucked, chewed, and swallowed face in Jonathan Demme's *The Silence of the Lambs* the year before. But that was a studio movie, and *Dogs* was an indie, and this was Sundance, sanctuary of the indie spirit. Violence was long regarded by Sundanistas as the special provenance of the despised Hollywood movie, so it's not surprising that Tarantino's picture was greeted by a mixed chorus of applause and outrage. Recalls Richard Gladstein, the Live Entertainment executive who shepherded the project, "Going in, I didn't realize—stupidly, foolishly, ignorantly—that Sundance didn't show films in this genre. Watching the movie with that audience was shocking. You heard these gasps." People rarely died in Sundance films, lest of AIDS, old age, or boredom, and in *Dogs*, they not only died, they died slowly, painfully, bloodily, with feeling. The soon-to-be-notorious ear slicing that Tarantino choreographed to the monotonous thrum of "Stuck in the Middle with You," provoked a firestorm of protest that eclipsed the furor over the New Queer Cinema, especially when Tarantino refused to give an inch in the face of angry catcalls from the sober guardians of indie film virtue who stood up at screenings to denounce *Dogs* for being socially irresponsible. Instead, he goaded and provoked his critics. At the last screening of *Dogs*, the big one at the Egyptian Theater that Tarantino ever after referred to as "the Faye Dunaway screening," because she was in the audience, a man stood up and asked, "So, how do you justify all the violence in this movie?" The director replied, "I don't know about you, but I love violent movies. What I find offensive is that Merchant-Ivory shit." He says today, "Violence is one of the greatest things you can do in cinema. Edison invented the camera to *do* violence, all right?"

Tarantino was raised in the 1970s, when the 1960s were still vivid. "The Vietnam War and Watergate were a one-two punch that basically destroyed Americans' faith in their own country," he observes. "The attitude I grew up with was everything you heard was lies. The president is a monkey. I remember my parents saying, 'Fuck the police, fuck the pigs.' " But his films have little explicit politics, as such. His rebellion was largely cultural, a bad boy aesthetic that embraced not only the street films of Martin Scorsese and the Grand Guignol of Brian De Palma, but TV sitcoms and kung fu movies he grew up with, everything that respectable mainstream culture abhorred. He may have loved Godard (Truffaut was too sweet), but Hong Kong was his Paris, chop-socky his New Wave. He was the Howard Stern of indies, and proud of it.

Gilmore had been worried about the violence in *Dogs*. In a final spasm of political correctness, the festival that year had turned down Nick Gomez's *Laws of Gravity*. Ditto *One False Move* from the team of Billy Bob Thornton and Tom Epperson because, like *Dogs*, they were genre films filled with mayhem. The official Sundance line was clear: "I'd gone to the theater one night during the . . . festival to see a few films . . . and I could barely eat for twenty-four hours because they were so loaded with violence," Redford commented. "There are too many films here that have token violence that's appealing to the commerciality of the marketplace. That's when I said, 'Let's be aggressive about finding edgier, more experimental, riskier films that don't depend on anything formulaic whatever.' " Tarantino just couldn't understand it. He recalls, "They didn't want to have two gun movies there? I'd buy that, if they didn't have six gay movies there. They could have changed the name of the festival to the Sundance Gay and Lesbian Film Festival."

Despite Tarantino's thinly veiled homophobia, *Dogs* had more in common with the kinds of gay films screened at Sundance in 1992 than he might have cared to admit. In some ways, *Dogs* was a (not so) straight version of those films and marked a seismic change in the direction of indie film, which was rapidly moving toward a more genre-inflected cinema—albeit with a transgressive and ironic, post-modern spin. Despite the success of *Poison*, the New Queer Cinema peaked in 1992, almost as soon as it began. There were many reasons for this, but not the least of them was that Tarantino had stolen its thunder. *Dogs* was as unsettling as *Poison*, without having to shoulder the queer baggage.

In Tarantino's nihilistic attitude toward "that Merchant-Ivory shit," i.e., "art films," lies the key to *Dogs'* impact. *Dogs* is an anti-art film art film, a canny amalgam of outsider and insider art. If the New Wave gallicized Hollywood B movies, Tarantino re-Americanized the French hybrids, reclaiming them, as it were, and by so doing imported both the sophistication and sentimentality of the French into homegrown indies. But by so doing, he also cut the umbilical cord that had linked the indies of the 1990s to their European art film predecessors and had kept them in their shadow. First Soderbergh, now Tarantino: American indies had come of age.

In opening the door to genre that had been slammed shut by Sundance in the 1980s, *Dogs* represented the return of the repressed, the revenge of the exploitation picture. By accepting Tarantino's film, Gilmore gave the festival's imprimatur to a much different kind of indie feature, closer to the tastes of the barbarians (read, Americans) outside the gates of Park City and—most fraught for the direction of the movement—potentially commercial. *Dogs* was everything Sundance wasn't: it was dark, downbeat, and irreverent. Like Harvey Weinstein, Tarantino was the anti-Redford, and such can be the power of a single film that it was Sundance that had to bend, not Tarantino.

Carrying that much freight, it was perhaps not surprising that *Dogs* was passed over at awards time. The Sundance politic was still very much in evidence, not only in its skittish stance toward genre films and violence but, as Tarantino had noticed, in Gilmore's programming preference for diversity over quality. And, so far as the awards went, in the nod toward films that "needed" a boost, as the director was told later, versus films, like his own, that didn't. The slight still rankles. "It was the thing about Sundance that I hated the most at that time," says Tarantino. "They were liberal in the worst sense. It wouldn't have been such a bad thing if I hadn't been told by everybody I was gonna win—something. But it hurt my feelings. I was sad, I was mad. When it was over I did a slightly less drastic version of storming out. 'Fuck all you!' " Later, when Tarantino became famous, recalls former festival programmer Cathy Schulman, "We were always trying to involve him in everything. We tried to get him on the jury. We tried to get him to work in the labs, as a resource person. He was never accessible to us. He was pissed off."

The jury bestowed the Grand Jury Prize on Rockwell's winsome *In the Soup*. Rockwell, of course, was delirious. "It changed my life," he recalls.

"All of a sudden I was getting CAA sending me little cookies at my hotel door, still hot. I signed with them, and I left them after about four months after realizing that they were not interested in independent films." Rockwell, Tarantino, and Anders hung out together, and subsequently referred to themselves as "the Class of '92." Recalls Rockwell, who was then married to actress Jennifer Beals, "When my film won the Jury Prize, there was some tension about *Reservoir Dogs*—some critics thought *it* should have gotten the prize. Quentin later came to New York and stayed with me. He was standing in my kitchen looking at me, and he said, 'I'm so happy you got the prize, I'm so proud of your movie,' and he came over and hugged me. With all my other director friends, you felt a little bit of resentment, they didn't want to introduce you to people who might finance your movie, but Quentin was not at all like that. He was the most generous and totally supportive guy I knew." Tarantino used their apartment for two weeks. "You didn't want to go into the room he was staying in, 'cause it was like a pop media bomb went off, with half-drunk Dr Peppers, board games, full-sized John Travolta dolls," continued Rockwell. "Quentin is intense."

Four
The Buying Game
1992–1993

- How Quentin Tarantino drew a line in the sand with the Weinsteins, who sold their company, if not their souls, to Disney, while Robert Redford left Steven Soderbergh at the altar.

"We don't want to grow up and be another Walt Disney."
— BOB WEINSTEIN, 1989

There are two kinds of executives in the independent film business. As Sony Classics's Tom Bernard puts it, "People like Michael Barker and me, or Ira Deutchman or Bingham Ray or Jeff Lipsky, we're in the business 'cause we love it, but a lot of the guys, like Amir Malin, put these companies together to get rich."

Lipsky and Ray flew to New York to meet with Malin, and had ample opportunity to see how he was spending the money Merchant and Ivory believed Cinecom owed them. Ray immediately recalled why he had disliked Malin so. "He was kind of dumpy, he could make an Armani suit look bad," recalls Ray. He continues, "If Amir told me the sun was shining, I'd look out a window. To this day I don't know if he understands how people regard him as just this side of an oil slick."

Ray and Lipsky stayed with him in his spanking new white brick McMansion in Oyster Bay Cove, where he lived with his wife, a dermatologist, and two children. Ray, who wasn't about to give Malin an inch, suspected that Oyster Bay Cove was a real estate agent's fiction, insisted that Malin's address was really Syosset, a considerably less distinguished location nearby, and to irritate him sent him mail there, noting with satisfaction that it always seemed to reach its destination. The furnishings—sleek, black oversized chairs, a huge projection TV—were new, trendy, and expensive. "It was nouveau with a capital N," says Ray. "This was not a simple guy, with simple tastes. He had some of the ugliest fucking clothes going. I've probably never in my entire life owned as many suits as Amir has thrown out or given to Goodwill. I was put in a small bedroom, like a hospital room, sterile, something out of Todd Haynes's film *Safe*."

Malin didn't allow smoking in the house, and Ray couldn't keep his hands off cigarettes. At night, the house was in lockdown. Ray continues, "He had this expensive alarm system hooked up to every nook and cranny. The guy was fearful of who knows what, he was Israeli, maybe Arabs coming to kidnap him. I wanted a cigarette, and I opened the window to blow smoke out, and of course, Whoop! Whoop! Whoop! He came in, 'Are you smoking in there?' It was like, Oh fuck, the smoke police are out to get me. I'm, 'How can you live like this? In fear. You're out in the 'burbs, Oyster Bay Cove slash Syosset!' "

"When Amir came into October, the only question was, Who's out first, Jeff or Bingham," says former Cinecom executive Richard Abramowitz. "Because you knew Amir was going to be the last man standing." As soon as word got out on the street, the phone started ringing. Their competitors, yet. Like Barker and Bernard. Recalls Ray, it was, " 'What're you, fucking crazy? Don't you know what this guy is like? He's gonna come after you. He's gonna kill you!' I said, 'Look, I'm not saying I can control him, but I'm not going to be his friend, I'm going to be his business partner. Even though he is loathed, he is respected. I think we're mature enough, it'll work out.' " Deutchman remembers, "There was plenty of word on the street about Amir at this point, but they chose for whatever reason to ignore it. I tried to warn them, and they kept insisting that he was a changed man, that he was acknowledging the mistakes that he made at Cinecom. And he did have a skill set that they needed." Ray confronted Malin at his office-in-exile, 850 Third Avenue, where he was tending the Cinecom library, keeping it warm, a hen on an egg. As Ray recalls, the conversation went this way: Ray said, "What you did to people at Cinecom, I know you're gonna try to do at October, and I'm just not going to let you do it."

Malin answered, "You're gonna have to give me the benefit of the doubt."

"Why? What have you done to earn the benefit of the doubt? Nothing. Your track record sucks. Leopards don't change their spots."

"I've really turned over a new leaf."

Continues Ray, "He'd tell you anything he thought you wanted to hear. He was the reason why everything worked, and other people were the reasons for everything being fucked up."

Ray may have had misgivings about Malin, but Lipsky was driving him crazy, and Malin was a willing ear. Ray would call him to complain about his partner, long conversations, forty-five minutes, an hour. Malin wondered what he was getting into.

Lipsky, on the other hand, was a good deal more upbeat about Malin. "I never had a negative encounter with Amir," he says. "I think he's one of the best dealmakers I've ever known. Is he duplicitous? Backstabbing? All these things that you hear from people? I've never been a victim. I think people are jealous of how shrewd he is." In any event, Ray and Lipsky agreed to take on Malin as a partner. Lipsky called Allen & Co. and crowed, "Great news. We just added a partner who started his own company, it was successful for a while before it went bankrupt!"

Unconvinced, Allen & Co. still refused to give them the keys to the car. *Life Is Sweet* had opened in October 1991, the first release of October Films-in-waiting. In December, the company that did not quite exist got a shot in the arm from the prestigious National Society of Film Critics, which named *Life Is Sweet* Best Picture of the Year. Says Ray, "Just two guys released that movie and it did over $2 million. That was the proudest moment of my life." Then Allen & Co. introduced them to John Schmidt, fresh from Miramax. He came with no baggage. He was like Switzerland. According to Ray, Malin had assured them he would be able to close, that is, secure the money they needed, but he hadn't. Just to irritate him, Ray used to stand in front of the door to his office and shout, "Who's the closer? Schmidt's the closer!"

Schmidt rewrote the business plan in March and April 1992, and closed the financing, appropriately enough, on October 5, 1992. Although there was a certain amount of euphoria, Lipsky and Ray were disappointed in Allen & Co. Instead of raising the $7 million they needed, the bankers raised a paltry $3.3 million and took a $300,000 fee, so October effectively began with $3 million of operational capital. "They were penurious," says Lipsky. "We weren't sure if they were just doing this to make us go away, or if they were testing our mettle, as if to say, 'If you're so cocksure of what you can do out of thin air, that's what we'll give you, thin air.' " Moreover, Lipsky couldn't help noticing that his equity and control had been progressively diluted, not to say, dissolved. He continues, "What began as me owning 100 percent of nothing, and me and Bingham owning 50 percent of nothing, then me, Bingham, and Amir owning one third of something worth nothing, then became four of us owning 25 percent of something worth nothing. And of course, once we made the deal with Allen & Co., we became glorified employees. You're all of a sudden reporting to a board, and we ended up with one seat out of eight people. Our autonomy—it wasn't compromised, it was eliminated."

Lipsky et al. found themselves in a financial straitjacket. He adds, "We had the ability to make whatever decisions we wanted up to a certain financial threshhold—$750,000 per title for combined acquisition and P&A—above which we would have to get board approval." And the investors, an assortment of bankers, "harped on how they were gonna make money, their exit strategy, how they were gonna get out. These people were not investing in the futures of Jeff Lipsky, Bingham Ray, Amir Malin, or John Schmidt. Their passion was money. Our passion, or at least Bingham's and my passion, was film. And we did a damn good job of merging those two passions—at least for the first couple of years."

By the fall of 1992, October Films was ready to rock 'n' roll. The pitch to filmmakers was, "October was the kinder, gentler Miramax. You're not going to get Harvey Scissorhands here. We're gonna let you make the movie you want to make." The first acquisition was Gregg Araki's *The Living End,* which had gone begging after Sundance. October acquired it for a trifle, $100,000 (the film only cost $30,000), opened it for no more than $350,000, and drove it to $1.4 million. They did well with a French film called *Tous Les Matins du Monde,* and *The War Room,* the D. A. Pennebaker documentary that made a minor star out of James Carville. At the same time, they exploited Malin's strengths. He made video and TV deals on titles like *Chain of Desire; Hold Me, Thrill Me, Kiss Me;* and *Free Fall,* while squeezing an annual $200,000 to $400,000 out of the Cinecom library. "It would have been very difficult to start October solely as an art film distributor," says Schmidt. "It was much more viable with a direct-to-video business. This was an important source of earnings for us." Even Ray had to give Malin his due: "The guy was really intelligent, he helped construct a lot of models of deal structures."

Still, it was tough going. Ray wanted to buy *Reservoir Dogs,* but couldn't come up with the cash. "It was frustrating when you can't compete," he says. "I wanted to have the money to go toe to toe with these guys. But we never had it, so I said, Okay, why drive yourself crazy? We're in a niche, we gotta be really smart in our niche, the films we can get." The most successful acquisition of those early years was John Dahl's *The Last Seduction.* October paid $300,000 for the North American rights in 1994, and launched it on a successful theatrical run in the fall after it had already played on HBO, almost unheard of. It grossed $5.8 million. If there was trouble down the road—and there was—the partners were too excited to see it.

QUENTIN TARANTINO, born on March 27, 1963, grew up in L.A.'s South Bay, a depressing sprawl of ticky-tacky tract houses near the Los Angeles airport. Raised by his mother with the help of a series of father surrogates, one of whom she married, her son, taking his new stepfather's name, became Quentin Zastoupil. He changed schools often. The eternal new kid, with a dorky name, Munster-ish looks, and aversion to sports, he was the oddball, the loner. "I was the dumb kid who couldn't keep up with the class," he says. Lonely and unhappy, he skipped school at every opportunity, hiding in the bathroom until his mother went to work, spending the rest of the day at home, burying himself in comic books and television—every mother's nightmare. He dropped out of the ninth or tenth grade when he was fifteen or sixteen, depending on which version of his life you believe, worked at a series of odd jobs, attended acting classes, and in 1984, he got a job at Video Archives in Manhattan Beach, a magnet for every movie geek in the South Bay. He was the avatar of a new wave of filmmakers raised on video, as opposed to the so-called movie brats of the 1970s, who went to film school and were weaned on the greats of world cinema. "I didn't go to film school, I went to films," he likes to say, confessing, "Film school was never an option for me. I didn't go to college. I didn't even start high school. My film school was trying to make my first film, *My Best Friend's Birthday*. I thought, Jesus Christ, people are paying small fortunes to go to college, and so I was always saying, 'Don't pay that money for tuition. Just go off and make a movie.'"

Roger Avary, a former friend and writing partner who also worked at the Archives, dropped out of the Art Center College of Design in Pasadena. "Before video, I would rent 16mm prints and read cinema books," he recalls. "You'd hear about movies described as if they were mythology. Every now and then one would breeze through town, and I'd rush out to see it—that's if I could get in. When video came along, all of a sudden you had a database of twenty thousand titles. One day I realized, What am I doing? Why go to film school to listen to somebody lecture about film in the old style when you can sit around for eight or ten hours a day and discuss movies with your friends. That was the greatest film school any of us could ever have."

With the advent of video, in other words, a culture of scarcity was transformed, almost overnight, into a culture of plenty, effectively stripping film of its hieratic halo, the mystique of the image that had inspired French Catholic film critics like André Bazin and through them a generation of American auteurs and would-be auteurs. (Scorsese had nearly become a priest.) Video heralded a cinema Reformation. Already the "democratic art," it democratized movies further, rendering, as Avary makes clear, the middlemen—the critic/teachers, the priests of the religion of the cinema—irrelevant. But the price of short-circuiting the film school route was the sacrifice of film culture, the "great tradition" academics made it their business to pass on to the students of the past. Blissfully innocent of civilizing influences, as it were, delayed adolescents like Tarantino preferred their martial arts movies to, say, Eisenstein or Renoir, and so video facilitated a new brutalism, of which Tarantino became the leading and most accomplished practitioner.

Avary, whose long blond hair tumbled down on either side of his face like cornsilk, first met Tarantino in 1984, at the Archives. "I didn't care for Quentin that much when I first met him," he remembers. "He was so much better a cinéaste than I was. He had an amazing encyclopedic brain. Photographic memory. We'd have shifts together. He'd pop a movie on, I'd resist it, only to challenge him, he'd explain to me what was so good about it, and why I sucked 'cause I didn't like it, then I'd realize I really did like it, and I would do the same to him, and after a while going back and forth like that, I realized, This guy is great." The gang at the store one-upped one another with movie trivia, argued violently—no film was too trashy to provoke a flash of temper or end a friendship over—and played pranks. There was an adult gay section tucked away in the back, and one day Avary, who is straight, was appalled to discover that his friend had posted a photograph of him in the section with a word balloon floating over his head that said, "Hi, I'm Roger, I work here at Video Archives, and I'd like to recommend X, Y, and Z titles." Avary remembers, "He actually talked me into leaving it up for a while. Quentin is full of snake oil, sellery, and shim-shamery."

All the while, Tarantino, like Avary, was writing feverishly. But he still didn't really consider himself a writer. He wrote to act, or better yet, direct. "It just seemed as an actor that I wouldn't have control over my own destiny," he says. "Unless I became some sort of major fucking star, I'd still be auditioning at fifty-five years of age or something, like a lot of my heroes who were character actors. And I also noticed that independent movies didn't do a hell of a lot for the actors that were in them. It was the directors that became known, not the actors. A director did an independent movie and he would go off and do another movie."

The Archives gang read each other's scripts, traded scenes and bits of dialogue. "We were going to be the Coen brothers, with him in Ethan's job and me in Joel's job," says Tarantino. When he asked his friend in 1987 if he could take a short script he had written called *The Open Road* and work on it himself, without hesitating Avary said yes. "By this time, I'd grown to love Quentin," he says. "Months went by, and then Quentin emerged with this stack of papers, handwritten—nearly illegible, words phonetically spelled, there was no real grammar or punctuation, pages had been cut and taped together and moved around. He literally put everything he ever wanted to do into this one thing, bits and pieces of *Reservoir Dogs, Natural Born Killers, Pulp Fiction*. But it was written as he spoke, so his voice was there. I was weeping by the end of it. It barely contained any of my original screenplay, but he had brought an emotional soul to it that was beyond what I had written. I said, 'You need to type it up, because no other person is going to suffer through this. And then you need to make it.' " It was *True Romance*.

In 1989, Tarantino decided, after five years of struggling, to strike out on his own. He recalls, "Every six months I would have my Quentin Detest Fest, where I would stay up all night and go through all the things that were wrong with my life, why I wasn't doing what I was supposed to do, like you're a fuck-up, you know? It actually always, like, helped me push forward. So I was, like, You're judging your rate of progress by your friends at the video store, and compared to them, you're doing a shit load, but they're not doing anything as far as, like, a career is concerned. You have got to get the fuck out of the South Bay. Go quit Video Archives. You need to move to fucking Hollywood because that's where it is happening. If you run with the fast crowd, you will run fast, even if you run last. By the end of the night I had decided that was what I was going to do."

In the fall of 1990, Tarantino and Avary decided to write a short, on the theory it would be easier to get made than a feature. But they quickly realized that nobody produces shorts, so the film became a trilogy, with one section by Tarantino, one by Avary, and one by a third director who never materialized. Each eventually expanded his section into a feature-length script, Avary's into *Pandemonium Reigns,* and Tarantino's into *Reservoir Dogs.*

Tarantino hooked up with Lawrence Bender, a former dancer and actor, to produce it. Bender got the script to Harvey Keitel, who committed, and with the help of director Monte Hellman *(Two Lane Blacktop),* the script eventually made its way to Richard Gladstein at Live Entertainment, the video company run by Jose Menendez until he was shot to death by his sons while he watched television in 1996. "Monte dropped the script at my house instead of my office, and as I was walking in I opened up the package and read the first page," Gladstein recalls. "It said, '*Reservoir Dogs,* Written and Directed by Quentin Tarantino.' It was a little startling to see that. It also said, 'Final Draft.' As I put my keys down, I started reading it, and I didn't stop until I was through. I was completely blown away." In their first meeting, Tarantino made it clear he was not going to be pushed aside. He said, "I'm making the movie, whether I make it in my backyard, with my own videocamera and my five friends, whether it takes me three days or three months or three years." That was fine with Gladstein, who had been so impressed with the script he had decided, I'm gonna do this movie with this guy unless he turns out to be a complete wacko.

In those days Live never budgeted scripts; Gladstein went to his boss and said, "For the video box, it's a bunch of guys with guns and Harvey Keitel, how many units can we sell if it doesn't go out theatrically?" The answer was fifty thousand units at $56 apiece. As Tarantino remembers, "Live was going to commit $2 million to make the movie with Harvey and somebody else—but we couldn't get anybody. All we had was 'Harvey and somebody else.' So it fell apart. Then Live said, 'Okay, if we can't get some-body else, we'll make the movie with Harvey at 1.3.' I was shocked. There's a big difference between 'You have a movie *if*' and 'You have a movie.' "

On one level, all movies are about themselves, and reading the *Dogs* script in the light of Tarantino's own history, his emergence, like an exotic butterfly, out of the Archives cocoon, it's hard not to see it as a story about its own creation. Filled with jokes, allusions, and fragments of dialogue culled from his five-year stint there, with the gang of color-coded Mr.'s standing in for the Archives crew, the heist for the big score, for making it, Tarantino—the one who got away, who actually directed a feature—is at once Mr. Orange, who betrays them, and Mr. White, the veteran thief who loves him anyway, and forgives him. *Dogs* expresses Tarantino's complex feelings of guilt toward his friends for first exploiting then leaving them be-hind, along with his hunger for absolution by a father figure he never had, but found in Keitel, who plays Mr. White as well as godfathering the film.

Right before he was slated to go into production, Tarantino went off to the Sundance lab for two weeks. "I thought that Sundance workshop was the greatest," he says now. "To actually get there, and realize that all those professionals, Sydney Pollack, Ulu Grosbard, all these resource people, all this money was being spent for me and eight other people, none of whom had ever really done anything before, just so we could put our best foot for-ward—I was overwhelmed. Nothing like that had ever happened to me be-fore, ever. I never had anyone really believe in me in my life."

But there was trouble in paradise. Tarantino shot his scenes unconven-tionally, in long takes. Stephen Goldblatt, the cinematographer (*The Cot-ton Club*), was one of the resource people. He stuck his head in the door of the editing room and Tarantino yelled, " 'Hey, we just got through editing the scene.' "

" 'Great, I'd love to see it.' We loved it. He hated it, said, 'You need to cut it up.'

" 'Fuuck, I wanted to experiment with long takes. When Godard—'

" 'I like Godard too, but enough of that!' He ripped it apart. And then said, 'The thing that scares me the most about this, is that you actually have your money to make the movie. And this is what you've done. I can guarantee you, if you do this on a real movie, you will be fired.' And that was my fear, being fired. 'Cause they don't let people like me make movies."

WITH *KAFKA* a flop, and the competing projects dead and buried, Steven Soderbergh was finally ready to begin *King of the Hill*. He was in L.A. work-ing on the script in late April, early May of 1992, during the South Central riots. The story, about a boy with an absent mother and intermittently present father essentially raising himself, had similarities to Soderbergh's own upbringing. His parents had had a bad marriage, and his mother was interested in the paranormal, giving readings, holding séances, etc. As Betsy Brantley once said, Soderbergh's mother is "the nightmare that looms in all of his sleep." "It had to be personal," recalls producer Barbara Maltby. "The book and what he saw in the book were two very different things. The book is a comedy about this upbeat, irrepressible kid. At our first story meeting, Steven turned it into a kind of tragedy. The kid had to be a version of himself." *King of the Hill* still wasn't a go project so far as Universal was concerned, and he needed Redford's support. There were a lot of meetings with Redford at the studio, some with Universal chief Tom Pollock and production head Casey Silver, arranged around the actor's schedule, that Redford nevertheless either canceled or just failed to show up for, perhaps irritated that Soderbergh had made him wait in line—or more likely, just living on Redford time. He sometimes phoned during meetings between Soderbergh and Maltby, had lengthy conversations with Maltby, telling her how he intended to call Soderbergh because he apparently felt guilty about skipping so many meetings, but he never actually phoned the director. Says Soderbergh delicately, "There were a series of decisions and actions on his part that I felt unhappy about, that I had trouble understanding."

Universal insisted that the budget not exceed $8 million, which meant that everybody had to take deferments, "as had been the case on *Kafka*, as had been the case on *sex, lies*," Soderbergh explains. "I was accustomed— being the filmmaker—to outlining what I felt the deferment plan ought to be. Redford wanted to defer at the same rate as everyone else. I wanted him to defer at a slightly higher rate than myself and the producers, since it was a project we brought to Wildwood. It had not been developed there, and nobody there was having to spend time working on it since it was not being physically produced through Wildwood." Redford refused, said he considered Soderbergh's request an insult. Days, weeks were spent on the issue, but he remained adamant. In the end, Redford being Redford, he got his way. Soderbergh registered his disappointment, and that was that.

Then one day, during pre-production, Baltimore Pictures head Mark Johnson asked Soderbergh if he would consider directing a project called *Quiz Show*, and sent him the script, which had been making the rounds for years with no takers. Johnson said, "I want you to read this, see if you like it."

Quiz Show was about the notorious cheating scandals that engulfed TV game shows in the 1950s. Soderbergh read it, called Johnson and said, "It's perfect, I would shoot this script right now, [the way it is.]" Johnson replied, "Great!" Soderbergh had conversations with Richard Goodwin, on whose book the film was based, met with Tim Robbins, who had agreed to play Charles Van Doren.

Meanwhile, Gail Mutrux, who worked for Johnson, must have shown the *Quiz Show* script to her husband, Tony Ganz, who happened to be head of Wildwood. Ganz must have shown the script to Redford, who decided that he, not Soderbergh, should direct it. Of course, Soderbergh was unacquainted with Redford's penchant for plucking the occasional project from the hands of the very indie filmmakers Sundance was supposed to be nurturing. If Denise Earle is to be credited, he did so with *The Giant Joshua*, and he did so again with *A River Runs Through It.* In 1983, producer Annick Smith optioned the book by Norman MacLean, with a $15,000 loan from Sundance. She brought in writer Bill Kittredge, as well as Richard Pearce, who had directed *Heartland.* Smith took a treatment to the lab in 1985. Two years later, when her option was about to run out, she heard Redford was interested. Her heart sank, because she knew what that meant. "When Redford gets control of a project, it's his project," she says. "He took over the show." Indeed, Redford went to MacLean and bought the rights. With Redford as director, Pearce was out. (Smith and Kittredge eventually got co-producer credit.)

"Redford works in such an Olympian fashion," says Pearce. "I don't know if he had any idea how much I wanted to make it. A friend told me something that helped me make sense out of it. He said Redford is like a beautiful woman who is oblivious to the chaos she creates when she moves through the world. But I will say one thing: if I had a project that one of Redford's companies would love, I'd hesitate to send it to them, because of what happened on *A River Runs Through It.*

Smith is resigned: "There's nothing sinister in it at all. He's not obliged to keep his hands off everything that's mentioned at Sundance. It doesn't all have to be done by the letter of the law—there is no law here." Adds former board member Howard Klein of the Rockefeller Foundation, "I had a rigid standard at Rockefeller when I was making grants: I never accepted a piece from an artist. But I'm not sure it was clear in Bob's mind that he wasn't supposed to touch the merchandise. There were so many gray areas, and he came from another world."

Redford, pacing the floor of his New York office in 1990, dismissed these charges. "This issue has been haunting us for ten years," he said. "There's been a lot of rumors about things we've done that I don't think are right or fair. They say, 'Well, Redford is taking the projects for himself.' I bend over backward not to try to get any of these projects for my own use." But it's less clear that he really hears the accusations. "I wasn't aware of moving anybody out," he says about *A River Runs Through It.* "We all joined forces. Now, in truth, I don't have a lot of success working with a lot of people. So

I said I'd just like to develop this myself. So am I going to be able to do that or not? Annick was very good about it and said, 'Yeah.' " Redford could not afford to be perceived as someone who would elbow aside a promising independent, especially not the director of a film he was producing, who was also busy flakking his festival. Nobody ever says what he means in Hollywood, especially when what he means is ugly, and therefore the message Johnson delivered to Soderbergh was something like, "We're sorry, but TriStar, which is financing *Quiz Show,* is ready to go. You aren't available because you're in production. We're submitting the project to other directors. We have a list." Beat. "Nobody on the list is available—but surprise, Bob Redford's interested. He can start right away." None of this made any sense at all to Soderbergh. He thought, That's a ruse. If you wanted to make a film right away and have it done quickly, you'd get Sidney Lumet, who moves fast, not Redford, who works at a crawl. Soderbergh said, "Oh." He was angry that Redford had not called him himself to tell him the bad news. After all, he thought they had a "relationship." He said, "It's a call I would have made; it's a call most people, I think, would have made." But there was nothing he could do. (Redford subsequently explained that he didn't phone Soderbergh because Johnson said that he would take care of it. But at the time, when several people called him on it, he acted surprised, said, "Well, if I'd known that Steven really wanted me to do it . . ." and promised to call him. He just never did.)

Soderbergh completed the *King of the Hill* shoot and had almost finished with post as well, when the phone rang one Saturday in February 1993, in the dreadful, three-room apartment on Elmer Avenue in North Hollywood Soderbergh was sharing with friends. He was still editing the film, tweaking and fine-tuning his cut. There were a couple of things he wasn't happy with, and he was planning some reshoots, mainly the ending. It was Redford on the phone. Referring to the awkwardness between them, he said, "Look, I know that we have a lot to discuss, and I want to have that discussion, but first is it possible for me to see *King of the Hill,* whatever state you have it in?" Soderbergh, somewhat at a loss, said, "Yeah. When do you want to see it?"

"Tomorrow."

"Lemme get on that, I'll see what I can do."

"Great, I'll look at the film, and then we'll talk." Tomorrow was Sunday, and Soderbergh had to do some scrambling to find a projectionist, but he managed to set up a screening at Skywalker Sound at Lantana over on West Olympic, near Bundy. Says the director, "That Saturday conversation was the last conversation I ever had with him." Redford never did talk to him about *Quiz Show,* never even got back to him about *King of the Hill.*

Later, word filtered back to the young director that Redford had not liked his film. "It's not my kind of movie," he is reported to have said. "It's not the way I would have shot it." This seemed to make sense, because according to Soderbergh he suddenly announced, "I'm gonna take my name off, I didn't do anything, I had one lunch with Hotchner, so I don't think it's a project for me to have my name on."

"Fine. But if you didn't do anything, do you feel it's really appropriate to take the remainder of your deferment? You can't have it both ways. You can't say you did nothing and get the rest of your fee. So which one is it?"

"Then I'll leave my name on and I'll take the money."

By that time, *King of the Hill* had been accepted to Cannes. "I was pissed off, and wasn't in the mood to be accommodating," Soderbergh recalls. He told Redford, "We're going to leave it the way it is, take your name off. And if my hand is forced, I'm going to be a fucking blabbermouth." He threatened to go public, and the issue went away. (Redford put the blame on Soderbergh. He claimed that by the time the production finally got started, he was off working on other projects. He said, "It took so long, I ran out of time for any involvement.")

In 1994, Soderbergh received a form letter from Redford, inviting him to a "best of" Sundance event in Tokyo. He didn't bother to respond. After Redford left footprints on Soderbergh's back, the honeymoon between the Sundance Festival and its most famous alumnus was over. Said Soderbergh, "The image that is given [of Redford]—as being a friend of the filmmaker—is not what I experienced."

WHEN THE SUNDANCE FESTIVAL ENDED, *Dogs* still did not have a distributor. Gladstein recalls leaving Park City doubting that the film would ever get a theatrical release. Still, Hoving and Tusk were eager to acquire it. Neither Weinstein had attended. As part of the belt-tightening, recalls Tusk, "They were making us do nonrefundable airfares. It was, I can't change the back–to–New York airfare, so, just go to L.A. So I carried the print of *Reservoir Dogs* from Sundance to the Carolco screening room in West Hollywood to show it to Harvey and Bob." Twenty minutes into it, Harvey was getting a little itchy. Tusk told him, "Sit still. Trust me." The movie ended. Harvey was dubious, afraid it would be a hard sell at the box office even if it got good reviews, which seemed questionable, given the carnage. Back in New York, the brothers screened it again, then went around the room, canvassing the staff. Ben Zinkin, an outside counsel, said, "That was probably the single worst movie I've ever seen."

"Russell?"

Russell Schwartz, head of marketing, replied, "Not my cup of tea. For me, it's a pass."

"Marty?"

"Actually, it could do *Blood Simple* business," said Zeidman. But several of the younger people were passionate about it. Recalls Gladstein, "Harvey said to me that it was really the enthusiasm of the staff that made him buy the movie. I felt it was more of a Bob acquisition than a Harvey acquisition." Harvey was particularly uneasy about the ear slicing scene. "I was afraid it would turn off women," he explains. He used his wife, Eve, and her sister Maude as guinea pigs in screenings the way he used everybody else. "When the ear scene came on, they were out of their seats like jumping jacks," he recalls. "Forget it, there go the women." On her way out, Eve turned to him and said, "I don't care how good the movie is, this is disgusting!" He thought, This is like my mother saying, "Brush your teeth and wash your face." Harvey wanted to impress Tarantino, but, he recalls, "They were circling outside the screening room, pissed off at me, pissed off at Quentin, pissed off at the movie. Angry." Embarrassed, he apologized to the director, who retorted, exasperated, "I didn't make it for your wife!" Eve and Maude stood outside the screening room for fifteen minutes. Then they returned and watched the rest of the film. "I thought you hated the movie, how come you came back?" Harvey asked them. Eve replied, "We wanted to find out what happened."

But Harvey wouldn't give up. Tarantino was incredulous, said, "What? You want to cut out the torture scene?!" The Miramax co-chairman had a way of getting behind a filmmaker, and then zeroing in on a signature scene, the one that best expressed the filmmaker's particular voice, that made the film; in this case, "a Tarantino film," and trying to get rid of it. "Without this scene, you have a mainstream movie," he told the director. "With this scene, you put it in a box. Without that scene, I could open this movie in three hundred theaters. As opposed to one! Thirty seconds would change the movie in the American marketplace."

"It's a problem if they're expecting it to be *Pretty Woman*," Tarantino replied. "This movie was never meant to be everything for everybody. I made this movie for myself, and everybody else is invited. Forget it, it's staying in." The director recalls, "I didn't have to cut out anything, because he bought the film the way it was. But that doesn't mean anything to him. He had one market research screening of *Dogs* at the Miramax theater. His minions were hanging around. He wanted to take out an invisible ten minutes. In particular the torture sequence. It was a moment with me and Harvey that really dictated our relationship." Tarantino thought back to his experience at the Sundance lab, when his scene was critiqued by all the resource people. He remembered, It was like a picnic table inquisition. It was a beautiful summer day, the birds were flying around and chirping, and all these people were just telling me, You suck! "I think most directors are pussies," he says now. "If you couldn't handle it at Sundance, with people who have the best of intentions, how're you gonna handle it when you gotta swim with the sharks, when you're trapped in a room with Harvey Weinstein and you gotta fight for your way, and fight in such a way that you're not alienating people as you fight, but you're doing your job, which is protecting your baby.

"He went, 'How 'bout this, let me give it to my guys, let them try editing it out. See if we like it. We're not touching your movie. It's on video. You hit erase and it's gone. Lemme just try it.' I knew that was the death of me, just letting anybody else get in there and fuck with it. But it was hard saying no. Because Harvey doesn't get his way by yelling and screaming like a maniac. A person like that is easy to fight with. He was being so reasonable, so nice, and he started dropping names of all the movies that he'd worked with. 'I took ten minutes out of Steven's movie . . . ' He was seducing me, and I didn't want to disappoint him. I wanted to be embraced and brought inside his family that had done so many good movies, I wanted to blurt out 'Yes' just to make him happy, but I couldn't. So I said, 'Harvey, no. I think the movie is perfect just the way it is. I think the torture scene—it does put the film into a smaller niche—but I think it's one of the best things in the movie.' There was just the tiniest bit of a pause, and he goes, 'Well, okay, then, and I want you to remember it was Miramax that let your movie go out exactly the way you wanted it!' It all comes down to little moments, and that moment decided my career for all time. With anybody and with everybody. It's that line in *The Color of Money*, 'If you you know when it's time to say yes, and when its time to say no, everybody goes home in a Cadillac.' "

Reservoir Dogs opened on October 23, 1992, in New York. Says David Linde, "When *Reservoir Dogs* came out, everyone was tense because Miramax had run out of hits and was trying to get this one movie to cross over." But it didn't. Although the Weinsteins were making their mark by distributing art films like mainstream movies, ironically, in the case of *Dogs*, the reverse was true, or at least that's the way Tarantino looked at it. He complained that Miramax marketed the picture like an art film. As he recalls, "Miramax had fucked Live up the ass with Madonna's *Truth or Dare*, that Live wanted for video the year before, so when the shoe was on the other foot, Live stuck it to Miramax," driving such a hard bargain that Miramax had little incentive to push the film. All in all, it was probably the least auspicious sendoff ever given someone who was destined to become a major filmmaker. *Dogs* only grossed about $2.5 million, despite a hurricane of press. Bender, his producer, wasn't happy. "I thought they could have done better," he says. "I wished they had put it out there more." *Dogs* did more than twice as well ($6 million) in England, where it was indeed opened like a mainstream movie. It sold very well on video, of which the Weinsteins only had a small cut, over 100,000 units in the U.S. and probably an equal number worldwide. (The video was banned in England.) As of the year 2000, *Dogs* had grossed about $20 million worldwide. Says Tarantino, "That's pretty fucking cool."

Tarantino more than paid Keitel back for his help. For the late-blooming actor, his memorable role in *Dogs* revived a career spent in the shadow of Robert De Niro. Keitel would also give a sensational performance in *The Piano*, and subsequently became a bit of a Miramax repertory player. But ironically, the Weinsteins turned out to be a stone in his shoe. Keitel and De Niro, two wild and crazy guys, had long lived next door to each other in Tribeca way before Tribeca was a happening place, when it was just industrial lofts, rats, and garbage. Years before Miramax moved in, they were the "Harvey and Bob" of the neighborhood. But there was room only for one "Harvey and Bob" in Tribeca, and as Miramax prospered, the Weinsteins were the ones who grabbed boasting rights to the names. When Keitel's assistant called over to Nobu to order sushi for the actor's lunch, it often ended up on Weinstein's desk, driving Keitel crazy.

Tarantino's success nettled the Archives guys who, with the exception of Avary, had become his ex-friends. In both *Dogs* and *True Romance*, ultimately directed by Tony Scott, they heard scraps of conversation, stories, and jokes that they recognized as their own. Tarantino had hoovered up everything around him without so much as a "May I?" and when he left his pals behind, they resented it. According to one, Rand Vossler, "There wasn't a day during those two and a half years that we weren't together working. Quentin and I were as close as guys could be. He slept on my floor. [But] he's Mr. Tarantino now. He became extremely difficult to get in touch with, because once the ball started rolling on *Reservoir Dogs*, it rolled fast. Quentin couldn't bother with anything that I was doing."

Allison Anders had asked Bumble Ward, the publicist she shared with Tarantino, to fix them up. Tarantino had had an on-and-off relationship with the love of his life, Grace Lovelace, and now they were off. He seemed to have fairly specific requirements in the girlfriend department. She had to like to sit in the third row. She had to like *Rio Bravo*. "Also, she shouldn't be a stickler when it comes to my personal hygiene," he added. "She has to cut me a little bit of slack. I'm not speaking about BO. But people have a natural smell, and she has to like my smell. If she has a big problem with it, that's sort of the beginning of the end."

In any event, the two filmmakers hooked up at a party for *In the Soup*. They bonded over their shared redneck history.

On their first date, they went to see *Passenger 57*, a Wesley Snipes movie, and then drove back to his apartment in the red, two-door Geo

Metro he bought with his *True Romance* money. On the right side, the fender was crushed like a beer can, and the inside was a mess, the floor littered with flattened Styrofoam coffee cups and blackened Q-tips that looked like they had been places you didn't want to go.

Tarantino was living in the semi-squalor of a single guy, occupying a cramped, funky apartment on Crescent Heights, below Sunset, filled with movie posters, movie memorabilia, dolls, and mounds of dirty laundry piled in corners. A portrait of Lovelace curled up asleep on a purple couch hung over the mantel, on which lay the straight razor that starred in *Dogs*. (The ear was in "storage.") The small living room was dominated by a big black Panasonic TV with a rectangular screen in the proper aspect ratio for viewing movies unscanned. He was deathly afraid that rats would overrun the apartment and took evasive action, sleeping in a different room every night.

Tarantino and Anders lay on the floor listening to music and playing Mystery Date and Mr. T, two board games Tarantino yanked out of a closet stacked from top to bottom with his vast collection based on TV shows and movies. Anders still hadn't seen *Dogs* and didn't really want to. She thought, Okay, date number three, I'm gonna have to watch this guy's movie.

Like so many others, Anders worshipped Scorsese. She told Tarantino she had sent him a copy of *Gas Food Lodging*. Tarantino said, "Oh yeah, he wrote to Miramax, said he really liked *Reservoir Dogs*."

"Oh really? He sent me a fax."

"To the company?"

"No, to me!"

"He sent you a fax?"

"Yeah, and I'm going to his house for dinner."

"He's cooking lasagna for you? And I wear this guy around my neck like a ball and chain?"

Tarantino had been riding the festival circuit, with its paparazzi, autograph hounds, and groupies. On one of their dates he said, "I'm thinking of doing this article on festivals—'A Young Filmmaker's Guide to Getting Laid at Film Festivals': first you choose your big festivals, then you go to the cool festivals, and then you go to wherever you like the girls. If you're into Swedish girls, you go to Stockholm."

"It doesn't work that way for girls," she replied. "You don't get that kind of groupie action. I get menopausal women. Following me around."

Tarantino and Anders were not meant for each other. It was the sixth week of their relationship, and they still hadn't slept together. After dinner at a restaurant, Tarantino asked her, "Do you want me to drive you home, or do you want to come back to my apartment and watch me alphabetize my videotapes?"

"You can't go out with other filmmakers," Anders observes. "Kathryn Bigelow said, 'Four times, no more.' I went out on dates with Quentin, I've been editing all day, and I was like, This guy can't be my boyfriend, he's telling me what's in his trim bin, what brilliant scenes are no longer in *Dogs*. I don't want to know this about you. It's like dirty handkerchiefs or something."

THE WEINSTEINS began to emerge from their funk in 1992, but box office did not rebound enough for them to claw their way out of the hole they had dug for themselves over the course of the previous two years, and the company's downward slide just seemed to accelerate. *Enchanted April*, directed by Mike Newell, was released on July 31, and became the year's big earner, grossing $13.2 million. *Mediterraneo*, which won 1991's sole Oscar for Miramax, did $4.5 million. *Delicatessen* grossed $1.9 million. But there were no breakout hits, comparable to Robert Altman's *The Player*, from Fine Line, and Merchant-Ivory's *Howards End*, from Sony Classics, each grossing nearly $25 million. The brothers' overhead was climbing too, at the same time that they were paying more for acquisitions because that market was overheating as a result of the blaze they themselves had started. Worst of all, most often the cash they were putting out wasn't paying off. *Dust Devil*, Richard Stanley's follow-up to *Hardware*, was never released, while *Tom and Jerry: The Movie* and *Love Crimes* both flopped. Harvey bought *Spotswood*, aka *The Efficiency Expert*, directed by Mark Joffe, because it was Anthony Hopkins's first film after *The Silence of the Lambs*. He recut it and watched it die in November, grossing all of $101,307—impressive next to Tom DiCillo's *Johnny Suede* which took in $13,477.

Variety quoted one exhibitor saying Miramax "has lost its edge from the early days because they've acquired too many films." According to the trade paper, as of September 1992 Miramax had a backlog of sixteen unreleased pictures that the company apparently couldn't afford to open. *Variety* got hold of audited financial statements showing that Miramax posted an after-tax profit of $2.64 million on revenues of $28.12 million in 1989. In 1990, the company enjoyed an after-tax profit of $4.04 million on revenues of $49.9 million; but in 1991, after-tax profits were nearly flat—$4.35 million—even though revenues had increased by 50 percent to $74.09 million. These numbers show how deceptive grosses can be in terms of the overall profit picture, and give a good indication of how much Miramax must have been spending in 1992 just to keep up with the previous year. Profit margins dipped from 9 percent to 8 percent to 5 percent over the three-year period. The movie business is cyclical, and studios, with their deep pockets, are able to withstand those inevitable cold spells, but it's very hard for a small indie company to survive a bad year, almost impossible to survive two or three.

All told, Miramax released twenty-two films in 1992 with a total gross of $39 million, or a mere $1.8 million a film. Its new Dimension division, known in-house as "Dementia," hit the ground running with *Hellraiser III: Hell on Earth,* which grossed $12 million, and *Children of the Corn II: The Final Sacrifice,* which grossed $7 million on a budget of $900,000. The two movies accounted for a little over a quarter of Miramax's profits. These figures—which don't include advances and expenses and don't address financing arrangements, ancillary profits, and so on—provide only a partial glimpse of the company's performance, but what they do show isn't good. Cash flow was nearly choked off. Recalls Tusk, "Creditors were knocking down the doors. We were being told, 'You've got $50 per day for Cannes.'" You couldn't buy a hamburger for that. Staffers were expected to turn over paper printed on one side and use the back for photocopying. Instead of replacing old toner with new, office workers recycled it into the copiers. They had to pay for their own coffee, water, and parking. Tusk continues, "You would hear they weren't paying vendors. Or they were trying to cut deals like, 'We'll give you 75 cents on the dollar.' We had always been urged, 'Read as many magazines as you can, keep in tune with what the critics are saying, read the feature press.' Suddenly it was, 'The other magazines are being cut off. You get *Variety* and *Hollywood Reporter.*'" Staffers ran to the bank with their paychecks, lest they bounce. (They never did.) Recalls Stuart Burkin, "Bob would come around and say, 'You guys want to work out of your homes the next few days? The lights are going off, and the phones.' The bills didn't get paid." As Bob himself recalled, "I used to go into Chase Manhattan Bank on my knees, to start out with, then I'd be on my belly, begging for money. You'd be trying to explain Jane Campion to bankers and, then, mid-sentence, you'd think, Why am I even talking?"

Miramax, in other words, was like one of those cantilevered California homes that threatens to slide down the hillside into the sea every time it rains. It was propped up on four wobbly legs: North American theatrical distribution, foreign sales, video, and pay cable. The theatrical leg was always weak because even in the best of times, the brothers were in a business where they had to spend a lot to make a little, where the more they made, the more it cost to make it, where they had to run fast to stay in place. Even with films that were "successful," it was questionable how much was left over in profit: the longer the pictures stayed in theaters, the more they had to pay for advertising, and the more the division of the box office receipts favored the exhibitors. Its deal with HBO, which paid 25 to

30 percent of its production costs, was soon to expire. This relationship was critical to the company, because the kind of specialty product Miramax distributed commanded an upscale, pay cable demographic, and therefore had little free television value. But even outlets like HBO were trying to broaden their audience with big Hollywood movies, and when HBO declined to renew its agreement, it was a disaster, especially since Miramax still owed money to several banks, including Midland Montague. Says CAA's John Ptak, who was hired by the Weinsteins to plug the HBO hole, "Harvey was up shit's creek."

But, to change metaphors, 1992 was like a roller-coaster ride, with gut-wrenching lows followed by breathtaking highs. Tony Safford, who had left Sundance to head acquisitions at New Line, had been unhappy for some time, and he chose that moment to jump ship to Miramax. "They're big on raiding other camps," he says. Safford was dubious about leaving a company that was thriving for one that was "always teetering on the edge, with a lot of films that weren't working, that had a lot of pictures on the shelf, banks looking over their shoulder, but I experienced [New Line's] Bob Shaye as a brooder, who would literally sit in his office as the sun went down, and even though it got darker and darker, he never turned on the lights. Harvey, on the other hand, not only wore his emotions on his sleeve, he played his emotions magnificently as the situation required. To be at Miramax during that period was exciting."

Although the Weinsteins' belt-tightening cinched the waists of their employees, they were not about to let it interfere with their own lifestyle. "They were the kings of T&E,"* says Schmidt. They loved luxe hotels, the Beverly Hills Hotel in L.A., the Savoy in London, the Hôtel du Cap in Antibes, the Ritz on Place Vendome. "They flew first class, then they started chartering their own planes, they had limos, car services," Schmidt continues. At the point when things were at their worst, PolyGram head Michael Kuhn ran into Harvey at the Beverly Hills Hotel, went up to his rooms, an expensive corner suite, and sat there dumbstruck as Harvey poor-mouthed, harangued him about reducing expenses and slashing staff. Incredulously, he asked, "Harvey, if that's the case, how come you are in this huge corner suite?" Harvey replied, "Well, I only pay a single room rate for it."

"How on earth do you manage that? I can never get anything like that on this floor."

"It's because I spend so much money here."

Miramax had brought *Reservoir Dogs* to Cannes that year. The French loved it, but more important, they adored Tarantino, who was becoming a

* "T&E": Travel and entertainment, i.e., expense account.

star on the festival circuit. He would talk to anybody who would talk to him. The Weinsteins marketed directors, and it was clear that in Tarantino they had a winner.

The festival also afforded the brothers the opportunity to unload some films Miramax had acquired but could not afford to release. Ptak, one of a handful of pioneers who had tilled the soil of foreign presales and co-financing, introduced Harvey to Jeffrey Katzenberg, with the notion of in-ducing the Disney chairman to buy the South African musical *Sarafina!*, which starred Whoopi Goldberg, along with Vincent Ward's *Map of the Human Heart*. Katzenberg watched forty minutes of *Sarafina!* and agreed to buy it, along with a package of five more films for video, for $13.5 million. "Miramax was the happiest bunch of people in the world," recalls Ptak. "They were about six to eight months from bankruptcy. When I came to their offices in New York the secretaries hugged me." (But it took CAA nine months to collect its commission on the deal.) In addition to selling Disney its package of pictures, Ptak engineered a first-look deal to produce larger budget pictures for Miramax, buying some time.*

The creation of Dimension, as well as the sale of *Sarafina!*, were regarded by the trades as acts of desperation, sure signs that Miramax was headed for the indie graveyard, which wasn't far from the truth. As Schmidt puts it, "Without *The Crying Game* in the picture, you're out of money." But *The Crying Game was* in the picture. Way back in the summer of 1982, Neil Jordan, whose *Mona Lisa* in 1986 had been an art house hit, hatched a tale he called, alternatively, *The Soldier's Story* or *The Soldier's Wife*. But Jordan was unable to resolve the story problems, and put it aside to work on *The Company of Wolves*, which Palace produced in 1984. Seven years later, Jor-dan and Steve Woolley found themselves at the Berlin Film Festival, which was screening Jordan's latest, *The Miracle*, an incest film. Over drinks with Woolley in a Berlin bar, Jordan brought up the unfinished script, asked, "What do you think if Dil, the girlfriend of the black soldier who Fergus looks up in London, turned out to be a man?" Woolley thought it over, de-cided it was a smashing idea, and assured Jordan he would produce it. He sent the script to the Weinsteins. "How the hell are you gonna do this?" Harvey asked.

"We'll find somebody."

"I don't believe it. Good luck."

According to Jordan, Weinstein, like everyone else, was afraid to touch it, with its combustible mix of race, politics, and sex. Harvey said "he'd do it if I cast a girl as the transvestite, because he thought audiences would find

---

* "First-look deal": In exchange for financial support, a production entity has the first crack at any project developed by a smaller production company, producer, director, actor, etc.

it too unacceptable and too revolting otherwise." Not easily discouraged, Woolley proceeded anyway, with the backing of Channel Four, British Screen, and a consortium of banks. Finding "a chick with a dick" to play Dil was proving difficult. Finally, director Derek Jarman's boyfriend recommended Jaye Davidson, a clubber and some-time fashion assistant. Jordan and Woolley liked Davidson's readings, but the search continued. Then, one day, Woolley called a halt. He said to Jordan, joking, "This is stupid. Jaye's so good and he's saying the lines so well. Can we just get on and cast him before I end up fucking him." The film was shot in the fall of 1991. With three films in production, all of which would become hits, Palace entered bankruptcy in August 1992.

Set in London against a background of IRA terrorism, Jordan's muted, melancholy film that begins and ends with death, tells the story of a man, Fergus, played by sad-eyed Stephen Rea, whose lover, Dil, indeed turns out to be a transvestite. Davidson, seductive, vulnerable, and scary, all at once, is absolutely convincing. Ironically, Jordan structured the film with the same fable of the scorpion and the frog that Matt Damon uses to gloss Harvey.

Jack Lechner, who was an executive at Channel Four at the time, saw a rough cut and walked out into the streets of Soho thinking, This is a really wonderful movie, and I hope twenty-five people go to see it. "It never occurred to anyone involved that it would ever be more than a lovely little British film that, if we were lucky, might make its money back," he recalls. "Cannes passed on it, and Venice did too. It seemed that the cards were stacked against it." Woolley and Powell set their sights high, deciding to take The Crying Game (as it was now called) to the studios instead of the art film distributors in February 1992. Typically, the executives didn't get it. They made and received phone calls during the screenings. Brandon Tartikoff, the Paramount chairman, took one such call just before the shot of Dil's private parts, and missed it entirely. When the screening ended, Woolley noted that he expected the film to be very controversial. Tartikoff, with a puzzled look, asked, "Why's that?"

Miramax saw the film at the American Film Market, two months before Cannes, at the Aidikoff Screening Room. Harvey liked it, but it was Bob who was blown away, and it was his enthusiasm that drove the deal. Both Weinsteins were convinced that they could prevail on the press to keep mum regarding Dil's member. But the question, as always, was money. Over and over the Weinsteins asked, "Is there any video value in light of the content?" They were worried that Blockbuster might blackball the film because of the premise. Finally they rolled the dice, decided to enter the mild bidding war for the picture. Miramax, which had shown zero interest in The Crying Game in the script stage, when it could have had North

American rights for well under $1 million, ended up bidding through the spring against Sony Classics for the North American rights. But the frugal Barker and Bernard refused to go the extra mile, and the North American rights went to Miramax for about $1.5 million. A lot of distributors, like Fine Line's Deutchman, walked away, and regretted it later. He recalls, wistfully, "I could have put Harvey and Bob out of business. I came very close to deciding to acquire that movie, but ultimately I backed off, assuming there was no way you could keep the surprise a secret, and once it was out no one would be interested in seeing the film."

Jordan, who felt that Harvey had dumped *The Miracle*, his previous film, insisted on severe terms. "I was nervous they would try to recut it and test it to hell," he says. Adds Woolley, "Neil was very bruised. We just didn't want to give it to somebody to chop up, and we were able to make sure they couldn't touch a frame, they couldn't change the title, they couldn't dub it, they couldn't test it—they had to just basically release the film." It was a good deal for the investors and a bad deal for Miramax. In return for its $1.5 million, the company was not getting any back end participation, only expenses and a 25 percent distribution fee. In other words, after Miramax took its fee, deducted its costs from what remained of its share of the gross, the balance belonged to the investors.

Throughout the fall of 1992, *The Crying Game* played festivals like Telluride and Toronto. Initially, Miramax, which was flogging *Strictly Ballroom* as its Oscar film, ignored it. Woolley, who had come up with the don't-reveal-the-secret strategy for the British release, was on his own. At Telluride for the first screening, the theater was deserted. "Nobody [at Miramax] had put any work into it," he recalls. "We were, Oh, my God!" But the next one was almost full, and the third was packed. Todd McCarthy gave it a rave review in *Variety* and it was off to the races. The tracking numbers were strong, and *The Crying Game* was looking like a winner. "Harvey did not create the phenomenon," says Woolley. "He managed the phenomenon, and as such he did a superb job."

As the British release date approached in October 1992, the IRA initiated a new round in its terror campaign in England, and *The Crying Game*, which had been retitled after a 1964 Dave Berry song to downplay the IRA angle, opened the same week. Despite respectable reviews, it did disastrous business, taking in no more than £300,000 at the box office, less than a seventh of its budget, forget P&A. In view of the grosses, Channel Four and Palace had little likelihood of paying the above- and below-the-line costs that had all been deferred.

The Crying Game opened in America on November 25 in only a handful of theaters in New York and L.A. Even at that point, Miramax was so disorganized that Woolley was appalled to see that it had not supplied posters for the theaters. But Harvey prowled the lobbies during the first weeks into release, buttonholing patrons, asking, "What happens in this movie? What's the big secret?" Says Woolley, "It was, 'You can sleep with my wife, but I'm not telling you the secret of *The Crying Game!*' The audiences were terrific. That's what sold the film."

In hock to the banks and barely able to put food on the table, here was the hit the Weinsteins had been praying for. They could practically taste the money. They redoubled their efforts to buy out Midland Montague, and they finally did so in December 1992, for $3.1 million and the assignment of a $2.7 million debt due to Miramax. As someone who was involved with the deal on behalf of Miramax put it, "We were struggling to find every nickel. The boys didn't have a pot to piss in." Bob was thrilled. He always used to say, "We made the best deal, fuckin great!" Says Harvey, "We never forced Midland Montague out; they wanted out. They were scared of us, that they were gonna lose their money, and they cited Avenue pictures that was going broke—Cinecom had gone broke—and they thought that this was not a worthy investment. They used the idea that Miramax was at its borrowing limit with Chase. Chase was not looking to extend further credit, and was in fact looking to have its entire loan paid off, so that we could not expand any further. They made a profit. And we were not in negotiations with Disney or anybody else during those negotiations."

But there was one big problem: "The reason we wanted to buy out *The Crying Game* investors was because we wanted to take the movie and expand it into a thousand theaters," says Harvey.

Acquiring the rights to *The Crying Game* was going to be a challenge. In December, with the grosses already well up in the teens, Bob went to London to offer a settlement to the various parties: Channel Four, which owned the international sales rights, had actually made the deal with the Weinsteins and therefore was the lead party for a group of investors that included British Screen; the creditors of Palace; the Berliner Bank; Poly-Gram; and the agents for the people with the approximately £500,000 in deferrals—everyone from Neil Jordan down to the grips. They gathered in the dim basement conference room of the old St. James's Club in London. For Miramax, the question was, What would make them sell? What would incentivize them?

According to Harvey, Bob told them, "We're gonna spend $10 million, *The Crying Game* is going to play those theaters in Nebraska where people go to to see all the Disney movies, all the Bruckheimer movies." The investors were appalled, replied, "We know what you're doing. You're just going to spend off our money."

"No, no, we're gonna expand the gross. And everybody's gonna make more."

"No, no, no, we're gonna make less."

In other words, the investors thought that Bob was just going to "gross up" the film by spending their share of the profits, behavior other producers had accused Miramax of in the past.

Bluntly, Bob said something like, "We're not gonna open the picture wide unless you guys sell out, because we have no incentive to do so." But he was too tough, made the mistake of presenting them with a lose-lose proposition that just infuriated everyone: either the investors retained their interest in the film, in which case Miramax would bury it, and they would get nothing; or they sold their interest to Miramax, in which case they would be unable to benefit from the big score, if there was one. The air in the room was thick with hostility and mistrust. Recalls British Screen's Simon Perry, "Bob was just aggressive and ill-humored. He threatened us: 'You have to do this, or you'll get nothing.' We smelled something big coming at the box office, and we thought, If they want to buy us out, they must know something we don't, so initially we turned him down."

With Bob getting nowhere, Harvey sent his financial consultant, Peter Hoffman, to join the negotiations. Hoffman had been a principal in Carolco, the Hollywood mini-major that had taken the *Rambo* and *Terminator* films to the bank before going down in flames. He had a reputation for being a brilliant tax lawyer with one of the sharpest minds in town, maybe too sharp for his own good. As one studio executive joked, "He was always talking about reverse self-liquidating mergers that we could do based on section 32E of the IRS code."

Hoffman played the good cop to Bob's bad. The dominoes that had to fall first were Channel Four and British Screen. Once they went, no one else was going to block the deal. Miramax knew that the mandate of Channel Four and British Screen was not necessarily to make a profit, but to nurture English filmmakers. For them, the goal was to get the deferrals paid, every last penny. Says Powell, "That was a big concern. Those people worked for next to nothing." Hoffman understood that, and he flattered them, made them feel good about selling. He said something like, "C'mon guys, this is the right thing to do. Don't get mad at Harvey and Bob and do the wrong thing. Keep your eye on the ball. You have all these good British boys who made this picture, and they should get their money."

Channel Four's Colin Leventhal was skeptical that the film would do all that well, and Hoffman seized on that too, played up the risk involved. According to one of the people who was in the room, he said, "The boys are taking a gamble, they're rash, who knows what's gonna come out of this." He tried to scare them, said something like, "Do you really think they're ever going to pay you anything? When you get done with this you'll be lucky if you get an accounting statement, much less get a check, and there'll be a bunch of garbage on it, who knows if they can even pay. Because they may have pissed all that money away on something else, and by that time, who knows where they'll be? They're up to here with the banks, this is a shaky situation. At the end of the day it's going to be a war."

This was not idle talk, and eventually, threats and cajolery did their job. Says the source, "It's hard to imagine that people actually do selfless things, but Leventhal and Simon Perry really sacrificed the interests of their companies to insure that no matter what happened, the people who had deferred their payments got paid." Sure enough, once Channel Four and British Screen fell in to line, the others followed.

When the negotiations had been completed, all the parties gathered to sign the deal, in which Miramax was going to buy out the U.S. and Canadian rights to the picture and terminate everyone else's participation for a payout that included a guaranteed amount for the back end, as well as bonuses if the film exceeded certain levels of U.S. box office performance. At the last moment, Powell said, "I don't know, I have to check with Neil to see if I can do this. Neil's worried about it." It was like he was finally waking up to the fact that he and the others had made a terrible deal. (It is worth noting that the deal was not without risk to Miramax. Although the film was doing well as an art house release in the U.S., it had yet to garner any broad commercial success.) Bob was so angry he looked like he was going to levitate himself across the room and strangle him. Hoffman interceded, said, "Bob, stop it. Calm down." Bob left the room muttering, "I'll kill him, I'll fucking kill him."

Ultimately, the momentum was just too great to stop the train. There was so much suspicion of Miramax—that they'd never pay out anything— and so much pressure for the deferrees to get their checks, that all the parties felt better with a bird in hand. Ultimately all deferments were paid, as well as the bonuses tied to the U.S. box office performance.

While the negotiations were going on, Jordan and Woolley were in L.A. doing publicity for the film, which was showered with honors—the Producers Guild, the L.A. Film Critics, the New York Film Critics, the Writers Guild, the Directors Guild—all of which were paving the yellow brick road to the Oscars. "I kept away from the negotiations because I felt there was something about it which didn't quite fit," says Woolley. "They took me out, they took Nik out, British Screen, everyone. It was a wipeout. Clever for Harvey to do that, but very strange. I left it to Nik. It was bad of me, but we were busy releasing the film, and it was out of my hands." *The Crying Game* did get six Oscar nominations. Harvey roared with glee—for maybe two minutes, then he was on to the next thing, in this instance a funk over Jaye Davidson, whose nomination he hadn't anticipated. After all, key to the film's continued success was preserving the fiction that the actor was a woman, and he'd been nominated for Best Supporting Actor. Now the press would be all over him, and he'd give himself away. Harvey hustled him out of the country—to Egypt—but only for a day, because Davidson couldn't find a place in that Muslim country to buy a drink.

The Crying Game grossed $62.5 million, finally shattering the $25 million ceiling that none of the indie blockbusters had been able to break. "When it began to make enormous amounts of money in America," says Jordan, "I definitely should have made $2 or 3 million. Having gone through this extraordinarily difficult process of making the film for almost nothing, I felt more annoyed at the stupidity of the English partners—the producers and Channel Four—for not protecting the ancillary rights and allowing this to happen so blatantly, than I was at Miramax. You kind of know they'll try to squeeze every penny out of everything. Harvey is what he is, isn't he, and Bob definitely is what he is. 'What do you think I'm going to do? I'm Harvey. Of course I'm going to sting you.' The pity of it is they're one of the only ports of call for independent filmmakers. I wish there were alternatives. On the other hand, they distributed the film brilliantly, and I wouldn't mind making more films for them at all." Indeed, says Harvey, "Our deal was never with Neil Jordan, it was with Film Four. If Jordan feels he's owed money, he should call them."

Miramax must have made in the neighborhood of $20 million on the picture, way more than it had made on any film to date. But the real importance of the success of *The Crying Game* wasn't the profit per se. Rather, it paved the way for a long-cherished dream to come true. Miramax became attractive enough to be coveted by a studio—Disney.

WITH *THE CRYING GAME* as their rainmaker, the heavens cracked open in a downpour of cash, bringing the Weinsteins' three-year drought to a watery conclusion. Even the brothers couldn't spend fast enough to burn through the film's earning power. And the success they enjoyed with Jordan's film seemed to irrigate everything else they released that year: John Sayles's *Passion Fish* opened on January 29, 1993, and grossed a very respectable $5.4 million. Baz Luhrmann's *Strictly Ballroom* followed three weeks later and rang up $11.7 million, spectacular for a small, clumsily shot, albeit charming Australian picture. Two months later, in April, Miramax released *Like Water for Chocolate.* "It was kicking around, no one really wanted it," recalls Eamonn Bowles. "Harvey did a radical restructuring, and it became one of the biggest foreign language films ever," grossing $21.6 million. He continues, "They call him Harvey Scissorhands, but he's helped way many films commercially."

In February, Miramax received twelve Academy nominations. In addition to *The Crying Game*'s six, which included Best Picture, Best Actor, for Stephen Rea, and Best Director, for Jordan, *Enchanted April* got three, *Passion Fish*, two, and *Close to Eden*, one, for Best Foreign Film. When the dust settled, Miramax won four Oscars. The brothers understood that if ever there was a moment to cash out, this was it.

Harvey, who talked to everyone and trusted no one, got into a conversation with Katzenberg, to whom he had unloaded *Sarafina!* Historically, of course, the studios had always disparaged the indie business as small change. Explains Katzenberg, "Investing a million to make $10 million would seem like a not very big business, but if you could do that four or five times a year, then it's a $40 or $50 million business, and suddenly it has size and scale to it." Katzenberg discussed Miramax with Ptak, who had first introduced him to the Weinsteins. Ptak advised him to go ahead, saying, "These guys don't quite know how to do it. They think that developing a friendship can be a sign of weakness, but I love them."

On April Fool's Day, Katzenberg phoned Chris McGurk, who was then CFO of Disney Studios, and said, "Hey, call Harvey Weinstein, let's talk to him about buying the company." McGurk had been an executive at Pepsico before coming to Disney, and he was a numbers guy, almost the definition of a suit, with a Grant Wood face, long and narrow, thin lips. He looked like he belonged behind the counter of a dry goods store in Nebraska at the turn of the century. But when he opened his mouth he revealed a dry, sardonic, slashing wit. McGurk threw knives, and enjoyed it when they drew blood. More important, he wasn't blinkered by the studio sensibility. McGurk called the brothers, said, "We're interested, make a proposal." Even though yesterday they had been on life support, the Weinsteins demanded upward of $90 million for their company.

According to McGurk, as Disney began to look at the deal, "We said, 'Hey, wait a minute, if they piggyback on the studio and we put them into our TV deals, put their product into our video operation, Jesus, we can increase their revenues by 30, 40 percent, dramatically improve their bottom line. This gives them a huge advantage in the marketplace, maybe there's something to this.' We laid out on a piece of paper how we would help Miramax take over the independent world and kill everybody. The big issue was whether these two guys could work with us, work within the system."

On the Disney side, everyone was worried about Eisner's take on it, given the Disney brand name and the parade of controversy the Weinsteins trailed in their wake. To their surprise, he went for it. Eisner had been uneasily watching his competitors get a foothold in television. Says Katzenberg, "Michael did not want to vertically integrate the company, he did not want to buy cable, he did not want to buy a network, because he felt we were too late. Our strategy was to extend our reach in terms of content. If we had a large enough control of the product being made—25, 30 percent—these so-called gatekeepers, the Rupert Murdochs, the John Malones, the Viacoms, the Time Warners that did own cable and network, would always have to deal with us. Miramax was a big building block in that strategy." Moreover, branding was something Eisner understood, and there was no question that Miramax had a brand name. Beyond that, "We'd had a couple of years of poor performance and he probably saw Harvey as a backstop in that regard, just as he brought in Joe Roth and gave him a producer's deal," McGurk explains. As for controlling the brothers, Katzenberg and Eisner had always been able to hammer anyone who got out of line, so he didn't think he needed to worry about that.

And Oscars—forget it. Disney couldn't buy one. So far as nominations were concerned, that year, Miramax outscored Disney twelve to five—and Disney's were all for *Aladdin,* an animated feature. If the studio were able to acquire Miramax for a song, it would be buying an Oscar factory with a track record of prestigious movies for adults. Compared to the other studios, Disney did not have much in the way of a live action film library. The Weinsteins, on the other hand, were building one at a rapid clip for next to nothing—by studio standards.

From the Weinsteins' point of view, the advantages were overwhelming. Harvey has always denied that Miramax was in financial trouble. But, he recalls, "The handwriting was on the wall, we kept losing talent. Jim Sheridan came in and left, Steve Soderbergh said, 'Hi and good-bye.' It was hand-to-mouth, and all of a sudden we'd have these resources."

Still, it was a gamble on both sides. As McGurk puts it, "You had a situation where the whole company was on the back of these two guys, and if something happened to one of them, you were out of luck. Plus, an uncertain profit stream, where they'd never made more than $5 or $6 million in any year. How were you going to justify paying even $70 million for this company? You had to go on faith that this model that we put together would work."

Disney president Frank Wells knew that the Weinsteins had always lived day to day, and feared that once they got a big payday they would lose their edge. He said, "You're gonna pay 'em $60 million, and they're gonna retire!" Katzenberg replied, "Not these guys." Still, one of the big incentives for Disney was that Miramax operated at a reduced budget level, and Wells was also worried that it was going to be harder for the brothers to plead poverty once they were feeding at the Disney trough. Neither its staff, nor the above-the-line talent could be expected to go quietly into the night of scale and deferrals.

Then, on Friday the 1st of May, the parties gathered around the big polished wood table in the sixth-floor conference room in Michael Graves's Team Disney building, the one with the nineteen-foot-tall seven dwarfs, on the Disney lot in Burbank, to sign the deal. Wells, on his way to chair a benefit for the Martin Luther King Foundation, was wearing black tie. Bob was skittish and upset. He was worried that they were making the biggest mistake of their lives, that they would lose their autonomy. "People were calling me and saying, 'They're never gonna keep their word,' " Harvey recalls. "We were terrified." The worst-case scenario, he continues, was that, "These guys were gonna say, 'You better do this, and you better do that, and if we didn't protect ourselves, we were gonna be in trouble.'"

Bob was reading the entire fifty-odd-page agreement himself, from cover to cover. Plus a fat attachment of schedules listing every movie in their library along with the rights they did and did not have. Getting more and more agitated by the minute, he was saying, "Wait, we don't have that, how'd this get on here?" Says former Disney VP of finance Rob Moore, "Bob suddenly started to fear that it was all a setup, and that once they signed the deal, we would attack the rights schedule, say, 'Hey, you told us that you had video rights in Latin America on this movie, you don't, so we're going to have to reduce the purchase price.' " Which, one suspects, is exactly what the Weinsteins would have done were they in Disney's shoes. Bob would look at McGurk or Wells and see himself. As Moore puts it, "Most people who had dealt with Frank could count on the fact that he would ultimately do the right thing. But that just didn't ring true to them, because that's not the way *they* work. These guys do what is in *their* best interests. And that means if they have leverage to screw a million dollars out of you, that's what they're going to try and do."

Ultimately, the pluses outweighed the minuses for both parties. The deal got done, and the brothers had a glass of champagne with Wells. Each side felt it had walked away from the table a winner. Disney assumed all the company's debts, including the payables, which amounted to about $22 million, and the bank lines, another $20 million. They had agreed to pay the Weinsteins a salary of about $1.5 million a year. All told, the deal was worth over $100 million to Miramax. Moreover, the brothers got what they valued most: their autonomy. "I said to Wells, 'I know it says it, but *I* really want to *say* it,' so I wrote it out and made Frank sign it next to me," recalls Harvey. "It's written on the contract in handwriting, ten times. If we lived within a cap of $12.5 million per picture, no one had the right to tell us how many to acquire, what to produce, or how many to produce. Nobody could tell us what to do." *

---

* The $12.5 million cap was not as restrictive as it sounds, because if they had, say, $5 million in foreign presales, that would offset $5 million more from Disney and they could do a $17.5 million picture, or if they had $15 million in foreign, they could do a $27.5 million picture.

"Eisner was so concerned that they would get money and turn into crazy men, he made a very smart deal in terms of keeping them in a financial box to force them to be profitable," says Roth. To make sure that they didn't just loot Disney, take the money and run, payments to the Weinsteins were doled out, little by little, over a period of five years if they showed up at the office every day, worked hard, and were as productive as they had been in the past. A clause was inserted into the contract that stipulated that if Miramax did not meet its projections for two years in a row, Disney could abrogate its autonomy. Although Disney now owned Miramax, the Weinsteins were incentivized not as producers, which would have given them a percentage of the gross and just encouraged them to spend Disney's money creating mammoth box office, but as shareholders in the company, with an interest in growing it. They were given a phantom equity position in the value they created over time. Beyond that, Harvey and Bob had escalators, which allowed them to take home a bigger and bigger chunk of their profits the more they made, starting at 15 percent of the company's pretax profits that exceeded the $10 million a year projection contained in their business plan. Disney didn't charge Miramax for operating capital, and there was no cap on the amount it could borrow from Disney to finance its operations. Disney wanted to take out life insurance policies on both brothers, but they had a hard time finding a carrier willing to write them. Bob got upset because Harvey's policy was larger.

By selling themselves to Disney, the Weinsteins laid the groundwork for the phenomenal success to come, but they would be haunted by their decision not to go public and build the value of the company, which in turn would fan the flames of animosity that consumed their relationship with their corporate parent. Says Schmidt, "What they do so well, scaling the next mountain that's in front of them in terms of the film release, would work well inside the Disney machine, but it never resulted in them creating that big company that would perhaps have enabled them to split $100 or $200 million between the two of them, instead of $60 million." The brothers would always feel cheated.

Indeed, when Miramax accepted Disney's hand in matrimony, it was clear the match was one of convenience, not affection, and most observers, dumbfounded, predicted it would end in a messy divorce. After all, Disney stood for everything the Weinsteins hated, or claimed they hated. Harvey said things like, "Michael Eisner can't make me do anything," a sentiment that was at once heartfelt and calculated, intended to reassure his constituents that he was still in the Miramax business. For its part, what would Uncle Walt have made of The Cook, the Thief, His Wife, and Her Lover, or Paris Is Burning? Or, for that matter, Reservoir Dogs? On the face of it, it would be hard to imagine two companies more ill-suited than the white-bread, wholesome, Burbank home of Mickey and Donald, and the two guys from Queens with their ragtag, anything-goes company in Tribeca. As a Disney executive put it, "When you see Bob or Harvey in L.A., it's like *Where's Waldo* in reverse: They are all you can see. . . . They seem like aliens from another dimension."

Now that Miramax was on its way to becoming a producer as well as an acquirer and distributor, the biggest question mark was whether the Weinsteins would be as skillful developing, shooting, and editing their own films as they had been acquiring those of others, which is to say, it's much easier to recognize in a finished film elements that can be exploited for an effective marketing campaign than it is to develop an idea from scratch and successfully see it through production. Not to put too fine a point on it, none of the films Miramax had produced up to that point had been any good.

While the Weinsteins were negotiating with Disney, Harvey was acquiring Jane Campion's *The Piano,* starring Harvey Keitel and Holly Hunter. Ptak was handling the sale of North American rights. He set up a screening in L.A. for all the distributors, but Jean-François Fonlupt, an investment banker who had just been hired to run CiBy 2000, refused to send a print to him in Los Angeles, and instead required him to fly to Paris. After flying all night, Ptak showed up at ten in the morning on a Tuesday at the Pathé screening room, and was nonplussed to come upon Harvey pitching Miramax to Fonlupt, when Ptak had promised the distributors back in L.A. that they would all see *The Piano* at the same time. Harvey wasn't any happier to see Ptak, because in Fonlupt, new to the job, he figured he'd found a pigeon, and had succeeded in convincing him to sell him the movie. Fonlupt asked for $3 million, and Harvey agreed to his price. During the negotiations that followed the screening, in front of nine or ten people, Weinstein promised an additional $50,000 bonus for each $500,000 of North American box office over $13.5 million, every once in a while darting a glance in the agent's direction. Ptak, who had been around the block and then some, asked him, "How many films has Miramax had that have grossed over $13.5 million in North America?" Weinstein stopped, looked him in the eye, and said, "Nine! Nope, ten! 'Cause we've got a movie out right now and I think it's going to hit the mark," and he continued his spiel. Later, during a break and away from the CiBy team, Ptak said, "Harvey, let me ask you a question: Why did you tell everybody that Miramax has had nine pictures that have grosssed over $13.5 million in North America?"

"Why, whaddya mean?"

"Because it's not true. You've only had three."

"You didn't tell 'em, did you?" Weinstein asked, turning pale.

"I had to, otherwise I'm lying to them too."

"Oh, no, this whole thing's gonna blow up—John, why'd you tell 'em?"

"What I told 'em was this was just an example of your creative enthusiasm, how much you wanted this movie." Weinstein threw his arms around Ptak, gave him a hug, and Miramax got the film. Ptak returned to Los Angeles to tell the other distributors that *The Piano* was off the table. He says, "Everyone was furious with me, but it was a real compliment to Harvey."

Soon after the deal was concluded, the Weinsteins took *The Piano* to Cannes, where it and another Miramax film, Chen Kaige's *Farewell My Concubine*, shared the Palme d'Or. In mid-November 1993, Miramax released *The Piano*, to rave reviews. It went on to gross an astonishing $40 million in the U.S. alone.

Like *Cinema Paradiso, Farewell My Concubine* was long. The version that won the Palme d'Or was just twelve minutes shy of three hours. Harvey took out his shears and lopped off ten minutes. Once again, there were howls of outrage—Harvey Scissorhands had cut up a film that had earned the international film world's most prestigious prize. Louis Malle, head of the Cannes jury that year, was incensed. He went so far as to challenge Miramax's claim, in its print ads, that *Concubine had* won the Palme d'Or. He said, "The film we admired so much in Cannes is not the film seen in this country, which is twenty minutes shorter—but it seems longer, because it doesn't make any sense. It was better before those guys made cuts." Still, the film grossed $5 million. The Weinsteins would get ten Oscar nominations that year, eight for *The Piano* and two for *Concubine*. And it would only get better.

Five
He's Gotta Have It
1993–1994

- **How Miramax knocked Bernardo Bertolucci on his ass, while indies like *Clerks* and *Spanking the Monkey* had their last hurrah, and Quentin Tarantino wowed Cannes with *Pulp Fiction*.**

"There's a bunch of people that don't think I'm a good filmmaker, just fucking hate my guts, and they can't understand why I'm able to keep making movies. But I'm not asking for a bunch of money to put what they deem crap up on the screen so, I mean, shit, I can go on forever."

— KEVIN SMITH

Christine Vachon was back at the 1994 Sundance Festival with a small, black-and-white lesbian film called *Go Fish*, directed by Rose Troche and produced by Guinevere Turner. John Pierson, who repped and partially financed the film, sold it to Goldwyn for $450,000. The sale of *Go Fish*, while relatively unremarkable in itself, was significant, because it was the first time a commercial transaction had actually occurred while the festival was in progress, and as such it became a marker, inaugurating the era of frenzied bidding that characterized the growth of the acquisitions bubble in the mid-1990s. Good Machine's Ted Hope arrived just after *Go Fish* had been sold. "That was a big deal, there was already that whole hysteria there is today," he recalls. "It had turned totally into being about the deal. Here was a movie that was never going to have much of an audience—two people in a room talking about their problems. And yet every distributor wanted it. It changed the whole tenor of the festival." According to Mark Tusk, it was Pierson as much as anyone who created the competitive atmosphere at Sundance. "It was that *Go Fish* screening, where that mantra of have your checkbook out kicked in. He was saying, it's gonna sell, it's gonna go quick. The intention was to make sure the Harvey Weinsteins, the guys who could pull the trigger, were at the screenings, not just the scouts." The competition was fierce. Says Ray, "In the acquisition world, seeing a film first, before your competitors, before Harvey, before Tom Bernard and Michael Barker, was what everyone got up each morning striving to do." Tusk adds, "This was the period when people would say, The way to get a deal with Miramax is to tell them that Goldwyn is interested."

After the conclusion of the deal with Disney in May 1993, Miramax went into overdrive, a Beetle with a Cadillac engine. With the studio supplying high-octane fuel, the Weinsteins didn't need to be goaded by Pierson to spend money. To switch metaphors, Harvey was like a hungry man at a buffet table laden with tasty dishes. He had always had the appetite, but now he had the means to eat until he was stuffed, then more. As former Miramax executive Eamonn Bowles puts it, "When Miramax got the Disney money, they just went on a slash-and-burn acquisitions rampage. It was like mad money to them. So they just went out and bought everything in sight. If they thought other people were interested in it, they would just swoop down and take all these films off the table and away from other companies." If New Line's motto was "prudent aggression," Miramax's could well have been "imprudent aggression." Concludes Bowles, "Just to get something away from Miramax in that era was a triumph."

Gone were the days when the acquisitions people from competing companies, who all knew one another—they went to the same festivals, traveled on the same flights, stayed at the same hotels—fraternized, and, God forbid, helped one another. Says Tony Safford, "There was a great suspicion of outsiders at Miramax. Very little socializing with them, let alone exchanging information, which was forbidden." The Weinstein acquisitions team was now comprised of Safford, Tusk, Hoving, and an army of junior people. Miramax had so many troops at the festival that many of them had nothing to do but call every filmmaker, chat them up—"We loved the script, Harvey's really interested in your movie"—and find out when and where they were going to be every minute of the festival. Each one was made to feel special, as if they were within a hairsbreadth of a Miramax deal. The Miramax soldiers used every trick in the book to get first look. Rumor had it that they bribed projectionists to smuggle them prints of coveted films between screenings, suborned lab employees, sneaked into cast and crew screenings pretending to be a friend of a friend, you name it. They even surveiled their opposite numbers to find out who they were speaking to. Miramax covered every conceivable base. They had Safford going to Australia repeatedly in the course of a year, and had people in China before Chinese films were on the map. One Miramaxer had flown to Hong Kong to get an early peek at *Farewell My Concubine*. As Tusk puts it,

"Hong Kong? At that time you might go to a festival there, but for one movie?" Continues Safford, "The motto at Miramax was, 'Do anything, go anywhere to get your job done.' We literally went to work with our passports in our bags, because we never knew where we were going to be that night."

Amy Israel, who had joined the company as Hoving's assistant, recalls, "After a whole day of screenings and dinners, we'd meet at midnight and watch more films till three in the morning. We'd watch the first reel, the third reel, the sixth reel. Usually Harvey picked up what his mother liked. Like *Passion Fish* was his mother."

But it wasn't just ego and appetite that motivated Miramax. There was a method to the madness. As Chris McGurk explains it, "Miramax could afford to pay $1 million or $2 million more for everything simply because they had all the Disney TV and video deals backing them up. So they bought everything, forty, fifty, sixty films, and nobody could touch 'em. The thing was to release as many films as you possibly could. Most of them lost money, a few broke even, and the one or two that broke out of the pack generated huge amounts of profit. Control the market, own more titles than anybody else, have an economic formula that they can't match, and you'll rule the world. It was great. It was the best of times."

Harvey understood the law of large numbers. His films were so inexpensive that he could afford to open three or four putative Oscar contenders in the late fall, wait and see which pulled ahead of the pack, and then throw his formidable marketing and publicity resources behind it, as he did with *The Crying Game*. Releasing more films than all the other indie distributors combined enabled Miramax to shut the competition out of theaters. Jack Foley came over from MGM later that year to succeed Marty Zeidman as VP of distribution. "My attitude was, we had forty movies a year, almost a movie a week, we were General Motors, we were going to dominate, and we did," he explains. The whole point was to eliminate the opportunity of the competitors to gain access to screens, so they couldn't do business. "Let's say a theater was making $5 million a year. Miramax was worth maybe 50 percent of that gross. So I could make threats like, Look, we made your theater, you owe us, give it to us! If you don't, you'll never see another Miramax sprocket hole again. It was always bullying and taunting and jiving and goading and pressing and molesting. If I could sustain a formidable, voluminous presence in the marketplace, then somebody else was gonna have a tough time getting theaters. Or, if they were gonna get in anyway, I could push them back, so that they had to wait seven weeks to open up a movie. So they lost momentum. Timing is everything. If they didn't get their openings, they wouldn't gross, and they'd be in trouble."

Paying most and buying more, Miramax was fast becoming the first stop for agents and producers' reps—unless they'd had a bad experience with the Weinsteins and had a good reason to avoid them, and even then they came back. Miramax was used to getting first look and other kinds of special treatment. If Harvey couldn't make a festival or a screening, he would want a print, or at the very least a tape, shipped to wherever he was, and usually the sellers were more than willing to accommodate him. In addition to the opportunity to make a first, or preemptive bid, he wanted to be able to make the last bid, to match or better anyone else.

The deep pockets consequent on the Disney sale, coming on top of the success of *The Crying Game*, and then *The Piano*, lent the troops a new swagger, a sense of entitlement. They were always trying to get that little extra bit of edge, push the envelope for Harvey. If they didn't get what they wanted, they would wheedle and bully, themselves become mini-Harveys. Typically, the seller would be told, "Harvey has to see it." Harvey would look at it, and word would come back, "Harvey thinks he'd rather wait and see. But if you're gonna sell it to somebody else, call us up, because you never know."

"No, I'm not going to call you back."

"Whaddya mean, whaddya mean?"

"If somebody else makes an offer based upon seeing the same movie, then it wouldn't be the honorable thing for me to then call you up and say, 'Hey, do you want to make an offer because somebody else made an offer?' "

"You gotta give us a shot, man, you gotta give us a shot."

"You had your shot, and if we decide to give everybody else a second shot, we'll show it to you as well."

"You can't do that. Harvey will be really fuckin' pissed off, man."

Miramax used its brawn to scare off the competition. According to video executive Larry Estes, Harvey was enthusiastic about Don Boyd's *Twenty-one* at Sundance in 1991, but, "after telling everybody else that the deal was on, they backed out." The filmmakers tried to sell it elsewhere but, "everybody was like, 'You made your bed with Miramax, sleep in it.' They acted like it was sloppy seconds." Occasions like that weren't oversights or accidents, they were policy, just business—Miramax style. In 1995, a picture called *The Young Poisoner's Handbook* played at Sundance. It was directed by a young British director, Ben Ross, and financed by Pandora, a company run by Ernst Goldschmidt. The film played at the Prospector Square. According to Mark Urman, who had been hired to represent the movie, "The Miramax people went nuts for it." Harvey orchestrated his arrival at the theater for the moment Ross emerged. Says Urman, who was there, "He threw his arms around Ben and said, 'Nobody gets near this guy.' Ben was summoned to go meet with Harvey and it was, 'They're buying the movie, they're buying the movie!' The festival ended, they hadn't bought it yet, but they're talking, they're talking, they toyed with it, they flirted with it, they sent out every possible signal that they were picking it up, they made it impossible for anybody else to get near it, and then they didn't do it. Which made it damaged goods. People moved on and didn't even realize it hadn't been picked up. It was too late to recover. Miramax always had its eyes open, like—who else is interested? At a certain point they would realize, nobody else is interested, maybe they shouldn't be interested either, and then they would walk away." In the great scheme of things, behavior like this may not seem that outrageous—after all, what's one film more or less in a crowded marketplace—but can have a devastating effect on the careers of young directors. Ross went on to win an Emmy, but features? Forget it. (Miramax denies it promised to buy his film, and maintains that the uninterest of other buyers confirms its judgement.)

The other distributors were not amused by Harvey's game of keep away. Sony Classics, October, Fine Line, Goldwyn—they hated Miramax and maligned the Weinsteins at every opportunity. Bingham Ray nearly came to blows with Harvey one year at Cannes. With typical bravado, Harvey laughed it all off. There's a "scene in *The Good, the Bad, and the Ugly* when the three banditos burst in on Eli Wallach and he's in the tub," Harvey told journalist David Carr, misremembering. (There's only one gunslinger.) "So just imagine, Michael Barker, Tom Bernard, and Ismail Merchant, the three of them, they walk in and they see Eli Wallach and he's playing Tuco, he's the Ugly. And they go, 'Tuco, you bastard,' in dubbed Italian. 'You shot up this guy, you got our gold, you have to die.' And then they reach for their guns, but he comes out of the bathwater with the gun and he shoots all three of them and says, 'When you talk, you talk, when you shoot, you shoot.' These guys are busy talking like old ladies about 'What is Harvey going to do? What is he going to do?' While they are talking, I am shooting."

As the competition geared up to respond, it set off a veritable arms race. Says Bowles, who was then with Goldwyn, Harvey's strategy "worked. It really dried up the opposition. If they weren't generating their own projects, there was almost nothing left for them to pick up." Companies like October, which didn't have money for production, were most vulnerable. Bowles continues, "Because all the product had been taken away from them, the other distributors beefed up their acquisition teams, and made all sorts of preemptive strikes, doing deals without seeing the films, putting up big money, in many cases with disastrous results." Besides driving up prices, this stampede had dire long-term effects. In a culture of caution, Harvey's edge was speed, decisiveness, and appetite for risk—he was so reckless that he became known for being "risk perverse." Acquisitions were getting so expensive that if a distributor got in at the script stage, it was both guaranteed and less expensive. In the old days, before Miramax upped the ante, the distinction between acquisitions and production was clear. But with companies going in earlier and earlier, the line between the two was becoming blurred. Acquisitions gave way to pre-buying, which gave way to production. Outside of a few big-ticket acquisitions, production is generally more costly, and these companies had to take measures to protect themselves. Says New Line's Janet Grillo, "As the risks became greater, we had to be more conservative, and that's when I started to see the death of independent film. The heartbreak was that it became harder and harder for films that were more personal or poetic. It no longer made business sense. Unless you had a tremendous cast behind you that was going to give you collateral." Indeed, indie distributors adopted the studio practice of hedging their bets with stars. Observes Ethan Hawke, who got his big break in 1988 with *Dead Poets Society*, "One of the things that's completely changed since I started acting is that almost 100 percent of film financing is cast-contingent. In those days, a director would get a go movie and then he would cast it. Now, you can't get a go movie *until* you cast it. It's not who's right for the part, it's who's right for the money. Miramax really started that."

But it wasn't just Miramax. David O. Russell's audacious and scandalous first film, *Spanking the Monkey*, a mother-son incest drama, which played in competition at Sundance in 1994, was a case in point. New Line's Bob Shaye liked the script and optioned it, but wouldn't make it without a major female star. Recalls Russell, "Shaye said, 'If you can get Faye Dunaway, I'll do it.' I went to her house, and she laughed in my face." The role was considered a career buster, and not a single actress would touch it. New Line let its option lapse.

Out of college, Russell had worked as a political organizer, and made a documentary about Central American immigrants living in Boston. "I felt like I'd missed out on the Vietnam War and the civil rights movement," he says. "Then I found myself the lone activist in the Reagan '80s and chicks weren't interested the way they were in the '70s. They were with the bankers and brokers. And I was in Maine organizing mill workers! On $6,000 a year. It was like, 'What happened?' " So he took a $40,000 NEA grant he had gotten, some donated 35mm film, and made the picture in Pawling, New York, using his college roommate's mother's connections. (He never told her what the film was about.) Russell edited the film on his dining room table. It cost $80,000 to get in the can, $150,000 more from an investor to finish, about $250,000 in all.

After *The Miracle*, Neil Jordan's incest film, "Harvey was like, 'No more incest movies for me!' " continues Russell. "It's not exactly box office fodder, and he was going in the direction of *Shakespeare in Love*. He didn't want anything to do with it at Sundance." In fact, Russell felt like a pariah there. "I made a movie that said, 'I hate my mother,' which is considered a heresy, certainly at Sundance at that time. A lot of people regarded me as a dirtbag. People in this country are so sanctimonious about the family. Harvey named his fucking company after his parents. He sentimentalizes them. But emotionally criminal things happen there, and why lie about them?" But *Spanking the Monkey* won the Audience Prize at Sundance, and was picked up by Ira Deutchman at Fine Line for $250,000. It grossed about $1.5 million.

Harvey hadn't been to Sundance in a while, and Miramax watchers interpreted his appearance in 1994 as a signal that he was still committed to indie films even after the Disney deal. *Go Fish* was bookended by its straight, male-bonding counterpart, another small, black-and-white film also repped by Pierson, called *Clerks*, directed by Kevin Smith. Harvey was so annoyed that *Go Fish* had gotten away, he told Pierson not to bother him about *Clerks*, give that to Goldwyn too. But Tusk was hocking Harvey about it, and Tusk had been right before.

Smith, short and broad—a fullback in a bottle—was a kid from a self-described working-class background in Red Bank, New Jersey. His father was a postal clerk. Smith shot the film in and around the Leonardo Quick Stop, a convenience store where he worked. Down and dirty, in ragged black and white with nonactor friends, *Clerks* exploded with testosterone-drenched trash-talk bent raunchily askew by Smith's twisted, adolescent sense of humor. Reviewing it in the *New York Daily News*, Dave Kehr nicely described it as Howard Stern crossed with David Mamet. Smith's I-can-do-that film was Rick Linklater's *Slacker*, which he saw at the Angelika multiplex on the corner of Mercer and Houston in New York in 1991, on his twenty-first birthday. "Seeing that movie was very empowering," Smith recalls. He thought, Wow, this counts as a movie? Nothing's really happening, just people walking around, no plot, just a lot of dialogue. Shit, if this motherfucker is making a movie in Austin, Texas, and I'm sitting here watching it in New York and enjoying it, why the hell aren't I making a movie in Jersey? I can fuckin' do this!

Like *Go Fish*, *Clerks* was the very definition of an indie film, the kind of shoestring production that comes out of nowhere with no sigificant money behind it, lacks stars, production value, finesse, and a video deal. It was the kind of film that was easy to overlook in the cascade of increasingly glossy indie product. But *Clerks* had what Sundance's programmatically regional films often lacked—a real, felt sense of place. It was clear these guys had never been out of Red Bank. And it was instantly evident that the film was the product of a wickedly inventive talent with a fresh and original perspective that had been successfully—and a bit miraculously—translated onto celluloid.

Clerks first screened at New York's Independent Feature Market in late

September 1993. Tusk, whose job it was to hang out at the Angelika, where the market was held, schmooze filmmakers, and see as many pictures as he could, had run into Smith's producer, Scott Mosier. The Disney deal had gone down. Mosier looked at Tusk's ID tag, and said, "This is not a Disney movie." Tusk was hearing his worst fears made real. He thought, Do they think that I'm working for Disney? He had championed *Paris Is Burning*, and he worried that he would be unable to acquire those kinds of films in the future. Tusk recalls, "The perception was that Miramax and Disney were oil and water. It was, Oh my God, are you guys not going to be allowed to screen certain things? Are our hands going to be tied?" This wasn't an idle question. Harvey had picked up a raunchy Martin Lawrence concert film called *You So Crazy*. It got an NC-17, and Disney made Miramax sell it—to archrival Goldwyn no less, which opened it unrated. Harvey was furious. "I lost all of Martin Lawrence's business, which would have been very fruitful over the years," he says. "He loved the company, and then didn't want to talk to me. That's when I said, 'We have to find another way.' "

Clerks was screening on Sunday morning. Virtually nobody showed up, except for a woman who collared Smith, said, "That's a really hateful little film you made."

"Yeah, thanks."

"I've got a theory that all the Nazis that died were reincarnated, they live in New Jersey. Your film proves it."

"Yeah, I hadn't thought of that theory."

Then she gave him her head shot. "The next day I was real depressed," Smith continues, "because it seemed like everything we'd worked for was a bust." But somebody suggested he enter his film in Sundance. Like many other filmmakers, Smith thought of Sundance as the *sex, lies* festival, and to him *sex, lies* was a real movie, slick, full of stars or near stars, beautiful women and lots of production value. "We never even thought about Sundance," he says. "That was not a festival that we were meant for." But, to his surprise, he was accepted. He was still working at the Quick Stop where *Clerks* was shot. "I was standing behind the counter, and I wanted to tell everybody who came in, but nobody knew what the fuck Sundance was, so it was wasted information." Smith hired Pierson to rep the film. "Pierson took us around to the five families," he continues. "We handed the tape to Sony, Fine Line, October, Goldwyn, and Miramax." Tusk recalls screening it at the Tribeca Film Center. Harvey passed. Smith was deflated. "Miramax was the premier indie label, the A Team," he explains. "This is where you wanted to be. But we figured we were dead at Miramax. The chairman didn't watch it. By the time we got to Sundance, everybody had passed."

Nor did Smith have high expectations from the festival. Pierson was ignoring them, focused on selling *Go Fish*. But audiences seemed to like

Clerks. The question-and-answer sessions after the screenings were full of energy. They loved the story about the filmmakers sleeping on the floor of the Quick Stop while they were shooting the film. They laughed out loud when Smith recounted how he'd lied to get discounted film stock from Kodak, saying he was in film school and then actually having to enroll in a course at the New School to get a student card. The buzz started to build. Tusk promised Smith he'd bring Harvey to the last screening. He buttonholed his boss, said, "I'm amazed that nobody else bought this movie. You're gonna sit down and you're gonna watch this movie with an audience."

"No way."

"Harve, way!" For a while it seemed like the Miramax co-chairman wasn't going to show up, because he had been attacked by a disgruntled screenwriter at a party and was rumored to have left town. But come Friday night, there was Harvey, puffing on a cigarette and gasping for lungfuls of the thin Park City air as he struggled up Main Street toward the Egyptian at the top of the hill.

The movie had barely started and already Harvey was getting fidgety. The acquisitions people had tricks for keeping him in his seat. He liked to sit on the aisle, so he could make a quick exit, but they wedged him in the middle, between Tusk and Hoving. He loved his chocolate-covered almonds, from Bazzini, that came in large cans. He'd pass them around, but they were warm and sticky by that time and no one could stand to touch them, much less eat them, so they would drop them on the floor under cover of darkness. He could eat his way through two cans, but on this occasion, there weren't any. Tusk told him, "Remember, think thirty-seven, you gotta stay until the number thirty-seven crops up, the blowjob stuff." (He was referring to a highly entertaining spat between one of the characters and his girlfriend over how many guys she'd had sex with.) That got Harvey's attention. Smith, standing in the back, heard one guy guffawing like a madman. He thought, Who's the incredibly rude fuckin' dude who's laughing like Max Cady in *Cape Fear*? Of course, it was Harvey. When it was over, Tusk introduced the director to his boss. Weinstein exploded, "Great fuckin' movie, I want to put a fuckin' soundtrack on it, and put it in the fuckin' multiplexes." Smith thought, Fuck, yeah. He replied, "Mr. Weinstein, it's an honor to meet you, I'm in awe of the movies that you've worked with, and I've seen this movie with an audience now four times, I've been taking notes, and I know the ten or twelve minutes that I would welcome the chance to take out." Intentionally or not, Smith was playing him like a fiddle. He says, "We'd read a lot about Harvey Scissorhands, but when you're trying to get your movie picked up, you don't give a fuck! If somebody wanted to cut it up, as Quentin says, like a kid cutting out paper dolls, it was, 'Here, take it, I don't care, go ahead!'"

Weinstein, Tusk, and David Linde herded Smith, Mosier, and Pierson over to the Eating Establishment across the street. They passed the October gang, Ray and Lipsky. Pierson asked Ray and Lipsky to speak now or forever hold their peace. They weren't interested. Harvey continued to lavish praise on the picture. "We dug on Harvey immediately, because he's a true vulgarian," recalls Smith. "I didn't know whether he was putting it on to talk to us or if that was him. Later on, I learned, that's him. He's just got potty mouth. He was smoking, like, nine cigarettes, eating fistfuls of potato skins. It was, 'This dude's in charge of the company? This is phenomenal.' " Pierson pulled them aside, said, "Their offer's not huge, but you guys didn't get into this business to make money, did you?"

"No, fuck no. I'd give 'em the movie for fuckin' free, I don't give a—it's Miramax, are you nuts?"

"Great! They're offering 200, I'm gonna get 'em up to 227." *Clerks* had cost $27,000. Weinstein said, "A hundred thousand dollars of that money goes to trimming the film, remixing, kicking it up to 35mm, whatever. The rest is yours." Smith thought to himself, Sure, they liked *Clerks*, but they picked it up because they've just been bought by Disney, and everybody's asking, "What does this mean? Will we still see movies like *The Crying Game*? Will Disney allow a guy to whip out his cock on film?" Buying *Clerks* sent a very clear message. "We're still Miramax, 'cause we picked up a grubby-looking black-and-white indie with a foul, foul fuckin' mouth." Someone produced a bottle of champagne. As Smith and Mosier left the restaurant, one said to the other, "Man, did you ever think we'd be able to pay the deferments? That's so cool." They went to the Miramax condo to party.

Jim Jacks, the producer at Universal who, along with his partner Sean Daniel, had financed Linklater's third film, *Dazed and Confused*, buttonholed Smith at the closing Sundance party. Jacks said, "Miramax bought your movie? That's a shame, because I would have liked to have taken it for Universal, and remade it." Says Smith, "I had no interest in remaking the movie, and I didn't want to make studio movies. *Clerks* never could have been made through a studio system. What they like is simple stories about overcoming adversity. But in *Clerks* it's a couple guys at work in a convenience store, hate their jobs, and by the end of the movie, they're still working there, and they still hate their jobs. Like, nobody overcomes anything, really. I wanted to be an independent filmmaker. I wanted to work at Miramax. In those days it was still, 'We *are* independent film.' "

Ironically, 1994 was probably the last year for genuine indies like *Clerks*, *Go Fish*, and *Spanking the Monkey*. The future lay with films like *Four Weddings and a Funeral*, which was distributed by Gramercy and went on to gross $53 million. Says Vachon, "You'd never be able to sell *Go Fish* now.

That was a genuine low-budget garage film. People's expectations for that kind of movie have really shifted. When they go to see a so-called independent film they want to see *Shakespeare in Love,* they don't want to see something that is really challenging, that's in black and white, where the sound is difficult to make out." Adds Hope, "No matter how grounded somebody is, once you have one Kevin Smith or Rose Troche instantly launched into a career and wealth, the expectation that this could happen to you—which is ironic because that is the title of a movie about hitting the lottery—is inescapable. Whereas once it was, 'Man, we just need to get our movie screened,' it became, 'Now's the time to make big score. To get what's ours.' "

Liz Manne, who was then head of marketing at Fine Line, noticed the change as well. "It felt like movies were being made for the wrong reasons. It was the independent-director-as-rock-star syndrome. These people were getting their auteur stripes based on one film. And it was no longer Andrew Sarris writing about them, it was some dipshit on E! sticking a microphone in the face of somebody in front of the Egyptian who's never seen a Bernardo Bertolucci film in his life, and would not know Antonioni if he bit him in the ass. It became a mockery."

THE SUCCESS OF the festival raised Geoff Gilmore's profile within the institute, cloaked him and his staff with an aura of untouchability, breeding envy and resentment among the other programs. On the other hand, the festival staff regarded the institute's other programs as parasites, siphoning off cash that it generated. As Cathy Schulman puts it, "The attendance was huge, and growing by leaps and bounds every year, and we would add up how many people bought tickets at these extraordinary prices, and we'd go, 'Where's all the money going?' There were rumors that it was being funneled into the failing ventures, like the resort."

The festival had become a double-edged sword. On the one hand, it became a sorely needed and extremely welcome profit center for the hard-pressed institute. "That '94 festival was a turning point in terms of getting more solvent and a bigger budget from Sundance," says Gilmore. "It was the first year we hard-bound our catalogue. Sundance was being written about as a national institution, and was being regarded by people inside the industry as playing an important role in setting the agenda for the independent universe. Even if they weren't buying the films, people came to the festival trying to figure out ways for young directors and young actors to cross over. All of a sudden those lines that had separated the industry from the independents a couple of years earlier blurred dramatically. The agents facilitated that. Robert Newman would bring Robert Rodriguez over to Columbia." Gilmore applauds the very thing—the erosion of the barriers between indies and the industry—that makes purer souls cringe. And indeed, the market element, dangerous as it was, did give filmmakers an unprecedented opportunity to sell their films for real money. If their distributors, Miramax and Goldwyn, were able to drive them into profit, so much the better.

On the other hand, everything Redford feared when he resisted taking over the U.S. Film Festival had come to pass. Not only were filmmakers pitted against one another in the competition, but "the competition was drawing Hollywood," says Schulman. "They liked to know that somebody was saying something's best." Gary Beer, whose job it was to raise money, favored the competition for the same reason Schulman opposed it. His goal was to grow Sundance, and at every opportunity, he screamed the word "branding." Worse, the market was cannibalizing the festival. Quality was being quantified—measured in dollars—and so desperate was the institute for money, that almost every nook and cranny of Park City had been sold off to the highest bidder—automobile companies, studios, magazines, vineyards et al. You couldn't walk three feet down Main Street without a goody bag being thrust into your hands filled with branded T-shirts, mugs, caps, maybe a CD or two, in fact, everything but Sundance gear itself—the sweatshirts, parkas, hats, pre- and après-skiwear that were sold in special kiosks at huge markups. The year before had seen corporate logos thrown on the screen at the end of the Sundance trailer for the first time. As former Sundance programmer Lory Smith puts it, "Gary Beer was really successful at attracting corporate sponsorship to the festival. Now you've got Mercedes-Benz and Hugo Boss and Piper-Heidsieck supporting independents. Yet on some level, it's almost like the heart and soul has gotten bled out of the organization. It's turned into this juggernaut." So many sponsors and underwriters had to be accommodated at the awards ceremony that there was no room for the filmmakers who had directed the shorts, some of whom would presumably return with features. Pierson, tired and disillusioned, stopped repping films after that year's festival, and the job would increasingly fall to agents and lawyers. Alexander Payne, who would attend the next year with *Citizen Ruth*, observes, "You have independent films at Sundance whose message is, Hire me, I want to be a commercial director, I want an agent and I want to come to Hollywood." Or, as Bingham Ray puts it, more succinctly, it became "a zoo, a circus, a pain in the fucking ass."

Even if the market aspect of Sundance has been good for filmmakers, it was not an unmixed blessing. As indie veteran, attorney Linda Lichter puts it, "In the beginning, there was a counterculture that supported an alternative point of view, either politically or artistically. That world is gone. Now, basically, it's about making it. At Sundance, the bulk of the pictures are about losing your virginity. It's babies making movies about babies. With some exceptions, the filmmakers don't really have a voice yet, and the place is so overpowering that they get eaten, chewed up, and spit out."

If, in 1994, Sundance was on a knife edge, and it was possible to argue about whether *Clerks, Go Fish,* and *Spanking the Monkey* represented the end of the old or the beginning of the new, Quentin Tarantino's next film would change all that, rewrite the rules of the game by making it very clear in which direction the indie movement was going.

QUENTIN TARANTINO, who had never before been outside the continental United States, had spent the better part of a year on the road, traveling around the world on the festival circuit with *Reservoir Dogs.* When he made pit stops in L.A., he would stay with Roger Avary at his apartment in Manhattan Beach. Jersey Films, Danny DeVito's company, gave Tarantino a $1 million development deal. He had been offered all kinds of things, but his mind kept coming back to the never completed anthology film he and Avary had written while trying to get *True Romance* off the ground. He told Avary, "What a great idea that was, except—I want to write all of the stories."

"Great! Do it!"

"Well, can I have the story you did?"

"Sure." Avary's story, "Pandemonium Reigns," the tale of the fighter who refuses to throw a fight, eludes some gangsters while retrieving his father's gold watch, constitutes about a third of the film Tarantino eventually directed. "When we originally ventured into *Pulp Fiction,* the agreement was that we would split the writing part of the back end participation, as well as screenplay credit," says Avary. Jersey had a deal with TriStar, then headed by Mike Medavoy. TriStar had no interest in Avary, and when the studio tried to get rid of him, Tarantino fought for his friend. He also used his new heft to help Avary find financing for his own film, *Killing Zoe,* by attaching himself as executive producer.

Exhausted by his grueling world tour, Tarantino finally went to ground in Amsterdam for three months, writing. Avary, who joined him in Amsterdam, recalls, "We took 'Pandemonium Reigns,' and rewrote it, although what I wrote and what he wrote are almost indefinable. We essentially raided all of our files, and took out every great scene either of us had ever written, put them on the floor, started lining them up and putting them together. I had my computer, so I would combine them into sequences. Quentin was being financed by TriStar, but I didn't have two pennies to rub together and had to make a living, so eventually I left and went to make *Killing Zoe.*"

Tarantino picks up the story: "We could have made *Pulp Fiction* for

TriStar for $8 million, and they really couldn't lose on the film, but they would have rather had me come to them with a star-driven piece of material that they could do for $25 million. I don't think they wanted to make a movie unless they thought they were going to make $100 million." TriStar looked at Tarantino and saw trouble. When he had the big meeting with the studio executives, their reaction was cool. He recalls, "They were talking about how dark and harrowing the movie was, and I went, 'Wait a minute, let me just get this straight, you didn't think it was funny?'

" 'Well, there were some funny lines in it, but—'

" 'A lot of it's really funny, guys, it's gonna be really funny, trust me.'

" 'Well, Quentin, uh, you're telling me it's funny, but I see a guy sticking a needle in his arm, and I don't think anyone's gonna laugh.' " According to Rick Hess, then a junior executive there, Medavoy thought it was "too demented."

Tarantino continues, "The worst-case scenario was, they weren't into it, didn't understand it, but were going, 'Well, we can't really lose money on it, and we don't want to be the idiots that pass on his second film,' so they'd make it anyway. I was prepared that if I got that vibe from them, to ask them not to make the movie. I'd say, 'Look, let me go and make it somewhere else. I want the marriage to be right.' So I told them, "We need you to say yes or no, right now, if we're going to get it done in time to show it at the Cannes Film Festival.' They thought about it and then they said no."

Medavoy put *Pulp* in turnaround.* Before going out with it, Tarantino's producer, Lawrence Bender, gave it to Richard Gladstein, whom Harvey had hired as head of production. Gladstein read it, and passed it along to his boss, who was in L.A. about to hop on the plane back to New York. It was 160 pages long, and Harvey gave him a look that said, What the fuck is this? This is not a script, it's a phone book. Gladstein exclaimed, "Please, just read it, it's Quentin's new script."

"Is it good?"

"It's great."

"You think we should do it?"

"I think we should do it."

"I have to read this on the plane tonight?"

"You have to read it on the plane tonight because we have a little window of opportunity before everyone else. It's not a big window, but it's a leg up. So let's have the leg up."

Three hours later, Weinstein called Gladstein. He had read the first

---

* "Turnaround": When a studio decides not to produce a project and instead sells it.

twenty pages, he said, "Ohmigod, this is brilliant. The opening of this is unbelievable. Does it stay this good?"

"It stays this good."

"Okay, don't leave the office, I'm gonna keep reading." Forty-five minutes later, he called back, and said, "The main character just died."

"Right."

"What happens in the end?"

"Harvey, just keep reading."

"Richard, is it a happy ending?"

"Yes."

"Ohmigod! He comes back, doesn't he? I'll call you back." When he in fact called back a half hour later, he exclaimed, "Fuck it. We have to make this movie. It's unbelievable. Buy the script, I'm making the movie."

Weinstein couldn't believe his good luck. "As opposed to many other people in this town, the Weinsteins trust their own opinion, work on a gut level," says Tarantino. "Harvey is like reading it on an airplane and halfway through, before he's even finished, he calls up and says, 'Make the deal. We've got to get this.' You can't argue with that kind of enthusiasm."

Compared to *The Piano* and *The Crying Game*, *Pulp* wasn't that risky. As Hess puts it, "Everyone had said, 'Goddamn, *I* wouldn't have bought a movie where the chick doesn't talk the whole damn movie, hats off to Harvey and Bob. I wouldn't have bought a movie where the guy shows his weenie in the third act, hats off to Harvey and Bob. *Pulp Fiction* was different. Yes, it had an unusual timeline, totally nonlinear in every way, but it had sex and drugs and rock 'n' roll, and violence, and that's something every studio would have [gone for]."

To bring in his pictures at a fraction of what a studio would spend to do the same films, Harvey had to convince actors to cut their rates. Everyone knew that indies were labors of love, and his attitude was, I'm doing God's work, and stars ought to defer, work for scale, and/or share the risk, taking percentages of the back end, the way they did for Woody Allen and Robert Altman. Before the sale to Disney, he couldn't afford not to. After the sale, when it became evident that Miramax was no longer really independent and could afford A-list prices, the fiction that it was independent became all the more important, a necessary shield to deflect the scrutiny of agents and unions. Hence, as Smith suspected, the acquisition of a film like *Clerks*. Agents, in particular, hated the Miramax co-chairman for talking actors into cutting their prices. "Harvey's always wanted to own a talent agency, as a way by which he could control talent and talent prices," says Safford. "I've been in meetings with him at agencies where he made the ugliest kinds of threats, saying he was going to start his own agency and walk out with half their clients." But the agents kept coming to the table.

Explains former marketing VP Marcy Granata, "Harvey's power base is the talent. They will do anything for him. Hollywood may resent the deals he strikes, but nevertheless, a major star or director or writer has put them at that table based on their loyalty to Harvey. A lot of talent, especially the young talent, has to adapt their personas to Hollywood's standards, and feel suffocated by it. So here's a guy they don't have to feel suffocated by. They don't have to act through an evening with Harvey, they can just be themselves."

Fortunately, Tarantino was so hot, and his script so cool, that actors were lining up around the block to work for scale. Underlining the affinity between the two men and their companies, the *Pulp* cast was shaping up to be a Katzenberg special: stars-in-trouble who needed career makeovers, like John Travolta and Bruce Willis; character actors, like Harvey Keitel and Samuel L. Jackson; barely proven up-and-comers, like Uma Thurman, and indie stalwarts like Amanda Plummer and Eric Stoltz. Tarantino rejected Daniel Day-Lewis for the role Travolta played, and Meg Ryan and Holly Hunter for the part that Thurman took, holding the budget down to a mere $8.5 million. Willis was coming off a series of big studio–busters like *Hudson Hawk* and *The Last Boy Scout*, and nonstarters like *Striking Distance*, but he was still a box office draw overseas, and on the basis of his name alone, Miramax sold worldwide rights for $11 million, putting itself in the black before Tarantino had a chance to yell, "Action!" As an index of how fast the indie world was changing, agent Cassian Elwes says that William Morris "packaged" *Pulp Fiction*. Morris clients included Tarantino, Avary, Willis, Travolta, Keitel, and Ving Rhames.

When he was going into production on *Pulp*, just into 1994, Avary was at the lab, CFI, supervising the color timing on his own film, *Killing Zoe*, when he was called to the phone. It was Tarantino's attorney, "frantic," according to Avary. He was faxing over a rider to Avary's *Pulp Fiction* contract according to which Avary gave up his co-screenwriting credit in exchange for "story by" credit. He wanted Avary to sign it and fax it back immediately. Avary called his friend and with a note of disbelief in his voice, said, "Hold on a moment here, Quentin. You want me to sign a paper that essentially says that I'm forfeiting my writing credit on the film, and take a 'story by' credit?" According to him, Tarantino replied, "Well, yeah, I want the credits to end with a title that says, 'Written and directed by Quentin Tarantino.'" The reason for that, says Avary now, was that "when you're positioning yourself to become a media star, you don't want people to be confused as to who the star is."

According to Avary, Tarantino tried to persuade him that this was a good deal, saying, "Yeah, but look, you'll get 'story by,' you and me, and the writing's for me, but the fact of the matter is, that middle story is yours, but this one attributes the whole story to you. That sounds really good." Avary thought to himself, He's very convincing. It's just like the time when he persuaded me to keep that picture of me in the gay section of Video Archives, recommending movies. But there are all sorts of things peppered throughout *Pulp Fiction* that are mine. Avary replied, "No, I'm not going to sign it." At that, Avary claims, "Quentin flew into a rage." He yelled, "Okay, fine, I'm gonna rewrite the script, and write all of your contributions out of the screenplay, and you're going to get nothing." Avary was not a member of the Writers Guild, and Tarantino promised him the equivalent of Writers Guild residuals, and an adjustment of the back end participation in his favor. Avary had just put everything he had into *Killing Zoe*, was facing credit card debts totaling $10,000, and was behind on rent. He thought it over, said okay. He signed the document, faxed it back, and took the money.

"I bought my house off that film, so I'm not complaining, but that was the moment when the fissure occurred in our relationship. I resented the fact that the call came first from his attorney instead of from him. The way Quentin suddenly attacked me was more startling to me than what he was fighting for, the credit. It was like an assault. For me, that was the moment when the fun of being two young guys coming up together, and writing for each other, completely vanished. I love Quentin, but things were never really the same between us after that. In that moment I realized that the '90s were no different from the '80s or the '70s. This business has a way of taking friendship and love and passion and excitement for just creating, taking that idealism, and just shattering it. What I want is for it to be the way that it was, and it's not money that would make it the way it was, it's just that I miss making movies for the love of making movies. And I just miss Quentin."

Counters Tarantino, "The things that Roger thinks are betrayal are just the natural way that things change. I had said, 'Let me buy 'Pandemonium Reigns,' I'll do a first pass, incorporate it into my material, and then you can come in, and we can do another pass on it. Well, that second pass never happened, because I pretty much did it all in the first pass. There was no reason to bring him in anymore. 'Pandemonium Reigns' could never have been produced. I just liked the basic idea of it, and a couple of incidents, and threw the rest away."

The Weinsteins were so infatuated with Tarantino or so convinced that *Pulp* was going to be a hit that they allowed him to flout what had become the First Rule of Miramax: "Thou Shalt Obey the Cards." * Says Taran-

* "Cards": Movies are routinely test screened for audiences, who check boxes on preview cards. The top two boxes are most important: excellent or very good, and are distilled into a numerical score. Such screenings often include focus group sessions.

tino, "It was a big, big thing when we made this deal, a make-or-break point, that I would not allow cards or focus groups or questionnaires. Basically, when I showed the movie to them, it was like, 'This is how it is.' When you hand out these stupid cards, and they say, 'What scenes did you like the most? What scenes did you like the least? Fill in the fucking blank.' You ask any director on the fucking planet who watches a movie with an audience and he knows where it's slow, where it's not funny, where they're confused. I'm not gearing it toward their opinions, anyway. I don't give a fuck what Mr. Hockenmayer thinks. I want to know what he feels!"

Harvey was a big believer in the publicity value of face time: personal appearances, interviews, what-have-you, and he exploited the potential Tarantino had exhibited at Cannes two years before. As director Alexandre Rockwell put it, "Quentin was born to be a celebrity." The protocol for a sneak preview is for the director to arrive after the film has started and lurk in the back or the lobby so as not to prejudice the audience. But Tarantino couldn't contain himself; he loved nothing more than stunning an audience of rubes in Nowheresville, Iowa, by appearing unannounced and putting on a show.

There was a screening in Portland, Oregon, at a sizable theater. The *Pulp* gang arrived, and was told that a theater functionary was going to introduce the movie. Tarantino said, "I don't want this fuckin' asshole to do that, I'm going to do it myself." Gladstein objected: "No, Quentin, you can't go in there and introduce the movie."

"Whaddya mean I can't?"

"Quentin, if you introduce the movie, you're gonna get this whole drama going, and you're not gonna get a real reaction."

"Richard, you mean, if I go in and introduce it, they might *like* it a little bit more? God forbid that were to happen!"

"We're already not doing cards—don't you want to see what they really think?"

Bob, who was watching them argue, broke in, said, "Fuck it, Quentin— you want to do it? Do it." Tarantino strode down the aisle, planted himself in front of the screen like he owned the place, and announced, "Okay, I want to make sure if I got the right audience here. I want to ask you a question. How many of you have seen *Reservoir Dogs*?" A third of the house raised their hands. He said, "Good." People were starting to realize, this was the man himself, Quentin Tarantino. You could feel the excitement coming off the house like heat lightning. Pacing back and forth, he said, "Wait a minute. I have another question. How many of you people out there have, lemme see a—raise your hands, how many of you have seen *True Romance*?" Half the hands went up. The place was abuzz with whispering: "It's Quentin Tarantino!" Looking out over the audience, he said, "Oh, wow, that's really, really good. But one last question before I go, How many of you liked *Remains of the Day?*" A few people shot their hands up eagerly, thinking they were going to get a pat on the head. He went, "Get the fuck outta here!" and strode up the aisle. The whole audience broke into wild applause, cheering, and screaming. The room went dark, the crowd went silent, and *Pulp Fiction* was screened for the first time.

Before *Pulp* opened, *The Crow* gave Miramax a taste of things to come. In May, Bob's Dimension opened Alex Proyas's film starring Bruce Lee's son Brandon, who had been killed during the production by an improperly loaded stunt gun, leaving his scenes unfinished. No one would touch the film but Bob, who bought and finished it. Says Foley, "In the first weekend, it grossed $12 million. They'd never gotten that much money in months, let alone in a weekend. That was the beginning. [Dimension] broke the glass ceiling. Instead of looking up at it and wondering, What goes on up there? they found out. They love money. It was, Oh my God, isn't this wonderful. And it came in so fast it was mind-altering." *The Crow* went on to gross $51 million and put Dimension on the map.

If the Weinsteins used to go to Cannes as small-time buyers, now they were not only big-time buyers, but sellers as well. They showcased three other films besides *Pulp*—*Fresh, Picture Bride,* and *Clerks*—and brought over two dozen or so *Pulp* actors and friends, plus the Weinstein entourage. Smith and Scott Mosier, who didn't want to go, preferring to stay in Red Bank, first saw *Pulp Fiction* at a special friends and critics screening Weinstein arranged at the Olympia Theater before the premiere. The film was running two hours, forty minutes. "We were blown away, we knew we had seen something huge," recalls Smith. "*Pulp Fiction* was just effortlessly cool, a movie you had to see and tell people to go see, and felt like you were in on something seeing it. But I said to Mosier, 'It's great, but who's gonna go to see this besides the five people who saw *Reservoir Dogs?*' When Miramax said they were going to go out on a thousand screens—which at that time was unheard of for an art house film—people were giggling, 'Oh my God, they're going up against a Stallone movie too, *The Specialist.*'"

Cannes was starved for celebrities that year—the only other picture with a star was Joel and Ethan Coen's *The Hudsucker Proxy* with Paul Newman—and the fans and paparazzi went mad over the *Pulp* bunch. Tarantino was already a festival favorite, and seemed to have as much of a following as the actors. *Dogs* had played at the Utopia Theater in Paris every night for a year, and it was still running.

Pulp premiered on Saturday night late, at 12:30 A.M. Festival officials

closed down the Croisette between the Carlton, where Tarantino was staying, and the Palais, where the premiere was being held. A caravan of two
dozen or so limos containing the *Pulp* gang, Miramax folk, Jersey Films's
people, and assorted hangers-on snaked through the street. Crowds four
deep lined the sidewalks, grabbing for the cars, chanting, "Quen-tin, Quentin, Oo-mah, Oo-mah." Observed Tarantino, who notices these things,
"Out of any group there was like fifteen people there for Bruce, and nine
people there for John and four people there for me."

Once again, on award night, the *Pulp* parade made the trip to the Palais,
seated themselves in the plush seats. As the prizes were ticked off, Harvey,
seated next to Tarantino, whispered loudly, "Okay, Best Screenplay, you
think you're going to get that?" Tarantino replied, "Yeah, I'm gonna get
Screenplay." But the award went to Michel Blanc for *Grosse Fatigue*.
Tarantino was beginning to get uneasy, but he thought he had a shot at
Best Director since he was convinced Krzysztof Kieslowski's *Trois
couleurs: Rouge,* also a Miramax film, would win the Palme d'Or and he
knew that the winner of the Palme d'Or could not take both. But Nanni
Moretti took the Director's Prize for *Caro Diario.* He thought, Oh wow,
that's off the board. It's any man's game now. Finally, the only prize remaining was the Palme. Weinstein, who was hopping up and down in his
seat like a walrus on a trampoline, barked, "Oh my God, you won the Palme
d'Or. You've won the fucking Palme d'Or!"

"Harvey, shut the fuck up. No, we haven't won the Palme d'Or." Tarantino imagined there was going to be a special prize for the actors, thought,
I'm gonna have to go up and accept an award for Bruce and John and Sam.
This is the in-between award. Eyes riveted to the stage, he watched as Clint
Eastwood strolled out and announced, "The next award is the Palme d'Or,
and the winner for 1994 is *Pulp Fiction!*" Slicing through the thunderous
applause like a knife was the voice of a female member of the audience
shrieking, "Scandale!" "Fasciste!".

When Tarantino won the Palm d'Or, his old friends worried. Rockwell
tried to have a heart-to-heart with him. He said, "Believe me, they're going
to descend on you like wolves on meat." Tarantino gave him a blank look,
as if to say, "So? What's your problem?" Rockwell thought, What a
schmuck, meaning himself, because his friend's evident incomprehension
made him feel like Mr. Paranoid, New York, versus Mr. That's a Great Opportunity for Me, L.A. Doggedly he went on, explained to Tarantino how
important it was to protect his integrity, said, "You're a great filmmaker,
don't compromise your vision. It doesn't matter how many people see the
films. Just make great films."

"No, no, I can do both," he replied. "I can be the next . . ."

Rockwell recalls, "I saw his eyes glaze over when I was talking about artistic integrity. I felt, My God, the guy's gonna sell out. Look at the '70s. Really great films were made by those directors. And then all of a sudden, they aren't rebels anymore. They *are* the system. People stopped being friends, people lost their artistic vision. A lot of my energy is 'Fuck you' energy. You know, if I was accepted, who am I gonna say fuck you to? Myself? We have to be rebels. But I felt it was almost as if I was speaking a foreign language to Quentin."

Allison Anders had better luck. She called her friend when he got back. "I was really scared, the way you are with friends, you think they're gonna get away from you," she explains. "I was in tears. He was just so great. He said, 'You didn't think I would change, did you?' I said, 'Why wouldn't you?' But I think he's gonna really be fine with it. It's frustrating, 'cause you sort of want to save him, but at the same time you realize he's got his head more securely fastened on than people imagine. I remember when he first got his PAL video player, he said, 'Ya know'—and he was dead serious—'I just figure if it doesn't work out with film, I can dupe tapes for people from PAL to NTSC.' It was, 'That's great, baby, I'm glad you got a backup plan.' "

KEVIN SMITH'S TINY FILM *Clerks* exploded out of Sundance. Smith was left scratching his head. "Life instantly changed, but at the same time it didn't," he remembers. "I was sitting there saying, 'Do I stay at the Quick Stop? Who knows if this thing is gonna work out or not.' I decided to keep working there. Of course, Miramax instantly went, 'You're still working at the convenience store?' Suddenly, it became an angle. They sent every journalist in the world there. 'Look at him! He is America! Working at a convenience store!' I was like, 'That's not why I went back to work—to be a symbol.' "

When Smith and Mosier returned to New York, Harvey told them, "I'm an old man, this is a young man's movie, I wouldn't even know what to tell you to cut, you say you got ten minutes, go do it!" He allowed Smith to make his cuts without interference. Then he made them take their dog-and-pony show on the road. "They introduced me to the notion of the grassroots campaign," Smith says. "We spent a year going from festival to festival, from Cannes down to the Colorado Film Festival, the first year of the New Orleans Film Festival, everywhere. We did the college tour as well. I got real comfortable being out there by doing it so fucking much. People would say, 'Do that dance you did in *Clerks*,' or 'Did you ever really try to suck your own dick?' and I sat there going, 'Okay, these are not the questions that Woody Allen gets if he goes to speak at a school, but that's fine, I'm not Woody Allen.' "

Smith was smart, personable, and very funny—a good performer. He was refreshingly frank and unpretentious about his own work. He refused to put on airs, and his fans felt he was one of them, which was more or less true. He was not quite megastar material like Tarantino, but he had his niche, and within it he shined brightly. He became the George Lucas of the self-abuse set, Red Bank his Skywalker Ranch. He had his own Web page from which he sold merchandise—T-shirts, posters, toys, whatever— and today he still spends four to five hours a day talking to his fans in chat rooms. He does college tours even when he doesn't have a new film out. He explains, "Miramax turned directors into rock stars because it was just easier to get the filmmakers to go out and talk about the movie than trying to negotiate with an actor or her publicist or agent, especially when they're on to their next picture."

Clerks opened on October 21, 1994, and grossed $3.1 million, exceeding *Slacker* and possibly *Reservoir Dogs,* two of Smith's favorite films, and then matched that worldwide. Not a bad business, when everything worked right. Smith had another script ready to go, a satiric evisceration of the Catholic Church called *Dogma,* but it was a bigger film, and he didn't feel up to directing it until he'd had more experience. He showed the script to Harvey, saying, "This is the next one I want to make with you guys." Harvey read it, came back, "Great, love it, we'll put it out on Good Friday!" Says Smith, "Years later, when we actually made the movie, he wasn't making Good Friday jokes."

Like Linklater, Smith couldn't resist biting into the apple, and did his second film, *Mallrats,* for Jacks and Daniel at Universal. He recalls, "Jacks kept pitching it as a smart *Porky's.*" That was fine with him. He continues, "I didn't grow up watching Eric Rohmer, I grew up watching John Landis. I wanted to make a teen tittie comedy that nobody makes anymore. Jim had the studio agenda in mind all the time. Initially, we wanted to make the movie for three million bucks. [They said,] 'You can't make a movie for three millon bucks.'

" 'Yeah, we can. We made a movie for $27,000.'

" 'That's not really a movie. No movie can be made for less than $6 million.' Later on, you find out that no movie can be made for less than $6 million if the producers are making $750,000 apiece! I didn't want to respond to some of the notes they gave me. For example, there . . . [was] a scene . . . [in *Mallrats*] where everyone is sitting around talking about scars they've gotten from eating pussy. We call it the *Jaws* scene. And they were like, 'You gotta take that out.'

" 'Why?'

" 'Because nobody will think it's funny, they'll think it's offensive, and you'll send them screaming from the theater.'

" 'You're just kind of hammering out what's original about the script.'

" 'It's not being hammered out, it's just about reaching the widest possible audience. Don't you want to reach the widest possible audience?'

" 'Yeah, I guess.'

" 'Don't you just want as many people as possible to see your movie? Can that be such a bad thing?'

" 'Yeah, I guess that makes sense.' And then later on, you figure out on your own, it's not like it's a bad thing, but it's not necessarily for everybody. It ain't about reaching the widest possible audience, it's about reaching *an* audience. There are some people that just like to tell stories, and it doesn't matter if a hundred million people identify with it, or a thousand people identify with it. There's a certain satisfaction, a certain artistic satisfaction—for lack of a better word—that kind of draws them to filmmaking. And I was one of those people. Independent cinema kinda allows anybody to pick up a camera and tell their story. I don't think of myself as an artist at all, but I think I'm just kind of pigheaded enough to want to do my stories my way, without any involvement, without any tips from somebody else."

The way Universal sold—or failed to sell—*Mallrats* says a lot about the differences between studio and indie marketing. "Dropped the ball is harsh, but there was no grassroots whatsoever," Smith continues. "One junket, and I'm talking to forty-, fifty-year-old journalists about a movie that's so not for them. Going through that experience, I learned that that's not where I wanted to be. So I was like, 'Oh fuck it, let's set up our deal at Miramax.' You slowly learn that Miramax is about as independent as Universal anyway. The big difference . . . is that you don't think of Miramax as a faceless corporation. There is a face on it. It's not a well-dressed, well-groomed fuckin' cover-boy-lookin' face. . . . It's a face you could see cutting your meat in the fuckin' deli."

BY THE MIDDLE OF 1994, in the aftermath of the Disney sale and the run-up to the release of *Pulp Fiction*, there were a lot of fresh faces at Miramax.

Although the Weinsteins undoubtedly drove the company, their employees contributed significantly to the success that culminated in the Disney buyout. Customarily, a company in Miramax's position would have given them bonuses. The Weinsteins called a meeting in the Tribeca screening room to announce the news, where they told people that they were indeed going to get bonuses, but somehow the bonuses never materialized.

The Weinsteins had always been skilled at assessing the strengths of the competition and luring away key executives with a combination of flattery, real or simulated passion, and an uncanny ability to suss out just what fantasy of success was lurking behind the eyes of the pigeon, what it would take to bring him or her over. It was the same gift for seduction that they exercised so successfully in bringing films and filmmakers into the fold. For example, when Pierson sold *Go Fish* to Goldwyn over Harvey's strenuous objections, he let Harvey know that Bowles had been a key player for his competitor. Harvey immediately threatened to hire him away, and he did so the following year. When Harvey ran into Bowles on the beach at the Sarasota Film Festival, in Bowles's words, "He came waddling up in a terry cloth ensemble, and rasped, 'That was textbook, that was beautiful, I loved it, I loved it. Awesome. Perfect, just a perfect job.'" Shortly thereafter, Bowles left Goldwyn for Miramax. "Fear runs through you at the thought of working for the Weinsteins because of their reputation, and I didn't want to do it," he recalls. "But at the same time it was something I was kinda looking forward to." At first, he loved it. "At Goldwyn, I'd throw out an idea, and the executives would say, 'That's too much trouble, let's not bother,'" he says. "When I threw out an idea at Miramax, it was, Bang! 'That's great, let's do this, let's do that, turn over every stone.' We worked like dogs. There was no sitting around the watercooler talking." Of course, once you took their money, they thought they owned you. They lost all respect, and the skills that had attracted their attention in the first place mysteriously evaporated. As good a job as you were doing at Goldwyn, or Fine Line, or Sony Classics, you were doing a lousy job at Miramax, and it was somebody else, somewhere else, who became the gold standard. Says one former employee, "It's like the guy who wants to make a sexual conquest, and the hunt is more intoxicating than the kill. Once they've gotten laid, they lose interest."

Nevertheless, the Weinsteins achieved a critical mass of extraordinarily gifted executives, who set the stage for the remarkable four-year run that culminated in *Shakespeare in Love* in 1998. In particular, the publicity and marketing departments were beefed up with Marcy Granata and Mark Gill coming over from Sony Pictures Entertainment, aka Columbia and Tri-Star. "We were asked to bring in the big-studio thinking," says Granata. "For example, you can be on David Letterman not just one night with one movie star, but six nights in a row with six different stars, like Sam Jackson and Uma Thurman, who had never been on Letterman. That was the new thinking: we can do it all."

Gill was quick, charming, and ambitious. In an industry built on spin, his silver tongue and reputation for frankness made him a favorite of journalists, although they sometimes got him into trouble. His relationship with the brothers was not so smooth as Granata's. According to Stacy Spikes, whom Gill had brought over from Columbia Records to help service a younger, hipper demographic through promotion of Miramax sound-tracks, "Gill would argue with them, say his piece, and they'd say, 'Well, Mark—why don't you quit!'

" 'I'm not giving you the satisfaction of quitting. Fire me.'

" 'No, quit. 'Cause you're terrible at your job, you're an idiot.'

" 'Fire me. Why don't you fire me. Don't you have the balls?' Mark would never quit, and they would never fire him. He knew how to walk that line and he could walk right up to the edge of it."

Spikes had problems of his own. He recalls his first day, when he was or-dered into the conference room. Bob popped a TV spot for some Miramax film into the VCR, and sat down next to him. Harvey was at the other end of the table. Bob said, his voice rising and falling with his signature singsong delivery, as if speaking to a child, "Stayyceee? Did you like that teevee spahht? Is that a good teevee spahht?"

"Yeah, Bob, I think it's a good TV spot."

"It sucks. It's horrible. How could you think that that's a good spot?" Harvey reminded Spikes of the Don Logan character played by Ben Kings-ley in *Sexy Beast*, the gangster who so petrified the other thugs that the prospect of a phone call from him was enough to make them soil their pants. No one could deny him. "There was no such thing as no," says Spikes. "We could be in a meeting waiting for Harvey to get there, and the people in the room were telling you eight ways they're gonna tell him no, and he arrives, and they leave saying yes."

Spikes left shortly for October.

In addition to Jack Foley, Donna Gigliotti, the highly regarded colleague of Michael Barker and Tom Bernard at Orion Classics in the 1980s, arrived in September 1993 as head of production. Jack Lechner was lured away from Channel Four in London via HBO to become executive VP of devel-opment. Cary Granat came from Universal to run Bob's division, Dimen-sion. And then there was Scott Greenstein, an attorney who came over from Viacom's Legal Department. The joke was that when Harvey audi-tioned lawyers, he pulled a signed contract out of the filing cabinet and said, "Okay, if you're so good, tell me how I can get out of this!" Greenstein looks like a Jewish Drew Carey, with a big, squarish head like a loaf of bread that broadens from forehead to chin until it bottoms out in a massive jaw. He was overweight and afflicted with a skin condition—psoriasis or eczema. Staffers didn't like him because he negotiated employment con-tracts. His condition became an occasion for ridicule. "When people made snow jokes around Scott, they did not refer to cocaine," says Tusk. "They were talking about his dandruff."

Greenstein grew up in New Jersey, and no matter how successful he be-came, he seemed gnawed by that bridge-and-tunnel sense of being not quite hip enough to play on the New York courts. He overcompensated in a big way, letting you know that he was on a first-name basis with "Bruce" (Springsteen), "Little Stevie" (Van Zandt), and Jon (Bon Jovi). He loved celebrities: sports stars, rock stars, movie stars, any kind of star. He tried hard to be cool, with his neon blue suits and oversized photo-sensitive glasses with gold frames that made him look like an owl. But he worked hard at getting it right, and eventually he did, more or less. After *Pulp,* he switched to Sam Jackson's shades. He was a shameless flatterer, and even though the target would see it coming and knew he did it to everyone, it worked anyway. He'd say, "Now look, [fill in the blank], this is just you and me talking. You're one of the few guys I can really trust about this. I can talk to you, because you can really understand this."

Still, Greenstein had a surplus of nervous energy—one colleague called him "a terrier on speed"—and quickly made himself indispensable to the Weinsteins. Says former Miramax head of production Paul Webster, who came from Channel Four around this time, "Scott was Harvey's attack dog." He would walk a step behind him, like a pilot fish. When Harvey looked to the right, he looked to the right. When Harvey looked to the left, he looked to the left. He always had a cell phone glued to one ear, while into the other, Harvey barked, "Tell 'im to go fuck himself," "Tell him I'll cut off his balls and shove them up his ass," or something less delicate. Greenstein was a fixer. Harvey would meet somebody at a party, go into his godfather mode, promising him or her the world. The next morning, it would be, "Whaddid I do that for? Scott, get me out of it." Scott would deliver the bad news, find some loophole, badger the guy, threaten, scare him, buy him off. It was as if he were following his boss with a bottle of Mr. Clean and a wet rag, tidying up after him. He was like Winston the Wolf, the character played by Harvey Keitel in *Pulp Fiction,* the crime scene laundryman who wipes the blood off the walls, scrapes the brains off the carpet. As Bowles puts it, "If there was a totally unpleasant, distasteful, almost impossible task to do, Scott would do it, by hook or by crook. He was an amazing weapon. That's what Bob and Harvey loved about him. He was the most relied upon, trusted person there. He executed." Eventually, Greenstein established himself as yet another "third brother."

But Greenstein had his partisans. He was a loyal friend to some Miramaxers, and they felt that beneath the bluster, posturing, and eagerness to carry the brothers' water, there was an insecure little boy unhappy about his looks, his weight, his dandruff. "I'm a big fan of Scott's," says Lechner. "Harvey would say, 'Go make this happen.' It wasn't easy, because Harvey was always asking for the impossible. But a remarkable amount of the time, Scott made the impossible happen. He was instrumental in setting up Miramax Books, and record deals, and trying to extend the brand." According to one source, "There was a lot that was very difficult for him, but people have different thresholds. He had a higher threshold than most."

But alas, although there was lots of competition, the third brother slot was also known in the company as the "whipping boy" position. The closer Greenstein flitted to the flame, the more often his wings got singed. The brothers heaped humiliation upon him. Harvey would shortly buy Jim Jarmusch's *Dead Man* for $4 million, sight unseen. Walking out of the screening in Cannes in 1995, one of the brothers turned to Greenstein and asked, "Whaddya think a'that, Scott?" Not known for his taste, or even interest in films, at that point in his career, and knowing that they had already paid a lot of money for it, he replied in words like, "God, I think it's the most brilliant film I've ever seen, absolutely sensational." Bob or Harvey replied, "Ya know, we think it really sucks!"

On another occasion, Harvey was standing by the elevators at the Miramax offices on his way to the screening room on the second floor, when Greenstein walked up. He got in the elevator with him. All of a sudden, Harvey said, "Scott, where ya goin'?" Greenstein replied, "I thought I'd catch some of the movie with you." With a look of disbelief on his face, like Greenstein had just said he could fly, Harvey asked "Why?" He wasn't being mean, he just couldn't comprehend why Greenstein would spend his time for which the brothers were paying him good money, watching a movie instead of sitting at his desk pulling out someone's fingernails.

Prosperity had not made the Weinsteins kinder or gentler. In fact, quite the opposite. With *Pulp*'s impending success a vote of confidence in his own perspicacity, Harvey Scissorhands became bolder. As Stuart Burkin puts it, "When I started there, before Disney, it was really about courting filmmakers. After Disney, it was another culture, arrogant." Harvey had picked up Bernardo Bertolucci's *Little Buddha*. Bertolucci, of course, was one of the towering masters of cinema, the director of *Before the Revolution, The Conformist, Last Tango in Paris,* and *1900.* He was not Robert Bresson; he had never displayed a taste for spare, economical narratives. He liked vast, sprawling canvases, rather like Francis Coppola. *Little Buddha,* starring Keanu Reeves, and shot in Nepal, Bhutan, and Seattle, had been financed by CiBy 2000 to the tune of $40 million. Bertolucci had had great success with his epic *The Last Emperor,* and Harvey was eager to be in business with him and his producer, Jeremy Thomas—like Saul Zaentz in America, one of the few consistent suppliers of quality films. He bought North American rights for $8 million after reading the script and watching a twenty-minute reel, which he loved. Jeffrey Katzenberg advised him against it, saying, "Harve, don't buy it. I've bought twenty-minute reels too. You're about to make the same mistake I've made."

"But it's Bertolucci!"

"You never had eight cents, much less $8 million, so now you think you can go out and make movies with Bernardo? If the movie's three and a half hours long, you could be on a collision course. You don't need that in your life."

"Jeffrey, I don't care if it's three hours long. *The Last Emperor* was long too. That didn't bother me."

"I guarantee it's going to be an unhappy chapter."

Says Harvey now, "I shoulda listened to Jeffrey on that. For me and Bernardo, it was an unhappy chapter." Weinstein's was not the best offer. But, says Bertolucci, "In Europe, we were very curious about this American distributor who was able to squeeze money out of movies that probably not even in Europe had been released in a proper way." Bertolucci thought, He is one of the few distributors who understands that there doesn't exist only one audience, that there are different kinds of audiences for different kinds of movies. Being smaller, being independent, he wasn't putting the movie in fifteen hundred theaters like a big studio, but in fifteen theaters, and widening it little by little. He adds, "I had some kind of fascination for that man, because it's rare to find someone different from all the executives you meet in Hollywood."

When *Little Buddha* was finished, the brothers went to London to get a look at "the film they had bought before seeing it," Bertolucci continues. "Harvey was brutal. He said, 'You have to cut at least twelve, thirteen minutes.' The tone was threatening. But at that point I was just at the moment of the mixing, the film was me, I was the film, so I couldn't accept any kind of [criticism]."

After the fever of mixing had broken, the director reconsidered. He met Harvey halfway: "Tell me what you want to cut. I'm not here to do the European auteur, in capital letters, with their big egos they faint with horror if somebody says to cut a frame of their film. If you convince me I'll do it." But Harvey couldn't convince him. A chill descended. Harvey sent letters containing lists of cuts, told him that he wanted to take the film wide, but he couldn't unless it were shorter, and threatened to send the film straight to video if Bertolucci didn't do as he wished. At one point during the winter of 1993–1994, Bertolucci and Thomas went to New York. Harvey tested *Little Buddha* in New Jersey. "You knew what the result would be when you saw the movie theater," says Thomas. "It was a multiplex in the middle of an industrial wasteland." Recalls Mark Urman, the publicist on the film, "They had recruited a bizarre group of people who were guaranteed not to like it. It didn't go well, and this was meant to be used as evidence for cutting the film." Says Bertolucci, "Previews are a terrible weapon in the hands of people like Harvey." (Miramax screened the film again in Manhattan to the same scores.)

According to Weinstein, "I couldn't get Bernardo to cut his hair, much less a frame of his film. They never listen to me. The only way to get some of these great directors to make changes is to get other great directors to tell them to. Jonathan Demme was the linchpin on Bertolucci. The minute Demme said it was too long, shit flew outta there." Bertolucci says it never happened: "It's another one of his fantasies."

The director was staying at a hotel in midtown. Accompanied by Thomas, Urman, CiBy 2000 head Jean-François Fonlupt, and a few others, he got into a stretch limo at 59th Street, and headed down to Tribeca for what he thought was just going to be a marketing meeting. It was snowing lightly, and the cars looked like they had been sprinkled with confectioner's sugar. In the movie business, it is customary to deliver bad news at the last minute, when it is impossible to do anything about it, and Fonlupt waited until the car had almost reached Tribeca to say, "Oh, by the way, we're going to see another version of the film, on tape." Shocked, Bertolucci, who contractually had final cut, exclaimed, "What are you talking about? I haven't made any cuts yet!" Fonlupt replied, "Well, *they* cut the film!" Says Urman, "They had some editor, some post-production person who did trailers—who knew who this person was, he was certainly not Bertolucci, nor Bertolucci's editor—do an abridged version of *Little Buddha*." Bertolucci announced, in heavily accented English, "This does not happen to me. I'm not attending any meeting." Turning to Thomas, he added, "Why did you let that happen? Why did you not protect me?" Urman continues, "Bernardo just flipped out. He was surprised that they would do something like that to a director of his rank, especially after he had indicated that he would be open to cutting it himself. He was Bernardo Bertolucci! He asked the driver to pull over, got out of the car, and disappeared for hours. We were worried about him, because he never showed up for the meeting."

"I found a bar," recalls the director, "and walking to the door, there was this very slippery patch, snow becoming ice, and I slipped, and ended up with my bottom on the ground, and I said, 'Okay, that's it, that's my situation.' "

Bertolucci never did look at the Miramax cut, but as months passed, in his words, "I realized that this movie wasn't coming out. So I told myself, these two or three years with Buddhists taught me to be modest. I said, 'Let's be Buddhists, let's give up the ego. So maybe the movie will come out. Otherwise we are going to go straight to TV or video.' I didn't cut twelve minutes, I cut eighteen minutes. I showed the movie to Harvey, and he said, 'Oh, thank you, you really did a great job, it's a great movie now.' He opened it, but he didn't really open it."

Little Buddha was released in the last week of May 1994. Despite the fact that Bertolucci had cut it, Miramax never did take it wide. The *Little Buddha* camp thought Miramax dumped it. The director and producer were crushed. "I dropped Bernardo in the shit," says Thomas. "I should have protected him better. But I didn't think it was possible that such a thing was going on behind my back. A film like *Little Buddha* is not like a normal film, it's a massive undertaking. You spend years to get into these places, into Nepal, these old monuments, costume all those people, it takes a toll on you, two or three years of your life, and it's even worse for a director. Bernardo was distressed by it. It took time [for him] to recuperate. It's just strange not to take care of a treasure like Bernardo, because he *is* a treasure. And you need treasure in cinema."

Bertolucci wonders now why Weinstein bought *Little Buddha* in the first place. "He's a snob," he says. "Snob means *sine nobilitate*, 'without nobility'—he is a snob because he has no nobility, so he wants nobility, and maybe he likes to go after movies that can make him look more noble. But then in my case it was just to punish the thing that can make you better. It's complicated. He had a certain kind of sense of smell for things. Then, as Harvey Scissorhands, he started to believe too much in himself as auteur of the film, and there's where he started to go out of [control] with that kind of megalomania. You cannot believe in a quality film made by personalities, like these movies are, and then go and overcome the personalities of the people who made the movies with your not very luminous ideas." Bertolucci has recently finished a film called *The Dreamers*, set in Paris in 1968. Did he offer it to Miramax? "No, I wouldn't offer a cup of coffee to Miramax. I wouldn't trust Harvey. I was watching *The Sopranos*, and I recognized certain mannerisms of Harvey." If he were making a biopic about the Weinsteins, would he cast James Gandolfini as Harvey? "Yes, but I don't think I would have him as the main character. He doesn't deserve it."

Six
The House That Quentin Built
1994–1995

• How October put Jeff Lipsky out on the street, Disney told Miramax that Larry Clark's *Kids* was too hot to handle, while Quentin Tarantino became Weinstein's Mickey Mouse.

"Miramax is a studio. There are no two ways about it."

—QUENTIN TARANTINO

Allen & Co. had always thought October's management structure—its quartet of partners—unwieldy. Worse, a year in, the company wasn't making any money. During a weekend retreat at Boca Raton in 1993, where the four partners were supposed to bond and strategize while playing tennis and golf, Amir Malin informed Bingham Ray and Jeff Lipsky at dinner that the board wanted him and John Schmidt to run the company. "The problem we had was that Bingham and Jeff were not businessmen, didn't care about dollars and cents," says Malin. "They just cared about their names being mentioned or about films that may have gotten good reviews but didn't make money. We were on a course for sinking the ship." He continues, "The board wanted me to run the company. I refused. I told them I would take more of a leadership role if John were involved."

Schmidt liked Malin more than Ray did, and disagrees with the characterization of him as a "pathological liar." "That's too strong a term," he says. "Amir's just one of these guys who carries his own reality around with him. I would characterize him more as someone who bends the truth. Shades things. You feel like you're in quicksand. Which is not a good way to work. But he's also someone with very sincere feelings about people, his friends, his family. In his own mind, there's nothing about any of that that's not completely genuine. And heartfelt." Still, Schmidt says it was he who derailed the board's attempt to elevate Malin, not Malin himself. "It was then that I began to believe in my heart what I had heard about him, that he would use the boards of these companies to oust his partners. Amir had maneuvered himself into a position where he was making a play to be the CEO. The Book of Amir is the opposite of the Book of Job. Everyone around him gets boils, but he doesn't."

In any event, highly agitated, Ray asked, in a loud voice, "Whaddya telling us? You're gonna fire us? From our own company? That we started, that we brought you into?" According to Ray, Malin just repeated, "Allen & Co. wants this, they want me to run the company." Ray continues, "We were no longer in the board's eyes equal partners. Malin and Schmidt were superior, and we were inferior. They were the finance guys and we were the lowly acquisitions, marketing, distribution grunts. Jeff and I were devastated." As time passed, Ray became convinced that "Amir's handiwork was behind the whole fuckin' thing. That was the beginning of his campaign to take over. Amir thinks his moves are invisible, but they're merely transparent. Why the board fell for Amir's [shtick] is one of the great mysteries of life. At the end of that street lies death."

The consequences of the management shake-up were serious. The roles of the two founders were changed. Lipsky took over marketing and distribution, Ray took over acquisitions. Explains Ray, "We became like place kickers." After the retreat at Boca, relations between Ray and Malin, never good, became worse. If Ray and Lipsky were a mismatch, Ray and Malin were from different planets. Ray continues, "There was open animosity between us in the office, in front of everybody, loud disagreements on almost anything, with Amir trying to impose his will and me not letting him."

Removed from acquisitions, Lipsky went his own way. "Jeff was not acting like a partner," says Ray. "He was doing cowboy things by this time, and really annoying John and Amir. He hated *The Last Seduction*, because he didn't have a say-so in its acquisition. He had been taken completely out of the loop. Jeff was so under the gun he started shvitzing, getting heart palpitations." Pale, shaking, and sweating profusely, Lipsky lay down one day on the couch in his office, said, "I'm having a heart attack, someone call an ambulance." Schmidt, who had never seen this before, was alarmed. Ray told him to ignore it, said, "He's just stressed out. It'll blow over, trust me," and it did. "Jeff is an extraordinary talent," he continues. "You can't get a more fiery, passionate guy about a movie, but the thing about Jeff is, he has one fucking speed. That's full-out, 150 miles per hour all the time. There's no curveball, there's no change-up, there's just a fastball at your head every single time. It works, but not for very long. He's so intense, so peculiar in the way he presents things to people, in the way he dresses, that these whiteshoe folks found it hard to take."

For his part, increasingly isolated, Lipsky could see things were going wrong. Malin, who initially had been content to remain in the shadows, as he had at Cinecom, was edging into the spotlight. In the spring of 1994 he came to Lipsky and said, "We're going to do this movie with Martin Scorsese," whose name—as executive producer—worked magic. Says Lipsky, "I was given a dreadful script called *Search and Destroy*. Illeana Douglas, who at that time was Scorsese's girlfriend, was going to be in it. I said, 'Wait a second, fellas, why are we doing this? You've got a first-time director, David Salle, an artist who's never gotten behind a movie camera in his life. You've got this script, based on a Broadway play'—I sent my assistant to the Donnell Library, 'Get me every review of *Search and Destroy* that you can find,' and she brought back ten reviews from the New York papers, some of the most scathing reviews I've ever seen in my life. It was crazy. It was our reputation. If you're going to dip your toe in the water like this, why choose this vehicle? There's got to be something better." But Malin ignored him. From his point of view, October's exposure was so small it was a no-brainer. "Production was Amir's destruction at Cinecom, but it was his passion and it still drove him at October," says Lipsky. The movie flopped.

While Lipsky was hunkered down in his office, Ray was increasingly out of town traveling to festivals, buying films Lipsky hated, felt were unmarketable. He recalls, "When Bingham and I started, we had determined that we would buy nothing that we didn't jointly have a passion for. One liked it, one didn't, we didn't do it. Then Bingham went off to France and spent $700,000 to acquire *Colonel Chabert*, a film I detested and couldn't sell. And *Cemetery Man* and *Bad Behavior*. I was compelled to support the decisions that he was making. This was when I had to say, October is no longer what I conceived of walking along the Thames River in London."

Lipsky had another problem, named Gary Siegler, the lead investor. Siegler was a hotshot venture capitalist. In Ray's words, "Gary's an arrogant, well-educated, extremely wealthy guy in his thirties who thinks he's got the world by the balls, and everybody should kiss his ass. You had to suffer Gary. Jeff didn't." According to Ray, Siegler was always complaining, his voice dripping with sarcasm. He would say, "This investment is really working out well. If I wanted this kind of return I could have invested the money in T-bills." Recalls Lipsky, "Allen & Co., I understood them. I didn't understand Gary. Siegler and I hated each other. He would become irate with me, because we would have benefit premieres for charitable organizations where we would charge people $250 a ticket, and we would save seats for all our board members and their guests. The movie would start, no Gary. Fifteen minutes into it I'd say to someone sitting on the steps, 'You paid $250, I guess nobody's coming, sit down there.' Gary would invariably show up twenty-five minutes after the movie started, with his girlfriend on his arm, and fly off the handle. Well, life's too short."

Ray continues, "Stupid, petty things like this were huge issues at board meetings. One time, when Jeff was going through the production slate, Gary went fuckin' ballistic. 'How dare you give my seats away!' When there was a little pause in the tirade, Jeff said, not in a terribly snide way, 'Are you finished?' And Siegler went, '*I am not fucking finished!*' Red-faced with anger. Rage. To show him, I'm fucking Gary Siegler, you're just a piece of shit. From that point on, it was death."

As 1994 became 1995, the October time bomb ticked away. If Ray was buying pictures Lipsky hated, Lipsky returned the favor. Like *Smoking* and *No Smoking*, two pictures directed by Alain Resnais, which he bought on his own in Paris. Says Ray, "Jeff was making decisions in a vacuum without involving anybody. He brought the films back, and everybody hated them, we didn't want to release them. 'What the fuck were you thinking, Jeff, when you bought these for $200,000? If they'd turned out to be *Hiroshima Mon Amour*, it might have been a different story, but they weren't. It led into a lengthy legal situation with the producers in France. Made us look really bad."

From the outside, people familiar with his MO suspected that Lipsky's skid was a Malin operation, the opening salvo in what would most certainly be an attempt to take out his three partners, one by one. But there was way more than enough combustible material there to start a blaze without Malin lighting the match; he just had to sit back and enjoy the show.

Despite the collapse of their relationship, Ray was the only friend Lipsky had at October. As Ray remembers it, in February of 1995, Malin and Schmidt came to him and said, "We're gonna fire Jeff. He's a danger to the whole company, we could really go down if Jeff isn't removed." Ray didn't disagree, but thought they should be able to deal with it. He said, "Why don't you let me talk to Jeff, and maybe there's a way he can get his shit together."

"No, no, no, it's not gonna happen." Ray thought, They just want to move him out, one fewer obstacle for Amir to take over totally. They didn't even want to be the ones to tell him. He said, "Well, I should tell him if you guys aren't." He went to Lipsky, said, "Jeff, they're gonna move on you. They want you out."

Lipsky was stunned, asked, "Where are you in this?"

"I don't want it to happen." But, according to Ray, both he and his friend were convinced that they were weak, their enemies were strong, and it didn't matter what Ray thought.

Schmidt, Ray, and Malin gave Lipsky the bad news over a weekend. He was ready to go, took it with grace. Later, he expressed his bitterness. Bingham Ray "betrayed me," he says. "I sometimes wonder if we were friends when we started. Maybe I was using him and he was using me to achieve a goal that we achieved. And that goal started dissipating almost as soon as we started compromising the original vision."

Lipsky had helped Ray on his way up, bringing him into two companies. "I've regretted it ever since," says Ray. "I allowed it to happen, I didn't stand up. I could have said, 'No, fuck you, you're not firing Jeff Lipsky, you fire him, then you gotta fire me too.' But I was a pussy, I got three kids, and so on. That was the beginning of Amir's campaign to take over. He got rid of Jeff with John's support, and my inability to act. I didn't want to take him down, it wasn't my idea. He blamed me for his downfall at October, put it on my head, he'll hold that against me for the rest of his life."

PULP FICTION WAS RELEASED on October 14, 1994. It was not platformed, that is, it did not open in a handful of theaters and roll out slowly as word of mouth built, the traditional way of releasing an indie film; it went wide immediately, into 1,100 theaters to such big numbers that the bad news about pictures like Little Buddha was simply obliterated. "I picked up where Marty Zeidman left off," says Jack Foley. "There was no theater that was not good enough or too good for this film or any film that can turn in money. This is a business. We sell art as a business."

Pulp grossed $9.3 million on the first weekend, just beating The Specialist, the Sylvester Stallone movie released in 2,300 theaters, the one that Kevin Smith thought would wipe out Pulp—or so Miramax claimed. By the time its run was over, it would gross $107.9 million in the U.S., twice as much as The Crying Game, and $212.9 million worldwide. Pulp became the first indie film to break the $100 million barrier. "Nobody saw that coming," says Smith. "Miramax had the vision to see that it was going to pop." Adds Foley, "Bob and Harvey had never had a $100 million movie before. That's lunacy money. There's so much you bathe in it. Consciousness changed in 1994."

Pulp's biggest impact was on Miramax itself, and therefore on the direction of indie filmmaking throughout the rest of the decade. Not for nothing does Harvey refer to his company as "the house that Quentin built." He says, "I never had to tell any filmmaker around the world anything other than one thing, 'We were the company that made Pulp Fiction.' Once we did that, we were home free." It cemented Miramax's place as the reigning indie superpower.

Tarantino gave Miramax its voice. With his épater le bourgeois flair, his dark humor abetted by his spooky facility with pop culture, he was the director Harvey dreamed of becoming when he stumbled about the set of

Playing for Keeps lo, those many years ago. Forget about third brothers; he became the son Harvey didn't have. The feeling was reciprocated. "Quentin loved Harvey," says Rick Hess, who before he moved to TriStar was a junior agent at the William Morris Agency, which represents Tarantino. "He felt Harvey was the master of the universe." Speaking about Miramax, Tarantino says, "If I put myself on the open market, I could write my own check. But I don't want to put myself on the open market. It's not just about the money. It's everything all together: the money, the autonomy, the creative freedom. I'm their Mickey Mouse. He could come by the set every day as far as I'm concerned. We just talk about how great we are!" Tarantino boasted that he could get Miramax to do anything he wanted, and he wasn't wrong. Continues Hess, "Harvey saw him as this guy who was his ticket outta there, meaning Quentin was going to take him to the next level." He used Tarantino's loyalty to bludgeon his agents. "He would call up and say, 'If you don't give me that deal, I'll call Quentin, I'll move him to ICM,' " adds Hess. "But Harvey's not dumb. He wasn't going to beat this one down, he wanted to secure the position, so he basically acquiesced on most of the big points. Quentin's deals were unprecedented. Huge. He got a percentage of video like no one ever had."

Tarantino, more than any other indie filmmaker of the 1990s, followed in the footsteps of the great New Hollywood directors of the 1970s, pop culture nerds who were virtually kids when they were touched by the wand of fortune and turned into frog princes of Beverly Hills. Says Weinstein, "He's the only one worthy of Marty Scorsese." Adds Smith, "Quentin became the face of *Pulp Fiction*, more so than Bruce fuckin' Willis, or Uma Thurman, or Travolta. When you see a director hosting *Saturday Night Live*, you're like, My God, what happened here? Something huge. Nobody ever called me a genius—I did get called a genius, but by people that I'm like, That and 50 cents will get me a cup of fuckin' coffee."

After *Pulp*, Tarantino's ego went off the rails. Said Alexandre Rockwell at the time, "Quentin is a video-geek-type character, who woke up in a candy store. All of a sudden, these women are interested in him who didn't even want to rent videos from him before. It was like a wildfire." As Hess describes it, "He had his fingers kissed by Tony Scott, and all the great directors, saying, 'I wish I did what you've done.' He had people parting the waters for him as he walked through. They wanted to use his name for a restaurant chain. It's pretty scary, heady stuff. Some directors run away from it, but he was really into it, fueled it. He said, 'Cool!' " Walking down the street in L.A. with a friend, approaching a newsstand, he would say, "Hey, man, if I don't find five magazine covers I'm on, or feature articles on me, I owe you 10 bucks. C'mon, man, bet me." Then he'd go through each one, and go, "Bingo, see? Five."

If kids were already going into filmmaking for the wrong reasons, the rewards of fame and fortune that *Pulp* so conspicuously conferred on its director made things worse. Says Miramax development head Jack Lechner, "There's just been so much hype, and so much press, with Quentin himself becoming the first independent celebrity director in a way that Soderbergh never was, that you get these people who in another world would be doing something else, because they're not driven by the same love of movies that Tarantino has." If imitation is the sincerest form of flattery, Tarantino quickly became the most flattered director on the planet. "There's always been imitation, even at the height of the old Sundance days, when you saw the tenth movie with haystacks, a drifter, and a small town," continues Lechner. "But I didn't see a lot of people imitating *sex, lies*. Because there wasn't yet that perception that this is a way to get rich, this is a way to gain fame and fortune. It really became rampant after *Pulp Fiction*."

Pulp kicked open the door of the indie hothouse and allowed a fresh breeze to agitate the languid petals of the exotic orchids within. Oddly enough, the Weinsteins' ambitions—art films for the multiplex audience—were not that different from Redford's. Sundance too tried to broker the marriage of indie and mainstream, but it didn't work, because Redford was so culturally puritanical that he more or less consigned films with any commercial elements whatsoever to the outer darkness. Miramax had no such inhibitions, and Tarantino fulfilled Redford's dream, a melding of art and commerce that yielded a financially successful indie film. As Soderbergh puts it, "Genre films are a great place to hide. You can play on two levels. The audience is there to see a film of a certain type, and take pleasure in the satisfaction that specific genres can provide. Meanwhile, you can indulge in some of your personal preoccupations without it becoming too pretentious or boring."

For indie filmmakers, Tarantino offered a new career path. The classic studio argument to filmmakers who considered themselves artists or auteurs was the one Paramount used on Francis Coppola in 1971 to convince him to do *The Godfather*, which, after all, was based on a trashy bestseller, namely, make a lot of money doing crap, and then you'll be in a position to make whatever you want. In other words, make one for us, and then you can make one for yourself. The assumption was, art and commerce don't mix. But after tasting the fruits of one for the studios, many filmmakers never get around to making the one for themselves. "I'm always being told that I have to do these movies that I don't want to do, so that I get to do the movies I do want to do," says Ethan Hawke, speaking as a sometime director and actor who faces similar choices. "When *Dead Poets Society* was done shooting, I was only eighteen years old, and I was at Disney for a meeting. I was taking a leak next to [Touchstone head] David Hoberman, and he said, 'Well, the real question is whether you got the guts to be a movie star, the guts to want it.' 'Guts' meaning to be a player. Because there's another kind of guts, the guts to try to do it without playing by his definitions. People try to make you feel bad, say, 'So you're happy being a fringe artist?' 'Yes! Yes I am. What kind of a real artist isn't a fringe artist?' So I don't buy it. I don't see that many people who become giant international movie stars that then go off and make all kinds of sophisticated, subversive, challenging adult films. Tom Cruise is in *Magnolia*, I admired that he did it, but I don't know that I could bear to make the other eighteen movies he had to make to get there. I have some of that romantic '70s thing going, a very anti-corporate attitude. I feel this generation plays too much ball. I see young actors right now, making so much money, getting sucked up into so many movies, it just scares me. If actors and directors have a corporate mentality, then who in the world doesn't have a corporate mentality?"

But, as it turned out, in the case of *The Godfather*, art and commerce mixed very well. It wasn't just one for them, it was one for him too; it was one for all of us, great popular art, meaning that it was that rare amalgam of art *and* commerce—cinematic cold fusion. But since that doesn't happen very often, the fate of Scorsese in the following decade is more common: after his personal projects either flopped (*Raging Bull* and *King of Comedy*) or were virtually unmakeable (*The Last Temptation of Christ*), he more or less adopted the either/or, one for them/one for him model: *After Hours* for him, *Cape Fear* for them. Every once in a while, he succeeded in giving his personal preoccupations popular expression, as he did in *GoodFellas*, mostly because his subject happened to be a commercial one, namely, the mob. Tarantino wasn't raised in Little Italy, but his interests—crime, drugs, violence—were similar. He was the first and only filmmaker of his generation able to transcend the Me/Them career path. As Hawke puts it, "The thing that's remarkable about Quentin is that he's as true to his own art as anybody. It's just his taste is very commercial. The reason *Pulp Fiction* broke the way it did is because you got a guy who's making a non-narrative piece, no real beginning, middle, or end, a movie with Godard references, breaking all these rules, but people are slinging guns around, shooting up heroin, so it's kinda titillating in a way that a lot of art house movies aren't. Most art house directors aren't interested in blowing somebody's head off."

While the Weinsteins were counting their profits, Hollywood, awash in red ink, was looking over its shoulder. *Hudson Hawk* had lost a pile of money for Columbia TriStar in 1991, ditto *The Last Action Hero* in 1993, and *Waterworld*, which would do the same for Universal, was bobbing up and down on the horizon. One hundred million dollars was a figure fast becoming more familiar to the studios as budget than gross. Jeffrey Katzen-

berg's notorious memo, in which he called on Hollywood to take stern measures to stem rising costs, had been circulated in 1991, and as CAA's John
Ptak understood when he introduced Harvey to the Disney chairman the
following year, the economics of the industry were becoming unglued.
Each studio had about $750 million available for production, and each had
to put about twenty movies a year into the pipeline to keep the exhibitors
happy. At an average cost of $75 million a feature, the numbers just didn't
add up. When *Pulp,* with its tiny budget, passed the $100 million mark—
not to mention $30 million more in cassette sales—it got Hollywood's at-
tention, transforming the industry's attitude toward the lowly indies and
spawning a flock of me-too classics divisions. With star salaries and P&A
costs skyrocketing, smart studio executives suddenly woke up to the fact
that grosses and market share, which got all the press, were not the same as
profits. Says Hess, "That's when they said, 'Shit, indies are a low-expense
business, negligible development costs'—which is the killer of all studios—
'and the movies cost in the teens,' so they looked very attractive." By 1994,
the lightbulb that went off in Katzenberg's head two years previous had
become a roman candle, and even studio executives who had missed Dil's
dick because they were taking calls could see the sparks.

Once the studios realized that they could exploit the economies of
(small) scale, they more or less gave up buying or remaking the films themselves, and either bought the distributors, as Disney had Miramax, or
started their own. Suddenly the Weinsteins faced stiff competition not
only from old nemeses Sony Classics, Goldwyn, October, and Fine Line,
but from new kids on the block, Universal's Gramercy, Fox Searchlight,
and even Paramount Classics. And of course, the studios wanted each of
their new divisions to become the "new Miramax." Like Fine Line, the
other distributors that had become more aggressive—beefing up their acquisitions staffs, writing Harvey-sized checks, and investing in production—now began to copy Miramax's marketing and distribution strategies,
not to mention their Oscar campaigns.

So great was the Weinsteins' success that the world of indie distribution
was remaking itself in Miramax's image. As Ray puts it, "The Miramaxization of the independents started when Harvey began spending advertising
dollars on TV, which did everyone a disservice. Spending all this money
has forced out the real, true indie, who can't compete anymore. So fewer
films are getting picked up, and fewer people are seeing those that are, because they're only responding to the ones that are paraded in front of them
in an aggressive way in terms of media advertising. And that's just bullshit."
Adds James Schamus, "If your little movie doesn't perform the first weekend, just like the big Hollywood movie, it's gone. So you have to wildly
overspend your marketing dollars in L.A. and New York in order to drive

your opening-week grosses. If you can't do that, you don't have much of a business. Suddenly you needed a company that could handle those kinds of releases. You needed enough people to book those movies, to collect the money from the theaters, oversee that large number of prints being shipped around the country, and then the morning after, when *Pulp Fiction* is off-screen, be thinking, Now, what's the next hit? The independent film business became a hit business, just like Hollywood."

As the studios stooped to conquer, the indies stood on tiptoes to reach the studio table. If the studios wanted to get into the Miramax business, Miramax and its peers wanted to get into the studio business. Indies increasingly divested themselves of the characteristics that distinguished them in the first place. Whereas initiates had debated the definition of independent in the past, now they threw up their hands in frustration. The convergence between studio movie and indie film created an identity crisis among the indies. Sure, indies had become more viable, but were they still indies? A phrase was coined, "Indiewood," to describe this new reality. In another sign of the times, that same year, the Independent Feature Project made sure that films with studio financing, e.g., Miramax films, qualified for its Independent Spirit Awards, IFP's answer to the Oscars.

With studio-sized pots of money being spent on marketing, studio-sized stars were needed to protect the investment. Like Miramax, they needed to cover their downside, and the Steve Buscemis of the world gave way to the Hugh Grants. Of course, indies had been kick-starting flagging careers at least since *Drugstore Cowboy* five years earlier, which had transformed Matt Dillon from a *Tiger Beat* cover boy into a (semi-) serious actor, but it wasn't until the mid-1990s that indies became obligatory pit stops along the career freeway, where actors staggering under a load of blockbuster baggage—be it Willis, or Stallone, soon to appear in James Mangold's *Cop Land,* or Pam Grier, mired in B movie hell, or Robert Forster, who was just nowhere—could launder or resuscitate their résumés. You couldn't have a trailer as big as a railway car, with a caboose for your Cybex machines, or bring your entourage of trainers, nannies, chefs, and best friends from high school—although increasingly, that wasn't so unusual—but it was just plain good for you, like carrot juice or mudbaths, or a month at Canyon Ranch.

But after seeing how much *Pulp* grossed, increasingly stars refused to cut their prices for these films, which brought studio budget creep to the indie world, with its attendant consequences. "The agencies and managers are totally complicit in blowing this thing out," says ICM's Robert Newman. "When the agencies started acknowledging that these were good places to put their clients, all of a sudden prices started going up. A movie that you should have made for $2 million, now cost $8 million, for no reason. And a movie that should have cost $8 million, now cost $20 million. And once you're at risk for $8 million or $20 million, you're totally different in the way you think about what you have to do to protect your interests. It's a much different animal when that much money is at risk." Increasingly, the indies and the studios met somewhere in the middle, forming what Arthur Schlesinger, Jr., in another context, used to call the "vital center." Sundance and studios, midwifed by Miramax, had become not so different after all.

Pulp became the *Star Wars* of independents, exploding expectations for what an indie film could do at the box office. By raising the bar, changing the rules of the game, *Pulp* caused Miramax gradually to lose interest in the kind of dinky, uncommercial films that are not amenable to big-money studio marketing strategies, that is, the kind of classic indies that maverick filmmakers liked to make. As Allison Anders put it, "The biggest thing was when *Pulp Fiction* had the outrageously good opening at the box office. We all saw it as something good for Quentin, and presumed that it was good for ourselves as well. But in fact, that victory was sort of the beginning of the end for the rest of us, because very few indie films can compete in that same kind of a way."

Miramax's competitors wanted their own *Pulp Fiction* too. Says Sundance festival director Geoff Gilmore, "The major guys are shooting for much bigger prizes. Harvey, Bob Shaye, Amir Malin, they want to be worth a hundred million dollars, so they change their agenda. Do they want a film out that will net $4 million? Or do they want a film that can do $20 million? Or $50 million?" Anders continues, "They set out to duplicate *Pulp*'s success. . . . It became a problem for nongenre, character-driven stuff . . . slow-moving tales with no violence, and no big stars. . . . And so that kind of put an end to the dream that we had in the early '90s."

Although *Pulp* cast a shadow over every other picture Miramax released that year, it was by no means the only hit. There was *The Crow* and Krzysztof Kieslowski's trilogy, *Red, White,* and *Blue,* and *Bullets Over Broadway,* the first of four Woody Allen films Miramax would release over the next few years. Nineteen ninety-four was such a good year—both in terms of revenue and the wide spectrum of films that Miramax was able to handle—that it made the Weinsteins look like geniuses not only to themselves but to everyone else as well. As Matthew Cohen, VP of creative advertising and one of the architects of the *Pulp* campaign, put it, "Miramax at that time felt, seemed, and truly was, invincible."

IN THE SHORT TERM, *Pulp,* like *The Piano* and the Weinsteins' other post-purchase hits, strengthened the brothers' hand at Disney. Breaking the bank with a film as scabrous as Tarantino's allowed them to continue in the vein to which they had become accustomed, picking up dark films like Atom Egoyan's *Exotica,* Peter Jackson's *Heavenly Creatures,* and Boaz Yakin's *Fresh,* all released in 1994. But right after the New York premiere of *Pulp,* Katzenberg abruptly resigned, after famously losing the battle to succeed Frank Wells for the number two heir apparent slot, after Wells was killed in a helicopter accident during a ski trip. Katzenberg's departure effectively ended, or rather, gave serious pause to, the honeymoon that had been based both on his warm relationship with the brothers, and on their success. Not that it was entirely cordial. "Bob yelled at me one day," Katzenberg recalls. "I said, Bob, you can always yell at me, just don't cross the line. Just don't threaten me, that's all. Once the words come out, you can't take them back."

After a few months, Katzenberg asked his marketing and distribution head, Dick Cook, to take charge of Miramax. Cook, a cherubic, gentlemanly, mild-mannered man cut from the cloth of the old, pre-Eisner Disney, was exactly the wrong choice to deal with the Weinsteins, who regarded themselves as Eisner's equals and were not about to defer to the likes of Cook or anyone else. At one point, Cook and Bob Weinstein almost got into a fistfight. Recalls Harvey, "Bob really got in there and soured Dick on us. Since I am my brother's keeper, I had to choose sides. I found myself in a terrible position, making me uncooperative with Dick against my will. Dick could have really been helpful to us, but quite honestly, Bob denied us both."

Since Cook and the brothers disliked one another, Katzenberg turned them over to Bill Mechanic, who was then head of international and worldwide video. Mechanic was a numbers guy from the business side, but a straight-shooter who knew the Weinsteins from a prior incarnation. Right away, he had to read Bob the riot act for massaging grosses. Says Mechanic, Disney caught Bob "floating high gross numbers, and I had to call him up and say, 'Bob, you're now part of a public corporation, it's actually a federal offense to report incorrect information, an SEC violation. I'm not going to jail for you, so—.' Bob denied it."

One of Mechanic's tasks was to help Miramax conform its business practices to the Disney model, which was roughly equivalent to turning post-Soviet Russia into a capitalist economy. According to Mechanic, Miramax did not provide their employees with retirement benefits. Again, Mechanic remonstrated, said, "You gotta do it, it's not a choice. Don't worry about it. Nobody lasts long enough to collect anything anyway." Indeed, Mechanic explains, "There was nobody there longer than three years, they were just churning people, so in essence, the retirement packages meant nothing anyway."

Mechanic left in the fall of 1994 to become chairman and CEO of Fox. Then Katzenberg followed, and the Weinsteins passed to former Fox production head Joe Roth, who replaced Katzenberg. Easygoing and laid-back, Roth was the opposite of his tightly wrapped predecessor. He prided himself on dressing casually—refusing to wear ties was his signature—and enjoyed a reputation for being a friend of talent. Roth admired the Weinsteins, at least in principle. "The big cost in the movie business, once you've made the movie, is how much you spend on TV advertising, and they just didn't do that," he explains. "What they were brilliant at was not going into the field and spending $20 million on TV until they knew it was going to work. Of the forty-odd movies they put out every year, they probably were in wide release on no more than three or four. So they didn't have movies that lost $30, $40 million, where studios have four or five of them a year. And every year they had some kind of a breakout."

One of the first things Roth did after assuming the Katzenberg mantle was fly to New York with Chris McGurk to break bread with the Weinsteins. To the Weinsteins, Roth was an unknown quantity. They were suspicious and mistrustful, looking for a reason not to like him. It didn't help that the brothers had aspired to Katzenberg's job, asked Eisner if they could take over the movie division, and were turned down. Harvey denies it, but says, revealingly, "To this day, it's our contention that had we been put in charge of the movies over there, we would have streamlined costs and made the place more profitable." The four men had lunch at the Tribeca Grill, the restaurant in the Film Center where the Miramax offices were. Intending to make nice, Roth said, innocently, "You know, you probably have a business—if we worked it all out—you could make $100 million a year." Bob, always eager to put the worst construction on whatever was said to him, started screaming, "Don't you dare pressure us like this, what we do is good enough, don't put expectations on us." Roth was very cool, just sat there and let it blow past him. He tried to interrupt several times, and finally said, "Can I talk? I know this is not at me, it's Michael and Jeffrey's thing, and you're gonna blame it on me. But I'm going to give you more freedom. I'm not going to micromanage you. You're going to say in two years, you don't miss Jeffrey." Now, he says, shaking his head, "That was my first encounter with these guys. I was trying to be complimentary, and Bob went through the roof."

The Weinsteins and the Disney executives spent the day together, and ended up at Elaine's at one in the morning. Before Katzenberg left, the brothers had been promised Hollywood Pictures, the Disney production division that had been struggling. (It was known as the "Sphinx that stinks," after its logo.) That would have been a big break for the Weinsteins, allowing them to step up to more expensive productions. But Eisner had his own candidate for the job, Michael Lynton, who had little experience in the film business. His mother was said to be a friend of Eisner's mother, part of the Park Avenue Mafia. McGurk warned Roth that there was going to be a problem, but Roth, who still didn't quite get it, brushed him off, saying, "Maybe we can amend their deal, give them the opportunity to produce two movies a year for Hollywood Pictures, and they'll get a producer's fee, and a percentage, and that'll solve the problem." McGurk, looking at the ceiling, said, "Yeah, right." The brothers, of course, had not forgotten the promise of so sweet a gift. In the middle of dinner, Harvey rumbled, "Whadabout Hollywood Pictures?" Roth looked about him uneasily, as if for help, cleared his throat, and replied, "I know you guys wanted Hollywood Pictures, but I gotta tell ya, we decided that we're gonna give it to Michael Lynton, but we'll amend your deal." You could practically see the steam start to pour out of Harvey's ears as his head swelled until it looked like it was going to burst, something out of David Cronenberg's *Scanners*. He bellowed, "You mean to fuckin' tell me that you and Michael Eisner think this fuckin' kid Michael Lynton can do a better job of running Hollywood Pictures than my brother Bob and me? Is that what you're saying?" Roth didn't know what to say. Backtracking, he stammered, "I didn't realize the depth of your feelings about this, I'll have to call you later on it." In the limo going back to the St. Regis Hotel, sitting with his hands on his knees, he turned to McGurk and said, "Ya know, Chris? When I took this fucking job I totally forgot about Bob and Harvey!"

Roth was charged with turning around Disney's feature film division, which was in desperate straits, but he found himself putting out fires the brothers had started. "If I heard that [ICM heads] Jim Wiatt and Jeff Berg were calling me together, I knew right away Harvey had threatened them with taking their clients over to William Morris or CAA or something like that, if they didn't get someone to work for free, get somebody off a picture, deliver a client, whatever the issue was." He adds, "Everybody else who was working at the studio was happy to be inside the box. Harvey and Bob always wanted to go directly to Michael. So that was a wild card for me. They were coming in and lobbing grenades from the outside."

Roth wished the Weinsteins would just go away, so he asked McGurk, who liked them, to be their minder. McGurk took up the cudgels on their behalf against their detractors, who were vocal and numerous. "Harvey was as good as it gets, creatively, and Bob was as good as the best in the industry, business-wise," McGurk says. "Stylistically they were just so different from your MBA or lawyer types, people didn't understand the great thing about Bob and Harvey, which was that everything to them came down to two things: 1) a passion about making movies, and 2) a passion about making money. If you could break any issue down to one of those two things, you could have an intelligent conversation with them, resolve it, and get on. But if you didn't understand that, it was like dealing with Attila the Hun and his younger brother. So it was battle after battle after battle. Sometimes I felt like I was a voice crying in the wilderness on their behalf against corporate Disney."

To Miramax, the Disney executives came off as arrogant suits, whose attitude was, We have to show you the way it's done. Recalls Foley, "You had this efficiency machine at Disney coming over into chaos-ville, saying, 'This is what you should do.' They put an audit on us, and the Disney auditors were truly the most Draconian, Machiavellian, Kafkaesque bureaucrats you'd ever want to meet in your life. They were trying to bash us."

Eisner supported Harvey but, says Roth, "They're enough alike to really not get along. They had some pretty big fights." The Weinsteins showed up at a corporate retreat one year wearing T-shirts that said, "Corporately Ir-responsible," which pretty well summed up their attitude. Continues McGurk, "Miramax was set up to be an autonomous business that lived outside the rules. To Disney executives they seemed to be this outlaw com-pany that leeched off the Disney divisions and made the executives look bad, because they were doing so well, so they hated that." Adds Roth, "Mi-ramax acted like Disney was just another company, and to Cook, it felt like he was being forced to support a competitor." For example, Miramax never paid the slightest attention to Disney's release schedule when they set their own. They routinely opened their pictures on the same dates that the parent company released its pictures. "They cared when they thought we had a stronger piece of product," recalls Roth. "Then they would call up and beg, borrow, and steal to get us to change." The Weinsteins' attitude was simple. As Disney VP of finance Rob Moore puts it, "People who did stuff for them, they liked, and people who didn't do stuff for them, they hated. You were their best friend or they wanted to run you over. There was no gray with them."

Almost everyone the Weinsteins dealt with, the middle-level bureau-crats—the foreign sales force, foreign theatrical, foreign TV, and video—regarded them as little better than dog hair. It was like the brother-in-law had moved in, Roger Clinton in the White House. Not only were they forced to piggyback Miramax product onto their own, they disliked the product, so different from Disney's. They felt it was dragging them down. At best it was an irritant and at worst it was cannibalizing their business. Says one former Disney executive, "Miramax had no brand identity, the packaging sucked, the trailers sucked, there was no awareness of their pic-tures because they were never distributed in the small towns between the coasts. Plus, Bob and Harvey were disagreeable sons of bitches to talk to over the phone. If you're a salesman at Buena Vista Home Video, and your bonus is based on how much you sell, do you want to push *The Lion King*? Or do you want to push *The Cook, the Thief*? Their video business was like a booger on your finger that you couldn't flick off!"

Disney had a video duplication deal with Technicolor. On one sixtieth of Disney's volume, Bob went out and negotiated better terms for Miramax, and as a result, Disney was able to renegotiate its own deal, saving the company millions of dollars. Eisner agreed to pay them a bonus of $8 million, which caused further resentment. As one former Disney executive puts it, "I thought it was a joke. Some of us were saving the company hundreds of millions of dollars every year and we weren't getting special bonsues for it. It was part of the job. It just showed how Michael, despite all this tough talk, was scared of these guys, afraid of losing them or pissing them off."

Another irritant was that the same year Disney bought Miramax, Ted Turner had paid $505 million for New Line, over seven times what the Weinsteins' company had fetched. The discrepancy between the brothers' payday and Bob Shaye's payday made them crazy. It was as though Shaye had become a billionaire and Harvey and Bob got a job, bolstering John Schmidt's contention that they would have done well to have gone public when they had the chance, as New Line did in 1986, raising $4·5 million in production money. Recalls Moore, "They got pissed off by the New Line deal, then had a couple of big hits and came in and said, 'Ya know? We're not happy with the deal we originally made.'" Roth adds, "They spent the entire time I was there renegotiating! These are guys where the deal is never really closed."

The jockeying between the two companies quickly took on the aspect of negotiations between the Israelis and the Palestinians, with threats flying fast and furious on both sides. The brothers waved DreamWorks in Disney's face; they would go join Katzenberg. Disney said, "Go ahead and walk, we'll hire one of those third Weinstein brothers, like Scott Greenstein."

Says another high-placed former Disney executive, "They drove McGurk insane. Dick Cook. Roth. I believe that they got extreme pleasure out of biting the hand that fed them. They still do. Psychologically, it makes them think that they're still independent, that they didn't sell out to a large conglomerate. But they did. They traded freedom for money. I immediately made it clear that I would not lift a finger to help these people. I just thought that they were troublemakers. I thought they had no respect, and I didn't get what people felt was so fabulous about them."

• • •

NINETEEN NINETY-FIVE was a relatively strong year in Park City, defying the diurnal waxing and waning of the festival. The hot ticket was not even entered in the competition, but was sneaked at the Egyptian in a midnight screening to a packed house of four hundred highly expectant people. The film was Larry Clark's *Kids*. The audience was not disappointed.

Gus Van Sant was an executive producer of *Kids*. He had met Larry Clark in San Francisco in 1993 while he was editing *Even Cowgirls Get the Blues*. Van Sant had been introduced to Clark's work in the late 1980s when he was preparing *Drugstore Cowboy*. Clark's *Tulsa* was a collection of photographs of street kids shooting up and nodding out that had been something of a bible a quarter of a century earlier for Scorsese and Paul Schrader, who dumped it into the creative cauldron from which *Taxi Driver* emerged. *Teenage Lust* was more of the same. *Kids* was going to be Clark's first film, and Van Sant agreed to produce it. But, as Van Sant says, he was a lousy producer, and after the project had been turned down by a few people, he lost interest, turned his attentions to his new film, *To Die For*.

Shortly thereafter, Christine Vachon got a call from a British producer. In a broad Cockney accent, she said, "There's this really cool kid, Harmony Korine, eighteen or nineteen years old, who's written this script, and this photographer, who wants to direct it." She described the film, a scabrous walk on the wild side down the Larry Clark street, a raw portrait of boozy, drugged-out teen zombies. Like somnambulists, they wander through a long hot summer's day in AIDS-ridden New York City. Oblivious to the dangers of infection, the boys are obsessed with deflowering "babies," the younger the better. As Clark put it, "Their idea of safe sex was sex with virgins." Telly, known to his pals as a "virgin surgeon," scores with a thirteen-year-old. The kids otherwise amuse themselves by drinking whiskey out of brown paper bags, peeing on the street, kicking cats, and stealing. This sounded like Vachon's kind of material, and indeed, she was intrigued. Her father had been a photographer, so she didn't need any introduction to Clark's work.

In May 1993, right after Miramax was sold, the script made its way to Mark Tusk, who passed it around the new Disney division. The consensus was, It's our kind of movie, the cost is right, let's go for it. At about the same time, through a friend, Korine's script had also made its way to Cathy Konrad, an attractive, wiry woman with a direct, no-nonsense manner who was then running Cary Woods's production company, Woods Entertainment. She recalls, "My friend said, 'This script is so dark, it's so dirty, ohmigod, I couldn't even finish it, made my skin crawl, I hated it, but you'll love it, the guy's really talented.' I read it, thought it was unbelievable, so raw, riveting, I never read anything like that."

Woods and Konrad also thought they could set it up at Miramax. Konrad recalls, "There was a lot of buzz about Miramax as a place to be, because it was taking chances on risky material with first-time filmmakers. Nobody was doing that then. Suddenly there were chances for people, other than mortgaging their parents' home to make a movie."

Clark recalls, "Miramax was gonna give us money to do *Kids*. Harvey put his arm around me, said, 'You're my next guy, my next star. We're doing this movie.' He was gonna give us a million bucks. And then they just dropped out completely. It was on, and the next day, boom, it was off. What happened was, they'd just made their deal with Disney, and they were just afraid." Gladstein called Vachon. He said, "If it was up to me, we'd make it. But it was Harvey and Bob." Vachon thought, They're blowing me off. It's the script, it's too risky, it's bad for Miramax's image, they're moving away from those kind of movies. She called Clark and told him, "Look, I still want to make this movie, but I don't have a company, I'm just one person, I have to go make *Safe* for Todd Haynes in L.A." A few weeks later, Clark called her up, said, "So I think we found this guy who says he can get us the money. This guy Cary Woods. Is that, like, cool with you?" She replied, "Well, if you can get the money for it, you should do it, right?"

Woods had met two twenty-four-year-old wannabe venture capitalists, one with $10 million of his father's money to fool around with, and of course they couldn't wait to blow it on the movies. Woods had intended to use the money to make Alexander Payne's *The Devil Inside*, later known as *Citizen Ruth*, but when he stumbled on *Kids*, he changed his mind, called Payne, told him he was going to use it to produce *Kids* instead, but not to worry, he would find a way to do Payne's picture too. (Woods says Payne's script wasn't ready and *Kids* was.) *Kids* went forward in the summer of 1994, with Woods and Vachon sharing producing credit with six other people.

Clark was adamant that it be cast with nonactors, and it was, save for Chloë Sevigny. The shoot, in the summer of 1994, was, according to Vachon, a nightmare. Often, when this is the case, it's the stars who are temperamental. On this set, the volatility was behind the camera, Clark and Korine. According to Vachon, Clark was inexperienced and paranoid, convinced that people were trying to take the picture away from him. In his mind, nobody knew "what the fuck they were doing," she says. He would look for a reason to hate somebody, invariably find one, and want him or her—more often her, since he seemed to get along better with men—fired. Says Clark, "She was used to shepherding first-time directors through their projects. The first day of filming she came up to me and made some suggestions, and I said, 'I appreciate it, but I don't want to hear it, I don't need any help, any comments, anything.' Everybody was looking at me saying,

'This guy doesn't know what he's doing. He's too close and he doesn't do any wide shots, no establishing shots.' But I was thinking, That's why your fucking films all look the same. Like cookie cutters. Leave me alone and let me make my film. After that, Christine did leave me alone and helped me. Anything I wanted she made sure I got it. I loved her."

There was already a lot of buzz around *Kids*, and when it was finished, Woods showed it to Harvey. He knew that *Kids* would most likely pull an NC-17, and that Miramax was the only distributor on earth that would have the guts to put it out. But he also knew that Harvey's hands might be tied by Disney. Miramax had already passed on the script once. He thought, If Michael Eisner sees this movie, it's all over. Woods showed it to Harvey at Todd-AO, in Midtown, off Ninth Avenue, at noon. Weinstein exclaimed, "Wow, congratulations, that's some movie you have there. What are you going to do with it?"

"We've been accepted to Sundance, I was thinking that I would just go there and see what happens, take bids."

"Well, what about me? What about us?"

"Look, Harvey, do you want me to talk to you as a friend?" Woods was close enough to Harvey to know what buttons to push. "As a friend, here's what I would say to you. You're part of the Disney family, you're doing really well, you're way too rich for—why do you need this headache? On the other hand, whoever puts out this movie is going to be the new Miramax!" Woods had spoken the magic words, better than "Goldwyn's interested" or "Fine Line's bidding." Harvey was not about to let another company become "the new Miramax." He said, "Be in my office at three o'clock." Woods appeared at the appointed time, and Harvey bought worldwide rights for $3.5 million.

Harvey, in other words, was schizophrenic. On the one hand, he understood Disney's sensitivity to projects like *Kids*, and he passed on it as a production, but then he turned around and picked it up as an acquisition. Explains Lechner, "Harvey the acquisitions guy and Harvey the producer were two very different creatures. Harvey would never have made *The Cook, the Thief*, but he was able to recognize it for what it was." The same was true for *Kids*. He wouldn't produce it, but he was ready to acquire it.

The 1995 festival not only showed *Kids* at midnight, but Haynes's *Safe*, in the competition, along with Bryan Singer's *The Usual Suspects*, Tom DiCillo's *Living in Oblivion*, Gregg Araki's *The Doom Generation*, Mike Newell's incest film, *An Awfully Big Adventure*. *The Brothers McMullen* won the Grand Jury Prize in the dramatic competition. It was acquired by Fox Searchlight, and went on to become a sizable indie hit, grossing $10 million. But it was a soft, sentimental film and came in for a lot of flak. Says Kevin Smith, "Ed Burns and *The Brothers McMullen* was the beginning of the end. It was a movie that absolutely could have been made by a studio. It had as much edge as vanilla ice cream, no name brand. Everyone wanted to get a *Brothers McMullen* underway. 'Cause everyone wanted that cheap but softshell picture that fuckin' reaches into the warm and fuzzies of the fuckin' average multiplex moviegoer while still being able to call it an independent. Even Harvey fuckin' talked to Burns about making a movie at Miramax. It made me heartsick for a year."

The revolving door that spun employees out of Sundance at warp speed in the late 1980s and early 1990s had slowed—at least for the moment. The institute rested, like a three-legged stool, on Gilmore, Michelle Satter, and Nicole Guillemet, the general manager. Still, the old problems persisted. As Cathy Schulman says, "It was a dysfunctional place. Since nobody was making a cent, people fought over power, and access to Redford. There was a lot of competition among Gilmore, Beer, and Guillemet for Redford's ear, who was going to get to have dinner with him." With some exceptions, Redford was well known for running hot and cold on people, and the composition of his inner circle—among them a handful of shameless groupies and sycophants—was chronically in flux depending on who had seized his fancy at any particular moment. Sundance wags referred to them as the "Bob whisperers." Says Sterling Van Wagenen, "Bob sees things in a very black-and-white way. He'd pick somebody out who for some reason he didn't think shared this mysterious Sundance vision. It was not an easy thing to confront him and say, 'You're wrong about this.' You're either in or you're out, and if you're out, don't expect to be invited to the tenth or twentieth anniversary party, or that there will be any sort of institutional memory that will acknowledge your contribution. And once you got on the other side of that fence, you just didn't get back." With a few exceptions, the people who do best at Sundance, and last the longest, are the ones who refrain from playing the Bob game, who are blessed with egos modest enough to be satisfied with basking in his reflected glow, rather than aspiring to shine themselves.

Despite the institute's unaccustomed stability through mid-decade, Redford hadn't changed much. He was still so passive-aggressive, still such a conflict avoider that it was almost impossible to know if he liked something or not, and if not, hard to assess the degree of his dislike. He was invariably polite, always prefacing his remarks with something complimentary, and whatever criticisms he then voiced were so mildly expressed you could leave the room thinking he loved your work when in fact he didn't. He would say, "I like the thinking, but I have a question," furrowing his brow and running his fingers through his tangled copper locks, adding, "Let's look at this further," or, "We gotta spend some time together," or, "We can get into that more later," leaving whomever feeling warm and fuzzy with the dreamy expectation of future meetings. But "later" never came, so decisions were postponed, and efforts to reach him failed because he was away on the set, otherwise preoccupied, or just unavailable, period, no reason given. And when he did get into it later, the way he did so was often by replacing the person responsible for the work he may or may not have liked. Redford, with his "Bobspeak," gave people he worked with the feeling that they were standing on sand.

The star was rarely around, and when he was, he would make a couple of oracular pronouncements and then vanish, leaving the staff to tease the meaning out of the tea leaves he had left behind. Says one former Sundance executive, "He'll disappear for six or nine months on a shoot, leaving you hanging out to dry. And if in the meantime you've been too independent, because that's what you thought was needed, when he comes back it's problematic for him." He was like a husband who frequently disappears on protracted business trips, leaving the care of home and family to the little woman. If she made a decision in his absence—moved his favorite easy chair or bought a new rug—when he got back, he filed for divorce.

Redford was just as suspicious as ever, more so, perhaps, since family ties had failed him—he never forgave Van Wagenen for trying to "leverage" him—so he increasingly surrounded himself with people of strong religious faith, a hazard, perhaps, of living in Utah. One of his long-term associates, attorney Reg Gipson, is the son of a missionary, and in the mid-1990s, Redford hired a colorful, highly successful advertising executive named Gordon Bowen as the chief "creative" officer for the Sundance Group. Bowen was best known for squishy ads that tugged the heartstrings. He was good at listening to Redford and articulating Redford's vision, but in the opinion of some, he just amplified the problem, which was, all vision, no execution. Bowen would kill people with encouragement, and then, like Redford, disappear, walk out in the middle of a meeting in New York, take a cab to the airport and return to Salt Lake City, where he lived.

In other words, the more things changed, the more they stayed the same. Gilmore's festival and Satter's labs were thriving, but Redford complained bitterly about the catalogue, the resort, and the other "entities." Some of that could be discounted as just Redford complaining, because he loved to complain. "No matter who you are in Bob's orbit, he complains about you," observes Van Wagenen. "In order to feel comfortable with people, he has to figure out where their limitations are, so everyone was relentlessly scrutinized. Bob is constantly analyzing what people do and why they do it, what their strengths and weaknesses are. It's an actor's talent, to analyze the character you're playing. After a while you think, Give it up, go with people and support their strengths and watch out for their weaknesses." As one former Sundancer puts it, "Bob is almost genetically impossible to satisfy. He is first and foremost dissatisfied with himself. And he will say that. He's so self-critical, it's sad. He thinks he's square and pedantic and boring. He's got an inferiority complex about his own intellect." But that notwithstanding, there were still real problems: the old questions about the financial health of Sundance were about to resurface.

WHEN AWARDS TIME rolled around at the beginning of 1995, Tarantino cleaned up. He won big at the L.A. Film Critics and the National Society of Film Critics. But there was the occasional thorn in those bouquets. When he won a Golden Globe for Best Screenplay, he neglected to thank or even mention Avary, who was already furious with him over the credits, and for appropriating his *Top Gun* riff for a cameo Quentin did in a film called *Sleep with Me*—without telling him. As Tarantino was walking past Avary's table, Avary's wife intercepted him, shouting, "Fuck you!" Says Avary, "He could have stood to learn a little humility, although humility is a hard thing to come by when everyone is telling you that you're the Second Coming."

On February 14, 1995, when the Oscar nominations were announced, Miramax got an astounding twenty-two, more than double the previous year. Most of this success was attributable to *Pulp*, which alone picked up seven, including Best Picture and Best Actor, some of it to the addition of Mark Gill and Marcy Granata to the company. *Bullets Over Broadway* also got seven, and Peter Jackson's *Heavenly Creatures* got one, and several other films shared the rest. Facing stiff competiton, mainly from *Forrest Gump*, Weinstein sang the little guy song. "I'm always going up against the huge Hollywood establishment, and this time it's no different," he complained at the time. "You have Bob Zemeckis and Tom Hanks, who could both be mayor of Beverly Hills."

On March 27, the big night, *Gump* thumped *Pulp*, showing that the Academy didn't get the joke. Miramax won only two Oscars, one for Dianne Wiest for Best Supporting Actress for *Bullets*, and one for Best Original Screenplay, which Tarantino shared with Avary. After the director, wearing a *Dogs*-style skinny black tie, made his remarks, Avary, who wasn't used to winning Oscars, thanked his wife and said, "And I really have to take a pee right now, so I'm gonna go. Thank you."

Tarantino wasn't amused by Avary's faux pas. "My whole thing was if, after Roger gets through thanking his wife, he thanks me, it will all be water under the bridge, he'll have said all that I ever wanted and would need to be said, in a sweet moment," says Tarantino. "He walked up there and thanked his wife and said, 'I have to go to the bathroom.' I said, 'Okay.' I expected no less. I was trying to take care of Roger, which finally made me feel like an idiot. Because I knew I was a better friend to him than he was to me. Roger would be working at an advertising agency right now if my mother never met my father. If I never existed. Roger never would have directed one foot of film, ever. And if I hadn't written *Pulp Fiction*, he would never have won an Oscar."

AS A PRETEEN, Steven Soderbergh was a Little League phenom, a pitcher with a 7 and 0 record, a no-hitter, and a .450 batting average. He dreamed of going all the way to the majors, but then one day he woke up and it was all gone. He couldn't pitch and he couldn't hit. The baseball gods had forsaken him. One year shy of twenty years later, it seemed like déjà vu. The precocious director of the hottest indie of 1989 had had two flops in a row and was well on his way to a third. Now everyone who had been looking for the next Soderbergh was looking for the next Tarantino, and it seemed that even he was not immune to the Tarantino bug. In 1994, he had done his own heist movie, *The Underneath*. He had written the script himself and was using one of his *sex, lies* stars, Peter Gallagher, but he hated it and he hated himself. "To sit on a movie set at age thirty-one and wonder whether or not you even want to do this, having no other real skills, is so terrifying and depressing," he said, adding, "I was bored, I was empty. I'd just run out of gas. I felt, If I have to set up another over-the-shoulder shot, I'm just gonna shoot myself."

The Underneath followed *Kafka* and *King of the Hill* quietly into the night. Not only was his career in the toilet, but his five-year marriage to Betsy Brantley ended in October 1994. Soderbergh had been in the habit of parking Brantley, along with their young daughter, at their farm in Charlottesville while he took off for distant climes, sometimes locations, sometimes not. According to Soderbergh, "The problem with my marriage was that I had not come to terms with the degree to which I had swallowed what I had seen growing up and then proceeded to reenact it." Brantley remembered, "At one point, I said to him, 'You are two different people. You have this secure, confident professional side. But personally, you're the most insecure person I've ever met.' He looked at me and said, 'You're just now figuring that out?' "

But now the professional side of him was becoming unhinged as well. He hadn't been having any trouble getting work. "People kept thinking, He might do *it* again," he recalls. "And I'm very comfortable disappointing people. It's like a really easy place for me to be. But I felt I was running out of time. What concerned me was, was I going to stay where I was and have the kind of career that is a footnote? I realized that I had a fear of success issue that I needed to confront. I was just lost. I didn't know what to do." He pauses. "Actually, I did know what to do, which was start over again, literally re-create the circumstances under which I made my first short films, which had a very Richard Lester energy to them. What the fuck happened to that? *The Underneath* is so sealed off, it's just somnambulant. How did I become a formalist? That's not how I started."

Soderbergh remembered the way it was when he lost his fastball, his timing at the plate, and everything else. He thought, Is that what's happening? Have I lost the *thing*? He decided that no, he'd just drifted off course, and the back-to-basics therapy he came up with for himself involved returning to Baton Rouge, where he'd made *sex, lies.* He called Rick Linklater in Austin, said, "Do you know any sound people?"

"Yeah, we got some around here."

"Do they have their own equipment?"

"Yeah . . ."

"Do you think they'll work for nothing?"

"Steven, I've gotten this call from grad students. I've never gotten it from a Palme d'Or winner and an Academy Award nominee! What the hell are you doing down there?" With used equipment, a crew of five, and a shoestring budget of $350,000, he was deconstructing his own life in an alternately amusing and self-punishing autobiographical fantasy of a kind that was unprecedented in the oeuvre of a major director. He called it *Schizopolis.*

Soderbergh admired Lester not only for his energy, but for "his eclecticism, the range of *Hard Day's Night, Petulia, Juggernaut, Robin and Marian,*" he explains. "I think that's what you do if you're not Fellini." But Lester did have a personal style, especially in his early films, and Soderbergh set out to make a Lester film. *Schizopolis* features himself in two roles, as well as his ex-wife and his young daughter. It was an indie *Rashomon.* He treats its subject (himself) with astringent wit, but its concerns are serious, if abstract and jejune, like a student film: the unknowability of others, the impossibility of relationships, the futility of communication. It bristles with fragments of his own personal history, including his marriage; satirical shafts aimed at a variety of contemporary targets; and allusions to other movies. In a jaw-dropping sequence, one of his doppelgangers masturbates in a men's room, as if to say, Soderbergh had been wasting precious time, if not bodily fluids, jacking off.

What with Soderbergh having just come through a painful divorce—"It was the worst I've ever felt in my life, ever!"—and directing his ex-wife, it was a stormy set. "We fought like cats and dogs," she recalled. "It was the one time I had him in a room he couldn't walk out of. He couldn't leave. He was the director." Looking back on it, Soderbergh says now, "What was that about? What would possess you to create a situation in which you are acting out surreal satirical variations on the marriage that is now over?" He continued, "I was so wrapped up in my own shit that I wasn't looking out the window. I was just hanging out in my own house with the blinds drawn and the music on and not answering the phone. *Schizopolis* was about detonating that house, blowing it up and putting myself in a position where I couldn't go back anymore." He adds, "I guess I wanted to be uncomfortable. I wanted it to be difficult. I wanted to be in a situation where I wasn't in control, entirely."

Weinstein offered him $1 million for *Schizopolis*, sight unseen. Soderbergh warned him off, saying, "Harvey, thank you, I'm flattered, you don't want to do that, see the movie first." Once the Miramax co-chairman did see the movie, he called Soderbergh and said, "Thanks. I really appreciate that." Reflects Soderbergh now, "It would have been a disaster for both of us."

DAVID O. RUSSELL was a director Harvey Weinstein very much wanted under his tent, and he came on very strong, pressing for Russell's next film, *Flirting with Disaster*. The filmmaker remembers, "It was like, 'This is the deal, it's good for like an hour. And after that, it's not on the table anymore." Russell grabbed the opportunity. It was the summer of 1994, and shortly after the phone call, he and his wife, Janet Grillo, found themselves on Martha's Vineyard, where Eve Weinstein's parents have their place. His lawyer told him, "You're going to go meet Harvey, sign the deal." Russell had spent every summer on the Vineyard as a child. He continues, "I went to this part of the island that I'd never been to, East Chop or West Chop, a gated community, WASP central. I met Harvey at the tennis club. Everybody was wearing tennis whites, except him, sitting on the porch wearing this blue T-shirt and too tight royal blue shorts, with his big gut, his balls bulging out, and his big hairy Jewish legs. I thought I would feel so uncomfortable here, but he just plops himself down, right in the middle of it. Everybody was coming up to him, all the preppies, the Chips and the Missys, saying, 'Hello, Harvey.' He'd given them, like, the 'Harvey Weinstein playground,' and I realized what a ballsy guy he was, the only Jew in the whole place, just sitting there like he was the mayor."

Russell was looking to get as far from the darkness of *Spanking the Monkey* as he could. "To me that incest material was really vile," he explains. "I didn't want to be that guy. I decided I wanted to make a fun comedy." Improbably, he fashioned his fun comedy from some rather unfun materials. It was the story of a young, adopted man searching for his biological parents. Right away, he had trouble getting Harvey's attention. "After we made the deal, that's when he was most excited, when he still had the smell of battle in his nose," he recalls. "Later he loses interest. He moves on to the next location of carnage. I couldn't even get a cup of coffee with him." The director wanted to cast Janeane Garofalo, and he had to make a commitment immediately or she was going to take another film. Garofalo was an actress, not a star. In Harvey's eyes she was about as glamorous as a bowl of cold oatmeal. Russell told him, "We better move fast, I don't want to lose her." Harvey opened the door of the Miramax conference room, and shouted down the hall, "Bob, sell the company! We can't get Janeane Garofalo!" Then he turned to the filmmaker and said, "I don't give a shit if we can't get Janeane Garofalo." And walked away. Harvey wanted John Cusack for the lead. He said, "I'll show you, lemme call John Cusack and wake him up." Cusack was in L.A.; it was six in the morning there. He got the actor on the line, went, "John, it's Harvey Weinstein and David O. Russell. Have you seen *Spanking the Monkey?*"

"Uh, no, but I, uh, wanna see it!"

"I want you to see it, and meet this guy." Says Russell, "Of course, that went nowhere. He wanted him, but he also just woke John Cusack up to prove that he could." Russell liked the look of *My Own Private Idaho.* He got on the phone with Harvey and said, "I want to use Eric Edwards, Gus Van Sant's guy, to shoot *Flirting with Disaster.*"

"Who cares? I hate Gus Van Sant's films. You're depressing me. You're manic-depressive. I hate talking to you!"

"Why are you speaking to me like this?"

"Because you're depressing." Harvey hung up. If Russell hadn't been depressed before the conversation, he was now. Later, of course, Harvey apologized.

On the basis of the script, Russell recruited an exceptional cast that included Ben Stiller, Patricia Arquette, Téa Leoni, Lily Tomlin, and Mary Tyler Moore, among others. The picture was shot on a shoestring budget. The actors had trailers, but Russell did not, to save money. He had to knock on the doors of theirs to use the toilet. There were the customary demands from Miramax. In the opening scene, in which Arquette undresses, Russell was asked to make sure he had some shots of her breasts.

When *Flirting* was completed, Miramax tested it in Ridgefield, New Jersey. Recalls the director, "The testing was a hideous experience. The movie did moderately well, in the high 60s and mid-70s, but there were some tests where it was down in the 50s, and I realized how subjective audiences are, and the insanity is that they're not audiences who would even choose to go to see my movie." Harvey thought he could raise *Flirting*'s scores by getting rid of some codas, brief shots under the tail credits. One showed the two gay characters in bed; another, Leoni's character pregnant, smoking and drinking. "He was hell-bent on this. He thought they would prevent the film from crossing over, which I disagreed with completely," says Russell, who was thinking to himself, That's a chickenshit attitude. The director knew he had final cut, and there was no way he was going to drop the codas. Out loud, he told him, "The movie's over by this point. You will have either liked it or not." Harvey replied, "Well, David, okay, I sat with"—he threw out a director's name—"and he was willing to work with me, so I'll be more passionate about marketing his film, and your film I'm not going to be as passionate about, because you're not willing to collaborate with me." Recalls Russell, "It was right on the eve of the release, and he was threatening me, saying he would not support the film. So out they came. Now I'd tell him to go fuck himself."

Miramax expected *Flirting* to do $30 million plus, but it plateaued at $14.7 million. Afterward, Harvey discarded Russell. "The thing that sickens me about Miramax is that Harvey isn't interested in having relationships. He's just interested in getting you when he wants you, and getting you to do what he wants you to do, and then he's on to the next person."

Russell's picture was a dry run. Harvey was only flirting with disaster. The real disasters were yet to come. Like *Kate & Leopold,* brought in by Cathy Konrad, with Sandra (*Speed*) Bullock attached, hardly a Meryl Streep, but eminently bankable. Although it was a script with problems— by a college buddy of Bullock's yet—Harvey was apparently blinded by the glare of Bullock's stardom. Recalls Konrad, "Harvey hungered to make movies that could compete with studio films. He said, 'This is going to be my big fat fuckin' commercial movie.' He wanted to taste what that was like." But he didn't want to drop studio-sized wads of cash on development. When costs flirted with the $2 million mark after an expensive rewrite by Carrie Fisher, Bullock dropped out, and Harvey refused to put any more money into it. The project stalled.

Meanwhile, throughout the spring of 1995, the controversy over *Kids* roiled the waters at the Tribeca offices at the very moment that the company and its parent, Disney, were entangled in a nasty tussle with William A. Donohue, president of the Catholic League, over a little film called *Priest* that Miramax had picked up at Toronto in September 1994 for $1.75 million. *Priest* had gotten a standing ovation at Sundance just a few weeks earlier and had picked up the Michael Powell Award for best British feature at the Edinburgh Film Festival. It was directed by Antonia Bird. Set in Liverpool, *Priest* is an angry story about a priest who is persecuted by the Catholic Church for being gay. The church is portrayed as rigid, small-minded, and hypocritical. And while the film is by no means graphic, there are a couple of scenes in which the priest makes love to another man, handled by Bird with tact and delicacy. *Priest* is about as far from exploitation as you can get, but the Catholic League, a conservative watchdog group always looking for a way to raise its profile, was spoiling for a fight, and Disney was a ripe target.

Harvey's first instinct, as it was with *Dogma,* was to go for the jugular and release it on Good Friday. It was like jabbing Donohue with a cattle prod. The league called on its constituency to tie up Disney phone lines with complaints and boycott Disney products. New York's Cardinal O'Connor, without having seen the film, denounced it for being "viciously anti-Catholic." (Today, of course, in the light of the Church's pederasty scandals, it looks woefully understated.) Disney had ridden out these kinds of storms before, but nobody had anticipated the virulence of this one. "It was overwhelming the amount of phone calls that came in, the faxes and letters, the death threats," says former Miramax executive David Linde. "The publicity chicks were losing their minds, because *Enchanted April* had been doing well, people were calling up going, 'Hi, I saw *Enchanted April,* can you tell me where that is, I want to plan a vacation.' 'Portofino!' And then this!" Harvey recalls, "Cardinal O'Connor lit the fuse. There's nothing as frightening as getting these letters that said, 'Dear Jew, Go fuck yourself, I'm gonna kill you.' My mother criticized me on top of everything else. You think that publicity always fuels the box office—not that kind of publicity."

Harvey apparently never gave the Good Friday release date a second thought. As Linde puts it, "Harvey perceived no boundaries. He'd do whatever the fuck he wanted to do. He would push the envelope as far as it would go. It didn't matter what Disney said, it didn't matter what anybody said. They fueled the fire, which is the way he marketed movies. He saw controversy as an opportunity to create greater publicity, greater awareness." Harvey told McGurk what he planned to do. McGurk thought, Oh shit, Michael's not gonna like this. He called Eisner to tell him the news. It was about nine months after the Disney CEO's heart attack. McGurk said, "I just want to tell you, there's an issue I'm trying to deal with."

"What's that?"

"Well, Harvey wants to release *Priest* on Good Friday! For the publicity." There was a dead silence on the other end of the line. McGurk thought, I hope he hasn't fainted. Eisner finally replied, "Whatever you do, you gotta stop him." Eventually, Harvey came to his senses, moving the release up to March 24, 1995. Says Bowles, "*Priest* was a turning point for Miramax in a lot of ways. That's when they saw the downside of controversy, and how it could come back to bite them. And now that they were in the Disney fold, there was much more at stake than just Bob and Harvey's film company. This was a global multinational corporation. Harvey isn't dumb. While he likes the controversy, likes the attention, he's not going to cut his own throat."

Some Disney executives were reportedly furious that Miramax acquired *Priest* and *Kids* in the first place, knowing they couldn't release an NC-17 film. They took it personally, the sense being that, as one executive puts it, "He was doing it just to fuck with Michael. It seemed hostile." Says Roth, "We had a couple of years, '94, '95, when it was rough going. The amount of controversy that was connected up to Disney was terrible. There was definitely a conversation about how do you continue a business and make a profit when you are so connected to these two guys."

On June 14, 1995, Miramax opened *Il Postino*, a charming story set in Italy about an unlettered village postman whose life is changed when he delivers mail to Pablo Neruda, in exile from his native land, Chile, then under the boot of the brutal Pinochet regime. Harvey had picked it up in Toronto the previous year. He was sitting in the back of the theater crying. Recalls Amy Israel, then Hoving's assistant, "He said, 'You know what I'm gonna do? I'm gonna republish Pablo Neruda in a book of love poems, and I'm going to have a CD of famous people reading Pablo Neruda.' In that one minute, he came up with the entire marketing plan for the movie. And that's what he did, put a CD out with Julia Roberts and Andy Garcia reading Pablo Neruda." Adds Amy Hart, a marketing coordinator, "If Harvey believed in a film, he did not base his decisions on the first weekend's grosses. He would say, 'We're gonna work it.' " *Il Postino* was one of those films Harvey wouldn't give up on. Recalls Peter Kindlon, who also worked in marketing, "First we pulled quotes from reviews, then we used every-body with a big name who ever had an opinion about anything. The ads practically shamed people into seeing the movie, like, You must see this movie and if you haven't, there's something wrong with you. They did pro-motions with Italian restaurants around the country—Bring in your ticket stub, you'll get a free glass of wine! Relentless." Harvey drove *Il Postino* to a remarkable gross of $20.7 million.

Il Postino represented the calm before the next storm, the one you didn't need the Weather Channel to predict. Harvey had gone too far down the *Kids* road to pull back. The film played at Cannes in May. Cannes director Gilles Jacob didn't want it in the main competition, recalls Larry Clark. "It was too controversial. They offered us the Directors' Fortnight, and I said, 'No, I want the main fucking competition.' Harvey threatened to pull all of Miramax's films out of the festival. He strong-armed them—for *my* film, so I'll always love him for that. I got to see *Kids* at the Palais on that gigantic screen, and after that, I said, 'I could die right now a happy man.' " The French went crazy for *Kids*, but Todd McCarthy, the influen-tial *Variety* critic, dumped a pail of ice-cold water on the Miramax parade. *Kids* "seems voyeuristic and exploitative of its young subjects," he wrote, "[and] will undoubtedly raise the spectre of kiddie porn." The red flag, of course, was "kiddie porn," as in "Disney Caught in 'Child Porn' Film Row," a headline in Britain's *Guardian*.

Meanwhile, back in the U.S.A., senator and presidential hopeful Bob Dole, whose wife, Elizabeth, claimed she was going to sell $15,000 worth of Disney stock because of *Priest,* referred to *Kids,* among other films, as a "nightmare of depravity," without, as usual, having seen it. Miramax screened the film for Roth. "I saw the movie, I said, 'There's no chance for it to ever get an R rating,' " he recalls. "I told them they couldn't do it." Harvey was humiliated. The Weinsteins bought the film back from Disney and formed another company, Shining Excalibur Films, headed by Bowles, expressly for the purpose of distributing *Kids.* "*Kids* was a hot potato," Bowles remembers. "The most shocking film ever made, blah, blah, blah. There were ugly rumors—child pornography, drug use, underage kids having sex on the set—which were not true, but they were out there. I put the phone in my wife's name and decided to do it." For Disney, the problem was how to prevent the Weinsteins from exploiting the situation for their own ends. Bowles insists that Shining Excalibur had its own staff, but the parent studio suspected it drew on Miramax personnel to work on the marketing. "It was all Miramax people doing the work and distributing it, except under the straw company," says Clark. But Disney could never prove it. Explains Roth, "It set a bad precedent. Anybody inside the company could then take a controversial film and manipulate the system so that they would get kicked out and then create a separate revenue stream for themselves. Disney didn't want Harvey to make a profit [on it]." Good luck.

Clark had hoped for an R rating, based on the absence of nudity, but on July 8, the Ratings Board slapped it with an NC-17, which meant writing off the big theater chains and theaters outside the major metropolitan areas, four hundred screens instead of eight hundred. The Weinsteins released the film unrated. "Harvey asked me to come in, and he said, 'We need a version for Blockbuster,' " Clark recalls. "We'll get another million dollars if we give them an R. If you could just clip a couple minutes out of the film, I will give you a check for $100,000, right now, under the table.' I said, 'Harvey, you can't buy me. And you have enough money anyway.' He looked me straight in the eye, said, 'Larry, you're right, I do have enough money, but it's not for me, it's for all the little people out there. All the secretaries in the cubicles, they have an interest in this film. That's who you're gonna hurt if you don't do this.' I thought, Man, is this guy sharp. He didn't miss a beat." To the press, Harvey said, "I just love movies. Other movie companies just love money. I cannot live, and nor can my brother, with the idea of artistic merit not being first."

Shining Excalibur released *Kids* on July 21 at New York's Angelika Film Center and Lincoln Plaza Cinemas, then rolled out the film to about thirty-five to forty markets on July 28. "Harvey and Bob did everything for that fucking film that could be done," says Clark. "We broke new ground. None of the chains played unrated films, and we got it into the Sony theaters. I flew back to Tulsa where I was born and went to see *Kids* with a bunch of my childhood friends. In a mall!"

The picture did not break any records. Still, it did about $7 million in domestic box office, on a budget of $1.5 million. Despite Disney's efforts to the contrary, the Weinsteins made out like thieves, according to Bowles possibly taking home a couple of million each. Clark, on the other hand, got next to nothing. "I got $40,000 to do *Kids*," he recalls. "I saw another hundred and a quarter when it was first sold. I never got a bonus. I had 10, 12 percent of the net, but according to their bookkeeping, the film never made anything, even though it made so much money all over the world. I just got fucked out of everything. But they were very nice to me. And man, I got to make my film." According to Miramax, Clark received all he was entitled to. Says Harvey, *Kids* was a risky movie, "it grossed $7 million, not $70 million. It did terrible overseas, and no payment was due him other than what his contract required."

Like *Priest* before it, *Kids* was a defining—or redefining—picture for Miramax. Says Vachon, "*Kids* was a Miramax before-and-after movie." The Weinsteins thought, Enough already! Although Miramax had indeed distributed a handful of daring, cutting-edge films, its reputation as a champion of the First Amendment was a carefully cultivated figment of its publicity department. As Tusk puts it, "While everyone thought we were battling the MPAA and doing all these transgressive films, the truth was, we were doing *My Left Foot*. We were doing *Hear My Song*, we were doing *Mediterraneo*." Adds Bowles, "Bob and Harvey were moving on to fry bigger fish. They were moving into the big-film game."

A year later, at the Independent Feature Project Spirit Awards on March 23, where *Kids*'s Justin Pierce won for best debut performance, the executives at the Miramax table refrained from coming over to the *Kids* table, where Clark, Van Sant, Korine, Sevigny, Woods, and Vachon were sitting to proffer their congratulations. Some of the *Kids* gang felt snubbed.

Harvey sent Clark a sweet note every time one of his films (infrequently) came out, but never produced or acquired one again. Says the filmmaker, "They were offered *Bully*, about kids who murder their friend who's a bully, and *Ken Park*," another unrated, scabrous look at teenage dysfunction, but, he continues, "they passed. They were tough films, and Miramax had changed."

Seven
Pumping Up the Volume
1995–1996

• **How Harvey Weinstein lost *Shine* but found *Sling Blade* and rescued *The English Patient*, while *Four Rooms* nearly broke up the Sundance Class of '92 and October scored some hits.**

"I'm not looking to make an NC-17 movie anymore. . . . The mantra at Disney is to keep the ratings 'R,' and I'm happy to do so. I don't want to cause Disney any problems. Why ruin a perfect relationship?"

—HARVEY WEINSTEIN

Quentin Tarantino was not one to flee from the fame that was thrust upon him in the wake of *Pulp Fiction*. "I always wanted to be a star since I was a little kid," he explains. He was quick to appreciate the perks. "The clubs and restaurants, I've been there when I've been the loser, and it's a lot better to be the winner: 'Okay, you motherfuckers, get up. Let these dudes sit down.' " He loved the limelight, the heat, the buzz. A fan himself, he felt a responsibility to the legions of people who worshipped him. But of course, celebrity like his exacted a price. No matter how much he gave, it was never enough. When Chasen's, L.A.'s legendary restaurant-to-the-stars, finally closed its doors, he wanted to be there. "I drove him over," recalls Robert Rodriguez. "As soon as he opened the door, people were already there with *Pulp Fiction* posters. Mobbing him. He said, 'Man, that guy, I signed his poster, and he looked at me like I was a dick, 'cause I didn't sign all ten.' "

Says Tarantino, "It was getting hard to do a lot of the things that I liked to do. I would think, If I was Neil Jordan, I could have twelve hookers and no one would know who the fuck I was. It was getting hard to just take walks. Everybody was a homeless person. I had to avoid eye contact. Because to make eye contact with somebody was to invite them to approach me. My regular-guy shit, going to a used record store and spending two hours on the floor, yanking out the boxes, looking through everything they have—all of a sudden I'm getting jacked and pimped by these people. I'd say, 'Dude, it's my day off, man, I just want to look through the fuckin' records. Like you.' "

Tarantino got acquainted with Mira Sorvino at the Toronto Film Festival in September 1995, where she was wildly acclaimed for her performance as the hooker with a heart of gold in Woody Allen's *Mighty Aphrodite*, for which she subsequently won an Oscar. When Tarantino finally broke up with his long-term girlfriend, Grace Lovelace, they started dating. "Mira and I were in Paris together for our exciting romantic week, and she had never been to the Rodin Garden, which was one of my favorite things," he recalls. "So we had a little picnic, and we were making out, and everybody was looking at us. It was like, Ohmigod, that's been taken from me. If I had to make the trade, yeah, I would, but goddamn, if I had known in advance, before I got famous, I would have gone to the Rodin Garden more. I woulda done a whole lotta shit more before I got famous if I knew I was gonna lose the option."

In addition to doing press for *Pulp* and campaigning for an Oscar, he had been polishing an old script called *From Dusk Till Dawn* for Rodriguez to helm, noodling an idea for a martial arts movie he called *Kill Bill*, which he had developed with Uma Thurman, and preparing to direct one "room" in a collaborative portmanteau film planned by Rodriguez, Allison Anders, and Alexandre Rockwell, called *Four Rooms*. *Four Rooms* was a project of the so-called Sundance "Class of '92." (Rodriguez, who attended the festival in 1993, was an honorary member.) Anders missed the sense of community that characterized the New Hollywood movie brats of the 1970s. With film school no longer the common thread, Sundance, with its labs and its festival, its moral and often practical support, was the closest shared experience for the 1990s generation. Says Rockwell, "Basically I'd been paying my dues alone in New York as an independent. Then I went to Sundance with *In the Soup*, and I met Quentin, I met Allison, I met Rick Linklater. All of a sudden I realized, Other directors aren't the enemy. There were a lot of new filmmakers coming up, there was a New Wave feeling—why not do a movie that celebrates that feeling. I was at a dinner party, and I said, 'How about this for a premise, a hotel, and a bellhop's misadventures on New Year's night.' I called Quentin, and he got excited by the idea right away."

Harvey was so high on *Pulp* that he would have financed Tarantino's laundry slips. Still, anthology films rarely work, and in similar circumstances, probably few other companies would have agreed to back *Four*

Rooms. This was Harvey doing what filmmakers loved him for, taking a flier on a nutty, unconventional project, even if it cost him a couple of million dollars. Of course, it was doomed to fail, and he made his own unique contribution to that failure.

Each filmmaker would write and direct a segment set on New Year's Eve spinning off from one common character—the bellhop, Ted, played by Tim Roth. (Originally, Linklater was going to do a fifth room, but he smartly dropped out.) "It was really exciting to go against the way that things have traditionally been done," explains Anders. "Nobody had truly collaborated before, so it was, Let's all make this film together, let's do it experimentally, let's not have to worry about movie stars. We'll just cast people we like. Everyone was going to be paid the same. But very quickly all that changed." Simply, there was an eight-hundred-pound gorilla sitting in the room that nobody wanted to acknowledge, and its name was Quentin Tarantino. "Once it went to Miramax, it became a whole different thing," continues Anders, "because Quentin became a whole different thing."

All four filmmakers collaborated on the script, and Tarantino handed in the first draft. "I was just kind of horrified," Anders recalls. "I was like, Wait a minute—we haven't finished this, we've barely worked on it yet!" But Miramax never asked for a rewrite. "The feeling was," she continues, "Quentin had just won the Palme d'Or, and they couldn't go wrong. Their attitude was, you can fix script problems in editing—but that's very, very misleading. Because if you haven't written it, you most likely won't shoot it."

Rooms went into pre-production during the fall of 1994, right at the time *Pulp* was exploding. Tarantino was becoming a star. How could they tell? For one thing, they discovered that no decisions could be made without his approval. Continues Rockwell, "I was the originator of the idea and one of the executive producers, but if I wanted to have a toothpick in the lobby or a coffee cup, there would be this, 'We'd better check with Quentin.' I was being second-guessed all the time." It wasn't easy to get Tarantino on the phone. Swept up in the publicity blitz for *Pulp*, he was always traveling. Rockwell continues, "I would find myself negotiating with Quentin's third assistant. When you have all these intermediaries, they have nothing else to do but to make everything a big deal. So you had the first intermediary calling the second intermediary going, 'Oh my God, Alex is freaking out because he thinks the hall should be painted blue. Find out from Quentin what he thinks. We have to do it quick because we've got to know by the end of the day.' The second intermediary goes, 'Emergency! Alex has timed it so you have only one hour to make a decision.' Then, by the end of the day, it's 'Alex is an asshole because he wants the hall to be blue.' The next day I would finally get a call from Quentin saying, 'What's going on?

You went ahead and painted the hall blue? I heard the wall looks like someone puked on it.' "

Tarantino's segment concerned a movie star spending New Year's Eve surrounded by sycophants who are exploiting him for all they're worth. It seemed transparently about his ambivalence toward his own post-*Pulp* fame. "It was very personal," says Anders. "There is one moment where he is just totally fed up with people that are just hanging around, sucking off of his fame, drinking up all of the booze. And yet he's there. This is who he's ringing in the New Year with, like, people that he doesn't even really know."

She adds, "Quentin would joke, 'My room should just be called "The One You've All Been Waiting For." ' And we'd go, 'Oh yeah, very funny, fuck off.' " They may have treated him like an equal, but nobody else did. "His set was like four times the size of ours," she continues. It wasn't that his story demanded a huge set, "his head demanded a huge set. All of our rooms could have fit inside his. It was a metaphor for what was going on. We teased him about it, and he'd always laugh at himself that way, but there was a level at which people didn't want to admit that he actually had that much more power than the rest of us. Which was not good for the film."

When *Four Rooms* came in at two hours, forty minutes, the filmmakers' hopes for the film came fluttering down like so many autumn leaves. Harvey, not unreasonably, pressured the directors to shorten it. But since Tarantino was untouchable and Rodriguez's room was virtually shot without cuts, the brunt of the pressure fell on the two most vulnerable filmmakers, Anders and Rockwell. Rockwell said to the Weinsteins, "Well, okay, I could cut my room—everyone is going to do some cutting, right?" They replied, "Who's going to tell Quentin he has to cut?" Anders complains, "My room ran twenty minutes. Quentin's room I think ran forty-five minutes. But we were the only ones that ever had to cut anything. Had Quentin not been so famous, had we just all been at the same level, he would have cut his down too." Rockwell thought, This is working with friends? Maybe I won't like these people at the end of this thing.

It didn't help that Harvey was openly contemptuous of the two filmmakers. He told Rockwell, "You're going to be an insignificant art film director for the rest of your life," which Rockwell thought was funny at the time. It also got back to the filmmakers that Harvey said, "You know what the problem is with this movie? It's working with two geniuses and two hacks." Anders continues, "The truth is, I don't think Harvey and Bob ever liked my stuff. The only reason I was included in the film was because Quentin wanted me. We had a lot of battles. Harvey would yell at me. I was scared, but I yelled right back at him, and then he would send me huge bouquets of flowers, and I'd be like, 'Fuck that, I'm going to throw these out the fuckin' window.' But I'm a real sucker for flowers, and I never did."

Weinstein played head games with Anders. She recalls, "He threatened me, said, 'I'm gonna gather all your actresses and I'm gonna show 'em all your footage, what you are, naked.' 'Well, go ahead.' (The only person who wants everyone to see all his footage is Quentin!) But the thing about gathering the actresses, like Madonna and Lili Taylor and Ione Skye, and Valeria Golino—I got really nervous about that, because he created this image in my head that was terrifying. I felt so exposed, and I thought, What's he going to say—that she can't direct her way out of a paper bag? That the film could have been better? It was absurd, something that would never happen in a million years, and later I thought, How fucking ridiculous is that? But he knew I was vulnerable, and somehow it was gonna scare me. He'd say, 'Is that the cut you want me to release? Are you sure? I'm gonna release it.' Even though that's actually what I wanted, I'd have second thoughts. He made me doubt myself."

Once, Harvey reached Rockwell while he was at the dentist. The filmmaker recalls, "My dentist went, 'There's someone on the phone for you.' I thought, Is there something wrong with my mother? Who calls you in your dentist's office? I'm getting a root canal! Harvey got on, I said, 'I can't talk, I gotta go'—I was dodging him 'cause he wanted me to make cuts in my episode. So he said, 'Lemme talk to the fuckin' dentist.' He told him, 'Knock all his teeth out, I don't give a good goddamn how much it is, I'll buy him a whole new set of teeth if he makes the changes.' "

The quarrels over the editing of *Four Rooms* put a chill on the friendship between Tarantino and Anders. On October 3, 1995, the day O. J. Simpson was acquitted, she left for a Sundance-sponsored trip to China that included Tarantino, Geoff Gilmore, Ira Deutchman, Michael Barker, Ethan Coen, Liz Manne, and others. The purpose was to introduce the Chinese to indie films. She brought *Mi Vida Loca*, Coen went with *Barton Fink*, and Tarantino arrived a day late with *Pulp Fiction*, but the time they spent together there did little to change Anders's feelings toward her erstwhile friend. "Quentin decided he was going to be the star in China, and he set himself apart from the rest of us," she explains. "He was sitting on this panel next to me, and he told me that he just had this dream, that he was fucking this beautiful Chinese woman, and I realized that the woman was China, like, Quentin was getting laid by the country of China! That pretty much sums up what he set out to do, and it bothered me enormously. He likes that kind of idolatry too much." The last night they were there, the Sundance group was invited to a ceremonial dinner at the Great Hall of the People. There was a large banquet table sumptuously appointed, but it quickly dawned on the guests that there weren't nearly enough chairs for all of them. Then they realized that they were not meant to sit at the table and partake of the dinner, which was intended only for Tarantino, Gilmore, and sundry Chinese dignitaries. Deutchman said, "This is an interesting concept, invite people to a dinner party so they can stand around and watch other people eat." Later, Tarantino confronted Anders, saying, "You were shooting darts at me while I was sitting at the table." She replied, "Well fuckin' A I was. Jesus Christ, where is your fuckin' loyalty? You're in a situation where the rest of the people who are your friends, your colleagues, are, like, standing?" (According to Coen, "Quentin was mortified.")

When they returned to L.A., Anders plunged back into *Four Rooms* hell. "Bob Weinstein called me, and very matter-of-factly said they had done a cut of my room on tape," she recalls. "I said, 'You recut my piece? I have final cut on this movie. You're joking, right?' I honestly thought it was a joke. He said, 'No, I'm serious. We'd really like you to have a look at it.' This fucker, their post-production guy, Scott Martin, was recutting and recutting and recutting. Alex told me Harvey was going to send Scott out here to L.A., and I'm like, 'Let's meet him at the airport.' And he goes, 'I'll dress up like a chauffeur, with one of those little cards that'll say "Scott," and flip the card down, have a gun and shoot him.' I complained to Quentin at one point, but I think everybody was out for themselves.

"When Miramax tested the film, they repeatedly asked audiences and focus groups which room they liked best, pitting the filmmakers against one another, a perversion of the spirit that inspired the project in the first place. That was exactly what they weren't supposed to do, and they did it every fuckin' time. You want to make a movie with your friends, and you have this idealism, and the first thing they do is go, 'This story's better,' or, 'Skip this one and go to the next one.' By the time it was all over, I was, 'Yuchh, God, let me out of this nightmare."

Despite their high hopes, *Four Rooms* turned out badly. A film that was supposed to cost $1 million ended up costing $4 million. A film that was supposed to be without stars ended up with Madonna, Bruce Willis, Antonio Banderas, and Salma Hayek. A film that was supposed to have been created by equals ended up a creature of unequals. *Four Rooms* was released on December 22, 1995, and flopped theatrically (it grossed $4.3 million), although Lechner claims it eventually got into net profit. At the end, the four friends were barely speaking. Says Anders, "Quentin and I had a tough time. Fifty years from now, I will still want to be his friend, but he's not going to grow if everyone's just kissing his ass. I said, 'Which do you want, we make a really great film, or we all kiss your ass? He said, 'I'd like a little more ass-kissing, actually.' The film was such a miserable experience for me, after a while, I just kind of shut off to it." Anders was so bitter she refused to publicize the movie, refused to go with it to the Toronto Film Festival. She says Miramax gave her a first-look deal as a bribe just to get her to go—she went for one night—but they were never interested in any of her ideas. She calls it a "first-pass" deal.

Anders (and to a lesser degree, Rockwell) was the conscience of the group, the adult, the superego, if you will. Rodriguez, who had a great eye, was, as his future films would confirm, in all other respects a delayed adolescent. He was the child, id, and Tarantino, who displayed elements of both, was in effect the object of a cultural and aesthetic tug of war between them. *Four Rooms,* with an assist from Miramax, marginalized Anders and Rockwell, an ominous sign of things to come.

WHEN THE MIRAMAX GANG—Mark Tusk, Trea Hoving, and Tony Safford, supplemented by Amy Israel and the rest of the acquisitions posse—rode into Park City on January 19, 1996, with Disney gold burning a hole in their saddlebags, they were confident that they could outbluff, outbid, and outmuscle any company foolish enough to lay claim to a place around the campfire. But this was going to be the year Miramax got its comeuppance, when the companies that the Weinsteins had pistol-whipped in the two and a half years since the Disney deal shot back.

That year's festival produced an unprecedented bounty of films. Among the pictures in the dramatic competition were *Welcome to the Dollhouse,* a first—really second—feature from an unknown director named Todd Solondz, which had already been picked up by Sony Classics; an unheralded Australian selection called *Shine,* directed by Scott Hicks; *I Shot Andy Warhol,* directed by Mary Harron and produced by Christine Vachon; *Walking and Talking,* a bright, twenty-something singles comedy written and directed by Nicole Holofcener; and a picture Miramax had already acquired, Alexander Payne's first film, *The Devil Inside* aka *Meet Ruth Stoops* aka *Precious* aka *Citizen Ruth,* produced by Cary Woods for $3.7 million.

The previous year's tempests over *Priest* and *Kids* seemed to have taken their toll on the Miramax co-chairman. He was more erratic and quixotic than ever. As Safford put it, "He can't be in a competitive environment without doing something that will piss somebody off." Payne was thrilled when *The Devil Inside* was accepted for Sundance. In classic Miramax fashion, his savage, Swiftian take on the abortion wars was calculated to offend everybody. Laura Dern reveals herself to be an accomplished physical comedienne in her turn as Ruth, a derelict, glue-sniffing, unwed mother of four, with a fifth on the way who, when a judge orders her to get an abortion, becomes the prize in the battle between pro-lifers and pro-choicers, each of whom tries to seduce her. The production had been pretty smooth, but recalls Payne, "A week before its premiere at Sundance, Harvey freaked out about the title." He thought it made the picture sound like a horror movie, which it did. He demanded Payne change it, and threatened to pull the film from the festival if he didn't get his way. Payne suggested *Meet Ruth Stoops*, as in *Meet John Doe*. But a real Ruth Stoops turned up and objected. When Payne arrived at Park City, he was greeted by posters picturing Laura Dern with Breck girl perfect hair, tumbling through the sky—in the film the character is dirty and disheveled—while the title Miramax had slapped on his film was now *Precious*, which had precious little to do with anything. Payne was mortified. Even more confusing, in the festival catalogue, the film was still listed as *Meet Ruth Stoops*. At the Q&A following the first screening, Payne listened patiently as audience members interrogated Burt Reynolds, who had a small role, about *Deliverance*. Then someone stood up and asked, "Who the hell is responsible for the poster and the title of this movie? Because it sucks." Harvey was standing in the back. Recalls Cathy Konrad, who was one of the producers, "All of us hated *Precious*. I looked up and saw the door open and close, and I knew Harvey had left. He knew it wasn't good—the thing about Harvey is that he knows." At subsequent screenings, the audience booed when it flashed on the screen, and Payne irritably repeated that it was something Miramax had slapped on the film against his wishes. Harvey accused him of stirring up trouble. (Harvey eventually approved a title Payne had previously come up with, *Citizen Ruth*.)

On top of the title flap, there was the ending, always something Harvey liked to tinker with because the indie films, with their downer, unresolved, confusing endings, always needed fixing. "He wanted a happier ending than the one which was on there already, one that shows Ruth's victory over the two opposing sides and has her running away with the money," the director recalls. There was no time to reshoot it, so Miramax came up with the idea of tacking a title card on the tail of the film. Payne objected, dragged his feet, and Harvey again threatened to withdraw the film. The director continues, "So at Sundance it played with a title card that suggested, albeit in a tongue-in-cheek fashion," that Ruth went to California and became a successful real estate broker, "that she improves her lot somehow." Woods wanted to call Harvey's bluff, threatened to call Redford, hold a press conference. But this was Payne's first film, and he told Woods, "Cary, they're gonna know it's the studio's thing. Let's just forget it." Suprisingly, a film calculated to offend everybody offended no one.

Meanwhile, the screening of *Shine* had been a huge success. It had played the first Sunday night, at the Egyptian. The film was financed in part by Ernst Goldschmidt's Pandora Films, and repped by veteran pro-

ducer Jonathan Taplin, the former Bob Dylan roadie whose producing career stretched all the way back to *Mean Streets* and *The Last Waltz*. Hicks
had flown in from Australia. When the screening ended, *Shine* received a
standing ovation; the film was so powerful that, recalls Taplin, "Even
agents were crying—really bizarre. Once in a while, you realize you've hit
it. Everybody was in my face. At 7:30 the next morning, my phone started
ringing. Fine Line, Searchlight, but nothing from Miramax, not a word."

On the previous Tuesday, four days before the festival was due to start,
Safford had seen the film. It was the perfect Miramax picture, a reprise of
My Left Foot, this time the story of a tormented piano prodigy, tetchily
played by Geoffrey Rush, driven mad by his controlling father, etched with
equal skill by Armin Mueller-Stahl. In both films, the functionally challenged artist improbably lives happily ever after in the arms of an even
more improbable bride. Like *My Left Foot*, *Shine* was prime Oscar material, guaranteed to tug at the heartstrings of the congress of ancients the
Academy was fast becoming with each passing year, but Harvey must also
have seen himself in their magnificent monsters, the frog prince transformed by a woman's magic kiss, as Eve had transformed him. Safford says
Shine impressed him, but Taplin thought otherwise, reported to Goldschmidt, "He obviously didn't give a shit for the movie, thought it was
worthless."

Around noon on Monday, Taplin learned that Harvey, who was in L.A.
for the Golden Globes, wanted to see it. He got a print over to the Beverly
Hills Hotel, where Harvey was staying, and around four o'clock that day,
Taplin finally heard from Safford: "We're in, where's the bidding at?" By
this time it had gone from $600,000 to $800,000 to $1 million, a million two,
a million four, so Taplin told him, "It's gonna be above a million five." Safford replied, "Okay, we want it, and we want to make the last bid." Taplin
demanded, "Based on what?" although he knew—based on the fact that
Miramax was Miramax. That Harvey had picked up the dice and joined the
game should have been good news, but Hicks had already told Taplin
about his first encounter with the Weinsteins' company months before,
when he was trying to raise money on the script. He'd flown from Australia
to L.A. at Miramax's request for a meeting. Hicks went straight from the
airport to the Miramax office, where he had been kept waiting for an hour
and a half. When he finally had the meeting, he wasn't offered so much as
a glass of water, which apparently made a big impression. He kept saying,
over and over, "They didn't even offer me a glass of water." Hicks made his
pitch and was told he would be called at his hotel. He went straight to his
room, went to sleep, and woke up the next day—no calls from Miramax.
Hicks returned to Australia, furious. Now, more than a year later, he was
still furious, but there was a difference: he had a hot film. According to

Taplin, Hicks told him, "Who the fuck do these people think they are? I don't like Miramax, I don't like their arrogance, I don't like anything about them." Besides, Goldschmidt's Pandora had also produced Ben Ross's *The Young Poisoner's Handbook*, which Harvey had killed with kindness the year before. The *Shine* folks would rather have taken less money than go with Miramax. So Taplin avoided Safford's calls.

For once, it was Fine Line, New Line's indie division, that was the most aggressive. There was, of course, the history between Fine Line and Miramax, not only Harvey's longtime rivalry with Bob Shaye, and Bob Weinstein's encounter with Deutchman five years earlier, but Safford, who had defected from New Line to Miramax. Around 4:30 in the afternoon, Fine Line's acquisitions team, Mark Ordesky and Jonathan Weisgel, literally moved into Taplin's condo with their laptops and printer, saying, "We're gonna do a contract right here." There they sat, at the bar, typing up a contract while Taplin was fielding calls from everybody on the planet, occasionally leaving for a meeting. The price was still going up, and around six o'clock, according to Taplin, Safford called, said, "We want you to wait till Harvey gets here."

"Tony, I don't think that's gonna happen."

"Here's my final offer, $2 million."

"Quite frankly, there's some animus between the filmmaker and yourselves, you guys have got ten other movies, you've got *English Patient*, there are other players who need this movie more, don't have divided loyalties, I don't think it necessarily looks good. Just sit tight, I'll call you if something changes."

Safford faxed Taplin a contract, but at the other end of the line were the Fine Line guys, who matched Miramax's offer. Taplin and Hicks put their heads together, decided, "Let's take it. These guys are totally there, they totally want to do it, they gave us a very good back end."* Taplin and Hicks signed the contract, shook hands with Fine Line, and went out to dinner.

Eamonn Bowles, who was also at Sundance for Miramax, insists that Weinstein was under the impression Safford had closed the deal. Harvey buttonholed Bowles when he finally made it to Park City, asked, "Did you like *Shine*?" Bowles replied, "I think it's a crowd pleaser." Harvey said, "Good, it better be, I just paid a fortune for it. Come on with me." They walked to a deli where they talked about how to handle the film, the campaign, when to release it, and so on. Harvey left, and Bowles thought, Okay, great, I can relax now.

It was a snowy night, the weather was miserable. Israel, Hoving, and Tusk were sent to look for Taplin, and tracked him down at the Mercato

---

* "Back end": participation in the revenues generated from the distribution of the film.

Mediterraneo, a not very trendy Italian restaurant at the bottom of Main Street, whereupon Israel called Safford on her cell, reported, "The eagle has landed." Apparently also under the impression that he had a deal, Safford went upstairs to find Taplin and came down again, ashen. Bowles, meanwhile, had made his way to a bar, where he had a couple of drinks. All of a sudden Harvey burst in, barked, "Fine Line got *Shine*! They fucked us!" Says Bowles, "Harvey was foaming at the mouth."

Back at the Mercato, Taplin was celebrating at the bar with some friends, attorney Linda Lichter; one of her colleagues, Carlos Goodman, who represented Tarantino; and Debbie Newmyer, who was married to Bobby Newmyer and was working at Steven Spielberg's Amblin production company. They were seated upstairs, having ordered two bottles of champagne. Recalls Goodman, "About a half hour after Tony left, worried about his ass because he hadn't gotten this picture, Harvey stumbled up the stairs." Taplin didn't see him. He was looking the other way when Harvey appeared to materialize out of nowhere—if such a thing were possible—and blindsided him. According to Taplin, he grabbed him by the shirt and bellowed, "You fuck! You fucked me! You told Tony Safford he had it. You bid me up, you're weren't going to—you fucker!" (Harvey claims, "I didn't physically touch him.") To Newmyer he sounded like a crazy person, repeating over and over that Taplin had lied to him. "He was about to throw things," she recalls. "He acted like a bombastic jerk." She looked up at Harvey and said, "For once in your life, Harvey, why don't you take the high road. You win some, you lose some. Could you just be a gentleman and leave?"

"Fuck you, bitch! You shut up!" Harvey yelled. At this point, Lichter, a slender woman no more than a fraction of Harvey's size, a toothpick beside a mighty oak, leapt up and pushed him, shouting, "You don't talk to my friend that way." Now everybody was on their feet, and a chorus of cries rang out: "Don't call her a bitch!" "Apologize to her!" Goodman went for the maître d', while Harvey shouted, "You're gonna need more lawyers than this because I'm gonna cut you a new asshole." Goodman came back with a waiter who said, politely, "Excuse me, sir, you're disturbing the clientele," and pushed Harvey away from Taplin, who sat down, saying, "Harvey, you can rant all you want, but we've already signed the deal." Undeterred, Harvey continued in a loud voice until the manager appeared with two burly waiters and escorted him out of the restaurant.

Hoving and Israel were parked outside in a Suburban. Taplin says Hoving told Harvey, "You shouldn't have done that to Deb Newmyer. You don't want to piss off Steven." In the car, Harvey had Hoving write a letter apologizing not to Taplin, but to Newmyer, explaining that he just couldn't stand people who lie to him, which he signed and sent in.

October's Susan Glatzer happened along, saw Harvey in the vehicle banging on the steering wheel. He was screaming loud enough for her to hear through closed windows, "I am too big and too powerful not to get that movie!" Now he says, contritely, "I ruined my reputation, I killed it forever with these people, and rightly so, because I behaved extremely badly—because I'm passionate about movies."

Taplin insists, "Tony totally screwed up. Nothing was ever put down on paper. He saw it four days before the festival, the only person to see it. He coulda had it for $600,000. If Scott Hicks had said, I want to wait for Miramax, we would have waited. Everybody knew about Harvey Scissorhands, that was part of Scott's calculation. All I was concerned about was that there be no cuts in the film. It was what it was. In hindsight, *English Patient* was Harvey's Oscar film that year for sure, that's where he was putting his money. *Shine* got as far as it got because it was the only thing Fine Line had to run with."

According to Safford, "We agreed on terms. Taplin said, 'Write it up, and I'll come sign it.' We wrote it up, and he then went south. Did Taplin lie? Absolutely."

Passing on a hot film was every acquisitions person's nightmare. Harvey hated to be beaten. He he was in a black mood, and returned to his condo with his troops in tow. There would be an inquisition, a trial, as there was anytime Miramax lost a movie, and Safford, who was the prime suspect, was in deep trouble. The next morning, Harvey emerged from the Stein Ericksen Lodge clutching a copy of an item from the *New York Times* faxed to him from the East Coast that mentioned the Mercato dustup. Harvey started firing questions: "So Tony, you had the print? You saw it? You didn't think it was for us? You told them that we'd wait to see how the response was in Sundance? Who went to the Sundance screening? Did anybody go up to Scott Hicks and say, 'Hey, I really enjoyed your movie?' "

"Well, no."

"NO! Do I have to do everything myself?" Harvey thundered, crushing the fax into a ball and hurling it into a snowbank.

"It was horrible," recalls one staffer who was there. It didn't matter that he was yelling at Tony, we all felt that we were getting it, and we were."

Later that day, Harvey, with Safford in tow, corralled Hicks for lunch. He was threatening to sue, made Safford write up a chronology of events leading up to the fiasco, and placed Israel at a nearby table as a witness. Hicks was going from the lunch to the airport. When he stood up to grab his bags, Harvey stopped him. "Oh no, Scott, you don't have to carry your own bags," he said. "Tony will carry them."

After all the Sturm und Drang, the awards were an anticlimax. *Care of the Spitfire Grill* won the Audience Award in the dramatic category, while

Welcome to the Dollhouse took the Grand Jury Prize. Tusk and Israel loved *Dollhouse*, thought it was perfect for the Weinsteins, another outsider-overcoming-adversity, if you could call what happens to its antiheroine, Dawn Wiener (Heather Matarazzo) overcoming adversity. It expressed a personal vision, it was uncompromising, just like *Muriel's Wedding* without the sappy ending, and a central character who was eminently unlikable. Solondz had originally wanted to call it *Faggots and Retards*, which perfectly captures the flavor of the film. In other words, the real deal. Which was, of course, the problem. Harvey met with Solondz in New York. It was a good meeting as these things go; instead of just charming the filmmaker and making a lot of promises that he might not keep, Harvey had a real heart-to-heart with him, until, that is, he said he wanted to reshoot the ending, sweeten it. Solondz refused, and that was that. Tusk and Israel were bitterly disappointed. It was no longer the old Miramax.

By the time the Superbowl arrived and everyone had gone home, the 1996 festival would go down as Ten Days That Shook the Indie World. Not only had Harvey made a public fool of himself, but Castle Rock, an "independent" company owned by Warner's and best known as the home of Rob Reiner and *Seinfeld*, had insanely overpaid for *Care of the Spitfire Grill*, a film Bowles described as a "Dr Pepper commercial," forking over $10 million when the highest competing offer, from a tiny company called Trimark, was under $1 million.

Only two years earlier the first deals had gone down at Sundance, when Goldwyn paid $450,000 for *Go Fish*, and Miramax $227,000 for *Clerks*. "Nineteen ninety-six, the *Shine* year, was a nodal point, the year in which more things were sold in six days than had been sold the whole year and a half before," says Gilmore. "It inspired the kind of buzz and interest where the industry and filmmaking community says, 'This is great, this is a door, something I can walk through.'" The energy, buzz, and press that in the past had swirled around the discovery of talented young directors or exciting new films now went instead to the flame of money burning through hot product. The dollar frenzy encouraged filmmakers, agents, and producers' reps to treat Sundance not as a place where they could find a distributor—that increasingly occurred before the festival started—but as a springboard from whence to launch films. Sums like this—insignificant by studio standards—dumped by the majors into this market through proxies like Miramax, Fine Line, and Castle Rock, shattered the economic foundations of the indie business, rendered acquisitions increasingly irrational, and further pumped up the bidding bubble. With the exception of Sony Classics, the studio-affiliated indies dramatically upped the ante, escalating the level of paranoia, aggression, and desperation already endemic to the acquisitions game. The days when Miramax could bend back the fingers of Fine

Line and others like it were over. Harvey had shown the way to the promised land of megabuck profits, but the question was, would his competitors harvest the profits before he did. Acquisitions wasn't fun anymore, it was a deadly serious business, and blowing one film, as Safford did *Shine*, could cost you your job.

The festival was so crazy that year that even Soderbergh turned up, with Gregg Mottola's *The Daytrippers*, which he had co-produced and Sundance had rejected. Says the other co-producer, Nancy Tenenbaum, who also executive-produced *sex, lies,* and later *Meet the Parents*, "Being rejected by Sundance was the kiss of death for that movie. It had this negative tailspin, where everyone then thought the movie was not very good." The filmmakers suspected that *Daytrippers* had become a victim of Soderbergh's feud with Redford. But the film was accepted by Slamdance, then in its second year. Slamdance had been started as an unofficial, guerrilla venue to fill the vacuum left when Sundance became gentrified. Running in Park City during Redford's festival, it accepted first films only, and only those without distribution. Redford had not reacted graciously to the upstart. The actor sourly complained that Slamdance was "a festival that's attached itself to us in a parasitical way." Said former Sundance staffer Lory Smith: "It's no secret Sundance tried to muscle Slamdance right out of Park City. . . . They went to the City Council to propose an ordinance that would preclude holding two film events at the same time. They tried to suggest that Park City couldn't cope with the influx." To some, Slamdance held aloft the flag of the old festival, before it became indistinguishable from a Mercedes dealership.

Soderbergh had been boycotting Sundance since his contretemps with Redford over *Quiz Show* and *King of the Hill*. He had stayed away in 1993, 1994, and 1995. "I responded to the whole sort of garage band attitude of [Slamdance]," he recalls. "Sundance's official reaction to it was inappropriately strong and negative: 'Oh, they're a parasite, blah, blah, blah.' I thought, Whoa, whoa, whoa. The whole idea behind independents is not waiting for permission, and not taking no for an answer. This was how the satellite events at Cannes started, so I didn't get it. When Sundance turned down *Daytrippers*, I said, 'Lets go to Slamdance.' " Soderbergh's participation lent the guerrilla festival instant credibility and provided a small measure of revenge for the *Daytrippers* gang. But it was short-lived. *Daytrippers*, as Tenenbaum puts it, then "got fucked again. We got an offer from Trea Hoving, who said something like, 'You have an offer, there's no question, it's definitely gonna be at least a million, possibly more, we definitely want to release this movie.' Then Harvey saw it and passed. We had based all our strategy on the Miramax negotiation, and then we couldn't give the movie away."

The repercussions of the *Shine* debacle lingered for months. Safford had been a favored child at Miramax, but afterward it was never the same. His contract was about to run out anyway, and he was ready to make a move. "I got tired of bringing in projects that would either languish on the shelf or fail to get the push they needed in the marketplace," he says. "It was not the way I wanted to conduct business. I saw so many films and film-makers treated poorly. At the opening of *Cry, the Beloved Country*, Harvey embraced the producer, Anant Singh, on the stage and said, 'This man is my brother.' The last straw for me was when I witnessed an attempt to go around Anant's back to get rights to a project that he had announced that he had, but didn't quite, and there was an opening for Miramax to blow through and get the rights. It was a bad thing to do to a good guy. I would see how Harvey would treat people, the insults, I'd see him reduce very good executives to tears."

The brothers, who valued loyalty above all things, never looked kindly on those who fled the bunker. It set a bad example for the ones who remained, and they were convinced the runaways were sure to feed trade secrets to the enemy. Feeling more sinned against than sinning, that he had been unfairly blamed for the loss of *Shine*, Safford had not bothered to inform the Weinsteins of his imminent departure.

The American Film Market in the third week of February is a mecca for every foreign buyer in the world, every distributor, every wannabe filmmaker, as well as scores of reporters. In other words, it was not a place to be embarrassed in front of your ill-wishing competitors by some pisher who works for you. Weinstein and Safford were sitting next to each other on a sofa in the Miramax suite when Harvey said something like, "I've heard you've taken the Fox job." Safford replied, "Yes, I've taken the Fox job." Furious that Safford would leave without giving notice, without giving him the opportunity to match the offer, Harvey erupted, ripping off Safford's badge, which was pinned to his lapel, and taking a sidearm swipe at him, clipping him on the chin with the back of his fist, after which he unleashed a string of invective. ("I acted badly again," says Weinstein. "I did take his ID badge off him, but I never touched him.") Then both Safford and Weinstein hit the phones. Safford called his lawyer. Harvey called McGurk, at Disney, to put out the fire. Many would have regarded this incident that involved the co-chairman of Miramax as an invitation to a life-time annuity, but much to Harvey's relief, Safford surprised everyone by settling for next to nothing. "They dumped my files, locked me out of my office," Safford says. "All I left with was my Rolodex and my personal effects."

•   •   •

In February, about a month after the festival ended, Redford unveiled his new Sundance Channel, a joint venture of the Sundance Group, Showtime, and PolyGram. The idea was to bring foreign films to quality-starved audiences who were suffering from the prohibition on subtitles that radically limited foreign film distribution on cable and video, as well as expose indie films to viewers in small-town America who otherwise would never get a chance to see these films. Like all Redford's ventures, the Sundance Channel proceeded at a snail's pace, and when it finally launched, a year after the announced start date, it found itself playing serious catch-up to IFC, a vigorous, edgier, and younger-skewing spinoff of Bravo that had debuted two years before and serviced a similar audience. At one point, the two channels had almost reached an agreement to enter into a joint venture, one channel instead of two. "But Redford wanted creative control, approvals over everything," says IFC president Jonathan Sehring. "In this business, you have to move fast, and here's a movie star, who's also a director, who's also going to be paying attention to the day-to-day issues that networks face?"

The Sundance Channel's handicap was worsened by the fact that it was run exclusively by cable people who had zero knowledge of or connection to the indie world, save for Gilmore, who was onboard as a part-time consultant. Says one former executive, "They were clueless." Nora Ryan, the president, came from Showtime, and Dalton Delan, the VP of programming, came from the Travel Channel.

Redford indeed tried to micromanage the channel, involving himself in the most insignificant decisions. Gilmore always complained that Redford, an artist as a young man, obsessed over the graphic design of the film festival poster, the look of the program, and the Sundance promos that preceded the films, while showing little interest in the films themselves. Similarly, at the channel, he was more concerned with the design of the on-air elements, the menus, trailers, and so forth, than he was with the programming. On the one hand, it was a blessing that he left the programming to the programmers, because had he obsessed over the selection of films the way he did over the posters, there simply would have been neither a festival nor a channel. On the other hand, says one programmer, "A huge element of what I was doing, which I thought was enormously creative, was almost invisible, like it didn't exist. It was demeaning."

John Pierson had come up with the idea for a weekly show about the wild and woolly world of indies called *Split Screen*, intended as a feisty collage of interviews and clips, anchored by himself, and dedicated to the proposition that filmmakers will do any loony thing they can think of to get their pictures in the can. He was unable to get Sundance's attention until he opened negotiations with IFC, and then, after being promised by Redford himself, he says, that the show would be "his vision" and would air on MTV as well as the Sundance Channel—Pierson wanted to preach the indie gospel to kids under twenty who had never seen a real indie film—he cast his lot with Sundance. In the pilot, one desperate director confessed he had staged a traffic accident to collect insurance money that he then put into his film, while another described how he launched his career with a phony résumé. The pilot also contained some footage from a work-in-progress Pierson was excited about called *American Movie*, Chris Smith's pitiless documentary about the crude attempts of a filmmaker named Mark Borchardt to launch his first feature, a stupefyingly awful horror movie about a coven of witches. The footage showed Borchardt shoving an actor's head through a kitchen cabinet door.

"It was obviously great material, and obviously funny," Pierson says, but "I couldn't get an answer [from Sundance], they were like a black hole." And far from finding the car crash anecdote amusing, Redford seemed to be afraid that the channel would be seen as endorsing the strategy of bilking insurance companies to finance movies.

Although Redford is blessed in many ways, a robust sense of humor is not one of them. He was smart enough to know that the channel had to be irreverent and hip, but irreverence and hipness did not come easily to him. Whenever channel executives tried, he criticized their efforts as "sophomoric" or "juvenile." He would always say, "Be funny, like Chekhov!" He used to cite the J. Peterman catalogue as an example of the kind of sophisticated writing he found clever. At their wits' end, they found a copy on eBay, but it wasn't much help.

After a three-month wait, word came back from Redford via Delan, referring to *American Movie*, " 'that this is not the kind of filmmaker we want to help promote,' " Pierson continues. "And then, of course, flash-forward three years, *American Movie* is finished, goes to Sundance, and it's a major sensation, somehow becoming a poster child for the spirit of independent filmmaking against all odds, the same spirit that Sundance presents itself as the embodiment of. All Redford wanted to do is chum around with Chris Smith and trade his war stories about how hard it was for him to make *Downhill Racer*."

Redford was less an artist-manqué than an advertising-executive-manqué. When he insisted, as he always did, that he wanted "creative" control over the entities under the Sundance umbrella, it seemed like he meant control over the look and image, that is, the packaging. *Split Screen*, Pierson's proposed program, was just a bad commercial for Sundance.

Eventually, Pierson and Sundance parted ways. He concludes, "I spent six months in the Sundance family, tearing my hair out." Delan, falling just short of a classic Sam Goldwynism, announced, "We pulled the trigger on stopping development." Just before Thanksgiving 1996, Pierson jumped to IFC, where *Split Screen* had a four-year run. (Pierson wound up using the car crash as a virtual logo for his show.) If you called Pierson's company around that time, you would have heard this message: "You have reached Grainy Pictures, the place where the words 'Sun' and 'dance' are never to be used in the same sentence."

BOB WEINSTEIN'S DIVISION, Dimension, was beginning to rack up huge profits. Just as the 1996 Sundance festival was getting underway, Dimension released *Don't Be a Menace to South Central While Drinking Your Juice in the Hood* in one thousand theaters. It went on to gross $20 odd million, and then a week later, on January 19, he opened *From Dusk Till Dawn*, directed by Rodriguez from an old Tarantino script, which before the year was out would gross even more, $26 million. It seemed like everything Bob touched turned to gold.

For Harvey, however, the year couldn't have started less auspiciously, with the humiliating loss of *Shine*, the ridiculous and very public dustup with Taplin, and then Safford's big "fuck you." But then Harvey stumbled onto a film that would more than heal the wound left by *Shine*, a specimen of Southern gothic called *Sling Blade*, written and directed by an original named Billy Bob Thornton, who also played the lead. *Sling Blade* was shot on an $890,000 budget in twenty-four days during the late spring of 1995. It tells the story of Karl Childers, a man for whom—before the age of political correctness—the term "village idiot" would have been appropriate. Karl has been consigned to a "nervous hospital" for decapitating his mom with a sharp instrument "some folks call a sling blade" when, as a child, he stumbled across her copulating on the floor of the kitchen with the town stud. But, appearances to the contrary, we quickly learn that Karl is a gentle soul, a bit of a holy fool, a misunderstood cornpone Frankenstein. Despite his homicidal bent, he's a bleeding heart liberal down deep, improbably befriending the town homosexual (John Ritter). He also strikes up a friendship with a cute, towheaded little boy who happens to have an attractive mother (Natalie Canerday), in turn plagued with an inconvenient boyfriend, an abusive, drunken lout played by Dwight Yoakam. Every once in a while, Karl gives vent to lines like, "I reckon I oughtta eat some biscuits. Thankee, uh-hum," the "uh-hum" being his mantra, punctuating his speech like the ticktock of a cuckoo clock. Yoakam's bad-guy boyfriend is the only character with any wit whatsoever, and when he screams early on, "If y'all don't shut up, I'm gonna go outta my mind," it's hard not to sympathize. When Karl finally takes a lawnmower blade to Yoakam's carotid artery—which in the moral universe of this film is oddly sanctioned—after two hours or so of "uh-hums" from somewhere deep inside Thornton's throat, we miss him.

Sling Blade was executive-produced by Larry Meistrich and his company, the Shooting Gallery. William Morris agent Cassian Elwes, who had been involved in launching the project and securing Morris client Robert Duvall's participation in a small role as Karl's father, was repping the picture. Bowles, who had liked the script and heard the buzz, pestered Meistrich to let him see it first. The producer finally agreed. When the competition screeched in protest, Meistrich and Elwes changed their minds, scheduling two screenings, one in New York and one in L.A., for all the buyers. Like the other Miramax staffers, Bowles was terrified of Harvey. He pleaded with Meistrich, "Larry, do you want me to get my head handed to me? You told me you'd do this for us early, I passed this on, now you're saying you can't? And not only that, Harvey's gonna be in Paris when your screening's going on. This is insane, like, I'm getting screwed here." Elwes and Meistrich set up the screenings in New York and L.A. for the same night. They agreed to run off a PAL tape for Harvey and courier it to him in Paris at 12:30 A.M. so he could see it at the same time as the buyers in New York.

On the big day, Meistrich turned to Elwes and said, "Okay, now it's your turn, dude, sell the movie."

"How much do you want for it?"

"I can't really take it off the table unless it's a really high number, because I asked everybody to come out. L.A. hasn't started yet, I'd burn a lot of bridges. Let's ask for the most amount of money that we can possibly think of." The highest amount that had been paid up to that point was the $10 million Castle Rock had just shelled out for *The Spitfire Grill.*

With its we're-all-human-under-the-skin message bleeding from every frame, its sentimental streak as wide as the Arkansas River, and its strict adherence to the ugly duckling formula laid down by *My Left Foot, Muriel's Wedding,* and *Shine, Sling Blade* was tailor-made for Miramax, and Harvey loved it. He thought, Whatever it costs, I've got to get this movie. Oscars dancing before his eyes, he must have seen a chance to kick Fine Line's butt. He called Bowles in New York from Paris, barked, "I'm a half an hour into this, it's fantastic! An American classic. We gotta get ahold of this." Then Harvey called Elwes in L.A., said, "Whaddya want for it?"

"Say a number."

"You say a number."

"Fox Searchlight, Paramount Classics, they're all bidding for it, seven, eight million." Harvey thought, He's bluffing me like crazy. "What'll it take right now?" "Ten million." Harvey started to laugh, as in, "Fuck you, you must be—" Elwes interrupted: "All right, then we're gonna wait until it screens in Los Angeles." The man who lost *Shine* wanted to close the deal before the rest of the buyers saw the film. "I'm gonna call you back." Harvey did call back about ten minutes later, saying, "I'm shakin', I'm shakin', but you got a fuckin' deal."

"Done!" By the time Bowles got back to the Miramax office, Scott Greenstein and Elwes at the Sunset 5 theater, where the L.A. screening had just started, were nearly done with the negotiations, tying up loose ends. Elwes took Meistrich out of the screening over to the Morris office to sign the contract, and then he returned to the theater as if nothing had happened.

Thornton, too antsy to sit still, was hanging out at the Wolfgang Puck Cafe in the Sunset 5 mall. He was so anxious and depressed about the prospects of his film that he was entertaining the notion of moving back to Arkansas. Elwes and Meistrich took him downstairs to the parking garage beneath Virgin Records. Meistrich said, "Cassian's got something to tell you, Billy Bob."

"What's that?"

"We sold the movie."

"Really? How much for?" He figured, like a million or two million, if he were lucky.

"Ten million." Thornton, who grew up dirt poor and wasn't a whole lot better off now, didn't believe them. Then he went white and burst into tears. The screening had just ended, with all the buyers really revved up, when word came back that Miramax had already bought the movie. The buyers flew into a rage. It was *The Piano* all over again. After all the bullshit about arranging screenings on the West Coast and East Coast, Elwes had tricked them, wasted their time. He had brought off a coup, but there was a cost. From that point forth he suffered a reputation for being in Harvey's pocket, and he would pay for it the following year. Harvey himelf was on the speakerphone at 4:00 A.M. talking about one distributor who was particularly incensed. Harvey chuckled, went, "Heh, heh, heh, you gotta be really quick to keep up with the fat man!"

Up to that point only a handful of agents bothered putting together packages and repping indie films, but the *Sling Blade* deal, coming as it did on the heels of the *Spitfire Grill* acquisition, created a frenzy. "The impact didn't really hit me until I was lying in bed that night," recalls Elwes. "I just kept thinking to myself, $10 million, an outrageous number, I'll never repeat this. But it woke me up to the fact that I had to be involved in the selling of these rights, because if we can get a percentage, then we can make a fortune from this. Because up until then, the agencies thought, Well, indies—the film's gonna be made for $3 million or less, the client gets paid $250,000, we make $25,000, what's the point? This showed there's a real business in this thing. And not only that, we could make stars out of our indie clients. This guy was a B TV actor and a writer, and now he's a multi-millionaire. *Sling Blade* changed the way people perceived the acquisitions business. It also got the studios to pay attention to these films, as opposed to just reading the scripts and saying, 'Yeah, maybe, no,' whatever."

As soon as the deal was signed, however, the trouble started. Some of the press coverage was critical of Harvey for overpaying. As Harvey admits now, "It was stupid, nobody was going to go to $10 million anyhow. I paid way too much." Stung by the bad publicity, and convinced that the film was too long, Harvey was determined at the very least to cut it. "Billy made it clear to me as a negotiating point that final cut was very important to him, and Harvey gave it to him," Meistrich recalls. "The next day Harvey decided he wanted to take that back. It was, 'You gotta cut twenty minutes.' That didn't go down well. Miramax is a company that plays leverage. It's like, 'Well, I want you to do this, and I'm gonna give you that, but if you don't, I'm gonna do this to you." Thornton didn't want to cut his film, so the first thing Miramax did, according to Meistrich, was torture them over the deliv-ery of the picture, stretching it out as long as it could, perhaps because once it accepted delivery, it had to pay up. "The Shooting Gallery had a produc-tion services business," Meistrich continues. "We were hired by other peo-ple to deliver, we knew what delivery was, we weren't freshmen. They just didn't want to pay. They'd come back with grammatical problems in the contracts, 'You gotta make this a semicolon, not a colon,' crazy shit like that. [Then it was,] 'We want three more movies from Billy.' It was a constant ne-gotiation, and then they still insisted on cutting it. Getting Billy to agree to that made for a brutal summer. I was in the middle between two lunatics."

Weinstein recalls, "We had one of those audience research screenings that was just like you wanted to cut your own wrists, much less the movie." But in Thornton he'd met his match. The director was an angry, unhappy, depressed man, just like Harvey. Continues the Miramax co-chairman, "It was a tempestuous relationship. I was Angelina Jolie before Angelina Jolie. Fights like fucking no tomorrow." Weinstein, who often talks about himself in the third person, says, "If Harvey was the fastest gun in the West, he had to shoot me three times. I said, 'Can't you just shoot me once?' " Adds Bowles, "Billy Bob is a very ornery, stick-to-your-guns guy. If you tell him to do something, he's gonna go, 'Fuck you.' " Harvey would call Thornton in the middle of the night, threaten to lock the film away in a vault where no one would ever see it. He screamed, "I'm a big, fat, hairy Jew worth $180 million"—or some such sum—"and I can do whatever I want." Says Elwes, "Weinstein said, 'I'm gonna sell the picture to HBO. You're not gonna get a Best Picture.' Billy Bob replied, 'Ah don't give a sheet. Ah made the movie fo' me, not fo' anyone else, ah've seen it and ah've enjoyed it, so fuck yuh. Yuh can fuckin' dump it onto video and yuh can bury it fo'ever, ah don't care.' " Thornton used to call Harvey and say things like, "Ah'm going to stick a fork in yo' neck, motherfucka. Yuh not so tough, ah'm Billy Bob, ah'm gonna kick yuh ass, take yuh out to the wagon and whup your butt."

"You're a redneck, an ignorant piece of shit."

"Ah'm gonna cut off a horse's head and put it in yuh bed."

"This is because I'm Jewish, right? Tell the truth, Billy."

"It is. Yuh one a'them Heebrews. Yuh from that tribe. An' down heah wheah ah come from, we don' like Heebrews." To hear Harvey tell it, at this point they both started laughing. These antagonistic relationships, like the one he developed with Daniel Day-Lewis, resolve themselves with hugs and kisses. But, according to Meistrich, this was not the case. "The fights were not happy hugs and kisses at the end of it," he says. "It was a series of very long, ugly battles. There were threats and threats and threats on both sides. It even got physical. They got into a stupid shoving match in a hotel, and me and the manager had to break it up."

Eventually, Harvey convinced Thornton to cut several minutes. "It was a war of attrition, a never-ending battle," Meistrich continues. "Billy was starting to move on to other things." In truth the film, which proceeded with all the speed of blood moving through a cholesterol-choked artery, *did* need twenty minutes out, at the very least. But Harvey never managed to get the rest of the cuts he wanted, and Thornton never did stick a fork in his neck. Explains Elwes, "They needed Billy to promote the movie. Plus they wanted to have a relationship with him, so they could manipulate him for the rest of time." Someone else who was close to the situation puts it this way, the Weinsteins "pay people to like them. They paid Billy to like them. It was, 'I'm going to fuck you, but I'll pay all your bills for three years.' " (Miramax denies that it "fucked" Thornton, and points out that all studios have overhead deals.)

Sling Blade wasn't the only picture sucked up by Miramax, whose acquisitions team was working overtime. *Trainspotting* had been a big hit in England, and Harvey acquired the North American rights. Fox bought the rights to filmmaker Danny Boyle's next picture, *A Life Less Ordinary*. Harvey had no claim on Boyle, but he wanted a piece of the new film. Bill Mechanic, still head of the studio, got a call from Jeff Berg at ICM, who represented Boyle. According to him, Berg said, "Harvey wants it, would you relinquish the rights?"

"I don't care what Harvey wants," Mechanic replied. "He didn't buy it, I did." Mechanic thought, This is an idiotic request, stupid. Berg asked, "Just as a favor, just talk to him. So I'm doing my job."

"Jeff, it's not gonna end well, but okay. He can call me."

Harvey did:

"We deserve half this movie. Split the rights."

"I don't even have all the rights. I only have America and a couple of territories."

"Well, split whatever you have. We made Danny Boyle, we deserve them."

"With all due respect, Harvey, you had nothing to do with this guy." (PolyGram had financed *Trainspotting*, and Miramax had not yet opened it in the U.S.)

"Well, we won't release the movie!" said Harvey, thinking this would damage *A Life Less Ordinary*.

"Well fine, go fuck yourself. I don't care. That's your problem, not my problem. I got a love story, you got a drug movie, and what you do has nothing to do with what I do, and if you choose to throw away your money, go ahead."

"Then we won't do any Oscar campaigns!"

"Great, I don't care."

"I gotta have half the movie, I gotta have half the movie."

Mechanic remembered that when he was still at Disney and Miramax had released *The Piano*, Harvey had taken an option on Jane Campion's next film. He said, "Okay, you still have the rights to Jane Campion's next movie? I'll give you half of *A Life Less Ordinary*, whatever that means, and I want the international rights to Campion's next movie."

"You'll make that deal?"

"Yeah, I'll make that deal."

"Lemme call you back."

Says Mechanic, "Of course I never heard from him again. He does this all the time. Over the years, Miramax got more and more pushy. Bad behavior doesn't get punished in this business, and theirs certainly doesn't. People just ignore it and say, 'They're good at what they do,' which they are."

On July 19, Miramax released *Trainspotting*, which grossed a very healthy $16.5 million.

In late summer, the 1996 edition of the New York Film Festival invited *Sling Blade*. As soon as the Miramax marketing team discovered Thornton's backstory, they knew they'd landed a live one. Thornton was—or could be made to seem like—a barefoot auteur, the "hillbilly Orson Welles," as his pal Duvall called him, more riveting by far than the film, his schmaltzy white trash anthem. With his shambling gait, aw-shucks drawl, veritable road map of tattoos (memorializing his ex-wives—"I can blame almost every one on Bushmills," he said), kit bag of behavioral tics, and gift for sound bites, Thornton was ready-made for the late-night talk circuit. The beauty of it was that most of the color was true.

Thornton was forty-one when *Sling Blade* hit. He indeed sprang from the hills and hollers of Arkansas, a small town called Malvern, and even there he was an oddball. "We were raised in the woods," he said. "We didn't really fit in. We're kind of like the Addams Family out there." Growing up, he wasn't too different from Karl, whom he plays in *Sling Blade*, geeky and strange, with glasses thick as ice cubes and a malocclusion straight out of *Francis the Talking Mule*. His boyhood pal and writing partner Tom Epperson used to call him "Silly Slob."

In 1981, Thornton and Epperson lit out for Hollywood. They didn't have friends in the industry, a cousin at Warner's or an uncle at an agency, so they nearly starved to death, and the black cloud that always seemed to hover over Thornton's head didn't make things any easier. His older brother died of a coronary, and he himself developed a hard-to-diagnose heart ailment. Then his house burned down. "I don't know why I'm so unhappy all the time," he wondered, rhetorically. "The human struggle or some shit. . . . I'm a chronic worrier, and a lot of my decisions were based on my level of worry. . . . Sometimes I start screaming, angry shit. Curses. I'll be in a theater, watching a movie, and then I'll be on my feet, shouting. Got a touch of Tourette's on top of it all, I guess." At one point, he was so broke that he lived on potatoes for weeks at a time.

Thornton paid his dues playing bit parts in schlock like *Chopper Chicks in Zombietown* or cable movies like *The Man Who Broke 1,000 Chains*. It wasn't fun. One day he went into his trailer and looked in the mirror. "I was full of self-loathing," he recalled, "and I was making faces at myself and saying, 'What are you doing out here? Why did you take this stupid job? You're just a failure—you're never gonna get anywhere.' I always felt like an outcast, and I always felt a lot uglier than I am." It was out of this toxic brew that Karl emerged like a homunculus.

Slowly, Thornton and Epperson rose through the sludge. They wrote *One False Move*, which also got made, in 1990, with Thornton playing a dope dealer. He recalled, "We worked our hearts out making *One False Move*, did everything for free, tried to make it good. Then it comes out, and a week or so later these agents are calling, saying, 'Great news! TriStar wants to remake *One False Move* with stars!' I had no option but to scream back, 'You fucking idiot! Do you have any clue what an insult that is?' The guy said he couldn't figure out why I was so upset. . . . I'm no Hollywood rebel, but the place sucks."

Sling Blade was joined in the New York Film Festival by Mike Leigh's new film, *Secrets & Lies*, distributed by October, which also had acquired Lars von Trier's *Breaking the Waves*. Bingham Ray had sat through a five-and-one-half-hour opus by the eccentric Danish director, called *The Kingdom*, at the Berlin Film Festival in February of 1995, when all the other buyers had stumbled out during the break, bleary-eyed and bored. With no idea how he was going to sell it, he bought the film for $150,000, thus adding von Trier and his Zentropa Films to October's growing stable of filmmakers, which by that time included Leigh, David Lynch, and Abel Ferrara, who was enjoying a brief time in the sun.

On the strength of *The Kingdom*, Zentropa sent Ray the script for *Breaking the Waves*. It was a bizarre story of an innocent girl whose life measures the short distance from rapturous love to sexual degradation. Ray knew that von Trier idolized Carl Dreyer, and saw this as his *Passion of Joan of Arc*. "Which intrigued the hell out of me," he says. "And it also fit the profile of the company. There was nothing else gonna be like this. One of a kind." Neither Amir Malin nor John Schmidt got it, but Ray insisted, "We're doing this fuckin' movie," and at Cannes that year he plunked down $800,000 of October's hard-won money for North American rights. One plus was the cast: Gerard Depardieu was slated to play Jan, the male lead, and "HBC" (Helena Bonham Carter), as Mike Leigh called her, was going to be Bess, the emotional center of the film. But about a week after Cannes, Zentropa called with bad news: HBC had dropped out, and if October wanted to do the same, they would certainly understand. Ray asked von Trier, "Who are you gonna replace her with?"

"I go for unknown."

"Which unknown?"

"English actress. I like her audition tape, Emily Watson. Emily Watson is going to be Bess." He couldn't supply a glossy of Watson, didn't have a bio, nothing, which didn't much bother Ray. "Having seen Linda Fiorentino's career resurrected by *The Last Seduction*, I always found it much more exciting to work with filmmakers and actors who no one's ever seen before or haven't seen for a long time," he explains. "They're brand spanking new, and for me that's the best." He went ahead.

Nine months later, Ray flew from the 1996 Berlin Film Festival to Copenhagen to see *Breaking the Waves*, which was finished. "That movie blew me away," he recalls. "There's no one there with you, and you just know you've got something really special. What it was, how it would do, if we're gonna lose money or make money, all I knew was it was gonna be a terrific ride."

October submitted *Breaking the Waves* to Cannes, along with *Secrets & Lies*. Both were accepted, and both were acclaimed by critics and jury members alike. Says Ray, "Going into Cannes, we were one kind of outfit, and coming out we were totally different."

In September 1996, *Secrets & Lies* opened the New York Film Festival and got enthusiastic reviews. Leigh's film was released on September 27. It did strong business through the rest of the year. *Breaking the Waves* opened weakly in November at a big Loews theater, got kicked out after two weeks, and moved to Talbot's Lincoln Plaza, where it played for months.

Miramax released *Sling Blade* and *Citizen Ruth* in December, for Oscar consideration. Although the brothers were still acquiring potentially controversial films like *Trainspotting* and *Citizen Ruth*, it was with considerably less enthusiasm, and often, like *Citizen Ruth*, they failed to release them in a timely fashion, if at all. Miramax held *Citizen Ruth* for almost a year, until after the 1996 presidential elections—because, suspected Jim Taylor, Payne's screenwriting partner, Harvey felt the subject was so controversial it would somehow embarrass Bill Clinton, for whom Harvey had conceived a fiery passion. Weinstein, a lifelong Democrat, had started to see himself as a player on the national political stage. He had joined Bill and Hillary's circle as a fund-raiser after the New Hampshire primary, and had begun to see them socially during summers on the Vineyard.

As the release date approached, the Miramax marketing department tried to sell the film as a wacky comedy. The ad, for reasons best known to the company, featured Dern as the Statue of Liberty, wearing a big smile and holding aloft a can of glue instead of a torch. Says Payne, "They send you stuff to look at and then they do what they want. It's, 'We did this film, we did that film, don't tell us what to do.' The director is the last person to know. I mean, people ask, 'What is the budget of your movie?' I still don't really know, they never tell you. All their machinations are cloaked. Okay, maybe they know something I don't, but I do know that the bait and switch rarely works, and I know that by putting a happy face on darker, more realistic films—I feel that realistic merely means dark—films which don't buy into these prettified myths of how people live, you turn off your true market. In the case of my films, egotistically speaking, the genre they're in is Alexander Payne films, and I love the idea that my films are difficult to categorize. It's unfortunate that they also become difficult to sell."

Adds Konrad, "I do think Harvey made promises about promoting the movie and promoting Laura Dern that he didn't ultimately make good on, but at the same time, how can you expect someone to keep putting money into something when it's not getting any traction. The marketing is the most crucial moment in the film's life. Films live or die by somebody's ability to create a world for them to come out into. What Harvey was famous for was taking movies that no one knew how to sell and making them gold. He had an amazing ability to take the darkest films and somehow make it seem like if you missed them, you missed out on the event of the century. So you wanted to believe that he was gonna spin that magic with your movie, and when he seemed to be doing a better job for other people, it was hard to understand. You'd ride the 'I know what I'm doing' wave for a while, but something's gnawing at you, something's making you feel like he ain't really delivering, but it's not like I had a solution, or Alexander had a solution."

Both Payne and Taylor felt that Dern's performance was Oscar material, but from their point of view, Miramax had decided to put its money on *Sling Blade* and dump *Citizen Ruth*. Says Taylor, "I was shocked because some other movies that I thought were completely marginal made three times as much. It would have been nice if we were out longer and won some awards. But I didn't feel I'd been gypped or cheated. I keep my expectations low." *Citizen Ruth* only made $1.5 million. "I didn't get one single protest letter from *Citizen Ruth*, not one," concludes Payne, with surprise. "I hope that we are entering an age where films throw grenades, where they question, don't just support the status quo, because that's what we used to have in the '70s, throwing grenades. It was like, What did I do wrong?"

Sling Blade was getting good reviews, but struggling nevertheless. The poster and ad campaign featured a picture of Thornton as Karl. The reaction was, "Who's that? Yuchhh!" Recalls Harvey, "You threw that spot in front of people with Billy going, 'Uh-huh, uh-huh,' and they went, 'I'm not going to see that movie.' I knew that any shot of him in character was death. The grosses were abominable."

Miramax thought *Sling Blade* might pick up a nomination or two, but their brightest hopes were pinned to *The English Patient*, which began life in 1994 as a Saul Zaentz production. Zaentz's company, Fantasy Films, is located in the Bay Area. Like the Weinsteins, he had begun his career in the music business; like Harvey, he was a ferociously independent character with a penchant for lavishly mounted but frugally produced upscale projects based on prestigious literary properties that appealed to the Academy, enabling him to scoop up Oscar nominations and sometimes, as in the case of *One Flew Over the Cuckoo's Nest* and *Amadeus*, the Best Picture Oscar itself. Says Bernardo Bertolucci's producer, Jeremy Thomas, "Saul, like all of us, is a buccaneer, one of those beacons for others which I hope I will be one day."

Zaentz was a man of strong opinions who saw the world in black and white. As he once put it, "My friends are my friends, and my enemies are my enemies." One of his friends was Anthony Minghella. A short, squarish man who wears his head shaved and his eyes shaded by dark glasses, Minghella was born of Italian parents, and grew up on the Isle of Wight. Despite his British accent, he has a whiff of indeterminate ethnicity about him—he could be from anywhere but England—and after September 11 he couldn't walk ten feet through an airport without being stopped and searched. Minghella is a cultivated man, a gifted conversationalist with a passion for music and poetry, cosmopolitan in the best sense of the word. Although Zaentz is pugnacious and Minghella rather more ingratiating, the two men had much in common. Like Zaentz, Minghella was a charmer, an animated dinner companion who spun spellbinding stories.

Each saw himself half reflected in the other. "*At Play in the Fields of the Lord* had just opened catastrophically badly, and he was so strong, and so decent about it, I was impressed," says Minghella, recalling one of his first encounters with Zaentz. "In a moment of profound failure, he said, 'This film was many years of my life, it was a project I absolutely believed in, but the movie doesn't work.' He was very stoic."

Minghella had just had a bitter taste of failure himself, and couldn't help noticing that Zaentz did not blame Hector Babenco, the director, the way he sensed Warner Brothers had blamed Minghella for *Mr. Wonderful*, his second film. He had unwittingly walked down a road taken by many indies before him, allowing himself to be beguiled and then toyed with by a studio intrigued with his first film, *Truly, Madly, Deeply*. It had ended badly, and undermined his self-confidence. "The studio lost faith in my ability to make a movie fairly early on in the process," he recalls. "I was in free-fall anxiety every second of every day. When I finished that film, I went home and made a decision that I would not make another movie unless I could make it on my own terms. That is why I instinctively gravitated toward Saul, because I knew that his whole mantra was to support directors, and in a sense the more of an outlaw the project was, the more he was attracted to it. The one special gift that Saul has is the ability to inject self-belief. He had no difficulty extrapolating from the small film that I had done to a bigger one that I might be capable of doing. Whereas I actually had a lot of difficulty imagining that."

Zaentz asked Minghella if he would write and direct his new project, *The English Patient*, an adaptation of a difficult and stubbornly uncinematic novel of the same title by Michael Ondaatje. Zaentz had always financed his films himself, with some combination of his own money—usually the profits from his previous film—and foreign sales. He would then sell North American rights to the finished film to a studio for the cost of production, and take a percentage of the back end as profit for himself. But after *Fields of the Lord*, as Minghella puts it, he "had determined that he wouldn't risk his own money in the same way again," which meant he was almost entirely at the mercy of outside financing. From the studio point of view, *The English Patient* was a bad bet. It was an expensive ($40 million odd) period piece set in and around World War II with Italian and African locations. The director was inexperienced, and the cast—Ralph Fiennes and Juliette Binoche—was conspicuously devoid of the Tom Cruises and Julia Robertses who make executive hearts go pitterpat. Then there was the story, about a badly burned man confined to his bed who tells tales to a French nurse in a ruined Italian villa. "Not a lot of laughs," says Minghella. "We met with polite indifference everywhere. I myself wouldn't have bought it."

Zaentz started the ball rolling with $5 million of his own money, and, making the rounds of the studios, finally wound up at Fox. After bitter quarrels over budget, script, and casting, Mechanic bought English language rights for $20 million. *The English Patient* went into pre-production in the summer of 1995. Locations were scouted in Italy, costumes designed in London, and so on. As was customary on his pictures, Zaentz persuaded the crew and cast, which now included Kristin Scott Thomas and Willem Dafoe, to take deferments. They went along, as they always did, because he made quality pictures and had a reputation for honesty. Everyone from Fiennes down, including Oscar-winning film and sound editor Walter Murch and costume designer Ann Roth, halved their fees. All told, $7 million in salaries was deferred.

What happened next is shrouded in a fog of selective memory and long-burning resentment. According to Minghella, Fox kept reducing its level of support. Zaentz was unable to make up the difference by selling the rest of the foreign rights. Eventually, Fox pulled the plug, and pre-production ceased. Mechanic denies this, saying that Zaentz failed to raise the remainder of the financing, preventing him from going forward. Minghella's friend and later partner, Sydney Pollack, and producer Scott Rudin called Harvey Weinstein. The brothers had already passed because they didn't want to meet Zaentz's asking price for the U.S. rights. But now the situation had changed. This was a fire sale. Says Pollack, "I called everybody in town when Anthony told me *The English Patient* was falling apart. Nobody wanted it. Harvey stepped up, spent the money, and promoted the hell out of it." Recalls Elwes, who was involved because Minghella was a William Morris client, and takes a more cynical view, "Miramax had been buzzing around, waiting till it all collapsed so they could come in and steal the whole thing, a classic move." He persuaded Fox to come back in. Elwes continues, "Once Miramax knew that Fox was about to close the deal, they went crazy, sent Scott Greenstein to L.A. to sit in our offices until the deal was closed for the whole film." Miramax bought world rights for about $28 million. Harvey insisted on $2.5 million worth of further deferments, which meant that Minghella, for example, deferred nearly four fifths of his salary.

After the acquisition of *The English Patient*, when Weinstein and Zaentz were romancing each other, Peter Jackson, whose *Heavenly Creatures* had been distributed by Miramax, told Harvey he wanted to make *Lord of the Rings*, which Zaentz had owned for thirty years and wouldn't sell. According to Jackson, Harvey said, " 'That's fantastic, I know Saul well, I'll speak to him.' He did do what everybody thought was impossible." In Harvey's words, "Saul was in love with me. I convinced him to sell the rights for it. He got a huge piece of the deal as the executive producer who didn't invest a dime. I put $10 million into the development of the film."

The plan was two three-hour films at $75 million for both, the first Miramax-Dimension co-production. Based on the budgets of their previous work, Jackson and his partner, Fran Walsh, believed they could do it. With Miramax's money, they completed most of the pre-production—scouting locations, building models, design work, and two screenplays over the course of eighteen months. But after the screenplays were finished, it became clear the budget would be more like $140 million, way over Miramax's cap. "Disney didn't believe in it, wouldn't give me the money to make the film," says Harvey. Continues Jackson, "Miramax was in a state of panic. Bob Weinstein was enraged because they'd spent all this money, and they were on the hook. He didn't understand the project and didn't have any confidence in it. Bob's lack of confidence was eating away at Harvey, who was trying to remain supportive. There were veiled threats of lawsuits against us, and I felt that Bob would have happily unleashed the lawyers on us, and tried to tie us up in some sort of legal hell, but Harvey moderated that." Harvey had his people reduce Jackson and Walsh's two scripts to one, saying, "We're too far down the line to pull out of this now, but we can't spend more than $75 million." Jackson goes on, "Fran and I were horrified at his. We argued that you'd be presenting a movie that anybody who had ever read *Lord of the Rings* would be severely disappointed in. They didn't want to hear that. Harvey said he wanted me to drop out of the script writing. Because he felt I was the impediment. He was going to send Hossein Amini, who wrote *Wings of the Dove,* to New Zealand to work on the script with Fran. Of course, Fran rolled her eyes and looked at me, This is never gonna happen. Then he said, 'Peter, if you don't want to be involved in this, then John Madden is lined up to step in and take over.' He had a plan, where Hossein Amini would write it, and John Madden would direct. We got home, decided this was not something that we wanted to do. We knew that decision could end our careers, but we thought, We could do TV films." The pair's agent, ICM's Ken Kamins, told Harvey, "They're pulling out, but there's one thing that you have to do: Peter and Fran brought this project to you. They worked on it for eighteen months. You have to at least give them a chance to shop the film somewhere else." Harvey did the right thing, but he attached such punitive conditions that the chances of their succeeding were near zero. "I gave Peter the worst turnaround in the history of turnarounds. 'Cause I didn't want to lose it. I gave him three weeks. And harsh terms, including 5 percent of gross for me and Bob, and more importantly, I said, I want all my money today! You had to pay me the $10.1 million back that minute. Which is never done on a turnaround. Usually you wait until the movie's made. I told Peter, 'Is this the worst deal you can possibly have?' He said, 'This is beyond horrible.' I said, 'Nobody's gonna buy it.' And then Bob Shaye said, 'Yes to three movies!' "

In the barrage of press that accompanied *The English Patient*'s Thanksgiving release, the tangled web that was the production history of this film was spun into a seductive fairy tale—part fact, part fiction—whereby the courageous indie rode in on a white horse to save the fair maiden from the clutches of the foxy old studio king who was ready to ravish her. Recalls Mechanic, "All of a sudden, I was reading some article about how Miramax stepped in when Fox tried to fuck this movie, Hollywoodize it," by demanding Demi Moore for the part that went to Kristin Scott Thomas. He continues, "I promise on my life—I am not a liar—Demi Moore's name was never uttered, Demi Moore was never in a movie while I was at Fox, Demi Moore was never offered a movie, much less *The English Patient*. We're not stupid." Mechanic believes the Moore story was "a round of lies . . . probably more Miramax than Saul, although Saul went along with it, and then, being pathological, started believing it. Complete, total lie!" (Says Minghella, "I know that Demi's name was always mentioned in the context of alternative casting.") Mechanic is still bitter: "Anthony would smile and say, 'It's not me.' But to me he was culpable, he could have told the truth. And if you asked Saul right now, he'd say we screwed them." But it would quickly become apparent that if Zaentz was screwed, which remains to be seen, it was not by Mechanic, but by Miramax.

Eight
Swimming with Sharks
1996–1997

• **How Dimension screamed its way to box office gold. Robert De Niro ignored Harvey Weinstein's script pages, while October sold out to Universal, and Steven Soderbergh hit bottom.**

"Scream's *opening weekend was a turn in the road that showed where Mira-max/Dimension was going, showed why no one can talk about their vast contri-butions to cinema culture any longer. They were going to out–New Line New Line.*"

—JOHN PIERSON

While Harvey was launching *Sling Blade* and *The English Patient*, Bob Weinstein was hard at work at Dimension, putting out movies like *The Crow* sequel, *The City of Angels*, at the end of August 1996, which would gross $8 million, and *Hellraiser IV*, which grossed $9 million. Meanwhile, an agent with whom Cary Woods had once done business gave him a spec script called *Scary Movie* by Kevin Williamson. Woods was not a fan of hor-ror movies, but people in his office loved it, said, "Don't worry, it's not hor-ror, it's really funny. It makes fun of the genre." He thought this script would be perfect for Dimension. He called Bob and said, "You gotta buy it." Bob took it off the table for $500,000, and Woods gave the script to Drew Barrymore, who committed immediately, to the part eventually played by Neve Campbell. With Barrymore on board, it was a green-lit movie, and they sent the script to Wes Craven, the legendary writer-director of *A Nightmare on Elm Street*, who was then ice-cold, as was the genre he practically invented, the slasher film.

Barrymore agreed to play the lead, then changed her mind, decided she wanted to play Girl 1, who's on-screen for two seconds before she's killed. Bob didn't like the title, *Scary Movie*. Craven, who was trying to crawl out from under the rock called "the horror guy," passed on it twice. But he loved the irreverence of it, the note of parody it struck, and finally relented. Recalls Cathy Konrad, who was still working at Woods Entertainment, "Bob felt strongly that in marketing the movie you had to play to the strength of Wes Craven, his core audience, and you couldn't sell humor in this kind of movie. We were just going, 'No, you don't understand,' and he was like, 'No, I *do* understand, you guys are just getting lost in yourselves trying to play it cute. I'm playing it smart.' He was very right."

"I didn't want it to be a parody," Bob recalls. He met with Williamson, the writer, and said, "Kevin, I want to make sure I bought the script that I think I bought. Is it a funny movie with scares? Or is it a scary movie with humor?"

"It's a scary movie with humor."

"Good, that is the way I saw it. But you got the wrong title." Bob continues, "My brother came up with the new title, from a Michael Jackson song out at the time." *Scary Movie* became *Scream*.

But Bob, who had not yet hit his stride as a producer, didn't trust Woods, Konrad, or Craven, and hired B. J. Rack to watch his back. Smart and tough, Rack had been around the block and then some, having produced, among other pictures, *Terminator 2*. She had a background in editing and special effects. Her skills were useful to the Weinsteins, they liked her, and since the early 1990s they had used her now and again as a hired gun. Rack similarly liked them, although she found Bob hard to deal with. "He has peaks and valleys that are really extreme," she says. "One second, he'll say to you, 'Yeah, that's a good idea,' and then, like that, without breaking eye contact, 'I hate it,' like a switch. His moods churn—they go in one direction and then in another direction. He can be charming and focused and great for hours, and then he can be negative and nasty. I was brought in as a hatchet man on *Scream*, to shove that budget down, go tell them to shoot it for less money."

Bob hated the rushes, thought they were flat, more pedestrian than frightening. During the second week, while Craven was shooting Barrymore, he started calling Konrad, who was supervising the production. Bob said, "I'm scared, I don't know about this." He started picking at details. Why was Barrymore wearing a sweater, shouldn't it be racier? Her wig looks terrible. Cary Granat, who headed Dimension, was a friend of Konrad's, owed her his job. He warned her, "Bob is not happy. This isn't going to get better, it's going to get worse." She replied, "What do you want me to do?" There was no answer. One day, Craven was shooting a scene with Liev Schreiber, who was doing a cameo as Cotton Weary, and Bob called the set, said, "Let me talk to Wes." Konrad interrupted Craven in the middle of a shot and said, "Bob wants to talk to you." She recalls, "Bob told him that he thought Wes could do better. Wes said to me, 'What kind of studio head calls a filmmaker in the middle of shooting and kicks him in the balls and expects him to work the rest of the day and do good work?' "

Twenty minutes later, Granat phoned Konrad, saying, "Bob just saw the stuff with the mask, and he thinks it's a joke. And he says he never signed off on the mask."

"Cary, that's just complete and utter horseshit. You're the president of the fucking studio, we sent you sketches of the mask. That mask was found by a location scout in a woman's attic, it is not a new revelation, and we all talked about how great it was, and how it looked like Munch's [painting] *The Scream*. I don't get it."

"Bob just doesn't like it."

"We're not shutting down!"

"Well, ahh, I'm gonna have to fly out there."

"I don't give a shit. Fly out here, but until you guys can tell us what we should be doing differently and so much better, we're just gonna keep doing what we're doing." A couple of hours later, Granat called again, saying, "Bob wants to review—do you know where all the other masks are that you submitted for consideration?"

"No, I don't know."

"Bob wants Wes to continue filming, shooting each scene with four different masks until he can decide which one he wants."

"Go to hell!"

Craven was mortified, asked, "What am I supposed to do? How do I tell an actor, we're gonna do this four times, with different masks?"

Says Rack, "They treated him very badly. There's no such thing as autonomy, except if you're Quentin. I've seen Bob bully Robert Rodriguez," who he was convinced was the new Spielberg. Adds Konrad, "They were trying to get us to keep shooting around the problem. We were going, 'You can't do that. The whole rest of our shooting schedule is around Ghostface. We are crippled without approval to shoot that. What do you want to do, shut us down?' "

"I thought the mask was goofy," Bob recalls. "People would laugh at it. I thought Wes was crazy. They told me they bought it in a store. I said, 'You bought it out of the store somewhere? You didn't design a special mask?' Because I forgot the Mike Myers' *Halloween* mask was actually a William Shatner mask that John Carpenter had bought out of a store. Had I been a smarter guy I woulda just said, 'Ah, Jesus, history is repeating itself.' We were going mask after mask after mask, choosing this and that, and finally I just relented. These guys were right, I was wrong."

In any event, Granat got on a plane for California. When he arrived, he convened a meeting in Craven's hotel room at midnight that included Konrad, the line producer, and a couple of assistants. Announcing, "We have reached an impasse," he told them how they could placate Bob. Konrad thought he was being disrespectful to Craven. Interrupting, she exploded with, "Wait a second. Who the fuck do you think you're talking to? You hired a guy who created the genre, basically, and you're telling him how to make the movie? The guy's made thirty-some odd movies, this is the most insulting thing I've ever seen in my entire fucking life! And frankly, you're not offering us any help. You're just telling us how to keep beating around the bush until someone who's invisible decides they like what they see. This is no way to make a movie. It's gonna cost a fortune, it's stupid, and we're not gonna do it!"

"Right, we're not going to do it!" Craven chimed in, as everyone in the room stared at them.

But Konrad realized, I can't just flat out say, "No, come and get me," because they will. I'm going to have to offer something in return. "Look, no one's understanding what they're seeing," she went on. "So the only way I know to solve problems when no one understands what they're seeing is that we cut together the first footage that we have, and if you like what you see, we never hear from you again. But if you don't like what you see, then we're going to all walk away happily, and you guys can make this movie with whomever and however you want to make it."

"That's a great idea," replied Granat, and flew back to New York. They cut together what they had, sent it to Miramax, and continued shooting. Pacing back and forth in front of the production office wondering, Are we going to live or are we going to die? Konrad took a call from one of Bob's assistants, who gave her an Elvis-has-entered-the-building play-by-play of the proceedings: "The footage is in the office . . . the footage is on its way down to the screening room . . . the footage has reached the projection booth . . . the footage is being threaded . . . Bob is on his way down . . . Harvey is now with Bob, they're both seated . . . the lights have gone out . . . they're starting—I'll call you back." Konrad was shaking. Craven poked his head in three or four times, asking, "Have you heard? Have you heard?" Then, ten minutes later, Bob called Konrad. He said, "That was fucking great, that was fucking great, Harvey levitated across the theater, it was unbelievable, Jesus Christ. You guys were right, I was wrong, I was so wrong it's fuckin' amazing, anything you guys want, anything!" She recalls, "That was it, we never heard from him again. I have to say it was one of the greatest calls I've ever received from a studio chairman in my life."

(Bob remembers it differently, says he never saw an assemblage until later, when Wes wanted [another] $400,000.) "He showed me forty minutes. I said, 'Yes, I like it, here's your 400 grand, it's great." From then on, adds Rack, "Wes was God. He was absolutely golden. When they get their comfort level up, they're fine."

By the summer of 1996, Dimension was a veritable beehive—perhaps roach motel is more accurate—of activity. While they were in post on *Scream*, they began work on *Mimic*, a horror movie that featured outsized cockroaches skittering about the New York City subway tunnels. It was brought in by Michael Phillips, best known for being half of a powerful New Hollywood producing team with his then-wife, the late you'll-never-eat-lunch-in-this-town-again Julia Phillips, who gave us *The Sting*, *Taxi Driver*, and *Close Encounters of the Third Kind*. Guillermo del Toro was attached to direct, with Phillips onboard as executive producer. Del Toro, a gifted young Mexican director, had made a stylish horror film called *Cronos*, distributed by October, which won the Grand Prize in the Critics' Week, 1993, at Cannes and nine Mexican Academy Awards. Stuart Cornfeld was slotted in as a producer. Bob called Rack. He asked if she wanted to work on *Mimic*. Unbeknownst to him, however, she was close to del Toro. She thought she might be able to watch his back. And she was also friends with Cornfeld. She asked, "Don't you already have a producer?" Bob said, "Well, I think there's room for you on the picture." Rack agreed. She had had plenty of experience working with abusive men. "I've worked with Paul Verhoeven and I've produced a Jim Cameron movie, but *Mimic* was the hardest professional experience I've ever had," she says. "I felt like I was in a prisoner of war camp."

Rack understood what she was getting into, or should have, and she has no excuses. As she puts it, "I knew everything, enough to have really failed that IQ test by coming onboard. Once they signed my deal, they asked me to fire Stuart." (Cornfeld eventually stayed on in a titular role.) Less than an hour into the very first meeting with all the principals, Phillips discovered that it wasn't the 1970s anymore when, after he had presented his notes on the script, by del Toro and his writing partner, 1970s veteran Matthew Robbins *(Batteries Not Included)*, Bob told him to be quiet, that they were the stupidest, shallowest notes he had ever heard. Recalls Rack, who was present, "Bob said, 'What are you talking about, that's stupid,' and then he said, 'You guys have to leave. I want to be alone,' and just shoved people out the door. When they were out of the room, he said, 'He's off the picture. I don't care what it costs, I never want to see his face again.' And he hardly had said anything."

Scream had come in at about $16 million, *From Dusk Till Dawn* at about $17 million, so at $22.5 million, *Mimic* was a stretch for Dimension, especially for a genre picture with a young, relatively inexperienced director. Bob wanted Rack to bring the budget down to $15, $16 million. Based on her reading of the script, she concluded that in fact $22 million, which included $3 million for special effects, was about right. She recalls, "Bob screamed at me, hung up the phone on me, and that was in the honeymoon period when he kept saying he loved me. It was incredibly brutal.

Normally, I would just say, 'I'm quitting,' but I could tell I was too deep into a co-dependent relationship. I'd pick it up again and say, 'Listen there's a way to fix this, take all these effects out. It doesn't have to be *Alien*. It can be *Jacob's Ladder*. Then I can get it down to 16 if you work with me.' It was, 'No! You're not listening to us, and we've asked you to deliver a budget for 16 and you're refusing. We're firing you.' There was no communication, I couldn't get anyone on the phone, and if I did, it was just screaming and yelling. There was so much chaos I couldn't organize meetings, I couldn't have conversations because somebody was screaming. When you say something Bob doesn't want to hear, he tells you, 'Shut up, shut up, stop talking, stop talking.' Harvey physically shoved me out of the room and into the elevator and made me go back to L.A. after I had made some innocuous statement that set him off. It was not like they were necessarily targeting me, they were just angry all the time, and screaming because it was not the way they wanted it. They're bullies."

Technically, Disney supervised the whole process. Rack's office was on the Disney lot, she submitted budgets to a Disney executive. They co-signed checks. After she produced a preliminary budget, she gave a copy to the woman at Disney to whom she reported, and sent one over to Bob. He called her, screaming, "I can't believe you sent this to them, how dumb are you?" He was so angry, she thought, If I was anywhere near him he would murder me, adding, "Bob and Harvey never dress up their act. They can't control their language, they can't control their bodies." But it worked for them, in that it seemed to Rack that the Disney people were afraid of them.

The script sessions, which took place in the cramped conference room at the Tribeca offices, were like nothing she had ever experienced before. There were five or so writers who worked on the screenplay, which changed continually throughout the production. The participants, some of whom had been flown in from the West Coast and put up at expensive hotels, were picked up by a car service at, say, 9:00 A.M., and delivered to the Miramax offices at 9:30, where they'd cool their heels in the tiny reception area opposite the elevators for a couple of hours until Bob and Harvey waltzed in at 11:00 or 11:30. Fifteen minutes into the meeting, Bob turned to an assistant, and speaking rapidly in his Queens-inflected singsong voice, puled, "A lox platter, okayyeee?" A few minutes later, the bagels and lox appeared from the deli around the corner. Harvey, who only attended occasionally, smoked cigarette after cigarette, filling the room with smoke and stubbing the butts out in the lox. If he was all out, he would pick up butts and relight them. The food sat around for hours because every time an assistant appeared to take it away, he or she got screamed at. When the platter was finally removed, Harvey began eyeing the leftovers on people's plates. He would turn to someone, ask, "Are you gonna finish that? No?" and help himself. Eventually, they would order lunch, which, like the bagels and lox, sat on the table for hours while the assistants who tried to clear it were shooed away. By four in the afternoon, Harvey was looking for leftovers again, asking, "Do you wanna finish that sandwich?" before reaching over and grabbing it. Dinner arrived around seven, and the meeting that had started eight or so hours earlier might continue until midnight.

But in the course of the process, Rack came to appreciate the Weinsteins' strengths. "They are incredibly good at what they do," she says. The kinds of studio story and script meetings she was accustomed to maybe lasted two hours, they'd talk in generalizations, and then they were over. The first meeting she went to with Bob and Harvey went on for eleven hours. She looked around the room, and saw that they had brought in everyone, vice presidents, assistants, people who had been there for a decade and people straight out of film school who arrived the day before. It was like a focus group. She thought, Well, we're just gonna breeze through, I've got my script notes, the director has his, the writer has his. But Bob started on page one, the first line, and then the second line, and he'd go, "Hey wait a minute. Would a female really be working down in the sewer? Could she really have a job as an anthropologist if she's only second year in college?" "Real questions," Rack recalls. "I had never seen that level of detail at a studio." According to former development head Jack Lechner, "Bob will talk for much longer, and in more detail about the script than Harvey will. There's a reason why *Mimic* went through that pileup of writers. That's never happened at Miramax." Adds Kevin Smith, "Bob is like, 'I wanna know exactly what I'm gonna get.' Harvey's whole thing is, 'Shoot it, and if something goes wrong, we'll fix it, we'll throw money at it.' Harvey works the talent more than Bob. Bob's movies are generally not talent-driven. He serves the concept, serves the genre."

Rack continues, "As soon as they got to something they didn't know, they'd scream, some minion would come in, and they'd yell, 'Go look up the MTA code for whatever.' Or we'd be at a story point and they'd scream, 'Go get *Alien* and give me a catalogue of the scares and at what minute in the film they come,' and then twenty minutes later they'd go, 'You don't have it? Why not? Get it right now! Get ten tapes of *Alien*, get ten people to take different parts, have ten more people type memos,' and forty-five minutes later it would be in front of them, so that they could use it as a reference: *Alien*, every single scare, bump #1, bump #2, bump #3. It's kind of impressive. Because for all the antics, for all the craziness, they have a lot of resources and they use them. And they just keep going, on to the next page, pounding on every detail. A lot of good things come out of pulverizing every line of the script, because those details always come back to bite you in the end anyway. It's not really a power thing. They didn't do that on *Scream* because the script was perfect. And even though they often don't know what they want, they recognize it when they see it. If Bob likes something and Harvey likes something, and there's that resonance between them, it's generally a brilliant idea. And you feel it. Because as badly as they treat their employees, they respect their opinions. And when everybody in the room is saying, 'Yeah, that's a great idea,' they go, 'Okay, great,' and they turn the page. They're tireless. Like, after the first two hours of the meeting, you think, Okay, we'll probably be taking a break, go to a really nice restaurant—no. They both remain focused in that stifling, stinking hot conference room, where you've had three meals in the last ten hours, and they're still pounding away at it. People are crying, people are screaming. They just shove and push and berate until they get what they want."

At one meeting that went on and on and on, at 10:15 or so at night, Bob or Harvey said, "Oh shit, turn on the TV, channel whatever," and he went, "Damn, they didn't put it right after the end of the show before the commercial like we said. They did it after the commercial, before the credits." It was a promo for *Scream*. They called the guy at home, woke him up and said, "You fucked us, why didn't you put it where we asked you to put it." Rack continues, "In other words, they're so on top of it, that they know exactly when the promo is supposed to go on, what channel, where it's supposed to fall on the show, and they know the guy's home number. That's the level of detail and control you want when you're distributing a picture, and that's why they get the venues they want, that's why the posters are right, why the commercials are right. They're really good at what they're really good at. Actually, they're good at everything."

Robbins who, with del Toro, was the original writer and did several drafts, based on a chilling short story about oversized, mutant cockroaches who walked upright and were easily mistaken for men in dark overcoats, was not amused by the process. "From the first day, every rough edge, every original notion, was attacked," he recalls. "The tenacity of Bob Weinstein is such that you really don't have any choice in the matter. He is all will power and no originality. People in Hollywood are very susceptible to the exercise of will, because most of them are too timid to have an opinion. This is not Bob's problem. What's disarming about him is his self-deprecation. And his excitement. He would say, 'God damn, this is going to be so great!' It is rare for an executive to expose himself like this. They're usually too guarded. He created the illusion that you are collaborating with him, and yet at the end of the day, in draft after draft, the idiosyncratic and unusual elements just disappeared. To this day, Miramax has the cachet of encouraging individual voices, and yet when you are in the room, it is that aspect that is most under suspicion. Any young filmmaker that goes into that factory is subject to the same grinding process. And if the filmmaker is susceptible to any private doubt, they will instantly locate that and play upon it, take charge of the project, and claim authorship afterwards: 'We made that picture what it is today.' Bob has enormous envy for creative people. He's like somebody who's bought the most beautiful piano in the world, a Bösendorfer, and can't understand why he can't play it as well as Vladimir Horowitz."

The script and budget turmoil continued, even after production on *Mimic* started in Toronto, a favorite Miramax location because it was cheap and could be made to look like New York. Bob would call Rack at four in the morning to complain that the dailies weren't scary. Del Toro was making an atmospheric, moody, cinematic movie, more like *Seven* than the Dimension staple, the *Highlander* series. At the beginning of the film, there's a noirish overhead shot of a hospital ward where children, infected by a disease spread by the cockroaches, lie in beds draped with towering tents of netting, lit from within, pools of yellow glowing in the shadows of the darkened room. Bob went ballistic, because, he insisted, no hospital in New York looks like that.

"Bob had a vision for the movie that was a B-picture," says Robbins, who had written dense characters appropriate to del Toro's style. They were eviscerated. "The final film was much more of an action film, chases, shootings, and explosions. Bob kept asking, 'Where's my war?' Given that it was a Dimension film, I'm sure it was totally appropriate." Despite all the meticulous prep work, the hashing and rehashing of the script, he and del Toro were making different pictures. Rack looked at the clock, said, "I have to go to sleep, 'cause we're filming tomorrow." Bob continued as if she hadn't said a word, talking about how you had to move the camera like this, you had to move the camera like that. "Make the camera go phoom! Go phoom!"

"What do you mean exactly, 'phoom,' show me the shot, what do you expect me to do? Tell him exactly how to shoot it?"

Bob started coming to Toronto himself. Rack had begged him not to have a tantrum in front of all the actors. He sat twenty feet back from the camera delivering his instructions for del Toro to her in a loud voice, whereupon she ran over to the director and told him what he was saying. "He really wanted to direct every shot," she says. A particular room would be dressed in a certain way. Bob questioned it, asked, "Why doesn't it look like *that*?"

"Well, because we were thinking of *this*."

"Well, I think it would be better like *that*."

Says Rack, "It wasn't like one idea was better than another, it was just, he always wanted his idea. I had just finished producing a movie that Sally Field had directed. I knew I could tell her, 'We really can't go two more hours into overtime because we don't have the money,' but I couldn't tell her, 'Can you do the dance number faster.' Bob would say, 'Do the dance number faster.' There's no boundaries for their input."

During one particularly acrimonious meeting in Bob's penthouse suite, Rack got angry because he wasn't listening to her, started raising her voice, and Bob, she recalls, "picked up a Coke bottle from the table, and pulled his arm back really fast, and made like to throw it at me, and caught it just before he let it go out of his hand. He looked at it and said, 'You make me so mad I almost threw a Coke bottle at your head. What the fuck is that? How could you make me so mad?' Bob used to come up and kind of punch me, and say [to Harvey], 'She makes me so mad I want to kill her, just like you and me fight.' And then to me, 'I've never gotten as angry as I get with you.' Like he was trying to compliment me. He kept saying, 'You're like part of the family.' " She thought, I have my own dysfunctional family, but they don't throw Coke bottles at my head.

Bob got into the editing room and looked at the rough assemblage before del Toro was able to work on it and decided it wouldn't do. He continued to call Rack from New York every night, waking her up, screaming at her until she turned her phone off, whereupon he would send one of his executives staying at the same hotel to pound on her door, waking up everyone on her floor. He flew up to Toronto yet again, this time to fire del Toro. He summoned the director to a meeting in his hotel room. Bob told him, "You're just not cuttin' it, and we have to let you go, I'm sorry I trusted you, I thought you were the right guy, that was my mistake, you're not the right guy."

Del Toro was crushed, said, "Maybe we're making two different movies."

Bob replied, "No, you're not making a *good* movie. That's it, you're going home tonight, we're gonna pick up the pieces tomorrow with somebody else."

But Bob was worried that this wouldn't sit well with the actors, who often rally to the side of their directors in these situations. Mainly, he was worried about Mira Sorvino. After her Oscar for *Mighty Aphrodite*, which Miramax had released the previous year, she had become the brothers' flavor of the week, a regular in films like *Beautiful Girls* and *Blue in the Face*. She was also going out with Quentin Tarantino, who was an occasional visitor to the set, so Bob had to be careful. In spite of having just given del Toro the boot, Bob wanted him to head off any potential resistance. "Mira's downstairs in the lobby, and you're gonna tell her that you couldn't cut it and that you're withdrawing from the movie," he instructed his now ex-director.

Rack said, in a loud voice, "That's not fair, I'm not going to let him go down there, he's in a state of shock over this, you can't put him up to this, he needs to get his agent." In effect, she was telling Bob he had to Mirandize del Toro. Bob yelled at Rack to shut up, instructed Dimension executive Granat to remove her from the room. She refused to budge, said, "I'm not leaving."

"You are leaving."

It went on like that for a while, then Bob changed tack, said, "Okay, we'll all go down together," because he didn't want her to go alone and contaminate Sorvino. Downstairs, del Toro walked up to the actress like a zombie and intoned, "I can't cut it, I've got to leave the movie. I just can't do it."

She saw through it immediately. According to Rack, without missing a beat, Sorvino, who had a lot to lose by antagonizing the Weinsteins, threw a spectacular tantrum, screamed at Bob, "You motherfucker, you're not doing this to him, you're not doing this to me, this is not the way you make movies, I'm not coming to the set tomorrow without Guillermo directing the movie. I won't work for anybody else. I'll split."

"You have to, it's in your contract," replied Bob.

"Well, then we're just gonna get into a big old fight! And you might win, but the movie ain't gonna get made."

Sorvino implied that she would get Tarantino to intervene if Bob sacked del Toro. Rack called him. "He was really supportive," she recalls. "He helped a lot, really terrific." Tarantino phoned Harvey.

"It was better to talk to Harvey about it, so I wouldn't have to confront Bob, and make him feel he was getting it from all sides," Tarantino recalls. "I said, 'Harvey, you did this [picture] for Guillermo, you liked his stuff, what's he doing that's so bad?' " But regardless, Bob hired another director, Ole Bornedal, a Danish filmmaker who made *Nightwatch* for Dimension, and then Robert Rodriquez to help him. The next day, Sorvino's agents flew in, and she carried the day, insisting, "This is not going to happen until we see an assemblage of the film, and we all sit down and make this decision together." Del Toro spent a weekend in the cutting room, putting his own cut together, flew to New York with his reel, and showed it to Bob and Harvey. Harvey turned to Bob and said, "I like the look. I wish our other pictures looked that good." Bob replied, "Yeah, okay." But Bob reportedly tried to make him work with Bornedal. Del Toro refused, and Bob gave in.

Says Tarantino, "Mira saved his job. She wanted to work with an auteur, put herself in the hands of a really good director. She wouldn't have done this movie in the first place if it hadn't been for *Cronos*. So if he were to get fired, there was no point. [For Bob], it was more of a reflex, this is something we can do, and she took that option away. She was able to do that because they weren't that against Guillermo. Because Bob's a tough guy, and if Bob really wanted to get rid of Guillermo, he would have gotten rid of him. He would have kicked Mira's ass for the fun of it, and reshot everything just to prove the fuckin' point." (Del Toro could not be reached for comment.)

Konrad had segued directly from *Scream* into *Cop Land,* based on a script by James Mangold that she had convinced Bob to buy in 1994 while she was producing *Things to Do in Denver When You're Dead.* Like *Denver, Cop Land* benefited from the guys-with-guns frenzy created by *Pulp Fiction,* but it lacked *Pulp*'s veneer of hipness. Mangold stood firmly in the tradition of American social realism, next door to James Gray, whose *Little Odessa,* a powerful portrait of a Brighton Beach (Brooklyn) Russian-Jewish family in decline that cuts so close to the bone it's almost painful to watch, had been released in 1994 by Fine Line. *Cop Land* was the small-town version of Sidney Lumet's big-city morality tales set in the sordid world of crooked cops—*Serpico* or *Prince of the City* meets *Fargo.*

Mangold, the son of Robert Mangold, a well-known painter, had grown up Jewish in Washingtonville, a conservative small town in the Catskills that seemed to be home to every angry white-flight cop who didn't live in Staten Island. Precocious and creative, he went to Cal Arts at seventeen and landed at Disney with a deal at the tender age of twenty-one. Eisner signed him, but Katzenberg let him go after he refused to fire his assistant when he was asked to. *Cop Land* was his way of going home again, as *Little Odessa* was for Gray.

"*Pulp Fiction* had just happened, and Miramax had this tremendous prestige," Mangold recalls. "I was excited that I wouldn't be working at a studio. Everyone wanted to be in the next *Pulp,* so I was able to meet almost anybody." Tom Hanks, Tom Cruise, Sean Penn, John Travolta, all expressed interest. But "Harvey was out to do what he had done with *Pulp,*" Mangold continues. "He didn't want to pay full freight for any these actors." His edge lay in making films at a price, making it possible for Miramax to produce pictures like an indie, but reap profits like a studio, the former the cause of the latter, which was the beauty of it all. Indeed, he had been very creative adapting the financial strategies he had learned in the indie trenches to more expensive movies, laying off the risk in co-productions and/or foreign presales. (The downside, of course, was that he had to sacrifice a chunk of his profit.)

But no matter how much heat was rippling off the company, actors were not so willing to cut their rates. Mangold and Konrad went down to Florida to meet Travolta at the Church of Scientology. Travolta said, "Look, I love the script, Harvey's talked to me about it, but he wants me to do it for no money because he thinks I owe him for *Pulp Fiction.* But I'd like to believe that I had a little something to do with its success, and I've already set aside the things I'm willing to do as a labor of love, and this is not one of them.

I've already told Harvey he has to pay me, and if he doesn't, it's just too bad." Harvey wouldn't pay him, and Travolta didn't do the movie.

But there were plenty of other falling stars who needed the Travolta makeover and who would slash their price. Sylvester Stallone came on-board to play the lead, a none-too-bright, deaf-in-one-ear small-town officer who has to decide whether to throw in with the bad cops or do the right thing. Stallone was loaded down with superstar baggage, but Mangold gambled on his doing for *Cop Land* what Travolta had done for *Pulp*. When Stallone signed on, what had been a small film became a much bigger film, especially when Robert De Niro, Harvey Keitel, Ray Liotta, and Michael Rapaport joined the cast as well. "I had wanted to make a smaller movie, but I had the feeling that independent film was like a floor that was giving way," explains Mangold. "Unless I had a vaultful of cash, which some filmmakers do, I didn't know how I could have remained outside the system. It had taken so long to get my first film, *Heavy*, I knew that was a hard road, and the kind of cynicism of the independent game had become depressing, so it wasn't something to cry over that I was suddenly cutting my teeth with big actors, and larger budgets. Here was a real opportunity to change the movies that were being fed to the general public, as opposed to changing the movies that were being fed to a kind of rarefied independent audience." But it wasn't long before Mangold decided he might have been better off working for a studio.

First, according to the director, Harvey called him up and told him that he had to hire an actor named Malik Yoba, who'd been featured in a Fox Network series, *New York Undercover*, to play a supporting role to De Niro's character. But Yoba wouldn't read for the part, and Mangold thought his show was awful. Harvey insisted, said, "He's the next Wesley Snipes, he's a friend of De Niro's, Bob's worked with him before, Bob loves him."

Mangold called De Niro, asked, "Have you ever heard of this guy Malik Yoba?"

"Malik what?"

"Malik Yoba, you worked with him before."

"I've worked with a lot of kids. Who?"

"He's the next Wesley Snipes, he's on *New York Undercover*. You don't know him?"

"I have no fuckin' idea who you're talking about. Why're you asking?"

" 'Cause Harvey wants him to play the guy who works with you, and he won't read, and—"

"Well, fuck 'im!"

When Harvey found out that Mangold had involved De Niro, he was furious: "You fucking asshole, you fucking prick, I'm trying to help you." Explains the filmmaker, "Because the thing that threatens him, the thing that pressed the button, is that he loves his relationship with talent. To them, Miramax is benevolent. It's a place that makes your dreams come true. Our responsibility, as directors or producers, is to keep the heavy combat secret from the talent. So when I involved one of the angels, and made him aware of what goes on behind the scenes, I broke the code, I tarnished Harvey's image, I committed a huge betrayal, especially with Bob De Niro, someone he truly adores. So then you get the call, 'You're gonna hire this guy, because I will fuck you on the next role if you don't play with me on this one.' Malik Yoba's in the movie."

But sometimes Harvey couldn't control himself, even with movie stars. As one Miramax executive put it, "He was desperate to be in the Al Pacino star-fuck business," and he frantically tried to acquire Looking for Richard, a behind-the-scenes glimpse of a production of Richard III, which the actor had directed. But Pacino gave the film to Fox Searchlight. He got Pacino on the phone, said, "Why didn't you give me the movie, I'm more passionate about this than anybody, I'm in New York, I know about these things, what do they know, they're Hollywood people."

"Well, my advisers felt that blah blah," replied Pacino, trying to be politic.

"I don't listen to advisers, I listen to me, and finally, you're the client, you're the one who has to decide. Why don't you just admit it, you're the one who didn't want to go with me."

"Well, my advisers thought it would be better if . . ." Harvey was getting angrier and angrier, and finally just lost it. "You know what Al? I've fuckin' had it with you. You suck!"

Cop Land was in production over the summer of 1996, while Mimic was still shooting in Toronto. Mangold shot the climactic gunfight between Stallone and the bad guys, in which Stallone loses his hearing in his good ear, in slow motion. While Mangold was cutting the picture, Harvey found out that he had never covered it in real time. Harvey was afraid it might be too slow and wanted to investigate the possibility of digitally speeding it up to normal. Mangold didn't want to hear about it, but Harvey wouldn't let it go, and it became a big issue, with Harvey calling and calling, insisting he wanted to see it at a faster pace. "Most studios don't get as intimately involved in every single decision," says Konrad. "Harvey will pop into the middle of a process that's already in midstream, he will undo decisons that are made, or that you believe were made, that everybody had said was okay, and then suddenly it's not okay." Mangold was so sick of his interference that he told his editor to remove the hard drives from the Avids. The director recalls, "I got on the subway, went up to my apartment, and called Meryl Poster."

Poster was a production executive who, like several others, began as

Harvey's assistant. As attorney David Steinberg, who worked in acquisitions for two years, puts it, "You have to be able to completely subordinate your own vision of right and wrong in order to succeed there. Grown-ups have a hard time doing that. That's why most of the senior people there started off as either Bob's or Harvey's assistants." She was "absolutely fearless, shockingly blunt, and the only person who could get Harvey to change his mind," says Lechner, but some neither liked nor respected her. According to Donna Gigliotti, "She didn't like film and didn't understand anything about it. She liked movie stars." Behind her back she was known as the "Bride of Weinstein." But in this case she rose to the occasion. Mangold continues, "I said, 'Meryl, we're ceasing work on the film. I don't know what's going to happen to your post schedule, but I ain't coming back until these issues go away.' Meryl went, 'Okay, I understand.' I got a call a minute later, 'I just caught Harvey in the elevator, he's says it's fine, the gunfight's fine, whatever.' There's all this brinkmanship, but if he likes you, sometimes he'll give in."

Mangold, says Konrad, "found a way to tap into the part that we all say we love about Harvey. Threats never work, you have to appeal to the filmmaker side of him, compare your idea to some film classic, some golden oldie. But you have to make sure you know what he likes and what he doesn't like before you get into a meeting, because if you bring up something that he thinks is a piece of shit, it's a bad meeting." Expands Mangold, "You have to be careful of your examples. You can't use a movie that bombed. You never want to say, 'It flips back and forth in time like Go.' The exec will say, 'Oh yeah, like Go, great! Gotta make it!' And you can't cast aspersions on a hit. If you say, 'Oh, you mean like, the reshoot of Fatal Attraction?' 'That would be a problem, making a movie that made $150 million?!' "

Then the test screenings started. Mangold remembers, "For me the most intense day in a movie's history is not a meeting with a star, or the first day of production, or the first screening for the studio, the most pivotal day is the test screening. It will determine whether you're stuck in that cutting room for the next year or whether you will be able to get out alive. It was frightening. The invitations to the screening said, 'Do you want to see the new Sylvester Stallone movie?' I stood in the back row of this theater on Long Island, and heard, 'Rock-y, Rock-y, Rock-y.' As Sly put it, 'My fans want me to pick up a gun and shoot the bad guy. They don't understand dialogue. It's the World Wrestling Federation crowd evaluating this movie.' My stomach twisted, because I knew, Rocky's gonna sit on his hands for the next ninety minutes in a paralysis of confusion." It scored in the low 40s. Harvey was ashen. Mangold continues, "The movie was written in my mind to play to a much more select audience than it suddenly was playing to—it ended with almost everyone dead, and our hero deaf. There wasn't much of a way around that reality."

But there was no way Harvey was going to let his Stallone movie, with Keitel to boot, and De Niro, especially De Niro, go down in flames, so Mangold was sent back to the editing room to tinker and trim. (One cut that Harvey insisted on was a low-angle shot of Stallone that Harvey thought made his butt look too big.) There was only one scene between Keitel and De Niro. The two actors had not been in the same picture since *Taxi Driver* in 1976, not since they'd become stars, and it seemed like putting them together a few more times might pump up the film. But Keitel nixed the idea on the grounds that if they someday did a movie built around the two of them, this would undermine its cachet.

Harvey insisted on reshoots and new scenes. "I thought I had been plunged back into this hell of studio filmmaking again," says Mangold. "There was pressure to inject some buoyant feeling at the very end, show that everything turned out okay, and the bad guys were punished. A scene was tacked on to that effect." At one point, he claims, somebody from Miramax called him up and told him, "Harvey has written a scene that he'd like to read to you."

"He's written a scene for the movie?"

"Yeah."

"But we've already agreed what we're shooting. I'm not getting into this." It was a feel-good scene in which De Niro, who plays an internal affairs investigator, gives Stallone an NYPD badge at the end. Mangold continues, "I found this scene awful, and everything I feared was suddenly coming to pass. The creative energy of this guy is insane, strangling. But I had learned a very big lesson, which was, Why play the bad guy?" Mangold called De Niro, and said, "Harvey has this scene he wrote."

"What is it?"

The director described it. De Niro just grunted, "Uh-huh," then asked Mangold, "Do you like it?"

"No."

"Well, I don't like it either."

"What do I do? He wrote it. He's gonna want—"

"We're not going to do it."

"What if he offers you more money than he paid you for the whole picture to do that scene? He wrote it, Bob."

"I won't do it." Mangold hung up thinking, There's no way that scene's gonna happen. He was right. To Harvey, he said, "If you can get Bob to do it, I'll think about it." But it never came up again. This was by no means the first time Harvey had written scenes and tried to get directors to include them. During Wayne Wang's *Blue in the Face*, a partly improvised spinoff of Wang's and writer Paul Auster's *Smoke,* set in a tobacco shop in Brooklyn, he woke up Auster, who was in Europe, in the middle of the night, and exclaimed, "It's Brooklyn, there's gotta be Jackie Robinson!" Initially, he wanted the whole Dodgers team to crowd into the shop, but Wang and Auster talked him down to just Robinson. It's the stupidest scene in a generally tepid picture, and once, when it was tested, someone piped up with something like, "That's pretty dumb." Knowing how Harvey revered testing, the filmmakers, who wanted to get rid of it, used this comment against him, but he dismissed it, saying, "What does he know."

Cop Land would be released on August 15, 1997. It ended up costing about $29 million, more than three times as much as *Pulp,* bad news for the Miramax business plan. Although it did pretty well, grossing $45 million, Mangold recalls, "I walked around feeling pretty shitty."

While *Cop Land* was in post, *Scream* was poised on the runway. Throughout the fall, it had been burning its way through test screenings. "It was a love-in," recalls Bob Weinstein. "The scores in the top two boxes were in the high 80s, 90s. 'Excellent and very good.' The 'definitely recommend' was in the high 80s. Usually you're excited when it's in the 60s. There was nothing to do, no notes, no meetings, no anything. We had a monster on our hands."

Says Konrad, "Harvey didn't pay a lot of attention to *Scream,* honestly didn't believe in it. He would always say, 'I don't really know what Bob's doing over there. He plays in his sandbox, I have mine.' " The combustible mixture of love and anger that one brother felt for the other was a constant fact of life at Miramax; it was the background noise, the elevator music against which all the other dramas played. As Bob built Dimension into a division that would eclipse Harvey's profit-wise, the noise became harder to ignore. Says Foley, "I think it's a spiritual/chemical thing, where what one likes the other one doesn't. There were occasions when they got into shoving matches with each other, like little brothers, in the middle of the conference room or in front of the staff at a meeting." Harvey intimidated Bob with his knowledge of the creative side of the business; Bob intimidated Harvey with his facility with numbers. Staffers noticed that the brothers couldn't bring themselves to look each other in the eye. Putting them together on the phone was next to impossible, because Harvey would never hold for Bob, Bob would never hold for Harvey. They would go for days without speaking to each other. Bob had to sign the checks, and when they were having a particularly bad spat, he wouldn't do it, bringing business to a halt.

But no matter how hard they fought, they always made up. They were knitted together, as tight as tweed. "I fight with my brother all day long," explains Harvey. "My dad ingrained us in this whole John Kennedy/Bobby

Kennedy thing—we had to be John and Bobby—he Svengalied us, said, 'You fight, and you forgive.' That's why I get into trouble all the time, because I fight and I don't mean it." Which is why, Tusk observes, "The worst thing anyone could do was try to play one against the other. They could be arguing in the hallway about something you were involved with, but if you tried to say something like, 'Oh, I only did that because Bob's office told me,' then Harvey, the same person who was bitterly arguing with his brother a moment before would turn and go, 'Baahb? Is that true?' 'No!' Then suddenly you had the two of them at you." Adds Foley, "Despite the fraternal psychodrama that goes on between them, they're only one person, always, always, always. It's primordial, before the sky and the earth were separated. And there's no one that's gonna get in between them and push open from the inside. It just ain't gonna happen."

Distribution was one of the worst jobs at Miramax. As Bowles puts it, "You can't do anything right. You have six screens in a complex, they want seven." Says Foley, "You'd open a Bob film, and you'd be going through hell with Bob, and then Harvey would enter your life, and he'd be doing Monday, Tuesday, Wednesday, Thursday, Friday, and Saturday quarterbacking. Second-guessing everything we did." Foley was ready to quit. "What I was dealing with was, every time I'd pick up the phone [with them], I'd be bleeding from my ears afterward for something or other, Bob or Harvey ripping my head off," he continues. "Then I'd put the phone down and another call would come in, one of the hundred or so I'd be getting every day, saying, 'You got a problem with this distribution situation in San Francisco or Seattle,' after I'd just been in a head-on collision. I'd just say, 'Oops, sorry, I know I'm bleeding from my aorta, but I gotta deal with this.' You were like a psychological playground for them. It was like the Invasion of the Psyche Snatchers. They played with you, they owned you, they crippled you, they broke you. Harvey would say these totally spurious things just to antagonize you, little things, seeking to demonstrate your ineffectiveness and ineptitude." When Foley arrived at Miramax, he had a spring to his stride. He was a snappy dresser, always seemed on top of his game. After a while, he acquired raccoon eyes and a hangdog expression. He lost weight. His clothes looked like they were three sizes too large for him, and his belt was cinched up to the last hole, the waist of his trousers gathered in bunches like beads on a necklace.

Harvey had been taunting him for weeks about a Dimension film called *Supercop*, with Jackie Chan and Michelle Yeoh, that had not performed to expectations. One night at a *Scream* test screening in Secaucus, New Jersey, Foley recalls, "He said to me, 'Do you know what such-and-such theater grossed on *Supercop*?'

" 'No, I don't.'

" 'Well, I do, 'cause I know everything. I read it on vacation.'

" 'Great, glad you could take a vacation, I haven't taken a vacation in three years. You're gonna nail me on some fuckin' theater in the middle of nowhere? What's that?' It was that viciously predatory thing." While Foley was sitting in the theater stewing, Bob or Harvey got up and walked out, giving him a look as he passed, walked back in again a few minutes later, got him out of the screening, and said, "We're checking you out." Foley thought, I've had it, I've had it, and said, "Fine, great."

"We're gonna pay out your contract."

"Fine." Foley knew that the brothers fired employees one day and re-hired them the next, and that they generally returned. He thought, I'm gonna come back to work, and Harvey's gonna go, "See, I can treat you this way, I can degrade you"? No. I'm gonna draw a line. "That's why I left," he says now. "I didn't have another job, but it was the last straw, because going back there, that ownership thing becomes demonic. When they die, people are going to talk about what great people they were. And they're not, they're cruel people. They're very, very sick people. They have contempt for humanity." Foley never did go back.

Bob had conceived the idea to open *Scream* Christmas week. "The [conventional wisdom] was, OK, Christmas—Christmas fare: the prestige pictures, the family-oriented movies, the softer, gentler kinds of things," he explains. Christmas is the time "every Miramax quote unquote prestige movie comes out. My attitude was, There's nothing for teenagers to see. Great, I'm going against *The Piano*." Wonders Lechner, "Who releases a bloody slasher movie on Christmas Day? Everybody in the company, everybody outside the company, everyone thought he was crazy." Bob said, "Everybody's telling me I'm wrong, Wes's agents, CAA, ICM, they're all calling me. But, we're doin' it." Adds Konrad, "Bob was adamant about it, and he had done his tracking. That guy knew everything about every movie. He had looked at all the competition and he had analyzed those numbers—his office was like the New York Stock Exchange. Counter-programming, niche programming—no one was thinking that way at Christmas."

One of Bob's most vocal critics was Cary Woods. Says Kevin Smith, who didn't like Woods, "Cary did the worst fucking thing imaginable, which was argue with Bob vehemently, and also publicly, about the release date of *Scream*. Bob can be a bigger bastard than Harvey if you fuck with him. Cary fuckin' tore him a new one, started saying, 'I'm gonna go to the press, and fuckin' tell them what an idiot you are. You're gonna kill it.' Cary was a star-fucker, he was worried about his relationship with Drew Barrymore. *Scream* opened Christmas, went on to make 100 million fuckin' dollars,

Cary looked like the idiot, and Bob looked like a genius, and they let him go. 'We're not renewing his deal.' Then just to fuckin' turn the screw, which I really respected, 'cause ultimately, if you're gonna be in the business, you gotta play it personal sometimes, they kept Cathy Konrad, who was his number two, and she went on to make two more *Screams*. Here are two guys who shouldn't make it personal because they're running the studio, but they still had the presence of mind to be like, 'Fuck him, let's keep Cathy just to fuck with him!' And they did! That was pretty ingenious. I can get behind guys like that."

Scream, which cost a mere $15.3 million, eventually did a good $173 million worldwide. Dimension was responsible for about 37 percent of the studio's total gross that year, $93.4 million on five films, or $18.7 million per film. Harvey, on the other hand, released forty-two films that grossed $160 million, or $3.8 million a film. Says Tarantino's attorney, Carlos Goodman, "You can almost look at Miramax as pre-*Scream* and post-*Scream*." As Bob's remarks indicate, he must have gotten an extra jolt of pleasure by going up against Harvey's "prestige" Christmas offerings and beating them. Indeed, while Harvey was playing in his own sandbox, Bob was building castles in his, and it wouldn't be long before Harvey tried to play there, too.

THE SUNDANCE FILM FESTIVAL of January past had been a watershed, what with the image of Harvey backing Jon Taplin up against the bar at the Mercato burned into everyone's brain. The 1997 installment was a real snoozer, especially since the previous year's star, *The Spitfire Grill*, had been a resounding flop, while *Shine*, despite the sound and fury, had failed to break out into the huge hit Fine Line expected. Over at Miramax, the core of the acquisitions team had left or was leaving, starting with Safford's abrupt departure in the spring of 1996. Mark Tusk, who had joined the company in 1988, left a few weeks later on April Fool's Day, unhappy with the changes at the company. "Two thirds of the time Harvey wasn't moving on the films I was recommending," he says. "It had become more difficult to corner him, to sit him down for a movie, get him to focus, because he was busy with all sorts of things." Trea Hoving, who had been there since 1989, followed in June of 1997. Amy Israel and Jason Blum moved up to replace them.

Still, if in retrospect it seems clear that as the sun set on the careers of the crack Miramax team, the Golden Age of acquisitions was over, it was not apparent at the time. Buoyed by the previous year's bidding wars, the agents and reps were increasingly reluctant to display their wares prematurely, hoping to spur a buying frenzy at the festival. Geoff Gilmore himself discouraged filmmakers from previewing their films before the festival, precisely, it seemed, to promote the Bloomingdale's-on-Presidents'-Day climate that increasingly pervaded the event. Buyers turning the Sundance soil could still find gems. Fox Searchlight picked up *The Full Monty*, which it released on August 13, 1997, to the tune of a $45.9 million profit. Neil LaBute's sulfuric portrait of single males on the prowl, *In the Company of Men*, which was acquired by Sony Classics, grossed a respectable $3 million, a momentary setback for the emerging consensus for feel-good films like *The Brothers McMullen*. But most of the films that were snapped up flopped, fueling the growing conviction that festivals were a poor indicator of commercial success. Says Sony's Michael Barker, "Those movies that were bought at Sundance lost so much money, it was a lesson for all of us."

After a disappointing pre-Christmas opening, Miramax had another go with *Sling Blade* in January. Dan Talbot had intended to boot it out of his Lincoln Plaza Theater, where it was playing to empty houses. Weinstein was in St. Bart's on vacation with his family. He called Talbot, said, "I don't care what the critics think. I don't care what anybody thinks, I don't care if I have to carry this movie on my back, I'm not giving it up. You cannot get rid of this movie. You'll see that audiences will come."

He redid the campaign, showing Thornton out of character, looking as little like Karl as he could be made to look. "I made TV spots of Billy in a work shirt against a gorgeous background, talking about *Sling Blade* over scenes from his movie." Thornton became the first director since Tarantino that Miramax made into a star from nothing. As Smith puts it, "They created instant recognition around a guy who made one movie. You don't look at *Sling Blade* and think, What a masterfully made film. Suddenly, it was, 'Oh my God, Billy Bob's interested in this movie, he'll bring some of that *Sling Blade* magic to it.' That was taking the marketing of the director to the next level. Not to say he's not a fantastic actor, but Billy Bob Thornton is an absolute fuckin' creation of Miramax."

Continues Weinstein, "The TV commercials ran in L.A. on cable as part of the Academy campaign, and grosses started to go up. Word of mouth started to build. Then I went to network. It turned around, went crazy." The film became a phenomenon, with people going around clearing their throats, Karl-style, grunting Uh-hum, uh-hum. "I think that if we hadn't sold it to them for $10 million, they would never have bothered to re-release the movie, and it would have gone straight to video," observes Cassian Elwes. "I have to give it to Harvey, for as crazy as he is, and unpleasant as he can be, he really is masterful when he wants to be in terms of marshaling his troops and forcing them to really focus on how to get a movie out."

Thornton's fortunes received another bump when the Oscar nominations came out in February 1997. He received two nominations for *Sling Blade*, Best Actor and Best Adapted Screenplay, while *The English Patient* racked up twelve, including Best Picture. Altogether, Miramax films picked up a phenomenal twenty-one nominations, only one fewer than in 1994, the *Pulp Fiction* year. The remainder were sprinkled among *Emma*, *Trainspotting*, *Marvin's Room*, *Ridicule*, and *Kolya*. But despite Miramax's muscular performance, the big news was that little October—only three years old in 1996—did just as well for its size, picking up six nominations, all in major categories, five for *Secrets & Lies*, including Best Picture and Best Actress for Brenda Blethyn, and one for *Breaking the Waves*, Best Actress for Emily Watson. For the first time, indies virtually monopolized the nominations. In addition to *Secrets & Lies* and *The English Patient*, the other Best Picture nominations went to the Coen brothers' *Fargo*, and Scott Hicks's *Shine*. Cameron Crowe's *Jerry Maguire* was the only studio picture to win a place at the head table. The message seemed to be clear: Cinderella had eased her foot into the glass slipper.

Thornton walked down the red carpet on Oscar night in March with his wife of four years, Pietra, twenty-seven, clutching his arm. She had posed for a nude spread in that January's *Playboy*, and now raised eyebrows by wearing a skintight dress that barely contained her ample bosom. "God gave me this body, and I shouldn't be ashamed of it. I'm a mother, not a loose person or anything," she explained to the press. "I just had breast surgery—they used to sag to the floor—so I've got these great new breasts and suddenly everyone's looking." But they didn't help her that night. At 4:00 A.M., she went home in a limo with Thornton's mother, leaving her husband behind at the Oscar party. The tabloids reported that he hooked up with Laura Dern.

When the ceremony was over, *The English Patient* walked away the big winner, with an astonishing nine Oscars including Best Picture, Best Director, and Best Supporting Actress (Juliette Binoche), with two for Walter Murch, Best Editing and Best Sound Editing. Thornton won for Best Adapted Screenplay. He quipped, modestly, "It's like taking one of those tests where one thing doesn't belong with the others. They'll have four kinds of fruit and, like, a buffalo. Well, I'm the buffalo here." Miramax won twelve Oscars in all. October won nothing. Bingham Ray was upset. Universal invited the October folks to sit with them at the Governors Ball, but he announced, "We're losers. I'm going to go back to the hotel."

On Oscar night, Anthony Minghella had invited Steven Soderbergh to the Miramax party, said, "Oh, you've got to come." Soderbergh had returned from Baton Rouge but had only been back in town for a couple of months. He was still looking for a distributor for *Schizopolis*, and neither that nor *Gray's Anatomy*, his subsequent film, had come out. He had worked on a polish of *Mimic*, was supposed to fix the romantic relationship between the two leads, but eventually he begged off, on the grounds that he was not qualified to write good relationships. He was also struggling in vain to set up a Charlie Kaufman script called *Human Nature* (since made by Michel Gondry) with a tiny budget, $9 million. He says, "That nobody wanted to make that movie at that price was a sobering moment, an indication of how cold I was."

The day of the Oscars he'd been shooting second unit for his friend Gary Ross on *Pleasantville*. "I got to the Miramax bash, circulated for a while, but couldn't find Minghella," he remembers. "Then I saw him through the glass in the special VIP section. The security guy wouldn't let me in. I said, 'There's the person who invited me.' He said, 'I don't care.' He was telling me there was no fucking way I was getting in that room, and literally, on a forty-two-inch screen behind his head inside the VIP room they were playing Miramax trailers from all their past films, and I was watching the trailer for *sex, lies!*" Soderbergh turned to his date, producer Laura Bickford, and said, "Yuchh—that's the sign that we're supposed to leave, we have to go now!" Soderbergh had skidded a long way downhill. He had just hit bottom.

Sling Blade's two nominations helped drive the domestic gross to $24.4 million. (Traditionally, it is the nominations more than the Oscars that boost box office.) Says Harvey, "We sold 240,000 cassettes. Sold foreign for $7 million. We made $20 million profit on the movie." The profit participants, of course, had net points, not gross, what Eddie Murphy once famously described as "monkey points," because studio accounting methods make it unlikely that net participants see any money, no matter how much the picture makes. Miramax was no different. "When you got a production statement, they'd claim millions of dollars in losses," says Larry Meistrich. "Which was a joke. I don't believe there were losses." Neither Thornton nor Meistrich ever saw a share of the profits. Says Elwes, "Harvey's like Pac-Man. He has to eat everything." Meistrich strongly considered suing, but decided against it. "In this business, it's not worth it," he continues. "I wasn't in it for how much I could squeeze out of that particular film. I moved on. Billy and I made another movie with Miramax, *Daddy and Them*, and I didn't want to hurt Billy's opportunity to do that. I preferred to take the fees I made on *Daddy and Them* than spend money on accountants fucking around." Retorts Harvey, "Meistrich didn't see any money because we paid him $10 million for the rights to a film that cost $1.1 million, giving him a $8.9 million profit up front."

Only three weeks after the Oscars, Thornton was again splayed all over the tabs and gossip columns, more grist for the Miramax publicity mill. On April 8, Pietra sued for divorce, charging that during their four-year marriage, he punched her in the face, choked her, tried to suffocate her, and bit her ear, making her fear for her life. According to the complaint, she said that he told her, "I'm going to kill you and then I'm going to prison and the children will be orphans." Thornton denied it and countered by claiming she threatened to kill him. So far as the biting was concerned, he said it was sexual fun. "His Marv Albert defense isn't going to work," she said. "I never once claimed he bit me during sex. . . . He maliciously bit me out of anger. Quite frankly, our sex life was pretty dull." One of the gossip columns reported he hit her with his Oscar, but he denied it. Pietra moved out to a new home in Malibu, where she devoted her time to praying. "Believe it or not, I'm a very devoted Christian woman," she told the press. "I probably read the Bible more than most pastors. All I talk about in the house with my kids is Jesus."

LIKE A LAB EXPERIMENT gone horribly awry, little October became the crucible in which volatile reagents—art against money, indies against studios—acted and reacted until they ignited, blowing the company to bits. Compared to Miramax's grosses on *The English Patient* and *Sling Blade,* October's figures for *Breaking the Waves* and *Secrets & Lies* barely made a ripple. Says Bingham Ray, a little defensively, "Those two films were the last films we handled in the old-fashioned way, the way I was schooled in, and we were profitable in both of them. Maybe they were stand-up doubles or triples sliding into third, but I considered them home runs, profitability-wise."

Still, with their nominations and awards, *Secrets & Lies* and *Breaking the Waves* put October on the map, and Ray justifiably could claim credit for both. Success, even modest success, has a way of changing the landscape of expectations. In the deathless words of Woody Allen in *Annie Hall,* relationships, like sharks, have to keep moving forward or die, and film companies are no different. As Ray explains it, "We had a breakthrough, and John Schmidt and Amir Malin started talking about how to 'grow' the company. We needed more financing to get to the 'next level'—I hated this expression, but I heard it every single day." Replies Schmidt, "It wasn't greed. The reality is, when you're an independent film distributor, you have to bring money into the company to continue to acquire and distribute films aggressively. New Line did it, Miramax did it. If you don't raise the capital when a window opens, you're a fool." The partners either had to get new investors to come in, thereby watering down their already diluted shares even further, or swim into the mouth of a bigger fish. Moreover, October was about to lose $6 or $7 million on David Lynch's *Lost Highway,* which Ray had convinced his partners to acquire.

"All the goodwill and all the profit we had earned in '95 and '96 went out the window," he says. Adds Schmidt, "If we did not do a deal, we would have been gone in three months. We couldn't afford to take a hit like that."

Of all the studios, Universal seemed like the best fit. Schmidt lived in Riverdale, an affluent zip code just north of Manhattan. One of his neighbors was Frank Biondi, CEO of Universal Pictures, whose wife was best friends with his wife, Wendy. Schmidt's partners told him, "If you're going to play the Frank Biondi card, now's the time to do it. Call Frank, John. Get him on the phone and see if he's interested." So in February 1997, the sheep called the wolf to ask if he was hungry. He was.

Chris McGurk, who baby-sat the Weinsteins at Disney, had joined the exodus from Disney at the end of 1996 and become COO of Universal Pictures. "I had a lot of experience with the upside you could generate in combining a studio with a specialty film company that employed a way of doing business—creative and marketing skills—that no longer existed in the big studios," he explains. "But I also saw how Miramax had begun to get away from the core business they had done so well with, that they were stepping up and producing movies for $15, $20, $30 million, making some really big bets, because Harvey didn't want to be just Harvey Weinstein, he wanted to be Louis B. Mayer. I saw that a void was being created. Add to that the fact that he and Bob had really aggravated everybody due to their dominance, and there was even more ill feeling toward them in Europe than there was here, and therefore Harvey hadn't penetrated that market as well as he could have. We saw an opportunity to take October Films and position it as the anti-Miramax, the Bingham Ray alternative, with Bingham the more talent-friendly Harvey Weinstein."

There was also interest from another quarter as well, Bain Capital, a hugely successful private equity group based in Boston. Bain, always on the lookout for companies to buy, had recently been sniffing about Los Angeles. Faced with a choice between the leather lingerie business or the video business, that is, Frederick's of Hollywood or Live Entertainment, it chose Live. Live owned a sizable library cobbled together from the inventory of defunct companies such as Carolco and Vestron. It contained a lot of junk, but it also had some gold, including *Dirty Dancing, Reservoir Dogs,* the *Rambos,* and a lot of Arnold Schwarzenegger films, like *Predator* and the *Terminators.* Bain thought this would make a good fit with October. This was a business plan Malin understood very well, and he aspired to a bigger role than just flipping movies to video.

Schmidt and Ray, on the other hand, preferred Universal. Even though Universal was like West Point compared to the October playpen, it was preferable to Bain. Ray was sick of investment bankers, and from his point of view, Bain was run by a bunch of arrogant guys in striped shirts and suspenders who drank a lot of Heineken beer. The plan was to sell 51 percent of October to the studio and use its deep pockets to grow the company.

The principals from the two companies celebrated their new partnership at a dinner in a private, upstairs dining room at Prego. The meal was over, they were sipping grappas. As Malin stood at the window looking at the twinkling lights of Beverly Hills, McGurk shouted, "Amir, so, listen, when this is all done, are you looking forward to running distribution?" As McGurk well knew, Malin's aspirations were much grander. Schmidt started to giggle, but, he recalls, "it was a knife to Amir's gut."

Then Malin did a stupid thing. Or at least it seemed like a stupid thing at the time. Through one of his friends on the board of October, he approached Universal CEO Ron Meyer, asked if he was the key man in the deal, if, in other words, were he not to go along, would they go ahead without him? Meyer, Biondi, and McGurk thought that this was a strange question. At the very least, it indicated to them that Malin had been negotiating elsewhere, most likely with Bain. They said something like, "We'd say you'd have to deal with your partners on that, that's not our business." McGurk and Malin had never liked each other. McGurk called Ray and asked, "What in hell does he think he's doing? I wouldn't want him to be my partner." According to Malin, "Bingham feared that by having gone in this circuitous way to Ron Meyer, I might have torpedoed the whole fucking thing." He says his intention was the opposite. "I did not want to see a scenario where if I decided to leave the deal might not happen. I just wanted to know that the deal would still go on." Once he was assured that it would proceed regardless, he felt free to leave.

Nevertheless, Ray and Schmidt were furious. They felt that Malin had tried to make an end run around them. "Whatever his intentions were, he backdoored us," says Ray. "It really pissed me off. His ego was always telling him, You're the key man here, fella, and if Universal had said, 'If you opt out, we're not gonna make this deal,' he would have tried to use that to restructure the whole partnership: 'That means I'm in charge. Fuck John, fuck Bingham, fuck October.' But he read the tea leaves wrong." Schmidt saw it the same way: "It was a destabilizing move. If Meyer had said, 'We won't make the deal without you,' he had the ammunition to make a move on us."

In any event, Ray continues, "I wanted to act swiftly to cut that fuckin' cancer out. I saw an opportunity, with Universal's blessing, to blow this fucker out." Says one Universal executive, "Amir took a well that was poisoned and made it toxic thirty days after we had made the deal. So then it was, Let's get rid of him." Ray phoned Schmidt at the Chateau Marmont, where he was staying in L.A., asked for his blessing as well. Schmidt said, "Well, whaddya wanna do?"

"I say we move on him. Right now. Lemme go fire him. I'm going down the hall!"

"Right now? I'll be back in the office tomorrow. I want to do it with you." They hung up. Five minutes later, Ray called again, said, "Like, right now! I'm gonna strike, right now!" Ray thought, John would rather not be ugly and confrontational, but I don't give a shit. I love confrontation, baiting people into confrontation. Schmidt told him, "Okay, I'm not going to stop you," and Ray marched into Malin's office, the big corner one, the largest on the floor, and closed the door behind him as dramatically as he could short of slamming it. As he tells it, "I sat down in that overexpensive, overstuffed, bullshit leather Italian chair in front of his pretentious glass-topped fucking stupid Italian knockoff desk, and I said, 'I just heard a very interesting story. That disturbs me. And John. Greatly. And I think we have to talk about it.'

" 'Wha . . . wha . . . what would that be? What story? What did you hear?' At first, of course, his instinct was to deny.

" 'Amir, I think you know what you have to do.'

" 'What do I have to do?'

" 'I think there's only one course of action for you to take, because we know exactly what you've done, what you've tried to do.'

" 'Whaddya talking about?'

" 'Don't make me tell you all of what you've been doing in the last ten days. Let it suffice to say that I know everything, John knows everything, and we both are in agreement that you should leave.' He tried to deny it, and I stopped him. 'Like I said, it's not working. No one, no one is going to let you off this hook. You're going to have to live with the consequences.'

" 'Okay, I'll go, all right, I'll go.'

"He was afraid of me, like I was going to hit him. He's one of the biggest pussies of all time. He was whimpering. He was trembling. He's a trembler. I'm gonna make a movie, call it, *The Trembler: The Amir Malin Story.* So we fired him. You know, there was a warm glow going up my spine that was what I imagined a heroin addict would feel when they're shooting up. I was taking a great amount of satisfaction sitting there in front of this fuck and doing him in. No one had done this fucker in before, and he'd done lots of people, good and bad, rightly and wrongly, mostly wrongly, and now he was getting his. He had tried to take us out, he got Lipsky, but he couldn't do the rest, and now he was falling on his own sword. It was one of the happiest days of my fuckin' life. I called John. I said, 'The deed is done. Satan is dead.' "

Malin maintains that he chose to leave October voluntarily. "I sat down with Bingham when I made my decision, and we talked," he says of his meeting with Ray. "It was not an easy discussion. But it was not a confrontation."

Then forty-five years old, Malin would pack his bags and leave for Live Entertainment, which would be renamed Artisan. Universal paid a paltry $14 million for 51 percent of the company. October had been the largest and most successful of the genuine independents. Now it belonged to a studio. But the deal enabled it to bump up its bank line from $25 million to $100 million, and the hope was to morph into a powerhouse so that in five or six years when Universal bought out the remaining 49 percent, the investors would make a killing.

October's future looked bright. The company had been the subject of a high-profile feature in *New York* magazine, where it was called—guess what—"the new Miramax," irritating the Weinsteins. When the distributors converged on Cannes in May of that year, right after October's deal with Universal had been announced, the inevitable occurred. Ray walked into a screening to find Harvey already there, three seats in from the aisle. "For years, everyone was more or less treated the same," recalls Ray. "Then this big division grew up between Harvey-the-mogul and the rest of us. The reps on the pictures were always sucking up to him shamelessly. It was just insane—they had seats, rows, saved for Miramax. I was standing in the aisle, and he turned to me and went, 'I guess we'll see how good you are now, eh?'

" 'Harvey, what is it about me that just kinda sticks in your craw? Whaddya, afraid of me?'

" 'What? Hah!' All of a sudden I was aware that the place had become deathly quiet. He shouted, 'I'm not—whaddya talking about, scared of you?'

" 'Harvey, why don't you just go fuck yourself, ya know? You start off, say hello to me, then boom, you're bustin' my chops. Go fuck off.'

" 'FUCK OFF? YOU TOLD ME TO FUCK OFF? YOU PIECE OF SHIT! Now we're gonna see if you're really talented, you piece of fucking shit slime. I'm gonna kick your ass all over town.' He was trying to get up, but he's a big guy, the seats were small, and he just couldn't get up to get in my face. I yelled, 'Can't you get up? GET UP!' But he could not get up. Afterward, as I came out of the movie, Tom Bernard walked past me. Bernard had never talked to me in his life except to give me shit in passing, and he said, 'Harvey was down, he couldn't get up. You shoulda hit him!' "

THE ENGLISH PATIENT was turning into a money machine, grossing $78.6 million in the U.S. and $150 million foreign, for a total of $228.6 million worldwide. The ancillary markets, mainly video, piled on even more millions. But the picture, recall, was Zaentz's baby, and six years later, Zaentz complained that hadn't seen a penny from Miramax, other than the $5 million Harvey had paid to the talent, but not Zaentz, early on. (On the day of the Golden Globes, Miramax reimbursed talent and crew for $2.5 million they were owed for the deferments Miramax had requested.)

Although Harvey wondered, rhetorically, in the *Los Angeles Times*, "Why should filmmakers live out of a sack and crews defer their salaries just because they work in the independent arena?," the crew and cast of *The English Patient* have never seen a penny of the remaining $7 million. Minghella was paid about $750,000 for writing and directing. Amortized over the four years he worked on the film, his remuneration amounted to $187,500 a year, half of which he deferred. He says, "I haven't had a cent since then."

According to sources, over the course of the six years, payment was always just around the corner. "You'll be paid in October." October came and went. "You'll be paid in April." April came and went. In the fall of 1999, Zaentz audited Miramax to determine, among other things, how much the company made from the ancillaries in order to determine when the film actually went into profit. Zaentz threatened to sue Miramax. Harvey's response was always, "Go ahead. We're the Walt Disney Co., we have two hundred lawyers here sitting around at their desks with nothing to do. You wanna pay $1 million to hire a lawyer? Be my guest."

"Harvey the monster," says Weinstein with heavy sarcasm. "We spent $42 million on P&A. Did we want the Academy Award? Yes! Did we overspend? Yes! We did whatever we had to do. What has irked Saul to this day is that I presold the foreign. I had never written a check that big for a movie, my hands were shaking, and I had to protect myself. In retrospect, that was one of the stupidest decisions anybody ever made, not only for Zaentz, but for us. As a result, the money that he thinks is there [isn't]. He keeps saying we owe him money. But he hasn't sued us. It's much more fun to dine out in the press all the time. What else are they going to ask Saul Zaentz about? His last movie? He will make $100 million personally on *Lord of the Rings*. Harvey made him a hundred fuckin' million bucks. If he thinks there's $5 million that he owes his crew on *The English Patient*, he should raise his hand and say, I made a fortune on *Lord of the Rings*, here's the fuckin' money. Just shut up already, and write the check."

"What's that got to do with the price of corn?" Zaentz retorts. "We have to pay 'em, but we have to get the money from him to pay 'em." He says in fact he plans to sue Miramax: "We're gonna do it. I wouldn't have spent the money we've spent or get lawyers like we have. He's full of shit as always."

It is, of course, possible that Miramax is right. *The English Patient* was acquired in a distress sale, and the Weinsteins no doubt drove a hard bargain. As Jeremy Thomas puts it, "You push the boat out, and often when you need a lifeline, you're incredibly weak and get into terrible jams."

Zaentz says Harvey "is a pushcart peddler who puts his thumb on the scale when the old woman is buying meat. When I talked with him about it, he says, 'I am a filmmaker; I'm not an accountant.' " Walter Murch, the gifted editor of *Godfather III* and *Apocalypse Now,* who won two Oscars for *The English Patient,* says he is still owed one third of his deferred salary. He describes himself as "angry slash philosophical" about his predicament, adding, "As far as the Oscars went, *The English Patient* won the Super Bowl that year, which was a very big thing for Miramax and Disney. Well, that was made possible not only by their own publicity machine, but by the people who made the *film!* And you would think that when you win the Super Bowl, you get a bonus or you get your ring, or something, and not only did we not get anything other than the Oscar—which I'm very happy to have—but we didn't get the money that we deferred in order that this wonderful film got made. So now we're all blinking in the daylight thinking, Oh, it's that trick again, it's the same old song. It was the first time I'd ever worked for deferments, and I got stung." Murch went on to edit *The Talented Mr. Ripley,* which Minghella directed and Miramax co-produced (with Paramount). "At the point that I agreed to do it, it was a little less than a year after *The English Patient* had come out. The idea was the money was coming, just hang on," he says. "I would have second thoughts about doing *Ripley* again."

The irony is, of course, that the people who are exploited in these situations are not the hacks or journeymen, but the good guys, the idealists, the passionate few for whom film is not just a job but a calling. The artists' best selves are turned against them. Says Murch, "Our dedication to the material always supersedes our own financial self-interest. If we didn't care, if we were just in it for the money, then we wouldn't get victimized." Miramax offered to pay Minghella the deferred salary he was owed, but the director refused to accept the money. "I have a very clear position on *The English Patient* in terms of money," he says. "I am not interested in getting my money until I know that my crew has been paid. I couldn't look at them on a film set knowing that I had some money and they hadn't." In 2000, Minghella signed on to direct *Cold Mountain,* a picture that Miramax was producing with MGM. Did the lingering, unresolved situation with regard to *The English Patient* color his approach to this project? He says, "It certainly makes it more difficult for me to go to my own crew, who I feel an enormous responsibility for, and say, 'We're doing *Cold Mountain,* would you consider deferring some of your fee?' I wouldn't ask them to do that. So there is a consequence to the fact that no money's been forthcoming, and it's an unfortunate consequence. Let me say, however, that the first round of deferments were at Saul's request, not Miramax's. However, the irony is not lost on me that had Saul financed *The English Patient,* I would be a very wealthy person now." Would Zaentz work with Harvey again? "No! Billy Wilder once said, about someone everybody disliked intensely, 'Don't even bother to ignore him!' He's abusive to everybody that he has a chance to be abusive to. He's an abusive man."

The critical and commercial success of Minghella's historical romance defined the "Miramax picture" for the rest of the decade and beyond. After *Pulp Fiction,* it looked for a while as if that's what the Weinsteins would do, pictures that were too cool and too hip for the studios. But *Priest* and *Kids* put an end to that. As much as the Weinsteins might love Tarantino, *Pulp Fiction* was never going to win an Oscar; it was just too weird. But *The English Patient* could. The Weinsteins would provide a steady diet of high-toned, Masterpiece Theater–style, Oscar-grabbing pictures often adapted from prestigious literary works. Miramax mined Jane Austen like a truffle-sniffing pig, and turned out frock pieces like *Emma* and *Mansfield Park.* *Emma* had been released on August 2, 1996. It was a delivery vehicle for Gwyneth Paltrow—the classy blonde who became to Harvey what Grace Kelly was to Hitchcock, a star he could parade in front of the public to burnish his own reputation. He used to refer to her as "the First Lady of Miramax." Tarantino noticed what was going on right away. He says, "Harvey knows that I hate that shit. Unwatchable movies from unreadable books. I told him, 'You really need some NC-17, or people will really think you've lost your balls.' But the thing is, Harvey made his name with *Enchanted April* as much as he made it with *Kids.*" Tarantino may have derided *Emma* as "shit," but to Miramax that shit was smelling sweet.

Nine
Ace and Gary
1997

• **How a couple of kids from Boston named Matt Damon and Ben Affleck launched** *Good Will Hunting,* **while October beat Miramax to** *The Apostle* **and found** *Happiness.*

"The mainstream sucks, and it always will, is the bottom line. Because they don't understand how to make movies—they went to Wharton. They're selling widgets. The thing I love about working for Harvey is that it's like the old studio system. He tells you right to your face to go fuck yourself."

—MATT DAMON

Good Will Hunting began in the early 1990s as a writing assignment Matt Damon turned in to his Harvard class in directing. Damon grew up in Cambridge, Massachusetts. The family lived on the wrong side of the tracks, so to speak, in Central Square, worlds away culturally and economically from nearby Harvard. A wannabe actor struggling through one disappointing role after another, he shoehorned his career into his on-again off-again stint as a Harvard student. He finally did what many actors in extremis do—he wrote a role for himself, and enlisted Ben Affleck to help him do it.

Damon and Affleck were childhood friends. Two years younger than Damon, Affleck was born in 1972. His parents were '60s people, anti-war activists. When he was growing up, they tried to take him to films they liked, mostly foreign. "They dragged me to movies where nobody spoke English," he recalls. "They wouldn't take me to movies that other kids were going to, that were fun. To me a real movie was, like, *The Terminator.* Or *Star Wars.* When I was five years old, I thought it was the greatest thing that had ever been done. It was the equivalent of *The 400 Blows* or *The Bicycle Thief* or whatever it was that made Scorsese fall in love with movies. I just thought, anything my mother likes, with her outdated view of the world, like Truffaut, or any of that boring shit, can't be good." Affleck's father, Tim, himself a sometime actor, used to ask Ben and Matt, "Why the fuck do you guys want to be actors? It's the stupidest fucking job in the world." But they ignored his advice, as kids will, and hopped onto the Hollywood merry-go-round.

When Rick Linklater cast him in *Dazed and Confused,* Affleck had few credits, mostly TV movies and one Hollywood feature, *School Ties.* "My agent said it was by the guy who did *Slacker.* I saw *Slacker* at an art theater in Waterville, Maine, when I was eighteen. I thought, This is a strangely nonlinear movie, experimental. I should like it more than I do, but you have to understand that at that time, *Lethal Weapon* was my favorite movie. It was the bad guy part. I didn't want to play the bad guy, but I figured I would do it anyway. Then Rick sent out the script with a note that said, 'If this movie is realized as scripted, it will be a massive underachievement. I want to solicit contributions from everybody,' and he was true to his word. I would write stuff, and it appeared in the movie. I felt empowered to have a voice in that, and it gave me the notion that you could make movies this way."

Dazed and Confused showcased an array of up-and-coming actors, and it gave some of them, like Matthew McConaughey, a leg up. But, recalls Affleck, frowning, "It didn't do anything for me. I was the only unlikable character in a movie full of likable characters. I was completely forgotten." He was losing parts to his peers—McConaughey, Chris O'Donnell, Brendan Fraser, whoever. He figured, There has to be another way. It was at this point that Damon brought him the concept, saying, "A movie where a kid from Southie is a savant would be cool." Affleck was familiar with indie films, thought, Yeah, *Clerks* was out there, *Slacker,* that didn't cost a lot of money. This seems, like, easy to do. "To me indies were a new way for guys to make your own shot," he explains. "You didn't have to sit around and wait for somebody to decide to cast you in *Billy Bathgate,* or as Robin in *Batman.* To do all these things that people like Brendan or Matthew were breaking with. You could make an end run, do a movie on your own, and then maybe someone will give you a shot to work with one of the great guys—De Niro, Scorsese, Coppola, Pacino, Hoffman."

As Affleck makes clear, for him, indie film had devolved into no more than just another way of getting your foot in the studio door. *Good Will Hunting* was never a pure blue flame burning in Damon's breast, a story that demanded to be told, a vision calling for expression. Although based on his experiences growing up as a townie in a university-dominated community, the script was simply a means to an end, intended to get them work. But it wasn't that the young filmmakers coming up in the late 1980s were more opportunistic than their predecessors, or that they didn't care about doing good work. A new generation gap had opened up. When *Dazed and Confused* flopped, Affleck noticed that Linklater just shrugged it off. After all, it was a studio film, and from where Linklater was standing, the studio blew it. Born in 1960, Linklater had that old-time religion, which is to say, that Us/Them, anti-studio mentality. "Rick's older'n me," Affleck observes. "He had a '70s deal going on, a kind of anti-authoritarian, throwback mentality, like, It's not about the money, man, people liked the movie. I really didn't have that, since I grew up in the '80s, with Reagan. My perspective at the time was, there is no 'Man,' nobody's holding you down. That worldview seemed anachronistic to me—'Get over it!' "

Affleck had never bought into the idea that indie films are necessarily superior or more virtuous than studio films. He aspired to do good work too, but for him, the question wasn't indies versus studios; it was good pictures versus bad pictures. Good pictures could be made inside the studios or outside, just as bad pictures could. A studio logo in front of a movie didn't automatically mean that he was going to reach for a tomato. After all, the great directors and actors he admired had entrenched themselves within the system. In fact, they *were* the system. Like so many of the younger filmmakers of his generation, the children of the flower children, he was oblivious to the bitter political and cultural battles waged in the 1960s and 1970s that put them there. He took the way things were for granted. It was the go-go '90s, and everything seemed possible. Like Quentin Tarantino, he thought, There's this brass ring out there, and it's exciting, glamorous, and fun—and you can be an artist too.

Not everyone, even in Affleck's generation, agrees. Says Ethan Hawke, who is only two years older and has acted in many of Linklater's films, "Ben's right in that art is valuable if its aim is true, even if it's inside the studio system. There's no rules about it. But it's not only that there are good movies and bad movies, but it's how the movies are made and what they're like that's important too. For me, the job of the artist is to be a maverick. If you cease to be a maverick, then you become Coca-Cola. I resented working for Time Warner when I did *Training Day*. It bugged me. I don't think it would bug Ben. Rick has an interest in being subversive, but I don't know how subversive Ben wants to be."

In any event, Affleck told Damon, "Yeah, guys are making these kinds of movies now, we can do this for $1 million." The original script they wrote was an amalgam of their favorite movies: *Midnight Run, Beverly Hills Cop, E.T.,* and *Searching for Bobby Fischer.* They knew they needed a good guy, a bad guy, a girl, and that it had to be cheap, people in rooms talking. The story had an action overlay that they thought would attract studio financing.

Damon and Affleck were inspired by other nobodies who had sold first scripts with themselves attached as actors. Of course the most celebrated example was Sylvester Stallone, who some two decades earlier had managed to star in his own script, *Rocky*. Recalls Damon, "We'd just say, 'Stallone, Stallone,' because he had $103 in the bank and a pregnant wife, and they offered him thirty grand if he would bow out and let Ryan O'Neal play Rocky, but he stuck to his guns. When the studios would balk, and go, 'Who the hell are these guys and why should they be in the movie?' at least our agent had some leverage to say, 'It's not a first-time thing, this happens.' Our feeling was, Don't let them draw a line in the sand, you do it, why not ask for it, demand it, insist on it—and maybe they'll give it to you."

Affleck and Damon's "I can do that too" pictures were not only *Slacker* and *Clerks*, but *Reservoir Dogs*. "I mean, this guy Tarantino worked in a fucking video store," says Damon. "It just made it doable, and it was shortly after seeing *Reservoir Dogs* that we started writing." But it was not so much how Tarantino made it as how he got to make it. "We heard the story about how Lawrence Bender had given Harvey Keitel the script in his acting class, and his name got that movie made," Damon continues. "It was worth $500,000 or a million bucks or whatever they got—because of Harvey Keitel. We said, Jesus, we need our Harvey Keitel." They tailored the part of the therapist to a Hollywood star, any star, gave him the best lines, made it small so he could fit it into his schedule. "We called it our Harvey Keitel part," Damon goes on. "We figured any great actor could step in and make it theirs. If it were Morgan Freeman we'd make the guy from Roxbury, or if it's a white guy, we were going to make him from South Boston. If it's Meryl Streep, that's a different kind of tension. But our mantra was, Keitel and Stallone."

Despite the Stallone precedent, nobody at the studios was thrilled with having to buy a ticket on the Damon and Affleck bus. Says Damon, "I'm sure these guys read the script and went, Oh, fuck, if we could only get rid of these two jackasses." All the two wannabes heard was "Brad and Leo, Leo and Brad." Director Michael Mann loved the script, but only with "Leo and Brad." During their first meeting with Castle Rock, Rob Reiner, who didn't know that they wanted to act in it, said, "This will be great, and we'll get Leo and Brad." One of the other executives jumped in and said, "No, no, it's these guys, it's these guys." Reiner's eyes widened and without missing a beat he said, "It's these guys? Even better, even better!" They could almost hear the wheels turning in his head: We won't have to pay for Leo and Brad! Paramount flirted, but Mark Wahlberg told Affleck that an executive there confided, "We got a great movie for you, we're just gonna buy their script, ice them, and put you in it." Wahlberg passed.

Affleck continues, "We agreed with whatever anybody said to us, went in and just said, 'Yes!' 'Yes!' 'Yes, we have some problems—it's not finished. We know we need a movie star, we know we're not famous, we're just happy to be here.' " In *Hoop Dreams*, there's a scene in which the father of a basketball prospect who has just been kicked out of prep school is being wooed by a recruiter who is giving him a song and dance about how his school builds character, and finally the father says, "Ah'm jus' happy somebody want da boy." And that was their mantra. They would say, over and over, "We're jus' happy somebody want da boy!" Still, Damon and Affleck had no illusions about the studios and expected, eventually, to go the indie route. But the problem was, the indies were passing too. Cary Woods had turned it down for Miramax.

While Damon and Affleck were writing and rewriting, their acting careers were showing signs of life. Affleck was trying out for Smith's studio film, *Mallrats*. "I wanted to meet Kevin Smith, although I still hadn't seen *Clerks*, but I thought maybe I could learn something about how they did that," he recalls. "I thought the script was really funny. Maybe that means I just have bad taste, I don't know. I got cast as another dumb bad guy—that was lame. I was thinking, No one's gonna like me. But I was so awestruck to be working with a director my age. The first day of *Mallrats*, at wrap, Kevin turned to the first AD and said, 'What's the protocol here? Shall I start grabbing boxes and stuff? And carry them downstairs?' The guy just chuckled, 'No, no, no, you're the director, you don't do that!' "

Damon went up for *Courage Under Fire* and got the part. De Niro–like in his zeal for prepping his role as a junkie, he lost forty-five pounds, threw his adrenal system out of whack, messed up his electrolytes, and nearly died. Afterward, he left L.A. and returned home to Cambridge. He thought, Fuck it! If that's what I gotta do to rise up in the pecking order of these fucking idiot young actors, then I don't care anymore. I'm killing myself. It was six months before he was ready to even think about another picture.

Luckily, Damon's agent sent *Good Will Hunting* out just at the time the town was in a frenzy over spec scripts. Everything screenwriter Shane Black (*Lethal Weapon*) put his name to was fetching millions of dollars. Eventually, using the proverbial smoke and mirrors, the agent created a bidding war over the screenplay. "The first thing we found out was somebody wanted to buy it for $25,000," Damon recalls. "We were like, 'We're fuckin' rich!' " Quickly, the price escalated. Linklater had a deal with Castle Rock and at his urging, Damon and Affleck accepted their offer of $600,000 in November 1994. Recalls Damon, "We were broke. That money changed our lives." They even got their pictures on the front page of *Daily Variety*.

Affleck had just broken up with his girlfriend and was sleeping on Damon's couch in his tiny apartment on Curson in West Hollywood. It was, "We need an advance, man, we gotta move outta this apartment, it's too small," he recalls. They found a bigger place on Glencoe Way, off Highland near the Hollywood Bowl. Affleck continues, "But we didn't have any credit, so in lieu of credit, we took the copy of *Variety* to the landlord, pointed to our pictures, and said, 'See we're good for the money, these checks are coming.' "

But the boys felt like their car had stalled at Castle Rock. Says Affleck, "We developed the script for a year there, which seemed like ten years. Things were going sideways in a big way. We went from euphoria to finding out how fast you can spend $600,000."

Each one got $300,000, down to $150,000 after taxes, down to $135,000 after the agents took their cuts. They bought matching $35,000 Jeep Cherokees. Affleck continues, "Top-of-the-line, the Sport Pac, because we were rich, right? With the leather, the CD player—'I want the kind that goes, "Whoop, whoop!" when you try the key.' We both wanted the same car, the black one. We knew this was just *wayyy* too Ace and Gary—the sketch on *Saturday Night Live*, the two guys, superhero pals but obviously gay, ride motorcycles together—we can't have the same car, it's too his-and-his, but neither one of us wanted to back down, so we flipped. Matt won, he got the black one, mine was green. Once I realized that other guys were going, 'Soo, you guys both have the same car?' it was worse than his-and-his, it was his-and-hers!"

The place on Glencoe Way became party central, Animal House. "Our million buddies instantly moved in with us, because it was high times on the hog," Affleck goes on. "We spent all the money buying beer and playing poker, and we would play video games and stay up until the wee hours. A guy named Bubba lived with us, and one time he just got up from the poker table, leaned over the balcony, vomited, and sat back down. It wasn't really a drug scene, it was a heavy drinking scene, because that was the way we grew up in Boston, you'd go out and drink all the time, mostly beer. When everybody turned twenty-five, all of a sudden we're all twenty pounds heavier than we used to be and we all bought treadmills."

Damon and Affleck were getting impatient. The two writers suspected the Castle Rock guys were not even reading what they'd been giving them. In one draft they put in a scene where the "Harvey Keitel" character, a psychiatrist, gives Damon's character, Will Hunting, a blowjob in his office. Recalls Affleck, "Nobody at Castle Rock ever said anything to us about it, and we were like, 'All right, I guess the blowjob scene works.' It was demoralizing." The screenwriters thought the script was there, but they were getting the three-billy-goat treatment. It was always, "The next draft, the next draft you'll get a director." Finally, one day, the song changed to, "Congratulations, we're gonna make the movie."

"Great! We have a list of directors we're gonna go to," They had in mind their favorites, Scorsese, Coppola, Redford, Gus Van Sant, Martin Brest, Peter Weir. They figured they would all pass, but you gotta try, right?

"Don't worry, we're not gonna need to go to directors. Good news, Andy Scheinman wants to do it!"

"Whaddya mean, Andy wants to do it? You told us we could go to directors." They didn't even know Scheinman, one of the Castle Rock partners, was a director. They thought that he was Reiner's producer.

"Watch Andy's movie."

Andy's movie was called *Little Big League*, a kids' picture, not exactly what they had in mind. Both Damon and Affleck were fans of a novel by Cormac McCarthy called *All the Pretty Horses*. In it there's a scene where a thirteen-year-old kid named Blevins gets his horse stolen, rides into a strange town to find the thief armed with a pistol bigger than he is, and gets himself killed. One of the other characters observes, by way of a testament, "I'll say this for 'im, he wasn't gonna stand by for no sonofabitch hijacking his horse." Says Affleck, "We knew that we would rather do the movie the way we wanted to do it and fail, than do it somebody else's way. No sonofabitch was going to hijack our horse!"

Castle Rock put *Good Will Hunting* in turnaround. "We didn't know anything about turnaround, but we found out soon enough," Affleck says. "It was standard practice to bill a lot of other overhead costs against the movie so the turnaround cost to another studio becomes [prohibitive]. The price they were asking was in excess of a million dollars. They gave us thirty days to sell it, after which it reverted to them. Andy would make it and we were gonna forfeit our right to be in it. We'd be lucky if we got tickets to the premiere." Undoubtedly, Castle Rock regarded this as a ploy to get rid of them. "It had to be bought by somebody who was willing to put me and Ben in those two roles, and fork over $1 million for what looked like a $3 million movie, and it just didn't make any sense," adds Damon. "Castle Rock thought that we wouldn't be able to make the deal, and they were almost right."

Universal's *Mallrats* was released in October 1995. With a budget of $6.1 million, it grossed only $2.1 million and got miserable reviews to boot. "It was yet another ugly disappointing failure that I was involved with," recalls Affleck. "Anybody in that movie with a line was on the poster. Except for me. I'm sure my character tested the worst. I was the anal rapist, whatever, and Sherman Oaks doesn't look fondly on anal rapists." Smith got blasted by his indie peers for "selling out." At the time, Smith was stung, although now the phrase has a quaint ring to it. It springs from the days, long gone, when indies and their films manned the barricades against Hollywood. Increasingly, through the second half of the decade, the barricades were sold off to make room for condos, and "selling out" lost its meaning. It was Affleck's view, not Hawke's, that prevailed. In any event, Smith called Affleck, said, "I think you can play a leading man, nobody's ever given you the chance. I'm writing a movie for you about a guy who falls in love with a lesbian." Affleck didn't believe him, thought, This has gotta be some kind of jerkoff joke. But to Smith, he said, "Well, great, I'll do it, I'm in!"

With *Good Will Hunting* in turnaround, the clock was ticking. All the companies that were ready to kill for it the year before passed. As Affleck puts it, "It's like, you thought you were going to the prom with the girl you really liked, when all of a sudden she drops you, and you're going back to the girls you said no to." It began to look like they were trapped in the Hollywood version of Chutes and Ladders, landing back at square one. Affleck continues, "The deadline was approaching, we were getting really depressed, we were three or four years into this thing, and now we were going to be screwed out of our movie. We couldn't believe it." But in the best tradition of tinsel town happy endings, just when prospects looked bleakest, the sun broke through the clouds.

In a desperate Hail Mary, Affleck gave the script to Smith, who had indeed written a film for him. After the failure of *Mallrats*, Smith famously called Harvey and said, "Can I come home now?" He made his deal for *Chasing Amy*, at Miramax. "*Chasing Amy* could never have been made at a studio," says the filmmaker. "At a studio, the boy and the girl would have wound up together at the end, and it would have had a lot less of the harsh subtext, where Ben's character proposes a three-way with his friend and this girlfriend. The studio would have been, like, 'Are you high? That's ridiculous.' " *Chasing Amy* almost wasn't made at Miramax either. Executive Meryl Poster called Smith, scolded him for casting Affleck: "This is business, Kevin, it's not making movies with your friends." But Smith stood his ground, and for the privilege of making movies with his friends, he had to agree to do it on an astoundingly low budget of $250,000. (When it was released in April 1997 it grossed $12 million, making the Weinsteins a tidy profit. Smith was golden.)

Affleck pleaded with him: "We're having trouble with Castle Rock. Please Kevin, you have a deal at Miramax, direct this movie. Please, man!" Smith read it, replied, "I loved it, I cried on the toilet, but I'm not gonna direct it, I don't want to direct anything I don't write, I don't think I'd do a good job, but what I can do, I can walk it into Harvey's office."

It was a very long shot. First, Woods had already thrown the script in the wastebasket. Second, Damon and Affleck were wary of Miramax. Recalls Damon, "Everyone warned us, they said, He's Harvey Scissorhands, he'll bite your head off." Their young producer, Chris Moore, who hid a considerable shrewdness under a goofy exterior, told the boys, "What I hear about this guy Weinstein is, you're going to hear everything you want to hear, and you get off the phone with him and you'll feel like your life couldn't be any better, but it remains to be seen what you'll get." Says Damon, "True to form, Harvey called up and said every single thing we wanted to hear, which was, 'I don't know who the fuck you guys are, but I love this fuckin' script, Kevin loves it, it's really fuckin' good, but this is too much money these guys at fuckin' Castle Rock want me to shell out, like, it's *Breaking Away*? And there's one thing'—beat—'you can't be giving him a fuckin' blowjob at the office, okay, guys? You think you're funny, you're not that fuckin' funny.' " Adds Affleck, "Immediately we loved him. He pulled the trigger." Within a day of getting the script from Smith, Weinstein offered $1 million for it, with Damon and Affleck attached. He did what he does best—he saw the potential, accepted the risk, met their price, and executed with lighting speed.

From the Miramax side, it looked like another one of Harvey's foolish impulse buys. "It was tainted goods," says former Miramax development head Jack Lechner. "You had to commit to let these two unknown actors star in the movie, you had to pay Castle Rock all their costs and then you had to spend another $18 million to make the movie. People thought he was crazy."

Harvey wanted to tie up Damon and Affleck with options for two future scripts and two acting gigs, for which Damon would be paid $600,000 and $800,000, and Affleck somewhat less, $350,000 and $500,000. Damon's agent told them, "You don't have to accept this many options." But filmmakers who are so desperate to make their film that they will do anything, even work for nothing, are like clay in Weinstein's hands. Damon thought, Well, Jesus, $600,000 is a fortune, way more than I've ever been paid, or I probably will ever be paid. If we're complaining about getting that much money in two years for a movie, then that's a pretty high-class problem, and shit, I'd like to do every movie for Miramax anyway, because Harvey is the only person crazy enough to buy the script. He told his agent, "We don't give a shit how many options they want, let's get this movie made." With no other offers on the table and about to lose the film to Castle Rock, it was a no-brainer. Says Affleck, "We knew that he supposedly fought with filmmakers, and it wasn't that we hadn't seen that side of him—'You fuckin' guys, you got your heads up your asses'—but I didn't mind it, I preferred it to the smiling and shaking hands and fucking you later MO of Hollywood. I liked Harvey, I thought he was funny, I got along with him. Besides, beggars can't be choosers, and we were jus' happy dey wanted da boy." In the fall of 1995, Weinstein bought the script.

Grateful as they were, Damon and Affleck weren't quite so pliable as

Miramax imagined. They had a relationship with Van Sant, whom they both admired. Van Sant had just finished the sensational *To Die For* when Mark Tusk showed him the *Good Will Hunting* script. Van Sant loved it. But Harvey didn't want him. Miramax production head Paul Webster told Harvey, "Harvey, let's hire him, he's perfect. He makes movies with good-looking boys very well!" Harvey said, "I don't think so," and started looking in earnest. But nobody wanted to do it with two unknowns. Finally it came back to Van Sant—at a quarter of his asking price. Van Sant was nervous. He had talked to Tarantino, who expressed little sympathy for the directors Weinstein had steamrolled, saying, "A lot of these guys, they can't fight for themselves, they just get pushed around, it serves them right. They're not standing up to him." Van Sant thought, Quentin is the type of guy who can stand up to him. I don't know if I can do that or not. Probably not. He decided to insist on final cut. Harvey refused.

At a meeting in the Tribeca offices, Harvey casually informed Damon and Affleck, "I just want you guys to know we offered the movie to Chris Columbus." They were stunned. Columbus was an okay director forever enshrined in box office heaven for *Home Alone* (and later the *Harry Potters*) but if it wasn't going to be Van Sant, the boys wanted a director whose films had played at the Orson Welles in Cambridge, where they had grown up. As Harvey rattled on, saying, "I offered him $5 million to direct, and he almost did it. He read it three times before he passed on it," Damon interrupted him, said, "Well, you're lucky, 'cause you would have been out $5 million!" The room fell silent. This was the first time they had ever talked back to him. The Miramax drones looked down at their notepads. As Damon recalls, Harvey went ballistic, shouted, "What? Who the fuck do you think you are? How fuckin' dare you talk to me like that? You're a no-body!" Through gritted teeth, Damon replied, "I'm a nobody, but I'm a no-body with director approval."

Weinstein continued to look in vain for a director, because he wasn't willing to give away final cut. At one point, Mel Gibson expressed interest. They met at the Four Seasons in New York, Damon, Affleck, Weinstein, and Jon Gordon, yet another of Harvey's former assistants who was climbing the executive ranks and whom he had assigned to the film. According to Affleck, Harvey said, "Wait in the hall, Jon," and Gordon did so while the others sat down at the conference table with Gibson. Then Gibson said, "Harvey, I just want to talk to the guys."

Harvey paused for a minute and said, "I know, I love these guys."

"No, just me and the guys."

"Okay, Mel, I understand, no problem, I mean, great," and he walked out in the hall to wait with Gordon. (According to Miramax, Gordon wasn't present.) Two weeks later, Gibson passed. Unable to find a director, and doubtless annoyed that the two wannabes were still insisting on Van Sant, Harvey turned his attention to other things. Like releasing *The English Patient*. "The thing sat for a year," says Damon. "You could just feel that the heat around the movie had dissipated. It was a horrible time. Our careers were going nowhere. We'd moved back to Boston to get ready to do the movie, it was the season to do it, and Miramax wouldn't make the deal. We were flipping out."

Then Damon caught a break, got cast in *The Rainmaker*, based on a novel by John Grisham. Damon sent Weinstein a fax telling him the news. Harvey called him up, said, "What the hell does that mean?"

"The Coppola movie."

"The GRISHAM?! Every one of those makes $100 million."

"Well, I'm gonna do it. I'm gettin' in my truck and going to Knoxville, man," where he intended to research his role. Webster had continued to press for Van Sant, and by the time Damon arrived, the next day, Miramax had met the director's price, a million and a quarter. *Good Will Hunting* finally got its green light.

Robin Williams had been talking to Van Sant about doing *The Mayor of Castro Street*, the Harvey Milk story. He liked the *Good Will Hunting* script and agreed to play the therapist. Bingo! *Good Will Hunting* was fast-tracked. Recalls Damon, "Once Robin got involved, a lot of the stuff just went so smoothly, because suddenly they had this movie they were making for a price with one of the biggest movie stars around. So they were thrilled."

Harvey tried to bump Chris Moore, Damon's and Affleck's friend and producer, off the project. He hired Tarantino's producer, Lawrence Bender, instead. When the two writer-actors protested, he agreed to keep Moore on as associate producer, but the damage had been done. "I love Lawrence," says Jack Lechner, who was involved in the film on the Miramax side. "He's a brilliant guy, but he's not Mr. Tact, and he didn't kowtow to Gus, and he certainly didn't kowtow to Matt and Ben, who were not yet Matt and Ben. Lawrence wanted to do more work on the script." Damon, who had been working on it for over half a decade, shouted, "FUCK OFF, Lawrence, we're not changing it, it's good how it is."

"Well, I called Quentin, and Quentin agreed—"

"Fuck you, I don't care about Quentin, I don't think you had anything to do with those movies." Bender wanted to fire them, give the script to Boaz Yakin (*Fresh*) for a rewrite. Affleck and Damon threatened to walk, and Weinstein had to choose between the producer and the nobodies. He chose the nobodies. Damon finished shooting *The Rainmaker* in February 1997. By April, he was in Toronto on the set of *Good Will Hunting*.

• • •

EVER SINCE EXECUTIVE DIRECTOR Suzanne Weil had been dumped in 1991, the Sundance Institute had functioned without an executive director until the arrival of Ken Brecher, hired in 1997. Brecher was a cultural anthropologist who came out of a museum background and knew nothing about film. Redford seemed to enjoy filling slots with people who had little or no experience to qualify them for whatever it was they were supposed to be doing. It seemed to be a way of keeping Sundance in turmoil and maintaining control over the organization. Although Brecher may have been a film illiterate, he seemed skilled at managing Redford, and he was the first director since Sterling Van Wagenen whose tenure exceeded the life of a fruitfly.

In 1997, Redford again disappeared from Sundance, this time to direct and star in *The Horse Whisperer*. *The Horse Whisperer* was co-produced by his feature film company, Wildwood, which had also been involved with Soderbergh's *King of the Hill* and Redford's own *Quiz Show*. Wildwood was run by Rachel Pfeffer, late of Castle Rock, whose claim to fame was that she had been executive producer of that company's hit Tom Cruise vehicle, *A Few Good Men*. Pfeffer was apparently not a favorite of Redford's. He was characteristically and unfailingly punctilious toward her—he would never raise his voice nor utter a harsh word to her face—but he constantly complained about her behind her back, saying things like, "Wildwood is such a mess, I have to do something about it." But he never did. Instead, he acted as though she didn't exist. His office scheduled meetings at half-hour intervals beginning mid-morning. However, he rarely drove his Acura down from his home in Malibu to his office on Montana, in Santa Monica, until one or two in the afternoon, at which point there would be a waiting room full of supplicants who had been cooling their heels for hours. By that time, Pfeffer, who, after all, ran his company, was frantic to see him. Her office faced the front door. But Redford sometimes used the rear entrance, slipping in and shutting his door so that she never knew he had arrived. After it dawned on her that he was in fact in the building, she would beg his longtime assistant, Donna Kail, "I gotta talk to Bob, I only need five minutes with him." Kail would reply, politely, "Okay, I'll tell him," but he would eventually leave—through the back door. Says a former Redford employee, "Why didn't he just fire Rachel when he said he wanted to? That was a pattern with everything: it would take forever. People were always asking him for things, and you knew the answer was going to be no, but instead of him just saying no, he would always say, 'Hold on, I'm not sure,' and then these people would call back later and say, 'Well?' And you'd say, 'He's not sure.' And then the process would get dragged out, and these people would be strung along forever."

In the third week of August 1997, Redford announced another ambitious and long-cherished initiative, a deal with General Cinema Corporation, which owned theaters in twenty-five states, to create Sundance Cinemas, a chain of movie houses devoted to indie film. Thanks in part to the institute's own success, and abetted by a booming economy, there seemed to be more than enough money to finance indie films; if anything, there was a glut on the market, making for fierce competition for screens. The days when a film could sit in one theater for weeks and build an audience through good reviews and word of mouth were long gone. With the chains consolidating, theaters traditionally devoted to indies were being bought up or squeezed out. Exhibition had become a bottleneck, potentially limiting the growth of the audience for specialty films.

Redford envisioned the construction of a chain of theaters in the U.S. and even internationally over the next decade, with work to start on the first few as soon as possible. The theaters, to be designed by top architects, were intended to be satellite Sundances, oases of film culture amidst suburban popcorn deserts, replete with piazza-like open spaces in which filmgoers could sit and talk, debating the fine points of the latest Coen brothers film; restaurants serving healthy food; art galleries; video facilities; space for panels and lectures; and last but not least, an (independent) bookstore. Think New York's Film Forum or Berkeley's Pacific Film Archive designed by Frank Gehry, catered by Alice Waters, programmed by Gilmore or Richard Pena of the New York Film Festival, with L.A.'s Book Soup next door. It was typical Redford: visionary and inspired, and it would have been wonderful—had it worked.

Redford's attitude toward any co-venture was that the potential partners should be thrilled to participate. What that meant in practice was that Sundance would supply the stardust, and the partner would supply the cash. But, according to Gary Meyer, one of the founders of Landmark Theaters, the pioneering art house chain, whom Redford had hired as a consultant, "Getting General Cinema in there as a partner was a big mistake." Many of its theaters were either inconveniently located for the patrons of art films, or in such poor shape that it would have taken as much money to renovate them as it would have to start from scratch. Sundance had a golden opportunity to buy Landmark instead. Says Meyer, "If they had, they would have been instantly in business with a successful company, 150 screens, and a management team in place, ready to go. By the time they finally decided to buy Landmark, they were literally two days too late. Silver Cinema bought it. And that was the case throughout the history of it, which is that everything [Sundance did] wound up being too late. If you're traveling around the world making movies, like Redford, it's pretty hard to be there to hear a plan or see a location. But he's a control guy, he wanted to be involved in those things. That meant that everybody had to stop and wait until he got back."

At one point, they had the chance to redo a General Cinema multiplex in Scarsdale, a wealthy suburb of New York City, in an area that was under-screened, with lots of parking and an adjacent building available for the café and whatever else Sundance wanted to pluck out of its goody bag. Meyer, realizing that it was a perfect location, exclaimed, "Man, let's grab this place right now." But Gordon Bowen, Redford's pooh-bah du jour, had to approve the site too. According to Meyer, he said, "No, there's a Borders bookstore across the parking lot. We don't want to be anywhere near a chain," and they passed on it. Meyer adds, "Bowen may have known some-thing about branding, but he knew nothing about the business that Bob wanted to get into and he wasn't willing to learn. Clearview took it over, and they're running it today as a successful art house." (Clearview is the ex-hibition arm of Redford's bête noire, IFC.)

In the same way that the institute was now run by a man with no back-ground in film, and the Sundance Channel was launched by two execu-tives similarly clueless, so the cinema project began, bizarrely, without anyone who knew anything about exhibition, let alone indie exhibition. "What really killed it was some of the people who got hired to actually run the business," says Meyer. "Doofuses!' " Redford always described himself as an artist jock, and he hired a former football player named Bill Freeman who worked for ESPN Zone. Freeman was a restaurant guy. Says Meyer, "Freeman thought because he'd created ESPN Grill, Fuddruckers, and a bunch of other pieces of shit, that he knew everything. Freeman didn't want anybody who knew anything about the business around, because he didn't want anybody to know more than he did."

Ground was actually broken at two sites, one in Portland, Oregon, the other in Philadelphia. Portland already had a perfectly good art house. In-stead of opening a dialogue with the community, Sundance just came in and started building, a competitor, rather than a partner. "It was arrogant," says a former staffer. Like out-of-control movie productions, the construc-tion on both theaters immediately fell behind, while Redford complained that design-wise, they were not what he intended. Concludes Meyer, "The stuff Redford wanted to do was fantastic. Anybody who loved movies would have said, 'This is where I'm gonna spend as many nights a week as I can.' But unfortunately, he didn't look at the bottom line. His scheme was too grand for the reality of the business world."

AS LONG AGO as 1993, in the aftermath of the Disney deal, skeptics won-dered whether the Weinsteins would turn out to be as effective developing and producing films as they were acquiring them. *Pulp Fiction, The English Patient, Scream, Good Will Hunting* (and later, *Shakespeare in Love*), all picked up in turnaround, did little to answer the question. Or maybe they did: perhaps the answer was, Harvey didn't need to develop and produce. "The movies that Harvey has done well with have not been developed by Miramax," says Cathy Konrad. "They were labored on at other studios for endless years, with a lot of money and a lot of passion, and he came in when he could get them cheap." Harvey let the studios do the heavy lifting while he reaped the rewards. He had become Hollywood's most skilled ambulance chaser.

But there wasn't enough in turnaround to fill a forty-film slate. As Miramax increasingly turned toward production in the second half of the decade, it did more and more of its own development. But, says Lechner, "Harvey is not as interested in development itself. He is not someone who goes out and plants a seed and waters it every year, and is willing to take ten years to let it grow into a healthy tree. He comes out of an acquisitions background, and the closer it is to being a finished film, the more excited he gets about it and the easier it is to sell it to him. The next easiest is a half-completed film, and the next easiest a screenplay with elements attached."

Moreover, Harvey is not a patient man. He doesn't have the temperament for development; he likes his gratification quick and cheap. He always boasted, "We don't develop movies. We make them." It was true, and it was a problem. "My biggest frustration as a producer with that company was that they were really bad at development," says Konrad. "So either you found something that you could shoot right away, or you didn't make anything." Adds Paul Webster, "Harvey is not the best developer in the world, and he's not good on script. When I made *The Tall Guy*, which Miramax distributed, on the very first day of principal photography, Harvey sent me and the director the same present—Ralph Rosenblum and Robert Karen's *When the Shooting Stops the Cutting Begins*. In other words, his message was, 'I'm gonna be there at the end.' Nothing's changed."

When he did develop, the results were often dismal. Take 54. Webster brought Paul Thomas Anderson's *Boogie Nights*—a dark, downbeat exploration of L.A.'s porn underground—to Harvey in the late summer of 1995. The timing couldn't have been worse. Miramax had just emerged, bruised and battered from the *Priest/Kids* fracases and, with or without an assist from Michael Eisner, Harvey was determined to avoid future dustups. Still, Webster walked into Weinstein's office determined to take full advantage of the fifteen minutes he had to make his pitch. "This is fantastic, this is a great script," he began, before Meryl Poster interrupted him. She said, "Harvey, don't even read it, it's disgusting, it's about pornography." Weinstein replied, "Oh, it sounds obscene, I don't want to do it." Webster recalls, "She was one of the few people that Harvey always listened to, and she has very sentimental taste, very soft. It was the porno thing that made him reject it out of hand. Harvey never read the script. Those controversial films don't make much money, and the direction of the company through the period I was there up to now was toward doing much more commercial stuff." (*Boogie Nights* was ultimately produced by New Line to great acclaim.)

54, on the other hand, was regarded by Miramax as *Boogie Nights* Lite. Written by Mark Christopher, just out of Columbia film school, it was a script about the glory days of Studio 54 in the late 1970s and early 1980s, when it was the epicenter of the gay cultural explosion in New York City. The script was full of raunchy sex and not-so-nice characters. It is the tale of Shane, a kid from New Jersey who sleeps his way to the top of the 54 pecking order, which means that he becomes one of the shirtless bartenders for which the club was notorious, golden boys who flexed and preened for the clientele of both sexes, occasionally deigning to grant sexual favors in return for money or drugs.

54 was just the script to bring out the worst in Miramax. It contained all the elements Harvey used to like—it was sexy, transgressive, and hip—but now these virtues had become vices—they scared him—creating a fatal ambivalence. Miramax had released a considerable number of gay-themed movies (*Paris Is Burning, The Crying Game, Priest,* etc). Still, in the gay community, Harvey was regarded with some suspicion, despite his very visible support of organizations like GLAAD and amfAR. A lot of people thought he was homophobic—there were only a handful of openly gay employees at Miramax—and the word on the street was that any gay-themed project would have a tough time there. Harvey had insisted on cutting a coda from *Flirting with Disaster* showing two guys in bed. "There was always a little question about homosexual content in Miramax movies," says Mark Tusk, his out-of-the-closet acquisitions executive. "Harvey and Bob weren't really homophobic, they just felt more comfortable around people they could watch the Super Bowl with. Harvey's a guy's guy. And when they realized that it was a niche audience, and that there was money to be made, they grinned and bore it." But in the grip of a dream come true, the filmmakers put their fears aside. After all, everyone knew Christopher was gay, the script was filled with gay material. Miramax was the fearless company that released *Paris Is Burning, Priest,* this, that. What could go wrong?

Trouble came quickly, disguised as good fortune. The filmmakers knew it was a tough, uncompromising script that was not for everybody and not particularly commercial. It was aimed at a young, sophisticated urban audience. For that reason, they wanted to keep the budget down, $4 million. But Miramax wanted a bigger movie at double the budget, $8 million. (According to Miramax, the budget was close to $5 million.) The filmmakers feared that a bigger budget would necessitate a bigger marketing push to attract a bigger audience to pay back Miramax for the bigger budget and bigger marketing push. A bigger audience would necessitate script changes to broaden the film's appeal, as well as "casting up" the picture. But more money is more money, and this was Christopher's first feature. Like Jim Mangold, he found it hard to say no. Christopher met Harvey, who, as he always does when he comes a-wooing, told him everything he wanted to hear, that he loved the script, and added something like, "We'll do it by Christmas."

Indeed, at the beginning, everything went smoothly. Christopher had the benefit of good producers—Dolly Hall, who had just finished Lisa Cholodenko's extraordinary High Art, and Ira Deutchman, who had exited Fine Line and was trying his hand at producing. While Harvey's career had flourished, Deutchman's had had its ups and downs, and although there was a time, during the dark days of the early 1990s, when Harvey was feeling so defeated he asked Deutchman to take over his company, he now treated him with condescension. Deutchman was somebody he'd left behind. For his part, Deutchman seemed to be looking to Harvey for some sign of respect.

Christopher also had the benefit of the Weinsteins' development and production teams. But what was Miramax's golden talent bank one minute became Miramax's revolving door the next. First Jonathan King left, who had brought in 54 in the first place. Alan Sabinson was brought in over Webster and Lechner. His story became famous within the company. He had sterling credentials, was working as VP of original programming at TNT in Los Angeles when the brothers approached him. Sabinson was happy where he was and knew he would not be a good fit with the Weinsteins. He told them, in essence, that he wasn't like them, he was a nice guy with few enemies, and he probably wouldn't fit in. They replied, "That's exactly what we want. We want to soften our image." Against his better judgment, he uprooted his family, his wife and two young children, and relocated to New York, with a three-year contract. As it turned out, Sabinson was right. The brothers didn't like him. Harvey would set him impossible tasks, like convincing Kevin Spacey to trim Albino Alligator after Harvey himself had given Spacey final cut. There was no way the actor was going to listen to Sabinson, and when the executive reported this to Harvey, he shouted, "You're a fuckin' moron, an idiot. What am I paying you for? Get outta my office, I don't want to see you here, you're a piece of shit." The Weinsteins quickly decided to get rid of him. Remembers Webster, "I witnessed him being slaughtered on a cross-country plane trip. Belittled. Harvey completely disregarded anything he said."

Eventually, Sabinson gave up, but he wanted them to settle his contract. They didn't feel like it. When he insisted, they threatened, "We'll wake up every day and go, How do we make your life miserable? We will keep you in Hong Kong, you'll be on planes all the time, flying all over the world, you'll never see your family." Sabinson believed them and resigned. Says marketing VP Mark Gill, who watched it all go down, "It was a kill or be killed environment, and he was never a person who wanted to kill, so he got killed all day long. The guy was target practice."

Then Webster left, in 1997, to head Film Four in England. Sabinson was succeeded by Poster, who was quickly moving up through the ranks. Deutchman was fired, and 54 fell into Lechner's lap. Miramax battled Christopher over the casting. The most important role was Shane, the kid from New Jersey. The filmmakers wanted to use an unknown, but Poster objected, shrieking into the phone, "We need to cast someone we can book on Leno, on Letterman!" Finally, they settled on Ryan Phillippe, a relative newcomer. Salma Hayek was cast as the female leg of the triangle. Continues the source, "Then we got Neve Campbell shoved down our throats. She is one of the nicest gals you would ever want to know, but she can't act her way out of a paper bag with a flashlight. She makes Salma Hayek look like Meryl Streep." Campbell had appeared in *Scream*. Harvey used to say to actors like Campbell, "Work for Dimension and you'll make your payday, then work for me on a labor of love." Her presence virtually guaranteed a big TV sale, so that even if the movie tanked theatrically, they wouldn't lose money. "It was more of a studio mentality—familiar faces," says Lechner. But Campbell's part was small, and the filmmakers figured they could live with her. And, in a stroke of good luck, Mike Myers, fresh from *Austin Powers*, agreed to play Steve Rubell. It was a great part, gave him a shot at a serious role, allowed him to stretch. When Myers signed up, Harvey green-lit the movie.

NO MATTER HOW MUCH the press touted October as the "new Miramax," it was still a small New York company whose successes—infinitesimal by Weinstein standards—were directed by relatively obscure foreign filmmakers from England, Denmark, and elsewhere. McGurk thought October could use a new Amir Malin. Not someone who could squeeze nickels and dimes out of the library, but an impact player who could help take the company to the "next level." There was a guy at Miramax McGurk knew well. He'd be perfect, McGurk thought. His name was Scott Greenstein.

Greenstein's deal with Miramax had expired, and he was dying to leave. There was no room for him to move up, and he was the target of nonstop abuse. But the brothers were apparently under the impression that they were negotiating with Greenstein to renew his contract, while he was using the skills he learned at Miramax to job-hunt. Says Bill Mechanic, "Scott came to see me at Fox, told me he was the third Weinstein, wanted me to fire Lindsay Law, who was head of Fox Searchlight, he should have

Lindsay's job, and all that. That was the end of the conversation. He obviously went back to Harvey—or however it got back to Harvey—and said I offered him a job, which I didn't, and I got one of those calls from Harvey, 'How fuckin' dare you steal our people . . . ' I said, 'You're being played.' "

Claiming he had an offer from Mechanic, Greenstein had also been knocking on Universal's door, where he got a warmer welcome. "Scott is a good dealmaker, he's got a real nose for talent, he's a good publicist, there are real things he brings to the party," says McGurk. "It made sense on paper. We were taking somebody who was the number three guy at this company that had increased its value tenfold over ten years, so he must know what the hell he's doing." Since Ray and Schmidt liked and trusted McGurk, when McGurk said, "Look, meet this guy, he'd be good for you. His contract is coming up, he's gonna be a free man, other outfits are all over him," they agreed to see him.

Greenstein was terrified that the Weinsteins would discover that he was talking to October, so on a weekend in June he drove up to Riverdale to meet with Ray and Schmidt in Schmidt's kitchen. Ray tried to recall what he'd heard about Greenstein. He says, "He was Harvey's hatchet man, ballbuster, dirty guy, like, Harvey doesn't want to lower the boom on some folks, Scott was the hammer."

Ray got there early. He wanted to figure out what kind of questions to ask, wondered how truthful they could expect Greenstein to be. He was apprehensive, didn't want to make a mistake with him the way he had with Malin. He had expressed his doubts to McGurk, who thought he was asking too many questions and had too many impressions, he didn't want to process that much information. He just wanted him to do what he wanted him to do. He said, "Stahhhp! Stahhhp! Meet this fucking guy. I want you to like him."

Greenstein drove up in a big, black GMC Yukon, chrome wheels. He was casually dressed. Schmidt made coffee, listened. Greenstein asked, "What have you heard about me?" Ray replied, "This is what I've heard . . ." Explaining away his role at Miramax, Greenstein essentially told them, It's unfair to call me the hatchet guy. I was cleaning up Harvey's and Bob's messes. I was the peacemaker. I was the one, when there was a problem, who tried to patch it up. He flattered them, claimed they were a burr under Harvey's saddle, but said nothing weird or offputting. Ray wanted him to be obsequious and fawning, an easy-to-say-no-to asshole, a Uriah Heep, but he wasn't. On Monday, Ray called McGurk, who asked, "So you guys hooked up, whaddya think?" Ray replied, unenthusiastically, "He seems okay, you can't tell after one meeting, John thinks you never know about a guy until you work with him." They called some people, did some homework. The report came back, he's in an unfortunate situation, the third

Weinstein, he's really a good guy and he's not a film guy, won't get in your hair, and so on. He was the hatchet man for two hatchet men, so nobody could separate the hatchets from the men, what Greenstein did at Miramax from what the Weinsteins made him do. Still, Ray and Schmidt were filled with misgivings. They wanted to run October themselves, they didn't want another Malin. Says Schmidt, "Based on McGurk's comfort with it, we signed off on it." They were going to try to make it *Enemies—A Love Story*, but it would turn out to be more like *Sleeping with the Enemy*.

Meanwhile, there was work to be done, films to acquire and produce. A few weeks earlier, Ray and Schmidt had gotten a script from Killer Films and Good Machine called *Happiness*, to be directed by Todd Solondz. Sony Classics had done extremely well with Solondz's previous film, *Welcome to the Dollhouse*. It had grossed $4.7 million—so much for Hollywood's fatwa against unsympathetic characters—and Solondz had been widely praised as an original talent. Solondz is short and slight. His voice rises and falls in a high-pitched, singsong cadence that is not unpleasing, although comparisons with Woody Allen are inevitable, and he dresses the role, geek chic, which is to say, slightly retro, with yellow socks and argyle sweater vests. A receding hairline has left him with a high forehead, and he wears industrial-strength glasses with heavy, black frames, behind which his eyes swim like guppies in a fishbowl, giving him a bewildered, lost look. He doesn't like to make eye contact, and his characteristic expression is a slight frown, as if he senses a headache coming on or has taken a bite out of something bitter. Solondz looks like someone out of a Wes Anderson film, *The Royal Tenenbaums*, perhaps, although colder, more calculating and self-protective than Anderson's hapless heroes.

Solondz grew up in Livingston, New Jersey, which he regarded at the time as "the ugliest place on the planet, the embodiment of banality, an aesthetic void," until he realized that almost everywhere else in America was the same. Talking about his childhood, he has said, makes him "sick." The son of a builder, he recalls his parents planting an imperfect privet hedge that failed to grow together and thus never quite managed to shut out the neighbors. He's still obsessive about his privacy, screens calls, doesn't like to be photographed. He sees a lot of movies, hates pretty much everything, is competitive with his peers. *Pace* his goofy, dazed, and confused demeanor, however, Solondz is as tough, wily, and as controlling as directors with longer track records and far greater success. Even his age comes as a surprise. Despite his adolescent look, he was thirty-seven when he made *Happiness*.

At NYU film school, Solondz made a short that got him a three-picture deal at Fox. Fox wanted him to direct *Revenge of the Nerds II*. Needless to say, he declined. Instead, he came back to New York and made a film whose title seems to sum up his worldview, *Fear, Anxiety, and Depression,* which he hated so much he gave up filmmaking, only to return in 1995 with *Dollhouse.* Solondz's unprepossessing appearance and clumsiness at sports made him a classic shnook, and he transformed the pain of his own adolescence into a biting, often unforgiving Diane Arbus-like vision of middle-class America at century's end, way darker than Kevin Smith and Hal Hartley, the other leading practioners of the East Coast mall school. Next to Solondz's theater of cruelty, Alexander Payne's *Election* or Miguel Arteta's *The Good Girl* or even Terry Zwigoff's *Ghost World* and Paul Thomas Anderson's surreal visions of the San Fernando Valley seem benign. In short, in an era of feel-good, over-the-rainbow uplift, like *My Big Fat Greek Wedding,* and smiley faces like Sandra Bullock, Solondz makes feel-bad films. In the indie coal mine, Solondz is the canary. So long as someone whose voice is as dystopian as his can continue to be heard, there's still hope.

The *Happiness* script had been making the rounds of distributors, but with its masturbation scenes and not altogether unsympathetic treatment of pederasty, everyone realized it would have to go out unrated or NC-17, and that made them nervous. (Even the Farrelly brothers—*There's Something About Mary*—called *Happiness* "sick.") They all said, "You gotta get rid of that child sex thing." Solondz didn't even bother with Miramax, because word that Harvey was no longer interested in controversial material had finally leaked out.

Ray and Schmidt had chased *Dollhouse* after it won the Grand Jury Prize at Sundance the previous year, and even though they lost it to Sony Classics, they thought that they had connected with Solondz. He told them, says Schmidt, that he "didn't like Amir," and that was the reason *Dollhouse* didn't go their way. The two men read the script of *Happiness* immediately and loved it. It was dark, almost painful—and nearly impossible to get made. But anticipating difficulty getting an American distributor, Good Machine's David Linde—he had moved over from Miramax in 1997—had already covered half the budget by selling foreign rights. Ray's reaction was, "This is right up our street, exactly the kind of film we should be financing, let's go get it." October sent the script over to Universal, which approved it. October told the *Happiness* folks, "The rating will not be a problem for us. We have total autonomy from Universal in what we want to do." Later, someone quipped, "The one mistake October made when Universal told them that they had total autonomy was they actually believed it!"

Like Ray, Christine Vachon was a fan of *Dollhouse.* "It was one of the few movies that I'd seen that I wished I had produced," she says. She had called Solondz, and invited him to lunch at the Time Cafe, near the Killer Films office, one day during the summer of 1996. At the end of the lunch,

Solondz told her that he wanted her to produce his next film, which turned out to be *Happiness*—with Ted Hope at Good Machine. According to Vachon, October approved a $5 million budget, with Patricia Arquette attached to play the Cynthia Stevenson role, the child molester's wife. But Arquette abruptly dropped out in June because her mother was sick. "The next day, Ted and I woke up to an extremely skittish October," Vachon says. "These were the same people who'd said in Cannes, 'We want to be in the Todd Solondz business. We don't care who's in this movie.' Suddenly, it was all about who was in the movie."

The script went out to twelve to fifteen actors to play the part of the pederast, including Jeff Bridges, William Hurt, Gary Sinise, John Goodman, and Bill Pullman. Uniformly, the reaction was, "It's compelling and interesting material, BUT—" "A but as big as Mount fuckin' Rushmore," says Ray, as in, "I'm a father myself, a father first and an actor second." Each one took weeks to decide, and Solondz wanted to start production on August 1. He couldn't get a straight answer out of October regarding the casting, and he began to feel the movie turning to sand and sifting through his fingers. Malin was still around, a lame duck. Says Vachon, "When we were dicking around going out to every A list star that existed, Amir was the one who gave us a figure," says Vachon. In desperation, Solondz finally asked, "How much will you let me make this movie for and not have to worry about this nonsense?" Malin instantly said, "Two point two million." Solondz replied, "Fine, then that's what I want to do." Continues Vachon, "Amir had a terrible reputation, but my feeling was that his assholeness was right there in front of you, which I'm fine with. Besides, I had enormous respect for Bingham, and I figured whatever was going on in this unholy alliance, Bingham would protect us."

Malin, according to Schmidt, "didn't want to leave. He called McGurk, and he said, 'I'm haunted by what I did. You've got to undo this.' McGurk replied, 'I can't. You did what you did.' " Greenstein joined October on August 14, 1997. It became clear very quickly that his exit from Miramax left a wound that was anything but clean and bloodless. When Harvey found out that the third brother, his lord high executioner and favorite punching bag, had wriggled under the wire and enlisted with a competitor, he nearly had the coronary everyone was expecting. Says one former Miramax executive, "I'm surprised that they let him get away. He didn't just know where the bodies were buried, he put them there. It was a real personal affront to Harvey when he left." According to *Variety*, Weinstein locked him out of his office and had him escorted from the building by security, which forced him to spend his last week working from home. As Ray describes it, "When Greenstein came over to join us, it was open war for eight months. Any defection from Harvey is a big deal. If you're a lowly little grunnybug, he gets pissed off. But if you're living in his pants for four years and the CFO—he gets nuts."

Right away, the phone on Schmidt's desk lit up as if it were on fire. It was Harvey, who, according to Ray and Schmidt, unleashed a baroquely inventive stream of profane taunts and threats, causing Schmidt to hold the phone at arm's length. He remembers, "Harvey just screamed obscenities and idiotic comments for forty-five minutes at the top of his lungs, things like, 'Our missiles are aimed at you! The rockets will be launched! You won't know what hit you! You open a film, we'll open three. We will put you out of business.' " It was too good not to share. Schmidt put down the phone on his desk and went to find Ray, shouting, "You gotta come in here, you gotta come in here right now." Ray recalls, "Standing in the door of John's office, you could hear Harvey yelling through the phone. He said things like, 'We're gonna bury you, Schmidt! That equity in your company that you love so much is not going to be worth shit. We're gonna take that company and we're going to fuckin' destroy it piece by piece. If you have one talented person there, I'm gonna raid you, and I'm gonna steal everyone you've got that you like there, and in two weeks you won't have a fuckin' company. And after we fuckin' bury your piece of shit fucking company, when you climb out of the rubble of what used to be October, John, then you can come crawling back on your hands and knees here and then maybe Bob and I will think, We like John, we'll give him his old job back. And Bingham, you worthless piece of shit, you think you're good at anything? Fuck you. You suck, I could blow you away with one of my weakest farts.' "

McGurk had always been loyal to the Weinsteins. He championed them to Disney executives like Dick Cook, who hated them, and he was then in the midst of lobbying Universal to sell them *Shakespeare in Love*. All of this counted for nothing. Bob called McGurk, threatened to break his legs, said he'd never work in this town again. As producer Larry Meistrich observed, the Weinsteins are all about leverage, and they cleverly provided entry-level slots for the children of some of their friends—Anthony Minghella and director John Madden among them—a practice that smacked equally of generosity and hostage taking. At the time Greenstein defected, Universal chairman Frank Biondi's daughter was working at Miramax as an intern. Biondi says that Bob threatened to throw her out on the street. Greenstein was petrified of his former bosses. According to Susan Glatzer, who ran October's West Coast office, "I've never seen him afraid of anyone except Harvey and Bob. At the Gotham Awards, he was terrified he was going to run into them."

Whereas Malin had operated in the shadows, avoiding premieres in favor of an evening at home with the wife and kids, Greenstein was a party animal, a backslapper and gladhander. Whereas Ray and Schmidt ran a casual, low-key operation—they prided themselves on taking the subway to screenings uptown, sort of a guerrilla mentality—Greenstein insisted on a limo and a driver, the way Bob and Harvey did it. "I could see where it was going," Ray says. "It was the Miramaxization of October. And I was an immediate and extremely vocal opponent."

Every September, the indie world flocks to Toronto for the film festival. The hot film that year, the film that no one had seen—no rushes, no rough cut, no twenty-minute reel—was *The Apostle*, written and directed by Robert Duvall. Duvall was—or pretended to be—a real cracker, and he was fascinated with things redneck, like charismatic preachers. *The Apostle* was the story of a flamboyant man of the cloth—the big house, flashy white Cadillac, expensive white suits, patent leather shoes—struggling with his demons. A tortured soul, part con man, part man of God, with one eye on Jesus and the other on the ladies, he had a streak of violence that ran down his back like an interstate highway. Duvall had written himself a great part, and he was desperate to make the movie.

But he was having trouble getting financing. The endless, 160-page script, full of eye-glazing fire-and-brimstone sermons, was not likely to quicken pulses in the movie business, and it had been making the rounds in L.A. and New York for thirteen years, to companies like Miramax, even October, with no takers. Duvall was represented by the Morris Agency. One day, Cassian Elwes was sitting around with Duvall, his agent, Todd Harris, and Duvall's lawyer. Elwes told Duvall, "I think you should put the money in yourself." He felt a kick under the table coming from the direction of Harris, who gave him a look that said, Cassian, that's the dumbest thing an agent can say to a client. We'll lose the fucking guy. But Elwes had committed himself, and he blithely continued, convincing Duvall that he could make the money back in foreign sales alone. Duvall thought about it, decided Elwes was right. *The Apostle* became an all-Duvall show; the actor wrote the script, played the lead, and paid for the movie, to the tune of $5 million.

The new October team went up to Toronto, their purses fat with Universal coin, eager to make a killing. Despite his misgivings, Ray was putting the best face on the Greenstein situation. Cary Woods bumped into him there, said, "Bingham, let me give you a little hint: Watch your back!" and mimed getting stabbed in the back. Ray brushed him off: "Oh, no, you've got it wrong, everything's working out great." Privately, however, he wasn't so sanguine. "There were flagpoles upon flagpoles of red flags going up, one after the other," he recalls. "And Toronto was the place where there was one too many fuckin' flagpoles."

There were enough agendas colliding in Toronto in 1997 to have flummoxed a session of the United Nations Security Council. In Greenstein's mind, *The Apostle* was the film Harvey wanted to buy, because his spies at Miramax had told him so. As Eamonn Bowles puts it, "Scott was trying to get out from under his former bosses and prove himself on his own. If they were interested in something, he was automatically interested in it. He had an incentive to beat Miramax." Although Greenstein was not famous for reading scripts, and if he had read any of *The Apostle*, he most likely had not read all of it, Ray had read it twice, and didn't like it. He thought, Being a godless individual, this kind of Middle American Bible-thumping stuff is not really me. Regional American shit doesn't play well foreign. *Sling Blade* did not play well foreign. So right from the start, he and Greenstein were on a collision course. Elwes, who was repping the film in Toronto, had his own potential nightmare. He was competing against himself, his big score on *Sling Blade* the year before, and, having encouraged Duvall to finance the film himself, he now had to make sure that at the very least, the actor got his money back or risk losing his agency a good client. Harvey was a wild card. He wanted *The Apostle*, and he also wanted to screw Greenstein, which he could do either by outbidding him for the film, or driving the price up so high that Greenstein could never make a profit on it. And last but not least, instead of being grateful to the man who had given him the inside track on *Sling Blade*, he doubtless blamed Elwes for making him look bad by inducing him to overpay for it. So he may have been out to settle that score as well.

Elwes decided to replay the strategy that had worked so well for *Sling Blade*. He arranged a screening for the buyers at the Uptown, the biggest theater in Toronto. Everybody was going to be there—the Miramax troops, Lindsay Law from Searchlight, Tom Bernard and Michael Barker from Sony, Ruth Vitale from Fine Line, even Malin from Live, everyone, that is, except Harvey. Harvey was on Martha's Vineyard, but he had tracked Elwes down, saying, "I want to see it."

"Of course you'll see it."

"I want to see it when everybody else sees it."

"How're we gonna do that? I've told everyone that it's a flat playing field."

"Send me a print."

"I don't want to do that." Then Elwes thought, Oh, fuck it, I'll get them to make another tape, and I'll have somebody bring it to his house at the exact moment it starts in Toronto, so he doesn't have an unfair advantage.

The screening was set to start at 9:00 P.M. The night before, Todd Harris, Duvall's agent, had called Elwes at his hotel room to remind him, in case he had forgotten, "If you don't sell the movie, he's leaving!" Elwes went to the bathroom and threw up.

The buyers crowded into the Uptown. But when people realized that the Fat Man was absent, they smelled a rat. Ray, in the lobby getting some popcorn, asked Elwes the obvious question, "Where's Harvey?"

"He's not here."

"So I guess we don't have to worry about Miramax."

"Oh, you have to worry about Miramax, all right, because all these other people are empowered to buy."

"Cassian, not one of these people that are here, Amy Israel, Jason Blum, no one can buy a movie without Harvey seeing it. So I have to assume that Harvey has seen the film already." Elwes refused to bite. But, says Ray, "That was the final fuckin' red flag." The screening was mysteriously delayed, apparently enabling Harvey, once again, to get the jump on everyone else. As Elwes was waiting around, Blum handed him a phone, saying, "Someone wants to talk to you." Without preamble, the voice Elwes knew all too well, growled, "It ain't *Sling Blade*."

"How much do you want to pay for it?"

"Pause it. You always get to the fuckin' money."

"Cuz I'm a fuckin' agent, whaddya want?"

"All right, here's the deal: I'll pay him back what he's got in it, and I'll get my gross corridor. That's the fuckin' deal!"

"He's not just gonna break even on it, he's spent his whole fucking life trying to make this movie."

"Well that's the fuckin' deal, and you have five minutes to go find him and tell him."

"The movie hasn't even started yet!"

"I don't give a fuck!"

"I'm gonna go inside and get the movie started, and talk to Duvall, and I'll come back and call you back."

"Right, five minutes, call me back." No matter how many times Elwes had dealt with Weinstein, it was always like root canal, and he could feel his shirt begin to cling to his skin.

Greenstein, Schmidt, and Ray were sitting together, on the left side, with Greenstein on the aisle. Elwes, worried that the picture was so long no one was going to stick it out to the end, got up a few minutes into it, and made his way through the darkened theater to the right side, where all the other buyers were clustered. Upping the figure by $1 million, he said, in a loud whisper, "Miramax just offered $6 million for the film, does anyone want to beat that?" He was met by a chorus of angry whispers, saying, "We haven't even seen the film yet, you motherfucker."

"I'm sorry, man, what can I tell you, they're trying to preempt the movie." Jonathan Weisgel, who had helped snatch *Shine* for Fine Line the year before, said, "Well, we don't have to watch the rest of the fuckin' movie then, right?"

"You can stay here for the pleasure of it, enjoy it."

"Fuck you!"

"I didn't say I'm taking it, I'm just telling you guys they made the offer." Then he walked back to where the October group was sitting, and whispered to Greenstein, "Harvey's offered $6 million. If you want to stay in the game, you've got to make a bid now." Elwes knew he'd said the right thing, because Greenstein jumped out of his seat like he'd been stung by a wasp, whispering hoarsely to the others, "C'mon, we gotta go," and crab-stepped up the aisle and into the lobby, herding Elwes and his lawyer, Craig Emmanuel, ahead of him. They all got into one cab, because they feared Elwes, left to go separately, would pull a fast one, and headed for October's makeshift office in the downtown Sheraton. Greenstein's theory of negotiation—really Harvey's—was, get in the room, shut the door, don't open it until you have the movie. Ray was uncomfortable. He felt he was being stampeded, wanted to watch more of the picture. Since Harvey wasn't there, he was wondering how he could have bid at all, much less $6 million. There was always a chance that Elwes had made it up, that there was no other bid. Still, they started hondling in the cab, Greenstein leading the charge. He topped what he thought was Harvey's offer, bidding the price up to $7.5 million for a movie of which they'd seen only ten or twenty minutes. This was way out of Ray's comfort zone, and again he asked, "Where the fuck is Harvey? How do I even know—how is Harvey seeing this movie?"

"He's on the Vineyard, I sent him a tape. He's watching now, same as everyone else."

"That's a total crock of fucking shit! Harvey waited until the screening was gonna start at the Uptown before inserting the tape in his VCR in Martha's Vineyard? You expect me to fucking believe that?"

"Yes! Harvey's a man of his word. He wouldn't see this before you."

Ray snorted derisively. This was so preposterous that he became convinced Elwes had manufactured the whole thing for their benefit. He thought, We're bidding against ourselves. There's just too much risk here. We're just being wound up big-time by a very skillful Cassian Elwes. But Greenstein had a high opinion of his own street smarts. His attitude was, No one can play me, I'm bulletproof, baby. Ray kept his mouth shut.

The October office was on the second floor, no more than a bare conference room with a round table on which sat a plastic carafe of water and some glasses. Emmanuel was putting the deal points down on paper when Elwes went, "Oh, shit, I forgot to call Weinstein back."

"What?"

"I told him I'd call him back in five minutes. It's an hour later now, he must be going crazy!" Greenstein fixed him with a look and said, "You can call him back *after* we close."

"No, I'm gonna call him right now. And tell him we're closing."

"Fuck you! No you're not, you're gonna call him after we close!" Elwes was holding the cell phone in his hand, and Greenstein made a lunge for it. They began to wrestle. Elwes cried, "Scott, c'mon now, man, we're fucking adults here. I'm gonna take my phone, and put it right down on top of the table here, you guys can all see it, let's all sit down." Accounts of what happened next diverge, although all the players agree that Elwes lost control of the negotiation. According to Schmidt, Elwes's phone rang. Everyone froze. A look passed among the three October executives that said, Harvey! One of them warned, "Cassian, if you walk out of this room with that phone, we withdraw our offer!" Elwes looked like he was going to cry, said, "I can't not answer this phone, it's my job to answer the phone," and he left. According to him, he put the phone down in the middle of the table, everyone calmed down, and suddenly he grabbed it and ran out of the room, speed-dialing Harvey as he went while the October guys chased him down the corridor as he was shouting, "Hello, hello?" Harvey picked up, asked, "What the fuck is going on?"

"I'm with the guys from October!"

"What! What the fuck are you doing?"

"Well, actually, I'm making a deal with them."

"You motherfucking—you closed!"

"I didn't fucking close."

Meanwhile, the October troika chased him down the hall, yelling, "He fucking closed! He fucking closed!" Elwes was getting to the end of the corridor, checking all the doors as he ran, trying to find one that was open. He barged through one, where there were two elderly ladies, and locked himself in the bathroom. The October guys followed him in, pounded on the door, shouting, "He closed! He closed!" while Harvey was screaming in his ear, "You fucking closed! You fucking closed!" when Elwes's battery died. Elwes said, "That's it, I'm not talking to any of you guys anymore." Elwes slipped out of the room and started down the corridor in the opposite direction. The October guys chased him again, out onto the fire escape. It was pouring rain. A man three stories down who apparently worked for the hotel yelled, "You can't be out on the fire escape."

"I'm talking to Harvey Weinstein!"

"Oh, okay!" Elwes ran down to the next floor, found an empty room, slammed the door, and changed the battery. Suddenly, the phone started to ring. Elwes, figuring it was Harvey, said, "Yeah, what the fuck do you want?"

"Oh, Cassian, it's Mike Simpson." Mike Simpson was his boss at William Morris. Elwes said, as casually as he could, "Hey, Mike, what's happening?"

"I just got the strangest phone call."

"What was that?"

"I got this call from Scott Greenstein, he said you were making a deal and you ran away."

"It's true."

"Well, they're really pissed off."

"They're right to be, I just didn't know what to do, I panicked. Weinstein's offering way more." He wasn't, but Elwes thought he would.

Meanwhile, the October guys locked Elwes's jacket and his PalmPilot in their office, knowing that when he finished talking to Harvey he'd have to call them to get them back. They left the Sheraton and went to the bar of the Four Seasons, for some serious drinking. Elwes called Harvey back, who instantly yelled, "I'll beat it, whatever the fuckin' number is, I'll fuckin' beat it." Elwes spit out $10 million, the magic *Sling Blade* number.

"Okay, you got a fuckin' deal."

Then Elwes called Schmidt over at the Four Seasons, said, "I have an offer from Harvey that I have to accept."

"Cassian, I don't even know why you're calling us, because we're not in this. We told you, you walk out of that room, we withdraw, so right now you have one offer and one offer only. And by the way, good luck closing." Schmidt knew very well, as he puts it, "Ten million from Harvey is not $10 million from anyone else. The Miramax negotiating technique is to chase everybody else out of the arena, either through bullying tactics or preemptively high bids, and then when the competition has walked away, ratchet down until sometimes there's no deal at all."

Indeed, what Harvey giveth, Harvey could taketh away. A few minutes passed, and Harvey, who must have realized that he had scared off October, or maybe suspected Elwes was playing him, or perhaps because he was repaying him for *Sling Blade,* called back, said, "I've changed my mind, I'm not buying the movie." (According to Weinstein, he never went up to $10 million at all. "I was out after $5 million," he says.) Elwes could taste the bile rising in the back of his throat. He was thinking, Ohmigod, I have no deal whatsoever, nothing. I'm going to lose my client. This is the worst night of my life. He was sick, drenched in sweat. He had to get to a midnight screening of another movie he was repping, *Orgazmo,* by two young filmmakers, Trey Parker and Matt Stone. He started calling the October guys, but they had turned their phones off, and he couldn't get through. He went to the *Orgazmo* screening, which went well, then started driving around town in the rain, looking for them in the hotel bars. He repeatedly called their rooms, no dice. Finally, at 4:00 A.M. he found them at the Four Seasons. Ray noticed that he was wringing wet, thought, He's wetter on the inside than he is on the outside. He said "You got a lotta fuckin' nerve walking over to us right now."

"Listen, Weinstein's trying to fuck me."

"Oh, big surprise."

"Here's the situation. We can sit down right now, and we can make the deal we talked about, and I'll close it right now, I won't call him, I won't call anyone, we'll sign the contract right here. And you guys'll have the movie, you can read about it in the trades tomorrow." Ray was skeptical. What Elwes was telling him just confirmed his suspicion that they had been bidding against themselves all along. Then Simpson called, told Ray, "This thing has cratered, we're nowhere, we need your help to put this back together. What will it take for you to do it?" The October guys went off and conferred among themselves, came back ten minutes later, said, "Okay, we'll make the deal. But it's gonna cost you $2.5 million." At 5:30 in the morning, they put the deal back together. October penalized the Morris Agency by dropping down to $5 million from their high of $7.5 million, but $5 million made Duvall whole. (They told the trades $6 million to help Duvall save face.) That same day, Elwes sold Greenstein and Schmidt *Orgazmo* over Ray's objections. Greenstein wanted a relationship with Parker and Stone.

Although *The Apostle* chase was among the looniest in the annals of acquisitions, everybody involved seemed to get what they wanted. Harvey taught Elwes a lesson. "I think he was really toying with Cassian," says Bowles. "Harvey takes affront at any perceived slight. Even people he really likes, if he thinks you're getting too big for your britches, he'll cut you down, make sure you're in your place." Moreover, Weinstein avoided the onus of another overpriced purchase. And his willingness to let the film go was yet another sign that Miramax's center of gravity had shifted away from acquisitions. By satisfying Duvall, Elwes avoided what would have been a personally embarrassing failure and worse, a defection from his agency. Greenstein came away the big winner, albeit at the cost of further angering Ray, who now blamed him for "cowboying" two films—*The Apostle* and *Orgazmo*. In the old days, recalls October executive Susan Glatzer, Ray used to say, "Amir Malin is Satan. That was before he'd met Scott Greenstein."

Ten
Crossover Dreams
1997–1998

• How Miramax took *Shakespeare* to the bank but got sued by its
own employees, while Spike Lee dissed Quentin Tarantino over
Jackie Brown, and Bingham Ray et al. lost *Happiness.*

*"He offered me a movie, said, 'I'll make you rich, I'll make you rich.' I was broke.
I gave all my money away, but I said, 'Harvey, it's not about the fucking money.
This movie is a fucking piece of shit. I'm not going to do it.' He was screaming at
me on the phone, 'Fuck you!' and he hung up on me."*

—MATT DAMON

Good Will Hunting was scheduled to open just before Christmas 1997, and
go wide in January and February. Miramax pretty much left director Gus
Van Sant alone, and he, along with Matt Damon and Ben Affleck, had a
good experience there. According to Damon, speaking in September 1997,
just a few months before *Good Will Hunting* was to be released, "There was
never a hiccup. It was like a joyride. As much as Harvey'll fuck you in the
cutting room—and I'm sure there will come a time when he will—he didn't
do it with us."

Harvey had seen Van Sant's cut, and simply said, "Great, let's test it." Affleck was in L.A. doing *Armageddon.* Producer Chris Moore called him,
said, "It tested 94."

"What does that mean?"

"That's good, the movie's a hit."

"The movie's a hit? The movie's not out yet."

"No, no, that kind of score doesn't happen, it's the highest they've ever
had, it's really good."

Based on the stratospheric test scores, Miramax moved *Good Will Hunt-*

ing up to December 7, going wide in the wake of *Titanic*. The boys went up to Weinstein's house in Westport, Connecticut, to screen James Cameron's movie, see what they were up against. According to Affleck Harvey said, "We got nuthin' to worry about. There's just this one scene with the boat sinking. We'll be fine."

As usual, the marketing department ran Damon and Affleck ragged. Recalls Damon, "Harvey's mentality was do absolutely everything to get your name and your face out there. Someone would call and say, 'We want to put you on the cover of this magazine.' I thought, Well, I don't want to do that anymore. Harvey would sit us down and say, 'Don't you want people to go see your movie? Aren't you proud of it? Didn't you just work on this for six fucking years? What's your problem? Do it, do all of it.' We'd go, 'Okay, Okay!' "

Impending success did nothing to change Affleck's and Damon's feelings about producer Lawrence Bender. According to Affleck, Bender told him and Damon, "Me and Quentin, we do a thing we call 'pushing power.' We push power."

"What the fuck is Lawrence talking about? Pushing power?" Matt or Ben asked Ben or Matt.

"In the press, we go out and say good things about each other in the press," Bender told them.

"Well, bro', that's you and Quentin, you probably don't try to fire Quentin! You'd better be careful Quentin doesn't fire you!"

In L.A., their film premiered in Westwood, at the Bruin. "The marquee had *Good Will Hunting* on it, and Ben's and my names up there, literally in lights, and searchlights on a trailer," Damon remembers. "We were hugging each other, really, really excited. The whole experience was overwhelming, very unhealthy. The first thing that happens is that somebody puts a camera in your face and asks you how you feel, and it's impossible to say, 'I'll tell you when you get that fucking camera out of my face so I can go and sit with my family for a little while.' I didn't realize that it was going to be over in a flash, that no matter who you are, if you don't have a movie in the theater that's making money, people will just think you're someone they went to high school with. I remember deciding that I was gonna not act in movies anymore, maybe just plays, because this was not a life."

When all was said and done, *Good Will Hunting* grossed $138 million domestic and $226 million worldwide, excluding network, cable, and video. With its modest budget of $20 million, the picture was phenomenally profitable for Miramax, one of its most profitable movies to date. Robin Williams had a huge chunk of the first dollar gross, starting at 10 percent and escalating to 25 percent when the film hit $100 million. Van Sant, who received no more than his directing fee, had approximately 2.5 percent of the adjusted gross, increasing to 7.5 percent. "If I was to guess, I'm sure there was a couple of million dollars owed me," says Van Sant. Replies Harvey, "Van Sant received everything he was entitled to under his contract."

If Van Sant didn't see anything from his cut of the adjusted gross, there was no way Damon and Affleck, who only had net points, were going to receive any money. Nevertheless, Affleck was incensed. He says, "The movie had done enormously well by then, but we had gotten an accounting statement that said the movie was $50 million in the red, and it was just like, This is fucked! You had to do some great accounting to hide net profits on that movie." With his acting fee added to his writing fee, Damon had been paid $650,000, Affleck a little less. *Good Will Hunting* was a film that Damon conceived, co-wrote, and starred in. While he was working on *Rounders,* before *Good Will Hunting* was released, Weinstein called him and Affleck, asked them to meet him at the apartment Damon was renting on Spring Street in lower Manhattan. Harvey said, "All right guys, you ever seen a million dollars before?"

"No." They were thinking, Holy shit, he's gonna give us each a million bucks.

"Here it is, Happy check!" It was two checks for $500,000 each, a million dollars together. He obviously thought, This is gonna make a big impression on these guys. They've never seen this kind of money. And it did. They were disappointed, but happy, especially since neither of them had a lot of cash.

It costs a lot to audit, and few are able and willing to go it alone. Van Sant says, "Matt and Ben weren't interested in auditing. They were in the Miramax camp, so whatever was going on with them was, like, in-house." Affleck retorts, "Gus is full of shit. He was like, 'Yeah, I'll audit.' We were, 'Gus, I dunno, man, you never get any money out of these audits, nobody gets net points, the last movie that paid out net points was *Three Men and a Baby!*' It was like we were gonna have to pay for the audit and we weren't going to get anything. Beside, Gus had already made a ton of money off the movie, and he was getting $5 million to direct *Psycho.*"

Given how much money the Weinsteins made from Damon and Affleck, Harvey could just as well have given them checks for $1 million each or even $2 million each, and still made a fat profit. Five hundred thousand dollars was small change, but Damon doesn't see it that way. "For two kids from Boston it was huge," he says. "When you're in a movie that big, your salary goes way up. Even if he hadn't given me a bonus check I wouldn't feel ripped off. Maybe if I had never worked again after that, I would feel, Jesus, I invented something in my garage and a big company patented it

Cannes, 1989: Steven Soderbergh, looking glum, holds his Palme d'Or as if it might bite him, as Jane Fonda looks on. He said, "When *sex, lies* happened, I martyred myself out of enjoying it. And it's disingenuous and borderline offensive not to enjoy it."
(© AP/Wide World Photos)

Bob (left) and Harvey Weinstein at the *Dogma* premiere in November 1999.
(© Eric Charbonneau/Berliner Studio/BEI)

The young Bingham Ray at Telluride, c. 1987, with hair. "I would come in from the suburbs, wearing a button-down shirt, to the Elgin, sit next to a guy in a raincoat," he recalls. "My father would say, 'You keep going to all these movies, you're going to turn into a bum!'"

A match made in heaven? The Weinsteins flanking Jeffrey Katzenberg, on April 30, 1993, announcing Disney's acquisition of Miramax. "People were calling me and saying, 'They're never gonna keep their word,'" Harvey recalls. "We were terrified." (© AP/Wide World Photos)

Todd Solondz and Sony Classics' Michael Barker at Telluride in 1994 for *Welcome to the Dollhouse*. Solondz wanted to call it *Faggots and Retards,* which perfectly captures the flavor of the film. Harvey wanted to sweeten the ending, reshoot it, so Solondz went with Sony.

"When *Pulp Fiction* had the outrageously good opening weekend at the box office, we all saw it as something good for Quentin and presumed that it was good for ourselves as well," said filmmaker Allison Anders. "But in fact, that victory was sort of the beginning of the end for the rest of us, because very few indie films can compete in that same kind of a way." (© Photofest)

Moment in the sun: the crack Miramax acquisitions team on the Miramax boat in Cannes, 1994: From left to right: Mark Tusk, Trea Hoving, Elli Jackson, Tony Safford, Patrick McDarrah, and Agnes Mentre. Little did they know that Miramax productions, like that year's Palme d'Or winner, *Pulp Fiction*, would make them redundant.

Bowling for October: John Schmidt (bottom left) and Bingham Ray (holding beer bottle, right), among others, raise the flag; Amir Malin (left) and Jeff Lipsky, inset. Although the partners fought like cats in a sack, the Little Company That Could scored big with *Breaking the Waves* and *Secrets and Lies*, and sold itself to Universal.

David O. Russell on the set of *Flirting with Disaster* in 1994 shows Mary Tyler Moore how to raise her shirt so she can say, "Look at these breasts! Are these the breasts of a fifty-year-old woman?" (© Barry Wetcher)

Bernardo Bertolucci coaches one of his actors on the set of *Little Buddha* in 1994, not one of Miramax's finer moments. Says Harvey, "For me and Bernardo, it was an unhappy chapter." Bertolucci recalls, "He started to believe too much in himself as auteur of the film."
(© Alessia Bulgari)

Quentin Tarantino and Roger Avary accepting the screenwriting Oscar for *Pulp Fiction* in March 1995. At the time, the two former friends were barely speaking. Avary memorably excused himself on national television to take a leak, and Tarantino was miffed because Avary failed to thank him. (© Gary Hershorn/Reuters/Landov)

Quentin Tarantino and Mira Sorvino at the Miramax pre-Oscar party. "Mira and I were in Paris together for our exciting romantic week," Tarantino recalls. "She had never been to the Rodin Garden, so we had a picnic and were making out, and everybody was looking at us. It was like, Ohmigod, that's been taken from me. If I had known in advance, before I got famous, I would have gone to the Rodin Garden more."
(© Eric Charbonneau/Berliner Studio/BEI)

Anthony Minghella and producer Saul Zaentz on the set of *The English Patient*. The picture made $229 million worldwide, but Zaentz never saw a piece of it. He called Harvey "a pushcart peddler who is more than happy to put his thumb on the scale when the old woman is buying meat. When I talked with him about it, he says, 'I am a filmmaker; I'm not an accountant.'"
(© Photofest)

Marisa Tomei and Quentin Tarantino taking curtain calls on the opening night of *Wait Until Dark* in the spring of 1998. The blood on Tomei's shirt might as well have been spilled by Tarantino, who was gored by the critics. "I tried not to take it personally, but it was personal," he says.
(© Henry McGee/Globe Photos, Inc.)

Ben Affleck and Matt Damon react to their Golden Globe for their *Good Will Hunting* screenplay in January 1998. Says Damon, "I didn't realize that it was going to be over in a flash, that no matter who you are, if you don't have a movie in the theater that's making money, people will just think you're someone they went to high school with."
(© Lisa Rose/Globe Photos, Inc.)

Marc Norman, Ed Zwick, Harvey, Donna Gigliotti, and David Parfitt accepting their Oscars for *Shakespeare in Love* on March 24, 1999. Says Norman, "Harvey came on like a linebacker from the backfield just as Zwick was moving towards the microphone, pushed him out of the way, and grabbed the mike."
(© Gary Hershorn/Reuters/Landov)

October's Scott Greenstein, Chris McGurk, and John Schmidt, c. 1998. In December, Greenstein waltzed into Schmidt's office and said, "I have good news and bad news. The good news is, Barry Diller wants to buy October. The bad news is, he wants me to run it!"

Kevin Smith and actor Jason Mewes on the set of *Jay and Silent Bob Strike Back*. Says Smith, "It came out that Jay's mom was HIV positive, flat-out dying of AIDS. Harvey said to him, 'I'm gonna give you my number, and you call me, and we're gonna set your mother up with this great doctor, the best HIV doctor in the city, if not the world. We're not going to let your mother die.' I was blown away."

(© Tracy Bennett/Photofest)

Director James Mangold and producer Cathy Konrad at the *Identity* premiere, April 2003. Says Mangold, "Harvey does both good and bad. But the problem is that the same personality type that has the hubris to face the wind and say, 'I looked in his eyes, and I believe in this guy,' is also the person who will look in that same kid's eyes and say, 'I saw your movie, and I don't believe in it.'"

(© Lester Cohen/WireImage)

Producer Christine Vachon and Todd Haynes at the Independent Spirit Awards in March 2003, where Haynes won Best Director for *Far from Heaven*. "Soderbergh had final cut on *Far from Heaven*, and I felt completely safe around that," says Haynes. "He got tough with me, but in a very constructive way, saying that whatever I ultimately decided, he would support."

(© Kevin Winter/Getty Images)

and sold it and made all the money. But it wasn't a one-time thing. I'm still benefiting from that experience."

Damon went on to get his $800,000 for *Rounders*, a sum dictated by his Miramax contract, $1 million for *The Talented Mr. Ripley*, and a big bump up to $5.5 million for *All the Pretty Horses*. Most often, actors who make a big score double or triple their asking price, and show no particular loyalty to the executive or company who gave them their shot. But by the force of his personality, and his aggressive use of options, Weinstein folded Damon and Affleck into the Miramax "family" (he used to refer to them as his "little brothers"), along with Quentin Tarantino, Gwyneth Paltrow, Wes Craven, and Kevin Smith, and by so doing was able to control their careers—at least in the beginning—and keep their salaries low. Says Damon, "He'll call me up and say, you're doing this movie, this is what you're getting paid, and he knows that he has the relationships with people that they'll [accept it.] Besides, you can make a deal with Harvey, and business affairs will get everything back."

It was the old story: they were going to make their payday on the next movie. As Van Sant puts it, "Those guys went from nowhere to everywhere. I went from somewhere to the next step up. Miramax worked hard. I don't think I would have been nominated without their push. If the film was going to get any nominations at all—it might have gotten three—they made sure it got nine. They get you that, they know it, they want something in return, and what they get in return is not paying [you] any more money. Obviously, it allows them to feel okay about keeping it. Except that it's a business, and when you think about it as a business, it's not right. But in the end, it doesn't really matter. It was easier for me to just do another movie than it was to try to get my money out of Miramax." Most people, like Billy Bob Thornton and Larry Meistrich, who have found themselves in Van Sant's position feel the same way, and the brothers know it. Still, when Weinstein offered Van Sant a three-picture deal, the director turned it down. "I wanted more independence," he explains. "I felt like I was going down a road that three years later, I'd come out at the end, having wasted time. Maybe made some money and done some movies, but maybe not the ones I'd wanted. I didn't want to be Lasse Hallström."

Adds Affleck, "The exchange is, they'll spend money promoting the movie, they'll spend money on an Academy campaign—they've had a movie nominated every year—and their reputation is they make better movies. But they're a nightmare to make a deal with. It's harder to make deals with them than anywhere else in town. If your movie fails, you can't make a deal because it's, 'Fuck you, you're a failure,' and if you're a success, they want to hang on to it and they'll fight you tooth and nail anyway. It's not a place you want to work if you want to get rich. It's a trade-off. And you know what? You don't have to work with them. It's like that scene in *Hollywood Shuffle,* man, there's always work at the post office! So yeah, we kinda got screwed, but when it came right down to it—it worked out great for us."

Still, there was a bitter aftertaste. Affleck and Damon had agreed to appear in their pal Smith's *Dogma,* but when Weinstein tried to get the two actors to work for scale, they balked. Affleck recalls, "What pissed me off with *Dogma* was, I thought, This is where we're supposed to get a better deal, this is the next movie. We realized that he knew we thought we owed Kevin, and I didn't like that he was using our friendship with Kevin to get us to do the movie without having to negotiate with us, putting us in a position where he could say, 'The guys are being difficult, they don't want to do your movie, Kevin,' forcing Kevin to call us. First of all, he had options on us, and if they have some leverage they'll use it. And if they don't have to pay, they won't. I was used to it, and I just assumed, if you want to get the money you have to battle like a bastard. So I called him and said, 'This is bullshit, man, look at how much stuff we've done, whoring for the Oscars, this is crazy. You dudes have made so much money off *Good Will Hunting,* we're not gonna see any of our net points, we're gonna have nothing to do with *Dogma,* we're not gonna promote it, we're never gonna work for you again! Unless we're paid $1 million each. In cash!' "

According to Affleck, Harvey got on a plane and showed up in L.A. carrying a *Jackie Brown* tote bag filled with Monopoly money. It was like, "Here's your $2 million, you greedy fucks!" Affleck thought he'd actually brought cash, until Weinstein threw the bag at him, yelling, "I'm not gonna give you assholes a bag of fuckin' cash." Whipping out checks, he said, "Here's two million dollars! You fuckin' happy now? Don't say I never did anything for you." The actor adds, "We *were* happy. We were very happy. I thought we should have asked for four. Who knows, he probably wrote it off by billing it against some other poor guy's movie."

Reflects Smith, "Ben is far more business-savvy than Matt. Matty's more about the art, the performance, he's a true actor. Ben is more of a movie star, and thinks like a movie star, and he definitely thinks about his paycheck. If you catch Matty on the right day, it's, 'I fuckin' hate Miramax too.' You catch anybody on a bad day, and they'll talk shit about Harvey. Because there's shit to talk. It's not like they're creating fiction. But I've never met anyone who breeds the kind of allegiance that he does. It's a real love-hate affair you have with the Weinsteins. So Ben to this day is smarting over the fact that they didn't kick them more cash on *Good Will Hunting,* and that he had to hold our movie hostage. That he had to get down to what he feels is their level. And threaten them."

A week after Miramax opened *Good Will Hunting,* Dimension released

Scream 2 on Friday, December 12. On the following Monday, the company reported that it had grossed $39.2 million over the three days, thereby grabbing the number one spot, and breaking the record for the biggest nonsummer opening, held by *Ace Ventura: When Nature Calls*, which had earned $37.8 million in November 1995. Rankings and records had become marketing tools because, as Spike Lee puts it, "People are going to see movies based on how much money they were making. You pick up the newspapers on Monday, and they give you the top ten grossers—not just *Variety*, but the *New York Times*, the *Post*, the *Daily News*." They were so important that the temptation to fudge was almost irresistible, at least for Miramax, which was caught padding the figures. On December 19 it backtracked, revising the gross downward to $33 million, claiming it counted 449 theaters more than the picture actually played in, and that it was an honest mistake. "I don't know how anyone misplaces 450 theaters and overreports $6 million," said Barry Reardon, head of distribution for Warner's. According to Joe Roth, former Disney Studios chairman, "Dick Cook told them after the fact that we felt they were overstating" the grosses. *Variety* reported "that it was well-known in distribution/exhibition circles that Miramax had inflated both playdates and grosses for *Scream 2*. . . . The company was probably legally obliged to make the disclosure, being part of the publicly traded Walt Disney Empire."

On Christmas Day, Miramax released *Jackie Brown*, Tarantino's spin on Elmore Leonard's thriller *Rum Punch*. The director turned *Rum Punch* into a homage to the blaxploitation movies of the 1970s he had grown up on. The two most substantial roles went to Pam Grier, a fixture in those pictures, then nearly fifty, and Robert Forster, best known as the photographer in Haskell Wexler's *Medium Cool*, released in 1969. Grier and Forster had plenty of help, including Sam Jackson, Robert De Niro, and Bridget Fonda, but hanging a picture on two less-than-A-list actors who had seen better days was a gutsy thing to do, especially in *Pulp Fiction*'s wake.

Jackie Brown had been a long time coming, four years after *Pulp* was shot. Although Tarantino seems to be a stranger to self-doubt, his friends came to believe that he had been almost paralyzed by the vexing question: What next? As one of them put it, "Quentin had done the movie that's launched a thousand films. It was Welles after *Citizen Kane*." There were distractions everywhere. He had always wanted to be an actor, now he had his choice of parts, like playing Richie, a psycho, in *From Dusk Till Dawn*. He moved out of his ratty apartment on Crescent Heights into a grand home in the Hollywood Hills near Universal, which some of his friends derisively referred to as "the castle." The place was filled with memorabilia from his films—posters, toys, stills, and models of his characters. Like many movie star homes, it became a shrine to himself, or at least his work. Recalls Rodriguez, "Quentin spent most of a year designing and building this home theater. He said, 'All my friends made a movie this year, I made a theater.'"

Tarantino also started making regular visits to Rodriguez's hometown, Austin, Texas, where he'd hang out with him and his filmmaker buddies, Rick Linklater and Mike Judge. Breezing into town like a latter-day Elmer Gantry of the Church of Movie Geeks, he'd get a room at the Omni, registering under the name of some B movie actor. Austin has a thriving film and music scene, and he quickly made his own contribution, holding ten-day-long, more or less annual "QT Fests," where he introduced and screened films from his collection, the obscure work of obscurer actors and directors, like Arthur Marx (son of Groucho) and Cy Endfield (*Zulu*). He resurrected William Witney, who directed many of the Roy Rogers and Dale Evans pictures, and conceived a passion for the couple and their horse, Trigger, whom he could talk about for hours—what a great horse Trigger was, what an amazing presence Trigger has, how Trigger owns the screen—and even Trigger, Jr., who appears in one of his favorites, *The Golden Stallion*. He wanted to name his first child Trigger and had been heard to say, "Trigger is the Uma Thurman of horses," or, "Uma Thurman and Trigger have pretty much the same profile!"—in his mind, flattering to both.

"I'd go over to his hotel room and talk movies," recalls Louis Black, publisher of the *Austin Chronicle* and a self-confessed film geek. "Rick, me, Harry Knowles, Quentin, and a couple of others. Everybody was kinda equal, you weren't dealing with Quentin Tarantino superstar. But if we were in a public place and a bunch of attractive women showed up, then it became the Quentin Tarantino Show, and we didn't really count anymore. The spotlights came on, the marching band arrived, and Quentin performed."

Tarantino had a friend in Austin named Dulce Durante. She scoffs at the idea that Tarantino had OD'd on celebrity. "He loved it," she says. "It was one motivation for him coming back to Austin. He's such a star here, he couldn't go anywhere without being stopped. He ate it up." She recalls that on one occasion, he told her, " 'If I take you shopping, you can help me pick some stuff out, because I have no sense of style, and I'll buy you a pair of shoes,' because he's got a huge foot fetish. He was always trying to get my shoes off. He wanted to stick my toes in his mouth." Recall the famous foot massage debate between Jules and Vincent in *Pulp Fiction,* or the scene in *From Dusk Till Dawn* in the camper where the camera lingers fondly on the feet of Juliette Lewis, or the Thurman toe fest in *Kill Bill.*

Durante continues, "He did buy me a nice pair of shoes, from this store called, interestingly enough, Fetish."

Tarantino was an inveterate pot smoker. Some of his friends joked about it, in the vein of, "So I called Quentin, and he said, 'Well, I'm working on my new script, phttt, phttt.' " After a couple of years of doing bit parts here and there, hanging out, visiting Austin, fixing up his new house, they began to suspect that, as one Austin friend puts it, "he would do almost anything not to have to make another movie, because he was nervous about doing a follow-up."

At least partly in response to the blizzard of attention to which he was subjected, and the incessant demands and requests, Tarantino went through periods of withdrawal. He'd hole up in his new home, stay up all night watching movies and smoking weed. "This was not Martin Scorsese watching Michael Powell's movies, where there's a reason to get excited by it," says an acquaintance who occasionally joined him. "I'm not even talking about something that's kitschy or trashy, an AIP picture. These were lousy made-for-TV movies, flat, one-dimensional, and still his eyes would be glued to the tube. After a while, I realized you could literally be showing him anything, you could turn it upside down and put it out of focus, and he'd be watching it like a kid with a pacifier, a lonely little boy in his living room, where he was safe. It was sad and beautiful at the same time."

Tarantino ducked out on commitments, driving people crazy who were depending on him for this or that. "There was a lot of volatility," says former agent Rick Hess. "He'd be gone for three weeks, and no one was quite sure where he was." As one friend puts it, "He's a genuinely nice guy. I've never seen him be mean or vindictive. But he's Quentin, and he does what he wants to do." Or, as Jennifer Beals puts it, "Quentin is not Jimmy Stewart. The shadow side is definitely there, and he lets it out only when he needs it, like some kind of beast that gets fed every now and again, and then gets put back. That's what makes the films great. That's where his genius is."

Every once in a while, the beast would escape. Two months before *Jackie Brown* was slated to open, Tarantino ran into producer Don Murphy *(The League of Extraordinary Gentlemen)*, with whom he had a tangled and troubled history that went back a decade. Says Tarantino, "Before I was famous, I didn't have people like Don Murphy, who started a career as my arch-enemy. He was always in the press making fun of me. It was kind of crazy, just short of stalking me. I'm just not a guy you do that to. I don't play by any Marquis of Queensberry rules Hollywood has. I thought about going to his house and fucking him up, but at the same time I thought, You know what? Hollywood's a real small place. I don't have to go knock on his door and propel myself into trouble—one of these days I'll walk into some place and he'll be there. And that will be the day I'll take care of it."

In the third week of October, Tarantino entered Ago, a hip Italian restaurant on Melrose in West Hollywood, where he was to lunch with Harvey. Murphy was seated on a couch near the entrance, waiting for a table. As Tarantino tells it, "I beelined right over to him. He stood up, and said, 'Hi Quentin.'

" 'Don't give me any of your fuckin' "Hi" shit.' " (Tarantino explains, "Whenever I get violent I turn into a black male.") " 'What's all this shit you've been talking about me?'

" 'I think you know.'

" 'No, no, you tell everybody on the planet, I'm standing in front of your face now, tell me.' " Tarantino recalls, "He started to talk for just a second, and I shoved him down, took one hand and grabbed him by his hair, and then slapped the piss out of him with the other hand. I just bitch-slapped him three times. And after the third slap, they started yanking me off of him." Tarantino slapped Murphy so energetically that his watch sailed off his wrist. The cops showed up, and shoved him into the back of a sheriff's car, from whence he blew kisses at Murphy, and he would have been taken downtown had not Weinstein intervened, convincing him to apologize and Murphy not to press charges. A few days later, Tarantino reenacted the incident as shtick on *The Keenen Ivory Wayans Show*, telling Wayans, "A little bitch slap don't hurt nobody." Murphy sued the filmmaker for $5 million. It was eventually settled out of court. Tarantino thoroughly enjoyed the whole episode, the fight, the press, the TV appearance.

When *Jackie Brown* was done, it was running two hours, forty minutes. Harvey thought it was at least a half hour too long. But in Tarantino's mind it was just right, and he and Harvey nearly got into a fistfight in the lobby of a Seattle multiplex at a test screening one rainy night. The filmmaker emerged from the screening elated, said, "Wow, it played great!" Harvey, who had been asking people, "Whaddya think? Whaddya think?" shot back, "That's not what the audience thinks."

"Fuck you!"

"You gotta cut the movie."

"I'm done with it."

"Well, fuck you!"

"Fuck you!"

"Okay, fine, go make movies for New Line. I don't need this shit anymore, I'm too rich." Harvey was screaming, "Try this, try that," while Tarantino just repeated, "No, no, no, no." As Tarantino recalls, "I probably started it, flying off the handle. But he was in there in a nanosecond, the minute I was. With me or Harvey, it always threatens to get physical. When it started to go that way, Bob got in here, and Lawrence [Bender] got in there." Bob's feeling was, it's not worth it. Even if this one's just okay, we're not losing money, we're keeping him happy, keeping him in the family. He sat Tarantino down, said, "Okay, Quentin, here's the deal. You cut it down to two hours, we make $70 million with this movie. You come out this long, it's going to affect the box office. Are you okay with that, Quentin? Are you going to blame us when we don't make $70 million?"

"No."

"You accept that deal?"

"Yes."

The filmmaker did, and made a brilliant job of it. *Jackie Brown* contains some of his best writing, with two scenes qualifying for those all-time best lists: one in which Melanie, Fonda's Valley girl, follows Louis (De Niro) across a parking lot, ragging on him for losing his car, until he turns around in a fit of thug pique and shoots her. In the other, Ordell (Jackson), in a dazzling display of verbal tap dancing, convinces a reluctant Beaumont (Chris Tucker), to climb into the trunk of his car, whereupon he pops him. And that's not counting the bravura opening sequence where Ordell and Louis sit on a sofa watching a chicks-with-guns video while Melanie languidly does her nails and smokes a joint. (The camera, needless to say, lingers on her toes.) All in all, the film is a more mature work than either *Reservoir Dogs* or *Pulp*; thanks to the performances of Grier and Forster, it's quieter and gentler, but Tarantino gets more deeply into his characters, gives the relationship between the two a resonance all the more moving for being unexpected.

Once again, as in *Pulp Fiction*, the n-word was used liberally, most often by Jackson. The spectacle of black actors calling one another "nigger" for a white director was too much for Spike Lee. He actually had an intern count how many times the slur was uttered. "I'm not saying he couldn't use the word, but the excessive use of the word was disturbing to me," Lee explains. "Just in that scene between Sam Jackson and Chris Tucker, it was like thirty-eight times or something. It was 'nigger, nigger, nigger, nigger, nigger, nigger.'" Lee had used Tarantino to good effect in the opening of *Girl 6*, playing a piggy director who bullies an actress into baring her breasts in a casting session. "Quentin was very good-natured to play that part knowing that he was basically playing himself," says Lee. But now Lee took him to task, attacking him in the press, calling him "ignorant," and accusing him of wanting to be "an honorary black man." Jackson sprang to Tarantino's defense, to which Lee responded, "I'm sorry, if he wants to defend Quentin Tarantino, he can. But for me, it's a lot like the house Negro defending the massa." Likewise, the Miramax co-chairman couldn't resist injecting himself into the fray, asking rhetorically, "Does [Lee] have anything nice to say about anybody's work but his own? I'm getting sick of this. . . . If Spike wants to take the gloves off with me, come on." According to Lee, all Harvey was worried about was the grosses. He said, "Spike, you gotta stop talkin' about *Jackie Brown*. You're hurtin' me."

Three years later, in his two-thirds brilliant, biting media satire *Bamboozled*, Lee revisited the issue by including a fatuous white network executive, energetically played by Michael Rapaport and clearly based on Tarantino, who thinks he's more black than the black writer (Damon Wayans) who works for him. He tells the writer, "I grew up around black people my whole life. If the truth be told, I probably know niggas better'n you. And don't be gettin' offended by my use of the quote unquote n-word. . . . I don't give a goddamn what that prick Spike Lee says. Tarantino was right. 'Nigger' is just a word."

According to Lee, "That's something Quentin Tarantino actually told me. I didn't make it up. I was in the Angelika Theater, waiting with my wife to see *The Blair Witch Project*, and he came up to me, gettin' in my face like he was gonna kick my ass or somethin'. Tough guy." Tarantino recalls, "He stuck his hand out, and I said, 'I'm not shakin' your motherfuckin' hand.' " Lee goes on, "He told me that he knows black people better than me: 'I grew up watching black exploitation films, I've always lived among black people, my mother had a black boyfriend . . . ' So I just laughed at him. Then he tried to wriggle out, sayin', Well, I didn't write that stuff, it was ad-libbed. Well, you can't put that shit off on somebody else, because the director decides what goes in, what goes out. He's the director. The guy's a good filmmaker. He tapped into something, but then it became something else—too much 'nigger, nigger, nigger, nigger.' "

From Tarantino's point of view, "It was almost like Don Murphy. He was workin' it. He was getting his name in the press a whole bunch. Which I think is what it was all about anyway. I took issue with the fact that if he genuinely had a problem, then he should have called me before he called the press. I thought he handled it like a real wuss. One of these days I'll walk into a place and he'll be there. And that will be the day that I take care of it."

Tarantino defended himself further, saying, "More or less every single thing I've ever done in film is about the division between black and white in this country. And how this division actually is a sham. . . . The poor blacks in Chicago have more in common with the poor hillbillies in the Appalachian Mountains in Tennessee than they have with affluent blacks living in Pasadena, California. They're at the same place." It's almost shocking to hear Tarantino ascribe a class analysis to his own work, after creating a cottage industry out of baiting and scandalizing liberals for most of his career, but it's not just posturing. He does in fact present a world where class trumps race, just as there is a message about class stratification buried in *Clerks*, or a disquieting look at the politics of the family marbled throughout *Spanking the Monkey*.

In any event, raising the flag of political correctness in the face of the Tarantino hurricane was like spitting in the wind. *Jackie Brown*, which cost $12 million, grossed $40 million and as much again overseas. But Bob was right. And because it didn't do *Pulp* business and was overshadowed at the box office by *Good Will Hunting* and *Scream 2*, it was regarded as a failure.

DARREN ARONOFSKY was a kid from Harvard who had put in his time at the American Film Institute's film school and then gone into a tailspin. In January 1996, he had gone to Sundance to give moral support to a pal from AFI who had a film in competition. While he was there, he saw *Welcome to the Dollhouse*. He says, "I thought it was such a unique, weird film, that it really gave me the courage to go back to New York and just try to throw something together." The film he threw together he called *Pi*. He figured he could raise $20,000, and did, by asking everyone he knew to invest $100. (Ultimately, it cost $60,000 to get it into the can and $120,000 to get it ready for theatrical exhibition.) By November of that year, he was shooting. "Our goals were very low," he continues. "Because it was an edgy black and white movie, we thought maybe we'd have a shot at being a midnight show at Sundance. The day the decisions were to be announced, I couldn't handle it, so I ran back to Brooklyn to my mom and dad's house. If I didn't get in, I just wanted to cry in my parents' arms. It was getting later and later—I had heard most people were finding out in the morning, now it was five, six o'clock at night, seven, I figured, It's all over. The phone rang, it was someone from Salt Lake City—'Can you fax over that information?'

" 'What are you talking about?'

" 'Oh my God, no one's called you to tell you?'

" 'No.'

" 'Oh, you're my first first.'

" 'Whaddya mean?'

" 'You're the first person I've been able to tell, You're in Sundance!'

"I was convinced it was a joke, one of my friends, I asked him, 'What's your area code?'

" 'Eight-oh-one.'

"I looked it up, then I started screaming. It was one of the great moments of my life."

Pi was a psychological thriller shot in high-contrast black and white. Talk about a cinema of poverty! But *Pi* had style, a distant echo of the between-the-wars German expressionism of Fritz Lang. In places it felt like an indie version of *The Cabinet of Dr. Caligari*. *Pi* was a disturbing, unpleasant, audience-unfriendly, virtually impossible-to-market film, but undeniably orig-inal and a great showcase for a director with real visual flair.

Aronofsky refused to show *Pi* to distributors pre-festival. He hired a pub-licist, and a rep, an attorney named Jeremy Barber. Aronofsky analyzed Sundance the way *Pi*'s "hero" tries to suss the stockmarket: one of the *Pi* gang actually prepared a booklet, *How to Behave at Sundance*, and they met beforehand to brainstorm about getting the film sold. One strategy was to "pi" Sundance, that is, plaster little stickers featuring a red pi on a white background all over Park City.

Aronofsky's film was screened first in a theater at the Sundance resort, forty minutes from Park City. "It was an all-industry screening," recalls Aronofsky. "It was following *Next Stop Wonderland,* a big hot film that Har-vey went to see. I saw him in the bathroom afterward. A legend. The thing was to have Harvey buy your movie. He couldn't figure out how to turn on the faucet. But I was too scared to say anything to him, invite him to our film. And it became clear to me that by 1998, Harvey wasn't in that busi-ness anymore, the *Clerks* business, of taking a weird edgy film and selling it. He refused to even scout our film. After *Pi* was screened, there was little ap-plause, if any, and I went up for a Q&A. There was not one question. I was devastated. Bingham Ray hated it, walked out." Eventually, *Pi* was pur-chased by Amir Malin et al. at Artisan, which did very well by it, and be-came a home for the filmmaker. "Amir treated me like a son," he says. "He was a mentor for me."

Sundance 1998 was a definite improvement over the year before. The features included Lisa Cholodenko's *High Art,* which October acquired, and Don Roos's wonderful picture *The Opposite of Sex,* picked up by Sony Classics. Miramax paid a staggering $6 million for *Next Stop Wonderland,* a not quite funny enough romantic comedy directed by Brad Anderson.

Weinstein looked at a two-hour rough cut of *54* in February 1998. The film, shot in Toronto, had wrapped in the fall of the previous year. During the shoot, Mark Christopher and company were more or less on their own. As Paul Webster puts it, at Miramax, "when you're in production, you're left entirely alone to make the movie. The company influence is felt most keenly during the casting, and post-production." Harvey flew up occasion-ally to kiss the stars. While he was there, he complained about the Studio 54 bartenders, asked, "Can't there be some girls behind the bar? Why can't these guys keep their shirts on?" Conversely, he reportedly wanted Hayek to remove her shirt in a scene where she and Shane make love in the bath-room. She refused.

When the lights came up, the Miramax co-chairman congratulated the filmmakers on the quality of their work, and painted a rosy picture of future success, especially since Ryan Phillippe was no longer an unknown. While 54 was in the editing room, his teenage slasher movie *I Know What You Did Last Summer*, written by Kevin Williamson, had grossed a cool $72 million, domestic, for Columbia. Suddenly, Phillippe, along with Mike Myers and Neve Campbell, made for a hot cast.

Harvey smelled money. Instead of an edgy film by a first-time queer director, 54 was going to be Miramax's summer blockbuster. Says Ira Deutchman, "In Harvey's mind, 54 was going to be a teen movie that could cross over to a wide youth audience for which the film was never intended." Weinstein test-screened 54 in a mall on Long Island early in 1998. Because the film had never been intended for mallrats from the 'burbs, the filmmakers were upset, and indeed the preview cards were terrible, with particularly poor ratings for Shane, who seemed unsympathetic. Says a source, "When a movie tests badly in the malls, nobody thinks, Okay, we tested it in front of the wrong people. They think, We've made the wrong movie."

The 54 gang was devastated. Harvey told Christopher to get rid of any suggestion of bisexuality in his lead character. Webster recalls, "Everybody miraculously became straight." It seemed clear that Weinstein was retrofitting the film for an audience of heterosexual suburban teenagers. To Miramax development head Jack Lechner, homosexuality was not the issue. "The fight was about how do you get anyone to give a shit about these characters," he recalls. "It was particularly unfortunate that the most explicitly gay scene in the film where Shane kisses his roommate and his roommate freaks out was badly acted, badly directed, just not believable. The audience burst out laughing. The problem was, you couldn't say that without someone coming back and saying, 'You're being homophobic.'"

In fact, this is exactly what the filmmakers suspected. Weinstein insisted that he wasn't homophobic and tried to get the filmmakers into a screening room to watch another Miramax film, *Velvet Goldmine*, produced by Christine Vachon and directed by Todd Haynes, that had just been completed. He explained that he had kept his hands off it, in his mind proving he wasn't reworking 54 because he was uncomfortable with the material. The very same day that Weinstein met with the filmmakers to purge the picture of the bisexual ambience that surrounded Shane, he accepted an award from GLAAD.

In any event, instead of trying to realize the director's vision and reshoot the kiss, Miramax took the film in the opposite direction. Continues Lechner, "The decision was made to make Shane nicer, but there was no point making a nice version of that story, because who wants to see a story about nice people at Studio 54, and that's not what was shot. If it had been my responsibility, I would have tried to do it better, instead of changing it."

But Lechner doesn't have much sympathy for filmmakers who go through the Miramax blender. "People moan and complain about Miramax's ruthlessness in recutting films, but for the most part, these are people who didn't make the film well enough in the first place. They blame Harvey because they don't want to blame themselves. When he's working with something that actually is good to begin with, his amazing attention and passion can help it to be great, but his weakness is that if it's lousy to begin with, he'll work as hard or harder, and it just never will be any good, because you can't turn a turd into gold. You only get a really polished turd. If you've made a lousy movie, you're better off at a studio, where they're not going to take the time and trouble to make your life hell."

At the studios, development is the Bermuda Triangle into which scripts can disappear forever, the no-man's-land known as Development Hell. A studio, continues Lechner, "would have ground the life out of it before it ever got shot. At Miramax, they let the filmmakers make their films," and *then* they grind the life out of it. It was Post-Production Hell. Films would languish in post for months, sometimes years. Harvey would pour so much money into post-production that by the time he was finished, the films were too expensive to make their money back, and rather than throw good P&A money after bad (post-) production money, he would either give them a token release or put them on the shelf before casting them into the netherworld of ancillaries like video and cable.

Throughout the second half of the decade, so many films were stalled in post-production that the gridlock resembled Times Square at rush hour. Recalls James Ivory, "An editor friend of mine went up to their editing room once, and there were like eight broken films lying on these various tables like plane crashes all around the room."

Meanwhile, the mantra of the Miramax executives was, "There's a $50 million film in here somewhere, we just have to find it." Then the filmmakers discovered that Harvey had given the film to his post-production department to recut without informing them. Christopher's crack editor, Lee Percy, who had cut *Kiss of the Spider Woman* and would go on to do *Boys Don't Cry*, resigned. Also, unbeknownst to the 54 folks, Harvey hired a second writing team, and even *Dispatches* author Michael Herr, who wrote the narration that rescued *Apocalypse Now* from incoherence, to fashion a voiceover. Christopher was locked out of the editing room. The new writing team produced twenty-five additional pages—nearly a quarter of the film—fleshing out the romance between Shane and Neve Campbell's previously minor—but straight—character, for whom Shane develops a sudden crush.

How could a script that gestated in the womb of the studio's development division for a year or more have needed such radical surgery in post?

"The root of everything was that Mark's vision of the movie and Harvey's vision of the movie were two different things," Lechner explains. "Harvey thought he was going to get *Saturday Night Fever*. He was reading that script and imagining it the way John Badham would have directed it, with John Travolta. When he reads the script, Harvey's looking at it as a potential acquisition, thinking, How am I gonna sell it? He's not as concerned with detail until he actually sees the movie." If, despite that, your film tests well, you'll be fine, but if it doesn't, at the very least it will be shortened, and at the most reconceptualized as the film that Harvey himself would have made—in fact, the film that he will now try to make, recut, revoice, rework in every respect, additional footage added as needed—with himself as the auteur.

As he became more and more successful, Harvey fell victim to a fatal ambivalence. "Harvey fell off the tracks when he started making a lot of money," says producer Peter Newman. "He began picking films that were tweeners, halfway between indies and the studios. The scores were almost good enough—in the 70s—and if you could get them to 80 or 90 you could make a lot of money. So he would shred the things that made the movie individualistic to try to broaden them out."

The filmmakers desperately wanted to believe that Harvey knew what he was doing, convinced themselves, "Okay, Harvey is very successful, he's made some really good movies, he must know what he's talking about." But eventually, Christopher refused to shoot the additional scenes. He threatened to take his name off the movie. Miramax came right back, counterthreatened to fire him. By this time he was on the edge of a nervous breakdown. As Donna Gigliotti puts it, "Harvey gets personal with people. And if you're susceptible to it, you'll begin to believe that you don't know what you're talking about, that you don't have any talent. He only wants to work with people that he can control. He'll rarely work with a final cut director. 'Cause he is just a frustrated director himself!" Eventually Christopher reluctantly agreed to oversee the shooting of the new scenes. When Christopher showed up at the sound studio to oversee the mix, he had not even seen the final cut.

Lechner was out the door before *54* was released. "Miramax had changed a lot by the time I left," he explains. "It was becoming more of a studio. I wanted us to do *Election*. It's a very edgy movie, an old Miramax movie, and Harvey, having had a rocky experience with Alexander Payne on *Citizen Ruth*, said, 'Let's let Alexander make his second movie somewhere else and he can come back and make his third one here.' I think Alexander was relieved. He didn't want to go through it again. I wanted to do *American Beauty*, but I passed on it because I felt, This isn't where we're at now. One day I just looked at the projects I was working on and I realized, I don't care about a lot of these things, they're just not my taste."

Cathy Konrad wanted to make *Election* as well, through her producing deal at Miramax. "Harvey read the script, but he passed. I was exclusive to Miramax, and I started feeling the exclusivity was hurting my chances to be involved with material I felt passionate about, because if he said no, I had to drop it. I didn't know what they wanted. One day they'd buy something obscure, the next day they'd buy something mainstream." Konrad left.

OCTOBER'S JOHN SCHMIDT is a nice guy. He can get along with almost anyone, and likes to think the best of people until experience teaches him otherwise. The first time it dawned on him that there might be something amiss with Scott Greenstein was in March 1998 at the Academy Awards, where Robert Duvall was up for an Oscar for *The Apostle*. "That's when it went bad," he says. "In poker you look for the 'tell,' the little gesture or the tic or the eyeball movement that tells you this guy's bluffing. For Greenstein, this was the tell." One of the October publicists called from L.A., said, "I don't know if you guys know about this, but Scott has asked to sit with Duvall at the Oscars." Says Ray, "In the *Secrets & Lies* year, we sat in Row 21, in the middle. Sumner Redstone was sitting two rows away. He's Sumner fucking Redstone! He's not sitting down in Row 3." It was like the time years before when Harvey tried to take Alison Brantley's seat next to Daniel Day-Lewis. According to Ray, when asked, Greenstein explained, "Oh yeah, Bobby asked that I sit with him. One of us has gotta be there, one of us has got to sit in the front row where Harvey is." Says Schmidt, "I checked with Bobby and his producer, Rob Carliner, and Rob said, 'Fuckin' bullshit, Scott just took my date's seat.' " According to Carliner, "It had nothing to do with Duvall. Bobby's an outsider. He would never ask to sit near a quote unquote suit under any circumstances. It was Scott working on me to sit in that row." Schmidt rarely lost his temper, but he did so now, exclaiming to Greenstein, "I can't believe you're fucking doing this. You should be sitting with us. You want to be on TV that much?" But Greenstein insisted, "got red-faced crazy," says Ray, and Schmidt thought, The three of us are partners in this company, but Scott is really out for himself, he's about Scott Greenstein, not about October. It's a real asshole thing to do, a complete Harvey move.

For Ray, it had been a long, hard road to the Dorothy Chandler Pavilion that year. At Chris McGurk's urging, October hired Jack Foley, who had exited Miramax two years before, figuring he would be more aggressive getting the films into theaters, as well as Dennis Rice, formerly of Buena Vista Home Video, and the marketing mind behind the phenomenal performance of Miramax's titles on video. Ray grudgingly went along. When the October team had returned from Toronto after the acquisition of *The*

Apostle in September 1997, his relationship with Greenstein, already frayed, proceeded to unravel completely. As one source puts it, "Bingham would yell at him. He wasn't coy about it. If he thought something was wrong, he would say it to his face, 'That's a stupid-ass, shitty idea.' He's just a person who doesn't have a governor." The two men clashed often and bitterly over the marketing of Duvall's film. As Schmidt explains, "If you look at two camps in the business of marketing independent films, you have Sony Classics's Bernard and Barker in one camp—the slow rollout, small ads, build your audience—and in the other, Harvey, which is push your budgets as high as you can, crowd out the market, take as many screens as possible, build the hype, in short, play more of a studio marketing game. Bingham was more the Sony Classics kind of marketer; Scott was more the Harvey kind of marketer. That was a fundamental issue which ended up tearing October apart."

Looking for the cheese, Ray, the old Sony rat, careful and conservative like Barker and Bernard, and Greenstein, the new Miramax rat, aggressive like Harvey, threaded their ways through the maze—until Greenstein knocked the box off the table. Because if Greenstein learned anything at Miramax, it was not so much business skills or marketing strategies, it was disregard for the rules of the game—anything goes.

Inside the company, the conflict between Ray and Greenstein played itself out in weekly marketing meetings, where they debated ad nauseam the number of screens, the size of ads (14" or 24"), whether to allocate an extra $10,000 or not. Where Greenstein wanted to spend, Ray wanted to save. When Ray objected, Greenstein threw up his arms and exclaimed, in his best Jersey accent, "It's pennies!" This became Ray's mantra. Every time somebody would complain about some expenditure, say, "That's another $6,000," Ray, from the other end of the table would throw up his arms and spritz, in a high-pitched whine, "It's *pennies!*" expelling the "p" from his mouth like a BB from a BB gun.

But they were divided by more than philosophical differences. According to several sources, Greenstein was actively working to undermine Ray and Schmidt. Says October executive Susan Glatzer, "Scott was always talking on his cell phone, and he'd go, 'I'm your guy, okay? Everybody else hates you, but I'm your guy. You gotta problem? Come to me!' " Adds Ray, "Scott was systematically, not just with talent, but with agents as well, saying, 'You gotta question? Come to me. Don't talk to Bingham, I'm your guy.' " Agrees Carliner, "Scott was an unabashed manipulator in that sense. He had the loudest voice and was certainly the pushiest. But when the dust settled, it was clear who really knew the indie scene and who didn't. It was Bingham who actually knew how to market a film and position a film, and Scott knew how to hustle. Bingham and John didn't really know who they were getting into bed with with Scott."

Although Greenstein had picked up *Orgazmo* the previous September at Toronto, Trey Parker and Matt Stone put a parody of him on their *South Park* CD, the parental advisory version. A dead-on impression of Greenstein's voice, identified as that of "Sid Greenfield," says, "Hello, Matt? This is just you and me talkin' here. I'm sitting here bleeding out of my ass. You want to know why? It's because of this Mousse T track."

" 'Horny, Horny, Horny?' "

"It's gotta go on the *South Park* album."

"Oh, no, we've already talked about this. We hate that song."

"I know you hate it. Everybody hates it. I'm the only one who agrees with you. I'm your guy. This song is the best song ever written!"

"How can you say that?"

"What did I say?"

"This song is the best song ever written."

"I agree with you, Matt. It is a great song. I know that."

"Hold on, Trey?! Trey! They want to put that Mousse T song on the album."

"No, dude, we said no."

"OK, Matt, listen. This is just you and me talkin'. Fuck Trey!"

"This is Trey! That song sucks, man."

"You know, I agree with you. I always agree with you. You said no, so I'm not going to put it on the album. You know why? Because I'm your guy."

According to some sources, Ray's filmmakers and Greenstein's filmmakers were entirely separate. (Greenstein had made deals with Michael Douglas and Sean Penn.) One person who knows Greenstein well says, "Scott never said 'I'm your guy' to a single filmmaker Bingham had because he never got to talk to them." Adds Sandy Stern, head of Michael Stipe's company, Single Cell, "That never was an issue with Scott, because my relationship there was with Bingham. I wouldn't have thought of talking to Scott."

The Apostle opened in December 1997 and became October's biggest hit, grossing about $23 million domestic, and twice that worldwide. October made about $5 million from foreign sales, and something like $12 million from video. All told, the company probably reaped a roughly $10 million profit from the film. Says Rice, "Nothing could have hurt Bingham more than that the *Apostle* campaign was successful. There was a sense that the world as he knew it at October was gone forever."

A large share of the credit for the film's success has to go to Greenstein. The picture badly needed cutting, and when Duvall refused to trim a frame, Greenstein came up with the idea of hiring Walter Murch, whom the director trusted, to lighten it by twenty minutes. In addition, *"The Apostle* benefited from the aggressive, multiple hundreds of screens, Miramax-type campaign that Scott orchestrated," says Schmidt. "He was really good at publicity. Bobby Duvall was everywhere, in places like *Parade* magazine. That eventually translated into playing for weeks and weeks and weeks in the heartland. Being able to do that was part of the formula that McGurk and I had envisioned when Scott came in. If his style and Bingham's style could have coexisted, we would have had a great deal more success, but you had two bulls in the paddock, and they tore each other apart. It wasn't, Stand back and let's do the right thing for the film, it was two guys digging in their heels to protect their turf, which was bullshit."

FOR MIRAMAX, *Shakespeare in Love* was the *Good Will Hunting* of 1998. It began life as a lightbulb that went off in the head of writer Marc Norman (*Oklahoma Crude*) in the late 1980s. Norman's idea was that the Elizabethan theater, with its neurotic writers, producers, and agents, its feuds, lawsuits, and backstage machinations, was just like Hollywood, and with it, he wrangled Ed Zwick, a friend and neighbor. Norman would write; Zwick, who had created, with Marshall Herskovitz, one successful TV series, *thirtysomething*, and had directed the critically acclaimed hit *Glory*, would direct, and the two of them would produce. Zwick didn't like the script that Norman turned in, but Julia Roberts did, and agreed to play Shakespeare's muse, Viola. Zwick brought in Tom Stoppard to rewrite Norman, who managed to hang on as co-producer. In late 1991 or 1992, the picture went into pre-production at Universal, where Zwick had a deal. They started making the costumes and building the Globe Theatre at Pinewood Studios, near London. Roberts had Shakespeare approval and wanted Daniel Day-Lewis. Day-Lewis, however, had committed to Jim Sheridan's *In the Name of the Father*, and had already turned them down. Roberts was confident she could change Day-Lewis's mind. She said, "Let me try," and along with Zwick and Norman flew to Dublin to see Day-Lewis over a weekend. She sent him flowers and commenced to woo him, but Day-Lewis remained firm, and on the following Monday, she flew back to L.A. and withdrew from the picture. While Universal head Tom Pollock is supposed to have quipped, "Couldn't she have waited to fuck him until we had his name on a piece of paper?," according to press reports at the time, the relationship amounted to no more than an innocent flirtation. Six weeks from the start of principal photography, Universal decided not to make the picture, but didn't want any other studio to make it either, and therefore put a staggering $9 million price tag on it in turnaround, half in hard costs, and half in soft. Zwick hit the pavement with the script, but of course none of the studios would bite. To them, it was an art film, and an expensive one at that.

Zwick, who proceeded to direct *Legends of the Fall* for Sony, had the *Shakespeare* script sent to Miramax, and screened his new picture for Harvey as a sample of his work. Harvey, who loved the *Shakespeare* script, professed to love Zwick's movie as well. Zwick recalls, "He flipped over it, said, 'Ohmigod, we're gonna do this, this is fabulous.' He picked up the phone, called Sony and told them, 'This movie is so wonderful, what can I do to help it? I want to attach a trailer to every Miramax movie.'" According to Zwick, he looked him in the eye and shook his hand, while assuring him that he would direct and produce *Shakespeare*. Harvey then tried to buy the script in turnaround, but he and Universal could not agree on terms, and the impasse lasted for several years until Harvey found himself with some leverage. Universal wanted Peter Jackson to do a remake of *King Kong*, but Harvey had an option on Jackson dating back to Jackson's *Heavenly Creatures*, which he had released in 1994. Harvey raised his hand and said, "I'll give you Peter Jackson if you sell me *Shakespeare in Love*."

By that time, Pollock was out, and Frank Biondi was in. Casey Silver was running the studio. They knew that if the film was any good, the Weinsteins would steal the glory—the credit and the Oscars—while they would get nothing. McGurk argued, "Who cares about their reputation? Let's ride on the shoulders of these guys, and we'll make a lot of money." Generally, in a turnaround deal, the buyer pays 10 percent down, in this case $900,000, and the rest later. But Universal was holding Miramax up for $2.25 million, probably because they didn't want to sell to the Weinsteins. "They were being greedy," says former Miramax executive VP John Logigian, who was negotiating with Silver. When Logigian informed Harvey, "He went a little nuts, said, 'That can't be,'" adding, "'You know what, I'll get the number down.'" In his mind, Silver was a pisher, and he was Harvey Weinstein. According to another source, he got Silver on the phone, shouted something like, "You know, I don't even know why I'm talking to you. I'm a chairman and you're just a president or something. Casey, let me tell you how to do your job. If you don't give me what I want, I'll go to Frank Biondi," whereupon Silver hung up on him. He knew Biondi would back him up, and he did. The word back was, "The hell with you, now the number has doubled," $4.5 million. (Silver doesn't recall the details of this conversation.) Logigian told Harvey, "That phone call cost us $2.25 million!" He recalls, "Then Universal said, 'There's one thing we have to put in this deal.'

" 'What is that?'

" 'You cannot take this from us and put a big star in the movie.'

" 'What's a big star?'

" 'Like a Julia Roberts.' A lot of people would have said, 'Ohmigod, I wanted to make this with Meg Ryan or Demi Moore,' but it didn't faze

Harvey, because he didn't feel he had to have a big star to make it work. He deserves a lot of praise, because he stuck with it even when Universal stacked the odds against him, raising the price to $4.5 million, and then limited the type of stars he could put in the movie. Most people would have run for the hills." Harvey adds, "It's the most incredible amount of money I've ever paid for a script or a project or anything else. It took guts to say, 'I'm gonna make it.' "

Zwick heard third hand that Miramax had bought the script and that he was out. "I don't think anyone was enthusiastic about Ed directing it," says Gigliotti. "I know I wasn't. Harvey wasn't. The truth is, we were all hiding behind the fact that we didn't think he could do it for the price, when in fact nobody wanted him." Zwick hired the powerful Hollywood attorney Bert Fields. In a meeting at the Peninsula Hotel with Zwick and his agent, ICM's Jeff Berg, Harvey was gracious and accommodating. It was carrot, not stick time. He apologized, said that he had been bad, that Zwick was an artist, a great artist, and that his role developing the script with Stoppard would be front and center of the marketing campaign. He offered him *Chicago* to direct and an Elmore Leonard property, *Rum Punch*, to produce. Zwick's producer credit was reinstated. He says, "Harvey was so contrite and so seductive, I chose to just believe it." Subsequently, Zwick was frozen out of the project.

Legend has it that Paltrow saw the script on Winona Ryder's coffee table and asked, "What's that?" but in fact, she had just done *Emma*, and didn't want to do another British period piece. At the time, she was all over the women's magazines—she loves clothes—and had a devoted following, but she was realistic about her career and recognized she had no more than a limited shelf life—not as an actress, but as a star. She was hot, and she wanted to take advantage of it. But, as usual, Harvey prevailed. Paltrow had been paid $3 million to play opposite Michael Douglas in *A Perfect Murder*, but Harvey knocked her salary down to $2.5 million, and she got a small percentage of the gross.

Harvey wanted Affleck to play Shakespeare. But the actor had a conflict; *Dogma* was shooting at the same time. Harvey told him, "Forget about *Dogma*, do *Shakespeare*." But Affleck was loyal to Smith and refused. (Harvey denies that he wanted the actor to play Shakespeare.) Harvey tried to persuade him to do a bit part as Ned Alleyn, which he could do after *Dogma* wrapped. At the time, Affleck had just finished his first mainstream picture, *Armageddon*, and this was a step backward, a small supporting role. The night Affleck and Matt Damon failed to win the Writers Guild award for the *Good Will Hunting* script, they drowned their sorrows at Elaine's with the Miramax co-chairman. When the subject of Alleyn came up, Damon argued against it. It was a bad idea, bad for Ben's career. Besides,

Ben and Gwynnie were an item, and everyone would say, "You're going to work on this movie just to be with your girlfriend? It's her movie, you're just the sidekick. Don't put yourself in that kind of place."

Turning to Affleck, Harvey retorted, "Forget all that Hollywood crap, this is about, you should show that you can be a leading man and a character actor too. You're funny. It's good for you to do a part that shows that you can be funny. Rupert Everett's not worried. He doesn't give a fuck. He knows he's not going to be Shakespeare, he took a bit part, he knows he's going to kick ass." Affleck gave in.

Miramax produced *Shakespeare* for a mere $24 million, and it looked like it cost twice that much. Harvey took a producer credit. According to former Miramax publicity VP Marcy Granata, he "was involved in every detail. He even knew what the leading lady should wear. He produced everyone else to produce. It was Selznick!" But studio executives rarely took producer credit, and Zwick, for one, was appalled.

According to Norman, the first time Harvey watched the picture with the titles, he became enraged when he saw Zwick's producer credit, shouting, "Get his name off the picture." His lawyers told him he couldn't do it, but Harvey found another way to make his point. In the title sequence, Geoffrey Rush, who plays the impresario Philip Henslowe, the Elizabethan version of a desperate Hollywood producer, is chasing around London looking for Shakespeare. At the moment the production credit for Bedford Falls, Zwick's company, flashes on the screen, Rush steps in a pile of horse shit.

Shakespeare tested well, near 80 in the top two boxes. But in Harvey's opinion, it could do better, and he told director John Madden and Gigliotti, who thought they were finished, to keep working. He said, "You have a good movie but not a great movie." Madden, unlike some of Miramax's other directors, was happy to comply, and he became one of Harvey's favorites. Says Lechner, "This was one case where the Miramax process functioned at its absolute best. The test screenings allowed us to focus in on what was holding the audience back. And we fixed it."

Test audiences complained that the film was too long, so it was cut. They couldn't understand why Viola didn't just run off with Shakespeare, why she had to marry Lord Wessex. This was clarified by means of revoicing. Every time someone turns his or her back, lines were inserted that explained that if she didn't marry Wessex, her family would be stripped of its lands and Shakespeare killed. The tests also revealed that the ending wasn't working, didn't have sufficient emotional punch. Audiences needed to feel that this was the love that changed Shakespeare's life, made him "William Shakespeare." Madden did an earlier scene over, where the two lovebirds are punting on the river, making the romance between them carry heavier emotional freight. Paltrow needed to be softened, she needed to cry, she needed to smile. Miramax was panicking. The opening was five weeks off and still there was no ending. Harvey pressed for a happy ending, where Shakespeare and Viola get together, completely at odds with the tone of the script. He kept saying, "We need more jokes, we need more jokes." Gigliotti understood that the female audience had to cry, that the film was, in the last analysis, a tear-jerker. Stoppard thought the ending was fine as it stood and refused to write a word. Harvey badgered him, flying back and forth to London. Eventually, the playwright grudgingly reworked it, they reshot it, reshot it again. Finally, Stoppard came up with the ending they went with, where Shakespeare complains, "I can't write anymore." Viola, with tears in her eyes, replies, "Here's the idea for the next play," which persuaded the audience. Eventually, the changes pushed the film into the 90s. But by the last test screening, at the end of November, the numbers were down. Weinstein was nervous, contemplated a limited release. But Gigliotti had heard the women sobbing at the test and was convinced the picture would work.

VACHON AND HAYNES were at Cannes in May of 1998 with *Velvet Goldmine*, the film Weinstein had cited during the *54* contretemps to prove that he wasn't homophobic. Although he wouldn't make wholesale changes in *Goldmine* the way he had in *54*, doing that film for Miramax was not an entirely happy experience for the filmmakers. *Goldmine* was a snapshot of the glam rock era focusing on the career of a David Bowie-like musician. Ewan McGregor, white hot off *Trainspotting*, was attached, as were Christian Bale, Toni Collette, Jonathan Rhys-Meyers, and Eddie Izzard. Shot in England, it was a difficult production. Vachon, who is famous for her formidable temper, was reputed to have terrorized the British crew. Some even compared her to Harvey. Haynes disagreed. "No! That's not true," he said. "There is no cruelty in Christine for the sake of cruelty. And there is in Harvey, believe me. She just doesn't kiss ass." Weinstein was eager to buy the North American rights, and he sat down with Haynes and Vachon, told Haynes what a brilliant filmmaker he was. He went out of his way to portray himself as a friend of gays, told them a story—something about homosexuals getting beaten up in a bar, and how their assailants were the kind of people who should see *The Crying Game*. Vachon thought it was a nice touch and found herself wondering, Did he get up this morning and go, All right, I'm meeting Todd Haynes and Christine Vachon, I gotta think up something good.

But the director and producer were ready to become believers. Although they had partial financing from CiBy 2000 and Film Four, they were desperate to make their budget, eager to take his $2 or so million off the table. As was his custom, Weinstein kept his hands to himself while Haynes shot the picture in London. Harvey "has a reputation for being homophobic, but he never pressured us to cut anything that was 'gay,' " says Vachon. "Miramax's notes were not stupid. They were constructive, and they were presented in an atmosphere of give-and-take. He really did not impose his will. He didn't threaten, he wasn't a bully. And he was extremely respectful of Todd."

But, also characteristically, post-production was another story. In an effort to extract more money from Miramax, Vachon showed the picture to Harvey, probably before she should have. He was under-impressed, insisted on testing it. Vachon's attitude toward test screenings was no different from that of any other indie. "Screenings are about 'the numbers,' " she says. "So trying to fit Todd's kind of round peg into a square hole made me feel horrible," adding, "Those NRG* screenings were probably the last nails in the coffin."

In the late spring of 1998, right before Cannes, Haynes and Vachon were summoned to a meeting in the Miramax conference room with Lechner and a few others. Haynes was wary, but Vachon gave him a pep talk: "Don't be threatened, don't be freaked out, just keep an open mind, like, Who knows? If it can make the movie better, then let's do it." The Miramax folks proposed various cuts that amounted to maybe thirteen minutes, but at some point, Lechner said, "Well, actually what we did was we—we thought the easiest thing to do would be to do the cuts on the film and show them to you. Right?" This was standard operating procedure at Miramax, but Haynes had never experienced it before. Lechner shoved a "cut/uncut" tape into the VCR, which showed a version cut by the Miramax post-production team, followed by Haynes's cut. Haynes had a well-earned sense of himself as an auteur, but he was nicely brought up, good manners, not the kind to blurt out, "What! You cut my movie? Are you out of your fucking mind!" So he said, "Okay," and they ran the tape. As Haynes watched, his eyes filled with tears. "Todd cried," says Lechner. "He cried because no one had ever touched his movies before, and I realized as soon as we did it, like, We have really been rude and insensitive." But the damage had been done. Vachon winced, thinking, Oh, God, this is just so not the right way to do this with Todd. This is going to backfire! Suddenly, Haynes interjected, still polite, "You know what? It's kind of difficult for me to really concentrate with you all in the room. May I just take the tape and go home?" And they were, "Oh sure!" Says Vachon, "It was awful. Because Todd is obsessive. He'd thought about every single cut, every single

* National Research Group.

frame, and to him, it was like somebody was taking his movie and just mashing it. It wasn't that their ideas were all wrong. It was just that they didn't have the sensitivity to really understand that you just can't do that to a filmmaker who is as much an auteur as Todd is. He was absolutely incensed, beside himself."

Vachon told Miramax, "That was a really bad move."

"Well, you know, we spent a lot of time on that tape, like John from post spent his whole weekend on it."

"Todd spent the last four years of his life on this."

When Haynes calmed down, he cut three or four minutes out of the film. *Goldmine* went to Cannes, and got a mixed reception—despite winning a Special Jury Prize. "There had been a certain sense of excitement about the movie [at Miramax] that literally seemed to evaporate," recalls Vachon. "I'd heard how when Miramax is 100 percent behind you, how wonderful it is, and I know that when a movie does badly, it's easy to blame the distributor, but I just felt that there was not a great deal of passion for it. Was it that they had too many movies? Was it that there was a concrete ceiling of what they thought the film could do, so why spend so much money on it? Todd wasn't pressured, but maybe we paid a price for that. The *Goldmine* experience was really awful. It's the tragedy of my life—it broke my heart."

Miramax was right; *Goldmine* wasn't working, but cutting was not going to help it. Vachon watched while *Goldmine* sank in a bath of lukewarm praise, but she had another bullet in the Killer Films chamber: *Happiness*. Generally speaking, October left Todd Solondz alone during production *and* post-production. Solondz had final cut up to two hours, but his version ran two hours, twenty minutes, and Ray felt it was too long. He kept after Solondz to trim it. But, unlike Miramax, October did not have a post-production facility, did not make Solondz test the picture in a mall, and Ray did not threaten to bury *Happiness* if he didn't get his way. Solondz did make a couple of cuts, tried this and tried that, but he usually ended up restoring the footage. Says Vachon, "It was like Ted Hope and I had to drag him in to have the will-you-cut-the-movie conversation. He dealt with the pressure by trying to avoid it as much as possible, trying very hard not to have himself in the room with the person making the request. You can't make Todd do anything he doesn't want to do. You just can't."

Ray finally agreed to let Solondz show his director's cut at Cannes. *Happiness* created a scandal at the Directors' Fortnight. Whether people loved it or hated it, it was the most talked about film of the festival. It was another triumph for October, which, with the success of *The Apostle*, Duvall's Oscar nomination, and *High Art*, was on a roll. It looked like McGurk's gamble was paying off. Ray says he thought *Happiness* was a work of genius, and he invited the Universal brass—Ron Meyer, Casey Silver, McGurk et al.—to a screening. But, he says, "They were there to open something real epic, like *Blues Brothers 2000*," and they never bothered to show up. *Happiness* walked away with the Critics Prize, and when they got back to the U.S., the picture was invited by the New York Film Festival.

Solondz ran the film again for the October guys. According to Ray, during one of the scenes between Bill-the-pederast (Dylan Baker) and his son, Greenstein's eyes started rolling around in his head like marbles, and he said, "Ronnie's gotta hear about this," referring to Meyer. Ray replied, "No, he doesn't. This has nothing to do with them. This is our movie, our business. We sent them the script, they've read it, and if they haven't read it, they have it, they know we're making this movie. We've been nothing but up front with them. Plus, the budget is so totally under their radar." Although he couldn't prove it, Ray suspected that Greenstein in fact alerted Meyer.

If he did, he needn't have bothered. On June 3, *The Hollywood Reporter* published an article drawing attention to the fact that October had four films on its slate—*Happiness, Orgazmo,* Lars von Trier's *The Idiots,* and Thomas Vinterberg's *The Celebration*—that could draw NC-17 ratings and lead to a potential clash with Universal. To Ray, it read like October was being branded as a renegade division making pornography; he concluded he was being set up by one of his competitors. Universal suddenly demanded to see *Happiness*. For reasons best known to himself, Ray thought this would be an easy problem to finesse. After all, *Happiness* was the kind of film October had been involved with in the past. "My attitude to Universal was, buyer beware. Tough shit, Sherlock, fuck you, you read the script, you knew the kind of company we were, this was the kind of film that you should celebrate, not censor. You should be embracing us, you shouldn't be kicking us in the ass. It was totally naive on my part." Meyer was quite conservative on issues of taste. Universal refused to buy *Arlington Road* because it opens with the image of a kid whose hand is burned. According to a source, Meyer saw *Happiness* and went crazy at the ejaculation scene. He said, "We can't release it. Sell the movie," and walked out of the screening. Meyer was furious with October because he thought it was courting controversy to raise its profile, the old Miramax trick. He exclaimed, "I don't want to understand the mind of a pedophile." He was appalled when he found out that Ray had allowed Solondz to use a snapshot of his young son Nicholas (named after Nicholas Ray the cult director) in the scene where Baker's character plays with himself in the back seat of the car, looking at a photo. Says Ray, "Ronnie thought I was a degenerate. He said, 'Bingham Ray must be a sick twisted fuck.' My feeling was, it's just a movie. Is it going to have a traumatic effect on my son for the rest of his life? No. Does it mean that I'm a pedophile, the New York chapter president of NAMBLA, the Man-Boy Love Association? No. But do I want to help a low-budget film because I believe in it? Absolutely. I thought it was kind of funny, to tell you the truth. No one else did! All of a sudden, people were saying, 'How could he put his son through that?' It wasn't like Dylan Baker was jerkin' off into his face. Come on."

By July, Ray continues, "the whole thing had unraveled into this ignorant, controversial, bullshit issue." Vachon got a call in the evening at home from Hope. He said, "Are you sitting down? I just talked to McGurk. Edgar Bronfman says Universal will not let October distribute this movie." Ray's response to Universal was, "We can release NC-17 films if we want, it's in the deal."

"No, it's not in the deal," replied a Universal executive.

"You're the studio that invented the NC-17 so that you could release *Henry and June.*"

"Things have changed. It's a shareholder issue now; Seagrams shareholders should not be subject to this kind of entertainment." Ray thought, Hey, you don't need me to drive the stock down. You've got Edgar for that. He says now, "It went down with all the aplomb of a fuckin' anvil. The fish stinks from the head, and that fuckin' stunk. *Happiness* was when the boat hit the iceberg. This is where we bottomed out, where the ideal was corrupted, the dream of being able to work within the studio system as some maverick, autonomous independent—it was just total horseshit. And if you're me, it was debilitating and disillusioning. 'Bingham, you don't get it.' I heard it eight thousand times in one month. Malin, at Artisan, was probably laughing through his asshole, saying, 'Ahh, I warned you.' Because if we had been private, no connection to Universal, there would have been no ratings issue, no anything issue. Nuthin'. It was awful, just torture. I was drinking too much, moody, inconsolable."

Ray was so addled he concluded his only alternative was to provoke Silver into firing him, whereupon he would distribute *Happiness* on his own. "If these guys didn't want that picture, I would do my own version of *Kids,* get the fuck outta Dodge, get fired from that shithole place," he recalls. That same month, after leaving the Holly Springs, Mississippi, set of Robert Altman's *Cookie's Fortune,* another October film, he called Silver on his cell phone from the baggage claim area of the Memphis airport. He yelled into the phone, "You ignorant piece of shit—you're just a fucking scumbag, asshole idiot, you never even read the fucking script, and you didn't see the fucking movie. How can you make a determination on a movie you didn't see? Only fucking scumbag Hollywood shitheads do that. I'm the one who doesn't get it? No, I don't think so, *you* don't get it!" Silver, who rarely lost his temper, lost it now. He hung up on Ray, burst into McGurk's office, saying, "I'm gonna fire that motherfucker." McGurk calmed him down, saying, "Casey, hang on a second, this is Bingham Ray we're talking about. What he's trying to do in his Fred Flintstone-like way is to get you so out-of-control mad that you fire him, because that's really what he wants. We can't give him what he wants."

Ray continued to protest, "You might as well just fuckin' eighty-six us right now, just put a fuckin' shotgun to the company's head and pull the trigger, because you're just gonna waste whatever credibility we have left. There's going to be a shitstorm in the media." The studio came back with, "No, there won't be a shitstorm in the media if you don't contribute to it, and you won't be able to contribute to it because you're gagged. Todd and Christine and James Schamus and Ted Hope aren't going to contribute to the shitstorm because they want what's best for the picture, and we're going to do a deal with them, and everything's going to be hunky-dory."

The deal was, Universal quietly did what needed to be done under the table for Good Machine to secure a bank loan that allowed it to distribute *Happiness*. The film played the New York Film Festival on a Saturday night in October and opened the following day. Despite a huge amount of publicity, most of it good, it grossed only about $3 million. Ray sat on the sidelines. "I'd cut my throat nine thousand times, I was all bled out," he says. Solondz made next to nothing. He was paid $30,000 for writing and directing *Happiness*, about $15,000 a year for two years' work. Says Vachon, "We weren't distributors. We didn't have the money or the muscle to really drive it all the way home. Bingham was worried about his reputation, Good Machine was worried about, Is our relationship with Universal going to be damaged by this? Everyone was getting absorbed by their places in the Greek tragedy, Oh, how does this reflect on me? and no one was saying, There's this movie that has two years of life and blood in it, let's get the movie out! It was really rough. Good Machine had a horrible time doing it, it was a big money suck, a lot of work for a little return. We so could have had a screenplay nomination, and we maybe even could have gotten Dylan Baker a nomination, but we didn't do a real Academy push. It was a missed opportunity."

This experience further alienated Ray. Greenstein didn't much care, saying, "There are other fights to fight, let's move on." Ray's attitude was, "Fuck that! When are you gonna stand up and fight the fight where if you lose, there is no tomorrow."

IN THE SPRING, a $1.4 million class action suit was filed against Miramax by former employees for unpaid overtime. Working conditions there were no better than they had been in the 1980s, and in some ways they were worse, despite or because of the Weinsteins' success. It was still an exciting place to be, especially for celebrity-starved New Yorkers. With the company's name in the papers every day—Liz Smith, "Page Six" of the *New York Post*, Rush and Molloy at the *Daily News*—staffers felt like they were at the center of the universe. Go to the men's room, and there was Sean Penn peeing in the next urinal. Step into the elevator, and there was Madonna. Sharon Stone wandered the halls looking fabulous. "I loved to drop the name 'Miramax' in a bar," says former marketing assistant Peter Kindlon. "It was very cool."

But whereas the old Miramax was small enough for everyone to crowd into a screening room, see a potential acquisition, and be grilled on their opinions, the new Miramax was big and impersonal. Harvey liked to think he had the common touch, traded on the fact that he was the son of working people—"I was born in Brooklyn, grew up in Queens, in rent-controlled buildings, didn't have the niceties of life," etc., etc.—but assistants, interns, floaters, and temps were treated like they didn't exist, or worse. Says Kindlon, "If Harvey and Bob didn't have to talk to you, they wouldn't. Harvey certainly knew who I was, but I could be in an elevator with just him, and he'd never acknowledge me." Robin Rizzuto, an assistant to Mark Gill, adds, "You could work at the company for three or four years and never really be acknowledged. If Harvey wanted something from me, and I was standing there, he never would have used my name. He'd say to Mark, 'I need an ashtray,' and Mark would say, 'Robin, could you get Harvey an ashtray.'"

Harvey had a driver who was devoted to him. One time, he was driving Harvey in from Teterboro Airport. Another car from the car service, Prime Time Limousine, left at the same moment headed for the same destination. Harvey noticed that the other car had beaten his to the city. He became furious with his driver, couldn't understand how the other driver had beaten him. He browbeat the man, shouting, "Just because you're merely a driver, don't you have any pride? Don't you care about the work that you do?" As one person who witnessed the incident put it, "It was as if he was trying to demean the fellow because he was a driver and not some fucking studio mogul."

Says former marketing coordinator Amy Hart, "I had worked at New Line, and if there was a hit, like if *Austin Powers* made a gajillion dollars on the first weekend, there was a champagne breakfast for us Monday morning, and everybody shared in the success. At Miramax, after working our asses off to win twelve [nominations] for *The English Patient*, we got an e-mail saying, 'No more expensing your lunches, no more car service home.' Our thank you was a big 'Fuck you!' That left a real bitter taste in your mouth, and that's why there was such a huge turnover. At the assistant level we just felt exploited. There was such a nastiness."

The atmosphere around the office was still abusive. Says one assistant, "The way to get respect in the office was to yell at people on the phone, a messenger fucked something up, a FedEx didn't arrive, you had to show how much of a prick you could be. People went, 'Oh, man, that was great, that was great.' It was a really sadistic environment." At another assistant who incurred his wrath, Harvey yelled, "You're a dildo! *You* are a dildo. Say it, 'I'm a dildo.'" The assistant did. Hart continues, "One time a floater, working for Harvey—he had three other assistants—really had to go to the bathroom. She waited and waited. Finally, she stood up, and he went, 'Where are you going?' 'I have to go to the bathroom.' 'You work for me now, siddown.'" He told one employee, "I hate the sound of your breathing." He told publicist Dennis Higgins he had to make something or other happen, adding, "Do you know what's going to happen if you don't?" "You're gonna fire me?" "I'm gonna kill you." Says Gill, "Every year at Miramax felt like a dog year, for mental distress and emotional cruelty."

The staff learned quickly enough that although Miramax may have been at the center of the universe, Harvey and Bob were at the center of Miramax. Life there revolved around them. "I remember waiting for Harvey to get off a plane or in from the airport, the whole place would shut down," Kindlon continues. "For hours, we'd just sit there in a meeting and wait. Then he would walk into the room, and God forbid you were laughing—the room would stop, everybody shut up."

People took huge pay cuts to work at Miramax. Marcia Kirkley, who worked in Harvey's assistant pool, had been earning $150,000 a year at IBM before she went to work at Miramax for $27,000 a year. Hart, a single mother, was expected to make ends meet in New York City on $25,000 a year. Not only was it impossible, it was galling, "especially when you knew," says Hart, "that they were just throwing money out the window, $100,000 for Gwyneth Paltrow to have a weekend in Paris just for the hell of it. He got her a private jet from New York to Paris, got her a Mercedes so she could have fun."

The brothers expected their staff to work long hours. Says Kindlon, "I literally went to my desk at 9:30 A.M. and never left it before 11:00, 11:30 at night. I was burned out, exhausted." Adds Hart, "It was like factory labor in a Third World country. We never got lunch breaks. Unless you smoked you never left that building." Even if you finished work by, say, 7:30 in the evening, it was considered bad form to leave, so staffers killed time for another couple of hours. Consequently, virtually nobody had a life outside the office—families, girlfriends, boyfriends. Vacations made the Weinsteins crazy, especially an extended weekend or a few days off during the winter holidays, admittedly a busy period for the company. It was always, "What do you mean you're going on a trip? People work here for a living.

You go, don't come back!" People were recalled from the airport as they were ready to board planes headed for sun and sand. One woman is said to have postponed her wedding. Says a source, "It was a question of control. When they lost the control, they lost you as a loyal player. And didn't want you there anymore."

Then there was the fear factor, still. Employees worked under the constant threat of losing their jobs. In a typical incident, Bob called a staffer who had just been hired in a senior position, whom he had never met. Her temp didn't know who Bob was, and she was on the phone with a director. Still, it took her no more than twenty seconds to pick up the call. He said, "Don't you know who I am? You never keep me on hold. You're fired."

"I have a temp who didn't know, Bob," the staffer remonstrated.

"Well, fire her." Abuse coming from the top was handed down the line. Says Hart, "Harvey has this negativity and ferocity, and it trickled down. People who left would say, 'I was turning into the biggest bitch in the world.'" Adds Kindlon, "There was a feeling at that time that if you didn't like it, there were plenty of people who would. I had a window, and I could look out on Greenwich Street, and I always imagined thousands of young people holding résumés yelling, 'Pick me, pick me!'"

In 1997, the Labor Department had investigated Miramax's employment practices for seven months. A settlement was reached without the agreement of the plaintiffs, which allowed them to go to court. In early spring of 1998, attorney Merri Lane, whose daughter Stacy was a former Miramax employee, gathered some thirty-five people in a midtown office and told them that she was going to launch a class action suit against the company. Kindlon remembers, "She looked around the table and asked, 'Is anyone willing to put their name on it?' Dead silence. Most of the people in that room, all of them except me, were afraid of retaliation, afraid to be associated with anything against Miramax. I raised my hand, because having been out of there for a while, I realized how much they had exploited me, and I knew I was doing the right thing. I said, 'Put my name on the suit.' I would never have done it if I had still been working there. I'm not that courageous."

On April 9, the suit was filed on behalf of about two and a half dozen former employees charging that Miramax owed back wages for overtime. The amount in question wasn't huge, but it was embarrassing and generated the thing the Weinsteins hated almost as much as losing money: bad press. "They intimidated everybody," says Lane. "None of the people who still worked there would sign up. They were convinced that they would be fired, be blackballed, that terrible things would happen. There were people who sent in consents to me and before I could have them filed they withdrew. There was one poor young woman whose father called me constantly saying that she wanted to join but she was terrified, and I couldn't guarantee that nothing would happen to her."

The case was settled for an undisclosed amount. Kindlon says he received about a year's salary, $25,000. Hart, who was also a plaintiff, recalls that she got between $7,000 and $10,000. By that time, Kindlon was at Fine Line. His salary was almost doubled, and he arrived at the office at 9:00 A.M. and left at 5:00 P.M. But, he says, "Fine Line was horrible at marketing films. I really loved working at Miramax."

Eleven
The Bad Lieutenant
1998–1999

• How Scott Greenstein sold out October, Harvey Weinstein won an Oscar for *Shakespeare*, made Rosie O'Donnell and M. Night Shyamalan cry, but got his knuckles rapped by Michael Eisner.

"I was a fuckin' stone idiot. Total moron. You don't get any stupider than that, not to have had the wherewithal to navigate these very tricky waters. I was in a canoe going around a whirlpool with no paddle and just getting sucked down by the whole thing."

— BINGHAM RAY

While 54 was being pinched and pulled to raise its scores, a Miramax executive told the filmmakers not to worry, they had fixed problems like this before, they had even solved *Wide Awake*. *Wide Awake* was an insipid, sugary piece of cotton candy, a prequel of sorts to *Touched by an Angel*, notable only for being the second feature of M. Night Shyamalan. Says Jack Lechner, who joined Miramax after it had already been shot, "Why did it ever get made? Beats me!" The saccharine script appealed to Harvey's sentimental side, now, apparently, ascendant. He thought it would be a huge family movie. Meryl Poster characteristically championed the project, and became the executive in charge. Shyamalan's conceit is that a twelve-or-so-year-old boy in a Catholic prep school, grieving over his grandfather's death, becomes obsessed with finding God, and actually succeeds in doing so. The story is semiautobiographical. Shyamalan, born in Madras, India, the son of two doctors, attended such a school as a child in Philadelphia. In the film, however, the surrogate for young Shyamalan is, naturally, fair-skinned, with blue eyes and tousled blond hair. So much for diversity in indie film.

In fact, Miramax had come a long way since Harvey wanted to open

Priest on Good Friday, and executives were not only worried that the story was silly, but worse, it was blasphemous, likely to agitate Catholic watchdog groups best left sleeping. The solution was to replace God with a more modest hierarch, and they arrived at an angel, over Shyamalan's objections. The executive, proud of the fix, told the 54 gang, "See, isn't that great? We've maintained the essence of his movie."

Right away, Shyamalan made himself unpopular by condescending to the Miramax folks. Even then, without a hit, Shyamalan was arrogant and stubborn. To them, his attitude was, "I'm Steven Spielberg, and this is a pit stop, and I'm going to blow past you guys. I'm writing a movie right now, called *The Sixth Sense*, which is going to be a $100 million film, and that's the business I'm interested in." The Weinsteins returned the favor. "They treated Shyamalan like shit," says a source. When Harvey and Bob first saw *Wide Awake* at the Tribeca screening room, Bob, according to former Miramax production head Paul Webster, told the young director, "I don't think this movie can be saved," while Harvey "made Night cry. Destroyed him, in front of everybody."

As was their custom, the Weinsteins slashed the budget way beyond a point that was reasonable, tormented Shyamalan for exceeding it, and then when their self-fulfilling prophecy was fulfilled, threw money at post-production, allowing Harvey to flex his producing muscles. Adds Lechner, "There was cut after cut, reshoots, rescoring, revoicing, but it was fucked from Day 1. It wasn't a good script, it wasn't a good movie, and you could have worked on it for another ten years and you wouldn't have made it into a good movie." Says Joe Roth, "Harvey was recutting it behind him. Shyamalan had a terrible time."

Rosie O'Donnell had a small role, a nun. Her television show became a hit during the course of the post-production marathon, and she was hot. She loved the director, loved the movie. Shyamalan called O'Donnell, said, "Help me." On the speakerphone to Harvey, Shyamalan, Poster, Cathy Konrad, who was one of the producers, and others gathered in the conference room at the Tribeca offices, O'Donnell said, "Listen, Harvey, you can't steamroll this poor filmmaker, you gotta live with what you make, I don't want you to release it unless it's Night's version. He's an artist. I'm an artist. You're just the guy who sells it." She didn't mean it in an insulting way, but she inadvertently pushed Harvey's we're-producers-not-just-distributors button. Says Konrad, "There are these moments where you can actually see smoke come out of Harvey's ears. He just snapped. He lost his mind." As a couple of people in the room remember it, he roared, "You're some fucking artist! You're just a fucking talk show host! Like you would fucking know. You bitch! You cunt!" Konrad recalls, "Rosie burst into tears. I was like, Excuse me, Rosie O'Donnell is crying?" (According to one source, Harvey called her "a big fat fucking cow." Harvey says, "I never used 'cunt' and I never said 'cow.' ") Konrad remembers him continuing in that vein, looking around the table and screaming, "You don't know who you're dealing with. I can take your film and put it in a closet with a lot of other films and it will never seen the fucking light of day! And you know why I can do that? Because I have a lot of money. So you need me more than I need you. And the way I'll show you that is I will make your work that's important to you invisible to everybody." She adds, "It was heartbreaking." Afterward, of course, there was a lot of backpedaling. Harvey was just in from London, he was jet-lagged, he wasn't prepared for the call, etc., etc. He sent flowers. But she was furious, said, "I want *Double Wish*"—another project she had at Miramax—"out of there. To my grave I will go, I will never speak to him again. I will never work for that man again. And I will not do press for that movie." Of course, not doing press for *Wide Awake* was an empty threat, because Miramax dumped it—which, actually, was a public service. And as for the rest of it, as Konrad says, "Everybody has this moment where they say they're never gonna talk to him again, they're never gonna make anything with them again, and then of course we all do. Because he's smart, he's a cinephile, he knows more about films and filmmaking than most people in Hollywood. It's a love-hate thing with Harvey."

Several years later, when Joe Roth took on *The Sixth Sense* at Disney, Harvey told him, "You can't let that guy direct that picture, look at the terrible job he did on *Wide Awake*." Still, Harvey had hired him to do a polish on his Freddie Prinze vehicle, *She's All That*. "I thought I had a good relationship with him," Harvey says, "but once *The Sixth Sense* got really really big, he let me know how he felt. I said to him, 'Why don't we restore *Wide Awake* to your original cut? Every scene just the way you wanted it! That way I can show what I had to deal with.' He didn't want to do that."

Explains Lechner, "The weirdness of being at Miramax was, on one hand, you have in the works at the same time, *The English Patient, Shakespeare in Love, Good Will Hunting*, where everyone agrees on what the movie is up front and you let the filmmakers get on with it, everything Miramax does helps it to be better, and it makes a zillion dollars. But ultimately, everyone at Miramax ended up spending more time on *Wide Awake, 54*, and *Talk of Angels*, which was in post for three years."

Indeed, it seemed that almost every picture in 1998 was a problem. Although Harvey had paid a fortune for *Next Stop Wonderland*, he made director Brad Anderson reshoot the ending. "Miramax will steamroller over you, if they can," he said. "I'd never been through that before. My assumption was that you sell the movie and that's the movie they buy. But they look at it as a product. A product needs to be reworked or altered in order to fit the consumer's needs. And you're just the obstacle in their way. . . . And of course, you don't get that shtick when they're buying your movie. It's like, 'We love it.' "

Meanwhile, *Dogma*, Kevin Smith's poke at the Catholic Church, was ticking away like a time bomb. After the success of *Chasing Amy*, he figured it was now or never. The film was shot in Pittsburgh. Like Anderson, Smith was annoyed that Harvey didn't deliver on a series of promises he'd made. "Bob is no bullshit, but Harvey will blow smoke up your ass," he says. "After he read the script, he said, 'We're gonna get fuckin' Roger Deakins to shoot it, Vittorio Storaro, I'll call him personally,' and you wind up with Bob Yeoman, who's wonderful, but not them. He'll promise you the sun, the moon, and the stars, and if you get a handful of earth, you're feeling pretty good, never remembering, Wait a second, where are the sun, the moon, and the fuckin' stars?"

When Smith emerged from the cutting room, he had a three hour and twenty minute cut. According to the filmmaker, Harvey said, " 'This is fantastic, you guys did a phenomenal fucking job, but I do think there's about ten minutes we can cut outta there.' We're like, 'All right,' and we cut out ten, fifteen minutes, and he said, 'Wonderful, it moves like a sonofabitch, but I really think there's probably another ten minutes we can dig out of there.' We got to two hours, and didn't even notice. Then he wanted to keep going. His whole theory was, you need to program it as many times as possible in one evening. At ninety minutes, you get two screenings. We finally said, 'No, this is it.'

" 'I'm telling you, five more minutes.'

" 'Harvey, there's not five minutes to cut, we're too close to the bone now.'

" 'No, I'm telling you, there's five more minutes, you should get in there and do the work.'

" 'Look, you have to stop with the cutting. We've cut it to the point we're gonna cut it, if you make us cut five minutes more I'm going to go to the press and scream like a raped child!'

" 'Okay.' And that was that." Harvey treated Smith, and his producer, Scott Mosier, a whole lot better than he had punching bags like Christopher, Shyamalan, Anderson, and the rest. Smith was family. *Clerks* was one of the last truly indie films Miramax had acquired. Says Smith, "You always read about people having horrible fuckin' experiences with Miramax, and clashes of egos and shit like that. 54? Reshooting and reshooting and finally ending up with a movie the director doesn't recognize as his own. From what I've seen, Harvey only takes movies away from people he has no respect for. We've never had that. He's never lost money on us, he's only earned off of us, and we've never gone through a period of defiance, 'Fuck you, Harvey, I'm in charge.' We always recognize that he is the man with the wallet that we listen to."

But if Smith provided Harvey with a way to channel the Miramax of yesteryear, he also served as a reminder of how much the company had changed. *Dogma* was yet another film that threatened to put Disney on a collision course with Catholic pressure groups, promising a return to the bad old days of 1995, which Disney and Miramax had both tried to put behind them. As Roth remembers it, "I told Michael Eisner, 'I don't see this as the same thing as *Kids*, this is a parody, this is fun, it's Ben and Matt and Chris Rock,' but Michael just said to me, 'I can't take this pressure. You may be right, but I can't take that chance here.' " Eisner called Harvey and told him, "If one person does not go to Disneyland because of this movie, that will be one person too many. I do not want you to release it." Adds former Disney CFO Rob Moore, "It became very clear to Harvey that it would be a huge problem between him and Michael if he forced the issue, so he agreed to get rid of it. Ultimately he had to deal with Kevin and Matt and Ben, who were basically like, 'We're at Miramax because you're willing to take these kinds of risks, now what's going on?' "

Smith thought it was a tempest in a teacup. As Harvey recalls, "Kevin said, 'What are you worried about?' So I sent him ten thousand letters that had come into the office by truck." They changed his mind. "We were in the middle of a shitstorm, with tons of hate mail," Smith remembers. One letter, from the "Hispanic Coalition of Catholic Warriors" was typical. It said, in part, "You Hollywood Jewish sons of bitches, all you are interested in is money and money at any cost. I advise you to spend your billions of looted gold in flak jackets. We are coming for you, I promise we'll get you somehow at office, at home, or anywhere you are seen." Continues Smith, "The Catholic League went right for Disney. They didn't even care about Miramax, so it was very easy to be like, I want to get as far away from Disney as I can get. Because it wasn't about our movie anymore. It was about the controversy of our movie. Nobody had seen frame one. *Dogma* was a cluster fuck for all involved."

Needless to say, none of the other studios would touch Smith's film. "We had Ben and Matt following *Good Will Hunting*, a movie that made $125 million, plus won them a writing Oscar," Smith continues. "MGM watched it and passed, Columbia watched it and passed. Universal watched it and passed. Edgar Bronfman, Jr., watched it himself, and was just, like, 'There's no way we can put out this movie without seeing our stock drop.' The unsung villain in all of this is Blockbuster Video. Because Blockbuster has made it their mandate that they won't shelve an NC-17 film, and when you have a company that takes up 85 percent of the video business, maybe more, it's tough. Every distributor who's looking to the ancillary market to make more money or make up what the film didn't make theatrically, has to take that into consideration." The moral of all this, of course, is that when studios gobble up indies, it's bad for the kind of freedom prized by these filmmakers and distributors. "Independent" became "dependent."

QUENTIN TARANTINO never appreciated *Jackie Brown* as much as he should have. On the contrary, it seemed to be a disappointment to him. As one of his friends put it, "He thought he really fucked up." Like Madonna, his antennae were always tuned to the twitches of the zeitgeist, aquiver with each ripple of the culture. Although he always claimed to be and behaved as if he were making his films exclusively for himself—refusing to tailor them to suit the Weinsteins' wishes or the comments scrawled on preview cards—he felt he had let down his fans. Tarantino even got his first taste of bad press. He would stumble on phrases like "the dangerously overexposed Quentin Tarantino," and think to himself, You're the motherfuckers that overexposed me. "I got sick of the way journalists, especially in a profile, kill you with their adjectives," he says. "He 'lumbered' into the room. 'Gesticulating wildly.' 'Manic.' You're getting your ass kicked by these little adjectives. After you suffer through your school years, most adults go through their lives and never have to hear or read anyone making fun of them ever again. That is officially gone out of your life. All of a sudden I was getting self-conscious about what it is that makes me me. I was hearing people say, like, 'He's a motor mouth,' 'Shut the fuck up, dada.' But that's what made me famous in the first fucking place. I started to feel like a piñata. Maybe I overreacted, okay? 'Fuck y'all.'

"The acting bug was very big on me at that time," Tarantino continues. "I was really chomping at the bit because I wasn't acting in *Jackie Brown.*" Soon after the film was released, director Leonard Foglia approached him about doing a revival of *Wait Until Dark*, on Broadway, taking on the role of a thug who terrorizes a blind woman, to be played by Marisa Tomei. Even though he hadn't done live theater since he was a teenager, and then only a little, he jumped at it. The play opened in the first week of April 1998, to awful reviews. Tarantino in particular got killed. Slaughtered. Eviscerated. He compared it to being tied to the back of a wagon and dragged through town while everybody flogged him with whips.

In the best of circumstances, Tarantino does not relish criticism, even friendly, constructive criticism. As one of his friends puts it, "Quentin needs you to deal with him on a fan club basis. He just doesn't like negatives. He's got that American disease where everything has to have a positive spin." But the reviews of *Wait Until Dark* were vicious. "It was tough," Tarantino continues. "It was the morning after opening night, every other person in New York City is reading the *New York Times*. They look up from the *New York Times*, and there I am. They see me. Me. I'm the one whose acting sucks. You try not to take it personally, but it is personal."

But the press was so bad that Tarantino began to wonder privately if the play hadn't been a foolish move. Years later, on the set of *Kill Bill*, he brought up the subject with David Carradine, who plays Bill, and who happened to have seen *Wait Until Dark*. "Tell me the unvarnished truth," Tarantino asked. "Don't hold back. Do I have what it takes to make it on Broadway?" The actor answered, evasively: "I think it was very brave of you to do that, but there is something in the back of my mind."

"What?"

"Why do you want to parade around on a stage in front of a bunch of blue-haired ladies who arrived on a bus? Because that's what Broadway is. Whereas what you're doing is making pictures that blow people away. What could you possibly get out of that compared to the other?"

Says Uma Thurman, who stars in *Kill Bill*, "You must never forget with Quentin that he wanted to be an actor. If somebody asked him to act in something while he was prepping *Kill Bill*, he would drop everything to go and act. His schedule was not being dictated by being a film director. He was much more interested in doing a guest spot on *Alias*."

Says one friend, "Part of him understood that he'd done something that was wrong. You don't just go from acting in little bit parts in your own movies to all of a sudden somebody taking advantage of you—although he was game for it—to make you the lead of a Broadway play. That was really horrible. He was like fodder, throw him up there to get the shit kicked out of him. He's like a little boy, he shares his enthusiasms, they're bubbling over, he trusts people, and he opens up and tries things, and then he gets burned, and he retreats. He was traumatized by that resounding slam that was delivered to him by the New York critics. He went into a tailspin. It scared him. He's a very wounded guy in that way."

Tarantino had rented an apartment in Greenwich Village for the duration of the play, but discovered that he couldn't even walk around the neighborhood in peace. He asked his downtown pals Thurman and Robert De Niro for advice. De Niro said, "You wear a baseball cap, sunglasses, you're fine, people don't recognize you."

"Well, that doesn't work for me," Tarantino replied. "I look like me, in a baseball cap. I'm not really that famous, I'm that recognizable. If you know what I look like, you're gonna know me when you see me." To Thurman, he complained, "If I take a walk by my house, past nine o'clock, I'm gettin' jacked all the time."

"Quentin, you wanted this," she replied, not very sympathetically. "Take your walks at eight!"

• • •

SCOTT GREENSTEIN was still riding high on the success of *The Apostle*. There was a deal with Albert Brooks for *The Muse*, at $15 million, a modestly budgeted picture with Angelina Jolie. Greenstein insisted on Sharon Stone instead. If Harvey had made a deal with Stone, he wanted her too. Even though the actress cut her salary, she—along with the addition of Andie MacDowell and Elton John—bumped the budget up $8 milllion to about $23 million. Almost overnight, *The Muse* went from a mildly amusing Brooks movie that was almost guaranteed to recoup on the basis of an estimated $20 million in foreign sales, to a not-nearly-funny-enough Sharon Stone vehicle that was almost guaranteed to lose money. Schmidt and Ray exchanged looks. Antically disposed, they had improvised a little ditty for the occasion. Set to the tune of "Fugue for Tinhorns" from *Guys and Dolls*, it went, "I gotta movie heah/Our aim is very cleah/We gonna make it for a price that isn't deah/Can't lose, can't lose/Our guy says *The Muse* can't lose/And heah comes Albert B/he meets with Scottie G/and the next thing ya know the budget's 23/Can't lose, can't lose/Our guy says *The Muse* can't lose/So Scottie grabs the phone/Says, Get get me Sharon Stone/Ya know it's time to throw CAA a bone/Can't lose, can't lose . . ." And on and on.

Already bad, the atmosphere in the October offices became acrid. Doors that had always stood open were now closed, and the sounds of shouting rocketed off the walls. Staff said, "Mom and Dad are fighting again." Ray could feel the company slipping away from him, and he felt powerless to stop it. He thought, I'm losing, and I know I'm losing, and I don't know what to do about it. He ran into Amir Malin in a mall in Toronto when they were both there for the film festival. Malin was on an escalator on his way to the top floor; Ray was on the adjacent escalator descending to the parking level. Ray was angry over something Malin had said in *Premiere* magazine, and as he passed him, he shouted, "Fuck you, you shithead," and gave him the finger. Generally, people in the film business are rude when they're on the way up. But this was Bingham Ray on his way down. Later, as his situation at October continued to deteriorate, the irony was not lost on him.

There were no secrets at October. Everyone spoke to everyone else, told everyone else what was being said. Greenstein talked to Chris McGurk nearly every day, said things like, "Bingham's not a businessman. He doesn't want to make money, he wants to make Danish-language art films, you can't get this guy to step up and think in a commercial way." No sooner would Greenstein hang up the phone than Ray would call, complaining that Greenstein was a Philistine, didn't give a shit about independent film.

According to one source, Greenstein wanted Ray to report to him, then openly urged McGurk to get rid of his partner. But there was no way McGurk was going to get rid of Ray. "Bingham was the creative essence of October Films," he says. "You went to Cannes with him, you walked down the street, he was there in Bermuda shorts and people were coming out of the woodwork."

It wasn't like October was the only thing McGurk had on his mind. Universal was staggering through one of the worst dry patches in recent memory, a virtual Death Valley of would-be hits, bleached by the sun and picked over by buzzards. Says former October marketing head Dennis Rice, "It was one fucking disaster after another that made October look like the pimple on the elephant's butt. McGurk's ass was on fire and he had to take a phone call from Bingham, who's bitching about the fact that we wanted a forty-two-inch ad instead of a twenty-one-inch ad." McGurk screamed into the phone, "I don't have time for this, Bingham, go figure it out. I don't give a shit, enough with this petty garbage bullshit, you're complaining about Scott, he's only been in there a year, don't you have anything better to do? Aren't you doing your job? *Don't call!*" McGurk was feeling less like a studio head than a therapist. Ray remembers, "Chris acted like I was Chicken Little, negative, not a team player, stuck in the old way, while Scott and John represented the new way." Eventually, McGurk stopped taking his calls.

As the months passed, September giving way to October and then November, Ray arrived at work later and later, shut himself in his office chain-smoking, with the Grateful Dead cranked up to such ear-splitting volume that it practically stripped the paint on the walls. Always high-strung, he became a screamer. Recalls Ray, "It was the single most painful period of time I've experienced in this business." He was still drinking too much, Absolut vodka martinis and single malt Scotches. "I was stressed out beyond all belief," he recalls. "I started seeing a therapist."

Meanwhile, storm clouds were gathering on the horizon. Decisions were being made in distant boardrooms that had nothing to do with October directly, but would affect its future. In 1998, Edgar Bronfman, Jr., had bought PolyGram for $10.6 billion, assuming a hefty debt. With Universal's feature division bleeding cash, he put PolyGram's film holdings on the block, as well as Gramercy, its speciality division. Greenstein went around dropping mysterious hints, telling favorites, "There's some things in the works, I can't really tell you about them, but hang in there, things will be fine, don't worry, you're in great shape, you're doing a great job."

Then, in the third week of December 1998, Greenstein waltzed into Schmidt's office and said, "I have good news and bad news. The good news is, Barry Diller wants to buy October. The bad news is, he wants me to run it!" Schmidt was flabbergasted. Greenstein asked him not to tell anyone, especially Ray. Schmidt replied, "Whaddya mean I can't tell anyone? First of all, you've got your partners, and number two you've got your board, Universal and the shareholders—it's ludicrous." He rushed into Ray's office, exclaiming, "Barry Diller's made an offer for October. He wants Scott to run it, and he wants us too. There's no fuckin' way I'm gonna work for Scott, and I know what your answer is going to be. But if it's a serious offer for the company, we've got to see if it plays out." Stunned, Ray looked at Schmidt and asked, "What? How has it come to this? This doesn't smell right to me. Why would anyone on God's fucking green earth think that I would ever, under any circumstances, report to this guy? It just would not happen. If I had no other job and no other recourse, and no other anything—as dumb as I am, you'd have to be dumber than me to do it." He called McGurk, said, "What the fuck's going on with this?" McGurk had been blindsided as well. Greenstein had told him nothing. Now, adds Donna Gigliotti, who would shortly work for Greenstein, "McGurk hates him. He spits nails when you mention Scott's name."

Greenstein had a weight problem, and according to a source close to him, was in the habit of taking long walks. It was during such a walk that he accidentally ran into Diller. He said to Diller, "Hey, howya doin', I'm at October, we're loosely affiliated, I'd like to sell *The Apostle* on the Home Shopping Network, 'cause I think it would have real good blue-collar appeal." Diller thought it was a good idea, and a relationship began between the two of them. Diller called Greenstein when he was in Dallas at a meeting at Blockbuster. He said, "Would you be interested in me buying October?" Then Greenstein went to Schmidt and said, "We need to deal with this."

Between Christmas and New Year's 1999, Schmidt and his wife, Wendy, along with McGurk and his wife, Jamie, converged on the Rays' home in Mount Kisco for dinner. It was all very festive. The tree was up, the kids were running around. The McGurks brought a nice glass ice bucket as a gift. According to Schmidt, McGurk was contrite, said, "I made a mistake. Bringing in Scott was the worst thing I could have done. He's an opportunist, a backstabber. Scott has ambitions that make Amir's pale by comparison. He wants to run the company." No one could figure out why Diller wanted to buy October, what he thought he was buying. Nor did they believe that Greenstein had run into Diller by accident. Says Schmidt, "I think they might have run into each other on the street, but I would assume one of two things, that Scott waited on that street corner for maybe three weeks until Diller walked by, or he really bumped into him and used it as an opportunity to say, 'Lemme come by and talk to you.' But either way he was looking for an opportunity to set himself up. Which he'd probably been doing from day one." To him, it didn't make any difference whether Greenstein suggested that Diller buy October or the reverse. "The right kind of partnership is all about sitting down with your partners and discussing, 'Hey, we've got a possible offer, should we pursue it?' Unless you want to promote yourself at the expense of others." According to Diller himself, "It may be a bit apocryphal that we ran into each other on the street. I have no memory of his talking about *The Apostle* and HSN. It could have happened, but it seems unlikely—it's such a weird idea. But I had the desire to build a film company, because the TV part of USA needed product. I had heard about Scott. I asked him to come and see me, and we started exploring purchasing the company, because it was kind of imploding. Maybe Allen & Co. brought it to us rather than Scott—I don't remember—but Scott was a bright guy and incredibly energetic. He will go anywhere, knock down any wall, call anyone, do anything, and I'm an admirer of that. We decided to back him instead of Bingham Ray."

However it happened, during that dinner, Ray managed to turn around both McGurk and Schmidt. They all understood that they had to fight. They even had Malin's support, who was still a partner, even though he had moved on to Artisan. "When basically Scott sold out the company from underneath Bingham and John, I sided with them," he says. "I called up John and told him, 'It strikes me the wrong way, you and Bingham can vote my vote for what you think is right.' "

Schmidt recalls, "We all came away from that dinner reaffirming the things we believed in deeply in terms of the kind of company we wanted, the morality of the company, what it stands for, how we treat people, friendship and loyalty—things that count more in the balance than taking a three quarter of a million dollar a year job from Barry Diller. I would have been the COO or the president of the new company, and Bingham could have been set up in his own division. That was a future that we basically said 'Fuck it' to that night, a future where there would be security for our families, the possibility of continuing to do what we did, but it was just wrong. Scott did something I regarded as dishonorable. You don't report to a guy like Greenstein, given where he came from. That was an intolerable ethical position."

In January, Diller offered $20 million for October, with a couple of hundred thousand dollars going to Ray and Schmidt after seven or eight years with the company. To the partners, it was an insult. None of the minority shareholders thought it was a good offer, but they were afraid to turn it down, afraid of saying no to Bronfman's friend Diller, embarrassing him. Nevertheless, they did turn it down. Greenstein apparently hadn't realized that the minority shareholders had the power to veto a sale, and for a moment, it looked like he might have overplayed his hand. He was on the verge of cleaning out his desk. He would come into Schmidt's office, say, "Can't we work something out?" Ray, who carried The Godfather around in his head like a metal plate, saw himself uncomfortably seated across a red checked tablecloth from Sollozzo, expecting to be shot at any moment, when suddenly the man says, "What are you worried about? I am the hunted one." Except he couldn't figure out whether he was Sollozzo or Michael Corleone.

Still, even though Greenstein was momentarily checked, the fate of October rested on a knife edge. Ray and Schmidt tried to carry on business as usual. They understood that Bronfman would probably find a way to sell their company one way or another, and that they had to locate a white knight. "Once you're put in play, alarm bells are going off. Die! Die! Die!" Ray says. "We were under the gun, because the company was weakened in the light of all this activity. Even idiot Bingham got that. But we went to Sundance."

"MIRAMAX IS BRILLIANT at publicizing its successes, but it's even more brilliant burying its failures," observes Dennis Rice. Many films, with titles changed once, twice, sometimes three times, tiptoed out on video, with maybe a cable airing as well. The company released, half released, or sent straight to cable and/or video a string of under-performers and outright disasters, including not only 54, Velvet Goldmine, Next Stop Wonderland, Wide Awake, Talk of Angels, but A Price Above Rubies, Martha, Meet Frank, Daniel and Laurence (released as The Very Thought of You), and The Wisdom of Crocodiles (starring Jude Law, released as Immortality), etc., etc.

Some of these films were homegrown productions developed at Miramax, some were acquisitions. It didn't seem to matter much. A case in point is the sad tale of The Hairy Bird, or at least that was the title its writer-director, Sarah Kernochan, gave it—it would have three titles all told. Kernochan, a tall, poised blonde, is married to playwright James Lapine. She won an Oscar for co-producing one of the big documentaries of the 1970s, Marjoe, the story of a young, charismatic preacher. (In 2002, she won another for a documentary short called Thoth.) Subsequently, she turned to writing scripts. "I was on the bottom of the A list or the top of the B list," she says, having written the excellent Impromptu, with Judy Davis and Hugh Grant. She had written for Tom Cruise and Steven Spielberg, who handed off one of her scripts to Robert Zemeckis. Zemeckis made it as What Lies Beneath, for which she got a credit. She recalls, "I had no problem getting work. I said no all the time."

As a teenager, Kernochan had attended Rosemary Hall, an exclusive girls' school in Wallingford, Connecticut, that was subsequently absorbed by Choate. At a reunion in the late 1980s, she found herself saying to her former classmates, "I'm going to make a movie about us for our daughters." She thought this would give her the opportunity to direct, as well as write. She finished the script in 1990, and five drafts later, she was ready to send it around town.

The Hairy Bird is an attempt to capture the secret life of adolescent girls at that fleeting, combustible moment when they experience the three-way collision between the rush of hormones, their own sense of empowerment, and the looming constraints of the adult world. Or, as Kernochan once succinctly put it, the film is about "the incursion of the penis in young girls' lives." Drawing on her own experience, Kernochan created a vivid, sharply etched picture of the highs and lows of life at a girls' prep school with the canniness of an insider. As Miss Godard's School fights a takeover by St. Ambrose, the boys' school nearby, her characters transcend their privileged, whitebread circumstances. The script weaves an unlikely tapestry of idealism and raunch, and in the process deftly touches on issues of family, class, adolescence, and education without allowing any of them to torpedo the high spirits of the narrative. The title comes from an exchange between two of the girls, in which one confesses, "I want to be an ex-virgin." The other inquires, "What have you been doing with Dennis all this time? Dry humping?" The first replies, "No, I ate the hairy bird!" meaning, of course, she gave her boyfriend a blowjob.

Kernochan finally connected with Ira Deutchman, who had partnered with producer Peter Newman to form an outfit called Redeemable Pictures. Deutchman and Newman persuaded Atlantic Alliance, a Canadian company that had deals with both Miramax and New Line, to finance the film. Kernochan cast Gaby Hoffman, Kirsten Dunst, Heather Matarazzo, and Rachael Leigh Cook, all of whom were virtual unknowns at the time, with Lynn Redgrave as the headmistress of Miss Godard's.

The Hairy Bird was shot in Toronto in the summer of 1997, and Kernochan brought it in for a modest $1.5 million. Alliance thought it had a commercial film, and Kernochan was pleased. In November 1997, Harvey was making one of his periodic visits to the set of *54* in Toronto, which went into production after *The Hairy Bird* wrappped. While he was there, he picked up David Cronenberg's *eXistenZ*, with Jennifer Jason Leigh and Jude Law. Perhaps as an afterthought, he also bought *The Hairy Bird* for $3.5 million. Alliance may have shown him Reel 5, the one that contained the drinking, barfing, sex, and fumbling attempts at sex during a dance Miss Godard's hosts for the St. Ambrose boys. Just as Harvey looked at *54* and thought, *Saturday Night Fever*, he probably looked at *The Hairy Bird* and thought, *Porky's*!

"I was jumping up and down," Kernochan recalls. "I'm an Academy member, so I'm on the receiving end of the Miramax Oscar campaign every year, I admired how they would bully themselves into people's awareness, and I was rooting for them. Because no writer really likes the major studios, and I thought independence means what it says, 'independence.' And Miramax, of course, was the king of the independents." It didn't hurt that Weinstein had plunked down more than twice the budget of the movie. Kernochan couldn't help noticing, however, that Deutchman and Newman did not look overjoyed. They wouldn't meet her eye, and she could see that they were steeling themselves—against what, she didn't know. She said, "What's the matter with you guys?" They replied, in unison, "Let's see what happens."

What happened was that Harvey insisted on testing the film at a mall in Mountainside, New Jersey. Nervous, Kernochan arrived at the theater before Weinstein, whom she had never met. By the time he finally emerged from a limo, followed by his marketing team, he was late, but had somehow found time to acquire a jumbo bucket of popcorn and was shoveling the contents into his mouth when her producers tried to introduce them, saying, "Harvey, this is the filmmaker, Sarah Kernochan." Harvey just brushed past her without a glance, saying, "C'mon, c'mon, let's go."

After the screening, as crowds of suburban Jerseyites milled about, he turned his back on her and huddled with his marketing team. This is standard operating procedure. Before the distributor chats up the filmmaker, he polls his own people, and gets the numbers. The numbers were bad. He began to lecture Alliance head Robert Lantos, executive Andras Hamori, and Deutchman and Newman about all the changes they were going to have to make, and when he was finished he said, "This was good, we'll have a meeting tomorrow, talk more about this, and when we take eight to ten minutes out of this thing, it's really gonna rock. Is 9:00 A.M. okay with everybody?" He still had his back to Kernochan, who was contractually entitled to final cut. She said, coolly, "Yes, and I'm very curious to know about all these changes we're to be making. I don't know where you'd find eight to ten minutes to cut." Whereupon he wheeled around, purple as an eggplant, and yelled, "*Fuck you!*" Building up a head of steam, he continued, "Fine, if you don't want to benefit the way—" and he threw out the names of several directors—"did, fine, fuck you, I don't need this, I'm a rich man, I have enough money. You filmmakers are the last people anyone should consult about how to market a movie, you don't know anything. We know, we're the experts, that's why they pay me the big bucks!"

Kernochan felt like she'd been hit by a truck, and when Harvey noticed her eyes darting to Deutchman and Newman as in, "Help me!" he bellowed, "Don't look at your producers, 'cause they'll roll over!" Then he pointed to them, shouting, "And you, you may be willing to roll over for these filmmakers, but I don't roll over for filmmakers, that's why I'm successful, and you're not. I'm so fucking rich—and you know what, I own your fucking movie now." In case anyone was feeling left out, he turned to Lantos and Hamori and continued, shouting, "You don't wanna play ball with me? I'll put it on TV. Because it's just another Canadian made-for-TV movie. See you on TV, Robert!" And he stormed off.

Recalls Kernochan, "I was dumbstruck. This man had never said hello to me, paid me any respect at all, or even acknowledged me. And it was my movie! He wasn't even the producer, just the U.S. distributor. The Canadians and Ira and Peter were totally silent. Nobody leapt to my defense."

The next morning, they met for breakfast at the Stanhope Hotel, opposite the Metropolitan Museum of Art. Kernochan hadn't slept. She recalls, "I dreaded seeing him face-to-face. Whenever I saw him my stomach just tightened up." Everyone was smoking cigars, to which she was allergic, but in the spirit of conciliation—"as if I'd done something wrong"—she pledged her cooperation. Harvey was effusively apologetic. He sent flowers, said, "I'm so sorry, this is a habit of mine, it's a terrible thing, I've been working on not having that happen, please forgive me." He explained, "Don't take this personally, I do this to everybody, except for Quentin Tarantino. I do it because I'm passionate about movies." Says James Ivory, who has had reason to think a lot about Weinstein, "He's passionate about films in the same way a dog is passionate about meat. Harvey has a canine appetite for dismembering his own movies." Adds someone close to the film, "That's always his excuse. 'I might have lied, I might have killed one of your children, I might have hijacked an airplane, but I'm passionate about movies!' Temporary insanity. It's part of his manipulative technique. He tries to scare the shit out of people, and the next day he sends the flowers." The source continues, "At one point, his nanny even showed up with his baby girl for a brief moment of, 'I love you honey, Poppa's with you,' before she was whisked away. It was *echt* Harvey—warm, sentimental, spontaneous. On the other hand, it seemed like a scene from a movie, scripted to make Harvey appear human. It was either, it was both—you never knew."

At breakfast, Weinstein turned on the charm, said everything Kernochan had been waiting to hear: "Your movie has a real teen appeal, but it's classy, it's got a message, it's empowering, it's gonna have a real effect on girls." She was thrilled that he "got" her film, listened raptly as he warmed to his subject, "This movie's gonna be so big, I'm gonna put it in hundreds of theaters, sixteen hundred theaters!"

Kernochan's mantra was, "He is not my enemy, he is my teacher"—which she repeated to herself several times a day. During the next few months, the two exchanged a lengthy series of faxes, which made it clear that Weinstein was giving the movie minute attention, watching it over and over again, cut by cut. The protocol of these communications involved insincere flattery on both sides, followed by insistent requests for excisions on Harvey's part and restorations on Kernochan's. The changes Harvey wanted were by no means confined to pacing. He wanted to alter the essence of the movie, recutting to a specific demographic. At one point he said, "We have to appeal to young males too, because the girls' audience is not big enough." She protested, "But this movie is written for girls. I put in enough interesting underwear so that the boys can have fun too." She adds, "Even though he said the test screenings don't tell the whole story, for him they do. He loves the game of seeing the scores go up. He's hooked on the numbers, almost like a gambler. It's a God thing." But the scores were not going up. It was clear that the Miramax fixes were not working.

Eventually, it became clear to her that Harvey was losing interest. It took longer and longer for him to respond to her faxes, sometimes as much as a month, although he still kept asking for changes, more cuts. It was as if he were second-guessing every one of her editing decisions, remaking the film vicariously through her. Says Kernochan, "It's not enough for him to be a great distributor. Now he thinks he's a great producer. He sees himself in the David O. Selznick mold. He wants to horn in on every decision. He wants to be the auteur."

Indeed, *Playing for Keeps* had done nothing to dampen Weinstein's ardor for directing. (In a *New York Times* piece published in 2001, he confessed that he wanted to direct a Leon Uris novel called *Mila 18*.) At the very least, he sees himself as the filmmaker's partner. In one fax to Kernochan dated February 19, 1998, Harvey wrote, "Virtually all of the films with the Miramax banner are the result of collaborative efforts with filmmakers, myself, our post-production team, etc." He complained that he never got credit for his contribution. "Our work is always anonymous," he wrote, "and almost always unacknowledged." Harvey was in a bind. Publicly, he had to defer to the filmmakers. Privately, he craved the credit he believed was rightfully his. Even Tarantino was not immune. Recalls Spike Lee, "He told me himself, he's the one that cut *Pulp Fiction*. 'I cut *Pulp Fiction*.' I'm not lyin'. He probably cut *Citizen Kane* too, right?"

The degree to which Miramax releases represented a "collaborative" effort was, of course, debatable. How collaborative could it have been with Harvey pressing the straight-to-video gun against Kernochan's temple? Weinstein's initial *"Fuck you!"* outburst had established the ground rules under which she labored. But there was some truth to Harvey's claim. His suggestions were not capricious; he had a rationale for every one, and to a degree he was amenable to reason, occasionally restoring footage when he recognized that his cuts hurt the picture. Says Kernochan, "I actually learned quite a lot from him in terms of editing. Not only did some of his cuts improve the momentum, but Harvey paid for a day of reshoots, which the Canadians never would have done."

Weinstein treated Lantos and Hamori with contempt. They had been paying for Miramax's test screenings, paying for Kernochan's editing team to stay on and implement Miramax's changes. Harvey was doing what he often does with genres he's not used to: he goes to school at someone else's expense.

Eventually Alliance grew fearful that this process would never end and pulled the plug. Then everything changed. Weinstein was not about to continue fussing with the picture on his own dime. Alliance set a date for the Canadian release. Harvey agreed to open it in the U.S. one week later, the last week of August 1998.

As spring 1998 rolled around, Kernochan was feeling pretty good. The film was locked, she thought she was finally going to get her 1,600 theaters. She met with the Miramax publicity department, Deutchman met with the marketing people. In April, Miramax sent her artwork for comment. Kernochan wrote an upbeat memo to Harvey in which she said, "I'm a lot like Pinocchio waiting for the Blue Fairy—I'm waiting for the legendary magic of Miramax marketing to give my film, at long last, its life." But alas, the Blue Fairy was otherwise engaged—perhaps in pre-pre-production for Spielberg's AI. May went by, June turned into July, and still there was no publicity. There were not even any plans for publicity. By the middle of the month, Kernochan finally realized there was never going to be any publicity. Miramax gave her release date to 54.

Alliance was humiliated. Lantos "felt very much like he had his balls cut off," says Kernochan. In a blistering letter to Harvey, he wrote on July 17, "We release thirty of your pictures theatrically *per year* . . . winners and losers. We do not junk the pictures we don't like. We get behind all of them. . . . The one time you have the opportunity to get behind one of our films, you choose instead to flush it down to the nearest video store. That is after five months of reediting, rescoring, and retitling to your specifications at our expense. . . . Furthermore, you have not paid us the minimum guarantee due on delivery." He referred to Harvey derisively as "the great champion of independent films."

54 finally opened in Kernochan's theaters on the weekend before Labor Day 1998. It opened to mixed, but generally scornful reviews. Whether Christopher's cut would have worked better than the film Miramax released is besides the point. Miramax, wrapped in the indie mantle, behaved like the studios at their worst. 54 did indifferent business, and as a result, Christopher's promising career went into turnaround. *The Mayor of Castro Street*, which he was supposed to direct for HBO, was canceled. Says one

person connected to the film, "This whole thing was so painful, it sucked so badly, it almost made me leave the film business. I'm embarrassed to be associated with it." Editor Lee Percy concurred. He says, "After 54, I was ready to leave the business." The only thing Christopher will say is, "No comment."

While 54 was being shot down in the U.S., Harvey was at the Venice Film Festival for the premiere of *Rounders*, directed by John Dahl and starring Matt Damon and Edward Norton. As was its habit, Miramax intervened during casting, trying to get Dahl to hire actors with whom Harvey wanted to forge relationships or who would help the picture overseas, but who weren't right for the parts. For the John Malkovich role, which demands an actor who can just sit at a table with a deck of cards eating cookies and still project menace, Harvey wanted an action star. When Dahl remonstrated, the Miramax executive on the film would say, in a shaky voice, "I don't know if Harvey is going to like this. He really wants this actor, why don't you just cast him. We shouldn't make Harvey mad."

"Well, if Harvey's going to get mad, have him call me, I'll talk to him about it."

"You don't want to get him on the phone, do you?"

Says Dahl, "When you get a phone call from Harvey Weinstein, I swear to God you'd think the president of the United States was calling. They try to use the threat of actually talking to Harvey like it's going to scare you."

On the whole, Dahl says he had a pretty good experience with Weinstein: "I have a tremendous amount of respect for him. He's not afraid to put his money where his mouth is. Unlike a lot of movie executives, he's not just trying to keep his job. They [Miramax] have a great handle on the testing process, they try to do what they can to improve the movie, at the same time they don't overreact." *Rounders* has an unconventional ending where the guy and the girl, played by Damon and Gretchen Mol, go their separate ways. To Dahl's surprise, Miramax left it alone.

"We did really bump heads over the music," he says. "I had found an old Miles Davis piece that I loved from the French film *Elevator to the Gallows*. They just freaked out. It was like, 'Oh my God, jazz, we can't have that.' I just said, 'Gee guys, I don't want to bore anybody but this is what seems right to me.' "

Damon was in the audience, seated near Harvey, when *Rounders* was screened in Venice. He recalls, "At the end of the movie the lights came up, and he turned to me and handed me a videotape. He said, 'Now that you've seen that, this is the real movie!'

" 'Whaddya mean?'

" 'I've changed 320 sound cues. All that jazz is gone.' "

Rounders turned out to be a terrific film, under-appreciated by the reviewers, full of great performances. "To me, *Rounders* was a classic, brilliant Harvey production," Norton says. "Matt, Malkovich, John Turturro, Martin Landau, and me, and it was an $11 million movie. Nobody else could pull that off." But Damon thinks Miramax dumped it, which may be the reason it didn't make more of a splash. "*Shakespeare in Love* was their Oscar movie that Christmas. I'm sure they said, we'll put our eggs in that basket, and let's just throw *Rounders* into this slot and see what happens with it." Nothing happened with it. *Rounders* died, after grossing $23 million.

After Venice, Harvey segued to the next big festival, which was Toronto, in the middle of September. The hot film that year was from Germany, *Run Lola Run*, directed by Tom Tykwer. Harvey had not yet arrived, and the Miramax acquisitions staff, Amy Israel, Jason Blum, and Andrew Stengel, had managed to keep the *Lola* gang in a hotel room in a marathon negotiation that went on for ten or twelve hours. "They try to get you into a spiderweb, and then at the end, Harvey just comes to pick the cherry," explains Tykwer. "There was huge pressure on us to immediately decide for them, but it just felt like a gamble." Eventually, the *Lola* team walked out.

When he arrived the next day, Harvey was furious, told them, "We need to meet, we need to meet." Tykwer continues, "When I got to the meeting, the air was thick and tense, not a nice situation. It was obvious that here was someone who wanted something, and if he wanted it, got it, and now he wasn't getting it, and was extremely upset about it. He was suggesting that this could mean real trouble for us. Legal trouble." According to Tykwer, Harvey said, "You've been sitting with us in a room for twelve hours, and you dare to walk away even though we made an offer and you already accepted our proposal."

"No we didn't."

"Oh yes you did."

"We didn't sign anything."

"Who gives a fuck about the paperwork. If we sit down at the table together, this means we are partners." Tykwer goes on, "Harvey stood up and started to scream at Stefan Arndt, my partner. I stood up and screamed back. I felt like an actor in one of those mob movies spitting out lines like, 'You're insulting my family.' I took Stefan and the lawyer and I said, 'We're going. Nobody screams at us.' We left, and I heard these footsteps coming down the hall behind us, boom, boom, boom. We got into the elevator, and these hands grabbed the doors at the last moment and forced them open. It was like Terminator 2 coming back at us."

Tykwer proceeded to meet with Sony Classics. He hit it off so well with Michael Barker that they quickly came to terms, even though Sony's was a lower offer, $600,000 as opposed to the million or so that Miramax had floated, according to the director. "Sony did a great job," concludes Tykwer. "And we even got money on top of the purchase price from the revenues. I don't know if that would have happened with Miramax."

Later, Harvey vented his displeasure on Blum, flicking a lit cigarette in his general direction. By chance, it landed on Blum's shirt, and the Miramax co-chairman apologized, saying he was aiming for the wastebasket.

Meanwhile, Harvey was getting ready to release Roberto Benigni's *Life Is Beautiful* on October 23. Despite stiff competition later from *Chocolat*, this film has to be considered the lushest bloom of Miramax's kitsch period, its largely successful campaign to inject glucose into the veins of middle-brow American culture. At one time, the spectrum of Miramax's releases was broad enough to include both a *Cinema Paradiso* and a film like *The Cook, the Thief, His Wife, and Her Lover*, and do well with each. But as American indies gobbled up a bigger share of the market at the expense of foreign films, only the sentimental, accessible ones survived. Explains Mark Tusk, the brothers have "strangled the same market that they've promoted."

Life Is Beautiful was the Holocaust version of Weinstein signature films like *My Left Foot* and *Sling Blade*, where being Jewish in Mussolini's Italy is the ethnic equivalent of cerebral palsy or mental retardation, and is no less anodyne. It is a film of such breathtaking moral imbecility that it makes sugarcoated studio efforts to deal with the Final Solution, like *Schindler's List*, look bold by comparison, up there with the truly great cinema of the Holocaust, such as Vittorio De Sica's *The Garden of the Finzi-Continis*, or the giants of documentary, Alain Resnais's *Night and Fog*, Marcel Ophuls's *The Sorrow and the Pity*, and Claude Lanzmann's *Shoah*. Owen Gleiberman, writing in *Entertainment Weekly*, called *Life Is Beautiful* "the first feel-good Holocaust weepie," while in *Time* magazine, Richard Schickel wrote, "Sentimentality is a kind of fascism too, robbing us of judgment and moral acuity, and it needs to be resisted. *Life Is Beautiful* is a good place to start."

The real beauty of *Life Is Beautiful* lies in the way its premise so witlessly mimics the realities of the movie business. When Benigni's character, Guido, and his son, Giosué, find themselves imprisoned in a Nazi death camp, Guido conceals the awful truth by cocooning Giosué in a fantasy. He convinces him that the camp is a game, which will be won by the first player to accumulate 1,000 points. When Giosué hears that children are being gassed, Guido assures him that it is a lie intended to convince him to drop out of the game. Substitute the soothing *Life Is Beautiful* itself for Guido's fantasy and, say, $60 million in grosses for the 1,000 points, and you get the picture. If the price is right, Harvey, the self-professed tough

Jew who told the *New York Times* that he preferred Jews who fought back to Jews who marched off to the camps, had no qualms about flakking a film that endorses the state of mind—denial—in which millions of Jews did just that, comforted by the same delusion this film sells, that, somehow, everything would turn out all right.

Driven by Miramax marketing, *Life Is Beautiful* would gross $57.6 million, way more than any Italian language film ever had before in the United States. *Shakespeare in Love* followed, going into limited release on December 11, and becoming an instant hit, racking up a domestic gross of $100.3 million, significantly less than *Good Will Hunting,* but remarkable nonetheless. (It did $50 million more in foreign, to Universal's delight.) But it is well to remember that out of the thirty-six pictures Miramax released in 1998, there were only two real hits.

SUNDANCE 1999 represented a distinct falling off from the previous year. There was no *High Art,* no *Pi,* no *Smoke Signals,* no *Buffalo 66,* no *Opposite of Sex.* Bingham Ray didn't see much that he liked. He walked out on one film, called *The Blair Witch Project,* snorting, "It's a piece of shit." Later, Artisan bought it. Never one to forgo the last word, Ray quipped, "The only thing scary about *The Blair Witch Project* is how much Artisan paid for it." (*Blair Witch* was "a piece of shit," but it grossed $145 million.) The hot picture was *Happy, Texas,* a mindless comedy starring Steve Zahn, Jeremy Northam, and William H. Macy about two bank robbers in a small Texas town masquerading as a gay couple. Cassian Elwes repped it, and he provoked a bidding war between Miramax and Fox Searchlight, the outcome of which provided a wacky end to the acquisitions bubble. Weinstein rode the bidding bronco, ultimately paying $10 million for the picture. But times had changed, and it was no longer cool to spend that much money for that kind of film. Harvey just looked silly, and actually tried to pretend in the press that he had spent a fraction of that, $2 million. Nobody believed him, especially when Tony Safford, now at Fox, went public with the truth, piling embarrassment on embarrassment. But Harvey was impossible to embarrass, and he turned around and picked up another clinker, *The Castle,* for $6 or $7 million.

After Sundance, encouraged by the rejection of Diller's offer by the October board, Ray and Schmidt continued to beat the bushes for a white knight. The good news was that October seemed to be hitting its stride. Ray was excited by his fall schedule, which included David Lynch's *The Straight Story* and Mike Leigh's latest, *Topsy-Turvy,* his biopic about Gilbert and Sullivan. "I thought we were gonna kick serious ass," he says. But *Topsy-Turvy* had come in at three hours, nineteen minutes, and

Ray wanted Leigh to cut it to two hours, thirty minutes. Ray told him, "Look, Mike, this is a great film, might be your masterpiece, but it's way too unruly to release theatrically and give us a shot at earning the money back." Leigh had final cut if the version he submitted did not exceed 120 minutes. Ray continues, "I had very specific ideas about what could go. And that's what Mike resented. Because I'm not a filmmaker, I'm a distributor, I'm not qualified to make these kinds of comments to people like Mike Leigh. He dismissed my suggestions as being ignorant or uninformed, or completely wrong, 'You don't know what you're talking about.' Mike is very dogmatic. Abrupt. He knows what he knows, and no one else knows as much. He was very upset. We had a lot of unpleasantness. Mike said, 'What're you, Bingham Scissorhands?' " Ray refused to accept the film at three hours plus. Leigh threatened to take his name off it if he were forced to cut it. Eventually, Leigh got it down to a length that he could live with.

But Ray's battle with Leigh was moot, because it quickly became clear that there was not going to be an October Films to release *Topsy-Turvy*. Bronfman had told McGurk, "The company is going one way or another, what the hell is your problem?" On February 25, McGurk took Ray to lunch at the Grill in the Universal commissary. The Universal executive felt that he had to give Ray a reality check. When he had something unpleasant to impart, he'd just blurt it out, no preparation. In this case, he said, "Bingham, you should get the special, the soft shell crabs, and by the way, we're selling October Films!"

Diller came back with a slightly higher offer, $24 million, and the October board approved it. It was all over. Diller combined October with Universal/PolyGram's Gramercy to form USA Films, headed by Greenstein. Not everyone was sympathetic to Ray and Schmidt. Says Donna Gigliotti, "For a smart guy, Bingham must have been really stupid to have lost his company to Scott Greenstein! He didn't help himself by drinking as much as he was doing. He was too old to be doing that kind of stuff. He needed to grow up. It wasn't the '80s anymore." Adds Stacy Spikes, who had left October a year or so before to head up the Urbanworld Film Festival, "No one was ever gonna walk into Miramax and take their company from underneath them. The brothers would put a match to it before you're gonna touch it. Bingham should have thrown a fit, 'Fuck you, I built this, I don't care what the paperwork says, tell the law to come in here and pry my dead cold hand off the helm!' In nature, the things that survive have claws and very sharp teeth. That was missing at October."

To some degree, Ray and Schmidt were just victims of bad luck, a regime at Universal run by a man, Edgar Bronfman, Jr., more interested in music than in film, and in the end, uninterested in either. In eighteen short months, the Universal executives who had godfathered the deal with October—Biondi, McGurk, and Silver—would be gone. As Schmidt puts it, "We had no protection." But in other ways, there was a logic, an inevitability to the decline and fall of October. As Eamonn Bowles puts it, "October had a bunch of private investors who wanted a return on their money. At the end of the day, money is always going to beat art." And of course, *pace* Spikes, Ray and Schmidt did not have nearly the power over the fortunes of their company that the Weinsteins had at one time over theirs. The truth is, October wasn't really their company. Once Ray and Lipsky took on investors, whether Allen & Co. or the studio, the name of the game became profit, and when the company had a few hits, it was the wrecked-by-success story all over again. The iron laws of the marketplace, especially the go-go '90s version, dictated that the company dared not stand still, but had to move forward, get to the "next level." And to do that, it had to attract studio money dispensed by studio executives, carriers of studio values that infected and transformed the culture of October as they had Miramax before it, so that before long the company became unrecognizable. "It's a paradox," says Schmidt. "To continue to grow and capitalize yourself, that's a requirement for success. But to do that is to basically endanger the very nature of the company." October either succeeded in becoming another Miramax and lost its soul, or it fell prey to corporate hustlers and became no more than a chip in a grander game of media poker. Either way, it was going to lose. Would Ray have done it the same way if he'd had it to do over? "I would have kept it private," he says. "I would not have said yes to Universal or to Bain." But, as Schmidt puts it, "If we hadn't done the Universal deal, and then released *Lost Highway*, we would have become extremely private, sitting at home with no place to go. We would have been out of business!"

IT WAS ONLY A DECADE since the brilliance of Miramax marketing had pushed *sex, lies* into the multiplexes of suburban malls and changed the business forever. But the assumption then was that mallrats, far from being the core audience for indie films, were gravy, icing, the difference between a $5 million film and a $10 million or $25 million movie. That's a big difference, and a decade later, the sweet smell of success stung Harvey's nose like a line of coke, and made Miramax turn this formula on its head. By 1998, the multiplexes were no longer gravy; they were his company's meat and potatoes. As the misfortunes of 54 and other Miramax films showed, they were being tailored for malls. Harvey wasn't going to be satisfied until he demonstrated that he could churn out teen movies with the best of them. Miramax began to release pictures like *She's So Lovely* (1997) and *Senseless*, a Marlon Wayans comedy, co-released with Dimension in 1998.

Ironically, it was Eisner himself who tried to call a halt. On the last weekend in January 1999, Miramax released *She's All That*, the Freddie Prinze picture, and won the weekend. On Monday the 30th, Harvey was in the ABC television offices conferring with Eisner, ABC Group chairman Bob Iger, and Kevin Smith on a pitch for an animated series based on *Clerks*. Smith had already had an offer from UPN for twelve episodes with an on-air commitment. Eisner proposed buying six episodes with no guarantee to run all of them. Smith was leaning to UPN, but Harvey told him to go with ABC. He said, "We're all in the same family, so it's in their interest to do well by the show. It's money out of their pocket into their other pocket. Go for it." Smith plumped for ABC.

According to the filmmaker, "Harvey was incredibly proud" of *She's All That*. Eisner said, "Congratulations on the top spot. You did $16 million on that movie, and nobody's in it."

"You see that?" Harvey replied. "I wanted to prove to them that I can make a piece of shit and compete on their level. And I did."

"Yeah, but I really think you should have done that movie through Dimension, at the genre label. Because your label means something. Miramax has value, a certain level of quality. We had the same thing with Touchstone back in the beginning. Then we started making really bad movies, and Touchstone didn't mean anything anymore. If people start to think that Miramax produces stuff like *She's All That*, you're fucking with the brand name." If Eisner understood anything, it was branding. He had a substantial investment in the Miramax name, and he knew that Harvey's ego had committed a crime against the brand—that was stupid and potentially costly.

Smith listened to this exchange with his mouth open. He continues, "It was really weird to see the guy who you consider the king of the world being lectured by his employer. Harvey listened, as opposed to, 'Oh, eat shit, fuck you!' It was more, 'Yeah, yeah, that's your theory.' There was an air of 'Say what you want, I have the number one movie this week.'" The box office spoke louder than Eisner—*She's All That* ultimately earned $63 million, domestic—and his words had little apparent effect. "Miramax, which many consider the hallmark of indie film, functions like a studio," says Smith. "It's no longer the home of independent film, seat-of-your-pants or garage band filmmaking. It's not really a low-budget filmmaking operation anymore. The outlaws have become the in-laws, or better, the law." Or, as Spike Lee puts it, "Miramax tries to play this, We're the little guy shit. They're a studio."

(Ultimately, ABC pulled *Clerks* after two episodes. "They fucked us," says Smith. "We tried to go back to UPN, and they weren't interested." Subsequently, ABC also bought and cancelled another Miramax show, *Wonderland*, written and produced by Kevin Williamson.)

Not only was Harvey doing the indie world a disservice, he was sabotaging himself. By virtue of going toe-to-toe with the studios, Harvey began to deny himself the very advantages that had contributed to Miramax's success in the past. As McGurk puts it, "The original business model was founded on them doing movies where the total investment was less than $15 million, and generally less than $10 million, and if they found a diamond in the rough, like *The English Patient,* they could spend a lot of money in marketing and their overall investment would still be lower than the average. Now the average cost of a Miramax movie has got to be $30, $40, $50 million. As they've gotten bigger and bigger, the old model might just as well be thrown in the wastebasket."

Take *Kate & Leopold,* the fish-out-of-water time travel romance which Cathy Konrad resuscitated by convincing Jim Mangold to rewrite and direct it. It represented a dramatic change of pace for a filmmaker who usually gravitated toward darker material, like *Cop Land.* Mangold had seriously mixed feelings about working for Miramax again. "The level of creative interference is so much more intense at Miramax than anywhere else," he says, "and it doesn't come with a brush and a beret, either. It's the most base kind of interference—about test scores, and 'This person is unlikable,' and so on." Still, he owed the Weinsteins two pictures, and this seemed like a painless way to burn off one of his commitments. But nothing at Miramax is ever painless. While he was writing *Kate & Leopold,* he left the nest to write and direct *Girl, Interrupted* for Sony in 1998, which won an Oscar for Angelina Jolie. Harvey didn't appreciate his boys winning Oscars for other studios, and when Mangold finally handed in his script, Weinstein complained, "It took you two and a half years to deliver this."

"Where's Quentin's World War II movie?" Mangold snapped, referring to Tarantino's yet to be finished screenplay, *Inglorious Bastards.*

"That man made this company!" Harvey yelled. "So you don't compare to him." But when Meg Ryan expressed interest in *Kate & Leopold,* all was forgiven. The old Harvey would have balked at her $15 million price tag, the way he had refused to meet John Travolta's price for *Cop Land* and turned to Sylvester Stallone instead. But times had changed. Says Konrad, "It used to be, talent would do his movies at bargain prices because he was doing risky projects no one else would make. But when you're doing a romantic comedy, you're in Meg Ryan's wheelhouse. Why should she give him a bargain for something she gets full freight on at six other studios in town? Where's the deal?"

Everything that the success of *Pulp Fiction* had augured had come to pass. Transforming itself from an acquisition-driven company into a production-based company, Miramax was forced to lay out more money for fewer films, turning away from its its high volume strategy, and therefore losing the protection afforded by the law of large numbers. Miramax had built its success on taking risks, but the costlier the pictures, the more risk-averse the company had become. Says Konrad, "At that point they were casting movies around who got talk shows. Harvey wanted anybody from *Saturday Night Live*." Paradoxically, however, the more Miramax attempted to avert risk by protecting itself with expensive casts, the more risky the pictures became.

Harvey had once been quoted as saying, "Michael Eisner can't tell me anything," and he never ceased trying to prove it. After he hit the jackpot with *She's All That*, he used that as a yardstick to measure other films, including *Dogma*. Says Smith, "Harvey's become very score-centric. When we tested *Dogma*, all he was talking about was the quadrants. After one screening, he said, 'Okay, we're killing these two quadrants, what we don't have is these quadrants up here, with the young girls. We're gonna need all four if we're gonna do what we did with *She's All That*.' " Smith, his voice rising on an updraft of disbelief, says he asked, "Did you just compare this movie on any level whatsoever to *She's All That*? Are you seriously talking about marketing this film in a way that you would market a throwaway teen movie? It's apples and oranges, man."

Under pressure from Disney, Miramax sold *Dogma* to Lion's Gate, the Canadian distributor. "Harvey had his chance to put it out on Good Friday, but he was more than happy to get rid of it," Smith adds. Although, he says, Weinstein nevertheless managed the marketing campaign: "I think a blind eye was turned to the fact that he was working on it."

Good Will Hunting had just finished its run, and Harvey wanted to splay Affleck and Damon all over the ads. "We had had all these deals governing how we appeared, and they totally screwed us over," Damon explains. "We said, 'This is an ensemble movie, don't put our names above the title, that's cheap and misrepresenting it, but they made me and Ben really large anyway. At the end of the day they were just doing what they were doing. It's appropriate to approach any relationship with Harvey with a healthy amount of cynicism, because he is what he is."

When *Jay and Silent Bob Strike Back* came out two years later, in which Damon had a walk-on, it happened all over again. Says Damon, "They offered me a whole lot of money to do a scene in the movie and appear on the poster. I said no because of what happened with *Dogma*. Also, I thought the cameo would be funnier if it's unexpected. 'The deal I'll strike with you is, I'll do it for free, if you don't use me on the poster.' They go, 'Okay, great,' because they don't have to write a check. So, deal! Six months later, I was in Argentina doing this indie movie with Gus Van Sant. We started getting these frantic phone calls from Miramax. Gus was laughing, going, 'Uh oh, they want something from you.' They said, 'We want to use you in the trailer.' I said, 'Guys, the whole point is that it's a surprise, so no.' Then the movie came out, and I got frantic phone calls—

when Harvey wants you, he will find you no matter where you are. They said, 'We want to use you in the TV spots. The cat's out of the bag, everyone knows you're in the movie now, so your argument doesn't hold water anymore. Do it for Kevin.' On the one hand, I wanted to say, 'No, no, no, because that was what we agreed on.' You don't want to reward that kind of behavior, but on the other hand I wanted to do what was right for Kevin. Harvey is very in tune with who's friends with who—'Just do it for him, help him out, it's not for me, I don't need this.' Then that way, he doesn't owe you a favor, the other guy owes you a favor. I caved. I went, 'Jesus, fine, just go ahead.' The next day, I'm flipping channels, and I saw the ads. They already had 'em cut and out."

Lion's Gate released *Dogma* on November 12, 1999. The film, which cost about $10 million to make, grossed $30.7 million domestically, and sold a phenomenal one million DVDs. "Harvey and Bob made out like fuckin' bandits on *Dogma*," says Smith. "We had our salaries up front, but we never saw a dime of that money. They'll send you profit participation statements where you're looking at it and going, 'Okay, on paper I can see that your byzantine labyrinthine logic has proven that I owe you money, somehow, for the movie that I know you fucking profited off of. I'm not stupid, I know that there's a lot of money we're not seeing. The *Chasing Amy* P&A, which they said was $7 million, I could never understand how, because we never went that wide, no more than five hundred screens. We didn't buy a lot of TV ads. They'll charge you for all manner of things, throw anything into your account." Responds Miramax, "*Dogma* incurred $20 million in production costs, including interest and overhead, and $16 million in distribution costs. In addition, Miramax had to pay distribution fees to other distributors. It performed weakly abroad. Kevin was paid everything he was entitled to. The P&A costs on *Chasing Amy* were almost $9 million, including $3.3 million on TV advertising."

Every time Smith reached the end of his rope, Harvey, a master of the extravagant gesture, managed to reel him in. "The kindest thing I saw that man do had nothing to do with business," he recalls. One night, Smith found himself in Harvey's company, flying out of Burbank on their way to New York in the Miramax jet, accompanied by his pal, actor Jason Mewes, who regularly plays Jay to his Silent Bob. "It came out that Jay's mom was HIV positive, flat out dying of AIDS, and had been for a few years," Smith continues. "Harvey said to him, 'When we get home, I'm gonna give you my number, and you call me, and we're gonna set your mother up with the best HIV doctor in the city, if not the world. We're not going to let your mother die.' I was blown away. Here was a dude—Mewes is not a real big earner for Miramax, he didn't know from fuckin' Mewes, and he certainly didn't know from fuckin' Mewes's mother. Most of us were waiting for her to kick, because she was a horrible woman, would send him out to deliver drugs when he was a kid, took him out stealing credit cards out of mailboxes when he was six, seven years old, got him into drugs and shit. So on the one hand, I was going, 'You're saving the wrong person, man, use it for somebody who really deserves it, not this horrible woman who's fucked this kid's life up from day one.' But for a guy in his position to give a shit about this dude's mom, I was floored by the gesture, because it wasn't a gesture, it wasn't, 'Gimme a call, we'll see what we can do.' He followed through, sent a fuckin' limo to pick her up, bring her into New York from New Jersey, set her up with the doctor. The humanity on display at that moment was displayed for nobody, it wasn't for show. It was the one moment I've seen him be him without having an ulterior motive or like, the world is watching—it was just three guys on a fuckin' jet in the middle of the night. Moments like that, I went, 'All is forgiven!' These people gave me a career. It's not even like they saved me from the studio system. Without them picking up *Clerks*, nobody picks up *Clerks* and I'm still working at the convenience store paying off that movie saying, 'I can't believe I put that on credit cards.' To me it's never been about cash. Call it loyalty, call it Catholic guilt, whatever. So I always feel like, rather the devil you know than the devil you don't."

This was by no means the only time Harvey helped friends, relatives of friends, and mere acquaintances in life-theatening situations, and the beneficiaries of his medical largesse are grateful and not about to look the gift horse in the mouth. But whether these gestures are as selfless as Smith likes to think is debatable. For someone as ego-starved as Harvey, it gives him the ultimate high: the power over life and death—or at least the illusion of it. Harvey had already placed himself at the center of a vast web of favors rendered and received by which he exercises a degree of control over a sizable sector of people who matter, and by extending his hand in this way, he merely ups the ante. Nor is he shy about calling in the chits. In the midst of a heated argument with, say, an employee whose child he has directed to a doctor or whose care he has paid for, he is perfectly capable of asking, "And how's your kid doing?"

Not everyone felt like Smith. It was getting harder and harder for Harvey to keep his young directors on the reservation. "He was giving us a break that others hadn't," explains Jim Mangold. "There's this incredible debt you feel when you're a first-time filmmaker, and Harvey plays on that. I felt sometimes that I was working with a historic character, some kind of Selznick or Zanuck. But the problem is the second you get some respect for yourself, you realize that some of your decisions work, and some of the things he was sure were asinine get a laugh he didn't think they would—and you understand he's fallible, and you've got to stand up to him. So the next time around, when other people would like to hire you,

you don't quite feel so beholden that you go, 'You're right, Harvey, I owe you everything.' It's not Frank Sinatra with the Don anymore, and you don't have to play Vegas this year if you don't want to."

ON FEBRUARY 9, when the Academy Award nominations were announced, DreamWorks's Spielberg-directed *Saving Private Ryan*, a powerful and in many ways bold departure from cookie cutter war films, despite occasional backsliding, was widely regarded as the front runner, picking up eleven nominations. *Shakespeare* rang up a surprising thirteen. (Miramax had two Best Picture nominations, the other being *Life Is Beautiful*, while several other Miramax films got one each, bringing the company's total to a record twenty-four.) The battle royal between the two companies, led by old friends Weinstein and Jeffrey Katzenberg, was only slightly less brutal than the images of carnage on the beaches of Normandy offered up by Spielberg's epic, and kicked off a long-running feud between Miramax and DreamWorks.

On March 15, 1999, film journalist Nikki Finke published a column in *New York* magazine. Calling *Shakespeare* "froth," she charged, "Miramax pays a fleet of ultraveteran Hollywood publicists (who also happen to be Academy members)—including Warren Cowan, Dick Guttman, Gerry Pam, and Murray Weissman—not to generate press coverage but to schmooze their prominent Academy colleagues. As cronies of the Academy's graying voters, they are paid not just during the five-month Oscar season but nearly year-round—a practice unheard of elsewhere in the industry." She also called attention to how much Miramax was spending. "True independents might spend up to $250,000 on an Oscar campaign; the majors, $2 million," she wrote. "Miramax is estimated by competitors to have spent at least $5 million on its campaign for *Shakespeare*." Worse, she accused Harvey himself of launching a Richard Nixon-style dirty tricks campaign against *Ryan* by telling critics that *Ryan* "peaks in the first twenty minutes." Weinstein denies it. "It is complete bullshit," he says. "I love that movie. I called Steven two days after I saw it and said that to him." Miramax believed that DreamWorks was behind Finke's piece, in particular DreamWorks VP Terry Press. "I always think that Terry Press is behind everything," he continues. "These people, they have to win everything. Me? I'm happy to be in the race, I'm that scrappy player who got invited into the game and was happy to shake things up. The point of it is, when I lose, I'm not a sore loser. I've spent my entire life coming up from nowhere, winning, losing, whatever. We never malign somebody else's movie."

In L.A., Cowan, the elderly former head of the powerful publicity firm Rogers & Cowan, arranged a series of dinners for Benigni with his influential clients and friends, including Kirk Douglas, Jack Lemmon, and Elizabeth Taylor. Says former publicist Mark Urman, "Benigni moved into L.A. for a month during the peak of the voting period, and every night somebody was having a party for him. Roberto made a lot of friends, and it won him an acting Oscar even though I think history will tell us that it was perhaps not deserved. He won it for his dinner performances."

The Academy Awards were held on March 21. By this time, *Shakespeare* had a poker hand of producers, Harvey, Gigliotti, David Parfitt, Marc Norman, and Ed Zwick, altogether too many for Harvey, who was trying hard to convince Norman and Zwick to drop their credits. He called Zwick in the middle of the night. According to Parfitt, his argument was, "Everyone knows you weren't there, didn't do anything. It's an embarrassment, people will laugh at you." Harvey thundered, "I'm going to ruin your career in Hollywood, you'll never work again. You don't know how many enemies you have in this town, you don't know who you're dealing with, you fucking . . . ," and so on. Norman recalls that Harvey, who believed that everybody had a price, offered him about $100,000 to withdraw his producing credit, and threatened to attack his writing credit as well. But both men held on. (Harvey denies having this conversation with Zwick.)

As the ceremony was coming to a close, Harrison Ford walked onstage to award the Oscar for Best Picture. A friend of Spielberg's, he seemed visibly shocked when he opened the envelope, and spoke the three magic words: "*Shakespeare in Love.*" The picture's five producers trooped up onto the stage to accept the Oscar. There had been plenty of discussion among them about handling the logistics onstage in the event that the film won the brass ring. Zwick understood that Gigliotti would speak first, then himself, then Harvey. But, says Parfitt, "There was never an intention to let Zwick speak." Indeed, according to Norman, "Harvey came on like a linebacker from the backfield just as Zwick was moving toward the microphone, pushed him out of the way, and grabbed the mike." By the time Zwick regained his composure, the music had come up and Harvey was beaming like the Cheshire Cat. The image of Weinstein regnant, basking in the refulgence of the bejeweled audience before billions of viewers worldwide, said it all: at last, as Smith put it, the outsiders had truly become insiders.

Terry Press was in the audience at the Dorothy Chandler Pavilion. She was confident that *Ryan* would win Best Picture. When she saw the Oscar awarded to *Shakespeare*, she felt her face begin to burn. She was convinced that the system had been manipulated and that an injustice had been done. (Miramaxers just scoffed. From their point of view, *Shakespeare* was an actors' piece, and the actors, who make up the largest voting bloc in the Academy, threw their weight behind it.) Afterward, as Press approached Harvey to congratulate him, she exchanged a glance with Katzenberg, her boss, and muttered, "Never again!"

John Madden found himself a very hot director, but Miramax held options on his next two pictures. In the movie business, options are currency, like frequent flier miles. Most studios show some flexibility in enforcing them. If a director wants to do a picture somewhere else, they "suspend and extend," explains former Fox CEO Bill Mechanic, "suspend for the duration of whatever movie they take [elsewhere], and then the option is extended out. When you enforce a relationship, more often than not, you burn bridges. So you don't use a hammer." Not Harvey. Madden had two projects at Miramax, but neither was ready. He got excited about a script, *Shanghai*, by Hossein Amini. It was owned by Sony, and Mel Gibson was interested. In exchange for allowing Columbia to use Madden, Harvey wanted to partner. But, according to Mike Medavoy, whose Phoenix Pictures had a share of the movie, "Sony didn't want Harvey," and cashiered Madden rather than join Miramax.

"In some ways it's an old-fashioned feudal system," observed the director. "One doesn't like to think of oneself as a bargaining chip. I like to think of myself as a filmmaker."

Then Universal offered him *Captain Corelli's Mandolin* after the director of choice, Roger Michell, had a heart attack while the picture was well into pre-production. Universal stood to lose millions, with the star, Nicolas Cage, signed to a pay-or-play deal. Miramax demanded an assortment of distribution rights, as well as domestic rights to *Bridget Jones's Diary*, even though Miramax held no options on the director or any of the actors on that film. According to Working Title's Tim Bevan, who had a piece of *Corelli*, Universal chairman Stacey Snider "didn't want to give up domestic [on *Bridget*]. She didn't want to give anything to Harvey." But she was backed into a corner. Observes Mechanic, "They gave up half the movie, which is insane. For me, you just move on to the next director." Weinstein's option strategy nicely supplemented his skill at picking up projects in turnaround. If he couldn't develop films himself, he could attach himself, limpetlike, to films developed by others. As he put it himself, sounding very much like the cat who swallowed the canary, "It's a wonderful opportunity. We get to do big movies with no risk."

Norman, who originated *Shakespeare* in the first place, walked away a happy man. He won two Oscars, but he failed to benefit from the success of the film. He had 7.5 net points, more than any of the other net participants. "Miramax spent a lot of money promoting the picture, and a lot of money on the Oscar campaign, and their argument has always been, 'We spent all the money,' " he says. "I came close to auditing them, but nobody was interested in going into it with me. All I know is, a picture that makes $300 million worldwide does not provide money for people with net points. I'm going to put that on my tombstone." Harvey, on the other hand, says, "I made a small fortune on the movie."

October's Oscar party was held at the Chateau Marmont, in the garden, tented for the occasion. It was a peculiar affair, a celebration for some, a wake for others, not unlike October's Thomas Vinterberg picture, *The Celebration*, in which a family gathering marking the birthday of the patriarch is transformed into something of a scandal. The winners—Greenstein and his loyalists—were shaking hands and quaffing champagne, while the losers—Ray, Schmidt, and the October gang—spent the evening looking the other way.

In July 1999, Ray made his exit from the company he had founded with Jeff Lipsky eight years earlier. Eight months later, on Monday, April 10, 2000, at 10:30 in the morning, a little more than a week after that year's Oscars, he drove his black Audi A4 into a tree less than a mile from his home in Mount Kisco, New York. Ever a child of the 1960s, he had been out late the night before at a Crosby, Stills, Nash, and Young reunion concert at the Meadowlands. He had been drinking, but his blood alcohol level was within legal limits. Six weeks earlier, however, he had quit smoking, and was taking Zyban to keep himself off cigarettes, which may have been a factor. In any event, he drifted across the narrow country road and into a tree. He was going no more than twenty-five or so miles per hour, but he was unbelted, and the collision was severe enough to throw him against the windshield and then down to the floor on the passenger side, with his legs twisted up in the wreckage. His left upper arm was badly fractured, and it was bleeding freely. Blood was flowing from his ears and massive lacerations on his forehead. Both the front and side airbags had deployed, some punctured by the sharp end of his exposed humerus, and all four were smeared with blood. His Audi looked like Princess Di's car. Ray had to be cut out and helicoptered to Westchester Medical Center in Valhalla, where he lay in a coma for three days. When he awoke, his nurse said, "I was the one who met the helicopter when you got in here. You looked like shit. We didn't think you were going to make it." Ray glanced down at his leg, which was hurting, and saw bone. The doctors had dug trenches on either side of his tibia to relieve the pressure from swelling under the fascia that connect it to the muscles and tendons. The trenches were so wide they couldn't be stitched up and had to be closed with skin grafts. The doctors had expected him to die, and one day he woke up to find a chaplain sitting by his bed with a clipboard, who said, "Hello, Ray!" Everyone called him "Ray Bingham." Flipping through his papers, the chaplain rattled on with forced cheeriness: "How'ya feelin' today? You feel like a chat?" Ray does not have much use for religion, and all he could muster was, "More morphine!" He observes, "I didn't come out of it with a spiritual thing, not me. If there was a moral to it, it was that I literally hit a wall. I was just asleep at the wheel."

Ray lay on his back with his right leg and left arm elevated for three weeks and then some. He was issued two tickets, one for driving at an unreasonable speed and one for driving without a seatbelt. One day a nurse saw him watching movies on a portable Panasonic DVD player that Schmidt's son had lent him. She asked, "Are you in the movie business?"

"Yeah."

"What do you do?"

"I used to run a company called October Films." He noticed her eyes glaze over, and he added, "You ever hear of Miramax?"

"Of course I've heard of Miramax."

"It was kinda like Miramax, but not so successful."

Twelve
The King of New York
1999–2000

• How Harvey Weinstein romanced Tina Brown, got sick unto
death, made Uma Thurman cry and Martin Scorsese crazy—while
Steven Soderbergh broke the *Traffic* gridlock.

"I told Marty, to make Gangs of New York, *'You really sold your soul to the
devil on this one. The devil himself. Satan! Lucifer!'"*

—SPIKE LEE

By 1999, it seemed that Harvey had become bored. Acquisitions had lost its
luster, and *Happy, Texas*, the previous year's Sundance prize with its embarrassing $10 million price tag, earned a meager $2 million when it was released on October 1. Its failure cut the thread that ran from *sex, lies*
through *Cinema Paradiso, The Crying Game, The Piano, Sling Blade,
Trainspotting,* and *Life Is Beautiful.* The company snapped its acquisitions
purse shut until 2002, when Miramax paid a mind-boggling $20 million-
plus for *Hero*, which Harvey thought would become the new *Crouching
Tiger, Hidden Dragon.*

Indeed, Harvey allowed his crack acquisitions division, which had been
the mainstay of the company for so many years, to deliquesce into a puddle
of mediocrity. Amy Israel and Jason Blum both left in 2000 to start their
own production company, an exit possibly—at least on Blum's part—ac-
celerated by the cigarette-flicking incident over *Run Lola Run* at the
Toronto Film Festival in 1998. As Geoff Gilmore puts it, speaking of their
successors, "They're not in contact with me anymore. These guys always
used to call me up and say, 'What's going on, what's good?' The new staff is
much less sophisticated about what makes films interesting and what
makes them breakout possibilities. I don't even know their names.
Harvey's competitors, his peers, are trouncing him."

For a while, Harvey didn't seem to care. At Cannes in 1999 he sat on his hands. The moral of *Shakespeare in Love* seemed obvious: why get your life threatened over a tiny film like *Priest* with virtually no upside, when you can make pots of money and get showered with praise, including an Oscar, for producing costume dramas, and meanwhile passing on pictures like *Kids, Boogie Nights, Election, Happiness, American Beauty,* and later, *Traffic*. It was a no-brainer. As Lechner explains, "When Harvey became largely a producer, he began working more than ever off his own taste. And his taste is for feel-good movies, movies about food, movies about World War II, movies about underdogs who triumph. And as Miramax got more successful, won more Oscars, he felt freer to be himself." Success allowed Harvey to be Harvey, and Harvey is a man who feels a good deal more affinity for Claude Lelouch than he does for David Lynch.

For indie companies, "Production is a trap," points out attorney Linda Lichter. "Once you start spending money on production, you have less money for acquisition. And acquisitions financed outside the system are generally made with more freedom, are genuinely independent. Doing a picture at Miramax—or any of the other mini-majors—became no different than doing a picture for Disney. They are subject to the same kinds of financial, risk-averse pressures that the studio is. You have executives who think they're producers, who nitpick the script, take the voice out of it, and remake it the way they want. And all of a sudden, it's denatured, it no longer has that verve and the charm that we all look for."

In other words, at the same time the indie world was being Miramaxed, Miramax itself was being Disneyized. Harvey took indie films and rubbed down their sharp edges, sweetened their voices, just as he had Americanized foreign films in the old days. Miramax became, as it were, a Trojan horse through which studio values came to permeate much of the indie scene. As John Schmidt puts it, "The game of making $30 or $40 million putative art films, with $25 or $30 million marketing campaigns, has infected everyone. Everyone's spending more, and everyone's making less." It was not a conspiracy; no one set out, exactly, to subvert the indie world. Like Disney, the Miramax folk were just trying to maximize return on investment, in short, make money. Everything else followed. Somehow, it all just "happened." Eventually it became clear that it wasn't Quentin Tarantino who was the voice of Miramax, it was John Madden and Lasse Hallström.

Despite the spats—the raised voices, thrown dishes, and slammed doors—Miramax and Disney had more in common with each other than either cared to admit. Disney was very much cast in the mold of Barry Diller's activist Paramount of the late 1970s and early 1980s, thanks to former Dilleristas Eisner and Katzenberg. Paramount kept a tight rein on costs, gave writers voluminous notes, thought nothing of rapping the knuckles of directors and stepping in itself, rewriting, reshooting, and re-cutting. So did Disney, and more important, so did Miramax. Miramax was making money, winning Oscars, and beefing up its library. As Disney exec-utive Rob Moore, who had taken over the Weinsteins when McGurk left, puts it, "Miramax was delivering, and Disney was delivering." Which is why the friction between them may have created a lot of smoke but not much fire. Both sides had strong incentives to make the arrangement work. Dis-ney understood that without the Weinsteins, Miramax was just an empty shell. For their part, the brothers knew that Disney owned the ground they stood on, which is to say, the name and the library, and that financing them from scratch would be an expensive proposition for any other studio. Be-sides, the way their deal was structured, they would be leaving too much money on the table to just walk away. After *Kids* and *Priest*, McGurk went to Eisner and said, "Hey, do you want me to go and sell Miramax, because I would love to get a multiple of 10 to 20 on what we paid for it. For the sport of it." Eisner responded, "As long as I'm around, we're never selling that company." Says McGurk, "He thought that they had built one of the best brands in the business, so all that talk of leaving was baloney, on both sides. Look what Disney did with their business. They couldn't get arrested from a profit standpoint before Disney bought them, and now they're making $150 million a year."

Miramax's first phase, its Bronze Age, lasted seven years, from 1979, when the company was founded, to 1986, when *Playing for Keeps* was re-leased and the handful of original employees, some burned-out and bitter, exited en masse. The second or Silver Age lasted six or six and a half years, from 1987 to the middle of 1993, when Disney bought the company and another sizable group of staff left. The third phase, the Golden Age, lasted five years, from the Disney sale in mid-1993 to the *Shakespeare* Best Picture Oscar. During this period, Miramax blew the competition away, and at the same time enjoyed enormous critical goodwill and commercial success picking up films in turnaround, while Dimension broke records with *The Crow* and the *Scream* cycle. Harvey succeeded in building his own stable of stars—Ben Affleck, Matt Damon, and Gwyneth Paltrow—and produced one superstar director, Quentin Tarantino.

But in the wake of *Shakespeare,* as Miramax veered to its right, out of the fast lane into the center lane, another group of key staffers defected. It wasn't only the acquisitions team; in the second half of the 1990s, Linde, Webster, Lechner, Bowles, Gigliotti, and Foley joined them. The third stage of the rocket fell away. The glory days were over, at least for a while.

But Harvey never charted a course he couldn't, or wouldn't change. No sooner had he turned his back on acquisitions than he was consumed with envy as he watched his competitors move into the vacuum. Recalls Kevin Smith, "We were in Harvey's office the Monday after *Blair Witch* had made a load of money, and *Time* magazine, with the film on the cover, was in his in-box. I pointed to it and said, 'What happened?' He was like, 'I have no idea.' He was really pissed off that it wasn't his. And pissed off that somebody could do a Miramax and not *be* Miramax." The old rivalries may have produced pangs of jealousy, but increasingly it seemed that his real competition was closer to home—namely, his brother, Bob, who was practically releasing a blockbuster a year. As Cassian Elwes puts it, "The success of Dimension changed Miramax into a company that was looking to make $100 million profits as opposed to $20 million profits. They went up to the next level." As Dimension soared, Harvey borrowed Bob's stars, like Neve Campbell, for movies like 54. Smith continues, "We were telling Harvey that we didn't want to make *Jay and Silent Bob* at Miramax, we wanted to make it at Dimension, because we didn't feel it was a Miramax movie. I said, 'Look, man, this movie is a genre movie, I know you're making genre movies over here now with *She's All That*, but I don't want to be the guy who contributes to the downfall of what Miramax means.' What Eisner said rang very true to me. Harvey was fine about it, said, 'You pick my brother to make the commercial movie with, I gotta make the arty shit.' But later on I heard that it bugged him that we went across the hall."

Harvey had his Oscar and had showed Hollywood that he could acquire, produce, and market with the best. In the process he and his brother had created a wildly profitable mini-major. Like Oliver Twist, albeit in somewhat less straitened circumstances and with considerably less politesse, Harvey cried, "Please, sir, I want some more!" But it wasn't so much success or money that he sought, it was power, influence, and respect. Harvey's tireless publicity troops splattered items about him across the canvas of the movie business, publishing, and shortly politics; he became a veritable Jackson Pollock of self-promotion. Says producer Scott Rudin, "You've got somebody who whenever he farts, he feels the need to issue a press release about it." Practically leasing space in the gossip columns of Manhattan's tabloids, he fancied himself the face of the city. To his enemies, he was just a hypocrite. "He tried to position himself as Mr. New York, the unofficial mayor," says Spike Lee. "So when he talks about what he does for New York—'Hey motherfucker, how 'bout you shoot some of your films in New York instead of taking all those runaway productions up to Toronto?' Nobody talks about that shit."

Harvey's big problem in this regard was that the city already had a mayor, the law 'n' order former prosecutor Rudolph Giuliani, so in his own mind, he became the "sheriff" of New York. (There's a poster for *Nevada Smith* behind his desk, Steve McQueen with his gun.) Still gnawed by whatever it is that gnaws you when you've been born in Brooklyn and raised in Queens, dropped out of college, and been shunned by the kings and queens of Hollywood who couldn't see the prince for the frog, he hungered to conquer new territories, lands that would give him entrée into what must have seemed to him to be the intellectually soigné worlds of magazine and book publishing. And he wanted Tina Brown, former editor of *Vanity Fair* and then editor of *The New Yorker,* as his hood ornament.

On July 8, 1998, Brown stunned the media world by "ankling" *The New Yorker* in favor of a new venture, a magazine to be published by Miramax. *Talk,* as it was to be known, created yet another rift between Weinstein and Eisner. The Disney chairman had his own relationship with Brown, and he was after her to do something for him. "The Tina Brown hiring was a big problem," says Joe Roth. "Michael thought he was a friend of Tina's and Tina kept trying to get Harvey to allow her to let Michael know that this conversation was going on—which was totally outside the business plan, and had to be approved. Harvey called Michael at ten o'clock the night before it was announced. Michael hit the roof. He thought having a movie company and a magazine, especially an expensive magazine, was a conflict, and he was against it. It was very different from the business that these guys had contracted for." Roth adds, "Harvey was worried that if he told him earlier, Michael would scuttle it somehow, so he took a chance, and probably sold Tina on the idea that he didn't have to ask permission." Eisner could have vetoed the deal, and initially he told Harvey, "I'm not gonna let you do it." In the end, Eisner was reluctant to humiliate Weinstein. Still, the two men virtually stopped speaking.

After losing the Brooklyn Navy Yard as a site for the *Talk* launch party when Mayor Giuliani discovered that Hillary Clinton, his likely rival in the race to become New York's new senator, would grace the cover of the inaugural issue, Brown secured Liberty Island instead. On August 2, 1999, the $200,000-plus, star-studded party was held at the foot of the Statue of Liberty, bedecked for the occasion with festive Japanese lanterns. If Harvey wanted to buy his way into the charmed circle of New York's celebrity intellectuals, he succeeded beyond his wildest dreams. Everybody who was anybody was there, 1,400 strong, from Salman Rushdie, just emerging from his fatwa-induced internal exile, to Madonna to Henry Kissinger. As the first round of fireworks blossomed over New York harbor in a spectacular display of fiery brilliance, George Plimpton exclaimed, "This one's for Harvey and Bob Weinstein!"

• • •

FROM THE START, Barry Diller was not happy when USA Films picked up Steven Soderbergh's *Traffic*. He didn't think there was a prayer it would make its budget back, much less go into profit. A $50 million art film, about drugs, to boot, at Christmas, with the director behind the camera. Sequences in Spanish, with subtitles. And with so many actors you needed a scorecard to keep track of them. With the story so convoluted, so full of double crosses and double double crosses it was almost incomprehensible. Of course, Diller didn't like anything on the USA slate. He didn't like *The Muse*, he didn't like USA's untitled Coen brothers project, known only as "the barber movie." He expressed himself to USA chairman Scott Greenstein in words something like, "Coen brothers movies do not make money. The biggest one, *Fargo*, made $35 million, and that had Fran McDormand on her way to an Oscar. She was pregnant. She was delightful. Billy Bob Thornton is neither pregnant nor delightful. Who's gonna pay to see him made up to look like Humphrey Bogart strapped into an electric chair, who dies at the end for a crime he didn't commit—in a black and white movie? You are crazy to make this." But that was Diller's way. Everything was shit, and it was the executive's job to convince him otherwise.

Greenstein generally tried to anticipate Diller's every whim. But somehow he had a feeling about *Traffic*. Soderbergh's career was on the rebound. Of course, it couldn't have gotten any worse for a director who was no longer a wunderkind, but was pushing forty and badly in need of a hit. *Schizopolis* had played Cannes in May 1997. The response, while not positive, was at least unanimous. Says the director, it was "four hundred people scratching their heads simultaneously. A lot of people walked out as soon as they realized there were no actors in it who were recognizable." The film opened around the country in the fall of that year at more or less the same time as his other new film, *Gray's Anatomy*, and promptly disappeared. *Schizopolis* "probably crossed the line from personal into private filmmaking," said the director. "My idea with *Schizopolis* was to make one of these every two years, and live off it. Whatever ideas I had about it being commercial enough to return its investment and allow me to make another film like it were total fantasy. If it had made $2 million, I'd still be making them."

Soderbergh's taste, at least at that time, was not commercial, and he had been following the classic indie model, like Jim Jarmusch, like John Sayles, like the Coens, like Tarantino even, making films for himself and assuming that somehow they would find an audience. Tarantino's did, but for Soderbergh, *Schizopolis* provided a rude awakening. As Ethan Hawke puts it, "Quentin doesn't play any ball. A lot of the rest of us are not so gifted that every little pee we take is gold." Soderbergh had to take a hard look at his options. *Schizopolis* taught him that he needed to play ball, at least a little.

"I knew I had to pull my head out of my ass, and start thinking about the economic realities of making films," he says. "I needed to make a decision about whether or not I was content working on the margins. Looking back on the first four films, it's sort of staggering how naive I was in thinking that people would want to see these. I just was in a bubble, like, I'm just going to make these things and I'll make 'em the way I want, and if people don't go, that's just tough." He opted for the one-for-me, one-for-them route. He'd been doing films for himself; now he started looking for a movie for them.

Casey Silver, over at Universal, had always had a soft spot for the director, who recalls, "Casey pulled me out of a fuckin' hat! I'd made two movies for him that hadn't made a nickel." Silver offered him *Out of Sight*, like *Jackie Brown* based on an Elmore Leonard thriller. He said, "This is an open assignment, go get it. You should do this." Soderbergh's initial inclination was to duck. He said, "It's perfect for me—I can't do it." Suppose he failed. The worst of all worlds was to do one for them and blow it—like, "I can't even sell out." Silver replied, "Don't be an idiot." Soderbergh thought about it some more: This is a wake-up call. My apprenticeship is over, and if I'm going to become something other than an art house director, it's time to step up. It's easier to stay where I am, but I need to get off my butt. He called Silver back, said, "You're right, you're right. I want to do it."

Soderbergh remembers, "*Out of Sight* was the most pressure I've ever experienced. All self-imposed. It was a conscious attempt on my part to enter a side of the business that was off-limits to me, because I had marginalized myself. I got up every morning with knots in my stomach. I had to block that out every day on the set and basically make decisions as though I was making *Schizopolis*. Because I knew if I failed, I was completely fucked."

Out of Sight, with a fine script by Scott Frank, was Soderbergh's second foray into Tarantino territory, and featured several actors Tarantino had used, including George Clooney and Ving Rhames, as well as cameos by Sam Jackson, and Michael Keaton, reprising the same character he played in *Jackie Brown*. Soderbergh believed his films had become too cold and cerebral; he was trying to become more like Tarantino, hot and cerebral, and with *Out of Sight* he succeeded, pulling off the best Tarantino clone to date, so good it doesn't feel like one. It's a wild and crazy film, chock-full of terrific performances Soderbergh got out of his cast, which included Jennifer Lopez. The supporting actors—especially Don Cheadle—are dazzling. Like Tarantino, the director experimented with temporal disruption—he even used tinted stock—all within the skin of a commercial movie. He started building a repertory company that included Cheadle, Luis Guzmán, and most importantly Clooney. *Out of Sight* also did *Jackie Brown* business, grossing about $37 million, but in a stark reminder of the differences between a studio film, even one directed by Soderbergh, and a Miramax film, it cost twice as much (about $40 million), so it was considered a failure. Still, Universal recognized that Soderbergh had delivered, and this led to *Erin Brockovich*.

Meanwhile, in September 1999, Soderbergh had run into Greenstein and USA president Russell Schwartz at the airport coming back from the Toronto Film Festival, where his new film, *The Limey*, had been screened. Soderbergh had done three films with Schwartz when the executive was at Miramax and then Gramercy—*Kafka*, *King of the Hill*, and *The Underneath*. The USA duo had both heard about *Traffic*, intended as a remake of a six-hour British miniseries on the drug wars, and said, "We don't think anybody else is going to make it. But we will." They were climbing out on a long limb. *The Limey*, which would lose money for Artisan, had not opened yet, and all they knew about Soderbergh's other new movie, *Erin Brockovich*, was that it was a big, $50 million Julia Roberts vehicle due out the following March. *Traffic* was set up at Fox, and there wasn't even a script. Soderbergh replied, "That's great to hear, I'll let you know what happens with Fox." It is questionable whether Greenstein had ever seen any of Soderbergh's films. Likewise, if Soderbergh knew Greenstein had October's blood on his hands, he didn't much care. "To be honest, since none of it touched me, it just didn't stick," he says. "In this business, the only thing you can count on is that people will act expediently in their own interest, so I try to set up circumstances in which my needs and their needs are close enough so that there's not going to be a problem."

Traffic would turn out to be a coup for USA's shaky new film division. With a lot to prove, Greenstein badly needed directors of Soderbergh's caliber. Neither Greenstein nor Schwartz inspired much confidence in the troops. USA was so chaotic that, according to another executive, "There was no list of who the deals were with, nor were any executives assigned to oversee the deals. It was easier to call, say, Michael Douglas's Further Films and ask, 'Do we have a deal with you?' than to query someone at USA." Greenstein's response to every project he was brought was always the same: "Can we put Harrison Ford and/or Leonardo DiCaprio in it?" Observes yet another USA player, "Everything Scott ever did was a parody of Harvey Weinstein. There would be a problem getting a response from an actor, so Scott would go over the head of the agent and call the head of the agency, thinking, This is what Harvey would do. Trouble is, Scott's not Harvey. He can't bully anybody. Harvey can back you against the wall at a party, and threaten you, and make it stick. Scott does it, and it pisses people off."

One studio executive describes Diller and Greenstein's dynamic as a "weird, love/hate relationship." Diller demurs. "There was never any love/hate. There was never any love"—he pauses—and "there was never any hate. It didn't have a big range. That went from great to terrible. Sometimes people are able to communicate with each other and have actual conversations. Unless you can have an actual conversation, it's hard. We weren't—because of background and temperament—able to have such conversations. So it was not an easy process, but out of it came some pretty good movies."

Diller understood that if USA were actually going to produce movies, he needed to hire a head of production, a new Bingham Ray, someone with good talent relationships, someone who could talk the talk. In mid-October 1999, he offered the job to Donna Gigliotti, who had left Miramax after *Shakespeare*. Gigliotti had worked with Greenstein while she was there, and was not tripping over herself to sign up. She recalls, "People said to me, 'You are insane. Do not do this!' " She met with Diller at his West 57th Street office, asked, "How does this work? What's the structure?"

"Scott runs the company, you report to Scott."

"Well, I guess that's the end of this meeting." She stood up.

Puzzled, Diller asked, "What are you talking about?"

"He doesn't know anything about what I do, why would I report to him?" Whereupon, she walked out. But Diller persisted. As one source puts it, "They threw everything at her but Fort Knox." Harvey advised her, "Say this number. If you get it, throw yourself on the sword." Finally, Diller gave her a "happiness" clause. He said, "Reporting, forget about it. If you're not happy in a year's time, I'll make you happy." She took the job.

According to Michael Jackson, formerly of Britain's Channel Four, whom Diller installed over Greenstein as CEO of USA Entertainment, the relationship between the two men took a dramatic turn for the worse after USA blew approximately $20 million on a Michael Douglas picture, *One Night at McCool's,* by going too wide too quickly. Says Diller, "By small-company standards that's a lot of money."

Gigliotti saw how Diller treated Greenstein, stepped on him like a doormat, she says. Says a former USA executive, "Every deal had to be approved by Diller, and executives were instructed never to reveal that fact of life at USA." Recalls Gigliotti, "Scott was terrified of Diller. In front of him, he babbled and talked double talk. Diller finally said to him, 'You are not addressing the United Nations, speak English!' " She adds, "Scott would say anything to keep anyone happy, and then couldn't. He was promising people things that he couldn't deliver, constantly undercutting everybody, making snap decisions that were stupid, overpaying for this, whatever."

Gigliotti thought Greenstein was afraid of her, with some reason. She in fact became his Bingham Ray. She screamed at him in front of his staff. As a result of years of abuse at the hands of the Weinsteins he had grown skin like a rhino, but Gigliotti gave it the old college try. In one instance that became legendary around the office, she picked up the phone and overheard him negotiating with Barry Mendel, a producer with a project at Jodie Foster's company called *Flora Plum*, which had been set up at USA with a $25 million budget before Gigliotti arrived. She recalls, "Scott was terrified of making the movie, even though he had bought the script and agreed to do it. He had called Barry without my knowing it, and he was hocking Barry about lowering the budget. I screamed, 'Scott, take it back.'"

Traffic, which Bill Mechanic at Fox eventually gave back to Soderbergh after it foundered there, went into production in March 2000, starring Michael Douglas, Benicio Del Toro, and Catherine Zeta-Jones. As it was getting underway, it became clear that *Erin Brockovich*, which was just opening, was going to be a huge hit. Greenstein treated Soderbergh like a delicate porcelain figurine. USA Films was so hands-off that there wasn't even an executive assigned to the movie. Essentially, Soderbergh could do whatever he wanted, which is just the way he liked it. "Soderbergh's a smart guy, he knows a lot about film," says Gigliotti. "If he thinks that you are desperate or weak, you don't want to take him on. He has disdain for you."

When Soderbergh screened his director's cut for USA, the reactions ranged from lukewarm to despairing. At two hours and fifty minutes, it was too long by forty minutes at the bare minimum, and was impossible to follow. There was pressure from the company to cut the film. At one point, appearing to make a sincere effort to comply, Soderbergh sliced deep into Douglas's character, even excised the climax of his big scene where he resigns from his post as drug czar. The director had lunch with Douglas before the screening, but neglected to prepare him for the extent of the cuts. When Douglas saw the film, he was extremely upset, threatened—or rather, suggested—that he might not be able to support the picture. Soderbergh restored the footage. Some USA executives speculated that Soderbergh had kept Douglas in the dark anticipating his reaction, then exploited it to silence USA.

Soderbergh denies this, saying, "No. I don't work that way. I don't need to be that devious. I was trying some radical shit, 'cause I was being told by everyone that the shorter the movie the better, and I wanted to see what it would look like if I stripped the movie down to its plot, and eliminated all the character stuff. Michael said, 'Look, it's your movie, but I just think you've gutted the character. In this version of the film, he's as much a cipher as he was in the first draft of the script that I read.' He was right. It's really true that you can make the movie seem longer by making it shorter because people don't know why they're watching certain things. You've removed motivation and reflection."

Finally, USA just gave up. The thinking was, This is one of those movies where you get the general gist of who the good guys and the bad guys are, and you just go with it. If you tried to fix it, it just wasn't going to work. You would have needed subtitles underneath people's heads to say, "General Salazar, bad guy." That was the end of the trimming.

BACK AT THE MIRAMAX RANCH, all was not well. *Shakespeare in Love, Life Is Beautiful,* and *The Faculty* provided a steady stream of profits, but outside of *She's All That,* there was no new *Shakespeare* in 1999, not even a *Life Is Beautiful,* although the Disney division brought out a dubbed version in hopes of squeezing the last cent out of its Holocaust fairytale. Release after release crashed and burned. *Holy Smoke, Human Traffic, My Life So Far, B. Monkey, The Lovers on the Bridge, Outside Providence, A Walk on the Moon, eXistenZ, The Castle, Mansfield Park.*

Even Dimension lost its footing. *Teaching Mrs. Tingle* (1999) cost $13 million and only grossed $9 million.

Six years after being purchased by Disney, Miramax was still chaotic. The company was dramatically larger, but it had grown like a weed in an untended garden, wild and promiscuous. Since so many of the staff had never worked anywhere else, they were innocent of rudimentary management skills. Bob and Harvey prided themselves on being tightfisted, but according to one source, there were literally millions of dollars that were being wasted in direct marketing costs alone. Inefficiency was rife. Harvey's office wouldn't release his schedule, so that staffers never knew when they would be summoned to a meeting. An executive would get a call from one of Harvey's assistants, saying, "Harvey wants you over right now."

"Okay, what does he want to talk about? What should I bring?"

"Don't know, bring it all!" The executive on the other end of the line, perhaps in the middle of a meeting with a filmmaker, cutting a trailer, checking out ad art, whatever, dropped everything, gathered up his or her papers, marshaled the troops—say, the entire marketing or publicity department or both—and marched them into the conference room where they might wait forty-five minutes while Harvey took calls, maybe one from President Clinton, making sure that everyone knew it. Or, after the meeting had finally started, Harvey would stand up and say, "I gotta go to lunch, guys, stay here, order yourselves something, I'll be back." Or it would be, "I gotta go downstairs and watch a little bit of a film." Sometimes there were four or five of these open-ended, marathon meetings a week. After which, staffers had to put in their ten-hour day.

Harvey had always been famous for his preternatural grasp of detail, but as the company metastasized, and he was preoccupied with *Talk* or politics, overextended and not paying attention or simply because he didn't want to admit he was wrong, he became increasingly prey to selective memory. Staffers learned to put everything in writing, create a paper trail because he either forgot what they said or pretended to. As had always been true, his bad ideas vastly outnumbered his good ones, but whereas in the past he could be talked out of the bad ones, now it became harder and harder to get him to change his mind or admit he was wrong. He was prone to outbursts like, "I am Ariel Sharon! You are the Palestinians with sticks and stones," or "I am the tank commander and you are the infantry and you're about to get run over," or "I am the king and the king decides." He would insist that anything that popped into his head be implemented. He had a picture called *Malèna,* directed by Giuseppe Tornatore, that he was convinced would be a hit. He would not hear anything to the contrary, and against all advice, he squandered hundreds of thousands of dollars before he gave up.

But tank commanders need to be able to give orders, whereas the Weinsteins were often mired in indecision, especially if they were rattled or scared they were about to release a loser. Bob was notorious for not being able to decide on creative material—particularly if Harvey was undermining or ridiculing him—until it was almost too late. People learned not to throw anything away because what he hated one week, he loved the next.

When the holiday season came around in the fall of 1999, Miramax came up short. Weinstein thought Anthony Minghella's *The Talented Mr. Ripley,* which he co-financed with Paramount, was going to be his Oscar film. When *Ripley* faltered, the only thing Miramax could salvage from the debris of 1999 was Lasse Hallström's tepid adaptation of John Irving's *The Cider House Rules,* which Meryl Poster shepherded through the company, and which paled before the audacity of, say, former Miramax director David O. Russell's Gulf War picture, *Three Kings.* Even though right-to-lifers bridled at the film's pro-abortion message, it was so tepid as to be nearly invisible. The reviews of Hallström's picture were respectful, if unenthusiastic. Among the dissenters was indie flame keeper Amy Taubin, writing in the *Village Voice,* who called it "paternalistic, puffed-up, and dull."

While Harvey had been dallying with Freddie Prinze, Jr., his rivals had not been idle. Fox Searchlight released *Boys Don't Cry,* Kim Peirce's stunning cross-dressing tragedy, while USA put out a holdover from Gramercy, *Being John Malkovich,* the delightfully antic film from relative newcomers screenwriter Charlie Kaufman and director Spike Jonze. And New Line financed the overblown but not uninteresting, frog-raining *Magnolia,* directed by Paul Thomas Anderson. Even the studios had released a flurry of offbeat films by indies or first- or second-timers that became Oscar contenders, like *American Beauty,* which had ended up at DreamWorks.

Warner Brothers put out *The Matrix*, shoved through the studio meat grinder by maverick executive Lorenzo di Bonaventura, despite its doubtful antecedents (the relatively unknown Wachowski brothers). Di Bonaventura also godfathered Russell's *Three Kings*, while Paramount released *Election*, by another Miramax alumnus, Alexander Payne, earlier that year. According to one source, once the picture was anointed by the critics, Harvey called Payne in for a meeting. Even though Miramax had passed on *Election*, "they beat the shit out of him, said, 'You owe us! We made your first movie. You gotta do a movie with us.' " Payne was stunned. Later, he reportedly said, " 'You know what? I was so naive that I thought maybe they were gonna say they realized they dumped *Citizen Ruth*, they were sorry about the way they treated me, and if there was any way they could get back into business with me—and I kinda wanted to hear it. But it was the exact opposite tack.' "

In other words, this was the year that the seeds sown by the *Pulp Fiction* hurricane finally bloomed. The studios were beating the indies at their own game. The new generation of executives who came of age in the mid-1990s—di Bonaventura at Warner's, Amy Pascal at Sony, Stacey Snider at Universal, and Mike de Luca at New Line and then DreamWorks—were, to some extent, moving away from the we-know-best, anti-filmmaker arrogance of the generation that preceded them, the Eisners, Lansings, Semels, and Daleys, and trying their hands at Indiewood films, either directly or through their indie divisions. As Ted Hope puts it, "The current crop of people who control the purse strings at the studios got into the business partially out of the love of the films that they saw in the '70s, and regret that they don't have the same sort of cultural feathers in their caps."

Although the results have been mixed, this class of executives isn't stupid; they realize they have little choice. Like their predecessors in the 1970s, they know that even teenagers get bored—especially teenagers—and no matter how much money they're making, the studios continually need to restock the talent pool and vary the product, shuffle the actor deck so audiences can see the occasional fresh face, Steve Buscemi in *Armageddon* or Ethan Hawke in *Training Day*. The studios were not only making deals with indie directors, but giving them a relatively free hand.

It seemed for the moment, anyway, as if this strange fruit, far from representing the co-opting of indies by the studios, represented the reverse. "I think something has changed," Russell said at the time, hopefully. "I think the Sundance culture has definitely had an impact on the audiences—they've become more sophisticated—and also the studios. Ten years ago *Three Kings*—a war/action movie—would have been *Heartbreak Ridge* with Clint Eastwood, or *Election*—a high school movie—would have been *Zapped.* There are executives who yearn to work with independent-minded filmmakers and make films that are different from the run-of-the-mill 'product.' Studios want to find that *Good Will Hunting* audience." Even producer's rep John Pierson, who had seen it all, added his voice to the chorus. "David O. Russell is like my hero right now because here's a guy who made a no-budget film, *Spanking the Monkey,* and then a mid-level Miramax screwball comedy, *Flirting with Disaster,* still very personal and really hilarious, and then *Three Kings,* probably the most political film of the year—inside the studio system, like a termite. Putting George Clooney in the film and getting Warner's to pay for it, that's great." But, he cautioned, "Let's not get carried away." Indeed, although the studios did continue to patronize a few indie directors—Wes Anderson and Spike Lee at Disney, Russell at Warner's, etc.—their hearts lay with *Spiderman,* *X-Men,* and *The Hulk.* It was the middle-range movies—the $40 to $60 million pictures—that they were turning away from, creating a new niche for Miramax.

Harvey, self-exiled from the feast, arrived at St. Bart's on Christmas Day for his annual holiday there. Two days later, on Monday, the 27th, he spoke to his office, said he wasn't feeling well, didn't want to be bothered by phone calls. He was running a 104-degree fever that he couldn't knock down. He saw a local doctor, then spoke to his physician in New York, who said, "Let's not take any chances, you'd better get back here." His assistants scrambled to find a plane, and he flew back. Bob met him at Newark airport, and whisked him to New York Hospital in a shroud of secrecy.

MIRAMAX WAS ALMOST INVISIBLE at the January 2000 Sundance Film Festival. Karyn Kusama's *Girlfight* picked up the most press, but flopped at the box office. On the other hand, Paramount Classics's David Dinerstein and Ruth Vitale scooped up Kenny Lonergan's *You Can Count on Me,* as well as Sofia Coppola's *The Virgin Suicides,* and both did respectable business. Artisan, which had captured lightning in a bottle with *The Blair Witch Project* the year before, acquired Miguel Arteta's second feature, the weird and beguiling *Chuck & Buck.* Arteta's opinion of the festival was upbeat. "To say Sundance doesn't matter is crazy," he said. "People like myself wouldn't even have a career if not for the chances that Sundance has been willing to take."

Boys Don't Cry had been workshopped at a Sundance lab, and after it opened to rave reviews, Robert Redford was reportedly stung when IFC Productions, which co-financed the film, and Fox Searchlight, which distributed it, got all the credit, while the institute's role was ignored. Increasingly, IFC had become an irritant and a goad. Reflects an executive, "He was massively competitive with the IFC and if the IFC went into film distribution, which they did, and if the IFC went into production, which they did, why couldn't Sundance?" It seemed as if the labs helped filmmakers develop their projects, the festival showcased them, the channel aired them, and the theaters would shortly exhibit them, but the production piece of the puzzle was missing. Sundance neither got kudos for the films it nurtured nor, more important, a chunk of the profits. As the source points out, "It's almost like Sundance has been so much a part of creating the independent phenomenon that Bob wanted to capitalize on it, not just for his own financial gain, but as ego fulfillment. He wanted his cinema chain, he wanted his channel, he wanted his new production company, he wanted to be in distribution, he wanted what other people had, he wanted what he wanted for whatever reasons he thought he wanted them. He has this intense appetite, an appetite that has increased in the last few years, maybe because his movies haven't been successful, maybe because he's aging, who knows. Sundance is such a large part of his identity that if it does well, then it will somehow fill this empty hole inside him. It's psychological."

Redford had used the festival as a platform to publicize new initiatives in the past, and this year was no different. He announced the formation of Sundance Productions, to be headed up by Jeff Kleeman, a veteran production executive whom Redford lured away from MGM. The new company, a division of Redford's for-profit Sundance Group, which also owned the resort, the catalogue, and Sundance Farms, which made scented candles and soaps, would enjoy the same autonomy as the festival and the channel. Redford was on the verge of making an extremely sweet deal with Paul Allen's Vulcan Ventures that would finance the new production entity; give him a controlling interest in the channel by buying out his two partners, Universal (which had inherited PolyGram's stake) and Showtime; take General Cinema out of the cinema center mix, leaving Sundance in sole control of that as well; and finance a Sundance Internet venture. Of this smorgasbord, it seemed that Allen was most excited by the channel.

There appeared to be so much money in the offing, that so far as Sundance Productions was concerned, Redford claimed to have financing for development and marketing. He even talked about buying a distribution company that, along with its theaters and cable channel, would make Sundance a real powerhouse on the indie scene, a one-stop shop that might even be able to go up against the big boys, and at the very least humble upstart IFC. The fact that this vertically integrated indie behemoth totally contradicted the vision of the early Sundance, which was structured precisely to insulate novice filmmakers from the demands of the market, seems to have bothered only the dwindling number of purists in the Sundance ranks. As Sydney Pollack puts it, "Now you're in the theater business? Now you got a TV station? Come on, the government broke up MCA for this reason!"

Sundance Productions envisioned a slate of twelve movies over four years. Some would be small, $1 to $2 million, and some might go as high as $20 or $25 million, but they would average out at $15 million. In the fall of 1999, Kleeman hired seven people away from good jobs to work for the new outfit, found space in L.A.'s Westside, and hired an architect to design the offices. He started meeting with American and European production and distribution companies, such as Good Machine, with which Sundance Productions hoped to establish alliances. Although they respected Sundance, executives expressed considerable skepticism toward Redford, whose reputation for toying and teasing was legendary. He was fast losing his luster as a star, and if he had made a lot of movies around town, he had also failed to make a lot of movies around town.

But by the spring of 2000, the new company had targeted several projects and appeared to be up and running. Only one thing was lacking: cash. Where was Paul Allen's money? The answer was, "It's coming, it's coming, just hold off a week or two. Hire a publicist, prepare the announcements." Sundance Productions hired a publicist and sent out a press release. A week or two passed, and still there was no money. The refrain was the same, "Just be patient, just wait, it's coming." Weeks turned into months, and by early summer, rumors were flying, mostly to the effect that the deal was ready to be signed, but Redford would not put his signature on the piece of paper. Why? According to the story that subsequently made the rounds, he was all set to close, but cautious as always, he consulted Ruth Bernstein, the "branding" person he had hired to help slap the Sundance name on appropriate enterprises. Over a meal, he asked her, "Do you think I should make this deal?" Placing a napkin on the table, she drew a picture of a big blimp, and said, "From my point of view, the deal is like a blimp. This blimp is going to land in your backyard, and you have no idea who's going to emerge from that blimp and come live in your house." As soon as she said that, Redford realized she was right. He needed to get to know these Vulcan Ventures people better. But that would have to wait a couple of months because he was in post on *Bagger Vance*.

Then, in June 2000, Vivendi, the French waterworks that was reinventing itself as an entertainment powerhouse, bought Universal. In a televised press conference, Vivendi head Jean-Marie Messier, ticking off the goodies he had just acquired, mentioned not only Universal, but the Sundance Channel that had piqued Allen's interest. In other words, the window of opportunity that would have allowed Sundance to buy Universal's stake in the channel with Allen's money had slammed shut. Running on Redford time, the actor had been accustomed to keeping people waiting. Finished with *Bagger Vance*, he apparently tried to resuscitate his relationship with Allen, only to find himself on the wrong end of the hourglass. Allen's people failed to return his calls, and gradually it became clear that the deal was dead. (Allen declined to comment.) "Bob's ambivalent," says Sydney Pollack. "How do you sell a big financial interest to someone and not have them take the control away from you?" This is true, but little consolation to the people who were recruited to run Sundance Productions, which died with the deal, along with the dream of taking control of the channel from the partners, and the cinema centers from General Cinema.

That winter, Redford fired his COO, Gary Beer, who had been at his side since Sterling Van Wagenen had left in the mid-1980s. It was Beer who negotiated the deal for the channel and for the theaters. Reportedly, Beer was notified by FedEx, just after he closed the channel deal. Speculates a former Sundance executive, "Bob falls out of love with people, even people who have been with him for many, many years, like Gary. They're not shiny new toys anymore. What he wanted from Gary was for Gary to be a rainmaker for him, and there was a limit to what Gary could do." Beer had "Sundanced" more than his share of people in his time, and now he had been Sundanced himself.

Meanwhile, the Sundance Channel had been struggling to keep up with IFC. It was the perennial Avis to IFC's Hertz, and it rankled Redford. Nora Ryan, the president, and Dalton Delan, the executive VP of programming, departed, and in January 1998, in an attempt to turn the channel around, he had hired Liz Manne, someone, at last, who knew her way around the indie film world. Under Manne, the programming improved, and subscriptions rose. Redford, however, was still picking fault. Like Harvey, no matter how rosy the prospect, he was dissatisfied. He wanted more, he wanted better. He would blue-sky, and the channel personnel invariably found themselves in the position of wet blankets, telling him why they couldn't launch this kind of original programming or acquire that Sundance award-winning film because they didn't have the budget. Of course, Redford didn't like to hear no. As one source puts it, "You can paint a painting, but you have to have a frame. By explaining over and over what the frame was, you get put in the position of being the boogeyman. And that's a bad position."

LIKE EVERYONE ELSE, Bob Weinstein thought Harvey was a heart attack waiting to happen. He even reportedly had meetings with VP of accounting Irwin Reiter where they tried to "what if" themselves into the scenario. Now it seemed that their worst fears might be coming true. The exact nature of Harvey's illness was a closely held secret, perhaps, as some speculated, because he was in the middle of renegotiating his deal—yet again—with Disney, but also because Eve reportedly preferred it that way. Eisner didn't find out that Harvey was in the hospital until he read it in the papers, and even then Bob wouldn't tell him which hospital Harvey was in. (He registered under a false name.) The first thing that occurred to everyone was that it was indeed a heart attack, although staffers were quick to joke, "Heart attack—what heart?" Rumors flew, ranging from lung cancer to flesh-eating bacteria, AIDS, drugs, you name it, but those few who knew weren't saying. Director James Gray referred to it as his "mysterious Kremlin leader illness."

Initially, a cat's-away-the-mice-will-play giddiness pervaded Miramax. But as it became evident that Harvey was seriously ill and would be out for some time, the worker bees, motivated by a mixture of compassion, loyalty, and, as always, fear, labored mightily to keep the ship afloat. Bob was at the helm, and everyone pulled together in an effort to operate as Harvey would have wanted them to. Then, on February 2, senior executives learned that he was coming home from the hospital, and would shortly be back in the office.

When Harvey returned to work just before the Oscar nominations were announced, he looked drained and weak, uncertain on his feet, with a tracheotomy scar at the base of his throat that he tried to conceal with a turtleneck shirt. He had lost forty pounds and given up smoking. Reduced to sipping miso and chicken soup, he returned in a foul humor. He was bitterly disappointed that *Ripley* hadn't done better, blamed Paramount for bungling the marketing when he wasn't around to supervise it. He seemed determined to prove that he was the same old Harvey, if anything, tougher than ever. "The films weren't working the way they should be working," recalls one of Harvey's assistants at that time. "He didn't sit back and say, This is just cyclical, it will come back around, just keep plugging away. His reaction was, I'm not doing enough, my people are not doing enough. When he came back, it was with the same type of viciousness, fixated on making sure everybody was three times as productive. Nothing was ever good enough."

For staffers who expected to be patted on the head for carrying on in his absence, or were expecting a Harvey who had seen the white light and returned mellow and chastened, it was a rude shock. He second-guessed their every decision and ridiculed their judgment as if to show that Miramax could not function in his absence. Such are the vagaries of the human heart that in the face of this blizzard of abuse, some staffers felt sorry for him. People made excuses: he was a guy who loves to dance but had spent that year's Oscar prom in the hospital; going cold turkey on cigarettes made him edgy. As one former executive put it, "People talked themselves into saying, 'You know what, their bark is worse than their bite, they always apologize.' Or, 'Harvey doesn't know any better. Don't take it personally, he treats everyone that way.' But then somebody else went, 'Bullshit. He does know better. Does he talk to Eve that way? Does he talk to his daughters that way? Does he talk to Gwyneth Paltrow that way? No! He absolutely does know better, and he doesn't give a shit.' "

Weinstein called a meeting at Elegant Film, Eve's production company, to review the Oscar campaign for *The Cider House Rules,* an uphill struggle what with the film's tepid reception. The marketing division, which had prided itself on two Best Picture Oscars in the last four years, had the most at stake. Says one member of the team, "It was like, All right, we're gonna show him what we're made of. We left no stone unturned so that Harvey would be totally proud of us and that we could get as many Academy nominations as we possibly could. We worked like dogs." They downplayed the controversial elements in the film—abortion, drug addiction, and so on—and used warm and cuddly images to sell the picture. But instead of being pleased, Harvey was sarcastic. He would turn to someone and say, "Let me do the thinking. I've done pretty well, haven't I? Haven't I? You think this company's done well with me here?" Recalls the source, "Harvey completely shit all over the Academy campaign for *Cider House Rules.* He told us that we would never get any nominations because we had fucked it up. The next day, we got seven."

The Cider House Rules was up against *The Green Mile, The Insider,* and *The Sixth Sense,* but the front runner was *American Beauty.* Once again, it was Miramax against DreamWorks, and once again, the fur flew. This time, DreamWorks had learned a few things, beefed up its ranks to Miramax levels. Having concluded that the company that spends the most money wins, DreamWorks proceeded to do so.

Meanwhile, under the heading of unfinished business, *The Hairy Bird,* which Harvey had renamed *Strike,* for reasons best known to himself, was still hanging around with no place to roost. It had come to be regarded as that dread demographic pariah, a "tweener," too much of an art film for the commercial audience, and too much of a teen comedy for the art audience. To fulfill its contractual obligation to Alliance, however, Miramax was forced to open it in the U.S. So they did, in Seattle, in 1998. The sixteen hundred theaters he had promised Sarah Kernochan had become one. The film opened, closed, and returned to its nest on the shelf.

Months passed. In the wake of *She's All That,* Harvey realized that he owned what could well be Rachael Leigh Cook's next picture. In the spring of 1999, he asked Kernochan and Nora Ephron, who was the executive producer, to write a voiceover. The two women spent a month writing the new material, sent it to Miramax, but never got a reply.

Kernochan wrote Harvey yet another letter, imploring him to open her film in New York and L.A. The message came back, "Harvey's willing to go along with it, but who's going to pay for it?" Kernochan emptied her savings account, spent $100,000 opening the film herself—for a week in New York, which was all she could afford. Eighty thousand dollars of that went to the *New York Times,* for ads. Now called *All I Wanna Do,* it finally opened on March 24, 2000.

The Miramax experience devastated Kernochan's career. "When I stopped taking screenwriting assignments in 1997 to direct my own movie, I saw that as a step up," she says ruefully. "I was feeling very good about myself." Reentering the script market three years later, she found that she had been forgotten. "It was like I had to start all over again," she continues. "I was having to audition for teen zombie movies. I couldn't even get the shit assignments. Just as a screenwriter. As a director, forget it!" When Miramax bought *The Hairy Bird* for $3.5 million, she was paid $100,000 for the script, and $100,000 for directing. Subtracting the $100,000 she spent to open the movie in New York, and amortizing the remainder over the three years that passed between the start of production and release (excluding the years of pre-production), she came away with the equivalent of a salary of $33,333 a year! Would she ever do a film with Miramax again? "Never. I'd rather eat glass!"

Three days later, on March 27, 2000, DreamWorks found its groove. *Cider House* got two Oscars, Best Supporting Actor for Michael Caine and the other for John Irving's screenplay, but *American Beauty* beat it for Best Picture and won five Oscars in all.

What with Harvey's illness, and the various distractions that competed with Miramax for his attention, the beginning of the new millennium seemed very much like the end of the old millennium. There was still no *English Patient,* no *Good Will Hunting,* no *Shakespeare in Love* in the pipeline. *Vatel,* a lush and lavish period piece directed by Roland Joffé, was an inexpensive pickup from the previous year's Cannes that Miramax hoped would get some craft nominations. When it tested badly, Weinstein dumped it. *Vatel* opened so quietly and was gone so quickly that the film's star, Uma Thurman, didn't even know it had been released. It was insulting to Thurman, but then Harvey seemed to take her for granted.

Thurman was also the star of Merchant and Ivory's *The Golden Bowl.* The two men had given Weinstein a wide berth since the *Mr. & Mrs. Bridge* fiasco almost a decade earlier. Says Merchant, "Years passed and years passed, we felt he'd mellowed a bit, and he wrote me a wonderful letter, a sincere letter, I think, about A *Soldier's Daughter Never Cries*, how much he liked it. So I thought, Maybe he's coming around a bit, and would leave us alone. So we went to him with *The Golden Bowl*. Never at any time did he say anything about the cast, or tell us to change the script, or do anything. There was never any kind of attempt to influence us in any way."

As was often the case, the honeymoon lasted until Harvey actually saw the picture. Says Ivory, "He said the usual kinds of things—'Great film-making guys, worthy of being up there in the Merchant-Ivory [pantheon],' all this stuff, but then we started hearing about problems that they had with it, his ladies wanted to give us some tips on how we should shorten it. Basically, he didn't like Uma. He thought she was over-the-top, overdra-matic, and he told her so at a party for her husband, Ethan Hawke's, *Ham-let*, directed by Michael Almereyda, in New York."

Harvey had financed *Hamlet*, and didn't like it either, and the "party," held at the beginning of May, was a courtesy screening for friends of the film at the Tribeca screening room. *The Golden Bowl* had provided Thurman with a meaty role that had Oscar potential, erasing the embarrassment of V*atel*. She was proud of the work she had done on the picture. Harvey swept in late in the evening, after he'd already had several contentious encounters elsewhere. His agenda was to enlist her in his fight with Merchant and Ivory over the length, as well as his attempt to keep the film out of Cannes, against the wishes of the filmmakers, who had submitted it. He wanted Thurman to say to them, "Don't put the film in Cannes, protect my performance, take some time, work on it some more." Usually actors (not unlike humans in general), like to hear they've done a good job before the bullets start to fly, but Harvey dispensed with the preliminaries. Continues Ivory, who was not there but heard the story from Thurman, "It was an awful thing. He publicly told her that he hadn't liked her performance, and it could be improved if only I would listen to him, but if I didn't do that he couldn't predict what the critics might say."

By the time he was finished, Thurman was in tears. She was shocked by his behavior. After all, she was part of the Miramax family, Tarantino's fa-vorite leading lady, already slated to star in his next film, *Kill Bill*. Says Hawke, "I've heard that so much, 'She's a part of the Miramax family!' Yeah, until your movie doesn't work, and then you're not part of the family at all. You're not even a distant cousin. It's really fraudulent. Uma's not part of the Miramax family, she has her own family, the Thurman family." Thurman refused to throw her weight behind Harvey's attempt to cut the film. She explains, "Harvey is notorious now for wanting to put his stamp on the films that he puts out. He was enlisting me for my own self-interest. He was saying in his own scary fashion that the movie could be an Oscar film, but that the way Merchant and Ivory were going to do it was going to fuck it up, but if he had his way, it would turn out great for me. It didn't matter to me who was right and who was wrong, I wasn't going to try to manipulate Jim—regardless of whether it was in my interest. I have too much respect for him. James Ivory is an auteur, an artist, and win, lose, or draw, you don't turn your back on a filmmaker."

But Merchant and Ivory were not mollified. "They chose the mall in Clifton Commons, New Jersey, to test *The Golden Bowl*," continues Merchant. "We said, 'Why New Jersey, why Clifton Commons? What is there about Clifton Commons that is good for *Golden Bowl*?' They said, 'There's a Barnes & Noble right by the movie theater, and we recruited our audience out of the bookstore!' The audiences for intelligent films, films of quality, are in the cities. If it goes to the malls, like we did with *Room with a View*, it goes only afterward, not before. If you open it everywhere, wide, there will be no audience for it, because they have not heard the word of mouth and the reviews they have not read. That's a very important thing, otherwise we are going to lose the battle." Merchant understood the metamorphosis that had turned Miramax upside down.

With the filmmakers' permission, Harvey made his own parallel or shadow cut. According to president of marketing Mark Gill, "Miramax took twenty-one minutes out of the movie and it was a lot better. It wasn't 'You must do this,' it was, 'Consider this. Call us to discuss.' They never called. They sent a one-sentence letter saying none of the cuts are approved. It was a big 'Fuck you!' " Indeed, Merchant and Ivory rejected the Miramax cut, saying, "Thank you, but we don't want it." Recalls Merchant, "Then they just went nuts. We have a close relationship with the exhibitors, so they called us, and said, 'What's going on? Your film has been pulled from the two cinemas where it was booked.' We said, 'We have no idea.' Then we got a call from his [Harvey's] minions, and they said that they will send the film to video and HBO."

Regardless of whether the film was too long or not, the question again is, Why did it happen? It is easy to tell from the length of the script approximately how long a film will be. But Harvey apparently ignored the script, ignored the production, and treated the film, as was his habit, like all acquisitions, confident that when the time came, he could muscle the filmmakers and fix it in the editing. But Merchant and Ivory were not Mark Christopher or Sarah Kernochan. They had made their share of clinkers, but had had long and distinguished careers. They would not give in, and ultimately bought the film back from Miramax for $5 million. Says Ivory, Weinstein "doesn't know what he has in his films. He's like a savage in the jungle walking along, and he sees some bright, shiny thing down on the ground, and he stops to pick it up, he looks at it, he doesn't know what it is, but he knows it's valuable, so he puts it in his pocket and goes on his way."

Would the two men ever work with Miramax again? "I don't think so," says Merchant. "We have almost bankrupted ourselves trying to raise that kind of money. Because we are not in that kind of league to write a check for $5 million. But we are Merchant-Ivory, and we have the backing of our own work, our library, we could survive. But someone else would have just collapsed. It was a nightmare thing." And Ivory? "Never!" he says. "It doesn't mean anything to Harvey that you've made films for forty years and that people know who you are. He has to be like the bully in the school-yard, bend your arm around behind you until you scream." Adds Hawke, "I told Jim and Ismail, 'You shouldn't have taken his money.' How many peo-ple have got to be crying in the corner from going to this guy's birthday party before you stop going to his birthday party. Jim and Ismail being angry about that is like being angry at the scorpion. I know he's one of the few people with the cash to do these kinds of movies, but it's a dangerous dance, because if Harvey falls in love with *The Golden Bowl, The Golden Bowl* makes $40 million, and is nominated for seven Oscars. If Harvey doesn't, he buries it. And he's got the money and the power to not worry about it."

As for *Hamlet,* which *New York Times* film critic Elvis Mitchell listed as number one on his year-end top-ten list, Harvey dumped it. As he has shown repeatedly, it's not the hacks he exploits, but the real filmmakers, the ones who are ready to make sacrifices for their art. As Hawke puts it, "Filmmakers shortchange themselves by making the movie cheaply. We made *Hamlet* for under $2 million, really inexpensive for shooting a movie in New York, and the reason we did that was we wanted complete creative freedom. I didn't get paid, Bill Murray didn't get paid, nobody got paid. We just did it because we loved it. If we'd made the movie for $10 million, they would have had to advertise it. And then the movie would have had a chance."

But spending more money afforded no protection either, as James Gray discovered on *The Yards.* Gray found himself damned either way. Like *Lit-tle Odessa,* the director's first film, *The Yards* was produced by former Miramax production head Paul Webster, after he left Miramax to head up Film Four in London. On the basis of his script, Gray had recruited an ex-ceptional cast that included one hot actor, Mark Wahlberg, coming off *Boogie Nights,* and two up-and-comers: Charlize Theron and Joaquin Phoenix, who stood out in a cast of standouts in Gus Van Sant's *To Die For*—as well as a flock of 1970s veterans, including Ellen Burstyn, James

Caan, and Faye Dunaway. On the basis of this cast, Miramax reeled in $15 million in foreign presales, which covered all but a fraction of the film's $17.7 million budget. Gray shot the film in late summer of 1998.

Like *Little Odessa*, *The Yards* has the feel of a 1970s film. It is deliberate, dark, and uncompromising, as it follows the inexorable disintegration of the handful of lives pulled under by the whirlpool of corruption whose physical vortex is a New York City subway yard. Gaunt, lost, and stripped of his swagger under Gray's direction, Wahlberg turns in the best performance of his career, abetted by similarly fine work from Phoenix and Theron. But it wasn't *Shakespeare* or *Cider House*. There was no genius-in-the-making or plucky orphan to root for; it didn't have a tidy, upbeat ending, at least until Harvey got hold of it. (After he returned from the hospital, Miramax script readers were told that the company would henceforth make only films with happy endings.) Gray told Patrick Goldstein, writing in the *L.A. Times*, that Harvey made "every major decision from beginning to end. It's all top down, starting with him." In order to get him to go with casting singer Steve Lawrence in a small role, "Gray had to guarantee the studio his salary against the days it would cost to reshoot the Lawrence scenes if they didn't work out." According to a source close to the production, Weinstein, as he had done with Jim Mangold, actually wrote a scene that he dictated to Gray over the phone. Worried that audiences would think there was an incestuous relationship between the characters played by Wahlberg and Theron, rendering them unsympathetic (they're cousins and the relationship is left ambiguous), Harvey wrote dialogue that makes it clear that they haven't had sex. With no Robert De Niro to back him up, Gray shot it, but managed to avoid using it.

Then *The Yards* plunged into post-production hell—for two years. Gray delivered his director's cut in September 1998. It scored badly. In May 1999, he and Harvey had lunch. "Harvey, spitting crab meat at me, kept yelling, 'I'm the master of the invisible cut!' " Gray recalled, but gave him money to do three days of reshoots. In exchange, Miramax demanded another film from him. The reshoots, of course, included a new, upbeat ending on which Weinstein insisted, where Wahlberg's character improbably brings the bad guys down in a hearing room packed with bureaucrats and politicians. The Miramax ending felt tacked on, something out of another film, another era, Marlon Brando finking on Lee J. Cobb a half century earlier in *On the Waterfront*. When Gray asked for another day of reshoots, for which he paid with his own money, Miramax again extracted a future commitment, leaving the director owing two pictures to the Disney division.

Weinstein was capable of spending generously on a good script—especially with a stellar cast attractive to foreign buyers—that was too expensive for anyone else, but then he would turn around and say, "I spent all this money on a film no one else wanted to do, and now we can't make our money back." In this case, having spent liberally on post-production, he suddenly woke up to the fact that the budget was pushing $23 million. "It's very difficult with Miramax when you're in that post-production nightmare," says Webster. "When I was there, we had a thing called the 'gold report,' printed on gold paper. It was a budget, and gave the financial status of every movie. It went on Harvey's desk each week, and my guess is he never looked at it. Not once. Harvey doesn't care about budgets—until he needs to care, and by then it's too late."

The Yards would probably have gone straight to video had not Cannes president Gilles Jacob loved it and invited it to the festival in May 2000. But the critics who saw it there panned it, so Gray was back to square one. Says former Miramax marketing head Dennis Rice, "Look at the story! You got disagreeable people, an antihero who's a loser who gets out of jail only to get into trouble again, and he's on the run because he's betrayed by his loser friend. Why would anybody who lived in Spokane, Washington, give a shit about the New York City subway yards?" Miramax held a screening in New York in early October. There was nobody there but Gray and Wahlberg. Gray was heartened to see a seat roped off with Harvey's name on it, but he also noticed that it was empty and remained so throughout the screening. But what Gray called "the so-called premiere" at the Writers Guild in L.A. "was really humiliating." According to him, "The place was half empty, and no one from Miramax showed up. I saw someone the next day who said, 'Jeez, that was maybe the worst studio premiere ever.'" The poached salmon, fillets of beef, and plump shrimp that Miramax lavished on luckier filmmakers had become bad finger food and Martinelli sparkling cider.

The Yards finally went out on October 20, 2000, in about 150 theaters, unsupported by TV advertising or anything else. Says Webster, "Miramax kept the film in post-production for nearly two years, and then abandoned it at the altar. Completely. They dumped the movie so utterly, it was like a public dis." The reviews were mixed, although Elvis Mitchell included it in the same year-end top-ten list that was headed by *Hamlet*. After six weeks, it disappeared, grossing under $1 million. But having saved on P&A, Miramax would eventually make a profit on Gray's film.

Observed Nick Wechsler, one of the film's producers, who subsequently produced *Quills* and *Requiem for a Dream*, "Both of those films have difficult and disturbing themes, yet both Fox Searchlight and Artisan have spent the money to support them. Most distributors would have given it a bigger push, but Harvey has moved past the point where he has the energy or need to be the kind of P. T. Barnum figure who can create a market for a movie even where there isn't one."

Companies push pictures that don't turn a theatrical profit all the time. Sales of videos and DVDs represent such important revenue streams that theatrical releases are often little more than loss leaders, trailers for the ancillary markets. Some companies regard theatrical marketing as an investment in talent relationships. But not in this case. Continues Webster, "Harvey took a very ruthless, cold look and said, James Gray is an artistically interesting but noncommercial filmmaker, Joaquin Phoenix is probably not going to be a movie star, Charlize Theron, I've already put her in half a dozen movies, I'm fine there. James Caan, good actor, but older, so what's the point? Mark Wahlberg was the key. If he had gotten Mark's next two movies, he would have supported the film. Harvey tried, but they didn't hit it off." Wahlberg didn't like the way Harvey had treated Gray. Concludes Webster, "As it was, he cut and ran. If Miramax don't want your movie, they will drop it like a stone. I stand by that movie, 'cause it's a good movie."

But Gray went public, broke the taboo against taking his case to the press. "I warned James against it," says Webster. "For a young filmmaker like that, who's got a career ahead of him, it was an incredibly naive thing to do. You can never beat those guys in the press, they just understand the media too well. The corridors of power are too dark and murky, and you get lost in them." A source close to Gray believes Miramax punished Gray by pressing its claim to two future films. Gray got an offer to write and direct from Warner Brothers, but Miramax threw legal obstacles in his way. He had to hire an attorney to get the company to back off. Gray worried he was going to be forced into bankruptcy defending himself against Miramax. He said, "Believe it or not, I'm not bitter. I got to make the movie I wanted to make. . . . It just would've made a big difference to me and to the actors if Harvey had acted as if he was proud of the movie and judged the film on its merits, not just on its salability." Would he make another film at Miramax? "I will because I have to."

Meanwhile, Mike Ovitz had started a new management company, Artists Management Group, after his very public ouster from Disney. One of his clients was Martin Scorsese, whom he had represented since the mid-1980s at his former agency, CAA. Two of his top executives, Rick Yorn and Cathy Schulman, who had long since left Sundance, flew to New York to meet with the director. They asked him, "If you could do anything, what would it be?" His answer was, "I would make *Gangs of New York*, a project that I've had for eleven or twelve years." He described it as an epic saga, a revenge story set in New York City during its Jurassic Age before and during the Civil War, when nativist gangs roamed its streets, taking on all comers, especially Irish immigrants. One of the reasons the project had never been made was because it rested on the back of a twenty-year-old character, and there never seemed to be an actor able to play that young who the studios thought was strong enough to carry such a leviathan of a picture. Yorn represented Leonardo DiCaprio, and he pricked up his ears. On the plane back to L.A., they read Jay Cocks's lengthy, convoluted script. "It not only dealt with the story of these gangs, but also the conscription riots, Lincoln's presidency, the city burning down—twice, immigrant policies, Tammany Hall politics, on and on," recalls Schulman. "It was, Ohmigod, how're we gonna deal with this? It was way too long. And way too dark. We did a couple of more drafts with Cocks, but we felt we weren't getting anywhere."

Still, AMG started selling the notion of a Scorsese *Gangs of New York* starring DiCaprio, whom everyone still wanted for everything. The early budgets were coming in around $84 million. The picture had been set up at Disney, where Scorsese had a deal, but *Kundun* had not made a dime there, nor had *Bringing Out the Dead* for Paramount nor *Casino* for Universal. Studios were cutting back on mega-budget pictures, and Joe Roth was having second thoughts. He put it in turnaround. Every studio turned it down. Then Initial Entertainment Group's Graham King, who was trying to put his company on the map and was unaware of *Gangs*'s checkered past, wrote a check for $65 million for foreign rights. With King's money committed, Roth reconsidered, and turned *Gangs* over to Miramax. Harvey was thrilled. *Gangs* seemed like the perfect film to kick off the new century. It was an enormously expensive period piece directed by the legendary Scorsese, a genuine auteur who, with the possible exceptions of Woody Allen and Robert Altman among directors still working regularly, best embodied the revolutionary New Hollywood of the 1970s. With DiCaprio headlining, it wasn't even all that risky, and Harvey was confident he could weed out the violent and controversial material Scorsese was famous for. If Harvey could add Scorsese, with his reputation for artistry and integrity, to his stable, it was a surefire way of stilling those ugly stories that swirled around Miramax once and for all. For Harvey, it would be a triumph of branding. With Quentin Tarantino apparently lost in his labyrinthine World War II script, *Inglorious Bastards*, Scorsese could take up the slack. He was a trophy director, Oscar bait, and brought with him the kind of legitimacy that not even the *Shakespeare* Oscar could confer. In fact, smelling Best Picture, Harvey took producer credit.

Bob Weinstein reportedly opposed his brother's involvement, thought the project was a sinkhole and didn't like the script, but Harvey was determined. He claimed his exposure was capped at $15 million, with Scorsese and DiCaprio liable for budgetary overruns, but nobody in Hollywood believed him. (One former Miramax executive in a position to know is sure Miramax was in for $32 million, a figure also reported by Laura Holson in the *New York Times*.) Scorsese's price was $6 million, the same rate he got for *Casino*, $3 million of which was deferred in case he went overbudget. As was his custom, Harvey wanted everyone to reduce their rates. DiCaprio took a small cut, $15 million instead of $18 million, with $4 million of that assigned to cover overages, while Cameron Diaz, who had a lesser role, worked for something under $2 million. Daniel Day-Lewis, who is not a fan of Weinstein's, was a reluctant participant. He said, "What he doesn't understand is that I did *Gangs* in spite of Harvey, not because of Harvey."

The Miramax co-chairman lost little time before he started drawing on the Scorsese account. He peppered his conversation with the director's name. It was Marty this and Marty that: Scorsese had voted for *Shakespeare*, not *Private Ryan*; Scorsese had invited him to his sixtieth birthday party, etc., etc. When Harvey disclosed to a rapt audience at the Learning Annex in New York City on April 30, 2003, that he intended to direct *Mila 18*, he said, "I'm going to have Marty next to me. I'm not going to take any chances." But those who knew both the strong-willed Scorsese and the short-fused Weinstein smiled. "Marty is only interested in making the right picture, and he's strong enough to fight for what he believes in," said Saul Zaentz. "Harvey's interest is . . . about making money." As one observer put it to journalist Kim Masters, "Harvey finally got the director he deserves, and it's a fair fight." In fact, the yoking of Scorsese and Weinstein set up an epic clash between the auteur-driven aesthetic of the 1970s and the studio mentality of the 1990s that threatened to eclipse the drama on-screen. Harvey had always imagined himself an Irving Thalberg, a David O. Selznick, and it was the old studio system he admired. "While I grant the '70s was a golden era of moviemaking," he says, "1939 kicks the entire '70s' ass in one year. It fucking blows all those movies from the '70s completely fucking away. From *Citizen Kane* to *How Green Was My Valley*." (*Citizen Kane* was actually released in 1941.) A Thalberg needs his von Stroheim, a Selznick needs his *Gone With the Wind*. Harvey's von Stroheim would be Scorsese, and his *Gone With the Wind* would be *Gangs of New York*.

Principal photography commenced late summer, early fall of 2000. Harvey, concerned that his meticulous and temperamental director might fall behind, became obsessed with the picture, spending a mind-boggling sixteen weeks on the set. Indeed Scorsese worked at a snail's pace, shooting less than a page a day and running the budget way over the projected $93 million. Harmonious sets have produced bad movies, and tempestuous sets good movies—witness *Chinatown*—but in this case it seemed as if the duel of wills between director and producer brought out the worst in each. "I'm sick of my image of killing and maiming!" complained Harvey. "It's complete horseshit!" Still, *Gangs* did nothing to mitigate this perception. The two men had a blowout over the way the director had made up Day-Lewis, especially his hair and the prosthetics on his face. "He was playing a really bad guy, and he had to look pretty ugly," Schulman explains. "Marty was going for the integrity of the character, and Harvey wanted to have a marketing campaign that featured a good-looking Daniel and a good-looking Leo. He didn't think Daniel looked sexy."

Miramax hired producer David Parfitt, who had successfully shepherded *Shakespeare in Love*, as a consultant to ride herd on Scorsese, but it was impossible. Says Parfitt, "Marty's in control, he's surrounded by his people, he's gonna do what he's gonna do. You can't go to Martin Scorsese and say, 'Hello, I'm David Parfitt, you should shoot it that way.' He's a great filmmaker and you know what you take on."

Although there was tension between the director and the producer throughout the production, Weinstein generally showed Scorsese a good deal of respect. Nevertheless, according to a colleague close to the director, "Marty feels that this was not his best work. He was unhappy with the film." Essentially, Scorsese blames Harvey, at least in part, for its failure. Scorsese, the source continues, "complained that Harvey, with his suggestions and his huge ego, was an enormous encumbrance upon his creativity. At each stage Marty felt he was being hampered from moving to the next stage, creatively. He felt Harvey stopped him from being able to see the total picture. Harvey was always saying, 'You need to do this, you need to do that, you should get rid of this scene, that scene'—Marty hasn't had a producer speak to him like that since he was a kid." Others say it was the director who rattled the saber. After one angry meeting in his hotel room, he threw a coffee table at a Miramax representative, which crashed into the door as it was closing. (Scorsese actually had mirrors affixed to the video monitors to alert him to Weinstein's approach.) "Marty's as mean and difficult as Harvey," said one executive. "He has an extraordinary temper, and he won't bend at all for anything." And a crew member added, "Marty more than once said, 'I'll walk away and let someone else finish it.'"

The shooting dragged on for so long that the next movie on Diaz's schedule, *The Sweetest Thing*, hove into view. Recalls Harvey, "That was the big fight that I had with Marty, where I had to release Cameron. Marty said, 'You can't do that.'

"'Marty, you can't have an actress who worked [practically] for free, stayed four and a half months straight, six months overall, and then about to come into a $15 million payday, and not release her.'

" 'I'm gonna talk to Columbia myself.'

" 'Do whatever the fuck you want.' He called Columbia, and they said, 'Fuck you.' He got mad at me, overturned what he thought was my desk, but he threw down [producer] David Parfitt's desk by mistake."

Gangs wrapped after seven months on April 13, 2001, eight weeks over. As is his wont, Weinstein became more aggressive during post-production, and it was then that there were several big blowouts—over issues of taste, length, and score. Scorsese produced a rough cut that came in at three hours, forty minutes. Weinstein threatened that he wouldn't release the picture unless the length was radically reduced. The Scorsese camp was furious because Miramax was trumpeting the long, early cut as the "director's cut," when it knew perfectly well it was merely a rough cut that Scorsese always intended to shorten. Miramax just wanted to spin its case that the director was out of control.

Harvey, betraying some bitterness—although he still says he loves the movie—claims he wanted to end it two-thirds of the way through: "When we finished the pagoda sequence, where DiCaprio reveals himself, I turned to Marty and said, 'We're done. Here! Dramatically, the movie is over. As far as I'm concerned, it's a race to end it. We should get through it in fifteen minutes.' " He thought he was going to be able to muscle Scorsese into dropping the entire draft riot sequence, provoking one of the most bitter confrontations between the director and the producer. Speaking of Scorsese's editor, Thelma Schoonmaker, Weinstein reportedly told Scorsese, "She's too old to do the job anymore. Dump her." According to Harvey, Scorsese refused to cut the sequence, saying, "This is how I conceived it." He continues, "That's an example of my power on that movie. Why should he listen? He's 'Martin Scorsese'!"

Ironically, as desperate as Harvey had been to get into business with Scorsese, once he succeeded, he tried to tone down Scorsese's voice, the signature touches that would make *Gangs* a "Martin Scorsese film." As he had done in the past, he tried to make the picture more audience friendly. If there is one thing Scorsese's films are not, it is audience friendly, and this one was no different. It contained three big battles between the gangs. Harvey wanted to eliminate the first one—which happened to be the best—because it was long, harrowing, and violent, in order to get to the story faster. The dialogue is filled with nineteenth-century slang, as when DiCaprio's character says of Diaz, "She's a prim-lookin' stargazer," meaning she's sexy. Harvey tried to insert translations for that and like locutions into the voice-over, but Scorsese objected. Then there was the jar of ears, souvenirs of battle displayed in a bar. "I tried to get that out of the goddamned movie three years ago," he complained. "I said, 'I hate that in the script.' Who wants to see a goddamned jar of ears? It's disgusting!" Likewise, there's a brief scene in which a dog chews up some rats. Weinstein wanted to say, "Marty, I promise you, you'll get your $3 million back if you take out the ears and the rats," but he saved his breath. Instead, he said, sourly, "He doesn't give a shit."

As the picture became mired in post-production, the money flowed like water from a broken main. But it wasn't only the money. As Cassian Elwes puts it, "Harvey put all the resources of that company, the entire Miramax machine, on that movie for two, three years. The hidden costs of that, in terms of the time taken away from making other pictures, are gigantic!"

Thirteen
All That Jazz Is Gone
2000–2001

- **How Steven Soderbergh became a one-man Sundance, while Harvey Weinstein threw a headlock on a reporter, paused Billy Bob Thornton's directing career, and vaporized Todd Haynes.**

"Miramax has been a blessing and a curse for the film industry. You have to give them credit because they made indie movies sexy. They showed you could make money off them. The curse is that they commercialized them."

—ETHAN HAWKE

Still not entirely recovered from his five-week stint in the hospital, with *Talk* magazine floundering and the presidential election just around the corner, Harvey kept up an exhausting pace. Despite the Oscar nominations for *The Cider House Rules*, there was little to cheer about. Not only had Harvey's reentry traumatized his staff, but there was the humiliation of having to acknowledge that Bob's Dimension division, which had released *Scream 3* on February 4, 2000, to the tune of an $89 million domestic gross, was propping up the company.

Dimension's slate included another movie for which Bob had high hopes, *O*, directed by Tim Blake Nelson, who had previously made a small picture called *Eye of God*. Nelson is a short, intense, articulate hyphenate (actor-writer-director) best known for playing unshaven, nose-picking white trash roles in films as disparate as Miguel Arteta's *The Good Girl* and Steven Spielberg's *Minority Report*. He grew up in Oklahoma, went to Brown University and then Juilliard to study acting.

O was essentially *Othello* set in a prep school. It was a violent film with several intense scenes, including the rape of a white girl by a black student, and a shootout in the school at the end. The cast included Mekhi Phifer, Julia Stiles, Josh Hartnett, and Martin Sheen. Eric Gitter, a lawyer turned producer, along with four co-producers, raised $3.5 million from an assort-ment of investors. Just before they were slated to go into production, Bob made a run at the film for Dimension. His pitch was, "We're the kings of marketing films like this, we've done every film Quentin Tarantino's ever made, we've done *Priest*, we've done *The Crying Game*." The Miramax mythology, the origins legend—the nod to Mom and Dad enshrined in the company name, the stories about Miriam and her rugulah, the life-altering impact of *The 400 Blows*, the appropriation of Tarantino, the controversies over *The Crying Game, Kids*, and so on—was key to maintaining the fiction that the Weinsteins were the little guys. The less independent Miramax was, the more important it was to insist that it was still in the indie film business. This was the fig leaf that made it possible to continue trading on the reputation of a company that no longer existed. Gitter and Nelson bought it. It didn't hurt that Bob made a very generous preemptive bid of $7.5 million, and pledged to release it on one thousand screens. Says Nel-son, "They clearly saw the commercial potential of the movie."

On April 20, 1999, while *O* was in post-production, twelve students and one teacher were shot to death at Columbine High School, in Littleton, Colorado, mimicking the ending of *O*. Sure enough, the Senate Com-merce Committee scheduled hearings on the marketing of violence to chil-dren, and Senator Joe Lieberman testified on May 4. Instead of sensing trouble, Nelson just felt Columbine made *O* more topical. Bob seemed to like what he was seeing and the director imagined that the brothers would charge fearlessly ahead, the way they had with all those other films Bob had mentioned. Bob said he loved the dailies, wanted to rush the picture into release on October 17, and if not then, Thanksgiving.

Nelson gave Bob a cut on June 4. Soon after, he got a "really sweet" call from him, in which he said, "I love the film. I can't wait to show it to my brother. I just wanted to call to let you know that." Bob had reason to be in a good mood. He was about to release *Scary Movie* on July 7, a picture that would burn through the box office like no Dimension movie before it, even *Scream*. At the end of its run, it would gross an astonishing $157 million do-mestic. At the same time, however, Lieberman was pressing his crusade against violence in movies. "I was getting these calls from Eric Gitter," Nel-son recalls. "He and Miramax were starting to fight about everything. Eric was saying, 'They're terrified of this movie. And they wish they'd never bought it.'"

Nelson delivered the film on March 17, 2000. As far as he could tell, Miramax seemed happy. Except for one thing: they would not release the picture. "The movie just sat there," he recalls. "It was going to open several different times over the year, and then they would cancel it."

Meanwhile, Harvey continued to raise his profile on the national political scene. He emerged as a major fund-raiser and cheerleader for the Gore-Lieberman ticket. All told, he and Eve between them gave various candidates $750,000 and raised an additional $14 million. Harvey was invariably respectful, not to say obsequious in the presence of the First Couple. It was always, "Mr. President," never "Bill." He wouldn't eat in front of them. And he never smoked in front of Hillary, because he knew she didn't like it. But afterward, he would gorge on Cokes, hamburgers, and French fries, and chain-smoke on the plane back to New York.

Harvey threw a fund-raiser/birthday party for Hillary Clinton's fifty-third at the Roseland Ballroom on October 25. With a multitude of celebrity egos, a million things can go wrong at events like that, and a few weeks earlier, at a Gore fund-raising concert at Radio City Music Hall, there had been at least one incident. The green room was packed with stars—Matt Damon, Salma Hayek, Bon Jovi, Paul Simon, etc.—all wanting to sit down, but there weren't enough chairs. A young assistant in publicity had been delegated the task of guarding a precious half-circle of space comprised of a couch, two love seats, and a small table, apparently so that Harvey and his guest, Julia Roberts, could have a tête-à-tête. First the assistant had to turn away the wife of VH1's John Sykes, who was eight months' pregnant. Not happy, she snapped, "My husband is throwing this event."

"Ma'am, I'm so sorry, I can't let you sit here. This couch is reserved for Harvey Weinstein." She stormed off. Then Jimmy Buffet, Harrison Ford, and his wife, E.T. screenwriter Melissa Mathison descended on the couches, all wanting to sit down. "I'm sorry, this area is taken, Harvey Weinstein is sitting here."

"Come on, let us sit down." There were closed-circuit TVs around the room, and it was clear that at that very moment, Harvey was on stage. They said, "Hey, look, there he is, he's not sitting here right now, we'll move as soon as he comes in." No sooner had they seated themselves than Harvey entered the green room with Roberts and made a beeline for the table as the assistant frantically pushed Ford et al. away, pleading, "Get up, get up, get up." They did so, balancing their plates on their glasses. Roberts took off, abandoning Harvey for Damon, while the Miramax co-chairman, smiling, barked at the squatters in a tense voice, "Hey, that's my seat." The assistant, mortified, fessed up, said, "Harvey, it's my fault, I'm the one watching this area." Furious, but trying to put a good face on it in front of his celebrity friends, he pointed at the cowering girl in front of Ford, Mathison, and Buffet, laughed, and replied, "Yeah, it's your fault, you're fired!" She thought, Ohmigod, Harvey just fired me. He found her two bosses and berated them in a low voice, whereupon they came over and started yelling at her, "You're so stupid, we can't even trust you with this.

This is the easiest thing in the world, watching a table. Go stand over in the corner." Hillary Clinton was in the vicinity but was swept away by Sykes so that she wouldn't be exposed to the spectacle of one of her most prominent fund-raisers beheading an underling. (The assistant was rehired the next day.)

Later that evening, the master of ceremonies, John Leguizamo, departing from his script, shocking the Gores, the Liebermans, and Hillary Clinton, all seated in the first row, with a series of off-color remarks. (Example: The reason Gore had chosen Lieberman as his running mate was because "All the women in New York know that a Jew can lick Bush.")

At Hillary's birthday party, Harvey, wound tight, reverted to music promoter mode, which meant he was killing everybody in his sight line. The master of ceremonies was Nathan Lane, working pro bono. Shortly before Lane was due to go on, Harvey decided to review his script to make sure there was nothing in it that would embarrass Hillary. He took exception to a silly joke about Mayor Giuliani's comb-over, and exploded, yelling something like, "This is my fucking show, we don't need you."

Meanwhile, Nelson and Gitter had concluded that Harvey feared releasing a violent film like O in the midst of Lieberman's jihad because it might expose the candidates as well as himself to the charge of hypocrisy. In November 2000, journalist Rebecca Traister, quoting an unnamed source, reported in the New York Observer that Gitter had been told "that no decision would be made on when O was [to be] released until after the election." But Dimension publicist Elizabeth Clark affirmed that Bob Weinstein "stands behind the film," adding that "the company has released difficult films before," and promised that the film would "be released next year."

Traister, then twenty-four, was a cub reporter working for "The Transom," a gossip column in the Observer. On the evening of Monday, November 6, the day before the presidential election, she found herself at the Tribeca Grand Hotel at a party for Karen Duffy, Revlon model/MTV vj/friend of Harvey, thrown by the Miramax co-chairman to celebrate her new book, Model Patient: My Life as an Incurable Wise-Ass. The Miramax publicists had been stonewalling Traister, and she was there in search of a quote for her story.

Duffy's book told the saga of her struggle with sarcoidosis, a rare inflammatory condition thought to be the result of an immune system malfunction. She credited Harvey with saving her life by getting her into the hands of the right doctors. Traister, accompanied by her colleague and then boyfriend, Andrew Goldman, found themselves swept along in Harvey's slipstream, only a few paces behind him, among the crowd of stylishly dressed well-wishers on their way in. Traister caught up to him, and clutching her tape recorder, she asked him about O. He brushed her off, saying, "I have nothing to do with that. That's Bob, my brother's [division]. I haven't seen the movie and I don't know anything about it." He wasn't very responsive but it was a quote, and she was done for the night.

Harvey, however, was not accustomed to being bearded by reporters and asked questions he'd prefer not to answer. His army of publicists was supposed to protect him from just such surprises, not that it was often necessary, given how skilled he was at carrot-and-sticking the press. When the Miramax marketing department bought ads, TV spots, and so on it had a justifiable expectation of getting what it paid for. But Harvey demanded his publicists get the same results for free, and more, exercise as much control over what was written about himself, his brother, and his company as he exercised over paid advertising. The publicists not only planted pieces, they routinely tried, and sometimes succeeded, in killing stories, spinning those they couldn't kill, and selecting writers. Of course, studio publicists have always planted favorable items and exercised damage control, but it is almost unprecedented for the chief executive to be as personally involved and invested as Harvey was—and is. Reviewers who panned a Miramax film could expect to get an irate call or letter from the Miramax co-chairman himself accusing them of "betraying" him, sometimes followed up by the customary bouquet. Nothing was too small to escape his notice.

Back in May 1995, after Harvey had acquired, seen, and hated *Dead Man*—in that order—at Cannes, he vigorously tried to persuade director Jim Jarmusch to recut it. Failing, he held the film for a year, until May 1996, and then released it without much enthusiasm. Recalls lead *Village Voice* reviewer Jim Hoberman, "*Dead Man* was Jarmusch's best movie since *Stranger Than Paradise*. But he stood up to them, and they were vindictive about it. [Publicist] Cynthia Swartz called me and told me what a terrible film it was. They were badmouthing their own movie!" In January of the new year Jarmusch, a presenter at the New York Film Critics Circle Awards, publicly rebuked Miramax, to the merriment of the assembled guests, saying that *Dead Man* had been seen at more private screenings than public ones, alluding to Miramax's failure to support the film. This incident provoked John Clark, a writer for the *Los Angeles Times,* to do a story. Among the people Clark interviewed was Hoberman, who recalls, "One of the things that I said to him, fairly innocuous, was that I thought that Miramax had gotten more conservative since they were bought by Disney." Then Hoberman traveled from his home in New York City to Santa Monica on a business trip. He continues, "I came back to my hotel room, and there was this series of increasingly hysterical messages on the machine from Cynthia Swartz calling on her cell phone from Sundance. In the last one, where she was very upset, she said something like, 'Everybody has retracted what they said but you. I really hope that you do, and so does Harvey, because if you don't retract it, he's going to be forced to take some sort of action that he doesn't want to take.' "

In early 2002, Patrick Goldstein raised Harvey's ire by devoting one of his columns in the *Los Angeles Times* to chastising Miramax for its behavior in that year's Oscar campaign. As Goldstein recalls, Harvey phoned him and said something like, "You're a piece of shit, your column is a piece of shit, no one cares what you write, they throw the newspaper away and wrap fish in it."

Then there were the treats. Harvey had provoked a minor scandal when he gave *New York* magazine editor Kurt Andersen a lift on the Miramax jet to Martha's Vineyard in 1994. (Andersen offered to pay his own way, at the commercial rate.) The Miramax co-chairman claims this was the only time that sort of thing happened, although it occurred at least once more, when he ferried the new *Premiere* editor-in-chief, Jim Meigs, from the Sundance Film Festival back to New York in January 1997. Says Meigs, "Later, I regretted it. It was unseemly."

It is well known that Miramax has some of New York's gossip columnists in its pocket. Says former Miramax publicist Dennis Higgins, "Harvey is obsessed with the columns. He would rather see something break in a column than put out a press release and have it appear in the trades." The most notorious example is Roger Friedman, who often uses his Internet gossip column, *411*, to tout (and very occasionally knock) Miramax films. Says Higgins, "There's no one in the pocket like Roger. It's almost, 'Whaddya want him to write?' We [even] got him to say *The Shipping News* is great." Harvey financed Friedman's documentary, *Only the Strong Survive*, on soul singers, and is unapologetic. "Roger Friedman is making me $1.5 million," he says. "He can come up to my office all day long. A. J. Benza, thrown out of the *Daily News*, was broke. I gave him fifty grand to write a book. Mitchell Fink, from the *Daily News*, is gonna write a book for us. I do not say to Mitchell Fink, take good care of me. He's roasted me so many fuckin' times, it can't be a conflict of interest."

Richard Johnson, the editor of the *New York Post*'s widely read "Page Six," was hired by Miramax as a consultant when Harvey decided to remake a French film called *Jet Set*, about the club scene. Says Johnson, "The idea was, maybe I would work with a writer. They lost their enthusiasm. No money ever changed hands." Had the project not stalled, would it have been a conflict of interest? "Sure!" Johnson responds. "It's hard to write negative things about people who are paying you. But can't I recuse myself? How much do I write about Miramax?" Paula Froelich, his colleague at "Page Six," has a deal with Miramax Books for "a book on using the rules of fame to get ahead," she explains. Some suspected that Harvey used the magazines he had money in to distribute largesse to those members of New York's Grub Street who were Miramax-friendly. Says a former *Talk* editor, "They were always thrusting pieces on us that these gossip columnists had written that were not assigned by the editors, but by somebody else. Maybe by Tina. But Tina considered herself a literary lion, and they were beneath her, so someone must have made her do it, like Harvey. It was clear."

But even though Harvey well understood that he could win more friends with honey, Traister apparently didn't understand the rules of the game Miramax had laid down, and when she buttonholed him, he just couldn't help himself. As she was preparing to leave, she felt a heavy hand on her shoulder. He pulled her around, growled, "You're not gonna use that stuff I gave you, are you?"

"Harvey, I wouldn't worry about it. You really didn't say anything that could be used against you in any way."

"You can't use any of it, not a word." He was keeping his voice level, but it sounded to her as though he was expending considerable effort to do so.

"I identified myself, you didn't tell me it was off the record, and you were talking into my tape recorder."

"Give me the tape recorder!"

"No, I'm not going to do that."

Poking his finger vigorously into her shoulder, and turning to include Goldman, who had made his way over when he saw the commotion, Harvey bellowed, "You guys don't give me a break, I can't believe you fuckin' did this to me, you come to this woman's cancer party I'm throwing out of the goodness of my heart, and you guys show up under false pretenses— you're fucking scum, reporters don't do this, you don't come to one event and ask about another story. You have to go through my office."

"Harvey, I called your office this week, I've put in requests to talk to you and that wasn't working."

According to a witness, still poking and pushing her, spittle flying from his mouth, he leaned into her face and screamed something like, "This bitch came in here, she lied, she said she was going to cover the party, she's not covering the party. She came to sabotage me."

Traister was petrified. She thought, If he can break up his own party by screaming and pushing us, well shit, now anything can happen.

Goldman, in his late twenties, and maybe a hundred pounds shy of Harvey, chose this moment to intervene, saying, "Harvey, hold on a second, I was invited to this party, I'm covering this party—"

"That's a lie, you brought this woman." Sweating heavily, his face red and engorged, Harvey swung around to him, and drilling a hole in his chest with his forefinger, screamed, "This is going to be you and me, I want this mano-a-mano, I'm taking you outside and I'm gonna fuckin' kick your ass."

Goldman was so scared he looked like he was going to soil himself. But he had the presence of mind to pull out his tape recorder. Speaking haltingly through dry lips, he said, "Let's forget about what happened with Rebecca, and let's talk about Karen Duffy." As Miramax publicists swarmed around Traister, profusely apologizing—"Oh, I'm so sorry, he's very stressed out, it's the night before the election, he's really worked up, call tomorrow, we'll get you a quote"—Weinstein subsided as suddenly as he'd erupted, as if a switch had been thrown, and the two men proceeded to have a perfectly tranquil conversation about the author. But thinking he had an opening with the newly quiescent Weinstein, Goldman made a mistake. He said, "Harvey, I really think it was unfortunate what you did to this girl. She was just doing her job, the paper has been really respectful of you in the past, I just don't see why there was any need for you to do this in front of all these people." He had inadvertently flipped the switch back again, and Weinstein began to tremble with rage. As the guests watched agog, martini glasses aquiver, Harvey shouted obscenities, screamed, "Kick these people out, they're here under false pretenses, they're liars, they're liars, we're never talking to them again."

"Harvey, I don't think you want to do this," gasped Goldman.

"I'm sick of shit like that in my life. If you guys fuckin' play like that, then I'm gonna deal with you as a guy and I'm gonna kick your ass. Okay? Somebody has cancer. That's bad taste. Then you'll deal with me. And you know what? It's good that I'm the fucking sheriff of this fucking lawless piece of shit fucking town. Somebody cares." He shoved Goldman, and pausing to point at Traister, shouted, "Keep your bitch colleague under control." At some point Harvey must have noticed that the record indicator on Goldman's tape recorder was blinking red. He bellowed, "You fuckin' getting all this? You fuckin' getting all this?" and made a grab for it. In the scuffle Goldman fell backward, and struck a woman, an actress, with the tape recorder. Pointing at the *Observer* reporter, Harvey shouted, "Look at what this fucking guy did, look at what this piece of shit did. He hit this woman at this party, I'm gonna take him outside and I'm gonna fuckin' kill him!" He put Goldman in a headlock and dragged him out the glass doors onto the street as the guests poured out behind them and paparazzi snapped pictures. Finally, the Miramax publicists, who were all over Weinstein like Lilliputians on Gulliver, grabbing at his arms and saying things like, "Let him go, let him go, Harvey, you're acting crazy," succeeded in separating the two men. Weinstein instructed the hotel security to seize the tape recorder. But they had no idea who Harvey was, and as he fran-tically yelled, "This is my party, this is my party," Goldman made his escape.

In addition to the paparazzi, there were several gossip columnists covering the event; Goldman and Traister fully expected to see the story splashed all over the tabloids the next day. After all, the head of a major division of the Walt Disney Company had attacked a journalist at a party in a posh downtown hotel in front of scores of witnesses. But there was virtually nothing. Those items that did appear blamed the victims and seemed to have been spun by Miramax, like the one on "Page Six" of the *Post* that went, "A couple of pushy reporters for the *New York Observer* pushed Miramax chief Harvey Weinstein to the breaking point, causing an ugly scene at what should have been a joyous celebration for former MTV veejay Karen Duffy." In *Inside.com*, one of the few outlets to accurately report the confrontation, a Miramax publicist denied Harvey had had Goldman in a headlock, admitting only that he was "helping" him leave. Miramax publicists continued to insist that they had agreed to give Traister the quote she wanted, and that her behavior was inappropriate. Traister told friends she believed that she was subsequently followed by a detective, and that Miramax called around to her former employers to find out if she had ever done anything reprehensible.

Later that night, Harvey got on a plane with Affleck, Robert De Niro, and Glenn Close to fly to Miami to join Jon Bon Jovi, Stevie Wonder, and other celebrities onstage with Gore for an election eve rally. The stars rarely see Harvey out of control, and of course he never mentioned the dustup at the Tribeca Grand. "Does Harvey intimidate journalists?" muses Affleck. "I didn't know anything about it. If he intimidates gossip columnists—good, they fuckin' deserve it. They print erroneous shit every fucking day. Some guy trying to do some body slam story on *O*, where Iago's monologue that's four pages long gets boiled down to Josh Hartnett saying, 'Watch your girl, bro,' and he got yelled at and thrown out of the party—it's not like we're talking about the world peace. Where his behavior is like Queens coming across the river, and he's still the concert promoter, I think it's kind of charming. Maybe not so charming if you're the one in the headlock, but Harvey is a tough bastard, his people skills are not all that good. And he doesn't have a lot of restraint, he's all id. But Harvey is not Suge Knight. People are different to different people, and I've seen only the human side of him. He supported me and Matt, and he's been a pretty good friend to me."

On election night, November 7, Harvey took over Elaine's and told everybody that the Clintons would be dropping by. But the night got so crazy, with the dead heat in Florida, that Hillary called over from the Sheraton, where the couple was staying, to say, "We just can't come." Weinstein was infuriated, and told her, "I'm bringing a group up to your hotel." Capricia Marshall, who had been the White House social secretary, chimed in, said, "You cannot bring any press, and please limit it." Harvey walked around Elaine's, saying, "You can come, you can't, you can come, you can't." Affleck, Tina Brown, Uma Thurman, and Ethan Hawke were among the chosen few, as well as Roger Friedman and a few other reporters, despite the ban on the press.

There was no question that the time and effort Harvey was putting into the political campaign, as well as *Gangs of New York*, was hurting his production slate. Jim Mangold and Cathy Konrad were prepping *Kate & Leopold*. Says Konrad, "Generally you walk into movies at Miramax going, 'I hope Harvey doesn't come around.' Yet, this time we were begging for Harvey to come around, and he never did, until it was too late." He seemed bored by the nuts and bolts of production. "He asked us if we knew what was going on with him," Mangold recalls. "He said, 'Ya know, I don't just make movies anymore. I'm changing the world!'" Konrad thought, What do you do with that? I know we sound stupid—we care about the world too—but we have to start shooting in two weeks and no one gives a shit!

BY THE FALL OF 2000, Scott Greenstein's perch had become precarious. None of USA's films had made much money, and with high overhead, the company was devouring cash. On the eve of the release of *Traffic*, *Variety* published a piece saying that it was only a matter of time before Barry Diller fired him. People were counting the days until the ax fell.

But Greenstein showed surprising staying power. And when Russell Schwartz had brought in the Coen brothers' *The Man Who Wasn't There*, or Donna Gigliotti snagged Neil LaBute's *Possession* and Robert Altman's *Gosford Park*, he was happy. Before you knew it, USA had developed a respectable slate of pictures, none of which had yet been released.

Soderbergh thought he had a shot at the Oscar, and wanted *Traffic* out before the end of the year, which meant bucking the holiday gridlock. It was up to Jack Foley to get the theaters. For a new, small company like USA, "The competition is so destructive, so sociopathically murderous, that going up against the big guys at Christmas is bordering on volunteering for electroshock treatment," he says. "Everything about this picture was a square peg. It was a drug film, cerebral, noncommercial, and America was looking for entertainment, *Meet the Parents*. So coming from Miramax, where you live outside the box—take your rules and shove 'em up your ass—I took the Avco in Westwood, which was available because it had fallen on hard times, and we won. We won huge."

Traffic was released on December 27, 2000, and started breaking records. While marred by the improbable Michael Douglas subplot (with some exceptions, only in movies do high-level government officials resign on the grounds of principle), it was a throwback to the great faux documentaries of the 1960s and 1970s, like Peter Watkins's *The War Game*, and filled with all manner of formal experimentation. "I spent a lot of time analyzing *Battle of Algiers* and Z—both of which have that great feeling of things that are caught, instead of staged, which is what we were after," Soderbergh explained.

Traffic improbably grossed $124 million, only a million and a half less than Soderbergh's big Universal hit, *Erin Brockovich*, and it stayed the blade that had been tickling the nape of Greenstein's neck. Soderbergh's two consecutive blockbusters, meanwhile, finally gave him some muscle. After an interval of a decade, he cashed in the *sex, lies* promissory note, partnered in a new production company called Section Eight with his *Out of Sight* star, George Clooney. He started calling filmmakers—Kim Peirce, James Gray, Lodge Kerrigan (*Clean, Shaven*), Harmony Korine (*Julien Donkey-Boy*), Alison Maclean (*Jesus' Son*), John Maybury (*Love Is the Devil*), Chris Nolan (*Memento*), Alejandro González Iñárritu (*Amores Perros*), Alfonso Cuarón (*Y Tu Mamá También*). He asked them, "What are you doing? Can I help?" Soderbergh explains, "I don't know what else you're supposed to do with whatever juice you've got at the moment other than get interesting movies made. We're trying to move as quickly as we can before that juice runs out."

Soderbergh's idea was to offer indies he admired a financial incentive to do more commercial projects. His assumption was that the studios, with their increasingly single-minded focus on blockbusters, had abandoned the center, the kinds of films they used to make. "I feel there's dissatisfaction at both extremes," he says. "People who go to see art house movies are frustrated with what they're seeing, and people going to the big star-driven vehicles are also disappointed with what they're seeing." He proposed another model: "There's a middle ground to be had as there was in the '70s. Movies that were being financed by studios with stars in them were being made by really interesting directors. I've always thought that I'd rather see a movie in four thousand theaters by Todd Haynes than some hack." As his Section Eight partner, Clooney, put it, "Part of what we're trying to do is say, 'Why can't we do the aesthetic that came from [the '70s]?' We just try to push an indie sensibility within the Hollywood mainstream."

Soderbergh asked filmmakers on the other end of the line, "Do you want to stay in the art house ghetto your whole life, or are you interested in working in an established genre with movie stars? Because there's a way to do what you do and not be bothered by the studio, but also make something that people might go to see." He explains, "One of the reasons *Memento* popped is that it was an art house movie but it was also a murder mystery that had a couple of actors that aren't huge stars but are known, and I feel audiences went, 'Oh my God, someone who wants to tell a story and wants to entertain me a little bit. It isn't like eating vegetables.' Most of the directors have said, 'God, yeah, I'm really tired of making movies that nobody sees.' "

Soderbergh felt confident in their answers; after all, he had been there himself. He was using his own career trajectory as a model. He had hit the bull's-eye before anyone knew a target existed, after which, donning the indie hair shirt, he stumbled off the path into the wilderness, where he lost himself for nearly a decade until he hitched a ride on the Hollywood freeway, turning away from the esoteric (read, personal) projects that characterized his early years. He explains, "It makes sense when you consider that the independent movement has been swallowed up by the studios, that I'd inevitably be some sort of hybrid. Maybe I was acting preemptively when I decided I'm going to move toward the middle, because I don't know that I had a career [outside the mainstream] anymore. Something must have felt like, That's not happening." In Soderbergh's Good Samaritan phone calls to his less fortunate brethren, he was preaching the gospel of St. Harvey and St. Robert. Almost every indie institution had become devoted to nudging filmmakers toward the commercial center, whether it be Sundance or Miramax or the Independent Feature Project's Spirit Awards or Damon and Affleck's Project Greenlight or the example of the exceptional career of Tarantino.

Yet he was asking them to do something he failed at himself. Soderbergh hasn't been a hybrid, like Tarantino, so much as he was of two minds, divided, following the more common, easier, one-for-me, one-for-them model. The hybrids are hard to pull off—when they fail, they're dismissed as "tweeners"—and in a decade and a half, Soderbergh has only found the zone twice, in *sex, lies*, which increasingly seems like a happy accident, and *Traffic*. After *Traffic*, he embarked on *Ocean's 11* for Warner's, an unapologetic Hollywood movie, with an all-star cast. It wasn't a pleasant experience. "For me, *Ocean's* made no sense," he says. "It was the hardest thing I ever did. It's a movie about absolutely nothing. I found it just brain-crushing. I never felt fluent, never felt comfortable. Every day I was hanging on by my fingernails."

No sooner had he begun his studio film than he wanted to do one for himself. "About two weeks into it, I was feeling like, I want to do a little, a guerrilla movie. I just need to wash this out of my system." Ironically, he described the movie he wanted to make as *Son of Schizopolis*. "*Schizopolis* was not designed to be understood by anybody," he continues. "I combined the energy of that with a more coherent throughline, a narrative spine that's more in line with *sex, lies*." He wrote it during the *Ocean's* production with a friend, Coleman Hough, a playwright. The film was called *How to Survive a Hotel Room Fire*.

In February 2000, Soderbergh had read an article in *The New York Times* about Godfrey Reggio and his unsuccessful, ten-year journey to find financing for the last of his *Qatsi* trilogy. He thought, That's just insane, this guy's, like, amazing. He called Reggio and offered to finance the initial phase of production with his bonuses from *Erin Brockovich* and *Ocean's 11*.

Soderbergh gave Reggio $1.7 million against a $6 million budget. But just at the moment *Naqoyqatsi* shifted into high gear, he started running out of money. He thought, MGM owns the first two *Qatsi* films. I'll go to them and say, If you'll put up the remaining $4 million for Godfrey's movie, I'll give you *How to Survive a Hotel Room Fire*. And I'll eat my share to make it more enticing. So he went to MGM. Executives there said, "Sounds great," but then nothing happened. Months passed. Finally, Soderbergh called his manager, Pat Dollard, and asked, "What the fuck's going on? I need to know, I'm outta money, we're in a crunch here." Dollard phoned MGM, came back and told Soderbergh, "They're running numbers." The director replied, "That's it, call Miramax and USA and make the pitch." Both of them responded, "Where do we send the check?" He went with Miramax because Harvey also said, "I'm taking you out of Godfrey's movie, financially. You should never put yourself in that situation. I'll pay the whole $6 million." Adds Soderbergh, "Forty-eight hours later we had a three-page deal memo, so Godfrey got funded, and we went off and made *Hotel Room Fire*." For Harvey, it was a twofer: he was dying to revive the relationship with Soderbergh, for the moment the hottest director going, as well as get into business with Clooney, now a huge star. The film, which became *Full Frontal*, was shot in eighteen days in November 2001 on a rock-bottom budget of $2 million by keeping costs down, about a third on film and two thirds in digital video. None of its all-star cast, including Julia Roberts, was allowed trailers.

Yet *Full Frontal*, a cat's paw for Soderbergh and Clooney's attempts to renovate American filmmaking by finding a middle way, seemed to offend everyone. Rather than applauding a filmmaker like Soderbergh, unlike so many of his peers who—dare we speak the words—have "sold out," the reviewers roasted him. They seemed to regard it as a stunt, as if a director who had a commercial hit like *Ocean's 11* couldn't possibly be sincere in wanting to go home again. As Ethan Hawke puts it, "They'd just gotten through celebrating the shit out of him, setting him up to be the great Hollywood director, and he was finally going to come through on the promise of *sex, lies* and be a 'player,' right, and then he went back to get some indie street cred, and they smelled a rat. They're crazy."

Purists, the "real" indies who had little interest in making films inside the system, didn't like it either. To them, Soderbergh must have looked like the mouse in a Pavlovian experiment. Each time he wandered off into indie territory, he got an electric shock that drove him back to the studio cheese.

Soderbergh had always rationalized his romance with commercialism by modestly insisting that he never aspired to be an auteur, and in this he offended some of the hybrids he has been trying to promote, the ones who made studio films on their own terms. "I was on a panel with him at the Hamptons Film Festival in 1997, and he said something that surprised me," recalls David O. Russell. "He said, 'I want to know who's gonna be the next Sydney Pollack!' I thought, Wow, that's a weird thing to say. Then I realized, That's him! He's become the next Sydney Pollack. He sees himself as a craftsman. That's very convenient for him, because somehow it becomes an excuse to say, 'I can make more generic movies, like *Ocean's 11* since, let's face it, I don't have any pretensions, I'm not a visionary.' But that's a pretty black-and-white way to look at it. Is Alexander Payne a visionary? Is Spike Jonze a visionary? I don't know. But I know they're not just craftsmen. I know they're making really ballsy movies, and that's what I'm interested in. I don't know that I'm a great artist, but I suffer over the choices I make, and I think it's okay to make a movie that takes more time and tries to thread the needle more."

Soderbergh is probably right; there *is* a middle ground between the marginal and the commercial. It is the way taken by Russell, Payne, Jonze, and the two Andersons, who have all managed, with the help of modest budgets and big stars, to make studio-financed films with as few concessions to the market as possible. Even Hawke, albeit speaking as an actor, has started to come around. "You can't piss upwind for that long before you're peeing all over your pants," he says. "To be honest, I felt really excited by *Training Day* because I made a movie that could play at the mall that I feel comfortable talking about, and it lets me know that I can do it, and I want to keep trying to do it. Rather than doing one for them and one for me, I want to try to find the one with them that I feel proud of. Maybe that will come."

But it's like walking a tightrope without a net. One false move can land the filmmakers back where they started, scrambling for money wherever they can find it, like the Coen brothers after the failure of *The Hudsucker Proxy* in 1994, when Warner's unceremoniously dropped them. Whether Soderbergh and Clooney's attempt to reinvent the 1970s model makes sense is questionable. The same economic pressures that have driven the studios into co- and co-co-productions with one another and almost any entity with a bank account may conceivably drive them to take more chances. But in the 1970s, they were nearly bankrupt and had no choice; now they do. Plus, in that decade, the studios' primary market, the counterculture, was much more uniform than the market for movies today, which is demographically diverse.

Besides, there are good reasons indies have shunned the studios even as the studios have shunned them. Russell, who was most successful in pushing a personal, even subversive vision through the studio Cuisinart, decided, after *Three Kings,* to do smaller films. "*Three Kings* was my bottom," he says. "It was so stressful and so unpleasant that I said, 'I will never, ever do that big a movie again.' I will only write things that are closer to my heart, that I can do on a smaller scale. Some filmmakers, like Soderbergh, decided, 'I'm gonna make some commercial films, and then I'm gonna make some noncommercial films.' I feel, 'I don't want to make that bargain anymore.' "

AS THE ALL-IMPORTANT year 2000 holiday season approached, Miramax's hopes were riding on its triumvirate of stars, Affleck and Paltrow, who were featured in *Bounce,* Affleck in *Reindeer Games,* and Damon, who led the cast of *All the Pretty Horses,* directed by Billy Bob Thornton, also, of course, a Miramax creation.

All the Pretty Horses was an expensive, elaborate production with a tortured history that Miramax shared with Columbia. John Calley had acquired the Cormac McCarthy novel on which it was based way back when he was head of MGM/UA, and had hired Mike Nichols, an old friend, to direct it. Nichols decided that he would rather produce the picture, which then needed a director. When Calley left MGM/UA and became chairman of Sony Pictures in 1996, he took the project with him, and mentioned Thornton to Nichols. One day, on the set of *Primary Colors,* Nichols walked up to Thornton in the catering tent and dropped the script in his lap, saying, "You have to direct this movie!" Thornton, no great reader, didn't know McCarthy's novel. But he did love Westerns. His favorite movie was *High Noon.*

Thornton had a history of not suffering suits easily, and he was skeptical about doing a big, $50 million studio movie. He reputedly told Columbia, "Let's all be very clear. Yuh know what kind of movies Ah make. If yuh want sweepin' vistas, then hire somebody who does that. Don't be hirin' me for this if you're gonna cut mah legs out." Indeed, Columbia didn't want to hire his director of photography, Barry Markowitz, who had shot *Sling Blade* and *The Apostle,* because they didn't think he had the visual flair for it. They said, "We need Roger Deakins, we need John Seale, we need Tak Fujimoto." Thornton replied, "Ah want mah whole crew, the guys who have slugged it out with me on these small movies, and not gotten paid." Columbia gave in, and Thornton took the job. Miramax, which held options on his next three films dating from *Sling Blade*, was then in a position to demand an equity position from Columbia in exchange for Thornton's services. Thornton hired his writing partner, Tom Epperson, to rewrite Ted Tally's script, which was 150 pages long, thirty pages over the average. So was Epperson's. "Billy didn't ask me to shorten it. It seemed to not be an issue that it was a long script," Epperson recalls. But, he adds, "that was the whole downfall of the movie."

Thornton wanted Damon for the lead. Thornton assured him, "Ah've had this talk with Columbia, and Ah can make the movie the way Ah wanna make it." At one point, he went to the studio and said, "Ah want to do this movie for $25 million, not $50 million, because Ah'm afraid that when you get into this $50 million thing that yuh not gonna want the movie Ah'm gonna give you, and yo' gonna get scared." Columbia replied, "No, no, no, no, this is our big epic movie." Says Damon, "That makes you wonder who read the book over there, because anybody who thinks that *All the Pretty Horses* is epic, just because the title makes you think about vistas, is wrong. It was a dark, dark story. It's not *Braveheart*. It's not even Larry McMurtry. It's the exact opposite."

After struggling to get the length down to manageable proportions, Thornton came up with a three hour, forty minute cut, which he showed to Calley and Nichols. Says former Miramax marketing head Dennis Rice, who also saw the three-hour-plus opus, "It was the most self-indulgent director's cut I'd ever seen. It was like torture to watch that movie." Affleck, who also saw the cut, says, "I thought it was brilliant, a masterpiece, but I'm willing to concede that my taste may be different from everybody else's, and maybe I'm wrong." Calley is reputed to have been effusive as well. Then he disappeared, and turned the movie over to Columbia Pictures president Amy Pascal. Pascal and Thornton did not like each other. Thornton is said to have brought a coloring book to one meeting with her, and sat there with a crayon, filling it in while she was speaking. (Pascal declined to comment.)

Still, Columbia was so high on *Pretty Horses* that in late 1999, Thornton was offered *The Shipping News*, based on the Annie Proulx novel of the same name, to direct. Thornton was seeing Laura Dern at the time and insisted on casting her in the role of Wavey Prowse. Columbia wanted Julia Roberts, Meg Ryan, or Julianne Moore, anybody but Dern, and turned her down. Fed up, Thornton, who had been fighting with Pascal over the length of *Pretty Horses*, dropped out of the project, whereupon Columbia, according to Weinstein, said, "We're not going to be your partner" on the movie. Lasse Hallström wanted to direct it, so Miramax bought the picture for him for $3 million.

Thornton had final cut on *Pretty Horses* up to two hours. Over that, the studio had the right to take it away from him. Columbia test-screened the picture at the Sherman Oaks Galleria—the studios' version of Miramax's New Jersey malls—during the Christmas rush. Women carrying shopping bags wandered in midway through the movie, watched for a few minutes, and wandered out again in search of holiday sales. In other words, the screening was a disaster. Pascal was still pressuring Thornton to cut the picture down. Explains Damon, "You can understand them freaking out, you can understand them not wanting to release a three-hour movie that's slow and thoughtful by today's standards. When you write a check for $50 million, you want the money back. Amy reportedly yelled at Billy Bob, 'I did not want to make a $50 million art film!' " The picture missed its Christmas 1999 release date.

Talking to Thornton about cutting his picture was like speaking to a deaf mute. Taking up the cudgels, Affleck argued, "If you reduce this thing, you're gonna be neither fish nor fowl. The critics aren't gonna respect the artistry, the genius of it, because you'll have truncated the movie, and audiences are not gonna pile in, because there aren't gonna be any Wookies or Hobbits." Meanwhile, Harvey was telling everybody who would listen, "Amy Pascal is just bustin' my ass on the movie, they just don't know how to sell it, they don't think we have an Oscar contender. It's long, but it's great. We can do something with it." By August 2000, Pascal had reached the end of her rope with Thornton. Columbia was afraid that it was going to take a big hit. According to Damon, the studio said something like, "Harvey, you handle it, you have the relationship with Billy, you know how to talk to him, you know how to release just about anything, release this fucker, good luck!" Harvey, thrilled to have the opportunity to be a White Knight, jumped at it, and Miramax took over the domestic release, while Columbia retained foreign. Harvey told Thornton, "I know exactly what to do, we're gonna get you all these Academy nominations," while Miramax publicity claimed that Harvey was the only person Thornton would listen to. That, of course, was pure spin. Thornton never had any particular regard for Weinstein's editing skills—he fought him bitterly on *Sling Blade*—and used to say derisively that Harvey thought himself another Orson Welles. According to one source close to Thornton, he had nothing to do with the decision to bring in Miramax on domestic.

In fact, after *Pretty Horses* went to Miramax, nothing really changed. Thornton complained constantly, "Harvey's making me cut the movie down." Weinstein claimed that he had no choice; he was bound by the terms of Thornton's contract with Columbia. Thornton and Damon never knew if this was true or not. Says Damon, "The cynical view is that because he didn't have any of the responsibility, he could point a finger at somebody else and say my hands are tied." Says a source at Columbia, "Contractually, there was an agreement on length between the two companies. But had he showed us *Lawrence of Arabia* at three hours and *Snow Dogs* at two, I'm sure he could have made a good case."

Weinstein forced Thornton to cut the film by one hour and twenty minutes, bringing it down to a (relatively) slim one hour and fifty-five minutes. Thornton said something like, "At least Ah'll retain two hours of what's mine," but he was desperately unhappy with it. "We were all unhappy with it," says Damon. " 'Unhappy's' not the word." Thornton asked Epperson to look at this cut with an eye to writing a voiceover. "The cut I saw did not work at all," says Epperson. "It was a Cliff's Notes version of the script that I was familiar with, truncated and episodic." Adds Damon, "It was like you bake a soufflé and somebody wants you to make it half the size, and you just chop the thing in half and try to mold it and make it look like that was how you made it to begin with. It can't work."

This was the version Weinstein released, after infuriating Thornton by replacing the score that he loved, composed by multi-Grammy winner Daniel Lanois, who had written the music for *Sling Blade*. Continues Damon, "In the end, there was a lot of animosity and anger directed at Harvey, because he ran the marketing of the movie, and he pulled the trigger on how it was released and what cut was released. He tried to make it look like a love story, so that teenagers would go see it. He made a trailer with me and Penélope Cruz swimming around in the water, skinny-dipping, with Bono singing, and Billy's going, 'Look, I love U2, but it's just not appropriate.' And on the poster, they put, 'Some passions can never be tamed,' which is exactly what the movie's not about. There is no love story, it's about unrequited love, it's about life being bigger than these people and just crushing the passion out of them. At the end, it was R-rated, so teenagers couldn't go anyway."

Harvey failed to attend the L.A. premiere of *All the Pretty Horses*. A Miramax executive read a statement from the Miramax co-chairman, who claimed his plane, on its way from New York, had turned back as a result of inclement weather. Later that night, when queried, the executive said he had not been informed that Harvey had ever planned to attend.

All the Pretty Horses opened on December 25, 2000, and went down with a thud. The picture recouped about $10 million (excluding foreign and ancillary sales) on an expenditure that may have exceeded $100 million, including the P&A.

All the Pretty Horses devastated Thornton. "He doesn't want to direct anymore," says Damon. "He said, 'It almost killed me.' He lost all this weight, went into the hospital with a heart problem, he was so stressed he couldn't sleep. He really took it personally and invested a lot of himself in the movie. He said, 'Ah have kids and Ah have a life, and it's not worth it to me to put that much of mah soul into something and have it ripped away. Ah can't ever go through that again. Because it will kill me.' " He had always credited Harvey for launching his career as a director. Now he blamed Harvey for ending it as well. "Harvey has a great gift with filmmakers, but like most of our gifts, they can be our curses," says a source familiar with his MO. "His need to be liked is gigantic, and it's what enables him to get actors to do things nobody else can get them to do. He goes to the clubs with them, gets them out of whatever scrapes they're in, and is the only person they can talk to, but then when he needs to be a businessman, he's betrayed them, and when it goes bad, it's personal and dramatic."

Almost every single one of Miramax's holiday movies flopped that year. *Reindeer Games* tanked, along with John Madden's *Captain Corelli's Mandolin*, on which Miramax was partnered with Universal. (*Bridget Jones's Diary* was a hit, but Miramax had relatively little to do with the development or the production.) *Bounce* was released just before Thanksgiving. It also failed to perform, grossing $37 million against a budget of $35 million.

When the dust settled, the only Miramax film left standing was, improbably enough, yet another Hallström chronicle, *Chocolat*. Like *Corelli*, *Chocolat* was an international confection that one reviewer referred to as "Euro pudding." Indeed, there was the Gallic flavor and setting, the Anglo-American script, the English-spoken-here by all the characters (no need for subtitles nor declassé dubbing), the United Nations cast featuring the American Johnny Depp, the French Juliette Binoche, the Swedish Lena Olin, and the British Judi Dench. That was the period when Harvey tried to give every role to Paltrow. Thinking she had gotten the part, Binoche said at the time, "I flew to New York and spoke to Harvey Weinstein about [the role]. He said, 'You have to ask me first.' I was taken aback, but asked, with my tongue hanging out like a beggar, and he said, 'Okay, the part's yours.' " Then, according to Binoche, he turned around and offered the role to Paltrow, who turned it down. (Earlier that year, in March, Diane Keaton had complained that Miramax was strong-arming her into using Paltrow instead of Parker Posey in *So Shoot Me*, a film she was slated to direct. "We want actresses with way more edge," she said, "but Miramax wants Gwyneth in every picture that comes to them.") As Paltrow put it, with some understatement, "He looks out for me."

Inoffensive in itself, *Chocolat* seemed like an ominous sign of things to come, a new wave of by-the-numbers Euro-American filmmaking, a picture whose every particular was dictated by the requirements of the international—albeit almost completely Americanized—market. In the vein of *Like Water for Chocolate*, it was right up Harvey's alley, an ode to the liberating properties of sweets. The critics generally liked it, although they treated it with some condescension. Somewhat less than complimentary was Elvis Mitchell in the *New York Times*, who called it "an art house movie for people who don't like art house movies. That's hardly a compliment." Even tarter was Lisa Schwarzbaum in *Entertainment Weekly*, who wrote, "Factory sealed to preserve freshness, *Chocolat* is the season's latest Euro synthetic confection, manufactured from a proprietary recipe based on focus group data about what consumers enjoy most in a Miramax movie. . . . [It was] directed by Lasse Hallström with the same marzipan glaze he applied to *The Cider House Rules*." Schwarzbaum went so far as to make fun of Weinstein for wangling endorsements from heavyweights like Jesse Jackson and Abraham Foxman of the Anti-Defamation League in his efforts to win an Academy nomination for the film. She was quoted in *USA Today* calling Foxman a "flack" for allowing himself to be used in this way. "Apparently Harvey went crazy," says Schwarzbaum. He reached her editor-in-chief, Jim Seymour, by phone in the middle of lunch at "21," demanded a meeting. Seymour refused. Shortly thereafter, Schwarzbaum went to Sundance. No sooner had she arrived than she got a call at midnight from one of the Miramax soldiers saying, "Harvey is looking for you."

"That's nice."

"He needs to meet with you."

The next morning, at the appointed time, he rolled into the lobby of Eccles, a screening venue where they had agreed to meet. According to Schwarzbaum he said, "How dare you call Foxman a 'flack,' that's crossing the line, this is a great man, I lost family in the Holocaust, how could you say this about Foxman."

"You don't want to go down that path of who lost more people in the Holocaust," she replied.

"I can take this all the way to the top, I can make life difficult for you."

She recalls, "He wanted me to attend a screening of *Chocolat* with him to see how much audiences loved the movie. This was when he was completely nuts. The next day, I received a gift from him, a book of Truffaut essays, with a note, 'There's room in the world for all kinds of movies, from Truffaut to *Chocolat*.' "

As the year drew to a close, it became evident that had it not been for *Scream 3* and *Scary Movie*, 2000 would have been disastrous. But thanks to Bob Weinstein's Dimension, according to one source, Miramax turned a $120 million profit.

SUNDANCE 2001 marked the twentieth anniversary of the institute. It was a solid festival, with *Memento, The Deep End, In the Bedroom*, and *Hedwig and the Angry Inch* all making a splash. But what was most interesting was that the best films didn't get picked up until much later, and then they only got perfunctory distribution. Indeed, buyers had grown so cautious that they insisted on testing films *before* they bought them. Fox Searchlight flirted with *Lift,* directed by that exotic flower, a black woman filmmaker, Khari Streeter, with DeMane Davis. Searchlight planned to test it in Pasadena, one of the least appropriate venues on the planet. It tested badly, and Searchlight passed. Rick Linklater's groundbreaking animated feature, *Waking Life,* went begging until it was finally bought months later by Fox. Henry Bean's *The Believer,* about a tortured Jewish skinhead, won the Grand Jury Prize, but was deemed anti-Semitic and too controversial by distributors. Six months later, it was still looking for distribution. (*The Believer* was finally bought by Showtime.) Likewise, the remarkable *L.I.E.* was shunned for its sympathetic treatment of your friendly neighborhood pederast. Despite an unsatisfactory ending, *L.I.E.* was in fact a dazzling debut film by Michael Cuesta, which featured an array of extraordinary performances, led by Brian Cox as the pederast. It was finally picked up some months afterward by Jeff Lipsky's new company, Lot 47, which didn't have enough money to give it the push it needed and deserved.

Where was Harvey's acquisitions team when these films—which the old Miramax would have scooped up—went begging? Buying Todd Field's *In the Bedroom,* for $1.5 million. Recalls John Penotti, whose company, GreeneStreet Films, cashflowed the film, along with *Good Machine.* "It was really hard to get people up for a Sissy Spacek movie, let alone the concept, but the minute the screening ended, Mark Gill and Agnes Mentre from Miramax said, 'This is an extraordinary movie, we want it.' " Harvey demurred. "Talk about a movie ripe for cutting, you guys gotta be crazy. This guy's never gonna let us do anything with this."

"He will, he will."

"Guys, this is going to be like one of these epic battles. I don't want to have anything to do with this. I'm gonna get tarred and feathered."

"Take the movie, he'll do what you want." Searchlight, Universal Focus, and Lion's Gate were interested too, "but the Miramax guys came to our condo and wouldn't leave," Penotti continues. The deal stipulated that in the unlikely event *Bedroom* grossed more than $10 million, Miramax had to pay GreeneStreet bumps that kicked in when the film hit specified thresholds, like $15, $20, or $25 million. As far as Miramax was concerned, this was just funny money because no one anticipated that the film would do that well.

Meanwhile, Robert Redford had his hands full trying to shore up his empire, which was crashing around his ears after the Vulcan Ventures deal collapsed. According to a source, he had told the personnel at Sundance

Productions to take a back seat while he dealt with the cash hemorrhage in the cinema centers. So they did, waiting in suspended animation for something to happen, while the star negotiated with chief executive Jeff Kleeman to expand his responsibilities at the same time as he planned to fire everyone at his other companies, Wildwood and South Fork. Then he disappeared, just as he had so many times before, ceasing to return his phone calls.

General Cinema, meanwhile, like all the other exhibition chains, had overbuilt. In the winter of 2001, it declared bankruptcy, capsizing yet another vessel in the Sundance flotilla. Two theater complexes, one in Philadelphia and one in Portland, Oregon, were half built. According to a former Sundance executive familiar with the story, the cinema project had been so badly managed on the Sundance side that even had General Cinema remained solvent, there would have been plenty of trouble. "Financially, the cinemas just spun out of control," says one Sundance source.

Toward the end of March, just weeks after the cinemas had gone belly-up, Redford acquiesced to the inevitable and finally closed down the new Sundance Productions, only a year old, and laid off the employees, Kleeman included, who were now free to join the cinema centers staff on the unemployment line. Subsequently, Kleeman had to go to court to collect the balance of what he said was owed him on his multiyear contract.

Redford commemorated the twentieth anniversary of Sundance by dismissing other key people. Liz Manne, who had brought the channel back from the brink of extinction, increasing the subscriber base from three million to ten million in three and a half years, was fired in 2001. He also dropped his publicist, Lois Smith, who had been with him since the 1960s, and terminated the head of the catalogue, Patricia Warren, who was widely credited with turning it around.

Working for Redford was so difficult and disillusioning that one young, idealistic staffer, after a year or two in his employ, gave up his dream of going into the film business. "Bob is considered one of the good guys, and he wasn't all that good," he says. "So I figured, it probably will only get worse." Former producer Barbara Maltby, who worked for Redford on and off for twenty years, explains the bitterness this way: "When Bob is good he's as good as it gets. He has real vision and has certainly served the greater good in terms of helping people in the movie business. He is extremely smart, has good intentions, and most unusual for the industry, he can listen. Fatally, he also has great charm and lives in the moment. When the focus of his gaze is on you, you feel like you've won the golden ring. But when his gaze moves off you, you're forgotten, because he's on to the next person. This is extremely hard not to take personally, and sometimes it is personal. You have not lived up to expectations—his. But not only have you failed him, you've failed yourself, because you've been snookered by your own narcissism, thinking you're special, more special than the hundred people who came before you. So there's a double sense of failure. He's very Clintonesque."

THE OSCAR SEASON was always a stressful time at Miramax, with its small marketing staff working around the clock, under the Weinstein lash. Harvey himself was coming off the disappointment of seeing the presidential election stolen from his friends and political allies by George W. Bush. Then came the Golden Globes, which had assumed more and more importance every year, having gone from a joke to a dress rehearsal for the Oscars. When Binoche lost to Renée Zellweger *(Nurse Betty)* at the ceremony on January 21, 2001, after *Chocolat* lost to *Almost Famous,* Harvey had a public meltdown. He gathered his publicity troops in the lobby of the Beverly Hills Hilton, lit into them, singling out favorite Marcy Granata for particular abuse.

February rolled around, and O was still sitting on the shelf at Miramax. Now that the election was over, Tim Blake Nelson assumed that Miramax would finally open the film. He met with both Weinsteins at the Tribeca offices. According to him, Harvey said, "We do not feel it is in our interest or the film's interests that Miramax release it. We would like to find somebody else to release it."

Nelson said to the brothers, "You're talking to the wrong guy. Talk with my producer, Eric Gitter, about the terms of the contract. I have to warn you, though, he takes contracts very seriously." At that, Harvey, who should have been in a reasonably good mood—*Chocolat* had made a comeback, improbably scooping up five Oscar nominations—lost it. According to Nelson, he shouted, referring to Gitter, "I will string him up, I will kill him, I will—he does not want to become my enemy, and he will become my enemy if he holds me to this contract. I will ruin him."

In a button-down shirt and suspenders, Harvey met with Gitter in early March at the posh Peninsula Hotel on Little Santa Monica in Beverly Hills. Says Nelson, "It was one of those famous Harvey meetings. It was ugly. Eric says he broke glasses. There were obscene threats." What precisely happened in that room is cloaked by a confidentiality agreement, but Gitter suggests that Weinstein overturned furniture, and says that although Harvey never laid a hand on him, he got close enough so that "I could smell what he had for lunch. It wasn't attractive." The producer says Harvey told him that "his agenda had changed specifically because of his work with the Democratic campaign." Gitter's response was, "Honor the contract. One thousand screens, $10 million P&A, or I'll see you in court."

True to his word, Gitter filed suit on March 19, amending it on April 17, 2001, asking for $17.85 million—$10 million for compensatory and $7.85 million for punitive damages. According to the *New York Observer*, the complaint alleged that unless the *O* team acceded to the transfer of the film to Lion's Gate, the Weinsteins "would see to it that the film was released on one thousand poorly venued screens at inopportune times with no public relations support," and that Harvey threatened to "invest the required print and advertising funds in an inappropriate manor [sic] and would 'bury' the film in the press." Gitter was quoted as claiming that Harvey threatened that "he and his brother would see to it that 'no one in Hollywood' would do any future business with Mr. Gitter, personally." Miramax settled with the plaintiffs out of court for an undisclosed amount. Lion's Gate opened *O* on August 31, 2001, almost two years after the fall 1999 release date originally envisioned, and the film, of course, flopped.

A few weeks after Harvey's meeting with Gitter, the Academy Awards for 2000 were held. Miramax, which had ten nominations, won nothing. For the second year in a row, DreamWorks walked away with the Best Picture Oscar, this time for *Gladiator*. *Traffic*, which had been nominated for five Oscars, among them Best Picture, won four, including Soderbergh for Best Director.

Among the projects Soderbergh and Clooney initiated were Clooney's *Confessions of a Dangerous Mind* at Miramax, Nolan's *Insomnia* at Universal, the Russo brothers' *Welcome to Collinwood*, and Kerrigan's *In God's Hands*. One of the filmmakers Soderbergh also called was Todd Haynes. Haynes, who had moved from New York City to Portland, Oregon, had not made a film in four years, since *Velvet Goldmine*. Now he had a project called *Far from Heaven*, an homage to Douglas Sirk, about a suburban housewife whose life changes dramatically when she discovers that her husband is gay, and she falls into a relationship with her gardener, who happens to be black. One thing led to another, and the two met for drinks in L.A. Soderbergh told Haynes, "I'm in a position to try to make it a little easier for people whose work I think is worth it, and I would really like to do whatever I can to help you with this." Soderbergh agreed to become Haynes's executive producer.

In June, Harvey found himself bidding against the former third Weinstein for Haynes's new picture, now budgeted at $12 million and change, with Christine Vachon producing and Julianne Moore playing the lead. Greenstein never gave any indication that he knew who Haynes was, or had seen any of his films. Says Haynes, "He was riding almost exclusively on Soderbergh's word, his creative instincts." Vachon knew that difficult as Harvey could be, at least he could be depended on to know who Sirk was, which could not be said of Greenstein. On the other hand, she felt uncomfortable assuring Haynes that she could protect him from Harvey, because tough as she was, she wasn't sure. Haynes himself was tilting toward USA, and indeed, that's where he made his deal.

But Harvey wanted a chance to make his pitch to Haynes anyway. And at that point, the deal could have been undone. The last thing the film-maker wanted to do was get on the phone with him. He was still bitter about *Velvet Goldmine*. "He made suggestions that I didn't follow, and then he just buried it," says Haynes. "Even afterward, they threw out a DVD, they didn't ask for a director commentary, my name wasn't on the cover of it, it was buried in the minuscule billing block. He can't even do the really small things that don't cost anything—he never shows any re-spect." But Vachon said, "Look, Harvey knows you made the decision to go with Scott at USA, he just wants to talk to you." As a courtesy, Haynes fi-nally agreed. He recalls, "Here I was in Portland, in my beautiful old arts and crafts house, surrounded by these fruit trees and flowers and vegeta-bles, and I had just spent the night with my friend making out in the fire pit in my backyard, and suddenly I'm on the phone with Harvey Weinstein who's in Capri, and is screaming at me and calling me names like I've never been spoken to by anyone in my life. It was brutal."

Haynes began what sounded like a rehearsed speech by saying, "Look, Harvey, I just want to thank you for your interest, and tell you that I'm not naive enough to think that you guys aren't seminal players in the world in which we all work, and that in the future there will be opportunities I'll look forward to exploring with you. On this one film I'd like to have a dif-ferent experience." If Haynes thought Harvey was going to pat him on the back and wish him well, he was mistaken.

"WHAT? YOU FUCKIN' MADE YOUR DECISION? You fuck, you didn't fuckin' give me a chance to fuckin' talk to you?" With sinking heart, Haynes realized there had been a misunderstanding somewhere along the line, and Weinstein appeared not to know he'd already made his choice. Harvey growled, "I've spoken to Christine and Julianne and they all want to go to Miramax."

"Harvey, if that's really true, it's the result of your intimidation. People don't tell you what they really think. You're a very powerful person." Then Haynes seized the occasion to unburden himself of the feelings he'd been harboring for four years, ending with, "I wasn't listened to on *Velvet Gold-mine*, why would I be listened to on this?"

"It's not my fault that *Goldmine* didn't do any business," Harvey bel-lowed. "I spent $2 million on that film, and we made back shit. You fucking little motherfucker, you're just a spoiled brat, you think you're such a fuck-ing genius you wouldn't, like, listen—you fucking prima donna, you fuck-ing arrogant prima donna." According to Haynes, Weinstein threatened to spend $10 million to keep Moore, who at the time was starring in Miramax's *The Shipping News*, from getting an Oscar nomination for *Far from Heaven*. Miramax VP Meryl Poster had been on the line the entire time, and she said to Harvey, "Well, Harvey, you've just alienated yet another director from the Miramax stable." Harvey replied, "It's good for the directors to hear that kind of talk. You know what your problem is, Meryl? You're too soft!"

Afterward, Haynes called Soderbergh, told him, "Man, I got this unbelievable tirade from Harvey on the phone."

"You'll get the basket. Of cheese, and gherkins."

Says Haynes, "I didn't get a basket, I didn't even get a fax apologizing for it. I got a call from him a couple of days later but I wasn't gonna take it. Later I wondered, Should I have just hung up instead of staying on the phone? Why subject myself to this? I don't need anybody to talk to me like that for any reason at all. I felt like I'd been in a car crash. Completely drained and physically impaired by it. It took the wind out of me."

Losing *Far from Heaven* to Greenstein was bad enough, but Harvey was faced with difficulties wherever he turned. *Talk* magazine was going down the drain, *All the Pretty Horses* lost him more money and face, a teen comedy starring Kirsten Dunst called *Get Over It* tanked, *Malèna* had done nothing, and *Chocolat* folded at the Oscars. During the contretemps involving *O*, the filmmakers got the impression that Bob Weinstein was no more happy with the situation than they were. He wanted Dimension to distribute the movie, thought he could make money on it, while Harvey, who had no personal stake in it, put his political connections first. For a while, the division of labor between the brothers—Harvey won the Oscars, while Bob made the money—seemed to satisfy both. But Harvey wasn't bringing home Oscars anymore, and he certainly wasn't making much money. On the other hand, the rise of Dimension had been so dramatic that it couldn't help but have affected the relationship between the two. Dimension's contribution to the Miramax bottom line rose from approximately 25 percent in 1992 to nearly 75 percent in 2000, when it ponied up $339 million in grosses on eight pictures, for an astounding average gross of $42.4 million per picture, to Harvey's relatively paltry $137 million on twenty-one pictures, representing an average gross of $6.5 million per picture. On the strength of *Scary Movie* and *Scream 3*, Bob for the first time was elevated above Harvey on *Entertainment Weekly*'s annual power list, 8th place to Harvey's 22nd. Staffers noticed that Bob began to stand up to Harvey more. In the past, the brothers had shared marketing and publicity staffs, but now Bob insisted on his own.

Some Miramaxers felt that the relationship between the brothers had sunk to an all-time low. Says one, "They didn't talk for a while. It was very tense, very ugly." Harvey would corner Bob, say something like, "You never give a shit about Miramax, you never watch any of my pictures. Are you coming to the research screening of *All the Pretty Horses?*" Bob replied, "Nahh, I'm goin' to the Knicks game." But he took a tape and watched it at home. The next morning, he told Harvey, "I hated it." It endlessly aggravated Bob that Harvey was trying to compete with him with teen comedies like *Get Over It.* "And Harvey couldn't wait to shit on Bob when he comes out with something like *Dracula 2000* or *Highlander-Endgame,*" says one staffer. "When *Scary Movie* did great, Harvey hated it. That he hadn't had a huge commercial hit in a long time was absolutely killing him." The Weinsteins had snapped up a Nicole Kidman vehicle, *The Others.* Harvey was heavily invested in the relationship with Tom Cruise, whose company, Cruise/Wagner, was to produce the film, and now with Kidman, who was coming up fast, especially since Paltrow, prone to dark, anti-Miramax moments, seemed like she might be the wrong horse.

Ultimately, it went to Dimension, but the decision poisoned the well even more. According to Kevin Smith, something of a Miramaxologist, "Harvey was pissed because Bob had a movie that was not a Dimension movie, it was clearly a Miramax film, and he felt like Bob didn't know what the fuck he was doing with it, it wasn't tracking. Harvey stepped in and took the marketing away from Bob."

Harvey knew the public was salivating over the Cruise-Kidman divorce, and he pulled off a publicity coup, managing to get the two of them together for the first time since the divorce announcement at the *The Others* premiere, creating a media frenzy. *The Others* was released on August 10 to a healthy $14 million opening weekend, and the picture went on to gross $96.5 million. It was another one of those inexplicable Miramax marketing miracles. Continues Smith, "If Harvey hadn't gotten involved, that movie did a quiet $40 million and slunk off. But it caused a lot of friction between the brothers. [Publicly] Bob said, 'Harvey came in and saved the day.' But the word was that Bob was pissed off because Harvey took over. They didn't talk for weeks. Bad blood. There were whispers, veiled threats about splitting up the company. Bob wanted to go off on his own. I don't think they'd ever come closer to severing ties than over *The Others.*" Splitting up Miramax was almost unthinkable, but Bob, who was responsible for most of the company's profits, was also sharing their performance-based bonus 50-50 with his brother and was losing millions.

Ever since Miramax had moved into 375 Greenwich in 1991, Bob's and Harvey's offices had been side by side on the third floor. The space was re-done, and during the construction in August and September 2001, both brothers moved up to the fourth floor. Staffers, used to reading the Miramax tea leaves, thought it was significant that when the renovation was completed, Harvey moved back down to his spanking new office, but Bob, who wanted a corner office like Harvey's, stayed on the fourth floor.

GOING INTO THE FALL OF 2001, Miramax seemed to be looking at an uptick in its fortunes. The only problem, in fact, seemed to be an embarrassment of riches. The Weinsteins still employed a modified version of their throw-it-against-the-wall-and-see-what-sticks strategy, carpet bombing theaters with Oscar wannabes backloaded into the holiday season, most of them bunched into the week between Christmas and New Year's. *Amélie*, a delicate meringue whipped up by the French director Jean-Pierre Jeunet *(Delicatessen)*, starring a saucer-eyed, Audrey Hepburn look-alike named Audrey Tautou, and boasting of digitally enhanced clouds in the shape of rabbits, seemed poised to become that year's *Chocolat*, at the very least sure to clinch Best Foreign Film. *Iris*, the Iris Murdoch biopic Harvey produced with Scott Rudin, starring Kate Winslet and Judi Dench, was a natural for a Best Actress nomination. *Piñero*, which showcased Benjamin Bratt's critically praised performance, was another acting nomination waiting to happen. Almost forgotten in the crush was that year's Sundance acquisition, *In the Bedroom*, which might conceivably earn a nod for Sissy Spacek. And if luck really smiled on the Weinsteins, she could face off against Nicole Kidman, who might be nominated for *The Others*. The eight-hundred-pound gorilla, of course, was the eagerly awaited *Gangs of New York*. *Gangs* had Oscar written all over it, especially since Martin Scorsese, who should have won for *Raging Bull*, if not for *GoodFellas*, had never been honored. And if for some reason *Gangs* stumbled, Miramax had another Oscar contender in *The Shipping News*, which had been entrusted to the sure hands of house director Lasse Hallström. Miramax couldn't lose.

Gangs had originally been scheduled for December 21, 2001. But with its limb-chopping violence and brutal anti-government riots, it was not deemed post–9/11-friendly. Moreover, the meticulous Scorsese was still editing and reediting, and it wasn't ready. Rather than try to force the issue, as Paramount had the ill-fated *Godfather: Part III* in 1990, Weinstein wisely postponed it, first to July 12, 2002, and then December 25, 2002.

But what looked in late summer like a Weinstein Chanukah, by the fall resembled *The Nightmare Before Christmas*. With the pole removed, the tent was about to collapse, bringing down Miramax's fall schedule with it, especially since *The Shipping News* was underperforming in the top two boxes. Harvey panicked.

Amélie, released on November 2 to generally favorable reviews, was doing brisk business, and *In the Bedroom*, which opened on November 23 to even better reviews, was also showing signs of life. But these pictures were too small to plug the *Gangs* hole. Casting about for a more suitable replacement, Harvey's eye fell on Jim Mangold and Cathy Konrad's *Kate & Leopold*, scheduled for release on Valentine's Day, 2002. Consistently scoring in the high 80s, *Kate & Leopold* was looking like a Meg Ryan, *Sleepless in Seattle*-sized hit. When the film was screened at Tribeca for the Weinsteins, "Harvey cried," recalls Konrad. "He said he hadn't seen a movie like this since—he invoked the great masters, Sturges and Capra, and told Jim he was a fucking genius. Bob, who is more reined in emotionally, took Jim outside and said, 'If this movie doesn't make $100 million, we're morons.'" After the movie received kudos at ShowEast from hard-bitten exhibitors, the Weinsteins towed it from its safe harbor right into the midst of holiday traffic, assigning it Friday, December 21. But *Kate & Leopold* never would meet the Weinsteins' expectations, its fate a function of Miramax's weaknesses as the company accelerated around the curve between the old century and the new, no longer the little engine that could, but the Acela Express, way too large, powerful, and swift for the old wooden tracks to which it clung.

When Mangold and Konrad complained about the marketing materials, which seemed to be aimed exclusively at women, they couldn't find Harvey. Says Konrad, "We screamed and we yelled and we demanded to know where Harvey was. We were banging the gong, going, 'Where's the guy who used to live and die by marketing, the man you always expect to turn onion soup into gold bullion. Where the hell is Harvey?' Harvey was deep into *Gangs*."

Be careful what you wish for. After *Kate & Leopold* was moved up, Harvey parachuted back into Mangold's and Konrad's lives. "Then," says Konrad, "our hell began. I get a lot of calls from filmmakers asking my advice about how to deal with Miramax. I always say, 'You're gonna get it up the ass at some point, it's just that when you do, it will be the biggest surprise of your life, and you'll go, Why didn't I see that coming?'" Now it was their turn. The couple had already had their press junket, and the movie had been reviewed in the long-lead-time magazines. According to Weinstein, one thousand prints had already been struck.

The film had premiered in New York on Mangold's birthday, Sunday, December 16, and the next day, four days before the scheduled release, the two filmmakers went to Harvey's office for what they thought was a marketing meeting.

Harvey led them down the short hall to the conference room, saying, "C'mere, I want to introduce you to some people." There were something like fifteen people squeezed into the room. Konrad recalls, "I started shaking, because I knew that something really, really horrible was about to happen. I'm always prepared for the worst, because that's what this business has taught me, but nothing could have prepared me for what happened in this meeting."

Harvey had an unresolved issue with the film that the filmmakers had ignored. Some of the reviewers had noted that the time hopping and the convoluted ancestry of the characters raised an incest question between two of the characters. Worse, the numbers had apparently tumbled into the 70s at the two previews, still not bad, but not good enough to withstand the holiday heat. *Harry Potter* was still going strong, *Ocean's 11* had hung in, and so too, to everyone's surprise, had *Vanilla Sky*. Harvey said, "We're up shit's creek. We underestimated the competition." Turning to one of his executive gofers, he said, "Get me the numbers on *Lord of the Rings*. This is tracking huge. I've never seen anything like it." Konrad thought, Duhh! We're coming out in four days, you're just getting the tracking numbers now? We fuckin' busted our humps for two years? And you haven't done your job? "I admit, I didn't know," Harvey continued. "The early screenings on *Lord of the Rings*—people were saying there were problems, but now—I've moved your release date back, you're coming out on Christmas Day. And you gotta cut four minutes!" Konrad was stunned. She thought, This is after two premieres! We're done, we're locked. Finished. The cutting rooms are gone. There's no Avid. Our editor is helping Adrian Lyne cut *Unfaithful*. We're about to release the movie! Prints have been struck. She looked up, and at the end of the table she recognized, as she puts it, "the Scissorhands with their cassette," referring to post-production veteran Scott Martin. She knew what that meant. *Kate & Leopold* was about to go under the eleventh-hour knife.

Recalls Mangold, "They showed me a shadow cut of the movie in which they had made devastating, awful hacks, losing one scene without which the movie made no sense. They literally butchered it." Ironically, the major cut was a self-referential, signature sequence in which the director registers his contempt for testing. Mangold felt cornered. "It's very hard, even for a star, to say, 'Never,' in the face of someone who's as influential as Harvey is, and who controls that much material," he explains. "I found myself having to make Sophie's choice. The only way out of the position he put me in was to give him four minutes that were my four minutes as opposed to four minutes that were his."

By now, news of the last-minute cuts had leaked to the press. In the trades, Mangold was quoted saying they were his idea. He was in another bind. "I felt I was being made to look like an absolute idiot," he says. "But I also felt that if I had gone public, and said these were forced down my throat, I was fucking my own movie three days before my release. It would become a huge story, and the movie would be destroyed. You can't do that. I was in tears." If *Kate & Leopold* indeed required cutting, it should have been done way earlier. Snipping four minutes at that late a date served no purpose other than to add Mangold and Konrad to the increasingly unselect club of ex-Miramax filmmakers. Even some hardened Miramax hands were shocked. Exclaims Kevin Smith, "You sit there going, *Kate & Leopold*—how does this happen?"

Kate & Leopold opened on December 25 against *Ali* and several other films. It got slaughtered. *Ali* grossed $14.7 million over the first weekend, while *Kate & Leopold* did $9.7 million.

What's the moral of this story? If the director and the producer are to be believed, their movie was the victim of Harvey's inattention, an overburdened marketing department, and the mismanagement of the company. Hobbled by a culture of chaos based on a cult of personality, Miramax was no longer the brash adolescent whose growth spurt, financed by Disney, enabled it to wipe the floor with the competition. Miramax had become a mature company with five hundred employees, spilling out across Tribeca into three buildings, far too large to be run as a mom-and-pop store—particularly if Mom and Pop were otherwise occupied. None of the senior executives, the so-called vice presidents, was empowered to make decisions, nor wanted to. At Miramax, the premium was on loyalty, not initiative.

But *Kate & Leopold* was a sign of a more serious problem: the failure of Harvey's attempts to ratchet himself up to the next level, to go up against the studios. "*Kate & Leopold* is the kind of movie that a major should have made," says Rudin. "Miramax is now in the business of making ersatz studio movies, and it's never been good at that. They spend half of what the majors spend on marketing. If you're gonna release a movie in 2,500 runs, you gotta spend competitively in 2,500 runs. You can't release it like it's in eight hundred runs." Adds a former Miramax executive, "The problem is that Harvey thinks that if he's spending more money for movie stars, that that's good enough, and he forgets that he still has to market the movie. He'll cheap out on those wide releases. He'll try to save the incremental $5 or $6 million that could be the difference between hitting critical mass or not. It's true Harvey used to have the reputation of a big spender in the independent world, but in the studio business, the level of spending is just a different stratosphere. He's not comfortable doing that. He's scared of Bob saying, 'Harve, you wanna gross or you wanna make money? You'll kill your upside.' "

Konrad is bitter: "So your movie comes out, it's floundering, it's the holidays, and Harvey doesn't even call. He loves you for a minute, and then he just steps on your face and you're a piece of shit again. What I don't like about Miramax is that they profess a loyalty to filmmakers, they talk the family talk, but family doesn't treat family like that. Family is not about only when things are good. Family is about when things are hard. Talent is not allowed to bark. You only get to beg. I've never spoken to them again. I can't speak to them, because it doesn't do you any good in this town to remind people of where they failed. Everybody just looks at you and says, 'Just get over yourself. It's a business.' "

Fourteen
Gods and Monsters
2001–2002

• **How James Schamus and David Linde took over Focus, saving Christine Vachon and Todd Haynes from the clutches of USA, while Miramax scored with *Chicago*, but humiliated Martin Scorsese.**

"Harvey is deeply in love with the arts. He's one of those people who thinks that through helping artists fulfill their dreams, he becomes part of the art, which in a way is true. Heaven, Gangs, Cold Mountain—*wouldn't exist without him. He dreams of the filmmaker's dream, but it will always stay the filmmaker's dream and not his own. And that is Harvey's tragedy."*

—Tom Tykwer

The 2001 Oscar campaign showed how agilely Miramax could shift its marketing assets from one square to another. *Kate & Leopold* and *The Shipping News* were perceived as failures, roadkill on the shoulder of the Miramax highway. But Todd Field's *In the Bedroom* was starting to look like that year's Hummer—or, more like it, Volvo. "He didn't really give a shit about us," recalls GreeneStreet partner Fisher Stevens. Then, "once he realized *Shipping News* was not gonna work, he put all his eggs in our basket." When Miramax bought it, it was ostensibly buying a finished film. But, as often as not, in the Weinsteins' hands, a finished film becomes a work-in-progress. "Going with Miramax, we were signing a deal with a company whose corporate culture is to cut films to shreds and not let anyone stand in their way," says Ted Hope, who produced *Bedroom* for Good Machine. "I dreaded it. I sat Todd Field down and said, 'You realize what this means? They are going to want you to recut your film. They're going to fight you tooth and nail for what they think is the right movie.'"

Indeed, Harvey wanted to cut thirty minutes. Despite what the Miramax co-chairman had been told, Field refused. Harvey mounted an elaborate campaign to pressure the director, using Martin Scorsese to bludgeon him. Scorsese watched *Bedroom* with his editor, Thelma Schoonmaker, and according to Harvey, told him, " 'What are you, out of your fucking mind? Cut twenty minutes out of the fucking movie.' They both said the last third just goes on forever." Still Field resisted. Then Harvey just disappeared, as he had on Jim Mangold and Cathy Konrad. Over the course of several months of inconclusive haggling with Miramax executives, "You could see Todd wasting away," says Hope, "going crazy that he couldn't lock this picture."

Finally, Field and Hope were granted a meeting with the Man. He sat them down in a room with two decks and two monitors, his cut and Field's cut. He encouraged them to explain what they liked or didn't like about each version, but insisted, "At the end of this conversation, what I say goes." When it was all over, to their astonishment, he let them off with no more than five minutes of trims. "We won," says Hope. "But we spent nine months to get a meeting that we could've had six weeks in. Todd got a bleeding ulcer. I think a lot of people wouldn't make that trade."

What Field and Hope didn't know was that the picture was the object of a tug-of-war between dueling factions within Miramax. One side lobbied to cut the film. The other side, sensitive to the bad press stirred up by James Gray the year before, ridiculing Miramax for brutalizing *The Yards*, favored leaving it alone. "Everyone had seen the James Gray thing go so badly," says a source inside the company. "James got his movie, but the process had been bloody, and it wasn't worth the public embarrassment it caused the company." The argument against cutting *Bedroom* ran, "You're Harvey Scissorhands, you've ruined one movie, you're gonna ruin another movie? Your big problem right now is that you're sliding down the mountain with the critics, the guys who used to adore you, and now they think you're really fucking up. You've got to get some integrity back. Don't mess with something they've already seen at Sundance and liked." It was a small movie for which Harvey had zero expectations, so he agreed and let Field off easy.

Miramax loved the numbers *Bedroom* was racking up, but it hated those box office bumps the contract required it to pay GreeneStreet. Harvey's people began to pressure Penotti and Stevens to renegotiate what it now realized was a bad deal. Miramax wouldn't take no for an answer. The calls from Miramax were so relentless and pressing that the two men felt they were being stalked. Penotti received one call at seven on a Sunday morning. But GreeneStreet held fast and wouldn't let Miramax renegotiate the deal.

There was more bad blood over *Piñero*, also produced by GreeneStreet. "That was another horribly painful experience," says Stevens. "They wanted Leon Ichaso, the director, who's made tons of movies, to do this, to do that, and Leon finally said, 'Fuck it, I'm done!' They threatened to bury it, and basically they did. As soon as Ben Bratt failed to get a Golden Globe nomination, that was it. They do things behind your back, like saying, 'We're thinking of pulling *Piñero* from festivals,' when they'd already pulled it from festivals." Stevens has mixed feelings about working with Miramax again. "I would do another film with them in a second," he says. "But I would go in completely not trusting them. They beat us down so much that it's made us real skeptical and bitter. Harvey's right a lot of the time. But it's the way they go about it that makes it really unpleasant. The worst thing was trying to get money back from us. From our little company that's struggling to survive. It was squeezing blood. John and I personally made zero. We didn't even take a fee, nothing. Ted Hope? Todd Field? Crap!"

Flat broke, Field was anxious to do a deal somewhere. Out of Sundance, he accepted an assignment to write a script for a small company called Catch 23. "I let Miramax know that I would like to give them the first opportunity to match the offer and enter into some kind of similar arrangement," he says. "I never heard back from them." Months later, after *Bedroom* became a hit, Harvey desperately wanted to sign Field. After all, if he couldn't reel in the director of a tiny film he was turning into a $30 million plus hit, with whom could he do a deal? He was anxious to announce it on the eve of the Oscar nominations on February 12. But it never happened. Says Stevens, who was close to Field, "The relationship was tenuous. It would not be Todd's first choice to work with them again, for sure." (Field refused to comment, other than to say, "I decided against it. I wasn't ready to make that kind of commitment to anyone at that point in time.") Ultimately, he ended up at DreamWorks.

The Oscar jockeying that year was unusually ugly. Universal had watched while DreamWorks clawed its way to two Best Picture awards in a row by cloning the Weinsteins' Oscar strategy. In late December, around the time of the Golden Globe nominations, Ron Howard's movie, the front runner for Best Picture, became the target of a smear campaign unprecedented in the history of the Academy Awards for its viciousness. The trouble began when a Miramax consultant directed the attention of an *L.A. Times* stringer to a Matt Drudge item pointing out that the movie had omitted material from Sylvia Nasar's biography of John Nash relating to his alleged homosexuality. Friends of Miramax beat the drum through the weeks leading up to the Oscar nominations, when *A Beautiful Mind*, Fox's *Moulin Rouge*, New Line's *Lord of the Rings*, USA's *Gosford Park*, and *In the Bedroom* were nominated for Best Picture. (For Miramax, it was the eleventh Best Picture nomination in ten years.) Then, on March 5, just after the Oscar ballots went out, Drudge struck again, writing, "Some Academy members are discovering shocking Jew-bashing passages found in the book on which the movie is based." When he heard this, Brian Grazer, whose company, Imagine, produced the picture, thought, We're dealing with a man who's been schizophrenic for forty years, and now you want to load him up in a wheel chair and push him onto the 405 Freeway? It's so antithetical to the point of the movie, which is to help destigmatize mental disability, not to compound this man's problems. You can't defend yourself against that kind of charge. I'm lost, I'm never gonna win this thing. It's so fucked up.

At the Globes, held on January 19, Sissy Spacek won Best Actress for a Dramatic Role for her turn as the grieving mother in *Bedroom,* and Miramax won two additional Globes, but considering the number of nominations it got, fifteen, the company was virtually shut out. Worse, *A Beautiful Mind* won Best Dramatic Film, and worse still, *Amélie* was beaten for Best Foreign Film by the lowly *No Man's Land*—Bosnian Danis Tanovic's absurdist black comedy about the bloodletting in the former Yugoslavia, distributed by UA Classics, now run by Bingham Ray. Ray had been hired by Chris McGurk after he left Universal to become COO of UA's parent company, MGM. Waiting for the elevator to go up to the UA party tent on the roof, Ray, who could barely contain his glee, said, in a loud voice, "We kicked the fat fuck's ass." With a bow in the direction of family values, *Variety* reporter Bill Higgins quoted him saying, "We kicked Miramax's ass." Even that was too much for Harvey, who cut the article out of the paper, circled Ray's words in red, and sent it to McGurk. McGurk buttonholed Ray, demanded, "Did you say, 'We kicked Miramax's ass?' "

Shaking his head vigorously, Ray solemnly replied, "No."

"Good. So you were misquoted?"

"No, what I said was worse!"

"What did you say?"

"I said, 'We kicked the fat fuck's ass!' "

McGurk put his head in his hands.

In a dark humor, Harvey made his way to the CAA after party at the restaurant Muse. Earlier that evening, he had apologized to Universal Pictures chairman Stacey Snider for the consultant's indiscretion—"He's somebody on my payroll, I'll fire him if you want," etc.—and now he found that his mea culpa was on everyone's lips. Moreover, he had just been informed that his bête noire, journalist Nikki Finke, was about to come out with a story in the *New York Post* accusing Miramax of masterminding the negative campaign against *Beautiful Mind.* Harvey blamed DreamWorks executive Terry Press, whom he still regarded as the author of all Miramax bad notices, for both indignities.

Fortunately for her, Press wasn't at the CAA party, but Snider, who weighs in at 5' 2", 105 pounds, no more than a throw pillow next to Harvey, was. Poking his finger in her face like an irritable woodpecker, he accosted her in the packed room, saying, "You're going to go down for this! Get your house in order. And clean up your act. Or otherwise we will." He denounced Press, and warned Snider that if she didn't watch herself, she would be caught in the crossfire. She thought, If you feel that it's Dream-Works, go tell DreamWorks. "He was yelling," Snider recalls. "He was very angry. He wouldn't come down from it. Usually, you can say, Let's relax, let's talk about this, we can figure this out. He just kept going." (Weinstein has said, "I never raised my voice to Stacey.")

Says one executive, "It was the second public display of rage that night. After the Globes he stood in the lobby of the Beverly Hilton Hotel and yelled at his staff. For losing *Amélie*. When you're young and scrappy, this *Mean Streets* behavior is accepted. When you're fifty, and you're a fat cat, you can do all the benefits you want for the city of New York, but how you carry yourself matters." Adds Snider now, "There were two things at play. Miramax had had a best picture nomination for nine or ten years in a row. That was something that the company was focused on preserving, and that goal is legitimate. But if you have a company whose culture is in service of one personality, if it's the Harvey Weinstein Company, and there's no means of checking that personality, that means you can have poking fingers and maligning films." Shortly thereafter, Barry Diller gave Harvey a very public spanking. According to *Variety*, Diller "lashed out" at Weinstein for "threats and intimidation."

On the phone the following day, DreamWorks executive Jeffrey Katzenberg accused Weinstein of stepping over the line. Katzenberg said something like, "You can't work this way. You are endangering my friendship, and you must apologize to Stacey," adding, "And I'm sick of you always pointing the finger at Terry. You think if it's raining outside, it's Terry's fault."

"Jeffrey, I am paranoid about that woman."

"She says she hasn't spoken to Nikki Finke in six months."

"She's lying."

"You are speaking about somebody who's family to me. So you better think before you call her a liar."

People around Katzenberg believed that the close friendship between him and Harvey was a one-way street. People around Harvey felt the reverse. As a former Miramax executive put it, "The relationship is 80 percent Harvey." Harvey himself says, "I have great fondness for Jeffrey, and I will

never forget that he brought me to Disney, where I think I've done unbelievably well for him, because he has an ongoing piece of my efforts. [But]
hundreds of people have come to me and said, 'You're getting screwed.' I've
had many reports that he has been disingenuous. However, when I confront Jeffrey and say, 'Have you been disingenuous?' he says he hasn't."

Outside of the incident with the consultant, the evidence for Miramax
being the source of the campaign against *Mind* was circumstantial. Even
Miramax publicists who are in a position to know aren't sure. Says one,
"When *A Beautiful Mind* opened, there was a reference in A. O. Scott's
[*New York Times*] review to things being left out. Harvey's reaction was,
'Can you believe what's not in this movie?' The inference was, People
should know about this. We were told, 'This should be pushed. Everyone
get on this case.' One Miramax publicist is very close to Drudge, and he
brought up the anti-Semitism within the first week or so, and then it showed
up in Drudge later. The connection is just too close. But with Harvey there
was a kind of denial. Even when there were a bunch of us in a room, or in
the car, there was never a point where he'd let down his hair and say, 'That
backfired.' It was always, 'We didn't do anything wrong.' Clearly, though,
we were not innocent." As former Miramax executive Tony Safford says, in
another connection, Miramax "works very hard on pictures, and they work
very hard against pictures. Every slur, everything imaginable, they'll throw
against a picture." But publicity VP Matthew Hiltzik denies Miramax in-
dulges in negative campaigning: "Harvey never roots for someone else's
movie to fail." And Mark Gill: "Our hands were pretty much clean. He is
terrified of people coming after him." And Weinstein adds, "It's Scapegoat
101: let's blame Miramax." (Universal publicly absolved the company.)

On March 4, Harvey took time out from the Oscar campaign to flame director Julie Taymor in a lobby full of startled moviegoers at New York's
Lincoln Square Theater, on 68th and Broadway, after a successful screening of her film *Frida*. A biopic of the legendary, uni-browed Mexican artist
and companion of famed left-wing muralist Diego Rivera, the project had a
long and difficult history, starting with Madonna and ending with Salma
Hayek. Harvey grudgingly agreed to produce the film, which featured
Hayek, Alfred Molina, Antonio Banderas, Edward Norton, and others, but
he extracted his pound of flesh. Every time it looked like he was about to
green-light the film, he would go back to Hayek and ask her for another op-
tional picture or cut her price or get her to do a cameo in something else of
his. After working on the project for eight years, Hayek's salary was the
SAG minimum $70,000.

The first cut of *Frida* came in somewhere between two and two and a
half hours. Harvey wanted it shorter. He said things like, "I was put on
earth to deal with artists, to take their work and make it better." But Tay-

mor didn't think he was put on earth to make hers better. He tested the film. Taymor and the Miramax bunch milled around the lobby of the big multiplex waiting for the audience to finish filling out cards. They went back inside for the focus group session, came out again. Someone from the NRG gave Harvey a summary of the scores. He looked at them, said, "These scores are very good." They were in the mid-80s, miraculous for a story about Kahlo, Rivera, and Leon Trotsky. He said to Taymor, "What did you think about what the focus group said?"

"They were confused about Trotsky, Communism in Mexico—we could answer those things, but none of us want to make the film longer."

"Well, we could solve that by looping lines."

"They enjoyed the movie, the film succeeded, I don't feel we have to answer every question that an audience might conceivably have about the Mexican Revolution. This movie is about Frida Kahlo." What Taymor didn't know is that you're in trouble if your film tests badly, but you can be in worse trouble if it tests well, because Harvey will think he can get it to test better. Which seems to be what happened in this case. For reasons best known to himself, at that point Harvey just exploded. He tore up the scores, turned to Taymor and screamed, "You are the most arrogant person I have ever met. This is what my brother told me, and he's right." (Bob had just met Taymor for the first time.) With a parting shot—"Go market the fucking film yourself, I'm selling it to HBO"—he made as if to go. Then he turned on his heel. Looking at Bart Walker, Taymor's agent, he roared, "Get the fuck outta here." He pointed at Elliot Goldenthal, Taymor's companion, an Oscar-nominated composer who wrote the music for the film, basically for nothing, and continued at the same volume, "I don't like the look on your face. Why don't you defend your wife, so I can beat the shit out of you." He then turned to the Miramax executives, who were watching in horror, the producer, and the editor, and screamed, "You're fired, you're fired, you're fired, you're fired," as if he were pinging targets with an air gun at a carnival concession. "It was all about power," says Gill. "I want it my way.' Showing who's boss. 'Make her fucking listen to me.' " Regarding the incident, Taymor said later, "I wouldn't call it a screaming fight if only one person was yelling." She continued, "I would have quit had it not been for Salma. I wanted to make this happen for her."

For many years, Harvey had been in the habit of showing films in various states of readiness to a posse of friendly journalists and film reviewers. As he had in so many other areas, Harvey had taken a dubious practice that had always existed on an informal, ad hoc basis—Pauline Kael used to read scripts and visit editing rooms dispensing advice—and mass-produced it. It was smart business, because it killed a whole flock of birds with the same stone: it gave Harvey an advance peek at how a film might fare with reviewers, suggested changes he could make that might incline the critics to smile on it, gave him ammunition in his fights with recalcitrant directors, and last but not least, enmeshed writers, reviewers, and editors flattered by Harvey's attention to their opinions in a web of complicity that could not but affect their judgment, no matter how much they denied it. In this case he showed Taymor comments by Rex Reed, Lynn Hirschberg, Graham Fuller, John Brody, Tina Brown, and several others.* Says Mangold, who strongly opposes this practice, "There is a kind of strange incestuous relationship between film critics, market testing, and studios, where the critic becomes complicit in an act of recutting, and puts the filmmaker in the grave. Now it's not just what the shopping mall said, we also know that Peter Travers liked the movie, but was bugged a little by this or that. It's a kind of *Alice in Wonderland* world you're living in." Harvey screened *Frida* for his posse, and used their comments to pressure Taymor.

Eventually, their differences were resolved, but the entire episode left a bad taste. What with the public tongue-lashing he directed at his staff at the Globes, the scolding he gave Stacey Snider, and now the outburst with Taymor, Harvey seemed more out of control than ever.

After Harvey exploded at Taymor, he vowed to seek help. "The morning after Julie's thing was when I talked to Meryl Poster, I said, 'We gotta deal with my anger management. All my movies got screwed up because of [my] personality. I have too bad a temper, this has to stop, now. God, what an asshole I've been.' "

On Saturday, March 23, Miramax's pre-Oscar party was held under a tent in the Sky Bar of the Mondrian Hotel on Sunset. In an effort to show that there were no hard feelings, Weinstein and Katzenberg entertained about seven hundred guests with a skit that poked fun at their "feud." It was an amusing idea, but what made spectators gasp was the X-rated material. As Universal and DreamWorks executives watched uneasily from ringside, exchanging glances as if to say, "What are we doing here?" the two studio chairmen, dressed like gladiators, confronted each other in "Snider's office," where she, played by Christina Applegate, was trying to broker a detente between them. A sampling, courtesy of the infamous Nikki Finke:

KATZENBERG (to Snider): Hello, darling. You look so beautiful today.
WEINSTEIN: I timed that, Jeffrey. Exactly two seconds till your first suck-up.
KATZENBERG: If you gained exactly one more pound, you could have come as Rome.

---

* In the interest of full disclosure, I, too, have occasionally looked at early cuts of films—for the studios, not Miramax.

SNIDER: I brought you here today because I have had enough. I can't take any more of the "he said, she said" bull.

WEINSTEIN: Who are you calling "she"?

SNIDER: First it was *Saving Private Ryan* against *Shakespeare in Love*. Now all this backbiting about *A Beautiful Mind*.

WEINSTEIN: I swear on the life of my driver, I never said any of this. But Nash was gay, wasn't he?

KATZENBERG: Hey, looking at you in that outfit, you ought to know.

WEINSTEIN: Shove it up your skirt, Sparky.

KATZENBERG: I think you seem to have forgotten. I bought your company.

WEINSTEIN: Yeah, in 1993, with Michael Eisner's money.

KATZENBERG: Lucky for you, back then he still had some.

WEINSTEIN: Not that you ever saw any of it.

KATZENBERG (to Snider): Does it turn you on when he talks dirty like that?

It went on—and on—in the same vein. If it was meant to smooth ruffled feathers within the two companies, it didn't work. As one DreamWorks executive says, "It was a setup. To have the Universal and DreamWorks people down in front, like props in a play. It was like, this entire thing existed to show people that we came to them, onto their turf. It was this fake all-is-forgiven thing. To put us down."

The following night, on March 24, the Oscars were held for the first time at the new Kodak Center on Hollywood Boulevard. *In the Bedroom* lost Best Picture to *A Beautiful Mind*; Sissy Spacek, who was nominated for Best Actress, lost to Halle Berry, for her performance in *Monster's Ball*. According to one source at the company, Harvey blamed Spacek for not doing enough to promote herself. Although *Amélie* had broken *La Cage aux Folles*'s record to become the highest U.S.-grossing French movie ever ($33 million), it again lost Best Foreign Film to *No Man's Land*. Harvey had to settle for a Best Supporting Actor Oscar for *Iris*'s Jim Broadbent. As if this weren't bad enough, the brothers became the butt of award show patter. Nathan Lane, doubtless evening the score after Harvey's display of ill temper at Hillary Clinton's birthday party five months earlier, presented the new Best Animated Feature Oscar. Referring to one of the nominated features, he quipped, "Up to now I thought *Monsters, Inc.* was a documentary on the Weinsteins."

Miramax had not mounted a serious Best Picture candidate since *Shakespeare in Love* in 1998, a three-year drought. It was not just the humiliation of losing that rankled: promising Oscars was one way Weinstein managed to snag actors on the cheap. If he couldn't deliver, they wouldn't cut their rates, and if they didn't cut their rates, the days when a *Pulp Fiction* or a *Good Will Hunting* rained gold would be over, which is to say,

Harvey's spécialité de la maison, the mid-range blockbuster, would become a thing of the past. The company was stumbling, and things would get worse before they would get better.

TODD HAYNES and Christine Vachon had put their eggs in the USA basket. *Far from Heaven*, executive-produced by Steven Soderbergh, was supposed to go for $12 million and change, brutally low for an ambitious film that was attempting to reproduce a glossy Sirkean melodrama, with its elaborate sets, meticulous costumes, and lush cinematography. But it was beset with problems that nearly sank it, including the pregnancy of star Julianne Moore, who insisted that it had to be shot in New York City, where she lived, which was promptly hit with 9/11, cutting weeks off preproduction and destroying about a quarter of the locations, all clustered in downtown Manhattan. When Vachon complained that she couldn't make that budget, Scott Greenstein made all the right noises, "We'll figure it out," but later it became an issue. It was the usual story; indies have to make films like this on their own backs, and when USA pressured Haynes and Vachon to throw in chunks of their fees, they did. The production was hellish throughout. The bond company ousted Vachon and took over because the film had gone over budget by $300,000. The bond company representative summoned Vachon to a meeting and, like a principal speaking to a naughty student, told her, "We are extremely disappointed in you."

"Okay . . ."

"We trusted you and you lied to us."

"I didn't lie to you."

"You know what I'm gonna have to do?"

"What are you gonna have to do?"

"I'm gonna have to cut the schedule."

"Well, we can't."

"You mean, you won't." If the bond company could show malfeasance, or that she was refusing to cooperate, it could remove her entirely and, worse, seize what little remained of her fees. It was unable to do so, but this was the first time in the course of a career that had spanned nearly two decades and thirty-eight films that a bond company had moved on her. Vachon was furious. "Am I ten? I'm forty fucking years old! I honestly felt the attitude, coming from USA and the bond company was, 'You just got in over your head, girlie!' and that if this had been Ted Hope, they would have been, 'Poor Ted, he didn't have good people working for him, therefore we will work with him to figure a way out of this.' With me it was just punitive, 'Who the hell do you think you are? We're gonna take away the E-ZPass from your car and we need you to give us the $22.80 in charges that we don't think were directly related to driving to the set.' There was such an atmosphere of dread. I could not believe that USA allowed this to happen to the movie. Scott did not return my calls, he didn't return Todd's calls."

By the time the production ordeal was over, Vachon had changed her mind about Miramax. "I wish I had done the movie with Miramax," she says. "I realized that an asshole who cares about movies is better than an asshole who doesn't."

USA wanted to test *Far from Heaven*. Vachon continues, "In my experience, the studio always tells you, 'Don't worry, it's not about the numbers, it's about finding who your audience is.' And then of course, when the numbers are bad, which they almost always are for movies like *Boys Don't Cry* or *Far from Heaven* or *One Hour Photo*, they freak, and of course it is about the numbers." (*One Hour Photo*, which barely registered, grossed $31.5 million on a budget of $12 million, becoming the most profitable film Vachon had ever done.)

Indeed, the scores for Haynes's film were low. Despite the success of *Traffic*, Greenstein felt his position at USA was fragile. Soderbergh was his greatest asset. "Scott delivered for Steven," says Vachon. "He got *Traffic* made for him, he got him the nominations, and he got him the director award. Steven and Scott made a good team. Scott could say something insane, and Steven could pull out the piece that made sense and translate it. When Scott is at his best, he can tell what the pulse points are, in a room or in a story or in a package. He kinda understands the essence of the thing he's supposed to sell." Still, he would get on the phone with Haynes and say, in a hysterical voice, "I'm gonna lose my job over this film," and quote from the preview cards—"Look, 20 percent of the people thought it's too slow"—pleading with him to edit it down. Two days before he was scheduled to begin principal photography on *Solaris*, Soderbergh flew to Portland, Oregon, to spend a day with Haynes going over the film. "Soderbergh had final cut on *Far from Heaven*," says Haynes. Steven says, "He got tough with me, but in a very constructive way, saying that whatever I ultimately decided he would support." Soderbergh suggested lots of cuts, some of them radical, and Haynes rejected most of them. "I needed to be able to make the film my way," he explains. "We're different filmmakers; we make different types of movies, which is why he supported me in the first place." Trying to be cooperative, Haynes called USA and said, " 'I had a great meeting with Soderbergh, but some of the things he suggested are kind of extreme and I have a feeling I may not follow them all.' Scott heard immediately that I was not going to do every single thing Soderbergh said, and he called Christine and got really tough with her on the phone, said, 'If Todd doesn't do every single thing Steven says, we're not gonna support this movie.' " He was only doing what he thought he had learned from Harvey. Indeed, says USA Entertainment CEO Michael Jackson,·"That may well have been a good call. Let's face it, Velvet Gold-mine hardly set the world afire. He may have wanted to put his foot down. I'm sure he was trying to get something that would work for an audience as opposed to being a home movie. And, actually, the film worked."

At 4:30 in the afternoon of Thursday, May 4, Vachon was at a party at Robert Altman's company, Sandcastle, where she ran into Julianne Moore, who took one look at her face and asked, "What's going on with the movie?"

"It's fine."

"It's not fine, what's the matter, what's wrong? What are they doing to you? Are they going to fuck this up?"

Vachon thought, I have to leave, I don't want to pretend to Julianne that everything's okay. She got a cab, and on her way downtown, her cell phone rang. It was Good Machine's James Schamus and Ted Hope, saying, "You won't believe this, but Scott just got fired, we've taken over USA." Vachon was thrilled. She called Haynes in Portland, and told him the news. He too was thrilled. "It felt amazing because James was someone I've known for years and think is so smart and feel I could talk to about anything," says Haynes. Adds Vachon, "The only person who wasn't thrilled was Soder-bergh, because he's always been very loyal to Scott, and was like, 'I don't think this is good for the movie.' "

As the *Heaven* drama had unfolded in the foreground, the big picture was changing in the background. In the early days of 2002, Vivendi had bought Barry Diller's film and television assets, giving him what would eventually be a controlling role at Universal. USA Films was folded into Universal Focus under Stacey Snider. It looked like Greenstein was slated to head up the new division. Indeed, a piece in *Variety* said exactly that. Everyone, Snider included, thought Greenstein had leaked it. This was not, in fact, the truth, although it didn't much matter. Perception is all. Good Machine's David Linde spoke for many when he said, "This is sui-cide."

But despite the story, it seemed unlikely that Greenstein would head Focus Features, as the new company came to be called. At USA, Diller made all the day-to-day decisions, from poster design to allocation of a film's weekly marketing budget. This made Greenstein a bad fit with the company Snider envisioned. For her, it made no sense to have an indepen-dent division if it wasn't independent, and in this spirit Focus was to have its own marketing and distribution divisions, separate from the parent stu-dio. Before coming to Universal, she had been an executive at Sony and had admired Sony Classics's Michael Barker and Tom Bernard from a dis-tance. Their attitude to the parent studio was, "You can come in and kiss our ass when the Academy Awards come around, but otherwise, 'Fuck you.' " Says Snider, "I loved that." She admired Good Machine, Christine Vachon, producer and indie attorney John Sloss, and the pre-Disney Miramax, "when it was Miriam and Max's company," as she puts it. "They're mavericks that have personality." She told Diller, "Scott's a great executive, but if I'm going to do it, I'm going to do it differently, which is not to hire an executive, but to hire filmmakers." Moreover, Diller had asked Jackson to look around for a replacement for Greenstein, which Snider undoubtedly knew. Diller doesn't recall this and says, "My position was, 'I'm not going to tell [the Universal executives] what to do, but I knew they never intended to give Scott the job. He didn't do anything wrong, and he didn't deserve to be used in that way."

Universal and Good Machine already had a relationship. Schamus had been hired by Universal to produce and co-write *The Hulk*, with Ang Lee, who was also directing. Snider stunned everyone by proposing to buy Good Machine and install Schamus and Linde as the co-heads of the new division, Focus Features. Schamus told Haynes, "Cut it whatever way you want to." He adds, "Three days later they screened the film for me and by the end of the film, I was in tears."

Increasingly it seemed that the small indie companies were being shuffled and reshuffled by the high rollers in the ongoing poker game of international capital for whom they had little intrinsic value and were no more than the jokers in the deck. Universal bought October, sold it to Diller, who transformed it into USA Films, which in turn was gobbled up by Vivendi and returned to Universal, where it was merged with Good Machine to become Focus Features.

Still, for the moment, the good guys had won. Hope left to form his own production company. He says, "It's nice to feel that for once you have a fully integrated film company that is essentially run by filmmakers, knowing that you might have the opportunity of speaking to someone about why the movie should get made out of passion, and not strictly about numbers. So much of the process on the studio side is about risk aversion, cover your ass to protect your job. Here it's let your ass hang out for all to see."

WEINSTEIN HAD PULLED OFF a miracle with *In the Bedroom*, driving it to a $35.9 million gross. But he spent a lot of money doing it, and Bob was rumored to have complained that he had spent so much he couldn't make a profit on it. "Is it rational to spend $20, $25 million to maybe make [a profit of] $5 or $6 million?" wonders GreeneStreet's John Penotti. "I don't know." If he spent too much marketing traditional indie films like *In the Bedroom*, he spent too little on their studio wannabes like *Kate & Leopold*. At one time, Harvey had achieved a delicate balance between studio and indie-style marketing, combining the best of both worlds, but over the last few years, it seemed like he combined the worst.

As 2001 became 2002, the numbers remained dismal. *The Shipping News* lost $10 million; *Piñero* was barely released; *The Four Feathers*, a co-production with Paramount, was a disaster, costing about $80 million and grossing a mere $18 million worldwide. Miramax stood to lose about $13 million. *On the Line*, with two kids from 'N Sync, cost $10 million and did only $4.4 million.

As usual, Dimension had picked up the slack with *Spy Kids*, released in March 2001, which cost $35 million and grossed $113 million, as well as *The Others*, released in August, making 2001 Miramax's best year ever, according to Harvey, with $170 million in profits. But the next fiscal year, which ended October 31, 2002, was one of the worst, and Bob's magic touch seemed to have deserted him. *Texas Rangers*, with James Van Der Beek for example, cost $38 million, and grossed a mere $623,000. *Impostor*, with Gary Sinise, which cost $40 million, made $6.11 million; *Below*, aka *Proteus*, co-written by Darren Aronofsky, was a $40 million horror movie that grossed $589,000; and *Equilibrium*, with Christian Bale, cost $16 million and grossed $1.2 million. In the New York Times, Elvis Mitchell called *Equilibrium* "a movie that could be stupider only if it were longer." Too cheap to use stars (Van Der Beek, Sinise, and Bale couldn't open a can of tunafish, much less a movie), Bob was suddenly unable to come up with pictures that packed the high concept punch of the *Screams*. And sans stars, some of these flops weren't even cushioned by decent foreign and ancillary sales. Miramax shoved a few of its pictures into the future to burnish the books. *Waking Up in Reno*, a stinker that kept getting elbowed from quarter to quarter because it was sure to drag down everything around it, was pushed to October 2002 and died there, grossing a minuscule $269,109. Then there was the $27 million (probably more) Harvey lost in the noisy collapse of *Talk* magazine in January 2002. And finally, Miramax got slapped with half the production and marketing costs for M. Night Shyamalan's *The Sixth Sense* and *Unbreakable*, which one source put as high as $80 million.* According to a fall 2002 New York Times article, over the course of the past five years, Miramax ranked no higher than seventh among the studios in box office revenue.

In the spring, the Weinsteins had ceased stocking the offices with sodas and bottled water, bagels and coffee cake. Car service was cut back. On

---

* In exchange for its option on Shyamalan, Miramax got a piece of both movies. Belatedly, Disney realized that if the brothers were going to profit on those films, they were going to have to share the costs as well, although it's not clear which fiscal year, 2001 or 2002, these costs were charged against.

March 15, they fired seventy-five employees in the first mass layoffs in the company's history. The damage was compounded by hemorrhaging of key executives, which began in October 2000, when longtime Dimension head Cary Granat left, followed by president of publicity Marcy Granata, who had been there seven years. VP of finance Bahman Naraghi followed suit, as did the head of physical production, Kevin Hyman, and the top echelon of the marketing department, including Matthew Cohen and David Brooks, all of whom apparently melted under the pressure to generate box office for films that weren't grossing. West Coast publicity head Janet Hill also left. Then, in the middle of October 2002, Mark Gill, who joined Miramax in late 1994 and had become president of the West Coast office, resigned and was escorted out of the building at Bob's behest by a lawyer from business affairs. "They're like Mafia dons," says Gill. "They dote on their family and murder everybody else."

Miramax realized that these highly publicized firings and resignations sent the wrong message—the company was in trouble—so when they were followed by another round of cuts, it was done so quietly that the press barely noticed. The upheavals of 2002 rivaled the turnovers of 1986 and 1993–94. In all, the workforce was downsized by approximately 25 percent.

But Harvey insisted that the "Where's Harvey?" problem was moot. Once Talk folded and the electoral campaigns ended, he would again be able to give the company his undivided attention, and indeed, the 2002 fall slate seemed to be the beneficiary. But no sooner did he swear off media acquisitions than he quietly made an offer to buy the New York Observer from Arthur Carter—and failed. And he still, as he boasted to Mangold and Konrad, harbored ambitions to change the world. Come the next presidential election will he be able to resist mixing in Democratic Party politics? Probably not.

Harvey didn't seem to care about alienating filmmakers like Taymor, Haynes, or any of the others he's left for dead along the way, but the list is a veritable Who's Who of young American directors—most of whom have returned the compliment. Despite its attempts to tangle up talent in options on future projects, Miramax has lost out on repeat business. As Donna Gigliotti puts it, filmmakers "vote with their feet. How many people go back to Miramax for a second movie?" Although the watchword in the film business is "never say never," the vast majority of the 1990s generation don't work there, like Alexander Payne, Todd Haynes, James Gray, David O. Russell, Larry Clark, Jim Mangold, Baz Luhrmann, P. J. Hogan, Julie Taymor and Todd Field, all of whom once did so.

Outside of the Miramax family, the "made guys," as Rick Linklater calls them, and the directors Miramax held and holds options on, the company became the port of last call for many of the filmmakers who emerged in the

1990s, like Ang Lee, Neil LaBute, Wes and Paul Thomas Anderson, Todd Solondz, Nicole Holofcener, Allison Anders, Lisa Cholodenko, Hal Hartley, Kim Peirce, Darren Aronofsky, and Miguel Arteta. Nor do the Irish and British directors whom Miramax once distributed—Jim Sheridan, Neil Jordan, Michael Caton-Jones, Danny Boyle—appear to be flocking to the company with any great enthusiasm, not to mention Mike Leigh, who avoided it from the start. Nor are the great international filmmakers, like Bernardo Bertolucci and Pedro Almodóvar, eager to throw in their lot with the brothers. This is all the more remarkable because Miramax is one of the few games in town. As Russell puts it, "Given who Harvey was, he could have cornered the market, he could have had every gifted young filmmaker lined up to work with him, saying, 'God, this is the place to be.' He could have made a factory there, with us. His gluttony for power and fame has hurt him. If he can't shove you in his mouth and eat you right now, if you're not a Matt Damon soufflé, he chucks you aside. He alienates everybody." Adds Mangold, "Harvey does both good and bad. He does give people breaks that they wouldn't have had, and that does take courage that others don't have. But the problem is that the same personality type that has the hubris to face the wind and say, 'I looked in his eyes and I believe in this guy,' is also the person who will look in that same kid's eyes and say, 'I saw your movie, and I don't believe in it.' " Harvey jumped through hoops to snag Soderbergh and Clooney, but Soderbergh's next feature is for Warner's *(Ocean's 12)*. Soderbergh is producing eight films, and only one of those is at Miramax, *Confederacy of Dunces,* which Harvey bought for him. Clooney's *Intolerable Cruelty* was for Imagine, with Joel Coen directing.

Says Vachon, "Harvey sends me four scripts a week. Romantic comedies." Ironically, she has become Harvey's Harvey. "He thinks, We can do this for $20 million, I bet Christine could do it for $12. The movies are set up, all I have to do is say yes and collect money, but I can't put Killer Films's name on that crap. I respect his ability, but if I'm gonna put myself through that, it has to be with something I care about. But I know I'll be making a movie with Miramax in the next year or two. Either they'll give me the right romantic comedy, or I'll come up with something they like."

But despite his oft-repeated claim that "there's a new Harvey in town," the "new" Harvey turned out to be pretty much the same as the old Harvey. He seemed stressed and resumed smoking. Some even claimed to have heard him mumbling to himself in the elevator. In May 2002, Harvey had an ugly run-in with Diller at Cannes. Still smarting from Diller's comments in *Variety,* Harvey demanded, "Why'd you call me a bully?" Diller, who thought they were going to get into a fistfight, replied, "You *are* a bully." The last thing Harvey needed was a tussle with Diller, yet another drop in the ocean of bad karma that was washing away the Miramax beachhead.

Bullying staff and pushing around hapless indie directors is one thing; threatening studio heads is quite another. By mid-2002, there was a growing consensus in Hollywood that he was too big for his britches. Says Scott Rudin, "I think the behavior has gotten completely out of hand. People have had their fill and don't want to deal with him anymore. They're tired of being bullied and threatened, and tired of the vendettas and the punishing and the ugliness. People go to great pains here to make this look like a business, not a candy store. His shenanigans are not good for the public perception of the industry, not good for people whose businesses are publicly traded. There's a tremendous amount of money to be made in Hollywood, and nobody wants to have their livelihood fucked with, and that's what he does."

It seemed like Harvey had run out of lives, that he was poised on a tipping point. Says one top studio executive, "He's done one horrible thing too many. When the cat shit gets bigger than the cat, get rid of the cat." Or, as Cassian Elwes puts it, "In Hollywood, everyone's favorite page in the trades is the obituaries. There's a natural tendency to want to see people fail as opposed to succeed, there's an enormous amount of jealousy that floats around. And Harvey's pissed off a lot of people." Harvey had become so weakened that it didn't seem like it would take much to topple him into the no-man's-land inhabited by the likes of Mike Ovitz.

For the Miramax co-chairman, the consequences of peeing in the Hollywood pond are more serious than not getting the right table at Morton's or the best suite at the Peninsula Hotel. The agents, of course, are his natural enemies, mongooses to his cobra. "He moved into the studio game, and on that level, agencies are not looking to help him by suggesting that their clients work for nothing for him," continues Elwes. "Anytime you see a $50 million budget, actors should not be working for scale anymore. Agents feel that if there are going to be difficulties ahead, their clients might as well be paid for their misery." Counters Harvey, "Agents are the people who malign me the most. They wear suits, and they are suits. There's no ripped T-shirt and cool sensibility underneath. They might as well be on Wall Street."

Harvey has been able to muscle his way into partnerships with other studios in the past, but his behavior has made it harder and harder for him to continue to do so. Take DreamWorks. Co-president Walter Parkes had asked Lasse Hallström to direct *Catch Me If You Can*. According to sources close to Hallström and DreamWorks, at the time he had no contractual obligation to Miramax, but Harvey demanded half the picture. Hallström was desperate to do the film, especially after he got Leonardo DiCaprio, whom he had directed years before in *What's Eating Gilbert Grape?* to commit. In an effort to create a quid pro quo, Miramax sent over script after script, including *Rent*. But nothing clicked. Harvey offered Hallström another movie, *An Unfinished Life*, and in case he didn't get the point, he "just beat the shit out of him, told him he'd never work at Miramax again," says a top DreamWorks executive. "It was pure bullying." (A source close to Hallström says he walked away voluntarily because post-production on *The Shipping News* made it impossible for him to make the *Catch Me If You Can* release date.) Hallström would find himself buying a ticket to see *Catch Me If You Can* in a theater. Subsequently, Miramax and Dream-Works partnered on *Tulip Fever*, and Miramax bought a few territories on another, *House of Sand and Fog*. As one highly placed DreamWorks source puts it, "Jeffrey is psychotically loyal to Harvey."

After the talks collapsed, DreamWorks executives were amused to see Miramax put *Rent* in turnaround, suggesting how little regard it had for the material in the first place. *Rent* had been optioned jointly by Miramax and Robert De Niro's Tribeca Films. Spike Lee was approached to direct it. "I thought because it was coming through the auspices of Bob De Niro and Marty Scorsese, that people were gonna look out [for me], but they didn't," says Lee, angrily. "We got fucked." Lee worked on the script throughout the summer of 2001. At one point, he needed to talk to Harvey. "I could not get him on the phone," he says. "I have a summer house in Martha's Vineyard, and I had to track him down there myself. He was fucked, because he picked up the phone and he could not hang up. I said, 'Harvey?' He said, 'Who is this?' 'Spike! Look, you have to meet me.' " Lee went over to his house, which overlooks the sound in Vineyard Haven. They sat on his porch and spent an hour going over the script, the budget, and the casting, while Harvey drank Diet Coke. According to Lee, when the meeting was over, Harvey smiled, shook his hand and said, "We're making this film, Spike!" Yet, it never happened. Lee had cast the picture, was ready to begin pre-production. "We were trying to hold our cast together, but they didn't give us any money," he continues. "Finally I said, 'Fuck it, I'm not doin' this anymore, I quit.' They tried to make it out a budgetary thing, but it was bogus. My thing is, if you don't want to make the motherfucker, just tell me. He had us hanging for a whole summer. And then at the end, for all the work we did on the film, we got a measly $50,000, which had to be divided up many different ways." Would he ever get involved with Harvey again? "No way in hell. I would rather sell tube socks, three for $5. There's a sayin', 'God don't like ugly!' The fucked-up shit he's done over his career, that's just gonna come 'round and bite 'im. He's a lyin' cocksucker! A fat bastard. A fat rat bastard!"

Paramount has probably done more co-productions with Miramax than any other studio, but that too has been a rocky relationship. Not only did Harvey blame the studio for *The Talented Mr. Ripley*'s mediocre performance, he also tangled with Rudin, then a fixture on the Paramount lot. Rudin has a reputation for volatility that rivals Harvey's own, and in him, the Miramax co-chairman met his match. According to the producer, Harvey used *Iris*, which they were co-financing, as a counter in their tug-of-war over *A Confederacy of Dunces*, which Harvey was trying to get away from Rudin on Soderbergh's behalf. Says Rudin, Harvey threatened, "If you don't sell me *Dunces*, I'm going to put *Iris* on the shelf."

Rudin responded, "Do what you want. I've made the movie, I've delivered it, I don't care what you do. You don't want to release this movie, I'll give you Judi Dench's number, you call her up and tell her you're gonna shelve it! 'Cause I'm not gonna be the guy delivering that message. Hope you have a nice phone call." Rudin continues, "After a year of torture, threats, blackmail, and after holding *Iris* hostage, he finally agreed to pay me. It was probably the single most painful and unpleasant thing I have ever been through in the movie business. Solely at the hands of Harvey."

Prior to the falling out over *Dunces*, Rudin and Weinstein had entered into a deal to co-produce *The Hours*, adapted from Michael Cunningham's novel about Virginia Woolf, starring Nicole Kidman as Woolf, and co-starring Meryl Streep and Julianne Moore. "It was charming Harvey coming after me every day, beseeching me to honor him with the project," recalls Rudin. "Of course, the minute he gets it, you're [toast]. He wanted Nicole playing Virginia Woolf to look like herself, and was determined not to let her wear a prosthetic nose. Nicole Kidman looking like Nicole Kidman playing Virginia Woolf would be laughable. But he was relentless in trying to get me to can this idea to the point where he sent somebody to London to see her. I posted a security guard on the set so this person couldn't get at her." (Harvey responds, "That's complete bullshit. I said, 'Don't reveal the nose on the poster. Save it as a surprise, à la *The Crying Game*. And then they go and put it in the fucking poster.'") Rudin adds, "Every time you finish there, you swear you'll never go back, and then sooner or later you want to make a specific kind of movie, and the road leads to him. But I don't think I could do it again. I've gotten to the point where I feel like there's no movie that's worth being put through what you get put through there."

On or about August 9, 2001, a large, square box wrapped in red gift paper arrived at Harvey's office. It sat on the floor in the middle of his rug while his four assistants eyed it suspiciously. When they opened it, they discovered it contained twenty-seven cartons of Marlboro Lights and a note that said, "Thanks for all the help on *The Hours*, Best, Scott." Harvey apparently composed a letter to Rudin saying, "Dear Scott, I'm working on a cure for cancer, you better hope your family doesn't need it!" (Harvey denies this.) Marlboro Lights are not his brand—he's been smoking Carlton— but he smoked them anyway.

Then there was the case of *Cold Mountain,* based on the dark-horse best-seller of the same name by Charles Frazier, directed by Anthony Minghella, and set up at MGM. MGM's McGurk decided that rather than doing it as a big studio movie, "spending $100 million, it would be smarter to do it as a co-venture with Miramax, which could bring it in for much less. We'll take international, let them take domestic and manage the Minghella relationship."

Indeed, *Cold Mountain,* which takes place during the Civil War, is essentially a story about a man walking through the woods, and there was a time when Miramax would have made it for $10 million or less. Initially, Harvey talked a $40, $50 million movie, but it quickly became an $80 million movie, with each company kicking in $40 million. Harvey blamed Minghella. Says Gill, "Filmmakers like Minghella, who used to be treated very well, were getting kicked in the mouth too. It's the difference between, 'We love working with you,' and 'We're gonna kill you.' " His script contained some expensive battle scenes. Trying to save money, Harvey wanted to use Civil War reenactors, but Minghella, according to him, insisted on actors. "Anthony said, 'No. It's got to be my way,' " he says. "His detail rivals Scorsese's. I didn't want *Cold Mountain* to be another *Gangs.*" But the director got his way.

Again, there was a time when Harvey would have cast the lead with a cheap up-and-comer like Hugh Jackman, pre-*X-Men.* But now he wanted Tom Cruise, the most expensive star in Hollywood, and he wanted him to cut his price, which was then something like $20 to $25 million against 20 percent of first-dollar gross. Cruise's people told him, "He's getting a divorce, he needs the money," and refused.

Cruise's price brought the price tag rocketing upward to way over $100 million, the figure that McGurk hoped to avoid. After a good deal of backing and forthing, Harvey offered the actor a third of the movie to cut his fee out altogether, but Cruise again refused, and then the talks died. "When Harvey finally did decide to come up as high as he could go, Tom lost interest," says Sydney Pollack, who, with Ron Yerxa and Albert Berger, produced the film. "Cruise said, 'There's been too much negotiating here, I don't trust this, and I don't want to do this.' " The actor reportedly felt that Harvey had treated him shabbily. Minghella and Miramax subsequently put together a cast (Kidman, Jude Law, Renée Zellweger, Donald Sutherland et al.) whose entire cost was substantially less than Cruise's cut would have been, and there were no big-gross players. But the film's price going in was about $90 million.

Harvey fought the budget down by shooting the bulk of the production in Romania, and lopped another $10 million off the cost with a sale-leaseback arrangement, reducing the budget going in to somewhere between $90 and $100 million. But the Romanian weather frowned on the production. It rained when it should have been sunny. MGM executives were having second thoughts. They wondered if a Civil War drama would do well internationally. They saw *Four Feathers*, also a period piece, crash and burn, while the budget of *Gangs* was apparently spiraling out of control. MGM bailed.

With MGM out, Weinstein had to shop the picture around town, hat in hand, looking for a partner. He was like George W. Bush trying to rustle up a coalition of the unwilling to invade Iraq. Despite its best-seller pedigree, A-list director, stellar cast, and stunning rushes, every studio turned him down. Harvey, or rather, Disney, was stuck with the whole package, and Michael Eisner was reportedly not happy.

Still, it's a business, and money is money, so some studios hold their noses with one hand and Harvey's with the other, trying to structure deals so that their exposure to Miramax is limited. Miramax got a piece of Fox's *Master and Commander*, but as Russell Crowe, the picture's star puts it, "It's best to keep them in a subservient position, and make sure there's no blood in the water." Universal, where there was a considerable amount of ill will in the wake of *A Beautiful Mind*, is co-producing *Cinderella Man* with Miramax, also starring Crowe. It was an old deal, pre-dating *Mind*. "We've never had a bad experience on the actual partnership," says Snider. "For the most part, when he's not been yelling at me, Harvey has been respectful." But Universal has constructed the deal in such a way as to keep Miramax at arm's length. "If you're not careful, and not just careful but paranoid, you can end up in having to grant a concession to a demand that never in a gazillion years should have been made in the first place," says a source there. "Harvey will do things that no partner would do to another partner, like competing against you by setting a release date on one of your dates, and extracting a favor in exchange for moving off it. You have to build a wall around your business so your movie is protected." In the case of *Cinderella Man*, Universal is overseeing the production and controls domestic distribution, while Miramax is taking international. Still, observes Mark Gill, "There's no such thing as keeping Harvey at a distance."

Grazer and Ron Howard, who are producing and directing, respectively, for Universal, were still smarting from the *Mind* fracas and entered the relationship with trepidation. "We were seduced by the idea of doing the movie, but we were equally scared of Miramax," says Grazer. "But as much as I hated them, I have enormous respect for what they've accomplished. I felt like if they're capable of being that effective for themselves, they can be that effective for us. Sort of what Spiro Agnew said to James Brown when Brown was invited to the White House. He said, 'If you can stop a riot, you can start one.' You should either do a movie with somebody or you should not do the movie and walk away. My choice was, I'm going to trust Harvey—until something else happens."

In a relatively brief span of time—the summer of 2001 to the spring of 2002—Harvey managed to antagonize Mangold, Konrad, Hallström, Field, Snider, Katzenberg, Taymor, Haynes, Scorsese, Penotti, Stevens, Cruise, Rudin, Ron Howard, and Brian Grazer as well as scores of agents and former Miramax staff.

Even Disney, struggling in an adverse economic environment, turned on Miramax, threatening to eat its own. With falling revenues and plummeting stock prices, Eisner didn't want anyone roiling the waters, and that's what the Weinsteins—whose deal is up in 2005—do best. He was skittish and in the mood to resolve his problems with them as amicably as possible. On the other hand, there is no denying the bad blood between Miramax and Disney. With friends like Katzenberg, McGurk, and Roth long gone, replaced by Dick Cook, with whom they have a history, the climate there has turned frigid. Among other things, Disney was unhappy with the size of the movies Miramax is making, and wanted the brothers to go back to a modified version of their original business plan, $20, $30, even $40 million pictures, not the $70, $80, $90 million pictures they've been making lately. Miramax's 2003 slate would include several budget busters like *Cold Mountain*; *Kill Bill*, which exceeded its schedule by at least three months and may have reached nearly $70 million; and *Duplex*, which escalated from about $35 million into the neighborhood of $60 million—for a mirthless comedy that takes place mostly in one apartment—after Miramax dumped its bargain-rate director, Gregg Mottola, and replaced him with the very expensive Danny DeVito.

The Weinsteins have been operating with an annual $700 million budget cap, which includes production and P&A expenses. According to Harvey, the company exceeded it when MGM left it holding the bag on *Cold Mountain*, and Disney has been trying to redefine how those expenses are calculated in an effort to squeeze Miramax and downscale the size of the brothers' bonus package. According to Weinstein, Disney was also trying to lower the budget cap to $500 million, in part by changing the formulas by which foreign sales can offset costs. From the Weinsteins' point of view, Disney was nickel-and-diming them, which had made them livid. "They're in financial trouble, and they're trying to renegotiate the deal," Harvey says. It has always killed the Weinsteins to share the profits with anyone—agents, producers, investors, filmmakers, or employees— and this must be even more true of sharing them with Disney. As Elwes puts it, "I'm sure at the back of their minds is that nagging thought that had they managed to remain independent and had the success that they've had over the last eight years, they'd be billionaires as opposed to multimillionaires."

Eisner ordered an audit of Miramax books in 2002—such audits are annoying, but fairly common—and the Weinsteins retaliated by hiring two high-powered attorneys, Bert Fields and David Boies, to find legal grounds for a counteraudit of the Disney books pertaining to their video and international TV distribution of Miramax product. "They of course audit us every minute," Harvey says. "They get to see my books all the time, so there's no hiding what we do. On the flip side, Bob and I's [sic] pay is determined by accounting from Disney. I don't get to see everything unless I ask for an audit. There's been some discrepancies in what we think we're owed. We've asked to see certain things, and they haven't been as forthcoming as we'd hoped."

The Weinsteins, who have always thought they could do a better job running Disney than Eisner and his team, are openly critical of Eisner's judgment, starting with his refusal to let Miramax produce *Lord of the Rings*. "Let's not forget who was the guy who believed in it first," i.e., himself, Harvey says, "and to his detriment couldn't get his own company to back his vision. With the way they exploit theme parks, that one decision cost the company maybe a billion dollars. Right now, instead of the stock being at $13, it would be like Viacom's," which was then trading at nearly three times that level. According to Miramax sources, Eisner has made other decisions that incensed the brothers, including turning down the TV show *The Weakest Link*, which became a hit for NBC, and vetoing a scheme to turn One Times Square into an entertainment mecca for tourists. Sources also derided Eisner for overpaying for the ABC Family Channel and for the ongoing brain drain at the studio, such as Jerry Bruckheimer's defection to Warner's Television with his hit *CSI* franchise in tow. The brothers have been talking to investment bankers about putting together a group of investors who would buy Miramax—which has been valued by Harvey at approximately $600 million—from Disney. But Eisner not only turned it down, he declined even to bring it to the board. In an attempt, perhaps, to inflame Eisner and provoke him into letting Miramax go, Harvey reportedly showed up at his office the Friday before the March 2003 Oscar ceremonies with Bert Fields in tow. Eisner hates Fields, who represented Katzenberg in his successful suit against Disney, winning about $275 million, and this gesture was roughly equivalent to bringing Yasir Arafat to the Knesset. Furious, Eisner is supposed to have said something like, "That's crossing the line, and you can't go back from it."

Even Smith, Affleck, and Damon have gotten caught up in the tangled relationship between Miramax and Disney. As Smith puts it, "Both Matty and Ben have expressed alternatively or together, 'I don't know if I can do this anymore, I don't know if I can stay there anymore.' Affleck's like, 'Get out of Miramax, fuckin' leave it, we can make so much money elsewhere.' "
Affleck and Damon made a deal for their company, LivePlanet, with Dis-

ney, not Miramax, because Harvey would not meet their price. And outside of *Jay and Silent Bob Strike Back* and *Jersey Girl*, both of which Affleck made with Smith, none of the ten features he's made since *Bounce* in 1999 has been at Miramax save for *Daddy and Them*, which he did as a favor to Billy Bob Thornton, and *Third Wheel*, which he did as a favor for a protégé, writer Jay Locopo. "With *Jersey Girl*, it was Harvey's chance to get Ben back in," says Smith. "Ben knew that too, and it was like pulling teeth with him to do it at Miramax. There was a period when Ben was just like, 'You know, you and I could take this out anywhere. And get paid like crazy.'

" 'Yeah, but, I'm set up at Miramax, rather the devil you know—I like those guys.'

" 'Dude, you gotta break the slave mentality. He pits us against each other. He knows I want to do the movie with you, he knows you want to do the movie with me, and he knows that I would like to go elsewhere and you want to stay there. So, we're fucked. Look, I love you to death, and you know I am gonna do it, but I just want you to stay out of the negotiations because I'm going in there and I'm gonna play hardball.' And he did. We're paying Ben more than the entire budget of *Pulp Fiction*.' "

Affleck got $10 million against 10 percent of the gross, a bargain, considering that his rate is in the $15 to $20 million range. Jennifer Lopez, in a small part, got $4.5 million against 4 percent of the gross. Continues Smith, "Me and Scott Mosier, my producer, are at $4 or $5 million together, so now you're at almost $20 million before you've shot a frame of film. So you've got $10 or $11 million to spend on the movie itself, as much as it cost us to make *Dogma*." *Jersey Girl* came in under $40 million—now cheap for a Miramax film. But, concludes Smith, "If we had taken it independent, we probably could have made it for about $12 million, gotten the same people to do it for nothing. This was a company that could get away with paying people a lot less than what their quote was. But not anymore, man."

Weinstein is not happy about the direction taken by his two "little brothers." He says, "When I first came into the business, the idea of actors like the Robert De Niros or Al Pacinos of the world saying, 'I need my tentpole, I'm gonna make a comic book franchise,' was anathema. Now I have Ben and Matt, guys who grew up with me—and wisely so for their careers—saying, 'I have to do the *Sum of All Fears*, I have to do *The Bourne Identity*.' It's the triumph of the agents. There's nobody walking around at the agencies saying, 'Wait a second, what are we talking about, their franchise property. What happened to the art of cinema? I'm gonna make sure that they make the coolest material.' "

"It's tough for Harvey to get his head around paying Ben $20 million when a few scant years ago, he had him for scale," Smith adds. "But once Ben and Matty became marketable beyond Miramax, in a world where they can make $15 million, no questions asked, versus struggling to get Harvey up to $10 million, for Ben especially, it's just, 'Harvey is a businessman, I'm a businessman.' " Smith thinks the seeds of the discord go all the way back to *Good Will Hunting*. "That film made $130 million, and Ben and Matt never really saw money beyond the initial payments. The *Project Greenlight 2* negotiations were pretty ugly as well. The first one had worked, and those dudes were out there dancing like chimps to sell the show. They'd made *Greenlight 1* at a deficit. They had lost money, but Miramax had made money. Harvey wanted to do the second series the same way, and Affleck kept saying, 'I don't care about making money, but at least I want to break even!' Ben started calling it 'Project Redlight.' Matty and Ben are two people that Harvey strives every waking moment of his life to be in business with. It was like *The Third Wheel*, a little $3 million movie Ben and Matt produced. Miramax releases tons of bullshit anyway, why wouldn't they release that?"

After finishing *Jersey Girl*, Kevin Smith had some time on his hands before starting *Ranger Danger,* his next picture for Miramax. Affleck asked him to direct his new starrer, *Ghosts of Girlfriends Past*, at Disney. Smith told Affleck, "Ordinarily I don't do pictures I don't write, but being that it's you and it hits at the right moment, it might be fun." A big, mainstream movie, it would have been a nice payday for Smith, working in L.A., his new hometown during some down time, with his pal Affleck. His overall deal with Miramax allowed him to direct other movies so long as he didn't originate them, so there was no contractual reason he couldn't do it. Never thinking they would say "no," he told the Weinsteins, "I would like to do it, but if you guys say 'no,' I will totally respect it." He continues, "Lo and behold, they said 'No.' They asked Disney for half the movie, which is what they do. Michael Eisner said no." According to Smith, Harvey and Bob said, "Why would you want to work for Disney? They fucked *Dogma*, they fucked the *Clerks* cartoon."

"I don't want to go to Disney, I just want to make a movie with Ben. But don't we all work for Disney anyway?"

"Not like that." Then Harvey gave Smith the Hallström treatment, showed a side of himself that Smith had heard about but never seen up close before. Says John Shestack, late of Artisan and one of the producers, "Harvey's a twisted father figure to Kevin, and he bludgeoned him into not doing it, used every weapon in his arsenal of emotional blackmail, basically saying, 'How can you do this to me, I won't work with you if you direct it.' " Affleck told Smith, "Look, man, Disney would probably make the exact same deal that you have at Miramax," but Scott Mosier, Smith's producer, reminded him, "Yeah, Disney wants you to direct this script, great, but what happens if you bring Disney *Dogma*? They're not gonna want to make it, and Harvey and Bob did." Says Smith now, "Ben wants what Ben wants. But Miramax is my home. I had to pass." Smith asked to do *Fletch* in October, and Harvey acceded, as well as agreeing to give Smith some of the money he believed he was owed on his past films. Recalls Harvey, "Kevin said, 'I feel this, I feel that,' I said, 'How much?' He said, 'A million,' and I said, 'OK.' I also gave him gross on his next two movies. He was torn between Ben Affleck and me. It wasn't like I was giving him a million to not do that movie. I gave him a million because he was loyal, he stood up for me." But the episode further poisoned the pond in which Affleck and the Weinsteins used to swim. "Ben was like, If you do this, Harvey, lose my phone number," says Shestack. "He went to war, and it didn't matter. Harvey just did what he wanted to do."

So far, Miramax has not had much luck nurturing a new crop of Afflecks and Damons. "Who do you replace them with?" wonders Smith. "Ashton Kutcher? *Good Will Hunting* was lightning in a bottle. To be honest, I don't see Miramax fostering those kinds of relationships."

After pulling back from acquisitions, Harvey was incensed that Miramax could not boast of any of the best ones of the last couple of years. In 1999, Searchlight took *Boys Don't Cry*, and Sony got *Run Lola Run*; in 2000, Paramount Classics scooped up *You Can Count on Me*, while Sony picked up *Crouching Tiger, Hidden Dragon*; in 2001, Searchlight released *Sexy Beast* and *The Deep End*; Lion's Gate acquired *Monster's Ball*, UA put out *Ghost World*, and IFC released *Memento*. Harvey may continue to pick up the odd film here and there, even the dark and controversial ones, because he needs the street cred they provide to maintain the company's bona fides, but whatever his motives, he deserves credit for releasing them. He acquired *The Magdalene Sisters* while financing the production of *City of God*. He also asked Tom Tykwer to direct *Heaven* from a script by the late Krzysztof Kieslowski, Says Tykwer, "After the first impression of him that was kind of horrifying, during that production I was completely free to do the movie I wanted to do, including even final cut. And it is exactly the movie I was hoping for. He had suggestions—my first reaction was, What is he talking about? But very often, if you get a strong reaction from him, there is often something true about it." But Miramax is unlikely to get back into the acquisitions business in a big way anytime soon unless Disney steps on its budget cap. In 2002, Harvey sat on his hands while Focus took the Palme d'Or, BAFTA, and César winner, *The Pianist*, UA bought Michael Moore's *Bowling for Columbine*, Sony took *Talk to Her*, IFC released *My Big Fat Greek Wedding* and *Y Tu Mamá También*, Paramount Classics, *Mostly Martha*, while Searchlight acquired *The Good Girl*. Says Rudin, "The smaller, more interesting independent movies are no longer the main business of Miramax. Other people do them better now, are hitting the numbers that used to be their sole province." Adds Elwes, "They've really ceded the independent game. It's about keeping their hand in now, it's not a business anymore."

Perversely, when Harvey did find himself with a valuable acquisition, he wouldn't release it. He had paid $5.5 million for the North American rights to *The Quiet American*, based on the venerable Graham Greene tale set against a background of American meddling in Vietnam. It featured a sensational performance by Michael Caine and a not so sensational, although serviceable, performance by Brendan Fraser as the ruthless CIA agent. Harvey had tested the film in New Jersey on September 10, 2001. It scored around 60, not good, but not bad either. Director Phillip Noyce and his producer had a meeting at Miramax the next morning. "As we turned the corner to Greenwich, about twenty to nine, we could see people running along the street pointing up in a very animated fashion," Noyce recalls. "I saw a hole six-eighths of the way up the building and what looked like a small commuter plane, its tail sticking out, embedded in the World Trade Center, with smoke just starting to rise from the collision that had occurred about half a minute earlier. We stood there for the next two hours as the tragedy unfolded, leaving when the second building collapsed. We finally had the meeting two days later. Harvey's kids sang 'America the Beautiful' to us."

In October, the film was tested again. The scores plunged into the 30s. Continues Noyce, "People were heard to comment in the bathroom that they didn't appreciate moviemakers taking a swipe at America." Harvey also showed it to some of his critics, who didn't like it. Noyce delivered the film in May 2002 but was unable to get a response from Harvey. Then, in the summer, Gill told Noyce that the film was going straight to video. (Gill denies that he or anyone else told Noyce this.) The director hired Mickey Cottrell, a veteran indie publicist. "People have put their lives into these creations, and then they're just locked up," says Cottrell. "It's like Hansel and Gretel. Harvey takes them into the wonderful candy house and then puts them in a cage." Cottrell organized some critics' screenings—against Miramax's wishes—and tried to persuade Harvey to screen the film at the Toronto Film Festival. Harvey refused until he got a call from Michael Caine, who was so anxious for *The Quiet American* to see the light of day that he said, in Noyce's words, "I will not do any publicity for *The Actors* [another Miramax film of his], and I'll never work for you again."

At Toronto, "There were no press kits at the press screening," recalls Cottrell, who mobilized critics to pressure Harvey to release the film. It worked, and *The Quiet American* opened in November. But the problems weren't over. "We had a horrible time when the film was released," Cottrell continues. "They fulfilled their contractual obligations to the bare minimum." Caine's performance was Oscar caliber, but, says Noyce, "The film could only be seen for two weeks and then it disappeared. People were asking me how they could see the movie, and I'd say, 'Haven't you got a screener?' * Outside of the actors' branch, the screeners didn't go out until a week before the voting for the nominations. They said they had problems putting the covers on." Caine was nominated anyway (although neither the film nor Noyce joined him), and the conspiracy-minded suspected that Miramax failed to support Caine because they wanted Best Actor for Daniel Day-Lewis.

The Quiet American went on to do so-so business, grossing $13 million domestic, $25 million worldwide. Says Cottrell, "It should have done that much in the U.S. alone if Miramax had supported it." Noyce is more forgiving. "Harvey is a tough guy, an egomaniac, draconian in his interpretation of the laws as he's made them, but despite the checkered history of *The Quiet American*, we're better off with him than without him."

In the fall of 2002, Harvey backloaded his release schedule once again, as he had done in 2001 and previous years. Miramax released *Frida, The Quiet American, Confessions of a Dangerous Mind, Gangs of New York, Pinocchio, Chicago*, and several other pictures. Given the turnover in marketing, and the nature and expense of the pictures, it was a high-risk strategy. His attitude was, "I can do it all." He seemed to feel that as long as the Miramax brand was on the movie, it would sell itself.

Given his success with *Chicago*—the film grossed more than $170 million—there may have been more truth in this than his detractors allowed. Rolled out slowly in a classic, old Miramax campaign, *Chicago* pulled away from the pack to become the biggest Miramax grosser ever. Still, the bottom line, not the awards, indicates that one film a profitable year does not make, and some of *Chicago*'s profits may well have been eaten up by *Gangs'* losses. According to Miramax production consultant David Parfitt, at the end of shooting the hard costs stood at $105 million. Add another $10 million for its year and a half in post-production, and $40 to $60 million for marketing, it could have flirted with $175 million, while the domestic gross just reached $80 million. *Pinocchio* cost Miramax $20 million and grossed a mere $3.5 million; *Confessions of a Dangerous Mind* cost about $35 million and grossed $15.9 million; and the $20 million *Hero* was postponed again. Miramax profited on ancillary markets, including the *Pulp Fiction* and *Jackie Brown* DVDs, enhanced and deluxed to the nth degree, as well as straight-to-video films like *Seventh Inning Fetch*, moneymakers that no one has ever heard of, but it's probably easier to parse the origins of the universe than to penetrate the inky clouds that obscure the company's financial picture.

---

* "Screener": Tapes or DVDs of the year's movies sent to Academy members and other interested parties for their consideration.

Gangs can almost serve as a case study in what has happened to Miramax as it has tried to move into studio-sized pictures. Instead of beginning with a finished script and moving on to casting, the way indies used to be made, Miramax gave the cast pride of place, and *Gangs* had to begin principal photography without a satisfactory script to accommodate the busy schedules of its high-wattage stars, in turn required by the big budget. "Everybody knew the script wasn't ready, but they thought they had no choice," says a former Miramax executive. "If they didn't go when they did, they would lose the cast and the director. But they went too early."

Despite a stunning opening in which the rival gangs, dressed like refugees from the Mad Hatter's tea party, face off, and a spectacular performance by Daniel Day-Lewis, the film was a mess, almost shockingly so, given who was involved. The most glaring problem, among many, was that DiCaprio was miscast as Amsterdam Vallon; he has neither the physical presence nor the acting chops to weigh in against Day-Lewis, and worse, his part was woefully underwritten, throwing off the dramatic balance between Vallon and Bill the Butcher Cutting (Day-Lewis). It's the Satan problem in *Paradise Lost,* namely, the villain is more human and appealing than the hero, the sulky Vallon, who comes off like a punk. It is Bill the Butcher we're rooting for. Vallon badly needs to rise to the stature of a tragic figure, torn apart by the conflict between extracting a pound of flesh from Bill for killing his father, and loving him for, in effect, becoming his new father. But he doesn't. Nor does he seem to have much of an inner life at all, and when Jenny Everdeane (Cameron Diaz) asks him, "Who *are* you?" she's speaking for the audience as much as for herself. We never do find out.

This is not rocket science, it's Filmmaking 101, but the army of great cinematic brains who worked on this movie was never able to put Humpty together. According to Parfitt, "The feeling at Miramax was that a lot of Marty's work in recent years had been cold, and not character driven, and what would save this film from just being brutal was if we actually fell in love with characters in spite of all their faults. They wanted a real romance between Cameron and Leo. And genuine affection between Leo and Daniel. Kenny Lonergan was brought in to work specifically on character and dialogue, but it didn't happen on the screen. That has to be between Marty and his actors." Adds one former Miramax executive, "They talked themselves into, 'Oh, it's not so bad after all. It's Leo, he's a movie star, and every bit of time he has on the screen will be great.' " And with the draft riots intact, *Gangs* resembled nothing so much as a snake trying to swallow a beach ball. Harvey was right. The draft riot is a spectacular set piece dramatizing an event driven by complex historical forces, but it belongs in another film. It's way too complex to explain with an embarrassing Monday Night Football–style voiceover.

In the epic confrontation between Scorsese and Weinstein, Scorsese won, but it was a Pyrrhic victory in which the worst of the New Hollywood asserted itself—the excess minus the drugs, presumably—with Scorsese in effect directing his *Heaven's Gate* instead of *Raging Bull*. The clash between the two men indeed threw off its share of sparks, but it was somehow an anticlimax—with the director and producer going through the motions, not unlike Vallon and Bill the Butcher listlessly wrestling in the dust at the end of the film—and both sides lost. It seemed that perhaps Affleck was right; there is no Us/Them anymore. Scorsese's insistence on his creative integrity as an artist seemed empty when the picture turned out to be so flawed, while Harvey's attempts to enforce his authority likewise seemed beside the point. If the *Gangs* fiasco proved anything, it is that the economics of the system of production trumps everything else: creative genius, experience, personalities, intentions. Karl Marx would have been pleased.

Harvey barely dodged a bullet with *Gangs*—had *Chicago* not worked, he'd probably be buying a plot in the corporate burial ground—but, apparently motivated by his celebrated passion for movies, a burning desire to show that he and Scorsese are buddies, a positive addiction to heat and buzz, and an apparent taste for self-immolation, he signed a new deal with Warner's and Graham King to market *Aviator*, a biopic of Howard Hughes, again starring DiCaprio, with Scorsese directing. This time the launching pad for the budget was set at $107 million, and if *Gangs* is any indication, who knows where it will end up. Reportedly, Scorsese was appalled to have Harvey involved once again, and made it known that the Miramax co-chairman was not particularly welcome on the set. "Graham King had nowhere else to go," says a source. "That movie was going to die if it didn't go to Harvey. That was the last resort of a desperate man."

As an Oscar contender, Harvey ignored *Chicago*, just as he did *In the Bedroom* the year before, until the film on which he had placed his bets, *Gangs*, foundered. In both instances, his gut, his instinct, misled him, but like a studio executive, he played the percentages, taking his cues from the marketplace, and moved his money when and where the numbers told him to. *Chicago* was hardly an indie film, but it was relatively inexpensive and entertaining, yet again the kind of movie Hollywood used to make. To hear Harvey tell it, "I had more input in the editing of *Chicago* than I did on *Gangs of New York*." Unlike Scorsese, *Chicago* director Rob Marshall "embraced collaboration. I could sit in the editing room with Rob and say, 'This should move faster, this can blow by.' "

Yet *Chicago* was the occasion for customary Miramax carnage. According to one source, Harvey "tormented" Marshall. One day, Marshall even collapsed on the set. Richard Gere called Harvey and said something like, "Back off and don't be so tough on Rob, don't do it in front of other people, it's demoralizing, it's embarrassing, have some class." Harvey told Gere to mind his own business. (Marshall could not be reached for comment.)

As awards season approached, *Far from Heaven* looked like a strong contender. The reviews were universally glowing, and at year's end, it had appeared on approximately twice as many critics' top ten lists as any other picture. It cleaned up at the New York Film Critics Awards, winning five, including Best Film. Recalls Haynes, "Harvey made his way over to our table, looking so contrite, and sheepish almost, he wouldn't even make eye contact with me. Finally, he said, softly, 'Todd, I . . . am . . . so . . . sorry.' Then he started to talk about the fact that he was seeking counseling or something, 'because I just can't allow this kind of thing to happen again.' " Moore, who had won Best Actress at the Venice Film Festival, and the legendary Elmer Bernstein, who wrote the music, seemed like shoo-ins for Oscars, while Best Picture and Director also appeared to be within reach. But both Haynes and Vachon felt that Focus threw its weight behind *The Pianist*, and as a result, *Far from Heaven* was virtually ignored. Recalls Haynes, "People would say, 'Focus isn't pushing it enough, don't you wish you were with Miramax?' I could only say no, because the most important thing for me, hands down, is to finish the film the way I want. And someone interfering in the production process, that's worse than a lackluster marketing campaign. On the other hand, I wanted to say, 'Dammit, guys, think bigger. You seem to be the last ones catching on to the fact that actually t his could be a serious Oscar film.' " Adds Vachon, "*Far from Heaven* just wasn't Focus's movie. It was a leftover, an orphan. Soderbergh was right." Counters Schamus, "As with the success of our marketing of *Far from Heaven*, so did everyone at this company kill themselves for those Academy awards. None of us had any possible motivation why we wouldn't. We tried. We lost. We'll try again." Regardless, the episode put a chill on an old friendship.

Despite brutal competition, *Chicago* did well with the awarding class—the screenwriters, producers, and directors, as well as the Catholic, New York, L.A., and national critics, and in particular the Foreign Press Association, laying track for the Oscars. At the January 26 Golden Globes ceremony, one awardee after another, including Scorsese, Zellweger, and most conspicuously Gere, did their best to dispel the gloom that surrounded Harvey, especially after a tough piece in *The New Yorker* by Ken Auletta. As Bob was overheard complaining that no one was giving him the time of day, Gere called Harvey "a kindly, lovable, gentle man who we all love, a little rough around the edges but with a heart of gold," and even ridiculed Auletta by name. (Gere's valentine was enough to make you wonder about the Dalai Lama. Says Rudin, "I think it cost him the nomination. Toady-ish.") Allowing for the fact that everyone who praised Harvey that night either was, is, or may in the future be on his payroll, those familiar with his MO know that he shamelessly heaps encomia on himself via proxies when the occasion calls for it, and suspected that he was doing so again, playing Edgar Bergen to Gere's Charlie McCarthy. Says one former Mira-max staffer, "They're coached to do that. It's like, 'Catherine Zeta-Jones, you gotta talk about Renée Zellweger and how great she is whenever you talk to the press. Renée, you get up there and talk about Catherine. Richard, you get up there and you talk about Harvey.' It's like a big circle jerk."

The next week, Miramax got so many Oscar nominations (forty) that the *L.A. Times* dubbed the ceremony "the Harveys." Three out of the five Best Picture nominations—*Gangs, Chicago, The Hours*—were Miramax films in one way or another, while the Weinsteins had an executive producer credit on a fourth, *Lord of the Rings*. (The fifth film was *The Pianist*.) Two Mira-max directors, Scorsese and Marshall, were up against Pedro Almodóvar *(Talk to Her)*, Stephen Daldry *(The Hours)*, and Roman Polanski *(The Pianist)*.

Harvey campaigned hard for Scorsese, had him putting in appearances and gratefully accepting tacky awards at every rubber chicken dinner be-tween Los Feliz and Santa Monica. As one of his competitors put it, "I mar-vel at Harvey Weinstein's ability to turn one of the greatest directors in the history of cinema into a guy who would wash your car for your vote." With his knack for overdoing it, Weinstein created a scandal and no small back-lash by inducing *Sound of Music* director Robert Wise, then age 88, and possibly none too compos mentis, to put his signature on a text written by a Miramax consultant praising Scorsese. (It would have been more logical for him to endorse Marshall for his musical, and indeed, Marshall seemed to have thought so. Already chafing at Weinstein's campaign for Scorsese, Marshall perceived this as a slap in the face, had words with Harvey over it, and was a no-show at the party Harvey threw in honor of the *Chicago* sweep of the Screen Actors Guild Awards.) The Wise endorsement caused such an uproar that had the story come out even a week earlier, *The Pianist*, which was coming on strong, might well have won the Best Picture Oscar. When *The Pianist* won Best Picture at the BAFTA Awards in London, Miramax panicked. Publicist Swartz began badmouthing Polan-ski, calling him a "child molester." The internet site *Smoking Gun* suddenly produced the nearly thirty-year-old deposition of Polanski's victim, a flame that was fanned by Miramax soldiers, like Roger Friedman on his site, and "Page Six" of the *New York Post*. This suggested to some that the disclosure revealed the hand of Miramax although this was never proven. Says

Schamus, "Harvey made two mistakes: he failed to drag us into the gutter, and he very publicly treated the Best Director Oscar as something he could give to Marty Scorsese because he just decided to."

When Polanski won the Oscar, it seemed for a moment that the Miramax express might be derailed, but *Chicago* won, giving Miramax its first Best Picture since *Shakespeare* in 1998, putting Harvey back on top. But with the *Pianist* upsets, it seemed to some people that Harvey came away a loser. After months of asserting that Scorsese was a lock, he did an about-face, claiming that he never expected the director to win after he lost the Directors Guild award to Marshall and that the critics did not like the film. Despite *Gangs'* flaws, it was a sad moment when Scorsese lost. His face, flashed on the TV screen for no more than a nanosecond at the moment Polanski's name was announced, was a tragedic mask of surprise, dismay, and pain. It was as if Harvey had been entrusted with a Ming vase and had dropped it.

Postscript: The Sweet Hereafter

If Miramax picked up its chips and took them to the bank, its legacy, nevertheless, remains. Not only did the Weinsteins transform distribution, they brokered a marriage of indie and mainstream that resulted in a novel kind of picture that did more than just cross over; it exchanged DNA with commercial movies. An amalgam of difference and sameness, personal and commercial, voice and genre, these films played like Hollywood movies while retaining the indie spirit, however vague and hard to define that may be. Indie filmmakers began to work in a more commercial idiom, and stars were increasingly willing to aid and abet them, not necessarily because they needed career liposuction, like John Travolta and Bruce Willis in the days of *Pulp*, but because Miramax had made indies, as Ethan Hawke puts it, "sexy." The 2002 crop of films like *Far from Heaven*, with Julianne Moore and Dennis Quaid; *About Schmidt*, with Jack Nicholson; *Solaris*, with George Clooney; *Confessions of a Dangerous Mind*, with Clooney and Julia Roberts; *The Good Girl*, with Jennifer Aniston; *Punch-Drunk Love*, with Adam Sandler; *Adaptation*, with Nicolas Cage, twice; *The Hours*, with Nicole Kidman; and *One Hour Photo*, with Robin Williams, speak for themselves. Ditto the 2003 films like the triad from Focus: *Lost in Translation*, with Bill Murray; *Sylvia*, with Gwyneth Paltrow; and *21 Grams*, with Sean Penn. They are all children of Miramax, even if their directors don't want to sit on daddy's lap.

Even Miramax's most vocal critics won't go so far as to say the indie world would have been a better place had the Weinsteins gone into, say, loan sharking, repossessing cars, or solid waste management. Says Spike Lee, "Miramax has been great. They do what they gotta do, above the table and below the table, to get those nominations." Rudin adds, "I don't think Miramax has had a bad influence. A lot of movies reached larger numbers of people than they otherwise would have because they were very aggressive marketing them." The director-driven star vehicles no longer seem to be a contradiction in terms, and it is a compelling vision, one that ignited the indie explosion of the 1990s, but it is still a fragile one, as the fate of *Far from Heaven* suggests.

Moreover, Harvey is not Michael Ovitz. The Weinsteins have built a viable infrastructure, however erratically managed, and created a valuable library of films. And of course Harvey has Bob to depend on. As 2002 proves, many of his assets have remained intact. He is still bold, aggressive, able to move quickly and decisively where the majors can't or won't. He still has an eye for finding gold in studio slag heaps. As Marcy Granata noted, stars are his meal ticket, and so long as meaty roles in studio movies become fewer and farther between, he will always have a shot at luring them into his stable as long as he is able to buy up the best material in town, dangle it in front of them, and promise them Oscars. Filmmakers are warier—he's more brutal with them—but if the stars come, the directors won't be far behind. Still, much depends on whether Harvey can stop me-tooing the studios and listen to his contrarian instincts. If he goes on the Atkins Diet, resists swallowing huge mouthfuls of high-carb pictures like *Gangs*, and instead sticks with finger food like *Chicago*, he'll be fine, at least from a commercial point of view.

The question is, Can he? Projects like *Cold Mountain, Aviator,* and his ostensible newfound interest in studio-type tentpoles like *The Green Hornet,* suggest that he may not. The movie marketplace is in constant flux; it's a shadow play of shifting shapes, nearly impossible to make out. Today's trend is tomorrow's garbage and the next day's nostalgia. To make matters murkier still, Miramax in particular is very much a moving target. Predicting which way the company will jump is never easy. Dominated by the will of two men, it can turn on a dime, reverse course, bob and weave. Still, no matter how much the Weinsteins twist and shout, you don't need to be a weatherman to chart their direction. It's like global warming, which is to say, despite local fluctuations in climate, an early frost here, a late winter blizzard there, we know it's coming. Now that Miramax has stepped up to the "next level" to compete with the majors, it will live or die by the economics that governs the studio system, and therefore may lose its edge.

But even were Miramax somehow immune from the logic of the marketplace, Harvey's biggest worry will always be himself. He long ago fell victim to his own notices, most often fashioned, ironically, by himself. Trapped in a forest of mirrors, all the talk of "I'm rich because I'm right" too easily slides into "I'm right because I'm rich." His festering sense of inferiority, his hunger to become an insider, his fierce competitiveness, his passion for celebrities and deep need to bask in their reflected glow—all propel Miramax toward the studio sun, making him a poor guardian of the indie flame—although guarding the indie flame was never what he was about. Rather, it was more like feeding the indie flame, fanning it into a conflagration. The danger is, of course, that the blaze may consume him. Regardless, indie filmmakers and distributors have entered the post-Miramax era. What does this mean for them?

Strictly speaking, by the new millennium, as Steven Soderbergh says, "The independent film movement, as we knew it, just doesn't exist anymore, and maybe it can't exist anymore. It's over." And Miramax killed it. With success. Success that was purchased at an enormous cost. Of course, that's an exaggeration, but even though "co-optation" and "commercialization" may be dismissed as no more than slogans from the 1960s, and an Affleck may say, "Get over it!," that doesn't mean they don't exist. Today they are even more potent than ever. In the past, it could take years for a filmmaker to get from a Sundance film to a big studio movie—for Soderbergh, a decade elapsed between *sex, lies* and *Erin Brockovich*—but today, directors like Bryan Singer go from *The Usual Suspects* to *X-Men* and *X-Men 2*, or the Wachowski brothers from *Bound* to *The Matrix* in a couple of years. Darren Aronofsky signed on for *Batman 5* after he did his second film, *Requiem for a Dream*, and now Christopher Nolan is directing it, just one movie away from his breakthrough, *Memento*. Doug Liman went from *Go* to *The Bourne Identity*, while Charles Herman-Wurmfeld went from *Kissing Jessica Stein* to *Legally Blonde 2*. The escalating profitability of indie films, or at least the illusion of it, along with the video boom and the skyrocketing 1990s stock market created the motive (profit) and the means (cash) that corporatized what once was a movement fueled by artists.

Two thousand two and 2003 had all the earmarks of bumper years, and they were, but it's important not to lose sight of what is not and cannot be produced in the one-step-forward, two-steps-back indie world. In today's market, Anthony Minghella most likely couldn't set up *The English Patient*, especially not at Miramax. He says, "Sydney Pollack and I are trying to make a movie, *The Assumption of the Virgin*, which is a mirror project to *The English Patient*, and it's been very, very hard to raise even $5 million in the U.S. for domestic distribution, never mind the $15 million we went to Fox for with *The English Patient*." Spike Lee always has trouble getting financed, as his difficulties on *Rent* suggest, and it's getting worse. His recent film, *25th Hour*, produced on a modest $15 million budget, was done for a Touchstone worried that it didn't have any Oscar-class pictures. The Disney division refused to make the film unless he attracted an actor like Edward Norton, who worked for a fraction of his asking price. Said Norton, "The whole thing that's happening to Spike is BS. He's suffering from the Woody Allen syndrome. People say, 'Oh, it's just another Spike Lee movie.' " Ditto John Sayles: "It's getting harder to get our movies financed. . . . Anything over $1 million or $2 million sends distribution companies into their litany of the five or six hot actors who can allegedly 'open' a picture."

To the degree that indie films have deteriorated, they mimic the devolution of studio films, with a time lag of maybe half a decade. First there was the rise of films dependent on stars. Then, as Ethan Hawke points out, "Even on the indie level, the middle-range film is disappearing. The movies that I would have been the lead of, even fifteen years ago, aren't getting made anymore. I probably got the best reviews of my life, bar none, for *Tape*. Nobody saw the movie. Andrew Niccol, who wrote and directed *Gattaca* and wrote *The Truman Show*, did a script that's phenomenal, and he can't get the money for it with me and Ewan McGregor attached. For under $20 million! I called up this producer and said, 'Why don't you want to do this movie, man?' He said, 'The script is great, if you like Beckett.' I said, 'Well, I do like Beckett. So, that's not a plus?' 'No, that's not a plus. I don't want to make a movie that plays at the Film Forum in twenty-five years.' It's funny, 'cause I do."

You don't have to worship at the Jarmusch shrine or get your nourishment from the granola Sundance to wonder what's happened to the indie movement. The not-ready and never-will-be-ready-for-prime-time films, the ones that Rick Linklater, Hal Hartley, Allison Anders, and Gus Van Sant (occasionally) like to make, and actors such as Hawke like to perform in, have almost disappeared. "You can't get a film made for $10 million," Hawke continues. "Linklater has this incredible screenplay of a Philip K. Dick story, 'Scanner Darkly,' and I want to be in it. After *Training Day*, I can get you $30 million if you want to do a cop movie, but we can't get anyone to give us $10 million for that. Getting great reviews and being a respected indie film director doesn't get you shit to do your movie." Now, of course, after *School of Rock*, Linklater has enough clout to make a follow-up to *Before Sunrise*, with Hawke (and Julie Delpy), but it's taken him a decade to get there.

Some, like Affleck and Matt Damon, approached their first film as a calculated career move, but if you aspire or presume to be an "auteur" with something to say and a distinct way of saying it, if you cultivate a personal "voice," the road to the Independent Spirit Awards, or just a theatrical playdate, is neither straight nor smooth. History rewards the winners—Soderbergh, Tarantino, the Andersons, Payne, Russell, and so on—and they will insist, as does Vachon, that good filmmakers always rise to the top, dismissing those that don't as losers or whiners or hacks. But the new rules of the indie game are weighted heavily toward box office success, with promising or even brilliant but uncommercial films failing to get picked up for distribution, witness the fate that befell *L.I.E.* and *The Believer*.

As a direct result of becoming "sexy," there is tremendous pressure from the bottom from new filmmakers coming up. As John Sayles puts it, "As the last ten years have progressed, many, many, many more independent features are being made, and so a much higher percentage of them never get a theatrical release. And a not much higher percentage of them even go straight to video." Adds Ethan Coen, "The big difference between then and now from our perspective is that then, if you had a finished movie in 35mm, you could get everybody to see it. Now, partly because it's easier to make a movie, it's more difficult to get people to even look at it. Because there are so many."

The ferocious competition, alongside the twin obsessions with the young and the new, means there is little opportunity to fail, and from failing to learn. There is no apprentice system. "Most of the '70s guys just shoveled shit for Roger Corman, learned their craft long before they found their voices," says James Schamus. "Spielberg did so much TV, people have no clue. Whereas these days, you say to some guy at NYU, 'Why don't you go make some TV,' it's like, 'Please. Out of my sight.' "

Sundance was supposed to fill this hole, but there's a big difference between working for Corman and a Sundance lab that lasts three weeks at most. There are few first novels in filmmaking, efforts that go into the drawer or up in flames, because there are no—or very few—second chances. Or, to put it another way, indie film is almost exclusively a cinema of first films. "The psychology of the American independent has supplanted the auteur psychology," Schamus continues. "There's no question to me that Sundance, as a culture, has dangerously infantilized auteurism, because the reigning assumption is that by the time you're seventeen or eighteen years old, you're pretty much an auteur if you're going to be an auteur, and if you're not, you're not. If you'd put that on someone like Coppola, I don't think he'd ever have been Coppola. What could that guy have said at the age of twenty? Your first independent film has gotta be *your* film, *your* voice. So now the pressure is really on from the time you're out of diapers to be an artist. It's become a grim kind of joke."

If the first film is successful, the director is overwhelmed with praise and offers he (or much less often, she) cannot refuse. Then, adds Kevin Smith, "An independent filmmaker has to produce something that lives up to the hype based on what he did last, that he himself has encouraged. There's a lot of fuckin' pressure, and life is too short to deal with it." If, on the other hand, the first film fails, raising cash for the next one becomes an unrelenting grind of begging and scraping. There are so many filmmakers chasing so little money that getting film number two or three made can be harder than number one. Either way, the filmmaker stops living life—as most people know it. While the first film was about "My life up to now," the subsequent films aren't about anything at all or, if you're Charlie Kaufman, they're totally reflexive, about screenwriting itself.

The indie landscape is littered with first (or occasionally second) films of promise—promise that has rarely been realized, not necessarily because the filmmakers have no talent, but because of the cultural and economic ecology of the environment in which they are working. Examples: Anders's *Gas Food Lodging* vs. all her subsequent work; Gregg Araki's *The Living End* vs. his; Aronofsky's *Pi* vs. his; Whit Stillman's *Metropolitan* vs. his; Neil LaBute's *In the Company of Men* vs. his; Billy Bob Thornton's *Sling Blade* vs. his; Nick Gomez's *Laws of Gravity* vs. his; Alexandre Rockwell's *In the Soup* vs. his; Bryan Singer's *The Usual Suspects* vs. his; Lisa Cholodenko's *High Art* vs. hers; Scott Hicks's *Shine* vs. his; Hal Hartley's *The Unbelievable Truth* vs. his; Rose Troche's *Go Fish* vs. hers; Larry Clark's *Kids* vs.his; and Boaz Yakin's *Fresh* vs. his. Says Linklater, "Once you proved you aren't the next George Lucas, then your stock goes down. It's, 'Oh shit.' It doesn't get easier, it gets harder, 'cause with each film you define yourself more, what your limitations are. If you haven't had big financial success, you get smaller and smaller. I remember seeing Altman talk in Houston in the late '80s, and he said, 'Any of you in this audience has a better chance of getting financing than I do.' I was like, 'That's insane, he's Robert Altman!' Then you go, 'Now I know, he was right.' "

Just a glance at the Sundance Film Festival program each year reveals that for every familiar name there are ten unfamiliar ones, filmmakers who were wounded and left for dead, and that's just Sundance, which accepts a tiny fraction of the films submitted. A where-are-they-now list nearly as big as the Salt Lake City phone book could be compiled of filmmakers who never made it. What happened to Leslie Harris, whose *Just Another Girl on the IRT* made a splash at Sundance in 1992, or Karyn Kusama, whose *Girlfight* was acclaimed in 2000, or Susan Streitfeld (*Female Perversions*), or Mark Illsley (*Happy, Texas*), for that matter. Judged by one of its original, loftier goals, an institute to help outsiders, Sundance has failed. Women, Native Americans, African-Americans, and the poor still don't have equal access to the camera. And so far as creating a nurturing environment sheltered from the commercial demands of Hollywood where filmmakers could grow, learn, make mistakes, and grow some more—the labs do a good job, but a lot of that good work is undone by the frenzy of the festival. Skeptics once feared that Sundance would be no more than a farm team for the majors, and it has become just that. "If you're an independent who wants to get your feature looked at by Miramax or Focus, then SD is a great mechanism," says Sterling Van Wagenen. "But what if you're a real independent who wants to go someplace that's really out on the edge, I suspect it is not the answer. If you'd said to me twenty years ago that this is where Sundance was going to be, I would have been surprised." The indies who were in on the beginning of Sundance—Victor Nuñez, Annick Smith, et al.— are not much better off than they were two decades ago.

Still, if Harvey Weinstein is like the Terminator, coming back from defeat after defeat stronger than ever, Sundance is like the headless horseman, picking itself up, brushing off the dust, and plunging ahead. Schizoid, the festival has always tugged the institute in the direction of Hollywood, but the labs—under the radar—have nurtured the original vision. As the labs have evolved, they have changed in scope, not concept, supplementing the original June directors' program with labs for writers and composers, as well as an annual producers' conference. If Sundance managed to sink its production arm, it still, according to Michelle Satter, the unsung hero of the institute, provides "ongoing support for projects through their entire life—including help with financing, casting, production services, etc.—aimed at leveraging films into production." And if the Sundance cinemas went bottom up, the Sundance Channel, in conjunction with the Loews theater chain, opened four corporately sponsored indie films in 2003, while at the same time arranging DVD distribution for films that premiere on the channel.

THE WEINSTEINS hopped aboard the Miramax balloon and vanished skyward to the huzzahs of its fans and catcalls of its enemies, ascending as fast and as far as hot air would take them. But in truth, the Weinsteins escaped the gravitational pull of the indie world many years ago, in 1998, after *Shakespeare in Love,* or even earlier, in 1994, after *Pulp Fiction.* And despite the many ways in which the brothers Miramaxed and Disneyized everything in sight, it would be a mistake to exaggerate their influence. The broad shadows the brothers cast should not obscure the fact that in many respects, Miramax is sui generis. True, they recast the indie landscape, but when the Weinstein spores landed at almost every single indie distributor in the business and tried to pod and body-snatch their new hosts into Miramax clones, most often they failed. Scott Greenstein surely tried with October, but he never did succeed in cutting its cloth to suit the fashion of his old home. Even though every studio wanted its infant indie division to become the "new Miramax"—the chorus has always been the same, "October, the new Miramax," "Artisan, the new Miramax," "USA, the new Miramax," and even now, "Focus, the new Miramax"—it never happened, because it takes a certain kind of personality to fashion a Miramax, a ruthlessness, a willingness to take scissors to films, to shelve them, "bury" them, as Harvey so often put it. The Weinsteins' methods ran counter to the way indie companies had historically conducted themselves, and most former Miramaxers didn't have the stomach for it. They discarded their Ghostfaces and fashioned kinder, gentler companies. The start-ups have generally defined themselves against Miramax.

Life after Miramax, then, without the Weinsteins to kick around anymore (or, more accurately, without the Weinsteins to be kicked around by anymore), may be less dramatic, but it will certainly be more civil, with the business recapturing some of the collegial sensibility it enjoyed in its infancy, especially with the reemergence of indie stalwarts like Bingham Ray, and the empowerment of sane players like James Schamus and David Linde and Mark Gill at the new Warner's Independent Pictures. "Now that Miramax has stepped out of it, other distributors don't have to pay as much for films they like," says Cassian Elwes. "Filmmakers and agents won't make as much money because Miramax is not overpaying, but at the end of the day the films are still going to get distributed. It's healthy for the business." With the frenzied competition that created the acquisitions bubble ended, at least for the foreseeable future, and absent the Disney dollars Harvey dumped onto the Sundance game board, real filmmakers, rather than heat-seeking wannabes, may even reclaim the movement. Maybe.

Indeed, more relevant to the future of the indie movement than the presence or absence of Miramax, perhaps, is the state of the studios. At the beginning of the decade, the indie world was largely reactive; how it looked and felt, its focus and attitudes were determined by what the studios did or didn't do. As the decade wore on, the two worlds reached out to each other—the studios starting their indie divisions and the indies responding with their Indiewood films—but it was a dangerous dance, at least for the indies. Despite the spate of "indie spirit" films released in 1999, or again in 2002 and 2003, it's a mistake for indies to look to the studios for more than the occasional handout. For one thing, studios are fickle creatures and don't have much in the way of long-term, coherent strategies. One year it's *American Beauty,* the next it's *Gladiator.* Indie films and studio movies converge only to diverge again. Studios are no more suited to marketing indie films than they ever were. And when the studios do acquire or create their own specialty divisions, they're often treated like orphans, starved and neglected. Nor is the bureaucratic studio culture suited to the risk-taking indie sensibility that has served the Weinsteins so well. The executives with the most longevity are the most conservative, like Paramount's Sherry Lansing. On the other hand, Bill Mechanic, who pushed the envelope at Fox, launching *The English Patient* and *Traffic,* along with *Bulworth* and *Fight Club,* was swept away by Rupert Murdoch's broom in a "regime change." *Pulp Fiction* aside, *Three Kings* was the most important film of the last decade, because it showed that an indie director could ram a major film with leftist politics and a daring aesthetic through a studio, Warner's, one of the most conservative. Lorenzo di Bonaventura, the executive who fought for it, got the sack after tangling with Warner's COO Alan Horn, who had criticized him for making films, such as *Training*

Day, that are "too dark." Ultimately, it may be easier, and certainly more profitable, for the studios to revert to form, focusing exclusively on the kinds of pictures they're good at: comic book pictures, sequels, broad comedies, and steroidal versions of golden oldie TV series. What with the economic squeeze, they're thinking about the bottom line, not about Oscars, modest profits, and luring new talent into the fold. They may lose interest in their classics divisions.

The danger, as always, is that if they do continue to make the occasional Indiewood film, the likes of Payne, David Russell, and the Andersons will be cannibalized by the studios. As New Line's Bob Shaye admitted, in case anyone was wondering, when he defended himself against the charge of recutting *About Schmidt,* "We are not a cultural temple."* Adds Ted Hope, "When I started working, the Jim Jarmuschs, the Hal Hartleys, the early Todd Haynes were aiming for a different level of art, and audiences seemed to be responding, but it became harder and harder to get money to make those movies, whereas the films that actually could step forward and compete at the Oscar level, you could raise money for. But then specialized film has become simply this Academy-qualifying low-budget cinema of quality."

Besides, there's a quota system for indie films at the studios, as Russell discovered. Before di Bonaventura left Warner's, Russell set up his new film there, *I Heart Huckabee's.* Miramax still had an option on him, but neither he nor Warner's wanted to partner with Harvey. However, says Russell, "He'll litigate. We squirmed every which way, and we decided to make a deal instead. We made Warner's the production partner so we wouldn't have to deal with Miramax. Since Warner's doesn't know how to distribute an interesting film, Miramax was going to distribute domestically. It was the best of both worlds." That is, until di Bonaventura exited, and Russell found that neither Warner's nor Miramax would step up for his project, modestly budgeted at around $22 million with a cast that includes Jude Law, Naomi Watts, Dustin Hoffman, Lily Tomlin, and Isabelle Huppert. "This is where the whole movie star fucking thing comes in," says Russell. "I said, 'How come you made fucking *Confessions of a Dangerous Mind*— which I had been offered to direct a couple of years ago and concluded that it was just not about anything but a guy who liked to fuck girls and say that he shot people in the head—just so you could get to get in bed with Clooney? Of course they'll make a movie with a movie star in a heartbeat, as Fox did with *Solaris.*"

---

* Even though Payne had final cut on *About Schmidt,* New Line forced him to eliminate the opening sequence and add a happy ending, a replay of his experience with Miramax on *Citizen Ruth.* When the New Line version scored lower than Payne's, he was allowed to go out with his director's cut, but had the recut film tested better, Payne's version would have been history.

Russell shopped his project. "New Regency spent $45 million on an An-gelina Jolie/Ed Burns romantic comedy, *Life or Something Like It,*" he con-tinues. "So now the company was in austerity mode, and I came with my picture, and asked for $12.5 million, and it's 'no.' I have to pay for your stu-pid mistakes? Same thing happened at Universal. They spent a lot of money on the Jonathan Demme remake of *Charade.* Much as I respect him, Demme burned through the independent capital there. Wasted it. Same with Payne at Sony. Sony had just spent over $50 million on *What Planet Are You From?*, and then Alexander couldn't get the time of day for *About Schmidt*, and they put it in turnaround. The climate for inde-pendent type pictures is not good unless they're made for under $10 million."

Finally he ended up at Fox Searchlight, which is doing Payne's new pic-ture as well, and scored in 2003 with films like Danny Boyle's *28 Days Later,* Catherine Hardwicke's *13,* and Gurinder Chadha's *Bend It Like Beckham.* "For sure, Miramax is not interested in making certain kinds of risky movies and movies that have to be sold with tender loving care," Russell continues. "No, Harvey has to get the movie star juice, he has to do a deal directly with the movie star, like with Clooney. He's just bored. Now Fox Searchlight is doing that business."

But the good news is that by the end of the decade, the indies had formed their own infrastructure, their distributors—both the studio-affili-ated divisions with deep pockets and the unaffiliated companies looking for the old-style, star-challenged indies—their lobbying arm, the IFP, their own media (indieWire, *Filmmaker*, and the like), and last but hardly least, their base in the agencies, witness William Morris Independent, run by Elwes. This institutional foundation for the first time gives them leverage with the studios, hopefully making, for example, the first-film syndrome a thing of the past. As attorney Linda Lichter puts it, agents like Elwes, Robert Newman, and John Lesher "have found money for them so that they're not scrounging for bucks for their next movie, but can really have a career."

The contradiction that has always bedeviled Sundance reflects the con-tradiction at the heart of the indie phenomenon: Is the indie world a place where the studios develop talent, a farm system for the majors? Or is it an autonomous world of its own, with its own values and aesthetic existing outside and even thrusting against the gravitational pull of the system? The remarkable success of indies in the 1990s, for which Sundance, Mira-max, Sony Classics, October et al. are largely responsible, is that it was both, and the one fed the other. "The purpose of doing a film outside the system is so that they don't fuck with you," Lichter continues. "And the movie you get is the movie that has your voice. Then, when the big people come calling, they do so because of who you are, what you can bring to them, not because they can control you. Rather than doing one for them and one for you, you can do one for you that both they and you want to make. The impact of the independents on the studio world is that all of a sudden, they want what we got. Of course, you have to see if you can do it on your own terms and not be eaten alive by the system. David O. Russell really did that with *Three Kings*. Whether anybody can do it again I don't know."

Nothing could have made the new clout of the indies clearer than the reality check administered by the studios to the indies on September 30, 2003, when Jack Valenti, ostensibly backed by the seven majors, plus DreamWorks and New Line, announced the decision to cease sending out screeners to Academy members, critics' societies, and the guilds. The decision came out of the blue on the runup to the 2003 Oscar race, already foreshortened by the removal of the ceremony itself from the end of March to the end of February 2004. The new policy, reportedly spearheaded by Warner's CEO Barry Meyer, who stayed in the shadows, and announced by veteran MPAA lobbyist Jack Valenti, 82 years old and on the edge of retirement, was aimed at stemming the kind of rampant piracy that has laid low the recording industry. But the effect of the ruling would have been, and still may be, devastating for indies, especially those owned by the seven majors, which depend on screeners to level the playing field. Some indies went so far as to charge the studios with a conspiracy to reclaim the Oscars for themselves by frustrating their ability to compete. Says UA's Bingham Ray. "It was fuckin' railroaded by Barry Meyer, pure and simple. It's all about, What's good for the goose is good for the gander. I think it's fractionally about piracy. But what we all know, and will never be able to prove, is that it is about the studios reclaiming the Academy process." Added Christine Vachon, "This is such a smokescreen. It's clear people are getting pissed that every year the independents are getting the lion's share of the recognition. There's not a doubt in my mind that the bigger issue here is to refocus attention on big studio movies." Outraged distributors also questioned the timing of the decision and the lack of consultation with those most affected, i.e., the indie divisions themselves. (Ironically, "real" indie companies without studio affiliations, like IFC Films, Lion's Gate, Newmarket, Strand, and Artisan, would have presumably been free to continue to send out screeners.)

But the most serious objection is the obvious one: it's not the tiny indie films—idiosyncratic in voice and local in detail—that are likely to be pirated; they most often don't travel well. Rather, it is the big-studio action movies, like the two Warner's released in the late fall, *The Last Samurai*, a Tom Cruise vehicle, produced by *Shakespeare in Love*'s Ed Zwick; and *The*

Matrix Revolutions, as well as *The Lord of the Rings: The Return of the King,* from a Warner's division, New Line.

The merits of the studio case aside, one fact became glaringly obvious: despite the explosion of indie power in the 1990s, the undeniable viability of their business model, and their increased visibility in the public eye— from the studios' point of view, their indie divisions were so inconsequential that they could just ignore them. "I only wish the studios noticed the specialized business enough to conspire against it," observes Ted Hope. "The whole way it came about just shows how little respect there is for us. We're just a blip on their flowcharts and their income and outcome P&Ls—they couldn't care less." Piracy was paramount, and if the screener ban did inflict some collateral casualties, did knock some indies out of the Oscar race, the studios were all too willing to sacrifice them on that altar of piracy protection, especially, as Ray, Vachon, and others supposed, if it cleared the way for themselves. Moreover, events seemed to prove that the illusion of independence these divisions carefully cultivated turned out to be just that, an illusion. When push came to shove, they were unable to act independently of their studio parents.

Still, a funny thing happened on the way to implementing the new policy. It raised a hue and cry among indies and their friends. Said producer Jeremy Thomas, "The people who have made this rule are in the Dark Ages. The specialty labels live by awards. It's the little bit extra that they get from a nomination that makes their business pay." An Oscar in a major category can mean $10 to $15 million in additional revenue for an indie distributor. "When I first heard about it, I thought it was a joke," added Artisan CEO Amir Malin. "It's a great injustice and a knee-jerk reaction to piracy." Robert Altman, who had been an outsider throughout most of his career, got it right away and was furious. He said, "This is a real Karl Rove move. It's just plain wrong." Far from being powerless, they mobilized talent, critics, and industry groups that stood to be damaged by the shock wave of the hasty and ill-conceived studio diktat. Valenti and the majors were taken by surprise. The counterattack was organized, needless to say, by Ray, with a little help from his friends. Soon after the new policy was announced at the end of September 2003, he got on the phone. "We talked to the IFP in New York and L.A., and they motivated a whole group of people, and it really snowballed," he says. "We had people write letters, Altman, Scorsese, Coppola. We called friends, and they called their friends. It was an honest-to-goodness, classic guerrilla grass-roots campaign."

Ray organized a sit-down at the Four Seasons hotel in New York of the six families, as Kevin Smith likes to call them, UA, Sony Classics, Focus Features, Paramount Classics, Fine Line, and Miramax, who buried their differences and got together in the same room for the first time. (Actually,

Tom Bernard could not quite bring himself to break bread with Harvey, and made himself available by phone. Paramount Classics's Ruth Vitale and David Dinerstein were on the phone as well.)

Initially, Harvey toed the studio line. He was quoted in *Variety* saying, "I will go along with this ban if it is for the reason of combating piracy." At the Four Seasons meeting, Harvey took a back seat, explaining that he was already on the Academy's watch list, and that were he to play a prominent role, the media would spin the story as a feud between him and Michael Eisner. "This should not become Harvey versus Disney," he said. "It's bigger than just me." But rumor had it that Harvey had dragged his feet in the beginning, thinking that Miramax was too big to be adversely affected by the ban, and only came around after his staff rebelled. Says Hope, who had produced two pictures released that fall that would be affected, Shari Springer Berman and Robert Pulcini's *American Splendor* and Alejandro González Iñárritu's *21 Grams*. "I found it weird that someone like Harvey would not take a [stand] when clearly it's an issue that the creative community is 100 percent behind. He's one of the biggest fighters and vociferous voices, but he hasn't stepped out on a limb. The way I read that is his business today is blockbusters like *Cold Mountain*, not specialized niche pictures. He could have rallied a lot of support. Truly, it's the passing of an era." Ray disagrees: "I think Harvey has done a really fine job."

Bernard thought the idea of Academy members pirating indie movies was ludicrous and suggested that they produce a cartoon picturing them with walkers and pirate hats, DVDs in hand, boarding a ship flying the skull and crossbones. Harvey said he knew the president of eBay and that if he asked him to stop selling films, he would. With Harvey on the sidelines, the group selected Ray as their spokesperson. But no sooner had they done so than the phone rang. Harvey picked it up. Looking at Ray and unable to pronounce the name of his boss, MGM Pictures CEO Alex Yemenidjian, Harvey stuttered, "It's Alex Yemen-yemen-yemenegian—" Yemenidjian was not easily ruffled. He had a reputation for rarely losing his cool, rarely breaking a sweat. He reminded Ray of his old boss, Sam Goldwyn. "You would actually have to murder Sam's wife in front of his eyes to get a reaction," he recalls. He got a reaction out of Yemenidjian, who was furious, and Chris McGurk, who was also on the line and who had taken heat from Yemenidjian on Ray's behalf. Ray explained to friends, including Bernard, that Valenti had apparently called Yemenidjian at six o'clock in the morning and said, "Hey, your man's on the front page of the trades, what the fuck is that?" Yemenidjian was embarrassed, as in, You can't control your own people. According to Bernard, Yemenidjian insisted it was a piracy issue. Ray said it wasn't. It got heated and ugly, and—still according to Bernard—Yemenidjian, without saying the words, gave Ray a choice between shutting up and getting out. There was a long pause. Yemenidjian asked, "Are you still there?" Ray replied, "I'm thinking." As he told Bernard later, "It's the Jack Benny line. 'Your money or your life?' Beat. 'I'm THINKING!' " Ray went home that night, and said to his wife, "So Nancy, how much money do we have in the bank?"

"Oh, no, more drama?"

"Yeah, there's always drama." He says now, "When Alex told me to back off, I backed off. I felt bad, like a total fucking sellout. But I got a kid to send to college."

Paramount's VP Rob Friedman reportedly called Paramount Classics's Vitale and Dinerstein while they were on the phone to the group at the Four Seasons and silenced them as well. The industry was looking for favors from Congress—better copyright protection, trade concessions, etc.—and no studio could afford to look "soft on piracy." Sony Chairman and CEO Howard Stringer reportedly never saw the logic of the screener ban and went along reluctantly, perhaps helped by a threat that he and his company would be targeted by an ad campaign saying he was pro-piracy. After all, Sony made the device used to copy tapes and DVDs.

The group selected James Schamus—probably the only one who'd graduated from college—to collect the suggestions and turn them into a 1,000-word "Dear Jack" letter they sent to Valenti. Then Schamus, Harvey, and Michael Barker got on the phone with Valenti. Schamus told him, "The consumer has a completely cynical attitude towards the companies that make the product, viewing them as gigantic greedy corporations who want to control everything. And stamp out anything of interest that's unique or individual. You just did that, for the movie business, man. Under the rubric of fighting piracy, in one week, you have created precisely the market conditions that have destroyed the record industry. "

Initially, Valenti's attitude had been, I'm retiring soon, I'll take the heat. Indeed, he had said repeatedly, "If there is a villain in the piece, it's me." But Schamus hammered home, "This is your legacy, Jack, this is what you're going to be remembered for, this is a defining moment, you shouldn't go out this way." Valenti is not a stupid man, and he was swayed by both arguments. A few days later, a provisional compromise was reached: tapes (not DVDs) would go out as usual to Academy members, but not to the guilds and journalists, as they had in the past, and the issue would be reexamined in the future.

The indie divisions let out a collective sigh of relief but, at the same time, were suspicious. In the absence of any systematic attempts to deal with the piracy issue, it struck many as a stopgap measure to shut them up so that, as Bernard puts it, "Jack can go off into the sunset in peace."

On October 31, Harvey weighed in with a robust denunciation of the new screener policy in a guest column in *Variety*. "This ban [is] a grave threat to the progress of bringing independent and foreign films to wide audiences," he wrote. "Losing potential awards recognition for these types of films directly threaten[s] their ability to reach the filmgoing public. We [can] not sit still and watch this happen."

The family feud left hard feelings. It suddenly became crystal clear that despite the incestuous mixing of vital bodily fluids that occurred during the 1990s reign of Miramax and Sundance, there was still a chasm between the studios and the indies divisions, not to mention the "real," unaffiliated indies. There was still an Us and a Them—which is probably a good thing. The indie divisions, albeit owned lock, stock, and barrel by the studios, were capable of delivering a reality check of their own. The people who run them are different in kind from the bean counters who guard the studio gates. After Ray's dustup with Yemenidjian, McGurk called him and said, "I gotta tell ya, Bingham, with you, it's never boring. It's exhausting. Ya know, you would be a problem and have a problem, no matter where you went, no matter who you were working for. Or with. It's just your nature."

"You just arrived at that, did you?" Continues Ray, "No matter where I go—the only thing consistent in this is me. I bring out the best and the worst in some of these people. This was all about money, and I still believe that there are decisions that you make that aren't motivated by financial gain. The independent world isn't like the Hollywood world. The motives are different, the goals are different, people aren't necessarily trying to get rich and powerful, they're trying to push art first while thinking everything else will take care of itself. That's the naive part of it, it doesn't happen that way. You can't even talk about that with a straight face or people will laugh you off the planet. But there's a big big part of me that really does believe that. And will always believe that."

Cast of Characters

Not everyone mentioned in this book is included. Only those people who appear repeatedly or in widely separated sections are listed, with partial credits, relevant to the period the book covers.

Ben Affleck: actor, *Good Will Hunting, Chasing Amy, Shakespeare in Love, Dogma;* co-writer, *Good Will Hunting.*
Allison Anders: filmmaker, *Gas Food Lodging, Mi Vida Loca, Four Rooms.*
Paul Thomas Anderson: filmmaker, *Boogie Nights, Magnolia.*
Wes Anderson: filmmaker, *Bottle Rocket, Rushmore.*
Gregg Araki: filmmaker, *The Living End, Totally Fucked Up, The Doom Generation.*
Darren Aronofsky: filmmaker, *Pi, Requiem for a Dream.*
Bille August: filmmaker, *Twist and Shout, Pelle the Conqueror.*
Roger Avary: co-story, *Pulp Fiction;* director/writer, *Killing Zoe.*
Michael Barker: co-president, Sony Classics; formerly of UA Classics and Orion Classics.
Gary Beer: at various times, president, Sundance Group; executive VP, Sundance Institute, etc.
Lawrence Bender: producer, *Reservoir Dogs, Pulp Fiction, Good Will Hunting.*
Albert Berger: producer, *King of the Hill, Election, Cold Mountain.*
Tom Bernard: co-president, Sony Classics; formerly of UA Classics and Orion Classics.
Bernardo Bertolucci: filmmaker, *Before the Revolution, The Conformist, 1900, Little Buddha.*
Frank Biondi: chairman and CEO, Universal Studios.
Jason Blum: senior VP of acquisitions and co-productions, Miramax.
Lizzie Borden: filmmaker, *Born in Flames, Working Girls, Love Crimes.*
Eamonn Bowles: senior VP, acquisitions and marketing, Miramax.
Danny Boyle: filmmaker, *Shallow Grave, Trainspotting.*
Alison Brantley: director of acquisitions, Miramax.
Betsy Brantley: actress, *Havana, Schizopolis.* Married to Steven Soderbergh.
Alan Brewer: childhood friend of Harvey Weinstein; musical director, *The Burning, Playing for Keeps.*
Edgar Bronfman, Jr.: CEO of Seagrams, Universal's parent.
Tina Brown: chairman and editor-in-chief, *Talk* magazine.
Stuart Burkin: post-production, Miramax Films.
Jane Campion: filmmaker, *Sweetie, The Piano, Portrait of a Lady.*
Vincent Canby: lead reviewer, the *New York Times.*
Simon Channing-Williams: producer of Mike Leigh's films.
Eve Chilton: married to Harvey Weinstein.

Larry Clark: director, *Kids.*

Joel and Ethan Coen: filmmakers, *Blood Simple, Raising Arizona, Miller's Crossing;* producers, *Bad Santa.*

Matthew Cohen: senior VP, marketing and creative advertising, Miramax.

Dick Cook: chairman, Walt Disney Studios.

Matt Damon: actor, *Good Will Hunting, Dogma, All the Pretty Horses;* co-writer, *Good Will Hunting.*

Daniel Day-Lewis: actor, *My Left Foot, Gangs of New York.*

Dalton Delan: VP of programming and creative director, Sundance Channel.

Guillermo del Toro: director, *Cronos, Mimic.*

Mike De Luca: president of production, New Line.

Ira Deutchman: founding partner and president of marketing and distribution, Cinecom; head of Fine Line Features.

Tom DiCillo: filmmaker, *Johnny Suede, Living in Oblivion.*

David Dinerstein: senior VP of marketing, Miramax.

Pat Dollard: agent; Steven Soderbergh, client.

William A. Donohue: director of the Catholic League for Religious and Civil Rights.

Jim Doyle: Buffalo friend of Harvey Weinstein, Miramax employee in the 1980s.

Denise Earle: filmmaker.

Steve Earnhart: post-production, Miramax; director, *Mule Skinner Blues.*

Cassian Elwes: agent, William Morris.

Larry Estes: senior VP of feature films acquisitions for Columbia/TriStar Home Video; financed *sex, lies, and videotape; Gas Food Lodging; One False Move.*

Nikki Finke: film journalist.

Jack Foley: president of distribution, USA Films; formerly, senior VP of theatrical distribution, October Films; president of distribution, Miramax.

Jean-Francois Fonlupt: chairman, CiBy 2000.

Alberto Garcia: competition director, Sundance Film Festival.

Donna Gigliotti: president of production, USA Films; formerly, executive VP, Miramax Films.

Mark Gill: variously senior VP of marketing and president of the L.A. office, Miramax Films.

Geoff Gilmore: director, Sundance Film Festival.

Eric Gitter: producer, O.

Richard Gladstein: senior VP of production, Miramax Films; formerly, VP of production and acquisitions, Live Entertainment.

Ed Glass: partner, Glass/Schoor Films.

Susan Glatzer: VP, October Films.

Ernst Goldschmidt: chairman, Pandora Films.

Sam Goldwyn: chairman, the Samuel Goldwyn Company.

Carlos Goodman: entertainment attorney.

Cary Granat: president, Dimension Films.

Marcy Granata: president, publicity and corporate relations, Miramax Films.

James Gray: filmmaker, *Little Odessa, The Yards.*

Scott Greenstein: chairman, USA Films; formerly, co-president, October Films; senior VP, Miramax.

Janet Grillo: senior VP, New Line, married to David O. Russell.

Ulu Grosbard: director, *Straight Time, True Confessions.*

Nicole Guillemet: VP and general manager, Sundance Institute.

Dolly Hall: producer, *54, High Art.*

Lasse Hallström: director, *Chocolat, The Cider House Rules, The Shipping News.*
Todd Harris: agent, William Morris, for Robert Duvall.
Amy Hart: marketing coordinator, Miramax.
Hal Hartley: filmmaker, *The Unbelievable Truth, Trust.*
Michael Hausman: producer, *Alambrista!, Heartland, Desert Bloom.*
Todd Haynes: filmmaker, *Poison, Safe, Velvet Goldmine, Far from Heaven.*
Rick Hess: agent, William Morris.
Dennis Higgins: senior VP of publicity, Miramax.
J. Hoberman: lead film reviewer, *Village Voice.*
Peter Hoffman: consultant to Miramax; formerly CEO, Carolco Pictures.
Nicole Holofcener: filmmaker, *Walking and Talking, Lovely & Amazing.*
Ted Hope: partner, Good Machine; executive producer, *Trust, Safe, Walking and Talking, The Brothers McMullen;* producer, *Happiness, In the Bedroom.*
Trea Hoving: executive VP of acquisitions, Miramax Films.
Amy Israel: senior VP of acquisitions, Miramax Films.
James Ivory: director, *A Room with a View, Howards End, Mr. & Mrs. Bridge, The Golden Bowl.*
Peter Jackson: filmmaker, *Heavenly Creatures, The Frighteners, The Lord of the Rings.*
Gilles Jacob: director, Cannes Film Festival.
Jim Jarmusch: filmmaker, *Stranger Than Paradise, Dead Man.*
Neil Jordan: filmmaker, *The Miracle, The Crying Game, Interview with the Vampire.*
Jeffrey Katzenberg: founding partner, DreamWorks, former chairman, Walt Disney Studios.
Dave Kehr: film reviewer.
Sarah Kernochan: filmmaker, *Marjoe, The Hairy Bird/Strike/All I Wanna Do, Thoth.*
Peter Kindlon: assistant, Miramax.
Jeff Kleeman: head, Sundance Productions; formerly, executive VP of production, MGM.
Howard Klein: board member, Sundance Institute, director for the arts, Rockefeller Foundation.
Cathy Konrad: producer, *Citizen Ruth, Scream* (1, 2, and 3); *Cop Land, Kate & Leopold;* co-producer, *Kids;* formerly of Woods Entertainment; married to James Mangold.
Harmony Korine: writer, *Kids, Gummo, Julien Donkey-Boy;* director, *Gummo, Julien Donkey-Boy* (uncredited).
Christina Kounelias: publicity, Miramax Films.
Jack Lechner: executive VP of production and development, Miramax Films.
Spike Lee: filmmaker, *She's Gotta Have It, Do the Right Thing.*
Mike Leigh: filmmaker, *High Hopes, Secrets & Lies.*
Martin N. Lewis: producer, *The Secret Policeman's Other Ball.*
Linda Lichter: entertainment attorney.
David Linde: co-president Focus Features; formerly, partner, Good Machine; executive VP, Miramax International.
Richard Linklater: filmmaker, *Slacker, Dazed and Confused, Waking Life.*
Jeff Lipsky: founding partner, October Films; formerly, Skouras Pictures, the Samuel Goldwyn Company, New Yorker Films.
Mark Lipsky: head of distribution, Miramax Films. Brother of Jeff.
John Madden: director, *Mrs. Brown, Shakespeare in Love, Captain Corelli's Mandolin.*
Amir Malin: partner, October Films; formerly, founding partner, Cinecom.
Barbara Maltby: producer, *King of the Hill.*

James Mangold: filmmaker, *Cop Land, Kate & Leopold.* Married to Cathy Konrad.

Liz Manne: executive VP, programming and marketing, Sundance Channel.

Todd McCarthy: lead reviewer, *Variety.*

Chris McGurk: vice chairman and COO, MGM; formerly, president and COO, Universal Pictures; president, Motion Picture Group, the Walt Disney Company.

Bill Mechanic: chairman and CEO, Twentieth Century Fox; formerly, president, International Distribution and Worldwide Video, the Walt Disney Company.

Larry Meistrich: founding partner, the Shooting Gallery; executive producer, *Sling Blade.*

Ismail Merchant: producer, *A Room with a View, Mr. and Mrs. Bridge, The Golden Bowl.* Partner, James Ivory.

Jason Mewes: actor, *Clerks, Chasing Amy, Jay and Silent Bob Strike Back.*

Anthony Minghella: director, *The English Patient, The Talented Mr. Ripley, Cold Mountain.*

Elvis Mitchell: film reviewer, the *New York Times.*

Rob Moore: senior VP and CFO, the Walt Disney Company.

Errol Morris: filmmaker, *The Thin Blue Line.*

Scott Mosier: producer, *Clerks, Chasing Amy, Dogma.*

Tim Blake Nelson: actor, filmmaker, *O.*

Peter Newman: producer, *Smoke, Blue in the Face, The Hairy Bird/Strike/All I Wanna Do.* Partner, Ira Deutchman.

Robert Newman: agent, ICM; former executive VP, Miramax.

Bobby Newmyer: producer, *sex, lies, and videotape, The Opposite Sex;* married to Debbie Newmyer.

Debbie Newmyer: executive producer, *The Little Rascals, How to Make an American Quilt;* married to Bobby Newmyer.

Marc Norman: screenwriter, *Shakespeare in Love.*

Edward Norton: actor, *Primal Fear, Rounders, Frida.*

David Parfitt: producer, *The Madness of King George, Wings of the Dove, Shakespeare in Love;* consultant, *Gangs of New York.*

Alexander Payne: filmmaker, *Citizen Ruth, Election, About Schmidt.*

John Penotti: founding partner, GreeneStreet; executive producer, *In the Bedroom.*

John Pierson: producer's rep, *She's Gotta Have It, Working Girls, Clerks.* Author of *Spike, Mike, Slackers & Dykes.*

Sydney Pollack: director, *The Way We Were, Tootsie;* board member, Sundance Institute.

Tom Pollock: executive VP, MCA; chairman, Universal Pictures.

Nik Powell: partner, Palace Pictures; co-producer, *Mona Lisa,* executive producer, *Scandal, The Crying Game, Little Voice.*

Terry Press: head of marketing, DreamWorks; formerly, senior VP of marketing, the Walt Disney Company.

John Ptak: agent, CAA.

B. J. Rack: producer, *Terminator 2, Mimic.*

Bingham Ray: president, UA; founding partner, October Films; formerly, Cinecom, Goldwyn, Island, Alive.

Robert Redford: Sundance Institute founder; actor, *Butch Cassidy and the Sundance Kid;* director, *Ordinary People, Quiz Show.*

Dennis Rice: president, marketing, Miramax; formerly, president, worldwide marketing, October Films; head of marketing, home video, Walt Disney Company.

Alexandre Rockwell: filmmaker, *In the Soup, Four Rooms.*

Robert Rodriguez: filmmaker, *El Mariachi, Four Rooms, From Dusk Till Dawn*.

Joe Roth: chairman, Walt Disney Studios.

Scott Rudin: producer, *Marvin's Room, The Royal Tenenbaums, The Hours*.

David O. Russell: filmmaker, *Spanking the Monkey, Flirting with Disaster, Three Kings*. Husband of Janet Grillo.

Nora Ryan: president, Sundance Channel.

Tony Safford: VP, acquisitions, Miramax; VP, acquisitions, Fine Line; program director, Sundance Film Festival.

Michelle Satter: director of feature film program, Sundance Institute.

John Sayles: filmmaker, *The Return of the Secaucus 7, Brother from Another Planet*.

Maria Schaeffer: executive director, Sundance Institute.

James Schamus: co-president, Focus Features; formerly, founding partner, Good Machine; executive producer, *Poison; Safe; Happiness; Crouching Tiger, Hidden Dragon*.

John Schmidt: founding partner, Content Films; formerly, partner, October Films; COO, Miramax.

Cathy Schulman: president, Artists Production Group; programmer, Sundance Film Festival.

Russell Schwartz: president, USA Films; formerly, president, Gramercy Pictures; executive VP, marketing, Miramax Films.

Bob Shaye: chairman and CEO, New Line Cinema.

Gary Siegler: president, Siegler, Collery & Co.; investor and board member, October Films.

Casey Silver: chairman and CEO, Universal Pictures.

Marjorie Skouras: acquisitions executive, Skouras Pictures.

Tom Skouras: president, Skouras Pictures.

Annick Smith: producer, *Heartland*; executive producer, *A River Runs Through It*.

Kevin Smith: filmmaker, *Clerks, Chasing Amy, Dogma, Jay and Silent Bob Strike Back*.

Stacey Snider: chairman, Universal Pictures.

Steven Soderbergh: filmmaker, *sex, lies, and videotape, King of the Hill, Schizopolis, Traffic*. Married to Betsy Brantley.

Todd Solondz: actor; filmmaker, *Welcome to the Dollhouse, Happiness, Storytelling*.

Stacy Spikes: VP, marketing, October Films; VP, marketing, Miramax.

David Steinberg: attorney, Miramax.

Fisher Stevens: founding partner, GreeneStreet Productions.

Quentin Tarantino: filmmaker, *Reservoir Dogs, Pulp Fiction, Four Rooms, Jackie Brown*.

Nancy Tenenbaum: executive producer, *sex, lies, and videotape*; producer, *The Daytrippers*.

Billy Bob Thornton: actor; filmmaker, *Sling Blade*; director, *All the Pretty Horses*.

Mark Tusk: VP of acquisitions, Miramax Films.

Mark Urman: executive, Lions Gate; publicist, Dennis Davidson Associates.

Christine Vachon: founding partner, Killer Films; producer, *Poison, Safe, Kids, Velvet Goldmine, Happiness, Boys Don't Cry, Far from Heaven*.

Gus Van Sant: filmmaker, *Drugstore Cowboy, My Own Private Idaho, To Die For, Good Will Hunting*.

Sterling Van Wagenen: executive director, Sundance Institute. Cousin of Redford's wife, Lola.

Lars von Trier: filmmaker, *The Kingdom, Breaking the Waves*.

Paul Webster: producer, *Little Odessa, The Yards*; head of production, Miramax.

Suzanne Weil: executive director, Sundance Institute.

Bob Weinstein: co-chairman, Miramax Films.

Harvey Weinstein: co-chairman, Miramax Films.

Tom Wilhite: executive director, Sundance Institute.

Cary Woods: founder, Woods Entertainment; producer, *Kids, Citizen Ruth, Cop Land, Scream.*

Steve Woolley: founding partner, Palace Pictures; producer, *Mona Lisa, Scandal, The Crying Game.*

Ron Yerxa: producer, *King of the Hill, Election, Cold Mountain.*

Saul Zaentz: producer, *One Flew Over the Cuckoo's Nest, Amadeus, The Unbearable Lightness of Being, The English Patient.*

Marty Zeidman: senior VP, distribution, Miramax Films.

Ed Zwick: producer/director, *Legends of the Fall;* producer, *Shakespeare in Love;* director, *Glory;* executive producer, *thirtysomething.*

Notes

A NOTE ON THE RESEARCH
This book is based on hundreds of interviews. Conversations are based on interviews with at least one of the participants. When thoughts are attributed to a principal, they are also derived from interviews.

AI = author interview.

PREFACE

PAGE
1 "Independent filmmakers don't" and following: Quentin Tarantino, AI, 4/30/03.
3 "A lot of people are afraid": James Ivory, AI, 7/9/01.
3 "No comment" and following: Ethan Coen, AI, 10/15/03.
4 "I'll speak my mind.": Spike Lee, AI, 11/8/02.
4 "return to [his] roots": Rick Lyman, "After *Talk*, Miramax to Refocus on Movies," *New York Times*, 1/21/02.
5 "Matthew, get in here!": From author's notes.
6 "What do you really want to write?" and following: From author's notes.

INTRODUCTION: THE STORY TILL NOW

PAGE
8 Epigraph: Edward Norton, AI, 8/8/02.
10 "He's not a": Confidential source.
11 "I knew what": Robert Redford, AI, 11/13/90.
12 "I'm here to listen and learn": Confidential source, nd.
12 "It was a combination": Liz Manne, AI, 10/5/01.
13 When the photo op: After Lory Smith, *Party in a Box: The Story of the Sundance Film Festival* (Salt Lake City: Gibbs-Smith, 1999), 38.
13 "You might not think" and following: Alan Brewer, AI, 4/2/00.
14 "So Harvey, what": Bingham Ray, AI, 5/19/99.
14 "It's the old tale": Matt Damon, AI, 9/26/01.
15 "He's the kinda": Jack Lechner, AI, 5/31/01.
15 "I've heard that story": Mark Lipsky, AI, 11/15/99.
15 "We're artists": Lynn Hirschberg, "The Mad Passion of Harvey and Bob," *New York*, 10/10/94.
15 "This business is": Peter Schweitzer and Rochelle Schweitzer, *Disney: The Mouse Betrayed* (Washington, DC: Regnery, 1998), 192.
15 "Are we gonna": Confidential source.
15 "You can't really": Mark Tusk, AI, 2/3/00.

16 "Financing really didn't exist": John Sayles, AI, 7/9/97.

17 "The studios were bidding": Ira Deutchman, AI, nd.

17 "Specialized film": Eamonn Bowles, AI, 6/7/00.

18 "Many of these startup": Deutchman, AI, nd.

18 "We followed the same theory": Tom Bernard, reduced from Eugene Hernandez, "Decade: Michael Barker and Tom Bernard—Another Ten Years in the Classics World," Part 1 of interview, 12/20/99, indieWIRE.com.

19 "Independent usually meant": Sydney Pollack, AI, 6/10/02.

19 "a clothesline": *My First Movie*, edited by Stephen Lowenstein (New York: Pantheon, 2000), 61.

21 "The original sin": James Schamus, AI, 7/2/02.

21 "It's like looking": Sayles, AI, 7/9/97.

22 "I remember the": Tod Lippy, ed., *Projections 11: New York Film-Makers on Film-Making* (London-New York: Faber and Faber, 2001), 9.

22 "I was just getting": Norton, AI, 8/8/02.

23 "It's so exciting": Allison Anders, AI, nd.

23 "I've been pretending": Bill Desowitz, "Puzzling Filmgoers, with Serious Intent: The Coolly Received Drama 'Solaris' Aims to Challenge Audiences with Tough Questions, Say Its Star and Director," *Los Angeles Times*, 12/3/02.

23 "I remember seeing": Richard Linklater, AI, 3/12/01.

23 "I certainly didn't feel": Steven Soderbergh, AI, 4/22/99.

23 "Most of the filmmakers": Schamus, AI, 3/4/99.

24 "A good deal is smarter": Ray Price, AI, 12/9/00.

24 "To make a film": Colin MacCabe, *Godard: A Portrait of the Artist at Seventy* (London; Bloomsbury, 2003), 97.

24 "Independent films punched": Kevin Smith, AI, 12/18/01.

25 "If I didn't exist": Elaine Dutka and John Clark, "Miramax Finds Success Breeds Admiration, Envy," *Los Angeles Times*, 1/30/97.

CHAPTER 1: MADE IN USA
PAGE

27 Epigraph: Peter McAlevey, "All's Well That Ends Gruesomely," *New York Times*, 12/6/92.

28 "Look at Jimmy": Terri Minsky, "Hot Phenomenon," *Rolling Stone*, 5/18/89.

29 "the skiing and the parties" and following: Smith, *Party in a Box*, 123.

29 "feel-good, socially responsible": Smith, *Party in a Box*, 89.

30 "People were passionate" and following: Marjorie Skouras, AI, 5/2/00.

30 "It read like" and following: Nancy Tenenbaum, AI, 10/2/99.

31 "I think you've made": Katherine Dieckmann, "Liar, Liar, Pants on Fire," *Village Voice*, 8/8/89.

31 "Is she going to have a problem" and following: Steven Soderbergh, *sex, lies, and videotape* (New York: Harper & Row, 1990), 206, 207.

31 "That's how confident" and following: Jeff Lipsky, AI, 10/4/99.

32 "You should really see it" and following: Marjorie Skouras, AI, 5/2/00.

32 "It got to the point": Minsky, "Hot Phenomenon."

33 "Bob's very paranoid": Maria Schaeffer, AI, 10/3/90.

33 "Sterling was a": Confidential source.

34 "Sundance started out": Annick Smith, AI, nd.

34 "He wants to": Confidential source.

34 "We'd convert the": Robert Redford, AI, 11/13/90.

35 "The script is worthless": Denise Earle, AI, nd.
35 "Redford was not there": Tony Safford, AI, nd.
35 "This project was like": Redford, AI, 11/13/90.
35 "It was a perfect": Sterling Van Wagenen, AI, nd.
35 "Redford said to": Michael Hausman, AI, nd.
35 "Redford never wanted": Earle, AI, nd.
36 "Maybe because so": Van Wagenen, AI, 10/22/03.
36 "In 1984, '85, and '86": Howard Klein, AI, nd.
36 "He was funnier": Suzanne Weil, AI, 10/10/90.
36 "The reason Gevy Beer and following: Schaeffer, AI, 10/2/90.
36 "Bob had blinders": Confidential source.
36 "is not like one": Gary Beer, AI, 11/15/90.
37 "it was never clear": Johann Jacobs, AI, nd.
37 "I worked there": Schaeffer, AI, 10/2/90.
37 "There was a lot": Cathy Schulman, AI, 4/25/02.
37 "We could have gotten": Schaeffer, AI, 10/22/90.
37 "It drove me crazy": Redford, AI, 11/13/90.
37 "To make Gary": Confidential source.
38 "Redford thought": Confidential source.
38 "I said, 'Don't" and following: Redford, AI, 11/13/90.
38 "Bob does have a": Van Wagenen, AI, 10/22/03.
38 "He said, 'Hey, look' ": Redford, AI, 11/13/90.
38 "slap in the face": Gary Burr, AI, 11/15/90.
38 "It was like Bob": Mary Cranney, AI, nd.
38 "Redford doesn't fire": Safford, AI, 12/6/90.
39 "Sundance": *Sundancer*, Christmas 1988.
39 "So what have you heard" and following: Deutchman, AI, 9/17/99.
40 "Can my girlfriend": Minsky, "Hot Phenomenon."
40 "flypapered" and following: Soderbergh, AI, 4/22/99.
40 "I was involved": Minsky, "Hot Phenomenon"; James Greenberg, "sex, lies, and Kafka," *Connoisseur*, 10/91.
41 "There's a zeitgeist": Norton, AI, 8/8/02.
41 "When I look at it now": Greenberg, "sex, lies, and Kafka"; Steven Soderbergh, *Getting Away with It* (London: Faber & Faber, 1999), 185.
41 "It was different then": Soderbergh, AI, 4/22/99.
41 "I've seen it and I loved it": Soderbergh, *sex, lies, and videotape*, 225.
41 "I got a toothache": Soderbergh, AI, 5/2/02.
42 "They're slime" and following: Minsky, "Hot Phenomenon."
43 "We're not as well-heeled": Bingham Ray, AI, 2/15/01.
43 "a packed audience": Bob Weinstein, "All thanks to Max," *Vanity Fair*, 4/03, 440.
44 "This is fantastic" and following: Martin N. Lewis, AI, 4/6/00.
47 "While they were still trying" and following: Robert Newman, AI, 6/13/00.
47 "retouched Ohana's chest": Reid Rosefelt, AI, 10/18/00.
48 "People said that they were crazy": Alan Brewer, AI, 4/2/00.
49 "I've always called" and following: Jeff Silver, AI, 6/14/00.
49 "It was, Okay": Confidential source.
50 "It wasn't limited": Silver, AI, 6/14/00.
50 "It was hard for them": Brewer, AI, 4/2/00.
50 "No one knew what" and following: Silver, AI, 6/14/00.
50 "It was amateur night" and following: Chris Mankiewicz, AI, 4/12/00.

51 "They were trying": Lewis, AI, 4/6/00.

52 *Playing for Keeps* definitely weakened": Brewer, 4/2/00.

52 "Their passion to make": Lewis, AI, 4/6/00.

52 "What was done": Tom Pollock, AI, 3/11/03.

52 "Really dumb people": Lewis, AI, 4/6/00.

52 "That movie was like": Ed Glass, AI, 10/23/00.

52 "Within days or weeks" and following: James Doyle, AI, 3/19/00.

53 "I called everybody I knew" and following: Mark Lipsky, AI, 11/15/99.

53 "If you said you worked": Stuart Burkin, AI, 4/29/02.

53 "Getting the phone answered": Mark Lipsky, AI, 11/15/99.

53 "They sat there for months.": Marty Zeidman, AI, 4/28/00.

53 "It seemed like not even a day": Mark Lipsky, AI, 11/15/99.

54 "I thought they genuinely" and following: Brantley, AI, 10/18/99.

55 "Harvey got the idea for Miramax": Paul Webster, AI, 10/20/01.

55 "I came out of the punk scene": Steve Woolley, AI, 2/26/02.

55 "Look, I want" and following: Harvey Weinstein, AI, 6/28/02.

56 "I would get": Lizzie Borden, AI, 10/25/00.

56 "He was squeamish": Mark Lipsky, AI, 11/15/99.

56 "No, Bob" and following: Confidential source.

57 "Distribution costs on": John Pierson, *Spike, Mike, Slackers & Dykes* (New York: Miramax Books, 1995), 97.

57 "They were trying": Christina Kounelias, AI, 4/5/00.

57 "Harvey was ranting": Zeidman, AI, 4/28/00.

57 "Their father was": Glass, AI, 10/23/00.

58 "This was a very small": Zeidman, AI, 4/28/00.

58 "We sold it as": David Dinerstein, AI, 10/22/99.

58 "It was one of": Zeidman, AI, 4/28/00.

CHAPTER 2: THE ANGER ARTISTS

PAGE

59 Epigraph: John Colapinto, "The big bad wolves of Miramax," *Rolling Stone,* 4/3/97.

60 "The sell was": Kounelias, AI, 4/5/00.

60 "Harvey was an outsider": Donna Gigliotti, AI, 2/14/01.

60 "Michael, you gotta": Angus Finney, *The Egos Have Landed* (London: Arrow, 1998).

61 "Steve, you're making" and following: Harvey Weinstein, AI, 6/28/02.

61 "I'm a kid": Harvey Weinstein, AI, 6/28/02.

61 "We re-edited *Scandal*": Glass, AI, 10/23/00.

61 "A lot of the movies" and following: Alison Brantley, AI, 10/18/99.

62 "Are you crazy?" and following: Brantley, AI, 10/18/99.

62 "When you're talking": Jack Foley, AI, 6/21/01.

62 "It pissed me off": Harvey Weinstein, AI, 10/3/02.

63 "Christine gazing": Finney, *The Egos Have Landed.*

63 "Thaat's a stupid answer.": Confidential source.

63 "It was easier to say": Tusk, AI, 1/31/00.

63 "Whaddya think?" and following: Tusk, AI, 2/3/00; 8/16/00.

64 "At that point it was": Tusk, AI, 1/31/00.

64 "People will say": David Linde, AI, 11/16/99.

64 "Everybody who called us" and following: Larry Estes, AI, 10/29/99.

64 "I'm not going back": Michael Fleming, "Miramax, Riding 'Sex' Wave, Storms on into the '90s," *Variety*, 1/31/90.

64 "At that time": Bobby Newmyer, AI, 4/20/99.

65 "seemed a little nervous": Tenenbaum, AI, 10/2/99.

65 "There was paranoia": Deutchman, AI, 9/17/99.

65 "It was one": Estes, AI, 10/29/99.

65 "Estes insisted that Miramax": Tenenbaum, AI, 10/2/99.

65 "At the time $1 million": Estes, AI, 10/29/99.

65 "The whole thing": Soderbergh, AI, 4/22/99.

65 "They probably did overpay": Mark Lipsky, AI, 11/15/99.

66 "Hearing that Harvey" and following: Janet Grillo, AI, 4/10/01.

66 "Up until then, companies": Safford, AI, 9/29/98.

66 "I looked around": Marjorie Skouras, AI, 5/2/00.

66 "With *Scandal* I realized": Zeidman, AI, 4/28/00.

67 "Nobody wanted to be": Mark Lipsky, AI, 11/15/99.

67 "I'd go in there": Glass, AI, 10/23/00.

67 "He was huffing and puffing": Confidential source.

67 "Bob sniped at her.": Mark Lipsky, AI, 11/15/99.

67 "you couldn't imagine": Confidential source.

67 "demanding, aggressive" and following: Brewer, AI, 4/2/00.

68 "Ach, your mother" and following: Brewer, AI, 4/2/00.

68 "Instead of growing up" and following: Rick Lyman, "Watching Movies with Harvey Weinstein," *New York Times*, 4/27/01.

69 "Miramax ran on fear.": Burkin, AI, 4/29/02.

69 "Anything anybody ever says" and following: Amy Hart, AI, nd.

69 "How can you treat": Confidential source.

70 "I was having a nervous breakdown": Myrna Chagnard, AI, 3/14/02.

70 "Working there was like": Eleanor Reznikoff, AI, 3/13/02.

70 "In the end" and following: Jeff Rose, AI, 4/28/02.

70 "There was very scary yelling": Mark Lipsky, AI, 11/15/99.

71 "Bob is the scary one": Webster, AI, 10/20/01.

71 "Bob scared me much more": Brantley, AI, 10/18/99.

71 "If you could consider Harvey": Confidential source.

71 "Bob's the one": Confidential source.

71 "You don't want to get": Bowles, AI, 3/24/00.

71 "When it churned up": Dennis Rice, AI, 8/27/03.

71 "He would kind of puff up": Brantley, AI, 10/18/99.

71 "I'm really susceptible" and following: Bowles, AI, 3/24/00.

71 "When Harvey": Mark Lipsky, AI, 11/15/99.

71 "He's obviously got": Bowles, AI, 3/24/00.

72 "His emotions are completely" and following: Safford, AI, 9/29/98.

72 "They drove everybody crazy": Mark Lipsky, AI, 11/15/99.

72 "Some days Harvey would": Rice, AI, 7/24/01.

72 "I had promised" and following: Mark Lipsky, AI, 11/15/99.

72 "There's a hesitancy": Safford, AI, 9/29/98.

73 "If you got on an emotional": Bowles, AI, 3/24/00.

73 "They were equal opportunity abusers.": John Schmidt, AI, 6/9/00.

73 "I always felt sorrier": Brantley, AI, 10/18/99.

73 "I'm gonna fuckin' throw": Confidential source.

73 "People hate working there": Rice, AI, 7/23/01.

73 "They were nuclear": Foley, AI, 6/21/01.

73 "Bob was constantly critical" and following: Van Wagenen, AI, nd.

74 "I'd heard filmmakers say": Redford, AI, 11/13/90.

74 "In the beginning": Linda Remy, AI, 12/20/89.

74 "Redford's name attached": Tony Safford, AI, nd.

74 "We could interview everyone": Remy, AI, 12/20/89.

74 "Redford took over the film": Remy, AI, 12/15/89.

74 "It might have worked": Richard Fischoff, AI, nd.

75 "Our investors were putting up": Kjehl Rasmussen, AI, 3/31/01.

75 "The problem was": Van Wagenen, AI, nd.

75 "The institute has really missed": Safford, AI, nd.

76 "It was helpful": Tom DiCillo, AI, 1/4/01.

77 "There was a mandate": Michelle Satter, AI, 11/13/90.

77 "They literally brought their own" and following: Urman, AI, 10/31/01.

77 "My impression of him": Alison Brantley, AI, 10/18/99.

77 "Paramount wanted me to change" and following: Lee, AI, 11/8/02.

77 "white-plight" and following: Soderbergh, *sex, lies, and videotape*, 239, 241.

78 "us confidence in the future of cinema": Scott Collins, "The Funk of Steven Soder-
    bergh: His First Film, 'Sex, Lies, and Videotape,' Put Him on Top of Hollywood's
    Hill. He Predicted Then That It Was All Downhill from There. Why Was He
    Right?" *Los Angeles Times Magazine*, 2/16/97.

78 "It's like a door opened": Soderbergh, *sex, lies, and videotape*, 241.

78 "You're John Lennon": Alex Simon, "Steven Soderbergh: Hiding in Plain Sight,"
    V*enice*, 7/98, 37.

78 "What's so heroic" and following: Soderbergh, *sex, lies, and videotape*, 247.

79 "He's extremely smart": Soderbergh, *sex, lies, and videotape*, 244.

79 "Both Redford and Pollack": Bobby Newmyer, AI, 4/20/99.

79 "What the hell's going on here?": Confidential source.

79 "I was going to get my head": Collins, "The Funk of Steven Soderbergh."

79 "Don't you trust me?": Confidential source.

79 "mature": Dieckmann, "Liar, Liar, Pants on Fire."

80 "He liked to bowl.": Greenberg, "sex, lies, and Kafka."

80 "Their marketing instincts": Deutchman, AI, 9/17/99.

80 "It was an exploitative": Manne, AI, 9/28/01.

80 "How are we supposed to sell": Deutchman, AI, 9/17/99.

80 "art house death": Soderbergh, *sex, lies, and videotape*, 244.

80 "I helped keep": Deutchman, AI, 9/17/99.

80 "Everybody wants to know me": Dieckmann, "Liar, Liar, Pants on Fire."

80 "Steven's one of those people" and following: Brantley, AI, 10/18/99.

80 "There's a difference between": Soderbergh, AI, 8/31/01.

80 "When *sex, lies* happened": Dennis Lim, "Having Your Way with Hollywood," *Vil-
    lage Voice*, 1/3–9/01.

81 "think the reason": Soderbergh, *sex, lies, and videotape*, 249.

81 "Up to that point": Foley, AI, 6/21/01.

81 "It was like pouring water" and following: Zeidman, AI, 4/28/00.

81 "you'd take a four inch ad": Ray, AI, 3/8/01.

81 "To earn $25 million": Estes, AI, 10/29/99.

82 "I'm stunned with how deeply": Fleming, "Miramax, Riding 'Sex' Wave, Storms on
    into the '90s."

82 "There was a sense": Geoff Gilmore, AI, 3/9/01.

82 "Maybe it's time": Redford, AI, 11/13/90.
83 "There aren't that many" and following: Frank Daniel, AI, nd.
83 "the very thing": Ulu Grosbard, AI, nd.
83 "I wasn't all that impressed": Gilmore, AI, 3/9/01.
84 "I just couldn't have it": Redford, AI, 11/13/90.
84 "I had a chance": Weil, AI, 10/10/90.
84 "It wasn't passive aggressive": Pollack, AI, 6/10/02.
84 "No matter how hard": Redford, AI, 11/13/90.
84 "I would wish": Garcia, AI, 10/20/90.
84 "A lot of people": Redford, AI, 11/13/90.
85 "Bob would have liked": Van Wagenen, AI, nd.
85 "I understood that" and following: Soderbergh, AI, 4/22/99.
86 "Harvey used to say": Burkin, AI, 4/29/02.
86 "We never tested": Harvey Weinstein, AI, 7/18/02.
86 "Miramax did market-research": Diana Tauder, AI, 6/9/01.
87 "We never put it like this" and following: Burkin, AI, 4/29/02.
87 "I just felt like it was taking": Tauder, AI, 6/9/01.
87 "I love Ruth": Harvey Weinstein, AI, 7/18/02.
87 "This is so wonderful" and following: Ivory, AI, 7/9/01.
88 "They thought it": Merchant, AI, 7/9/01.
88 "It got a bad": Harvey Weinstein, AI, 7/18/02.
88 "We have to make changes" and following: Merchant, AI, 7/9/01.
88 "This film's intended": Ivory, AI, 7/9/01.
88 "God, that's pretentious": Harvey Weinstein, AI, 7/18/02.
88 "Harvey went mad": Betsy Sharkey, "The Brothers Miramax: Harvey and Bob," *New York Times*, "Arts and Leisure," 7/24/94.
88 "I'm taking film away" and following: Merchant, AI, 7/9/01.
89 "withheld the last payment": Ivory, AI, 7/9/01.
89 "He got pretty nasty": Howard Feinstein, AI, 10/10/03.
89 "No one should be surprised": Woolley, AI, 2/26/02.
89 "Are we gonna" and following: Burkin, AI, 4/29/02.

CHAPTER 3: RISKY BUSINESS

PAGE
91 Epigraph: Bernard, AI, 11/15/99.
92 "We have to keep up" and following: Jeff Lipsky, AI, 10/4/99.
92 "We were tired": Ray, AI, 2/15/01.
92 "I would come in": Ray, AI, 12/16/98.
92 "Why ties?": Ray, AI, 3/8/01.
93 "If you locked Bingham up": Pierson, *Spike, Mike, Slackers & Dykes*, 90.
93 "I always wanted us": Ray, AI, 3/8/01.
94 "Jeff is an extraordinary" and following: Ray, AI, 2/15/01.
95 "We were not going to make": Jeff Lipsky, AI, 10/4/99.
95 "I was never an entrepreneur": Jeff Lipsky, AI, 10/4/99.
96 "Amir was the first guy": Michael Barker, AI, 11/15/99.
96 "I always considered Amir": Bart Walker, AI, 12/7/00.
96 "Basically, everybody who comes in contact": John Shestack, AI, 12/11/00.
96 "the money that we": Ivory, AI, 7/9/01.
96 "When we called Cinecom's accountant": Ismail Merchant, AI, 7/9/01.
97 "I could kill you": Ivory, AI, 7/9/01.

97 "It's the filmmakers' money": Merchant, AI, 7/9/01.

97 "We stopped making films": Ivory, AI, 7/9/01.

97 "I don't remember": Amir Malin, AI, 10/22/03.

97 "I would never": Walker, AI, 10/22/03.

97 "All those years": Richard Abramowitz, AI, 2/14/01.

98 "I think what you guys" and following: Ray, AI, 2/15/01.

98 "Let's fly to New York": Jeff Lipsky, AI, 10/4/99.

98 "The tapes are what did it" and following: Harvey Weinstein, AI, 7/18/02.

99 "You create evening social activity" and following: Urman, AI, 10/31/01.

100 "I'd love to work": Confidential source.

100 "I'm surrounded by people": Hirschberg, "The Mad Passion of Harvey and Bob."

100 "Alie, I just can't" and following: Brantley, AI, 10/18/99.

101 "It was an experiment.": Tusk, AI, 2/3/00.

102 "The Italian films in particular": Bernardo Bertolucci, AI, 5/26/03.

102 "He owes us at least": Kees Kasander, e-mail, 6/6/03.

102 "modest success": Harvey Weinstein, AI, 11/11/03.

103 "I look like a fuckin' ": Earnhart, AI, 5/21/02.

103 "Eve will smell this": Confidential source.

103 "You better be here" and following: Confidential source.

103 "We went out to one": Harvey Weinstein, AI, 7/18/02.

103 "Miramax was maybe" and following: Schmidt, AI, 5/25/01.

105 "New Line was cleaning up": Schmidt, AI, 5/25/01.

105 "People take for granted": Norton, AI, 8/8/02.

105 "It was initially almost impossible": Pollack, AI, 6/10/02.

105 "the place where films": Estes, AI, 10/29/99.

106 "contains humiliation, abuse": John Lyttle, Independent, 3/1/91.

106 "AIDS was a life and death" and following: Todd Haynes, AI, 3/23/02.

106 "The regional filmmaker": Gilmore, AI, 3/9/01.

107 "I didn't grow up" and following: Christine Vachon, AI, 10/20/00.

107 "They were so sanctimonious" and following: Vachon, AI, 10/20/00.

108 "That movie was an epiphany": Vachon, AI, 10/16/00.

108 "We watched that movie": Haynes, AI, 3/23/02.

108 "Todd was this" and following: Vachon, AI, 10/16/00.

109 "That's when Ang" and following: Hope, AI, 10/15/03.

109 "Christine and I would go": Haynes, AI, 3/23/02.

109 "With great reviews": Vachon, AI, 10/16/00.

110 "wasn't personally motivated": Vachon, AI, 10/20/00.

110 "Roger Ebert met Todd": Vachon, AI, 10/16/00.

110 "Right after Truth or Dare": Bowles, AI, 3/24/00.

110 "We proceeded to try": Schmidt, AI, 5/25/00.

111 "Congratulations" and following: Deutchman, AI, 3/10/00.

111 "Let's compete against": Claudia Eller, "What About Bob?" Los Angeles Times, 4/6/01.

111 "It was a profitable film": Rasmussen, AI, 3/31/01.

111 "After incurring": Harvey Weinstein, AI, 11/11/03.

111 "What they were then": Mark Lipsky, AI, 11/15/99.

111 "The smarter filmmakers": Safford, AI, 9/29/98.

112 "Here's a million dollars back": Bobby Newmyer, AI, 2/18/99.

112 "In a deal for an acquisition": Steinberg, AI, 2/21/00.

113 "We inserted": Lichter, AI, 10/2/98.

113 "The reasons": Bobby Newmyer, AI, 2/18/99.

113 "We don't want": Schmidt, AI, 5/25/00.

113 "Newmyer signed a deal": Harvey Weinstein, AI, 11/11/03.

114 "David, you closed" and following: Tusk, AI, 2/3/00, and confidential source.

115 "They communicated": Schmidt, AI, 3/27/01.

115 "There was a constant": Schmidt, AI, 8/7/03.

115 "They couldn't accept the idea": Confidential source.

115 "Like all IPOs": Schmidt, AI, 5/25/00.

116 "The fact that": Schmidt, AI, 8/7/03.

116 "I couldn't believe it": Jami Bernard, *Quentin Tarantino: The Man and His Movies* (New York: Harper Perennial, 1995), 215.

116 "People would gush": Anders, AI, 6/14/94.

117 "Obviously, I think Park City": John Anderson, *Sundancing* (New York: Avon, 2000), 1.

117 "When you had movies": Vachon, AI, 10/16/00.

117 "It was becoming clear": Gilmore, AI, 3/9/01.

117 "It was an insane": Vachon, AI, 10/16/00.

118 "Everybody liked Allison" and following: Ray Price, AI, 12/9/00.

118 "She's a human mood ring": Peter Biskind, "Four Rooms," *Premiere*, 12/95.

118 "Critics are harder": Ray Price, AI, 12/9/00.

118 "Everybody was freaked out": Linde, AI, 11/16/99.

119 "Going in, I didn't realize": Richard Gladstein, AI, 6/4/02.

120 "the Faye Dunaway screening" and following: Tarantino, AI, 4/30/03.

120 "The Vietnam War": Tarantino, AI, 6/10/94.

120 "I'd gone to the theater": *Deseret News Archives*, 12/26/96.

121 "We were always trying": Cathy Schulman, AI, 4/25/02.

121 "It changed my life" and following: Alexandre Rockwell, AI, 7/13/95.

122 "You didn't want to go": Bernard, *Quentin Tarantino: The Man and His Movies*, 220.

CHAPTER 4: THE BUYING GAME

PAGE

123 Epigraph: Lisa Gubernick, "We Don't Want to Be Walt Disney," *Forbes*, 10/16/89.

123 "People like Michael Barker": Bernard, AI, 11/15/99.

123 "He was kind": Ray, AI, 2/15/01.

123 "If Amir told me": Ray, AI, 3/19/01.

123 "It was nouveau" and following: Ray, AI, 2/15/01.

124 "When Amir came": Abramowitz, AI, 2/14/01.

124 "There was plenty": Deutchman, AI, 10/4/99.

124 "What you did to people" and following: Ray, AI, 3/2/01.

125 "I never had a negative" and following: Jeff Lipsky, AI, 10/4/99.

125 "Just two guys released": Ray, AI, 2/15/01.

125 "Who's the closer?": Schmidt, AI, 7/30/03.

125 "They were penurious" and following: Jeff Lipsky, AI, 10/4/99.

126 "October was the kinder": Confidential source.

126 "It would have been": Schmidt, AI, 6/9/00.

126 "The guy was really": Ray, AI, 2/15/01.

126 "It was frustrating": Ray, 2/15/01.

127 "I was the dumb kid": Tarantino, AI, 4/9/94.

127 "I didn't go to film school": Tarantino, AI, 4/30/03.

127 "Before video, I would" and following: Roger Avary, AI, 5/2/02.

128 "It just seemed as an actor": Tarantino, AI, 4/9/94.

128 "We were going to be": Tarantino, AI, 4/4/94.

128 "By this time": Avary, AI, 5/2/02.

129 "Every six months": Tarantino, AI, 6/10/94.

129 "Monte dropped the script" and following: Gladstein, AI, 6/4/02.

129 "Live was going to commit": Tarantino, AI, 1/26/94.

130 "I thought that Sundance" and following: Tarantino, AI, 4/30/03.

131 "the nightmare that looms": Collins, "The Funk of Steven Soderbergh."

131 "It had to be personal": Barbara Maltby, AI, 6/14/03.

131 "There were a series" and following: Soderbergh, AI, 4/22/99.

132 "When Redford gets": Annick Smith, AI, nd.

132 "Redford works": Richard Pearce, AI, nd.

132 "There's nothing sinister": Annick Smith, AI, nd.

132 "I had a rigid": Klein, AI, nd.

132 "This issue has been" and following: Redford, AI, 11/13/90.

133 "We're sorry, but TriStar": Confidential sources.

133 "It's a call I would have made": Collins, "The Funk of Steven Soderbergh."

133 "Well, if I'd known": Confidential source.

133 "Look, I know that" and following: Soderbergh, AI, 4/22/99.

134 "It's not my kind of movie": Confidential source.

134 "I'm gonna take my name off" and following: Soderbergh, AI, 5/2/02.

134 "It took so long" and following: Collins, "The Funk of Steven Soderbergh."

134 "They were making us" and following: Tusk, AI, 2/3/00.

135 "Harvey said to me": Gladstein, AI, 6/4/02.

135 "I was afraid" and following: Harvey Weinstein, AI, 7/18/02.

135 "I didn't make it for your wife!": Tarantino, AI, 4/30/03.

135 "I thought you hated the movie" Bernard, *Quentin Tarantino: The Man and His Movies*, 161.

135 "What?" and following: Tarantino, AI, 4/30/03; and Bernard, *Quentin Tarantino: The Man and His Movies*, 160.

135 "It's a problem": Tarantino, AI, 4/30/03; Harvey Weinstein, AI, 7/18/02; and Bernard, *Quentin Tarantino: The Man and His Movies*, 164.

135 "I didn't have to cut" and following: Tarantino, AI, 4/30/03.

136 "When *Reservoir Dogs* came out": Linde, AI, 11/16/99.

136 "Miramax had fucked": Tarantino, AI, 4/30/03.

136 "I thought they": Lawrence Bender, AI, 2/3/03.

137 "That's pretty fucking cool": Tarantino, AI, 4/4/94.

137 "There wasn't a day": Vossler, AI, 7/11/94.

137 "Also, she shouldn't be a stickler": Margie Rochlin, "Quentin Tarantino, Filmmaker: Interview," *Playboy*, 11/94.

138 "Oh yeah, he wrote to Miramax": Anders, AI, 11/17/98.

138 "I'm thinking of doing" and following: Bernard, *Quentin Tarantino: The Man and His Movies*, 218; AI, 11/15/99.

139 "has lost its edge": John Even Frook, "Miramax Paradiso," *Variety*, 9/21/92.

140 "Creditors were knocking down" and following: Tusk, AI, 1/31/00.

140 "Bob would come around": Burkin, AI, 4/29/02.

140 "I used to go into": Hirschberg, "The Mad Passion of Harvey and Bob."

141 "Harvey was up shit's creek.": John Ptak, AI, 10/21/99.

141 "They're big on raiding" and following: Safford, AI, 9/29/98.

141 "They were the kings" and following: Schmidt, AI, 5/25/00.

141 "Harvey, if that's the case": Finney, *The Egos Have Landed*, 274.

142 "Miramax was the happiest": Ptak, AI, 10/21/99.

142 "Without *The Crying Game*": Schmidt, AI, 5/25/00.

142 "What do you think if Dil" and following: Finney, *The Egos Have Landed*, 7.

142 "he'd do it if I cast": Neil Jordan, AI, 5/6/03.

143 "This is stupid." and following: Woolley, AI, 4/16/03; Finney, *The Egos Have Landed*, 13.

143 "It never occurred to anyone": Lechner, AI, 5/31/01.

143 "Why's that?": Woolley, AI, nd.

143 "Is there any": Confidential source.

144 "I could have put Harvey": Deutchman, AI, 9/17/99.

144 "I was nervous": Jordan, AI, 5/6/03.

144 "Neil was very bruised" and following: Woolley, AI, 2/27/02.

145 "What happens in": Confidential source.

145 "It was": Woolley, AI, 2/27/02.

145 "We were struggling" and following: Confidential source.

145 "We never forced": Harvey Weinstein, AI, 11/11/03.

145 "The reason we wanted": Harvey Weinstein, AI, 11/11/03.

145 "We're gonna spend" and following: Harvey Weinstein, AI, 7/18/02.

146 "We're not gonna open": Confidential source.

146 "Bob was just aggressive": Simon Perry, AI, 3/5/02.

146 "He was always talking": Confidential source.

146 "That was a big": Nik Powell, AI, 2/23/02.

146 "C'mon guys" and following: Confidential source.

147 "I kept away": Woolley, AI, 2/27/02.

148 "Our deal was never": Harvey Weinstein, AI, 11/11/03.

148 "It was kicking around": Bowles, AI, 3/24/00.

149 "Investing a million": Jeffrey Katzenberg, AI, 5/23/02.

149 "These guys don't": Ptak, AI, 10/23/99.

149 "Hey, call Harvey Weinstein" and following: Confidential source.

149 "We said, 'Hey": Chris McGurk, AI, 5/1/01.

149 "Michael did not want": Katzenberg, AI, 5/23/02.

150 "We'd had a couple": McGurk, AI, 5/1/01.

150 "The handwriting was": Harvey Weinstein, AI, 8/9/02.

150 "You had a situation": McGurk, AI, 8/27/01.

150 "You're gonna pay 'em" and following: Katzenberg, AI, 5/23/02.

151 "People were calling me": Harvey Weinstein, AI, 8/9/02.

151 "Wait, we don't" and following: Rob Moore, AI, 5/1/00.

151 "I said to Wells": Harvey Weinstein, AI, 8/9/02.

152 "Eisner was so concerned": Joe Roth, AI, 5/1/00.

152 "What they do": Schmidt, AI, 8/7/03.

152 "Michael Eisner can't make me": Ken Auletta, "Beauty and the Beast," *New Yorker*, 12/16/02.

153 "When you see Bob or Harvey": Hirschberg, "The Mad Passion of Harvey and Bob."

153 "How many films has Miramax" and following: Ptak, AI, 2/9/99.

154 "The film we admired so much": Louis Malle, interviewed by James Greenberg, c. 1994, unpublished.

CHAPTER 5: HE'S GOTTA HAVE IT

PAGE

155 Epigraph: Smith, AI, 2/15/00.

155 "That was a big deal": Hope, AI, 6/10/01.

155 "It was that *Go Fish*" and following: Tusk, AI, 2/3/00.

156 "In the acquisition": Ray, AI, 3/8/01.

156 "When Miramax got" and following: Bowles, AI, 6/7/00.

156 "There was a great suspicion": Safford, AI, 9/29/98.

157 "Hong Kong?": Tusk, AI, 2/3/00.

157 "The motto at Miramax": Safford, AI, 9/29/98.

157 "After a whole day": Amy Israel, AI, 5/1/01.

157 "Miramax could afford": McGurk, AI, 8/27/01.

157 "My attitude was": Foley, AI, 7/13/01.

158 "Harvey has to see it" and following: Confidential source.

158 "after telling everybody": Estes, 10/29/99.

158 "The Miramax people went nuts" and following: Urman, AI, 10/31/01.

159 "scene in *The Good*": redacted from David Carr, "The Emperor Miramaximus," *New York*, 11/26/01.

159 "worked. It really dried up" and following: Bowles, AI, 3/24/00.

160 "As the risks became greater": Grillo, AI, 4/10/01.

160 "One of the things": Ethan Hawke, AI, 10/28/02.

160 "Shaye said": David O. Russell, AI, 8/30/01.

160 "I felt like I'd missed": Russell, AI, 10/25/02.

160 "I made a movie that said": Russell, AI, 10/25/02.

161 "Seeing that movie": Kevin Smith, Pierson, *Spike, Mike, Slackers & Dykes*, 173–74; AI, 12/18/01.

162 "This is not a Disney movie": Tusk, AI, 2/3/00.

162 "The perception was that": Tusk, AI, 2/3/00.

162 "I lost all of Martin Lawrence's business": Harvey Weinstein, AI, 6/8/02.

162 "That's a really hateful" and following: Kevin Smith, AI, 12/18/01.

162 "Miramax was the premier" and following: Kevin Smith, AI, 12/18/01.

163 "I'm amazed that nobody" and following: Tusk, AI, 2/3/00.

163 "Great fuckin' movie": Kevin Smith, AI, 12/18/01.

163 "Mr. Weinstein, it's an honor": Tusk, AI, 2/3/00.

163 "We'd read a lot" and following: Kevin Smith, AI, 12/18/01.

164 "I had no interest": Kevin Smith, AI, 12/18/01; *Frontline* documentary, 5/01.

164 "You'd never be able": Vachon, AI, 10/16/00.

165 "No matter how grounded": Hope, AI, 6/10/01.

165 "It felt like movies": Manne, AI, 10/28/01.

165 "The attendance was huge": Schulman, AI, 4/25/02.

165 "That '94 festival": Gilmore, AI, 3/9/01.

166 "the competition was drawing Hollywood": Schulman, AI, 4/25/02.

166 "Gary Beer was really successful": Lory Smith, AI, 4/8/99.

166 "You have independent films": Payne, AI, 2/21/00.

166 "a zoo, a circus": Ray, AI, 12/16/98.

166 "In the beginning": Lichter, AI, 10/2/98.

167 "What a great idea that was" and following: Avary, AI, 5/2/02.

167 "We could have made" and following: Tarantino, AI, 1/26/94.

168 "too demented": Rick Hess, AI, 10/23/98.

168 "The worst-case scenario": Tarantino, AI, 1/26/94.

168 "Please, just read it" and following: Gladstein, AI, 6/4/02.
169 "As opposed to many other": Tarantino, AI, 1/26/94.
169 "Everyone had said": Hess, AI, 10/23/98.
169 "Harvey's always wanted": Safford, AI, 9/29/98.
170 "Harvey's power base": Marcy Granata, AI, 12/16/02.
170 "packaged": Cassian Elwes, AI, 10/26/00.
170 "Hold on a moment here" and following: Avary, AI, 5/2/02.
171 "The things that": Tarantino, AI, 7/11/03.
172 "It was a big, big thing": Tarantino, AI, 4/9/94.
172 "Quentin was born": Rockwell, AI, nd.
172 "I don't want this fuckin' asshole" and following: Tarantino, AI, 12/07/02.
173 "In the first weekend": Foley, AI, 6/21/01.
173 "We were blown away": Kevin Smith, AI, 12/18/01.
174 "Okay, Best Screenplay" and following: Tarantino, AI, 6/10/94.
174 "Believe me, they're going" and following: Rockwell, AI, 7/13/95.
175 "I was really scared": Anders, AI, 6/14/94.
175 "Life instantly changed" and following: Kevin Smith, AI, 12/18/01.
176 "Sony spent $200,000": Linklater, AI, 3/12/01.
176 "We wound up shouldering" and following: Kevin Smith, AI, 12/18/01; *Frontline* documentary, 5/01.
178 "He came waddling up" and following: Bowles, AI, 3/4/00.
178 "It's like the guy who wants": Confidential source.
178 "We were asked to bring": Granata, AI, 12/16/02.
179 "Gill would argue" and following: Spikes, AI, 7/23/01.
179 "Okay, if you're so good": Confidential source.
179 "When people made snow jokes": Tusk, AI, 8/16/00.
180 "Now look": Confidential source.
180 "a terrier on speed": Confidential source.
180 "Scott was Harvey's attack dog.": Webster, AI, 10/20/01.
180 "Tell 'im to go fuck himself" and following: Confidential source.
180 "Whaddid I do that for?": Confidential source.
180 "If there was a totally unpleasant": Bowles, AI, 6/7/00.
180 "I'm a big fan": Lechner, AI, 2/8/00.
181 "There was a lot": Confidential source.
181 "Whaddya think a'that" and following: Confidential source.
181 "Scott, where ya goin'?": Confidential source.
181 "When I started there": Burkin, AI, 4/29/02.
181 "Harve, don't buy it." and following: Harvey Weinstein, AI, 8/9/02.
182 "In Europe, we were very curious" and following: Bertolucci, AI, 5/26/03.
182 "You knew what": Thomas, AI, 4/11/02.
182 "They had recruited a bizarre": Urman, AI, 10/31/01.
182 "Previews are a terrible": Bertolucci, AI, 5/26/03.
182 "I couldn't get Bernardo": Harvey Weinstein, AI, 11/18/02.
183 "It's another one": Bertolucci, AI, 5/26/03.
183 "Oh, by the way" and following: Urman, AI, 10/31/01.
183 "Why did you": Jeremy Thomas, AI, 4/11/02.
183 "Bernardo just flipped out": Urman, AI, 10/31/01.
183 "I found a bar" and following: Bertolucci, AI, 5/26/03.
184 "I dropped Bernardo": Thomas, AI, 4/11/02.
184 "He's a snob." and following: Bertolucci, AI, 5/26/03.

CHAPTER 6: THE HOUSE THAT QUENTIN BUILT

PAGE

185 Epigraph: Hirschberg, "The Mad Passion of Harvey and Bob."

185 "The problem we had": Malin, AI, 8/6/02.

185 "That's too strong": Schmidt, AI, 3/27/01.

186 "Whaddya telling us?" and following: Ray, AI, 3/2/01.

187 "We're going to do" and following: Jeff Lipsky, AI, 10/4/99.

187 "Gary's an arrogant": Ray, AI, 3/2/01.

187 "Allen & Co., I understood them": Jeff Lipsky, AI, 10/4/99.

188 "Stupid, petty things" and following: Ray, AI, 3/2/01.

189 "betrayed me": Jeff Lipsky, AI, 10/4/99.

189 "I've regretted it ever since": Ray, AI, 3/2/01.

189 "I picked up where Marty": Foley, AI, 6/21/01.

189 "Nobody saw that coming": Kevin Smith, AI, 12/18/01.

189 "Bob and Harvey had never had a $100": Foley, AI, 6/21/01.

189 "I never had": Harvey Weinstein, AI, 10/3/02.

190 "Quentin loved Harvey": Hess, AI, 10/23/98.

190 "If I put myself": Tarantino, AI, 4/4/94.

190 "Harvey saw him as this guy" and following: Hess, AI, 10/23/98.

190 "He's the only": Harvey Weinstein, AI, 7/18/02.

190 "Quentin became the face": Kevin Smith, AI, 12/18/01.

190 "He had his fingers": Hess, AI, 10/23/98.

190 "Hey, man, if I don't find": Confidential source.

191 "There's just been so much hype": Lechner, AI, 2/8/00.

191 "There's always been imitation": Lechner, AI, 2/8/00.

191 "Genre films are a great": Chris Gore, "Soderbergh Unleashed," *Film Threat,* 1–5, 2/18/01–6/17/02.

191 "I'm always being told" and following: Hawke, AI, 10/28/02.

193 "That's when they said": Hess, AI, 10/23/98.

193 "The Miramaxization": Ray, AI, 3/8/01.

193 "If your little movie": Schamus, AI, 7/2/02.

194 "The agencies and managers": Robert Newman, AI, 6/13/00.

195 "The biggest thing was when" and following: Anders, redacted from *Frontline* documentary, 5/01.

195 "The major guys are shooting": Gilmore, *Frontline* documentary, 5/01.

195 "Miramax at that time felt": Matthew Cohen, AI, 12/10/01.

196 "Bob yelled at me": Katzenberg, AI, 5/23/02.

196 "Bob really got in there": Harvey Weinstein, AI, 8/9/02.

196 "floating high gross numbers": Bill Mechanic, AI, 5/2/01.

196 "You gotta do it" and following: Mechanic, AI, 5/2/01.

197 "The big cost in the movie business": Joe Roth, AI, 5/1/00.

197 "To this day": Harvey Weinstein, AI, 8/9/02.

197 "You know, you probably" and following: Joe Roth, AI, 5/1/00.

198 "If I heard that" and following: Joe Roth, AI, 5/1/00.

199 "You had this efficiency machine": Foley, AI, 6/21/01.

199 "They're enough alike": Joe Roth, AI, 5/1/00.

199 "Miramax was set up to be": McGurk, AI, 5/1/01.

199 "Miramax acted like Disney" and following: Joe Roth, AI, 5/1/00.

199 "People who did stuff for them": Moore, AI, 5/1/00.

199 "Miramax had no brand identity": Confidential source.

200 "I thought it was": Confidential source.

200 "They got pissed off": Moore, AI, 5/1/00.

200 "They spent the entire time": Joe Roth, AI, 5/1/00.

200 "Go ahead and walk": Confidential source.

200 "They drove McGurk insane": Confidential source.

201 "There's this really cool kid": Vachon, AI, nd.

201 "Their idea of safe sex": Marc Fisher, " 'Kids': The Darker Side of Disney," *Washington Post*, 8/6/95.

201 "My friend said" and following: Konrad, AI, 6/10/02.

202 "Miramax was gonna": Larry Clark, AI, 10/22/03.

202 "If it was up to me" and following: Vachon, AI, nd.

202 "She was used": Clark, AI, 10/22/03.

203 "Wow, congratulations": Confidential source.

203 "Harvey the acquisitions guy": Lechner, AI, 5/31/01.

203 "Ed Burns and *The Brothers McMullen*": Kevin Smith, AI, 6/6/02.

204 "It was a dysfunctional place": Schulman, AI, 4/25/02.

204 "Bob sees things": Van Wagenen, AI, 10/22/03.

204 "I like the thinking" and following: Confidential source.

205 "He'll disappear for six": Confidential source.

205 "No matter who": Van Wagenen, AI, 10/22/03.

205 "Bob is almost genetically": Confidential source.

206 "Fuck you!" and following: Avary, AI, 5/2/02.

206 "I'm always going up against": Bernard, *Quentin Tarantino: The Man and His Movies*, 240.

206 "And I really have to take a pee": Bernard, *Quentin Tarantino: The Man and His Movies*, 243.

206 "My whole thing was": Tarantino, AI, 7/11/03.

207 "To sit on a movie set": Collins, "The Funk of Steven Soderbergh."

207 "I was bored": Soderbergh, AI, 5/2/02.

207 "The problem with my marriage" and following: Collins, "The Funk of Steven Soderbergh."

207 "People kept thinking" and following: Soderbergh, AI, 5/2/02.

208 "Do you know any" and following: Linklater, AI, 3/12/01.

208 "his eclecticism" and following: Soderbergh, AI, 5/2/02.

208 "We fought like cats and dogs": Collins, "The Funk of Steven Soderbergh."

208 "What was that about?": Soderbergh, AI, 5/2/02.

209 "I was so wrapped up": Lim, "Having Your Way with Hollywood."

209 "I guess I wanted" and following: Soderbergh, AI, 5/2/02.

209 "It was like": Russell, AI, 8/30/01.

209 "You're going to go meet Harvey": Russell, AI, 12/08/02.

209 "I went to this part": Russell, AI, 8/30/01.

209 "To me that incest material": Russell, AI, 10/25/02.

209 "After we made the deal" and following: Russell, AI, 8/30/01.

211 "The thing that sickens me": Russell, AI, 10/25/02.

211 "Harvey hungered to make movies": Konrad, AI, 6/10/02.

212 "viciously anti-Catholic": Schweizer and Schweizer, *Disney: The Mouse Betrayed*, 212.

212 "It was overwhelming": Linde, AI, 11/19/99.

212 "Cardinal O'Connor lit the fuse": Harvey Weinstein, AI, 7/18/02.

212 "Harvey perceived no": Linde, AI, 11/16/99.

212 "I just want to tell you" and following: McGurk, AI, 8/27/01.

212 *"Priest* was a turning point": Bowles, AI, 3/24/00.

213 "He was doing it": Confidential source.

213 "We had a couple of years": Joe Roth, AI, 5/1/00.

213 "He said, 'You know' ": Israel, AI, 5/1/01.

213 "If Harvey believed in a film": Hart, AI, 9/17/02.

213 "First we pulled quotes": Peter Kindlon, AI, 10/4/02.

213 "It was too": Clark, AI, 10/22/03.

213 "seems voyeuristic and exploitative" and following: Richard Brooks, "Disney Caught in 'Child Porn' Film Row," *The Guardian,* May 28, 1995.

214 "nightmare of depravity": Bob Dole, speech delivered 5/31/95.

214 "I saw the movie": Joe Roth, AI, 5/1/00.

214 *"Kids* was a hot potato": Bowles, AI, 3/24/00.

214 "It set a bad precedent": Joe Roth, AI, 5/1/00.

214 "I just love movies": Mark Jolly, "Growing Up Fast: *Kids,*" *The Times* (London), 7/30/95.

214 "Harvey and Bob did" and following: Clark, AI, 10/22/03.

215 "it grossed $7 million": Harvey Weinstein, AI, 11/11/03.

215 *"Kids* was a Miramax": Vachon, AI, nd.

215 "While everyone thought": Tusk, AI, 2/3/00.

215 "Bob and Harvey were moving": Bowles, AI, 3/24/00.

215 "They were offered": Clark, AI, 10/22/03.

CHAPTER 7: PUMPING UP THE VOLUME

PAGE

216 Epigraph: Bernard Weinraub, "Mavericks Adapting to Power of the Studios," *New York Times,* 6/24/96.

216 "I always wanted": Tarantino, AI, 4/30/03.

216 "I drove him over": Rodriguez, AI, 6/14/03.

216 "It was getting hard": Tarantino, AI, 4/30/03.

217 "Basically I'd been paying my dues" and following: Biskind, "Four Rooms," 12/95.

218 "It was really exciting" and following: Anders, AI, 11/3/98.

218 "I was the originator" and following: Biskind "Four Rooms," 12/95.

219 "It was very personal" and following: Anders, AI, nd.

219 "Well, okay, I could cut": Biskind, "Four Rooms," 12/95.

219 "Who's going to tell Quentin": Ibid.

219 "My room ran twenty minutes": Anders, AI, 6/13/00.

219 "You're going to be an insignificant": Bernard, *Quentin Tarantino: The Man and His Movies,* 230.

219 "You know what the problem is": Anders, AI, 11/17/98.

219 "The truth is, I don't think" and following: Anders, AI, 6/13/00.

220 "My dentist went": Rockwell, AI, 6/11/03.

220 "Quentin decided he was going" and following: Anders, AI, 6/13/00.

221 "This is an interesting" and following: Anders, AI, 11/3/98.

221 "Quentin was mortified": Coen, AI, 10/15/03.

221 "Bob Weinstein called": Anders, AI, 6/13/00.

222 "He can't be in a competitive": Safford, AI, 9/29/98.

223 "A week before its premiere": Payne, AI, 2/21/00.

223 "Who the hell is responsible" and following: Konrad, AI, 6/10/02.

223 "He wanted a happier ending" and following: Payne, AI, 2/21/00.

223 "Cary, they're gonna know": Confidential source.

224 "Even agents were crying" and following: Jonathon Taplin, AI, 2/2/99.

225 "Did you like *Shine?*": Bowles, AI, 3/24/00.

226 "The eagle has landed": Israel, AI, 5/1/01.

226 "Fine Line got *Shine!*" and following: Bowles, AI, 3/24/00.

226 "About a half hour": Carlos Goodman, AI, 10/2/98.

226 "You fuck!": Taplin, AI, 2/2/99.

226 "I didn't physically": Harvey Weinstein, AI, 8/9/02.

226 "He was about": Debbie Newmyer, AI, 4/20/99.

226 "For once in your life": Lichter, AI, 10/2/98; Debbie Newmyer, AI, 4/20/99.

226 "Fuck you, bitch!": Taplin, AI, 2/2/99.

226 "You don't talk": Goodman, AI, 10/2/98.

226 "You're gonna need more lawyers" and following: Taplin, AI, 2/2/99.

227 "I am too big": Susan Glatzer, AI, 4/26/00.

227 "I ruined my reputation": Harvey Weinstein, AI, 8/9/02.

227 "We agreed on terms": Safford, AI, 9/29/98.

227 "So Tony, you had" and following: Tusk, AI, 2/3/00; Confidential source.

227 "Oh no, Scott": Tusk, AI, 2/3/00.

228 "Dr Pepper commercial": Bowles, AI, 3/24/00.

228 "Nineteen ninety-six, the *Shine* year": Gilmore, AI, 3/9/01.

229 "Being rejected by Sundance": Tenenbaum, AI, 10/2/99.

229 "a festival that's attached": Kenneth Turan, *Sundance to Sarajevo* (Berkeley: University of California Press, 2002), 33.

229 "It's no secret Sundance": David Geffner, "Surviving Park City: Do the Craziest 10 Days in January Still Matter?", *Moviemaker*, 2001.

229 "I responded to the whole": Soderbergh, AI, 4/22/99.

229 "got fucked again": Tenenbaum, AI, 10/2/99.

230 "I got tired of bringing": Safford, AI, 9/29/98.

230 "I've heard you've taken" and following: Safford, AI, 12/04/02.

230 "I acted badly again": Harvey Weinstein, AI, 8/9/02.

230 "They dumped my files": Safford, AI, 12/04/02.

231 "But Redford wanted creative control": Jonathan Sehring, AI, 7/24/00.

231 "They were clueless": Confidential source.

231 "A huge element": Confidential source.

232 "It was obviously great material": Pierson, AI, 11/26/01.

232 "Be funny": Confidential source.

232 "that this is not the kind" and following: Pierson, AI, 11/26/01.

234 "Larry, do you want me": Bowles, AI, 3/24/00.

234 "Okay, now it's your turn" and following: Elwes, AI, 10/26/00.

234 "I'm a half an hour into this": Bowles, AI, 3/24/00.

234 "Whaddya want for it?" and following: Elwes, AI, 10/26/00.

236 "It was stupid": Harvey Weinstein, AI, 8/9/02.

236 "Billy made it clear to me" and following: Larry Meistrich, AI, 5/13/03.

236 "We had one of those" and following: Harvey Weinstein, AI, 8/9/02.

236 "Billy Bob is a very ornery": Bowles, AI, 3/24/00.

236 "I'm a big, fat, hairy Jew": Confidential source.

236 "Weinstein said" and following: Elwes, AI, 10/26/00.

237 "Ah'm going to stick a fork": Confidential source and Harvey Weinstein, AI, 8/9/02.

237 "The fights were not happy hugs" and following: Meistrich, AI, 5/13/03.

237 "They needed Billy": Elwes, AI, 10/26/00.

237 "pay people": Confidential source.

237 "Harvey wants it" and following: Mechanic, AI, 5/2/01.

238 "I can blame almost every one": Johanna Schneller, "*Us* interview: Billy Bob Thornton," 8/98.

239 "We were raised": Matthew Gilbert, "Southern Discomfort," *Boston Globe*, 2/7/97.

239 "Silly Slob": Richard Corliss, "Billy Bob . . . Olivier?," *Time*, 2/10/97.

239 "I don't know why I'm so unhappy": Schneller, "*Us* interview: Billy Bob Thornton"; Mark Jacobson, "Citizen Billy Bob," *Esquire*, 4/97.

239 "I was full of self-loathing": Patrick Goldstein, "A Story That Hits Close to Down Home," *Los Angeles Times*, 11/24/96.

239 "We worked our hearts out": Jacobson, "Citizen Billy Bob."

240 "Which intrigued the hell" and following: Ray, AI, 3/2/01.

241 "They send you stuff to look at": Payne, AI, 2/21/00.

241 "I do think Harvey made promises": Konrad, AI, 6/10/02.

242 "I was shocked because" and following: Jim Taylor, AI, 10/18/01.

242 "I didn't get one single": Payne, AI, 2/21/00.

242 "You threw that spot": Harvey Weinstein, AI, 8/9/02.

242 "Saul, like all of us": Thomas, AI, 4/11/02.

242 "My friends are my friends" and following: Anthony Minghella, AI, 10/30/01.

244 "I called everybody": Pollack, AI, 6/10/02.

244 "Miramax had been buzzing around" and following: Elwes, AI, 10/26/00.

244 "That's fantastic, I know": Peter Jackson, AI, 11/12/03.

244 "Saul was in love": Harvey Weinstein, AI, 8/9/02.

245 "Miramax was in a state" and following: Harvey Weinstein, AI, 8/9/02.

245 "I gave Peter": Harvey Weinstein, AI, 8/9/02.

246 "All of a sudden" and following: Mechanic, AI, 5/2/01.

246 "I know that Demi's name": Minghella, AI, 10/30/01.

246 "Anthony would smile": Mechanic, AI, 5/2/01.

CHAPTER 8: SWIMMING WITH SHARKS
PAGE

247 Epigraph: John Pierson, AI, 1/13/02.

247 "Don't worry, it's not horror" and following: Confidential source.

248 "Bob felt strongly": Konrad, AI, 6/10/02.

248 "I didn't want it" and following: Bob Weinstein, AI, 11/5/03.

248 "He has peaks and valleys": B. J. Rack, AI, 12/1/99.

248 "I'm scared" and following: Konrad, AI, 6/10/02.

249 "They treated him very badly": Rack, AI, 12/1/99.

249 "They were trying": Konrad, AI, 6/10/02.

249 "I thought the mask": Bob Weinstein, AI, 11/5/03.

249 "We have reached an impasse" and following: Konrad, AI, 6/10/02.

250 "He showed me forty": Bob Weinstein, AI, 11/5/03.

250 "Wes was God." and following: Rack, AI, 12/1/99.

253 "Bob will talk for much longer": Lechner, AI, 5/31/01.

253 "Bob is like": Kevin Smith, AI, 12/18/01.

253 "As soon as they got" and following: Rack, AI, 12/1/99.

254 "From the first day" and following: Matthew Robbins, AI, 11/8/03.

255 "I have to go" and following: Rack, AI, 12/1/99.

257 "It was better to talk to": Tarantino, AI, 4/30/03.

257 "This is not going to happen" and following: Rack, AI, 12/1/99.

257 "Mira saved his job." and following: Tarantino, AI, 4/30/03.

258 "*Pulp Fiction* had just happened" and following: James Mangold, AI, 6/10/02.

260 "He was desperate": Confidential source.

260 "Most studios don't get as intimately": Konrad, AI, 6/10/02.

260 "I got on the subway": Mangold, AI, 6/10/02.

261 "You have to be able": Steinberg, AI, 2/21/00.

261 "absolutely fearless": Lechner, AI, 2/8/00.

261 "She didn't like film": Gigliotti, AI, 2/14/01.

261 "I said, 'Meryl'": Mangold, AI, 6/10/02.

261 "found a way to tap into": Konrad, AI, 6/10/02.

261 "You have to be careful" and following: Mangold, AI, 6/10/02.

263 "It's Brooklyn, there's gotta be": Confidential source.

263 "That's pretty dumb": Confidential source.

263 "I walked around": Mangold, AI, 6/10/02.

263 "It was a love-in": Bob Weinstein, AI, 11/5/03.

263 "Harvey didn't pay a lot of attention": Konrad, AI, 6/10/02.

263 "I think it's a": Foley, AI, 7/13/01.

263 "I fight with my brother": Harvey Weinstein, AI, 10/30/02.

264 "The worst thing": Tusk, AI, 2/7/00.

264 "Despite the fraternal psychodrama": Foley, AI, 7/13/01.

264 "You can't do anything right.": Bowles, AI, 3/24/00.

264 "You'd open a Bob film" and following: Foley, AI, 7/13/01.

265 "The conventional wisdom": Bob Weinstein, AI, 11/5/03.

265 "Who releases a bloody": Lechner, AI, 2/8/00.

265 "Everybody's telling me": Confidential source.

265 "Bob was adamant about it": Konrad, AI, 6/10/02.

265 "Cary did the worst fucking thing": Kevin Smith, AI, 12/18/01.

266 "Two thirds of the time": Tusk, AI, 2/7/00.

267 "Those movies that were bought": Barker, AI, 1/14/99.

267 "I don't care" and following: Harvey Weinstein, AI, 8/9/02.

267 "They created instant recognition": Kevin Smith, AI, 12/18/01.

267 "The TV commercials ran in L.A.": Harvey Weinstein, AI, 8/9/02.

267 "I think that if we hadn't sold": Elwes, AI, 10/26/00.

268 "God gave me this body": Ann Oldenburg, "Pietra Thornton Bares Body and Soul," *USA Today*, 12/8/97.

268 "It's like taking one of those tests": Steven Rosen, "Billy Bob Thornton's Anonymity at an End," *Denver Post*, 2/16/97.

268 "We're losers": Confidential source.

268 "Oh, you've got to come" and following: Soderbergh, AI, 5/2/02.

269 "We sold 240,000 cassettes": Harvey Weinstein, AI, 8/9/02.

269 "When you got a production statement": Meistrich, AI, 5/13/03.

269 "Harvey's like Pac-Man": Elwes, AI, 10/26/00.

269 "In this business": Meistrich, AI, 5/13/03.

269 "Meistrich didn't see": Harvey Weinstein, AI, 11/11/03.

270 "I'm going to kill you": "Wife Sues 'Sling Blade' Star," *Times Picayune*, 9/20/97.

270 "His Marv Albert defense" and following: Rosen, "Billy Bob Thornton's Anonymity at an End."

270 "Those two films were the last": Ray, AI, 3/2/01.

270 "We had a breakthrough": Ray, AI, 3/2/01.

270 "It wasn't greed": Schmidt, AI, 7/30/03.
271 "All the goodwill": Ray, AI, 9/29/01.
271 "If we did not": Schmidt, AI, 7/30/03.
271 "If you're going to play": Ray, AI, 3/8/01.
271 "I had a lot of experience": McGurk, AI, 5/1/01.
272 "Amir, so listen" and following: Schmidt, AI, 7/30/03.
272 "We'd say you'd have to deal" and following: Ray, AI, 3/8/01.
272 "Bingham feared" and following: Amir Malin, AI, 8/6/02.
272 "Whatever his intentions" and following: Ray, AI, 3/8/01.
272 "It was a destabilizing": Schmidt, AI, 7/30/03.
272 "I wanted to act": Ray, AI, 3/8/01.
272 "Amir took a well": Confidential source.
272 "Well, whaddya wanna do?" and following: Ray, AI, 3/8/01.
273 "I sat down with Bingham": Malin, AI, 8/6/02.
274 "For years, everyone": Ray, AI, 2/15/01.
275 "Why should filmmakers": John Clark and Elaine Dutka, "Miramax Finds Success Breeds Admiration, Envy," *Los Angeles Times*, 1/30/97.
275 "I haven't had a cent": Minghella, AI, 11/1/01.
275 "You'll be paid in October.": Confidential source.
275 "Go ahead": Confidential source.
275 "Harvey the monster": Harvey Weinstein, AI, 8/9/02.
275 "What's that got": Zaentz, AI, 11/6/03.
275 "You push the boat out": Thomas, AI, 4/11/02.
276 "is a pushcart peddler": David Carr, "The Emperor Miramaximus."
276 "angry slash philosophical" and following: Walter Murch, AI, 11/14/00.
276 "I have a very clear position" and following: Minghella, AI, 11/1/01.
277 "No! Billy Wilder": Zaentz, AI, 11/6/03.
277 "Harvey knows that I hate": Tarantino, AI, 4/30/03.

CHAPTER 9: ACE AND GARY

PAGE

278 Epigraph: Damon, AI, 9/12/97.
278 "They dragged me": Ben Affleck, AI, 2/21/02.
279 "Why the fuck do you guys": Damon, AI, 9/12/97.
279 "My agent said it was" and following: Affleck, AI, 2/21/02.
280 "Ben's right in that art": Hawke, AI, 10/28/02.
280 "Yeah, guys are making": Affleck, AI, 2/21/02.
281 "We'd just say" and following: Damon, AI, 9/26/01.
281 "We agreed with whatever" and following: Affleck, AI, 2/21/02.
282 "The first thing we found out" and following: Damon, AI, 9/26/01.
283 "We need an advance" and following: Affleck, AI, 2/21/02.
283 "We developed the script" and following: Affleck, AI, 2/21/02.
284 "It had to be bought": Damon, AI, 9/26/01.
284 "It was yet another": Affleck, AI, 2/21/02.
285 "Can I come home": Smith, AI, nd.
285 "*Chasing Amy* could never": *Frontline* documentary, 5/01.
285 "This is business, Kevin" and following: Kevin Smith, AI, 12/18/01.
285 "Everyone warned us" and following: Damon, AI, 9/26/01.
286 "Immediately we loved him": Affleck, AI, 2/21/02.
286 "It was tainted goods": Lechner, AI, 2/8/00.

286 "You don't have to accept" and following: Damon, AI, 9/26/01.
286 "We knew that he supposedly fought": Affleck, AI, 2/21/02.
287 "Harvey, let's hire him": Webster, AI, 10/20/01.
287 "A lot of these guys": Van Sant, AI, 10/18/01.
287 "I just want you guys" and following: Damon, AI, 9/26/01.
288 "I love Lawrence": Lechner, AI, 5/3/01.
288 "FUCK OFF, Lawrence" and following: Affleck, AI, 2/21/02.
289 "Wildwood is such a mess" and following: Confidential source.
290 "Getting General Cinema" and following: Gary Meyer, AI, 11/27/01.
291 "It was arrogant": Confidential source.
292 "The movies that Harvey": Konrad, AI, 6/7/02.
292 "Harvey is not as interested": Lechner, AI, 2/8/00.
292 "We don't develop movies.": Corie Brown, unpublished *Newsweek* piece, c. 2/00.
292 "My biggest frustration": Konrad, AI, 6/10/02.
292 "Harvey is not the best developer" and following: Webster, AI, 10/20/01.
293 "There was always a little question": Tusk, AI, 8/16/00.
294 "We'll do it" and following: Confidential source.
294 "I witnessed": Webster, AI, 10/20/01.
294 "We'll wake up" and following: Confidential source.
295 "It was a kill": Gill, AI, 2/11/03.
295 "We need to cast": Confidential source.
295 "Work for Dimension": Confidential source.
295 "It was more of a studio": Lechner, AI, 5/31/01.
295 "Scott came to see me": Mechanic, AI, 5/2/01.
296 "Scott is a good dealmaker": McGurk, AI, 5/1/01.
296 "Look, meet this guy" and following: Ray, AI, 3/8/01.
297 "Based on McGurk's comfort": Schmidt, AI, 5/9/00.
297 "the ugliest place" and following: Hirschberg, "Crabgrass Gothic," *New York Times Magazine*, 9/27/98.
298 "You gotta get rid of": Hope, AI, 6/10/01.
298 "didn't like Amir": Schmidt, AI, 7/31/03.
298 "This is right up our street" and following: Ray, AI, 3/19/01.
298 "The one mistake October made": Hope, AI, 6/10/01.
298 "It was one of the few movies" and following: Vachon, AI, 6/1/01.
299 "It's compelling and interesting": Ray, AI, 3/19/01.
299 "When we were dicking around" and following: Vachon, AI, 6/1/01.
299 "didn't want to leave": Schmidt, AI, 7/31/03.
299 "I'm surprised that they": Confidential source.
299 "When Greenstein came over": Ray, AI, 12/16/98.
300 "Harvey just screamed obscenities": Schmidt, AI, 6/9/00.
300 "Standing in the door": Ray, AI, 12/16/98.
300 "I've never seen him afraid": Glatzer, AI, 4/26/00.
301 "I could see where": Ray, AI, 3/8/01.
301 "I think you should put" and following: Elwes, AI, 10/26/00.
301 "Bingham, let me give you": Woods, AI, 11/30/99.
301 "There were flagpoles": Ray, AI, 3/8/01.
302 "Scott was trying to get out": Bowles, AI, 6/7/00.
302 "I want to see it" and following: Elwes, AI, 10/26/00.
303 "Where's Harvey?" and following: Ray, AI, 3/8/01.
303 "Someone wants to talk to you" and following: Elwes, AI, 10/26/00.

304 "Where the fuck is Harvey?" and following: Ray, AI, 3/8/01.

304 "Oh, shit, I forgot" and following: Elwes, AI, 10/26/00.

305 "Cassian, if you walk": Schmidt, AI, 5/25/00.

305 "What the fuck" and following: Elwes, AI, 10/26/00.

306 "Cassian, I don't even know" and following: Schmidt, AI, 5/25/00.

306 "I've changed my mind": Elwes, AI, 10/26/00.

306 "I was out after $5 million": Harvey Weinstein, AI, 10/3/02.

306 "You got a lotta fuckin' nerve" and following: Elwes, AI, 10/26/00.

307 "This thing has cratered": Ray, AI, 3/8/01.

307 "Okay, we'll make the deal": Schmidt, AI, 5/25/00.

307 "I think he was really toying": Bowles, AI, 6/7/00.

307 "Amir Malin is Satan": Glatzer, AI, 4/26/00.

CHAPTER 10: CROSSOVER DREAMS
PAGE

308 Epigraph: Lynn Hirschberg, "The Two Hollywoods: The Man Who Changed Everything," *The New York Times*, 11/16/97.

308 "There was never a hiccup": Damon, AI, 9/26/01, 9/12/97.

308 "Great, let's test it": Van Sant, AI, 10/18/01.

308 "It tested 94" and following: Affleck, AI, 2/21/02.

309 "Harvey's mentality": Damon, AI, 9/26/01.

309 "Me and Quentin" and following: Affleck, AI, 2/21/02.

309 "The marquee had *Good Will Hunting*": Damon, AI, 9/26/01.

310 "The movie had done enormously well": Affleck, AI, 2/21/02.

310 "All right guys, you ever" and following: Damon, AI, 9/26/01; Confidential source.

310 "Matt and Ben weren't interested": Van Sant, AI, 10/18/01.

310 "Gus is full of shit": Affleck, AI, 2/21/02.

310 "For two kids from Boston": Damon, AI, 10/3/01.

311 "He'll call me up": Damon, AI, 10/30/01.

311 "Those guys went from nowhere" and following: Van Sant, AI, 10/18/01.

311 "The exchange is" and following: Affleck, AI, 2/21/02.

312 "Ben is far more business-savvy": Kevin Smith, AI, 12/18/01.

313 "People are going": Lee, AI, 11/8/02.

313 "I don't know": Len Klady, "*Scream 2* Debut Coin Overstated," *Variety*, posted 12/21/97.

313 "Dick Cook told them": Joe Roth, AI, 5/1/00.

313 "that it was": Klady, "*Scream 2* Debut Coin Overstated."

313 "I'm not gonna tell anyone": Confidential source.

313 "Quentin had done": Confidential source.

314 "Quentin spent most": Rodriguez, AI, 6/17/03.

314 "Trigger is the": Confidential source.

314 "I'd go over": Louis Black, AI, 6/05/03.

314 "He loved it" and following: Dulce Durante, AI, 6/17/03.

315 "So I called": Confidential source.

315 "he would do": Confidential source.

315 "This was not": Confidential source.

315 "There was a lot": Hess, AI, 10/23/98.

315 "He's a genuinely": Black, AI, 6/05/03.

315 "Quentin is not": Jennifer Beals, AI, 7/2/03.

315 "Before I was famous" and following: Tarantino, AI, 6/30/03.

316 "Wow, it played great!" and following: Tarantino, AI, 2/3/03.

317 "I'm not saying" and following: Lee, AI, 11/8/02.

317 "ignorant": "Quentin's Race Slurs Spark Brawl," "Page Six," *New York Post,* 5/5/98.

317 "I'm sorry, if he wants" and following: Kevin Merida, "Spike Lee, Holding Court," *Washington Post,* 5/1/98.

318 "Spike, you gotta stop" and following: Lee, AI, 11/8/02.

318 "That's something Quentin": Lee, AI, 11/8/02; S. F. Said, "Getting Spikey, *The Context* interviews Spike Lee, director of *Bamboozled,*" thecontext.com, 4/6/01.

318 "He stuck his hand": Tarantino, AI, 6/30/03.

318 "It was almost like": Tarantino, AI, 6/30/03.

318 "More or less every": Quentin Curtis, The Arts: Why I'm Not afraid of Failing in New York," *Daily Telegraph,* 6/19/98.

319 "I thought it was such" and following: Darren Aronofsky, AI, 12/11/01.

320 "when you're in production": Webster, AI, 10/20/01.

320 "Can't there be": Confidential source.

321 "In Harvey's mind": Deutchman, 3/1/00.

321 "When a movie": Confidential source.

321 "Everybody miraculously": Webster, AI, 10/20/01.

321 "The fight was about" and following: Lechner, AI, 5/31/01.

322 "An editor friend of mine": Ivory, AI, 7/9/01.

322 "There's a $50 million" and following: Confidential source.

322 "The root of everything": Lechner, AI, 5/31/01.

323 "Harvey fell off the tracks": Peter Newman, AI, 6/1/01.

323 "Harvey gets personal": Gigliotti, AI, 2/14/01.

323 "Miramax had changed a lot": Lechner, AI, 5/31/01.

324 "That's when it went bad": Schmidt, AI, 5/9/00.

324 "I don't know if you guys" and following: Ray, AI, 3/19/01.

324 "I checked with": Schmidt, AI, 6/9/00.

324 "It had nothing": Rob Carliner, AI, 10/20/03.

324 "I can't believe": Schmidt, AI, 6/9/00.

324 "got red-faced crazy": Ray, AI, 3/19/01.

325 "Bingham would yell": Confidential source.

325 "If you look at two camps" and following: Schmidt, AI, 6/9/00.

325 "Scott was always talking": Glatzer, AI, 4/26/00.

325 "Scott was systematically": Ray, AI, 3/19/01.

325 "Scott was an": Carliner, AI, 10/20/03.

326 "Hello, Matt?": *South Park* CD.

326 "Scott never said": Confidential source.

326 "That never was": Sandy Stern, AI, 10/20/03.

326 "Nothing could have": Rice, AI, 7/23/01.

326 "*The Apostle* benefited": Schmidt, AI, 7/31/03.

327 "Couldn't she have waited" and following: Confidential source.

328 "He flipped over it": Ed Zwick, AI, 8/29/03.

328 "I'll give you": Gigliotti, AI, 2/14/01.

328 "Who cares": McGurk, AI, 6/18/03.

328 "They were being greedy": John Logigian, AI, 10/30/03.

328 "You know what": Gigliotti, AI, 10/3/01.

328 "You know, I": Confidential source.

329 "I don't think anyone": Gigliotti, AI, 2/14/01.
329 "Harvey was so contrite": Zwick, AI, 8/29/01.
329 "Forget about *Dogma*": Kevin Smith, AI, 6/6/02.
330 "You're going to work": Confidential source.
330 "was involved in every detail": Granata, AI, 12/16/02.
330 "Get his name": Norman, AI, 8/13/03.
330 "You have a good movie": Granata, AI, 12/16/02.
330 "This was one case": Lechner, AI, 5/31/01.
331 "We need more jokes": Gigliotti, AI, 10/3/01.
331 "No! That's not true": Rebecca Traister, "All This Gray Hair Is from Far from Heaven: Christine Vachon Her Magnificent Obsession," *New York Observer*, 11/6/02.
332 "has a reputation for being" and following: Vachon, AI, nd.
332 "Well, actually what" and following: Lechner, AI, 5/3/01.
332 "It was awful" and following: Vachon, AI, nd, and *Projections*, 152.
333 "It was like Ted": Vachon, AI, 6/1/01.
334 "They were there to open" and following: Ray, AI, 3/19/01.
334 "My attitude to Universal": Ray, AI, 5/19/01.
334 "We can't release it": Confidential source.
334 "I don't want to understand": Hirschberg, "Crabgrass Gothic."
334 "Ronnie thought I was": Ray, AI, 9/29/01.
335 "the whole thing had unraveled" and following: Ray, AI, 3/19/01.
336 "We weren't distributors": Vachon, AI, 6/1/01.
336 "There are other fights" and following: Ray, AI, 3/19/01.
337 "I loved to drop" and following: Kindlon, AI, 10/4/02.
337 "You could work at the company": Robin Rizzuto, AI, 7/27/00.
337 "Just because you're merely": Confidential source.
337 "I had worked at New Line": Hart, AI, 9/17/02.
338 "The way to get respect": Confidential source.
338 "You're a dildo!": Eugenia Peretz, "Celebrity's Little Helper," V*anity Fair*, 7/00.
338 "One time a floater": Hart, AI, 9/17/02.
338 "I hate the sound": Confidential source.
338 "Do you know what's going to happen": Dennis Higgins, AI, 4/26/02.
338 "I remember waiting": Kindlon, AI, 10/4/02.
338 "especially when you knew": Hart, AI, 9/17/02.
338 "I literally went to my desk": Kindlon, AI, 10/4/02.
338 "It was like factory labor" and following: Hart, AI, 9/17/02.
339 "It was a question": Dinerstein, AI, 10/22/99.
339 "Don't you know" and following: Confidential source.
339 "Harvey has this negativity": Hart, AI, 9/17/02.
339 "There was a feeling" and following: Kindlon, AI, 10/4/02.
339 "They intimidated everybody" and following: Merri Lane, AI, 6/12/01.
340 "Fine Line was horrible": Kindlon, AI, 10/4/02.

CHAPTER 11: THE BAD LIEUTENANT
PAGE
341 Epilogue: Ray, AI, 3/19/01.
341 "Why did it ever": Lechner, AI, 5/31/01.
342 "See, isn't that great?": Confidential source.
342 "I'm Steven Spielberg, and this": Confidential source.

342 "They treated Shyamalan": Confidential source.

342 "I don't think this movie" and following: Webster, AI, 10/20/01.

342 "There was cut after cut": Lechner, AI, 5/31/01.

342 "Harvey was recutting": Roth, AI, 5/10/00.

342 "Listen, Harvey, you can't" and following: Konrad, AI, 6/7/02.

342 "You're some fucking artist!": Harvey Weinstein, AI, 11/18/02; Konrad, AI, 6/7/02; Confidential source.

342 "Rosie burst into tears": Konrad, AI, 6/7/02.

343 "a big fat fucking cow": Confidential source.

343 "I never used 'cunt' ": Harvey Weinstein, AI, 11/18/02.

343 "You don't know who" and following: Konrad, AI, 6/7/02.

343 "You can't let that guy": Roth, AI, 5/1/00.

343 "I thought I had": Harvey Weinstein, AI, 10/3/02.

343 "The weirdness of being": Lechner, AI, 5/31/01.

343 "Miramax will steamroller": Anthony Kaufman, "The Six Million Dollar Man Strikes Back; Brad Anderson Survives with Two New Movies," IndieWire, 8/10/01.

344 "Bob is no bullshit" and following: Kevin Smith, AI, 12/18/01.

345 "I told Michael Eisner": Roth, AI, 5/1/00.

345 "If one person does not": Confidential source.

345 "It became very clear": Moore, AI, 5/1/00.

345 "Kevin said, 'What' ": Harvey Weinstein, AI, 7/18/02.

345 "Hispanic Coalition of Catholic Warriors": Read by author.

345 "The Catholic League" and following: Kevin Smith, AI, 12/18/01.

346 "He thought he really": Confidential source.

346 "The acting bug" and following: Tarantino, AI, 4/30/03.

346 "Quentin needs you": Confidential source.

346 "It was tough": Tarantino, AI, 4/30/03.

347 "Tell me the unvarnished truth": Tarantino, AI, 4/30/03, and David Carradine, AI, 6/30/03.

347 "You must never": Thurman, AI, 6/27/03.

347 "Part of him understood": Confidential source.

347 "You wear a baseball cap" and following: Tarantino, AI, 4/30/03.

348 "I gotta movie heah": Schmidt, AI, 6/9/00.

348 "Mom and Dad": Glatzer, AI, 4/26/00.

348 "Fuck you, you shithead": Ray, AI, 3/2/01.

348 "Bingham's not a businessman.": Confidential source.

349 "Bingham was the creative": McGurk, AI, 5/1/01.

349 "It was one fucking disaster": Rice, AI, 7/23/01.

349 "I don't have time for this": Confidential source.

349 "Chris acted like I was" and following: Ray, AI, 3/8/01.

349 "There's some things": Confidential source.

349 "I have good news": Schmidt, AI, 5/9/00.

350 "Whaddya mean I can't" and following: Schmidt, AI, 7/31/03.

350 "McGurk hates him.": Gigliotti, AI, 1/4/01.

350 "Hey, howya doin'": Confidential source.

350 "I made a mistake." and following: Schmidt, AI, 7/31/03.

351 "The right kind": Schmidt, AI, 8/7/03.

351 "It may be a bit": Barry Diller, AI, 10/28/03.

351 "When basically Scott": Malin, AI, 8/6/02.

351 "We all came away": Schmidt, AI, 7/31/03.

352 "Can't we work something out?" and following: Ray, AI, 3/19/01.

352 "Miramax is brilliant": Rice, AI, 7/16/01.

352 "I was on the bottom" and following: Sarah Kernochan, AI, 5/14/01.

353 "the incursion of the penis": Pam Grossman, *salon.com*, 5/17/00.

353 "I was jumping up and down" and following: Kernochan, AI, 5/14/01.

355 "He's passionate about films": Ivory, AI, 7/9/01.

355 "That's always his excuse": Confidential source.

355 "Your movie has": Kernochan, AI, 5/14/01.

356 "Virtually all of the films": memo, Weinstein to Kernochan, 2/19/98.

356 "He told me himself": Lee, AI, 11/8/02.

356 "I actually learned": Kernochan, AI, 5/14/01.

357 "I'm a lot like": memo, Kernochan to Weinstein, 4/7/98.

357 "felt very much like": Kernochan, AI, 5/14/01.

357 "We release thirty": memo, Lantos to Weinstein, 7/17/99.

358 "This whole thing": Dolly Hall, 4/18/01.

358 "After 54, I was ready": Lee Percy, AI, 5/12/01.

358 "I don't know if Harvey" and following: John Dahl, AI, 5/6/99.

358 "At the end of the movie": Damon, AI, 9/26/01.

359 "To me, *Rounders*": Norton, AI, 8/8/02.

359 "*Shakespeare in Love* was": Damon, AI, 9/26/01.

359 "They try to get" and following: Tom Tykwer, AI, 6/1/03.

360 "strangled the same market": Tusk, AI, 2/3/00.

360 "the first feel-good": Owen Gleiberman, review, *Entertainment Weekly*, 10/30/98.

360 "Sentimentality is a kind": Richard Schickel, "Fascist Fable: A Farce Trivializes the Horror of the Holocaust," *Time*, 11/9/98.

361 "It's a piece of shit," and following: Ray, AI, 3/19/01.

361 "I thought we were gonna" and following: Ray, AI, 9/29/01.

362 "The company is going" and following: McGurk, AI, 8/27/01.

362 "For a smart guy": Gigliotti, AI, 1/4/01.

362 "No one was ever gonna walk": Spikes, AI, 7/23/01.

363 "We had no protection": Schmidt, AI, 7/31/03.

363 "October had a bunch": Bowles, AI, 6/7/00.

363 "It's a paradox": Schmidt, AI, 5/9/00.

363 "If we hadn't done": Schmidt, AI, 7/31/03.

364 "We're all in the" and following: Kevin Smith, AI, 8/19/03.

364 "Miramax tries to play this": Lee, AI, 11/8/02.

364 "They fucked us": Kevin Smith, AI, 12/18/01.

365 "The original business model": McGurk, AI, 10/23/02.

365 "The level of creative interference" and following: Mangold, AI, 6/7/02.

365 "It used to be": Konrad, AI, 6/10/02.

366 "At that point they were": Konrad, AI, 6/7/02.

366 "Michael Eisner can't tell me": Auletta, "Beauty and the Beast."

366 "Harvey's become" and following: Kevin Smith, AI, 12/18/01.

366 "We had had all these deals" and following: Damon, AI, 9/26/01.

367 "Harvey and Bob made out" and following: Kevin Smith, AI, 12/18/01.

367 "*Dogma* incurred $20 million": Harvey Weinstein, AI, 11/11/03.

368 "And how's your kid": Confidential source.

368 "He was giving us a break": Mangold, AI, 6/7/02.

369 "Miramax pays a fleet" and following: Nikki Finke, *New York*, 3/15/99.

369 "It is complete bullshit" and following: Harvey Weinstein, AI, 10/3/02.

370 "Benigni moved into L.A.": Urman, AI, 10/31/01.
370 "Everyone knows" and following: David Parfitt, 6/17/03.
370 "Harvey came on": Norman, AI, 8/13/03.
371 "Never again!": Confidential source.
371 "suspend and extend": Mechanic, AI, 5/2/01.
371 "Sony didn't want Harvey" and following: John Horn, "Signed, Sealed, and Delivered," *Premiere*, 1/00.
371 "They gave up half": Mechanic, AI, 5/2/01.
371 "It's a wonderful opportunity": Horn, "Signed, Sealed, and Delivered."
371 "Miramax spent a lot": Norman, AI, 8/13/03.
372 "I made a small": Harvey Weinstein, AI, 10/3/02.
372 "I was the one who met" and following: Ray, AI, 3/8/01.

CHAPTER 12: THE KING OF NEW YORK
PAGE

374 Epigraph: Lee, AI, 11/8/02.
374 "They're not in contact": Gilmore, AI, 3/9/01.
375 "When Harvey became largely": Lechner, AI, 5/31/01.
375 "Production is a trap": Lichter, AI, 10/2/98.
375 "The game of making": Schmidt, AI, 5/9/00.
376 "Miramax was delivering": Moore, AI, 5/1/00.
376 "Hey, do you want me" and following: McGurk, AI, 5/1/01.
377 "We were in Harvey's office": Kevin Smith, AI, 12/18/01.
377 "The success of Dimension": Elwes, AI, 5/1/03.
377 "We were telling Harvey": Kevin Smith, AI, 12/18/01.
377 "You've got somebody": Scott Rudin, AI, 6/7/02.
377 "He tried to position himself": Lee, AI, 11/8/02.
378 "The Tina Brown hiring" and following: Joe Roth, AI, 5/1/00.
378 "This one's for Harvey": Judy Bachrach, *Tina and Harry Come to America* (New York: Free Press, 2001), 315.
379 "Coen brothers movies": Confidential source.
379 "four hundred people scratching": Soderbergh, AI, 5/2/02.
379 "probably crossed the line": Dennis Lim, "Having Your Way With Hollywood."
379 "My idea with *Schizopolis* was": Soderbergh, AI, 5/2/02.
379 "Quentin doesn't play any ball.": Hawke, AI, 10/28/02.
380 "I knew I had to pull my head" and following: Soderbergh, AI, 5/2/02.
381 "There was no list": Confidential source.
381 "Everything Scott ever did": Confidential source.
381 "weird love/hate": Confidential source.
381 "There was never": Diller, AI, 10/28/03.
382 "People said to me" and following: Gigliotti, AI, 1/4/01.
382 "They threw everything": Confidential source.
382 "Say this number" and following: Gigliotti, AI, 1/4/01.
382 "By small-company": Diller, AI, 10/28/03.
382 "Every deal had to be approved": Confidential source.
382 "Scott was terrified of Diller" and following: Gigliotti, AI, 1/4/01.
383 "Soderbergh's a smart guy": Gigliotti, AI, 1/4/01.
383 "No. I don't work": Soderbergh, AI, 8/31/01.
384 "Harvey wants you over" and following: Confidential source.
385 "I am Ariel Sharon!" and following: Confidential source.

385 "paternalistic, puffed-up": Amy Taubin, *Village Voice*, 12/8–14/99.

386 "they beat the shit out" and following: Confidential source.

386 "The current crop of people": Hope, AI, 7/19/02.

386 "I think something has changed": Russell, AI, 2/24/00.

387 "David O. Russell is" and following: Pierson, AI, nd.

387 "Let's not take any chances": Confidential source.

387 "To say Sundance": Geffner, "Surviving Park City."

388 "He was massively competitive" and following: Confidential source.

389 "Now you're in the theater": Pollack, AI, 6/10/02.

389 "Do you think I should make": Confidential sources.

390 "Bob's ambivalent": Pollack, AI, 6/10/02.

390 "Bob falls out of love" and following: Confidential source.

391 "mysterious Kremlin leader illness": Patrick Goldstein, "Scrappy Miramax Disappears on 'Yards' Marketing," *Los Angeles Times*, 11/28/00.

391 "The films weren't working": Confidential source.

392 "People talked themselves into saying" and following: Confidential source.

393 "Harvey's willling" and following: Kernochan, AI, 5/14/01.

394 "Years passed and years passed" and following: Merchant, AI, 7/9/01.

394 "He said the usual kinds": Ivory, AI, 7/9/01.

394 "Don't put the film": Confidential source.

394 "It was an awful thing": Ivory, AI, 7/9/01.

394 "I've heard that so much.": Hawke, AI, 10/28/02.

395 "Harvey is notorious": Thurman, AI, 6/27/03.

395 "They chose the mall": Merchant, AI, 7/9/01.

395 "Miramax took twenty-one minutes": Gill, AI, 2/11/03.

395 "Then they just went nuts": Merchant, AI, 7/9/01.

395 "doesn't know what": Ivory, AI, 7/9/01.

396 "I don't think so": Merchant, AI, 7/9/01.

396 "Never!": Ivory, AI, 7/9/01.

396 "I told Jim and Ismail" and following: Hawke, AI, 10/28/02.

397 "every major decision" and following: Goldstein, "Scrappy Miramax Disappears on 'Yards' Marketing."

398 "It's very difficult with Miramax": Webster, AI, 10/20/01.

398 "Look at the story!": Rice, AI, 7/23/01.

398 "the so-called premiere" and following: Goldstein, "Scrappy Miramax Disappears on 'Yards' Marketing."

398 "Miramax kept the film": Webster, AI, 10/20/01.

398 "Both of those films": Goldstein, "Scrappy Miramax Disappears on 'Yards' Marketing."

399 "Harvey took a very ruthless" and following: Webster, AI, 10/20/01.

399 "Believe it or not": Goldstein, "Scrappy Miramax Disappears on 'Yards' Marketing."

399 "If you could do anything" and following: Schulman, AI, 4/25/02.

401 "What he doesn't understand": Biskind, *Premiere*, 11/02.

401 "I'm going to have Marty": David Rooney, "Harvey Set to Helm Again," *Variety*, 5/1/03.

401 "Marty is only interested": Laura Holson, "Two Hollywood Titans Brawl Over Gang Epic," *New York Times*, 4/7/02.

401 "Harvey finally got": Kim Masters, "Harvey, Marty, and a Jar Full of Ears," *Esquire*, 7/02.

401 "While I grant the '70s": Harvey Weinstein, AI, 10/30/02.
402 "I'm sick of my image": Masters, "Harvey, Marty, and a Jar Full of Ears."
402 "He was playing a really": Schulman, AI, 4/25/02.
402 "Marty's in control": Parfitt, AI, 6/17/03.
402 "Marty feels that": Confidential source.
402 "Marty's as mean and difficult" and following: Masters, "Harvey, Marty, and a Jar Full of Ears."
402 "That was the big fight" and following: Harvey Weinstein, AI, 4/11/03. According to Parfitt, Weinstein was not involved in this incident. Scorsese was angry with him and overturned his assistant's desk by mistake.
403 "When we finished": Harvey Weinstein, AI, 4/11/02.
403 "She's too old": Confidential source.
403 "This is how I": Harvey Weinstein, AI, 4/11/03.
403 "She's a prim-lookin' stargazer" and following: Masters, "Harvey, Marty, and a Jar Full of Ears."
404 "Harvey put all the resources": Elwes, AI, 5/1/03.

CHAPTER 13: ALL THAT JAZZ IS GONE
PAGE

405 Epigraph: Hawke, AI, 10/28/02.
406 "We're the kings of marketing" and following: Tim Blake Nelson, AI, 10/4/01.
407 "My husband is" and following: Confidential source.
408 "that no decision would be made" and following: Rebecca Traister, "The Story of O, Weinstein Style: High-School Othello Is Held Up," New York Observer, 11/13/00.
409 "I have nothing to do" and following: Confidential source.
409 "Dead Man was Jarmusch's best movie" and following: J. Hoberman, AI, 3/12/02.
409 "One of the things": Hoberman, AI, 3/12/02.
410 "Harvey is obsessed" and following: Dennis Higgins, AI, 4/26/02.
410 "Roger Friedman is making": Harvey Weinstein, AI, 10/3/02.
410 "The idea was": Richard Johnson, AI, 11/13/03.
411 "a book on": Paula Froelich, AI, 11/14/03.
411 "They were always thrusting": Confidential source.
411 "You're not gonna use that stuff" and following: Confidential source.
413 "A couple of pushy reporters": "Page Six," New York Post, 11/08/00.
413 "Does Harvey intimidate": Affleck, AI, 2/21/02.
414 "Generally you walk into movies": Konrad, AI, 6/10/02.
414 "He asked us if": Mangold, AI, 6/7/02.
414 "The competition is so destructive": Foley, AI, 7/13/01.
415 "I spent a lot of time": Anthony Kaufman, "Man of the Year, Steven Soderbergh Traffics in Success," Indiewire, 1/3/01.
415 "Part of what we're trying": Bill Desowitz, "Puzzling Filmgoers, with Serious Intent: The Coolly Received Drama 'Solaris' Aims to Challenge Audiences with Tough Questions, Say Its Star and Director," Los Angeles Times, 12/3/02.
415 "Do you want to stay" and following: Soderbergh, AI, 8/31/01.
416 "It makes sense": Soderbergh, AI, nd.
416 "For me, Ocean's" and following: Soderbergh, AI, 8/31/01.
417 "They'd just gotten through": Hawke, AI, 10/28/02.
418 "I was on a panel with him": Russell, AI, 10/25/02.
418 "You can't piss upwind": Hawke, AI, 10/28/02.

419 "*Three Kings* was": Russell, AI, 10/25/02.

419 "You have to direct" and following: Damon, AI, 9/26/01.

420 "Billy didn't ask me": Epperson, AI, 8/29/01.

420 "Ah've had this talk" and following: Damon, AI, 9/26/01.

420 "It was the most self-indulgent": Rice, AI, 7/24/01.

420 "I thought it was brilliant": Affleck, AI, 2/21/02.

420 "We're not going to be": Harvey Weinstein, AI, 11/18/02.

421 "You can understand them": Damon, AI, 9/26/01.

421 "If you reduce this thing": Affleck, AI, 2/21/02.

421 "Amy Pascal is just bustin' ": Kevin Smith, AI, 12/18/01.

421 "Harvey, you handle it": Damon, AI, 9/26/01.

421 "I know exactly what to do": Confidential source.

421 "Harvey's making me cut" and following: Damon, AI, 9/26/01.

421 "Contractually there was": Confidential source.

422 "The cut I saw": Epperson, AI, 8/29/01.

422 "It was like": Damon, AI, 9/26/01.

423 "Harvey has a great gift": Confidential source.

423 "I flew to New York": Jeanette Walls, AI, 2/26/01.

423 "We want actresses": "Gwyn and Bear It," *Toronto Sun*, 2/3/02.

423 "He looks out": Auletta, "Beauty and the Beast."

424 "an art house movie": Elvis Mitchell, " 'Chocolat': Candy Power Comes to Town," *New York Times*, 12/15/00.

424 "Factory sealed to preserve": Lisa Schwarzbaum, review, *Entertainment Weekly*, 1/16/02.

424 "Apparently Harvey went crazy" and following: Schwarzbaum, AI, 3/20/02.

425 "It was really hard": John Penotti, AI, 4/15/02.

425 "Talk about a movie": Harvey Weinstein, AI, 11/18/02.

425 "but the Miramax guys": Penotti, AI, 4/15/02.

426 "Financially, the cinemas": Confidential source.

426 "Bob is considered": Confidential source.

426 "When Bob is good": Barbara Maltby, AI, 6/16/03.

427 "We do not feel" and following: Nelson, AI, 10/4/01.

427 "I could smell" and following: Eric Gitter, AI, 10/9/01.

428 "I'm in a position to try": Haynes, AI, 3/23/02.

428 "He was riding almost exclusively" and following: Haynes, AI, 3/23/02.

430 Dimension's contribution to the Miramax bottom line: *Daily Variety*, 10/30/01.

430 "They didn't talk": Confidential source.

431 "You never give a shit" and following: Confidential source.

431 "Harvey was pissed" and following: Kevin Smith, AI, 12/18/01.

433 "Harvey cried" and following: Konrad, AI, 6/7/02.

434 "They showed me a shadow cut" and following: Mangold, AI, 6/7/02.

435 "You sit there going": Kevin Smith, AI, 12/18/01.

435 "*Kate & Leopold* is the kind": Rudin, AI, 8/7/02.

435 "The problem is that": Confidential source.

435 "So your movie comes out": Konrad, AI, 6/7/02.

CHAPTER 14: GODS AND MONSTERS
PAGE

437 Epigraph: Tykwer, AI, 7/13/03.

437 "He didn't really give a shit" and following: Fisher Stevens, AI, 6/23/02.

437 "Going with Miramax": Hope, AI, 7/19/02.
438 "What are you": Harvey Weinstein, AI, 11/18/02.
438 "You could see Todd" and following: Hope, AI, 7/19/02.
438 "Everyone had seen" and following: Confidential source.
439 "I let Miramax know": Todd Field, AI, nd.
439 "The relationship was tenuous": Stevens, AI, 6/23/02.
439 "I decided against it": Field, AI, nd.
440 "Some Academy members": Tom O'Neil, www.GoldDerby.com.
440 "We kicked the fat": Ray, AI, 8/7/02.
440 "We kicked Miramax's": Bill Higgins, Variety, 1/21/02.
440 "Did you say" and following: Ray, AI, 8/7/02.
440 "He's somebody on my": Confidential source.
441 "You're going to go down": Stacey Snider, AI, 4/26/02; Auletta, "Beauty and the Beast."
441 "He was yelling": Snider, AI, 4/26/02.
441 "I never raised": Auletta, "Beauty and the Beast."
441 "It was the second": Confidential source.
441 "There were two things": Snider, AI, 4/26/02.
441 "lashed out" and following: Craig Offinan, "Diller Defends Viv U Chief Messier, stox," Variety, 5/13/02.
441 "You can't work": Auletta, "Beauty and the Beast."
441 "And I'm sick of you": Confidential source.
441 "The relationship is 80 percent": Confidential source.
441 "I have great fondness": Harvey Weinstein, AI, 4/11/03.
442 "When A Beautiful Mind opened": Confidential source.
442 "works very hard": Safford, AI, 9/29/98.
442 "Harvey never roots": Matthew Hiltzik, AI, nd.
442 "Our hands were": Gill, AI, 6/4/02.
442 "It's Scapegoat 101": Harvey Weinstein, AI, 11/18/02.
442 "I was put on" and following: Confidential source.
443 "It was all": Gill, AI, 6/4/02.
443 "I wouldn't call it": Ben Kaplan, "Action Painting," New York, 9/9/02.
444 "There is a kind of strange": Mangold, AI, 6/10/02.
444 "The morning after": Harvey Weinstein, AI, 4/11/03.
444 "Hello, darling. You look": Nikki Finke, salon.com, 3/28/02.
445 "It was a setup": Confidential source.
447 "Scott delivered for Steven": Vachon, AI, 6/10/03.
447 "I'm gonna lose my job" and following: Haynes, AI, 6/13/03.
448 "That may well have": Michael Jackson, AI, 10/27/03.
448 "What's going on": Vachon, AI, 6/10/03.
448 "It felt amazing because": Haynes, AI, 6/13/03.
448 "The only person": Vachon, AI, 6/10/03.
448 "This is suicide": Confidential source.
448 "You can come in" and following: Snider, AI, 10/21/03.
449 "My position was": Diller, AI, 10/28/03.
449 "Cut it whatever way": Schamus, AI, 4/30/03.
449 "It's nice to feel that": Hope, AI, 7/19/02.
449 "Is it rational": Penotti, AI, 4/15/02.
450 "a movie that could be": Elvis Mitchell, review, New York Times, 12/6/02.

450 According to a fall 2002 *New York Times* article: Laura M. Holson and Rick Lyman, "Miramax's Big Screen Test," *New York Times*, 11/4/02.

451 "They're like Mafia dons": Gill, AI, 2/11/03.

451 "vote with their feet": Gigliotti, AI, 6/10/01.

452 "Given who Harvey was": Russell, AI, 10/25/02.

452 "Harvey does both": Mangold, AI, 6/7/02.

452 "Harvey sends me" and following: Vachon, AI, 6/10/03.

452 "Why'd you call me": Auletta, "Beauty and the Beast."

453 "I think the behavior": Rudin, AI, 8/7/02.

453 "He's done one": Confidential source.

453 "In Hollywood, everyone's" and following: Elwes, AI, 5/1/03.

453 "Agents are the people": Harvey Weinstein, AI, 8/9/02.

454 "just beat the shit": Confidential source.

454 "Jeffrey is psychotically": Confidential source.

454 "I thought because it was" and following: Lee, AI, 11/8/02.

455 "If you don't sell me" and following: Rudin, AI, 8/7/02.

455 "That's complete bullshit": Harvey Weinstein, AI, 11/18/02.

455 "Thanks for all the help" and following: Confidential source.

456 "Filmmakers like Minghella": Gill, AI, 10/23/02.

456 "Anthony said": Harvey Weinstein, AI, 11/18/02.

456 "He's getting a divorce": Confidential source.

456 "When Harvey finally did decide": Pollack, AI, 6/1/02.

457 "It's best to keep": Russell Crowe, AI, 9/4/03.

457 "We've never had": Snider, AI, 10/21/03.

457 "If you're not careful": Confidential source.

457 "There's no such thing": Gill, AI, 2/11/03.

457 "We were seduced": Confidential source.

458 "They're in financial trouble" and following: Harvey Weinstein, AI, 4/11/03.

458 "I'm sure at the back": Elwes, AI, 5/1/03.

459 "They of course audit": Harvey Weinstein, AI, 4/11/03.

459 "That's crossing the line": Confidential source. See also Paul Tharp, "Big Trouble at Disney—Weinstein Weighs Split as Feud Grows," *New York Post*, 3/4/03.

459 "Both Matty and Ben" and following: Kevin Smith, AI, 5/26/03.

460 "When I first came": Harvey Weinstein, AI, 8/9/02.

460 "It's tough for Harvey" and following: Kevin Smith, AI, 5/26/03.

461 "Ordinarily, I don't" and following: Smith, AI, 8/19/03.

461 "Harvey's a twisted": Shestack, AI, 10/20/03.

461 "Look, man, Disney" and following: Smith, AI, 8/19/03.

462 "Kevin said, 'I feel' ": Harvey Weinstein, AI, 11/11/03.

462 "Ben was like": Shestock, AI, 10/20/03.

462 "Who do you": Smith, AI, 5/26/03.

462 "After the first": Tykwer, AI, 7/13/03.

462 "The smaller, more interesting": Rudin, AI, 8/7/02.

463 "They've really ceded": Elwes, AI, 5/1/03.

463 "As we turned" and following: Philip Noyce, AI, 10/17/03.

463 "People have put": Mickey Cottrell, AI, 9/22/03.

463 "I will not": Noyce, AI, 10/17/03.

463 "We had a horrible": Cottrell, AI, 9/22/03.

464 "The film could only": Noyce, AI, 10/17/03.

464 "It should have": Cottrell, AI, 4/22/03.

464 "Harvey is a tough": Noyce, AI, 10/17/03.
465 "Everybody knew the script": Gill, AI, 2/11/03.
465 "The feeling at Miramax": Parfitt, AI, 6/17/03.
465 "They talked themselves": Gill, AI, 2/11/03.
466 "Graham King had nowhere else": Confidential source.
466 "If the budget spirals": Elwes, AI, 5/1/03.
466 "I had more input": Harvey Weinstein, AI, 4/11/03.
467 "tormented": Confidential source.
467 "Back off and don't": Confidential source.
467 "Harvey made his way" and following: Haynes, AI, 6/13/03.
467 "a kindly, lovable, gentle man": Rick Lyman, " 'Chicago' a Big Winner at Golden Globe Awards," *New York Times,* 1/20/03.
468 "I think it cost": Rudin, AI, 3/4/03.
468 "They're coached": Confidential source.
468 "I marvel at Harvey Weinstein's ability": Confidential source.
468 Already chafing at: Rick Lyman, " 'Chicago' Is a Hit After Feuds," *New York Times,* 3/19/03.
469 "child molester": Confidential sources.
469 "Harvey made two mistakes": Schamus, AI, 4/30/03.

POSTSCRIPT: THE SWEET HEREAFTER
PAGE

470 "Miramax has been great": Lee, AI, 11/8/02.
470 "I don't think Miramax": Rudin, AI, 8/7/02.
472 "The independent film movement": Soderbergh, AI, 5/2/02.
472 "Sydney Pollack and I": Minghella, AI, 11/1/01.
472 "The whole thing that's happening": Charlie LeDuff, "Box Office He Wants, Not a Drink," *Los Angeles Times,* 12/15/02.
472 "It's getting harder": "10 Questions for John Sayles," *New York Times,* 10/23/03.
473 "Even on the indie level" and following: Hawke, AI, 10/28/02.
474 "As the last ten years": Sayles, AI, 7/9/97.
474 "Most of the '70s guys" and following: Schamus, AI, 3/4/99.
474 "An independent filmmaker": Kevin Smith, AI, 12/18/01.
475 "Once you proved": Linklater, AI, 3/12/01.
475 "If you're an": Van Wagenen, AI, 10/22/03.
476 "ongoing support for": Satter, AI, 7/25/03.
477 "Now that Miramax": Elwes, AI, 5/1/03.
478 "We are not a cultural temple": John Horn, "Safer Movies, Less Moxie at New Line," *Los Angeles Times,* 12/9/02.
478 "When I started": Hope, AI, 10/15/03.
478 "He'll litigate" and following: Russell, AI, 10/25/02.
479 "have found money" and following: Lichter, AI, 10/31/03.
480 "It was fuckin' ": Ray, AI, 10/17/03.
480 "This is such": David Rooney, "The Battle of the Ban," *Variety,* posted 10/1/03.
481 "I only wish": Hope, AI, 10/15/03.
481 "The people who": Cathy Dunkley, Dade Hayes, "The Last Picture Show?" *Variety,* posted 10/5/03.
481 "When I first": Andy Seiler, "Small Guy May Fall to MPAA's anti-Piracy Ban," *USA Today,* 10/2/03.

481 "This is a real Karl": Jean Smith, Devin Gordon, "Hollywood Family Feud," *Newsweek*, 10/20/03.

481 "We talked to the IFP": Ray, AI, 10/17/03.

482 "I will go along": David Romey, "Ben Triggers Niche Bitch," *Variety*, nd.

482 "This should not": Ray, AI, 10/17/03.

482 "I found it weird": Hope, AI, 10/15/03.

482 "I think Harvey": Ray, AI, 10/17/03.

482 "It's Alex Yemen" and following: Bernard, AI, 10/23/03.

482 "Hey, your man's" and following: Ray, AI, 10/17/03.

483 "The consumer has": Confidential source.

483 "If there is a villain," Patrick Goldstein, "The Big Picture: Screeners: Behind the Ban," *Los Angeles Times,* 10/7/03.

483 "This is your legacy": Confidential source.

483 "Jack can go off": Bernard, AI, 10/23/03.

484 "This ban [is] a grave threat": Harvey Weinstein, *Variety*, 10/31/03.

484 "I gotta tell ya": Ray, AI, 10/17/03.

Index

A NOTE ON THE AUTHOR

Peter Biskind is the author of three previous books, including *Easy Riders, Raging Bulls: How the Sex-Drugs-and-Rock'n' Roll Generation Saved Hollywood*. He is a contributor to *Vanity Fair* and formerly the executive editor of *Premiere* magazine. He lives with his family in Columbia County, New York.